COMPARATIVE POLITICS
Democratic Representation in Europe

COMPARATIVE POLITICS

Comparative Politics is a series for students and teachers of political science
that deals with contemporary issues in comparative government and politics.
As Comparative European Politics it has produced a series of high-quality books since its foundation
in 1990, but now takes on a new form and new title for the new millennium—Comparative Politics.
As the process of globalization proceeds, and as Europe becomes ever more enmeshed in world
trends and events, so it is necessary to broaden the scope of the series. The General Editors are
Professor Alfio Mastropaolo, University of Turin and Kenneth Newton, University of Southampton
and Wissenschaftszentrum Berlin. The series is published in association with the European
Consortium for Political Research.

OTHER TITLES IN THIS SERIES

Democratic Representation in Europe
Diversity, Change, and Convergence

Edited by

MAURIZIO COTTA
and
HEINRICH BEST

OXFORD
UNIVERSITY PRESS

OXFORD
UNIVERSITY PRESS

Great Clarendon Street, Oxford OX2 6DP

Oxford University Press is a department of the University of Oxford.
It furthers the University's objective of excellence in research, scholarship,
and education by publishing worldwide in

Oxford New York

Auckland Cape Town Dar es Salaam Hong Kong Karachi
Kuala Lumpur Madrid Melbourne Mexico City Nairobi
New Delhi Shanghai Taipei Toronto

With offices in

Argentina Austria Brazil Chile Czech Republic France Greece
Guatemala Hungary Italy Japan Poland Portugal Singapore
South Korea Switzerland Thailand Turkey Ukraine Vietnam

Oxford is a registered trade mark of Oxford University Press
in the UK and in certain other countries

Published in the United States
by Oxford University Press Inc., New York

British Library Cataloguing in Publication Data
Data available

Library of Congress Cataloging-in-Publication Data
Democratic representation in Europe: diversity, change, and convergence/edited by
Maurizio Cotta and Heinrich Best.
p. cm.
Includes bibliographical references.
ISBN 978–0–19–923420–2 (alk. paper)
1. European Parliament. 2. Representative government and representation—European Union
countries. 3. Democracy—European Union countries. 4. Europe–Politics and
government—1989– I. Cotta, Maurizio, 1947– II. Best, Heinrich.
JN36.D44 2007
328.4'07334—dc22 2007021609

Typeset by SPI Publisher Services, Pondicherry, India
Printed in Great Britain
on acid-free paper by
Biddles Ltd., King's Lynn, Norfolk

ISBN 978–0–19–923420–2

1 3 5 7 9 10 8 6 4 2

Contents

List of Figures

Graph

List of Tables

Notes on Contributors

Heinrich Best is currently Professor of Sociology at the University of Jena. He is also Director of the multidisciplinary collaborative Research Centre, 'Societal Developments after the End of State Socialism: Discontinuity, Tradition and the Emergence of New Structures' funded by the German Science Foundation, and was Co-director of the Scientific Network, 'European Political Elites in Comparison: the long road to convergence' (EurElite) funded by the European Science Foundation. Professor Best's publication list entails 27 books and 105 journal and book contributions as primary author and editor. His recent publications include 'Parliamentary Representatives in Europe 1848–2000' (OUP 2000); Elites in Transition: Elite Research in Central and Eastern Europe (1997); Functional Elites in the GDR: Theoretical controversies and empirical evidence (2003).

Verona Christmas Best has a Ph.D. from the Institute of Education, London University and has been a Research Associate at the University of Jena, Germany since 1996. Her research interests are women's vocational training and career development with a special area of focus on differences between East and West Germany and on women in atypical careers. Related to the latter she has written on women as political representatives and presented on this topic in London, Moscow, and Balestrand, Norway, as well as working with the DATACUBE project.

Maurizio Cotta is Professor of Political Science and Director of the Centre for the Study of Political Change at the University of Siena. He was Co-director of the Scientific Network, 'European Political Elites in Comparison: the long road to convergence' (EurElite) funded by the European Science Foundation and is currently coordinator of the European 6th Framework Programme Integrated Project 'INTUNE Integrated and United: A quest for Citizenship in an ever closer Europe'. He has written extensively on parliaments, executives, and Italian politics. He has co-edited *Il gigante dai piedi di argilla. La crisi del regime partitocratico in Italia* (1996), *Party and Government* (1996), *The Nature of Party Government* (2000) (2006 in Chinese), *Parliamentary Representatives in Europe, 1848–2000* (2000), *L'Europa in Italia* (2005), *Political Institutions in Italy* (with Verzichelli 2007).

Valerie Cromwell is an honorary Fellow of the Institute of Historical Research at the School of Advanced Study in the University of London having been Director of the History of Parliament, 1991–2001. She is currently researching and writing the history of the History of Parliament. She is a Vice-President of the International Commission for the History of Representation and Parliamentary Institutions and has published numerous articles on British parliamentary history.

Kjell A. Eliassen is Professor of Public Management and Director of the Centre for European and Asian Studies at the Norwegian School of Management—BI in Oslo and professor of European Studies at The Free University in Brussels. He is also honorary professor at the Fudan University in Shanghai and at the Jiaotong Xian University. He has published eighteen books and many articles on the EU and European affairs, public management, telecommunications liberalization, and political elites, including, *Foreign and Security Policy in the European Union* (1998), *European Telecom Liberalisation* (1999) (2002 in Chinese), and a new edition of *Making Policy in the European Union* (2001) (2002 in Chinese).

Stefaan Fiers is Assistant Professor of Comparative Politics and Director of the teaching training programme in social sciences at the Catholic University of Leuven, Belgium. His main research interests include civic education and the recruitment of political elites, especially within the framework of multilevel governance. He has authored and co-authored several articles in Dutch and English on the recruitment of MPs, the selection of party leaders, the direct election of prime ministers and the presidentialization of the Belgian political system.

Daniel Gaxie is Professor of Political Sociology at the University of Paris-I Panthéon-Sorbonne. Among others, he has published *Le cens caché* (1993) and *La démocratie représentative* (2003).

Laurent Godmer is Assistant Professor in Political Science at East-Paris University. He is currently completing *Le Principe Représentation.*

Gabriella Ilonszki is the Head of the Elite Studies Research Centre at the Institute of Political Science at Corvinus University Budapest. Her research interests include the analysis of political elite—including women—and their role in maintaining or transforming regimes. Her more recent book is *Parlamenti képviselők Magyarországon (Parliamentary Representatives in Hungary)* (2005) and she edited *Women in Decision-making. CEE Experiences* (2004). She is currently working on the theme of the governmental elite in Hungary.

Miguel Jerez Mir is Professor of Political Science at the University of Granada. His main research interests are political and economic elites, interest groups, and political science as a discipline. His publications include three single authored books: *Elites políticas y centros de extracción en España, 1938–1957* (1982), *Corporaciones e intereses en España* (1995), and *Ciencia política, un balance de fin de siglo* (1999).

Ulrik Kjær is Associate Professor at the Department of Political Science at the University of Southern Denmark. His main research interests are political recruitment, political leadership, and local democracy. Recent books include *De danske folketingsmedlemmer* (with Mogens N. Pedersen, 2004) and *Den danske borgmester* (with Rikke Berg, 2005).

Juan J. Linz is Sterling Professor of Political Science at Yale University. He has published extensively on the processes of regime change, democratization, presidential systems, federalism, and national identity. His books include *The Breakdown of Democratic Regimes* (co-editor with A. Stepan, 1978), *Problems of Democracy in Developing Countries* (co-editor with L. Diamond and A. Stepan, 1988–9), *The Failure of Presidential Democracy* (with A. Valenzuela, 1994), *Democratic Transitions and Consolidation in Southern Europe, Latin America, and Post-Communist Europe* (with A. Stepan, 1995).

Carmen Ortega is Associate Professor of Political Science at the University of Granada. Her main research area is electoral systems and electoral behaviour. She is the author of *Los sistemas de voto preferencial. Un estudio de dieciséis democracias*. Madrid, Centro de Investigaciones Sociológicas, 2004.

Mogens N. Pedersen is Professor of Political Science at the University of Southern Denmark at Odense. He has published widely in the fields of legislative behaviour, political elite recruitment, parties and party systems, local politics, and methodology. Among his recent publications are *Kampen om Kommunen* (co-editor J. Elklit, 1995), *Leksikon i statskundskab* (co-editors K. Goldman and Ø. Østerud, 1997), *Party Sovereignty and Citizen Control* (co-editors Hanne-Marthe Narud and Henry Valen, 2002), and *De danske folketingsmedlemmer—en parlamentarisk elite og dens rekruttering, circulation og transformation, 1849–2001* (co-author Ulrik Kjaer, 2004).

Ilkka Ruostetsaari is an acting Professor of Political Science at the University of Tampere, Finland. His special fields of research are elites, power structures, professionalization of politics, local governance, and energy policy. He has published, among others, *Valta muutoksessa* (2003) and 'Social Upheaval and Transformation of Elite Structures. The Case of Finland' (*Political Studies* Nr 1, 2006).

Michael Rush is Emeritus Politics Professor at the University of Exeter. He is author, co-author, and editor of a number of books and articles on British politics and of articles on Canadian politics. His most recent books are *The Role of the Member of Parliament Since 1868: From Gentlemen to Players* (OUP, 2001) and *Parliament Today* (Manchester University Press, 2005).

Ineke Secker is Lecturer in Constitutional and Parliamentary History at Leiden University, the Netherlands. Her research interests focus mainly on governing and legislative elites. Her publications include a study on the background of the Dutch cabinet ministers from 1848 to 1990 and several biographical contributions. She is co-editor of the Dutch Parliamentary Yearbook.

Pedro Tavares de Almeida is Professor in the Departamento de Estudios Políticos of the Faculdade de Ciências Sociais e Humanas of the Universidade Nova de Lisboa. He has written extensively on the Portuguese Parliament and on ministerial recruitment. Among his recent publications : *Eleições e Caciquismo no Portugal oitocentista* (1991); *Who governs Southern Europe? Regime change and ministerial recruitment, 1850–2000* (2003): *Recruitment and Role of the Portuguese Administrative Elite: The Directors-General, 1851–1910* (2005); *Ruling the Portuguese Empire, 1820–1926: The Colonial Office and Its Leadership* (2005).

Filippo Tronconi holds a Ph.D. in Comparative and European Politics from the University of Siena. He is currently Assistant Professor of Political Science at the University of Bologna. His main research focus is on ethno-regionalist parties in Europe.

Luca Verzichelli is Professor of Political Science at the University of Siena. His main research interests are on political elite and parliamentary institutions in Europe. Recent publications include *Il parlamento* (with Chiara de Micheli, 2004), *L'Europa in Italia* (edited with M. Cotta and P. Isernia 2005), *Political Institutions in Italy* (with M. Cotta 2007) and several articles in Italian and English.

Preface

Why a new book centred on the parliamentary class? The answer seems to us straightforward. In spite of all the tremendous changes that have taken place over the last century and a half, the political life of parliamentary democracies still centres significantly upon national elections. And national elections are fundamentally about selecting members of parliaments. Parliamentarians have not ceased to be an important product and at the same time a crucial actor of representation processes. As long as contemporary poliarchies continue to take the form of representative democracies, studying those who are elected offers therefore a significant key for understanding its working.

Quite a number of years ago the 1988 ECPR meeting in Rimini and then a seminar at the Certosa di Pontignano near Siena (1991) convinced the editors of this book, together with a small group of scholars, that, in spite of a strong empirical tradition of country studies, research on national parliamentary elites had not yet been sufficiently developed in a comparative perspective. It seemed also to us that the growing integration of the national political systems of Europe into a continental polity made it even more interesting to systematically study variations and convergences in the long-term developmental patterns of elite recruitment across European countries. With a previous book, *Parliamentary Representatives in Europe, 1848–2000. Legislative Recruitment and Careers in Eleven European Countries* (published in 2000 by Oxford University Press), we had provided a detailed country by country exploration of the developmental trends that had affected the parliamentary elites of a large sample of European countries and had tried to provide at least a synthetic comparative view of the main similarities and differences. Yet it was clear to us that, in order to attempt to provide an answer to some of the scientific challenges that we had set to ourselves, we had to go beyond that stage and develop a more systematic comparison of some of the crucial features of representatives and put to a test a number of hypotheses capable to explain long term change and its variations.

The new task proved even more challenging than expected and more than once, as happens to mountain climbers, the peak of the mountain seemed to disappear amid the clouds and to be beyond reach. More meetings had to be arranged, more versions of the chapters had to be written, and the original group of scholars was broadened to include fresh blood. In the end also the second book of this enterprise is now finished.

Over the years the debts of gratitude we have accumulated have grown to a staggering level and we apologize in advance if we have inadvertently forgotten some. The European Science Foundation with its generous grant *(EURELITE: European Political Elites in Comparison: the long road to convergence)* has simply made all this possible and Mr Stronkhorts and Ms Eckert have constantly sustained our efforts from Strasburg. The German Science Foundation (SFB 580) and the Italian Ministry of University (MIUR) have added further financial support. The Universities of Jena and Siena and our departments there have continued to believe that our activities were relevant and have provided the facilities for organizing conferences and smaller meetings. Special thanks goes to Sylvia Juhasz on one side and Marina Borgogni on the other, together with all the other members of the two staffs. The Universities of Siena (October 2001), of Jena, of Southern Denmark at Odense (June 2002), of Granada (June 2003) and of Leuven (March 2004) have brought our little academic circus to enjoy the pleasures of these wonderful European cities and to explore advances and limits of European convergence.

There is no need to say that this book would not have been possible without the common effort of all the people that have written the chapters, yet everything would have been much more difficult and even more imperfect without the continuous work offered generously by Luca Verzichelli and Stefan Jahr in keeping the dataset up to date, checking for mistakes, looking for possible improvements. Michael Edinger in Jena, Silvina Cabrera, Francesco Marangoni and Licia Papavero in Siena have also provided help in the work of data analysis and in many other ways. From Oxford University Press the unfailing support of Dominic Byatt and then of Elizabeth Suffling and Natasha Forrest has enabled the transformation of our often messy files into the more reassuring and solid shape of a book.

Now that Book 2 (as it was called in our jargon) is accomplished and Book 3 on the development of representative elites in post-communist Central and Eastern Europe is near to completion, we feel a bit 'jobless'; but as time goes by, sooner or later someone will perhaps think that it is time to update, improve, broaden our dataset (DATACUBE), and to look for a more sophisticated interpretation of changes in parliamentary representation in an increasingly unified Europe. Our collective effort will maybe help other younger scholars to push our knowledge of representative elites a little further.

MC and HB

Siena and Jena, May 2007

Parliamentary Representatives from Early Democratization to the Age of Consolidated Democracy: National Variations and International Convergence in a Long-term Perspective

Maurizio Cotta and Heinrich Best

1.1. A LONG-TERM PERSPECTIVE ON THE DEMOCRATIZATION OF EUROPE: POLITICAL REPRESENTATION AND THE GREAT CHANGE OF EUROPEAN SOCIETIES

In the spring of 2004, following the latest enlargement of the European Union (EU), democratic parliamentary elections have taken place, on the same day in twenty-five European countries, to elect representatives to the European Parliament. We can rightly consider this date, whatever the immediate practical effects of these elections, a crucial symbolic point in the political development of Europe. This point in time provides us with a challenging perspective over the approximately 150 years of European history that have elapsed from the revolutionary year of 1848 to this day.[1] This historical period can be seen as the period of construction, diffusion, and consolidation of representative democracy to practically the whole of Europe, and at the same time as the period during which a regional system of fiercely competing nation states was in the end, if not completely displaced, undoubtedly contained and constrained through a supranational community, which also increasingly defines itself on the basis of the principles of representative democracy.

Apparently, the two dimensions of change are separate and distinctive: the first concerns developments pertaining to the internal political space, the second, aspects of the international space. Yet these two dimensions, which had traditionally been considered as the preserve of two strictly separate scientific domains, one that of comparative political science, the other of international relations, have today become much more tightly interconnected as a result of the process of European integration (Hix 1999). The EU itself, with its representative institutions (the European Parliament above all and the European Commission which is responsible towards the European Parliament, but also the European Council and the Council of Ministers since they are both the indirect product of representative processes, albeit at a national level), its ongoing process of constitutionalization, the diffusion of referenda on its treaties, can be increasingly seen as an extension to the international space of processes of political transformation (democratization) which were previously typical of the internal one. If this phenomenon has become particularly relevant today (but as the result of a process launched in the first decades after the Second World War), we should not forget that Europe, even in the age of the so-called sovereign states (Krasner 1999), was always a very 'dense space' where the internal processes of transformation, taking place within one country, had inevitably important reflections upon the other countries. Positive and negative examples, particularly when coming from the most influential countries (be they the big threes—Britain, France, or Germany—but also at some points, Italy and Spain and even in certain cases the smaller countries), have always triggered reactions and repercussions in the political life of the other countries. We should also not forget that 1848, the symbolic starting point of our research was at the same time a challenge to the internal order of states and to the international equilibrium of Europe.

This view of Europe, as a 'dense space' of interconnected polities, was clearly behind Stein Rokkan's ambitious research programme to analyse the processes of democratization in Europe, not just as a problem of comparative politics (whereby independent cases are compared in order to find general explanatory factors), but also as a problem of interpretation of a comprehensive process of change affecting Europe as a whole (Rokkan 1970*a*, 1970*b*, 1999). In this view, Europe, even before the processes of supranational integration of the post-Second World War period, was to be considered, at the same time, as an area composed of independent units but also as a political space sharing common processes. Using the terminology of International Relations, one could say that Europe, in its *westphalian* phase was still under the influence of many *pre-westphalian* elements of a transnational nature that made for important commonalities (the unifying force of a common religion, common legal traditions, the large-scale bonds of the Sacred Roman Empire, etc.); at the same time, it was preparing the ground for *post-westphalian* developments, whereby national sovereignty would have given way to supranational governance. In fact, one could read the past two centuries of European history as a political process evolving through the stages of national independence, interpenetration, and integration.

This historical period, from mid-nineteenth century to the beginnings of the twenty-first century, which has seen the ascendance of representative democracy in Europe, has been a period of deep changes affecting most dimensions of society. In the sphere of political life, we may simply mention three major processes of transformation affecting its fundamental dimensions of *politics*, *polity*, and *policy*.[2] In the domain of *politics*, we can highlight democratization, as the process through which the whole population has been incorporated as an active participant in the political process and political power has been limited and made responsible and responsive to the people (inclusion and liberalization in Dahl's parlance) (Dahl 1970); in the domain of *polity* nation building and nationalization of politics, as the processes by which a national identity has been firmly established and political life has acquired a predominantly national dimension (Bendix 1964; Rokkan 1999); in the domain of *public policy* the building of a developed welfare state as the process through which the central political authority has increasingly taken responsibility for the re-equilibration of social inequalities and the assurance of equal opportunities (Flora and Heidenheimer 1981). On top of this, at the economic level, the processes of industrialization and later of post-industrialization have deeply changed for the greatest part of the population the material bases of life and produced wide territorial displacements of population and wealth (Flora et al. 1983). And on the social and cultural level, the passing of traditional society with its static and hierarchic system of relations has opened the way to a more mobile, egalitarian, achievement-oriented, and dynamic society.

Today, at a point in time which is surely not Fukuyama's 'end of history' (1989), but undoubtedly marks a very distinctive high point in the diffusion and consolidation of democracy throughout Europe, and also the beginnings of its extension to the supranational perspective, a comparative assessment of this long-term process from the perspective of representation seems, for more than one reason, important.

The first reason is of a theoretical and normative nature. If democracy and democratization are the key concepts through which we interpret retrospectively this long-term socio-political change of the European landscape, but also the key values which have come to dominate our normative evaluation of the political and social phenomena, we must remember that representation—more precisely parliamentary representation—has become a central component of the contemporary interpretation of democracy (Schumpeter 1954; Sartori 1987). In fact, as a careful historical and theoretical overview of the theme has well established (Manin 1997), this conception of democracy is the result of the overcoming of an old contraposition which originally had democracy and representation as two opposed and conflicting (normative and analytic) models. Through a political and conceptual process of hybridization, the two have become so completely enmeshed that today (electoral and parliamentary) representation is often used as a synonym of democracy and our conception of democracy is predominantly based on the mechanisms of representation. The study of representation offers thus a crucial point of view for our understanding of contemporary democracy. And, for this purpose, the long-term perspective is particularly relevant as this identification between democracy and representation was the result of a long and difficult historical process, not of an immediate and easy convergence.

On a second and more empirical ground, the institutions and processes of representation offer, we surmise, a strategic point of view for observing the great transformations we have briefly sketched. They are a crucial connecting link between the different streams of change and in particular they work as an interface between socio-economic and political change. Representation means the complex and delicate institutional mechanisms and the connected processes through which identities, interests, demands, and opinions, originating from within society (in its many possible meanings) are transmitted to those who govern. It is also the process through which the responsibility of those who govern is enforced. Representation, however, is not just a one-way road from society to politics, from below to above; it is also a process from above to below, from politics to society, whereby representative elites (i.e. political elites who are produced and made responsible through the electoral processes) take the initiative to address the demos proposing ideas and solutions, shaping interests and identities and asking on these proposals the consent of the represented. Because of their intermediary position we expect that they have felt directly the impact of these changes but, at the same time, that they have mediated their effects (in some cases reducing and delaying them, in other cases inflating and accelerating them; in most of the cases not only reflecting but also interpreting them). On the long term, we can expect also that the essential elements of representation—who and what is to be represented (the nation as a whole, territorial or functional interests, social identities, groups, etc.), but also who is to play the role of representative (individual Members of Parliament, parliamentary parties, extra-parliamentary party organizations, etc.), and the meaning itself of representation as a relationship between two sides (Pitkin 1967) could not be left unaffected by the transformations mentioned above.

There is also a third reason that makes today a retrospective assessment of representation worthwhile. At the same moment when representative democracy is celebrating its triumphs in a unified Europe (and elsewhere), the spreading of feelings of dissatisfaction and distrust vis-à-vis the representative institutions, and the men and women embodying them, has become a crucial theme of political and academic debate (Norris 1999a, 1999b; Pharr and Putnam 2000). It is not a case also that the discussion about alternative or complementary models of democracy, which go beyond the principle of representation, has become over the last years more intense (Cain, Dalton, and Scarrow 2003). To what extent the new models of democracy (direct or participatory democracy, deliberative democracy, and advocacy democracy) will pose in the future a fundamental challenge to representative democracy is today difficult to forecast. It is rather obvious, however, that some manifestations of the new models already coexist with the old one (Dalton, Cain, and Scarrow 2003; Warren 2003). A fuller understanding of the itinerary of representative democracy and of the stage of development it has reached, by projecting a better light on its potential and limitations, can contribute to the debate on the present and future configurations of democracy.

This book, however, does not pretend to offer a comprehensive comparative and developmental appraisal of 150 years of representation in Europe. Its more limited purpose is to cover in a systematic way one aspect of representation: the production of parliamentary representatives. It is obviously only a partial perspective, but a strategic one if we follow Schumpeter's account of contemporary democracy as 'that institutional arrangement for arriving at political decisions in which individuals acquire the power to decide by means of a competitive struggle for the people's vote' and 'the deciding of issues by the electorate is secondary to the election of the men who are to do the deciding' (Schumpeter 1954: 259, 269).

1.2. RESEARCH BASES

The empirical base for the research leading to this book is the DATACUBE, the largest collection, assembled so far, of data concerning the characteristics of national legislators in European countries.[3] In our study, we have focused on three main sets of attributes: those that indicate legislators' positions in the framework of hierarchically and functionally differentiated societies (such as social status, occupation, education, and gender), those that are more specifically and directly related to the range of positions offered by the political system (such as involvement in party offices, elective positions at local and regional levels, and government offices), and those that refer to their parliamentary career, such as their age at entry into parliament and the number of elections for which they had stood successfully.

These features of legislators can be viewed as traces of complex and multilayered recruitment processes, involving selectorates, electorates, and contenders with their respective norms, values, and interests, and taking place within changing settings of opportunities. At the same time, characteristics of legislators both as individuals and as parts of collective groups (such as parties) may be considered as important components of the input for parliamentary decision-making, indicating (although for the most part indirectly) legislators' political ambitions, strategies, and resources.

Our study extends the established ways of social and political background research on political elites, by pursuing comprehensive diachronic and cross-national comparisons, providing, for the first time, continuous time series extending from the nineteenth century to the present day, and a set of identical or at least equivalent indicators covering a wide range of European polities.

This leads to the database that forms the common denominator of our project and which provides the empirical basis for the detailed analyses conducted in the chapters of this book. We designed our research as a comparison of *aggregate* data related to the political and social backgrounds of European legislators. Starting from national data collections at an individual level, our database has been constructed as a three dimensional data-matrix, whereby the sides of this DATACUBE are formed by time, countries, and variables (Best and Cotta 2000, fig. 1.2). Its basic entries are percentages and means for all the members of the parliament of a country for a given legislative term. These data can then also be broken down into the main party families. A typical entry into the DATACUBE would be the mean age of Danish Members of Parliament (MPs) elected in 1920, or the percentage of female members of the Social Democratic Party in the German Reichstag of 1928. Comparisons can thus be carried out in a nation by nation, party by party, or party by nation mode. Presently the DATACUBE consists of 48 indicators for 12 European countries and covers a maximum time span of approximately 150 years, from the commencement of European parliamentary democracy in 1848 to the present days. While the entries for France, Denmark, Great Britain, Italy, Germany, the Netherlands, Norway, Hungary, and Finland are, to all extent and purpose, complete, for some countries participating in the project (Belgium, Portugal, and Spain) it has not yet been possible to produce fully comprehensive time series for those periods in their history when they enjoyed competitive elections at a national level. At this stage, the integrated data collection covers only western European countries, with the exception of Hungary which has been inserted with the purpose of introducing some elements of comparison with the countries that had been part for forty years of the Soviet block. In the future, however, also other countries of Central and Eastern Europe will be included in the data-set making it possible to conduct a systematic comparison of the different areas of Europe.

As it happens when one attempts to cover such a long period for such a big number of countries, the data-set is necessarily characterized by some degree of '*géometrie variable*'. The starting point of the process was not the same for all the countries and not all the countries were characterized by a continuous development of parliamentary representation. For longer or shorter periods, representative democracy was overcome by authoritarian and totalitarian regimes and, by 1940, had disappeared in most of the continental European countries covered by our study. It took until 1949 before a first group of these countries managed a successful comeback into the family of European representative democracies, the mid-seventies for a second group, and the nineties for Hungary (and the other countries of Central Europe). Technically, the non-simultaneous start of time series and the democratic interruptions will mean that when aggregate measures for European parliaments (like the arithmetic mean or the standard deviation) will be used in some of the analyses they will be often based on different groups of countries. In interpreting aggregate time series, we need to keep the effects of changes in the composition of the relevant country groups in mind.

In the first book, based on this empirical data-set (Best and Cotta 2000), we had documented for each country the transformations of the parliamentary elites and analysed domestic variations across party groups. This work had enabled us to scrutinize in details country peculiarities in the developmental paths of electoral representation, and more precisely to delineate the specificity of conditions at the starting of the process, to identify the main phases of the long-term transformation, and to assess the tempo of change. Moreover, the country-based chapters had attempted to develop some first hypotheses on the factors which could have affected these transformations. However, the country-based design of the book, which had been required for conducting the first detailed exploration of such a large quantity of data, had not enabled a more systematic comparison of the transformations of representation across countries and a more serious testing of explanatory hypotheses. In the conclusions, a summary of results of the country studies and a first sketch of a comprehensive model of the transformations of parliamentary representatives across countries and across time was included (Cotta and Best 2000). The present book which is based on a systematic cross country comparison of trends of change is therefore the natural follow up of the first.

1.3. THEORETICAL PERSPECTIVES

As we have said, this book proposes to move one step ahead in the analysis of the great transformation of political representation, taking place during the last 150 years, through a systematic comparison of the changing profiles of parliamentarians across a large proportion of the European states. The European space provides a particularly favourable ground for a systematic comparative effort (Lijphart 1971; Sartori and Morlino 1991). It offers a number of cases that is adequate for this type of research; on all these cases there is a substantial amount of sophisticated background knowledge that can complement our data; and finally the differences among the cases are balanced by the existence of important similarities. We have therefore the opportunity not only to conduct an in-depth comparative description, but also to attempt an explanatory analysis of the transformation of representation in Europe, of its cross-temporal and cross-country variations.

Given the position of political representation at the crossroads between society and politics, we have started from two main theoretical perspectives and traditions which can provide inspiration for our research efforts. The first is modernization theory, the second is democratization theory. We will briefly recall their main contents and their relevance for our theme.

1.3.1. *Modernization Theory and Its Expectations*

The long-term transformations of representation and, in particular, the democratization and professionalization of political representatives can be easily related to the wider conceptual framework of modernization theory which has been routinely used as a basis for explorations into the change of European societies and polities since the eighteenth century and which still provides the theoretical framework of current debates on democratic change (Dalton and Wattenberg 2003). Although modernization theory has been never developed into a fully codified set of testable hypotheses, it can be used as a starting point for a deductive argument from which further propositions can be derived. Empirical evidence can be then confronted with what is to be expected according to the benchmarks set by the theoretical model.

In a very broad sense, modernization can be understood to be a profound transformation of societies and polities that involves their different levels and functional areas. It is expected to be a configuration of progressive, irreversible, and global processes in which less developed societies acquire the characteristics of more developed ones. Within a given society less advanced sectors should catch up with the development of more progressive ones (Huntington 1968). If we have a set of time series that are supposed to depict modernization, their trace lines should be linear, progressive, and unidirectional. Regression, stagnation, divergence, and cycles should not occur, at least not as persistent and enduring patterns. Partial modernization, which leaves important areas of societies untouched and produces an incoherent structure of progress and stagnation, is considered to be a source of societal tension and conflict. These are strong assumptions and it remains to be shown to what extent our data have conformed to such a model. However, before we can enter into a synoptic inspection of the data it has to be clarified what modernization actually means with regard to parliamentary recruitment, and which indicators can therefore offer themselves as measures.

Some propositions can be drawn from the concept of 'political development' that was introduced as a focused adaptation of modernization theory to the sphere of politics in the late 1960s. It was Samuel Huntington (1968), in particular, who amalgamated some pivotal elements of established political theory and turned them into a comprehensive developmental concept, which postulates the nature and direction of institutional and attitudinal change in the order of political life. According to Huntington, a central feature of political modernization is the replacement of rural and agrarian elites, often from aristocratic backgrounds, by a political elite recruited from the urban middle classes. Thus, the centre of gravity of the power structure shifts from rural to urban elites and to middle-class standards and values. This process is complemented by an extension of participation—namely by a transfer of suffrage and eligibility to formerly disenfranchised categories of the population: the abolition of property requirements and gender barriers furthers the democratization of society. A third feature of political modernization is the differentiation of structures that can be associated with the establishment of a centralized and functionally differentiated power structure. The development of the modern state, the separation of powers, and the emergence of the professional politician can be subsumed under this heading. Finally, Huntington includes the rationalization of authority in the dimensions of political modernization. *Inter alia*, this refers to the replacement of the 'divine right' by more secular principles for the legitimization of authority. The shift from ascriptive to achievement-based criteria for elite recruitment and subsequent access to power can also be included here.

Such developments change the basis of the power structure of polities and societies and, therefore, should be particularly well reflected at the level of political elites. Thus, the declining significance of a prestigious family background as a criterion for political recruitment, the emergence of specialized political roles (such as the professional politician), the shifting presence of interest groups in representative bodies, and the opening of political careers for previously disadvantaged categories of the population (such as workers or women) are directly connected to these four lines of political development and can be taken as indictors of political modernization.

The main agent and the decisive context of political development is the nation state within whose perimeters the creation and redistribution of wealth, the acquisition and attribution of power, the definition and assertion of collective identities, the institutionalization of norms in legal systems, the formation of large bureaucratic structures, the aggregation of interests, and the emergence of platforms for collective political action (e.g. parties) are all performed. If political development is path-dependent, it was the nation state which paved and maintained the way. This is a claim which can be extended to legislative recruitment and its outcomes, since the formal structure of opportunities for access to offices, such as electoral laws and eligibility rules, the supply of and the demand for contenders, the composition and the mode of operation of selectorates (such as caucuses or parties) were all defined by the national boundaries of polities and societies, although the actual act of recruitment might have taken place on a local or regional level. No wonder, therefore, that political elites have been expected to represent the national distinctiveness of polities and societies.

The question is, of course, was (and is) this assumption true? Could (and can) a particular polity be identified by scrutinizing the makeup of its political elite? The concept of globalization has led to the claim that national boundaries are losing their significance and that the (relative) integrity and self-sufficiency of national states and societies, as well as their capacity to set and apply the rules of the game, is fading. If the process of *modernization* has followed distinctive national paths, *globalization* has changed this situation and subjects societies and polities to the growing impact of transnational interdependencies. Empirically we should be able to recognize the effects of globalization by a decreasing degree of national distinctiveness and an increasing amount of transnational exchange. Although, in the sphere of politics, the competition for representative offices is tied to national citizenship and, since citizenship is still mainly granted to nationals, is institutionally anchored to distinctiveness, it is, however, far from closed to external inputs. It is sufficient to mention the broad transnational diffusion of political ideas and models and the international links among parties of the same family. The current territorial range of our database—twelve countries which are, with the exception of Norway, all member states of the EU—must necessarily restrict the scope of our findings. However, this limitation also has advantages, since a decrease in distinctiveness should be seen most clearly in a cluster of countries which are already unified economically, and which share common values and institutions. If globalization has an impact, European integration should have anticipated it.

1.3.2. *Democratization Theory: The State of the Art*

The second main theoretical perspective to which we refer in our work is democratization theory. To a large extent, it would be right to say that, in the early stages of comparative political science, democratization theory was the product of the broader theory of modernization and had been conceived as a specification of the former with regard to one sector of society: the building of democracy was to be conceived as *the* political face of modernity. In this perspective, democracy has often been assumed to be a linear and inevitable process and its explanation has tended to fall under the spell of economic reductionism: democratization would be essentially an effect, a dependent variable of economic modernization (industrialization, urbanization, etc.) (Lipset 1958; Vanhanen 1997). It is true, however, that other versions of modernization theory have stressed also more political aspects (models of authority, development of institutions, etc.) (Huntington 1968). It is not the place here to open a long discussion on this point; it is sufficient, however, to mention that at a closer look the correspondence between modernity and democracy is far from being unambiguous. It is possible to contend on the one hand that contemporary representative democracy counts among its sources significant elements of pre-modern politics. Parliamentary representation is indeed a crucial case in point: it is not unwarranted to consider it a 'medieval' solution that, after having been displaced by the *modern* absolutist and bureaucratic state, was revived (and transformed!) precisely in opposition to these developments.[4] On the other hand, the totalitarianisms of the twentieth century, which have been the most dangerous challenge for democracies, were very much part of modernity. For these and also for other reasons, the empirical theory of democratization has in general moved away from too broad and linear theories of society (such as modernization theory). The role of chance, choice, and discontinuity has been recognized at the expense of determinism (Almond, Flanagan, and Mundt 1973). And the attention has concentrated on the search of more specific political factors for explaining successes, failures, and variations in the process leading to the building of democracy.

What is the state of the art of democratization theory and which points are more relevant for our perspective? If we expect from a theory of democratization that it provides a general and comprehensive set of explanatory instruments for understanding how the process was set in motion, through which stages it developed and reached its culmination, why the process in some cases did not start or was delayed and why variations occurred across countries in the sequence and timing of stages and in a number of specifications of the institutional model, why failures and interruptions happened, then the answer is that we do not have yet anything of the sort. We have at best some important pieces of such a scheme. Serious efforts have indeed been made for specifying and describing the different components of the democratization process, their possible combinations, their variable sequences (Dahl 1970; Rokkan 1970a, 1970b). Very substantial progresses have been made also in shaping the conceptual tools for evaluating the different stages in the developmental process of democratization (Rokkan 1970a, 1970b), varieties of democratic institutions (Lijphart 1999), or the evolution of the crucial actors of democracy-parties (from Max Weber and Michels to Katz and Mair 1995). With regard to explanations, more than a general and comprehensive theory, we have middle-range theories that are geographically and temporally defined, or that cover partial sectors of the democratic process. Understandably, the most developed field of middle-range theories concerns the more recent transformations within stabilized democracies, as for instance those explaining changes in electoral mobilization (Inglehart 1977, 1984; Dalton, Flanagan, and Beck 1984; Norris 1999a, 1999b; Dalton, Cain, and Scarrow 2003; but also in a more long-term perspective Bartolini and Mair 1990; Bartolini 2000a, 2000b) or transformation of parties (Dalton and Wattenberg 2000). To these, we should add the attempts to specify (but essentially with regards to Europe and the US) favourable and unfavourable conditions for the crisis of the *ancien régime* and the setting in motion of the process of democratization (Bendix 1964; Moore 1966; Rustow 1970)[5]; to explain sequences and timings of the crossing of thresholds in this process (Rokkan 1970a, 1970b); to explain breakdowns of democracy (in Europe and Latin America) in the conditions of the twentieth century (Linz and Stepan 1978). Probably the widest extension in terms of the cases taken into consideration and of the geographical spread of them is to be found in the theoretical debate on the explanation of re-democratization and democratic consolidation after authoritarian and totalitarian regimes (O'Donnell, Schmitter, and Whitehead 1986; Linz and Stepan 1996; Morlino 1998). Within this debate a particularly important attention has been assigned to the role of political elites.

An interesting attempt in the direction of a more general theory of democratization is the one pursued by Field, Higley, and their associates using the elite perspective and the concepts of elite unity/division as the crucial tools for understanding consolidation or lack of consolidation of democracy (Field and Higley 1980; Higley and Gunther eds., 1992). With all its heuristic potential, even this important contribution has not yet produced a fully articulated theory capable of answering satisfactorily to all or most of the points mentioned above.

In short, more than a systematic theory of democratization (or a set of contending theories), what we have is something that could be described as a construction site, where there are some plans of the building, many still disjointed pieces but also a number of important blocks of a future construction which are already assembled. The building, however, is not yet in place. We cannot therefore draw a well-defined and coherently connected set of hypotheses to be tested but rather a number of interpretative keys and guidelines. The following points seem particularly significant for a long-term comparative exploration of representation:

1. the need to distinguish among different dimensions of the process of democratization (the development, legitimation, and consolidation of the institutions and procedures of limited and responsible authority on one side; the mobilization of a mass citizenship and its incorporation in an ordered system of representation on the other side); these dimensions, although linked by important connections, have some degree of reciprocal autonomy which explains why their developments are not always synchronized.
2. the possibility of specifying within these dimensions of democratization a series of discrete steps along the process leading to the full expansion of their democratic potential, and to identify a variety of possible combinations in the sequences of these steps;
3. the potential non-linearity of the paths leading to democracy due to the possibility of resistances, crises, and breakdowns;
4. the significance of variations in the tempo of the processes of democratization and thus the possibility of very substantial leads and lags between developmental stages in different countries; and
5. the acknowledgement of the fact that (successful) democratization has to do with the pressure of unsatisfied demands, challenges of new social strata, and new political movements and parties, but also with the ability of political elites to consolidate themselves and to provide continuity in the functioning of central institutions of democracy, to smooth and co-opt revolutionary challengers; that certain steps forward of democratization from below may disrupt a previously acquired equilibrium in the institutional dimension of democracy and, if not properly, channelled and harnessed may even produce democratic breakdowns.

The analysis of the long-term itineraries of transformation of the profile of parliamentary elites can well incorporate these indications and provide, on its side, important elements for shedding light upon the processes of democratization. The position of elected representatives at the crossing point between democracy from below (the inclusion and mobilization dimensions) and democracy from above (the dimension of the construction and consolidation of the institutions and procedures of limited and responsible power) offers undoubtedly a strategic point of view for an observation of the variability in these processes. The profile of parliamentarians must be expected to reflect on one side the progressive opening of the political system to increasingly wider strata of society and their mobilization in defence of interests and identities, on the other side the transformation of the institutions of central government. At the same time, their profile cannot be considered only a reflection of these processes but also as a factor shaping the way representation of society takes place, and affecting the functioning of the central institutions of democracy.

The study of representatives seems also a particularly apt field for reflecting on the delicate balance between continuity and change in the process of democratization. If democratization presupposes an openness of the political system to innovation (coming from society or from within the political sphere itself), consolidation of democracy requires also a degree of continuity that enables the build up of reciprocal trust among actors, transmission of rules, socialization in institutional roles, etc. The recruitment of parliamentarians with new profiles may be seen as a response to and also an instrument of innovation; at the same time some crystallization of the new recruitment patterns and the stabilization of elites become critical factors of continuity.

1.4. PREVIOUS FINDINGS: VARIATIONS AND COMMON TRENDS IN THE LONG-TERM CHANGE OF EUROPEAN PARLIAMENTARY RECRUITMENT AND CAREERS

The results of our long-term study into European legislative recruitment have shown so far that trends in our data can hardly be fitted into a linear conception of political development (Cotta and Best 2000). Even if we apply the most general notion of this concept which asserts that the broad direction of this development 'must be that of an opening of political societies' (Blondel 1997: 96) and an 'expansion of choice opportunities' (Apter 1965: 6), we see at least a contradictory picture. In some areas, recruitment patterns developed in a linear way, while in other areas resisted the pressure of general social change for decades, followed a cyclical course or diverged, while there was no diffusion of modernity. Just to mention some cases, Britain and France, the two 'model polities' for parliamentary democracy in Europe, maintained distinctly traditional features in their parliamentary recruitment patterns over extended periods (Best and Gaxie 2000; Cromwell and Rush 2000). On the other hand, the Weimar Republic displayed the most 'modern' parliamentary representation of the time, dominated by political professionals and closely tied to powerful party organizations (Best, Hausmann, and Schmitt 2000). However, if this was modernity, it was by no means a contribution to the stability of German democracy because it ushered in its breakdown of 1933. Seen in comparison, one might even speculate whether structural conservatism in parliamentary recruitment is directly (and positively!) linked to stability of parliamentary democracies (and thus to institutional modernity).

Although it is not appropriate to describe the long-term change of European legislative recruitment patterns as one coherent, homogeneous, synchronic, and progressive process of 'modernization', we have seen also some developmental patterns which were unidirectional. The fact is that developments followed paths which were directed both by democratization, that is the extension of the social niches from whence the electors and the elected were drawn, and by professionalization, that is the establishment of a fairly autonomous field of political action with specific (although mostly informal) rules for access and reward. These two trends are at least in part contradictory, since democratization is socially inclusive, while professionalization is exclusive, in that it creates a division between spheres of insiders and outsiders. While European parliaments have for long ceased to be exclusive clubs for the wealthy and high born, while women increasingly find their ways into the assembly halls, we have seen other barriers rise, replacing those of class and gender (Best and Cotta 2000; Best 2003). These new barriers and filters are no longer translating status hierarchies and value systems which prevail in societies at large into modes of recruitment, but they are now located within the narrower realm of political systems. The gradual exclusion from the ranks of MPs of those who have only a background in productive or distributive economic activities (like entrepreneurs, managers, workers, and agriculturists), the corresponding increase (for some time) of officials of pressure group organizations and parties and even more of public servants, the growing cumulation (sequential and simultaneous) of local and regional offices, and the increasing embeddedness of contenders into the ranks of party hierarchies point into this direction. The abolition of formal barriers of access to European parliaments was thus complemented by the establishment of an informal insider–outsider differential, firmly guarded and perpetuated by selectorates and party organizations. Today, those who are available (in terms of their time budget and the security of their jobs) for elective public offices, whose qualifications and skills are useful for a political career (preferably certificated by an academic degree of some kind) and who are willing and able to implant themselves in local or party offices, stand a preference chance to penetrate the filters and overcome the barriers on their way to a parliamentary seat.

The establishment of an insider–outsider differential combined with an (informal) careerization of access to parliamentary recruitment forms the basis of political professionalization. However, the political profession resulting from this process still bears some unusual traits: the taking over of a fully paid elective office and the transformation into a full-time politician takes place at an average age between 40 and 45, normally preceded by a professional career in non-political occupations. As a rule, the political professional has started and for a long time pursued his or her career as a political amateur. This career pattern, in addition to the before-mentioned entry criteria, favours clearly contenders from the public service, which has become the modal professional category in European parliaments after the Second World War, superseding the self-employed, those in distributive or productive economic functions, and even competing successfully with party and pressure group functionaries.

The re-rise of the public service (after its early heydays in the nineteenth century and its decline between the World Wars) as the preferred supplier of European representatives can be associated with the emergence of the cartel party which relies 'increasingly for [its] resources on the subventions and other benefits and privileges afforded by the state' (Katz and Mair 1995: 19f.). With the goals of politics becoming more self-referential and politics becoming a profession in itself, representatives with a background in the public service incarnate the fusion between party and state: while their public employer sponsored them when they were amateur or half-amateur politicians through generous exemptions, he offers a safe haven when their political career gets into trouble. On the other hand, their background and actual interest disposes them to act as 'agents of the state' in their representational role (Katz and Mair 1995: 18). Contenders from other professional backgrounds do not enjoy the same privileges and have to face a disproportionately unfavourable risk–benefit relationship when they pursue their political careers. Full-time party functionaries who might offer an alternative to public servants with regard to the compatibility between public office and 'private' occupation are a costly option for their employers and are probably harder to 'sell' to the voters as suitable representatives than state officials who can still capitalize on the (somewhat faded) aura of impartiality and competence attributed to the public service. However, the rise of the public service to become the main societal sector for parliamentary recruitment does not only reflect the cost-benefit calculations of selectorates and contenders, but can also be linked to the main challenge Western European polities faced in the bipolar world after the Second World War: the establishment of consensually unified polities and societies as a condition for the containment of social conflicts and the threat of communism. The mediation of conflicts and the integration of societies was the order of the day, corporate interest mediation and particularly the extension of welfare state benefits were the most important consensus creating politics. The 'consensus challenge' found a response in parliamentary recruitment: redistribution specialists, who are predominantly found in the public sector, prevail since this time.

A challenge-response model can in fact be seen as a fruitful springboard for interpreting the long-term transformation of European legislative recruitment. Rather than a linear development, following the transformation of social structure in general, we see a pattern of change in parliamentary leadership groups which reflects the sequence of main challenges for polities and societies since (Western) Europe entered the era of democratization and industrialization. Thus, the first period of public service dominance in many national parliaments during the nineteenth century coincides with the era of state and nation-building. During this period, specialists in the application of executive power, which were to be found in the higher ranks of the public sector, had a dominant role. The second challenge had to be taken up in the period of accelerated economic change when most European societies faced the full impact of industrialization. In this period, specialists in the creation and appropriation of wealth, such as entrepreneurs and landowners, or their delegates (lawyers and free professionals) prevailed in parliament. The third challenge was the incorporation of the new enfranchised masses into democracy through the accumulation of ideological and organizational power outside the state apparatus (as in parties and pressure groups). This period saw the rise of specialists in mass mobilization and in the running of intermediary organizations. Again we can establish here a link to Katz and Mair's typology of parties, with the 'Elite party' providing a political arena for high-ranking state officials and the economic elites (like entrepreneurs and large landowners), the 'Mass party' providing the career opportunities for party and pressure group officials of the Michelsian type, and the 'catch-all party', forming the seedbed for the 'redistribution specialists' from public service stock, who finally take over in the 'Cartel party'. The convergence of legislative recruitment and career patterns across (Western) Europe after the Second World War can therefore be attributed to a growing synchronization of developments in party systems and of the main policy alternatives faced by European polities, while the impacts of changes in the formal structures of opportunities (like electoral laws and eligibility rules) or societal transformations at large have lost momentum.

Within these broad trends, the more detailed coverage of the country-specific developments conducted in the previous book had shown the importance of national variations. This volume attempts a more precise comparative mapping and interpretation of national variations and common European trends.

1.5. MAPPING DIFFERENCES AND SIMILARITIES: RESEARCH QUESTIONS AND GUIDELINES FOR THIS BOOK

As we have said before, studying parliamentary representatives and their profile is a partial but strategic approach to the understanding of representation, how it varies across countries, and how it has changed over time. But what aspects of the profile of a representative are relevant for the understanding of representation and why or (to put it in another way) what is the relationship between the identity of the representatives (in its many components) and representation?

In order to define who a representative is, three different sets of attributes have been considered in this book as particularly relevant: the attributes that indicate his or her relationship with the object of representation (i.e. society in its many possible meanings and specifications); those that show his or her control of the skills and resources that are useful for winning a role of representative and for a successful performance of the function of representation; and those which specify the relationship of the representative with other representatives (i.e. the belonging to a collective group as a party) and with the institution of representation. Information about social status (such as being part or not of the nobility), type of occupation before entering parliament, links to a broad economic sector, religious affiliation, and gender of the representatives is particularly relevant for the first set of attributes, as it offers indications of personal linkages with different structural dimensions of society and might consequently be assumed to indicate the sharing of the same interests, views, and identities. Education also, to the extent that it is to be considered a privilege dependent on the stratification of society (as it often was and to a lesser extent still is) can add further elements of information along these lines.

With regard to the second dimension, that of skills and resources for the competitive game, some of the same variables concerning social background, but in particular age, education and certain types of occupational background, can be interpreted as indicating the control of resources of prestige, social connections and the possession of special skills that are valuable for being selected as a representative and to prevail over competitors. In this perspective, variables concerning social background would not be interpreted as, necessarily, indicating the sharing of the same interests with the corresponding sections of the population. They rather suggest the role of social background as a stepping stone for building a career as representative (an example would be a representative who exploits his upper class or nobility status not so much to represent the interests of his class, but to establish himself thanks to his social prestige as representative of much broader strata of society). A further group of variables relevant for this dimension refers to the resources and skills that have been gained in the sphere of political life rather than within society: offices in local government, in party organizations, governmental positions, positions in other parliamentary-like assemblies provide a measure of the importance of political experience and of an articulated career through different types of political offices for being selected first as a candidate and then to be elected as a representative.

As for the third dimension, which has to do with the relationship of a representative with the other representatives and with the parliamentary institution, that is with the collective dimension of representation, the variables pertaining to the party affiliation and to the parliamentary career of representatives are especially relevant. Other variables not related to the individual representatives but to the collective organizations they belong to and providing information about their cohesiveness, will also be relevant.

When interpreting the meaning of the profiles of representatives, we should be aware that the relationship between the attributes of representatives and their performance of a representative role is not absolutely fixed. It may indeed change with the prevailing models of representation (which in turn may change with time, space, and conditions of political life). Similarity of social background and personal characteristics constitutes the basis for an important and traditional model of representation: *representation by peers*. This model plays indeed a very powerful role under specific social and political circumstances: it is especially important when only a limited (and privileged) part of society has access to representation (the upper classes will obviously require to be represented by their peers: who could share better their interests and values?), or when a group which perceives its position in society as oppressed or endangered defines itself essentially on the basis of certain aspects of its identity (language, religion, and gender) (if Catalan speakers, Catholics, women, etc., feel like a threatened minority or an oppressed majority, they will want to be represented by Catalan speakers, Catholics, women, etc.). Together with its obvious strengths, this model has also some important weaknesses. These have to do mainly with the problem of resources and skills. Peers may not always be the best qualified ones to represent effectively the interests of a group: similarity is indeed a rather simplistic and unsophisticated instrument of representation. The recourse to representatives that are qualified not so much for their similarity but for the resources and skills they control may become a preferable option, or even a necessity, when representation becomes a more complicated game. When, with the extension of suffrage, the larger middle and lower classes enter for the first time into the representation game their peers are simply not enough qualified in terms of the skills and resources the game requires. For representation to be effective, a more qualified personnel seems necessary. Representation becomes then a more indirect game; it increasingly requires specific structures and dedicated personnel to make it work. In such a situation, the law of increasing distance between represented and representatives begins to apply (Putnam 1976). Similarity gives way to professionalization; the qualities of the representatives are defined more by the requirements of the political profession of representation and by competition among professionals than by the need of exhibiting a direct linkage with the represented. *Representation by professional agents* takes the place of representation by peers. In this context, there is a progressive substitution of societal characters with political characters as the crucial elements of the profile of representatives. The extreme case is reached when the 'pure politician' comes to dominate representation: at this point social background and other social characteristics have become almost completely irrelevant and political career and positions are the only significant elements. This type of representative, which shows enhanced abilities to navigate the institutional complexities of contemporary democracy, is, however, susceptible to a new type of criticism: his distance from society, the collusion among fellow politicians in defending their own specific interests at the expenses of those of the 'common citizens' may fall under attack. The voters may come to reject them as too distant, too separate: when this characterization starts spreading, there is obviously a problem for representatives who by definition must create a link between society and politics. The cycle of professionalization of political life which has unfolded during the past century might be approaching if not to a full reversal, perhaps to a levelling of its progression. The demand for members of 'civil society' as representatives increases again.

In order to analyse the changing realities of electoral representation, the following points and questions will be addressed in the book through a systematic exploration of the variables of our data-set across countries and across time:

1. *How much change overall?* The process that has lead from non-representative regimes to the first steps in representation and, finally, to the consolidation of a fully developed system of democratic representation in Europe, has been long and far from linear. The distance covered from the conditions existing

at the beginning of the process to those at the end is indeed impressive. The actors involved, the institutions, the modes and style of political life, the issues at stake have undergone an enormous change. From the politics of early parliamentarism, when the newly created representative institutions were in most of the cases still uncertain of their role vis-à-vis a well-established monarchical authority and developed state bureaucracies fully conscious of their strengths, and had to mount a difficult fight to establish their role at the centre of the political system, and when citizenship was *de iure* or at least de facto restricted to small sections of a society still largely dominated by pre-modern conditions, to the age of full-fledged party government and universal conditions of citizenship, where monarchical authority has disappeared from the scene (or at best has been preserved as a politically neutralized symbol of national unity) and the state apparatuses have been deeply reshaped by democratic demands and often penetrated by partisan inputs, in the context of a fully industrialized society, to the first steps of what might be called post-modern politics (with much weaker parties, strong role of the new mass media, personal leadership, etc.) and within the framework of a post-industrial society, the representative function has necessarily undergone very deep transformations under the challenges coming both form the demand and the supply side of its equation.

The study of this long-term transformation of representation has been conducted from many different perspectives: studies of electoral behaviour, of political parties and party systems, of legislative behaviour and of policymaking have offered important insights for its understanding. Yet a crucial view into it must obviously be offered by an analysis of those who are the products of the representative process and who carry every day directly on their shoulders the function of representation. How much they have changed over time, with regard to the main dimensions that define the profile of the parliamentary representatives, is therefore the first question to which this book tries to answer.

2. *Which paths and stages of change?* Taking for granted that over the long term the amount of change in the features of the parliamentary class has been deep, we propose to specify better how the process of change has taken place. We attempt therefore not only to gauge the global distance covered between the starting point and the end result, but also to describe and evaluate the paths followed to reach the final result.

General studies of democratization have shown that the paths through which a fully developed democratic system has been reached were significantly diversified. At some point in time during the twentieth century, it even seemed that such paths would lead to highly divergent results: democratic regimes in some cases but stable undemocratic regimes in other ones. Only during the last decades of the past century it has become clear that, in Europe at least, non-democratic regimes were to be considered only a temporary interruption (albeit a very long lasting one in some cases) in a difficult process of democratization rather than a permanent alternative to representative democracy, and that their strengths were counterbalanced by very serious weaknesses (while, on the contrary, the so often exposed weaknesses of democracies were balanced by some less visible strengths). Even leaving aside such dramatic variations between cases of continuous and cases of discontinuous democratization, other significant differences among processes of democratization are easy to detect. As suggested by Dahl with his distinction of the processes of liberalization and inclusion (1970) and Rokkan with his thresholds of democratization (1970a, 1970b), the definition and consolidation of the principles and institutions of political competition and the expansion of citizenship, which are the two crucial dimensions of modern liberal democratic regimes, have developed with variable speeds and sequences. And the same can be said for two other important aspects: the consolidation of parliamentary control over the executive and the diffusion of Proportional Representation (PR) in electoral systems (Rokkan 1970a, 1970b). On another level, we might mention the timing of the building of strong party organizations and of the freezing of party systems as yet another dimension of differentiation across European countries. All these elements concur to a very substantial diversification of developmental paths of democracies (and to an extent also to persisting differences across countries).

With this general background in mind, how can we describe the changes in the profile of MPs? Was it incremental and linear or on the contrary discontinuous, irregular, and non-linear? Was the global change the result of limited and incremental transformations moving in the same direction or, on the contrary, characterized by periods of stability followed by abrupt changes, or perhaps reversal of trends? Is it possible to identify, through an internal analysis of the variables available to us, distinctive stages in this transformation process? And in general, how countries compare on these dimensions?

The mapping of these developmental paths and the comparison of them across countries is a prerequisite for an analysis of the relationships between the transformations of representation and the other dimensions of democratization mentioned above, both in a configurative perspective (assessing how changes in different aspects of the process of democratization cluster together over time) and in an explanatory one (determining what is the impact of the different aspects upon each other). The following ones are some of the relevant questions waiting for an answer. Which degree of correspondence can we establish between the process of suffrage extension (its gradual or abrupt enlargement, its early or late timing) and the changing social background or political careers (and resources produced through them) of MPs? Or between the increasing control gained by parliament over ministerial recruitment and the professionalization of representatives? What relationship between the political mobilization of certain social groups and the decline of some characters of MPs or the rise of other ones? Between interruptions of democratic continuity (through democratic breakdowns and then re-democratizations) and changing social profiles of parliamentarians?

A crucial aspect to be analysed in this context is that of the lags occurring between elite level change and other transformations under way in the political system. The existence of these lags is a crucial sign of the relatively autonomous dynamics of the processes of production and reproduction of representative elites and of their ability to filter and delay challenges coming from other sectors of the political and social system.

3. *How convergent or divergent are the developmental trends?* The end result of the long-term process of political transformation in Europe is a fundamentally common type of political regime—representative democracy of a parliamentary type.[6] The many different national clocks of political life in Europe seem thus to have reached at the turn of the millennia a high level of synchronization. Undoubtedly, they appear better synchronized now than they were forty years ago when at least a third of the same European states were under non-democratic regimes of one type or another, or sixty years ago when an even larger proportion was in the same situation. We might continue this exercise retrospectively and we could perhaps find that differences were on the contrary smaller at earlier stages among the existing units. During the last decades of the nineteenth century political differences between Italy, Germany, and Spain on one side, and Belgium, Denmark, the Netherlands, the UK, France, etc. on the other side were surely less serious than in the thirties of the twentieth century. Even without a detailed discussion of this theme, it is sufficiently clear that the history of parliamentary democracy over the last 150 years does not fully correspond either to a process of convergence or to a process of divergence. We can rather say that phases of greater convergence were followed by other ones of divergence and vice versa. This was particularly due to the non-linear character of the developmental trend of a number of countries but also to the different speeds in democratizing.

The analysis of the profiles of MPs throughout this period can be used to check to what extent the institutional picture is paralleled also at the level of the representative elites: more concretely, to what extent differences across the whole range of the variables analysed in this volume show convergence or divergence. The analysis conducted on a country-by-country base in the previous volume had shown that the national profiles of representatives seemed to converge broadly towards a common model, that of the professional politician sharing a number of rather standardized features (a middle-class background that suggests the limited relevance of strong social identities, a rather high level of education, a long commitment to a political career, and the dependence from political offices as the basis for the accumulation of skills and resources) (Cotta and Best 2000: 523–4). In this book, we are able to assess much more precisely how far this convergence towards a common model has gone and which elements of difference persist within a basically common model. The same can be done with the other models of representation sketched for the preceding stages of development.

4. *Similarities within and variations across party families?* In contemporary democracies the processes and institutions of representation have nurtured the growth of parties as a crucial actor in this field of political life. Parties, in turn, have increasingly gained control over the process of representation and over representatives themselves (their selection and training and the direction of their actions) (Katz 1986). Parties have become the main channels through which different social groups with their specific interests, demands, identities have been mobilized (Bartolini 2000*a*, 2000*b*), and represented. We have therefore explored to what extent this has meant also different profiles of the representatives selected by each party. Since for purposes of comparability it has become common to regroup parties across Europe within a relatively limited number of party families (Rokkan 1970*a*, 1970*b*; von Beyme 1985; Gallagher, Laven and Mair 2001) on the basis of ideology, position on the left-right spectrum, linkage to cleavage lines, representation of specific interests and international links, we have explored how homogeneous, across countries, these party families are in the profile of their parliamentary representatives, and how significant are differences across families. More concretely the questions that have been addressed are the following: are representatives of Socialist parties (or Christian Democratic, Liberal parties, etc.) of different countries more similar among themselves than to those belonging to other party families of the same country? To what extent the distinctiveness of a party family was maintained or declined over time? Did the passing of time and the long-term integration in the parliamentary institution stimulate a process of homogenization across party families? And, in particular, did this take place with party families that were at first peripheral (or excluded) and have become later fully included in the parliamentary game (and in government coalitions)?

1.6. SEARCHING FOR EXPLANATIONS

The purpose of this book is not only to map carefully similarities and differences in the profile of parliamentary representatives across countries and changes across time (but also persistence over relatively long periods). It is also to explain these trends. All the points and questions mentioned in the previous paragraph have a fundamentally descriptive nature. Yet each of them obviously poses an explanatory problem. Why differences and why similarities in the global picture of representation in Europe and in its transformations over time? Why trends of different types? Why the persistence of the original patterns has varied across countries? Why the tempo of change has not been the same? Why the degree of homogeneity across party families differs?

The explanatory model of representation as a mirror image of a society, whereby the changing composition of society would be reflected in a similar changing composition of parliament (the decline of nobility in society would be followed by a similar decline in parliament, the rise of the working classes would be translated in a parallel rise, the granting of political rights to women would change the gender balance of the representative assemblies, etc.) is obviously too simplistic: it forgets of any autonomous role of politics. The data at our disposal do not confirm it or at best suggest that its scope is limited: the mirror image model of representation applies only to special situations. As society changes, the profile of the parliamentary elite changes too, but in general a clear parallelism between the two cannot be established.

Representation as the connecting mechanism between the sphere of society and that of politics requires a more elaborate explanatory model. The point is that democratic representation cannot be considered a simple and direct reflection of society, a photographic or statistical process, but is rather a highly complex political phenomenon involving the active role of political actors. It requires first of all that social change becomes politicized, that is to say that transformations of society produce interests and demands that are directed towards the political sphere. This, by the way, should not be taken for granted: societal interests and demands may to a significant extent be directed and find satisfaction elsewhere (for instance in the economic process or within the family or in other societal structures). The second requirement is that political entrepreneurs come forward to propose the electoral platforms and the candidates capable of representing the mobilized interests/identities. Representation can thus be interpreted very much as a demand/supply model, whereby both demand and supply functions require a specific understanding (Norris 1997*a*, 1997*b*; Best and Cotta 2000). The factors, that we must take into consideration for explaining the profile of parliamentary representatives, must be related therefore to the demand and the supply aspects of the model and to the mechanism through which equilibrium is established between the two. On the demand side, we will have first the transformations of society that provide the background factors for the development of new interests, identities, and values, but also and crucially the development and the behaviours of the political agents (leaders, movements, and parties) that are responsible for the politicization of the former. On the supply side, we will have to consider the dynamics of political competition and the transformations of the institutions of representation which will affect the production and selection of potential representatives for matching the demands from below.

1.7. THE PLAN OF THE BOOK, CHAPTERS, AND THEIR CONTENTS

Attempting to answer at least partially to the descriptive and explanatory questions set in the previous pages, with regards to transformations covering a fairly large number of cases over such a long period, has posed to the team of researchers involved in this effort very serious substantial and methodological challenges. Clarifying the meaning of the specific variables used to define the profile of parliamentarians; putting together a more comprehensive view on the basis of different elements; assessing the role and weight of a variety of explanatory factors has required to analyse our data from a variety of different viewpoints. The structure of the book reflects these competing preoccupations.

The first part of the book is devoted to an in-depth exploration of some of the main variables used to define the profile of MPs. The purpose of these chapters (2–7) is to specify the meaning of variables, analyse trends of change, and offer preliminary explanations of variations over time and across countries. As it happens in any large and chronologically 'stretched' comparative empirical research, interpreting the meaning of the data collected is rather obviously a major challenge: a close up on specific variables is an attempt to provide an answer to this problem. The variables chosen for this exploration are those that were thought to offer the most crucial points of view for understanding, through the different stages of the evolution of parliamentary representation, the relationships between representatives and society, and between them and democratic politics.

In the second chapter of the book, Michael Rush examines the role of the nobility, a variable which from the contemporary point of view seems the most marginal for elected parliaments, but in a longer time perspective is a crucial element for understanding the early steps of modern representation and its connections with the pre-modern tradition. The comparative analysis explores to what extent an aristocratic status, having been one of the strongest basis of political power under the *ancien régime*, could maintain in many countries an important role during the first stages of representative government. Its decline will lead in the end in all the countries to the irrelevance of this factor, but this process developed with fairly different speeds in the various countries. The next variable discussed—a background in the public sector—offers a window for exploring the relationship between democratic representation and the bureaucratic state, that is the overarching structure of contemporary polities. In Chapter 3, Maurizio Cotta and Pedro Tavares de Almeida discuss the meanings and implications of the significant weight of this variable in the profile of parliamentary representatives and analyse the peculiar temporal trend of this feature according to which its initial importance has at first progressively declined (yet without ever losing some significance) and then, in the last decades, has experienced a new substantial upturn. In Chapter 4, Verona Christmas and Ulrik Kjaer examine one of the most visible characters of parliamentarians: the fact that their gender has been predominantly male. If this was easy to explain when women were deprived of active and passive franchise, how is it that for many decades after they overcame this exclusion the gender ratio in most of the parliaments has remained dramatically unbalanced? Yet, not only this delay requires an explanation, but also why the gap between the two gender shows a more marked decrease in the last years in some countries than others. The temporal and spatial variations of this specific feature of representatives offer an interesting ground for testing different social and institutional explanations of representation and also for an exploration of its variable meanings. In Chapter 5, Daniel Gaxie and Laurent Godmer analyse the role of education among the resources that play a significant role for the career of parliamentarians, but also as one of the strategic element for the construction of the identity of elites. The two other chapters of Part I are devoted to the exploration of the central political aspects in the recruitment of parliamentarians. In Chapter 6, Ineke Secker and Stephan Fiers, focusing on the role of party as the main selector of representatives, analyse how a career within the party organization has become with time an increasingly dominant element in the formation of parliamentarians. In Chapter 7, Mogens Pedersen, Ulrik Kjaer, and Kjell Eliassen centring their attention on the persisting territorial dimension of representation assess the role of local attachments in the recruitment of parliamentarians.

In the second part, the book moves to more comprehensive analyses of the profiles of parliamentary representatives. To do this the next chapters (8–13) bring to the centre of the picture the crucial actors in the processes of political representation of contemporary democracies, that is parties. In view of their role in the representation of different interests, opinions and social identities and at the same time in the recruitment of representatives, these analyses start from the assumption that the profile of the parliamentarians will vary significantly according to the different party families they belong to. In these chapters, each devoted to one party family—with Valerie Cromwell and Luca Verzichelli studying the conservatives, Ilka Ruostetsaari the liberals and agrarians, Luca Verzichelli the Christian democrats, Gabriella Ilonszky the socialists and communists, Juan J. Linz, Carmen Ortega, and Miguel Jerez Mir the extreme right, and Filippo Tronconi and Luca Verzichelli the most recent streams of green, new left, and regionalist parties—the authors put this assumption to an empirical test by exploring, on the basis of a broad range of characteristics of the parliamentarians, to what extent each party family shows a relatively homogeneous parliamentary profile across countries or, on the contrary, cross-country differences make for internal diversity within the same family. The analysis is also extended to assess how the profile of one party family compares with that of the others (and in particular of the ideologically neighbouring ones). The purpose of this part of the book is not only descriptive and configurative—a dimension of research which is far from being irrelevant if we want to understand the meaning of parties in political life—but also explanatory. On the one hand, it contributes to establish to what extent party identities differ across party families, not only in terms of ideological and programmatic platforms, but also of representative linkages and organizational models, with the significant traces they have left in the features of parliamentarians, and in what measure these identities are transformed with time and with the changing position of parties in the competitive game. On the other hand, it offers some important instruments for explaining changes in the global outlook of parliamentary elites (and of representation), making it possible to ascertain to what extent these changes are linked to the rise and the decline of different party families.

The third part of the book attempts to provide a synthetic overview of the transformations of political representation, and of its relationship with societal and political changes. In Chapter 14, Heinrich Best discusses the relationship between societal cleavages and parliamentary representation and the intermediary role of parties. In Chapter 15, Maurizio Cotta and Luca Verzichelli analyse the complex relationship between the process of democratization and the transformations of representation. Variations across countries in the patterns of democratization—from the timing of the steps in the expansion of suffrage to that of the establishment of parliamentary control over the executive, to the rise of mass parties, to the continuity or discontinuity of the democratic regime—are tested as explanatory factors for the differences in the profiles of parliamentary representatives. In the conclusion after a brief summary of the main results the attention is directed on some of the paradoxes of the transformation of representative democracy.

ENDNOTES

1   There is no need to say that 1848 was not a common starting point for all the European countries but rather the critical juncture of the final crisis of the *ancien régime* and of the quest for a new regime.
2   With the word *politics*, we will designate here essentially the aspects of political life pertaining to the problems of power, its distribution and the institutions, processes and actors connected to it; with the term *polity*, the aspects pertaining with the political community and its creation, maintenance and transformation; with the word *policy*, the programmes of action issued by public authorities.
3   The DATACUBE was built and updated over the last fifteen years thanks to a large cooperative effort of scholars from different European countries. This effort has been made possible thanks to the generous support of the European Science Foundation and also many other national research funds. It is available to scholars from the websites of the universities of Jena and Siena.
4   We should never forget the importance of the links between pre-modern and modern parliamentarism. Both the exemplary and contrasting cases of Britain and France testify to it. In Britain, because of the incremental continuity between old and new; in France, because the great revolution which opened the way to constitutional and parliamentary democracy was set in motion precisely by the re-convocation of the dormant *Etats Généraux* of medieval origin.
5   A variety of studies have attempted to specify the political conditions of democratization from above (such as the elite structure—unified or divided—the resources of elites and their calculations of costs and benefits—cost of repression, costs of liberalization—pacts among elites, etc.) (Dahl 1970; Rustow 1970; Higley and Gunther 1992, etc.) and from below (with special attention to processes of mass mobilization) (Rokkan 1970*a*, 1970*b*; Bartolini 2000*a*, 2000*b*).
6   With an increasing frequency in the recent democracies of hybridizations with the presidential system (Elgie 1999).

Part I

Dimensions of Variation

2

The Decline of the Nobility[1]

Michael Rush

2.1. INTRODUCTION

The impact of the aristocracy on and in Europe has been long and profound,
economically and socially and in the exercise of power and influence. Indeed,
it is probably difficult to exaggerate the historical importance of the nobility
in European society. Even powerful, so-called absolute monarchs ruled with
and through the nobility. Ownership of land and, moreover, control of those
who worked on the land gave the nobility immense economic power, but noble
power and influence extended well beyond the economic sphere, intertwining
with the social and the political. The aristocracy was part of an elaborate social
hierarchy in which deference and patronage played a major role. Crucial as
noble power was to each and every locality, it also extended in a significant
number of cases to the national level, particularly in the holding of civil and
military office. Noble power and influence was also important in the growing
towns and cities and, although it increasingly came under challenge with the
development of the bourgeoisie, the aristocracy often showed considerable adaptability to changing economic and social circumstances. Legislative representation
was no exception, but it needs to be seen as part of more fundamental changes
in European society, involving changes in the values that underpinned those
societies. Thus the nobility both challenged and was challenged by royal power,
by parliamentarianism, by mass politics, and by democracy. The challenge of
royal power could be met by the counterclaim of hierarchy, that of parliamentarianism by the concept of representation, but mass politics and democracy
challenged the very idea of aristocracy and turned representation against the
nobility. The more ideas about equality and universal rights, popular consent
and control penetrated European societies, the more the position of the nobility
was undermined, especially economically and politically. What had been its
strengths and had assisted in its survival, became its weaknesses: the advantages of hierarchy and deference became disadvantages under the impact of the
drive for equality and democracy (Spring 1977; Mayer 1981; Bush 1983, 1988;
Lieven 1992).

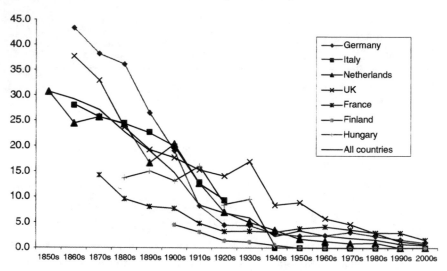

FIGURE 2.1. The weight of nobility among European MPs

The political challenge was particularly strong and is clearly reflected in the DATACUBE data for legislative representation (Figure 2.1). On the one hand, the data shows a marked decline in the representation of the nobility, to the point where it becomes non-existent or negligible, but, on the other, to considerable variation in the rate of decline and, indeed, in the maximum levels of aristocratic representation. This is shown in sharper focus in Table 2.1.

All six countries now have levels of aristocratic representation of 2 per cent or less, but the highest levels recorded range from Germany's 43.5 per cent and the UK's 37.7 per cent to France's 18.9 per cent and Finland's 5.5 per cent. Furthermore, the rate of decline varies considerably: only Finland (from a very low base) and France had less than 5 per cent before the First World War, whereas the remaining four were still had more than 10 per cent, but, by the end of the Second World War, only the UK was above the 5 per cent threshold. Similar

TABLE 2.1. *The decline of the representation of the nobility in six European countries*

Country	Highest	<20%	<15%	<10%	<5%	<2%	0	Lowest
Finland	5.5 (1908)	1907	1907	1907	1913	1916	1948	0.0 (1948)
France	18.9 (1871)	1848	1876	1893	1914	—	—	2.1 (1997)
Germany	43.5 (1868)	1903	1912	1919	1919	—	—	2.3 (1948)
Italy	29.5 (1861)	1904	1919	1919	1946	1946	1946	0.0 (1946)
N'lands	35.3 (1853)	1913	1917	1922	1946	1959	1994	0.0 (1994)
UK	37.7 (1868)	1906	1945	1945	1974	1992	—	(0.7) (2001)

Source: DATACUBE data-set.

patterns can be found in three other countries: Hungary, Portugal, and Spain, except that each was characterized by long periods of non-democratic regimes. In Hungary, the mean level of noble representation in the lower chamber of the parliament averaged 13 per cent between 1848 (when it was only 6%) and 1910, but rather than showing a steady decline actually increased after 1885, when restrictions on aristocratic membership of the upper house 'contributed to pushing the aristocracy towards the House of Representatives' (Ilonszki 2000: 201, 203). However, regime change, the semi-democratic regime of the inter-war period, and the period of communist rule between 1949 and 1989, first undermined and then eliminated the aristocracy. Representation of the nobility in Portuguese Chamber of Deputies averaged 9 per cent between 1851 and 1890, declining from 11 per cent in 1860 to 7 per cent in 1890 (Tavares de Almeida 1995: 160), but the Republican Revolution of 1910 led to the abolition of noble titles. Similarly, in Spain the proportion of nobles in the Chamber of Deputies was 18 per cent in 1879 and averaged 12 per cent between 1907 and 1914 (Linz, Gangas, and Jerez Mir 2000: Tables 11.3 and 11.11). Norway is an extreme case in that the nobility as a social class was abolished in 1821; in Denmark the nobility was similarly abolished in 1910. France represents yet another variation: abolished in 1790 in the early stages of the French revolution, the aristocracy was revived under Napoleon, abolished again in 1848, only to be revived again under the Second Empire in 1852, but surviving only in name after the establishment of the Third Republic in 1870. Similarly, the proclamation of republics in Portugal in 1910 and Spain in 1931 inevitably undermined the position of the aristocracy, as did the turmoil experienced in both countries through much of the nineteenth century and part of the twentieth. Regime discontinuity undoubtedly played its part in Germany, too, with a precipitous drop in noble representation from 14.3 per cent in 1912 to 2.2 per cent in 1919, and in Italy, where Mussolini's fascist regime left the monarchy and nobility largely discredited and, with the proclamation of a republic in 1946, it was formally abolished. However, discontinuity or, perhaps more accurately, regime interruption in Finland (1939–45), France (1940–5), and the Netherlands (1940–5) had no discernible affect. This would suggest that internal regime discontinuity is much more important than regime interruption caused by occupation by external forces. Thus, within the general pattern of the decline of noble representation, significant variations are found, as Table 2.2 shows.

What is also striking about the levels of aristocratic representation is just how varied it was, from just over 5 per cent at its highest in Finland to more than two-fifths in Germany, and how persistent it was in countries like Germany and Italy until the end of the First World War and well beyond in the UK. Indeed, in the cases of Germany and the UK, it is all the more surprising given how advanced both were in the process of industrial transformation, vividly illustrating that economic change is not necessarily swiftly translated into wholesale social and political change. Part of the explanation is undoubtedly that a numerically substantial and determined nobility is in a better position to resist and adapt to

TABLE 2.2. *Variations in the patterns of noble representation in six countries*

Country	Base level	Rate of decline	Regime discontinuity/ interruption
Finland	Low (5%)	Slow	Interruption
France	Medium (19%)	Fluctuating, followed by steady decline	Discontinuity and interruption
Germany	High (44%)	Fluctuating but steep decline, followed by slow decline	Discontinuity
Italy	High (30%)	Fluctuating but steady decline	Discontinuity
Netherlands	High (35%)	Fluctuating but steady decline	Interruption
UK	High (38%)	Steep decline, followed by steady decline	Neither

Source: DATACUBE data-set.

social and political change than are its smaller counterparts, as clearly seems to be the case in the four Scandinavian countries. A further illustration of variation is the level of noble representation in countries directly affected by the 1848 revolutions: in France, Germany, and Hungary. These were significantly lower than in the next relevant elections and also lower than those in the Netherlands and the UK *c*.1848.

Thus some factors affected all or most of the countries studied, others were peculiar to one or some countries but not all. Understanding aristocratic representation and its decline, however, also requires an understanding of the role of the nobility before mass politics and democracy and of the sources of power and influence open to the nobility, as they sought to meet the challenge to their societal and political dominance.

Barrington Moore, Jr., in his classic study *Social Origins of Dictatorship and Democracy* (1967), argued that whether and how parliamentary democracy developed depended to a significant extent on the attitude and actions of the nobility, especially in its relations with other social classes. In particular, he examined the cases of England, France, and Germany, arguing that the role of the nobility was significantly different in each. In England (and it was what happened in England that largely determined what happened in the UK), the landed aristocracy, or at least a substantial proportion of it, forged an economic and political alliance with the emerging bourgeoisie against the crown and played a major role in the development of parliamentary democracy. The peasants or agricultural working class became increasingly detached from the land through enclosure, many migrating to the growing towns and cities to become the industrial proletariat, most of those remaining in the countryside becoming wage labourers. The nobility therefore had a vested interest in the growth and maintenance of parliamentary government and used parliamentary representation as a means of defending their interests much longer than in other European countries. In particular, they sought to limit the extension of the franchise and the growth of democracy. In France, however, the nobility largely abandoned the land to the peasantry but failed to establish

TABLE 2.3. *Variations in noble representation in 1848 and subsequently (%)*

Country	1848	Next relevant election
France	14.8	18.9 (1871)
Germany	15.3	43.1 (1867)
Hungary	6.0	13.3 (1861)
Netherlands	20.6 (1849)	20.2 (1850)
UK	36.3 (1847)	32.1 (1852)

Source: DATACUBE data-set; Ilonszki 2000: 201; UK parliamentary archive (ESRC Data Archive at the University of Essex).

common economic and political interests with the bourgeoisie. The revolution of 1789 almost destroyed the aristocracy and its subsequent revival under Napoleon, the restoration and the second empire was limited. Moreover, the aristocracy remained in conflict with both peasants and bourgeoisie. Continued but limited representation of the nobility was therefore largely a matter of defending aristocratic interests rather than playing an important role in the development of parliamentary institutions. In Germany, the nobility, especially in Prussia, also failed to establish common interests with the bourgeoisie, which was relatively weak in any case, but, in contrast to France, the nobility subordinated the peasants to the land and saw and sought to use legislative representation as a bulwark against the development of parliamentary democracy (Barrington Moore 1967: chs. I, II, VII, and VIII).

Applying Barrington Moore's theories to all the countries covered in this volume is beyond the scope of this chapter, but their applicability to the UK, France, and Germany is clear and a further variation can be found in Italy, where the nobility played a significant part in the development of parliamentary government in Piedmont and retained economic and political influence until the advent of fascism. Elsewhere the nobility was either very small or was less successful in forming economic and political ties with other social classes.

2.2. THE PRE-DEMOCRATIC ROLE OF THE NOBILITY

2.2.1. *The Size of the Nobility*

Although there are definitional problems in comparing the nobilities of different European societies, they do not prevent meaningful comparison, as Michael Bush's massive two-volume study of the European nobility illustrates (Bush 1983, 1988). As he points out, membership of the nobility in the widest sense extends beyond titles, the ownership of land, and various privileges; it is also a matter of status. However, status itself goes beyond formal rank and the nobility may also include members of noble families, particularly second and later sons (Bush

TABLE 2.4. *The size of the nobility in selected European countries*

Large: at least 3%		Intermediate: 1–3%	Small: less than 1%	
Poland:	6–8% (16th cent.)	England	Bohemia:	0.8% (early 16th cent.)
	8–10% (18th cent.)	Scotland	Denmark:	0.4% (1660)
Spain:	12–18% (1700)	France		0.2% (1720)
	4% (1797)	Portugal	Sweden:	0.5% (mid-17th cent.)
	4.8% (1788)	Prussia		0.7% (1711)
Hungary:	5.5% (1842)	Piedmont		0.3% (mid-19th cent.)
	4.5% (1580)	Savoy	Norway }	
Venice:	3.7% (1642)	Bavaria	}	smaller
	2.3% (1790)	Austria	Finland }	

Source: Compiled from data in Bush 1988: 7–8.

Notes: Nobility as a percentage of the population.

1988: 30). Moreover, although historically and usually associated with ownership of land, noble rank also came to be acquired as through the performance of civil or military service to the state. Most countries developed hierarchies of noble rank, while the numerical size of the nobility varied considerably, both from country to country and over time. Ultimately, membership of the nobility depended on the prevailing norms within each society, norms not only of rank and status but also of the privileges associated with that rank and status. To impose a common and rigid definition of nobility would distort any attempt to explain the decline of aristocratic representation in European parliaments; it is the variations in the nature and characteristics of European nobility that help explain why parliamentary representation varied and its decline followed a varied path.

Table 2.4 demonstrates just how much the size of the nobility varied in different parts of Europe and over time in the same societies. The latter are, of course, partly the function of an expanding population, but the data also reflect changes in the nature and role of the nobility. In particular, it is clear that the Scandinavian countries had small nobilities, but the substantial decline in the size of the Spanish nobility should also be noted. Thus it was in countries with numerically and proportionally larger aristocracies that substantial noble representation of the levels shown in Table 2.1 are found. Those with small aristocracies found it increasingly difficult to maintain their social and therefore their political position.

2.2.2. *The Structure of the Nobility*

Most noble titles were originally linked to land and often carried seigneurial privileges bestowing political and administrative authority over particular areas and sections of the populace. Over time, the structure of the nobility became more complex, with the introduction of ranks and the development of royal appointments to the nobility not linked directly to land (even though land might be granted with the title) but to the holding of office. There were other distinctions, too: in France, for example, there was a significant distinction between the *noblesse de robe*, whose status depended on the holding of office in the royal administration, and the *noblesse d'épee*, whose distinction rested on military tradition. In Finland, there were rival Swedish and Finnish nobilities and the latter's status was also based on military service (Ruostetsaari 2000: 54). By the late eighteenth century, only the Basque nobility in Spain did not constitute a hierarchy and a further distinction existed between noble titles created under different regimes, as in France or in Spain, with the pre-1808 *old nobility* and the post-1808 *new nobility* (Linz, Jerez Mir, and Corza 2003: 99–101). What the nobilities in different countries had in common, however, is that their membership was hereditary, though significant expansion took place through the creation of new titles—ennoblement by royal fiat. The Netherlands, for instance, provides an interesting case: 'Two centuries of republicanism had thinned out ancient nobility considerably' (Secker 2000: 280), but the uniting of the southern Netherlands and the United Provinces and the creation of a monarchy established a new situation. William I (1813–40) ennobled many Dutch *regenten* (descendants of families whose wealth stemmed from commerce and finance and those involved in city government) as a counterbalance to the Belgian nobility (Secker 2000: 281). In Britain during the nineteenth century both Conservative and Liberal governments, in the name of the crown, used noble titles to reward prominent supporters, including many from the newly rich entrepreneurs of the industrial revolution (Cannadine 1992: 297–307). However, the British case offers yet a further dimension: the nobility extended beyond those holding peerages (and the members of their immediate families) to those who held hereditary knighthoods, known as baronetcies. Originally, many of these were landed gentry, but increasingly baronetcies were also conferred on the nouveau riche. Furthermore, numerically baronets were as numerous as holders of peerages, considerably extending the pool of nobility available for election to the House of Commons. In addition, there were the holders of Scottish and Irish peerages (as distinct from UK ones), most of whom were not eligible to sit in the House of Lords. Ultimately, the relationship with the crown was historically crucial, and in cases where the monarchy disappeared noble titles no longer had formal recognition. This was the case in Portugal from 1910, Russia from 1917, Germany, Austria, Bohemia, and Poland from 1918, Spain in 1931, and Italy in 1946. In Hungary, with the restoration of the monarchy under the Horthy regency, titles were revived and remained until 1940, while Spain actually revived titles in 1947, though not the privileges that formerly went with them. Of course, in a number of these countries titles were still used, but had no political significance, whatever their social cachet (Bush 1983: 136).

There were also considerable variations in the extent of land ownership and wealth, from the ownership of vast estates to the landless and from the immensely rich to nobility who had fallen on hard times. Wealth, whether in land or other assets, was concentrated by the practice of primogeniture in western and southern Europe, but in eastern and northern Europe the practice of divided inheritance dispersed wealth and led to a proliferation of titles. Where primogeniture was the norm, younger sons often sought other positions in society (in the church, the military, and, increasingly, the bureaucracy). These were important, not least because they provided alternative careers for members of the nobility, away from the direct involvement with the exercise of political power.

As a social group or class, the nobility had a common interest in maintaining its cohesion and solidarity against other classes, but this did not prevent conflict within its ranks. Much of this, of course, stemmed from individual rivalry, but there was also conflict between different strata and different political factions. Conflict between *noblesse de robe* and *noblesse d'épee* was common in France, the latter regarding itself as superior. Similarly, different monarchical factions emerged in France and English politics came to be dominated by the rival political but noble-based factions of Whigs and Tories.

2.2.3. *Noble Power and Influence*

Membership of the nobility invariably carried with it not only status and wealth, but political power and influence (Bush 1983: 2–25), as well as a range of privileges that set them apart from the population at large. As already noted, in some cases this involved the exercise of political and administrative authority, but it also extended to the raising of taxes and administration of justice in particular areas, monopolies over various products, commercial and other economic activities, even their tenants' right to marry, move, change their occupation or hold land. Other privileges gave the nobility tax exemptions and other fiscal concessions, membership of diets or parliaments, access to various offices of state, military rank, and to education and the church. Not all such privileges were available to all members of the nobility, normally depending on rank but usually hereditary.

More importantly from the point of view of changes in parliamentary representation from the nineteenth century onwards, the nobility played a 'particular part...in the development of representative systems and government....Parliaments originally developed in conjunction with the establishment of national systems of taxation' (Bush 1983: 23). However, although parliaments were seen as a means of curbing royal power, they also helped preserve noble privileges, but crucially 'the nobility helped to uphold the idea that the authority of the state should rest upon the consent of its subjects as well as upon the divinity of the king, and that subjects as well as governments should have rights' (Bush 1983: 24). Such parliaments were mostly in the form of estates assemblies or diets, representing the aristocracy, the clergy and the wealthy towns and cities. Before nineteenth century parliamentary reform, local diets operated alongside national and provincial diets in a number of European states, but local diets rarely consisted of more than one estate and many were exclusively noble. However, from at least the fourteenth to the early nineteenth century most national and provincial diets consisted of several estates. Nobles had either the right of personal attendance or to elect members to the aristocratic estate, but whereas local diets usually involved personal attendance, national and provincial diets often involved deputations. Moreover, where personal attendance existed, it tended to be limited to the higher nobility and, even where all nobles were entitled to attend, limits were placed on the right to speak and vote. In some estate parliaments there was one noble chamber (e.g. Sweden, a number of German states, the Tyrol, Sicily, Naples, Catalonia, Valencia, England, and Denmark), in others there were two, one representing the higher nobility, the other the lesser nobility (e.g. Hungary, Poland, Aragon, Bohemia, East Prussia, Savoy, and all the Austrian territories except the Tyrol). However, estates parliaments had largely disappeared by 1850, surviving only in Sweden until 1866 and two German states (Mecklenburg-Schwerin and Mecklenburg-Strelitz) until 1918 (Myers 1975; Bush 1983: 93–100).

Only a few estates parliaments exercised the right to control government— sixteenth- to seventeenth-century Poland, Sweden for part of the eighteenth century, but more significantly England and the Dutch republic from the mid-seventeenth century. Between the fifteenth and seventeenth centuries other diets won and lost the right to intervene in foreign affairs; the Bohemian Diet had control over legislation between 1310 and 1627, as did the Swedish Riksdag during the sixteenth and seventeenth centuries. Tax-granting powers also existed, but they were not very important, since governments could raise much of their revenue without needing parliamentary consent. Furthermore, estates parliaments met mostly in response to the royal summons and therefore met irregularly (Bush 1983: 103–4).

By the outbreak of the French Revolution, in most European states, laws tended to be made by royal edict, taxes tended to be levied either without parliamentary consent or with a right of consent which failed to alter the government's demand, and policy tended to be decided by ministers who were solely responsible to the Crown (Bush 1983: 104).

In short, estates parliaments or diets became the victims of royal absolutism. The polish Sejm and local diets in Poland secured extensive rights, but these were all swept away by the partitions of Poland in the late eighteenth century. Parliaments survived only in Hungary, England, Scotland and Ireland, and the Dutch Republic. However, the Hungarian Diet did meet between 1765 and 1867, the Scottish Parliament was abolished in 1707, and the Irish Parliament was dominated by England from 1495 and abolished in 1801, leaving only the parliament of the UK.

2.3. THE NOBILITY AND DEMOCRATIZATION

2.3.1. *Changing Opportunity Structures*

An inevitable consequence of democratization in Europe was a broadening of the opportunity structures in political recruitment, but whereas this broadening benefited most of the population, however slowly, it was to the disadvantage of the nobility. In some cases, opportunity structures available only to the nobility were removed or attenuated, notably with the decline and eventual disappearance of estates parliaments. However, it was the growth in electoral competition that was crucial. On the one hand, the eligibility criteria for parliamentary candidacies were widened and, on the other, the extension of the suffrage facilitated the growth of parties, particularly those on the left of the political spectrum, all of which militated against the parliamentary representation of the nobility. Thus, political recruitment shifted from a narrow, less competitive process to a broader, much more competitive one.

The eligibility criteria for standing for election were remarkably wide in a number of European countries in the nineteenth century. Of course, in no case were women eligible—the earliest being Finland in 1907, others later, some much later (the UK 1918, Spain 1931, France 1944, Italy 1946, and Portugal 1975). Nonetheless, male eligibility applied to all those aged 25 or over in Italy from 1846, France from 1848, Germany from 1867, and Spain in 1869,[2] and to those of 30 or more in the Netherlands from 1848. There were some exclusions, such as holders of civil service and ecclesiastical offices in Italy, of official and judicial positions in the Netherlands, and of various posts in France. In the UK, males over 21 had long sat in parliament, but until 1858 all MPs were subject to a property qualification. In other countries, such as Denmark, Hungary, Norway, and Portugal, eligibility in the nineteenth century was more restricted, not widening until the early twentieth century or even later.

The extension of the suffrage helped foster the growth and development of political parties. Universal male suffrage was no means a prerequisite of party development; lesser extensions of the suffrage were no less important, but universal male suffrage undoubtedly fostered more and a wider range of parties across the ideological spectrum. The development of parties was driven by two major factors: ideology and expanding electorates. Both within and outside legislatures groups of ideologically like-minded individuals came together to advance and defend shared values and interests, essentially following Michels' dictum that the organized have an advantage over the unorganized. The need for organization also became increasingly important as electorates expanded: soliciting support from small electorates (whether by traditional loyalty, persuasion, coercion, or corruption) required less organization than was needed for large electorates. Furthermore, as parties came to dominate the electoral process, so there was less and less focus on individual candidates; more and more electors voted for parties rather than candidates. For the nobility, this increasingly meant joining or becoming associated with a political party.

In most European countries parties and party systems developed in the late nineteenth century; this was certainly the case in Denmark, Finland, Hungary, Italy, the Netherlands, Norway, Portugal, and Spain. However, there were important exceptions in the cases of France, Germany, and the UK. In France parties existed in the period of the Second Republic (1848–52), but there were clearly ideological divisions and groupings in the various elected bodies and assemblies that followed the 1789 revolution and the Restoration of Louis XVIII in 1814. Similarly, in Germany party groups existed in the ultimately abortive Frankfurt Parliament and, more importantly, in Prussia from the 1848 revolution onwards. However, in the UK parties and factions go back further than in either France or Germany, certainly to the 'Glorious Revolution' of 1688 and, arguably, as far back as Tudor times. Nonetheless, in all cases parties developed gradually rather than suddenly and the development of significant extra-parliamentary organization was, in most cases, related to the expansion of the electorate. Some measure of the pace of that development can be gained from the fact that in France 'the membership of parliamentary groups was very uncertain, and until 1910 deputies were allowed to belong to more than one group' (Mackie and Rose 1982: 109) and that in Italy it was 'only after the election of 1919 that parliament can be said to have been structured predominately along party lines with formerly recognized parliamentary groups' (Cotta, Mastropaolo, and Verzichelli 2000: 229). However, while the development of parties tended to reduce the opportunity structures available to the nobility by widening those structures, their slow development tended to help the nobility maintain a legislative presence in elected chambers and in greater numbers than would otherwise have been the case.

Ideologically, the nobility was, not surprisingly, for the most part attracted to the right of the political centre rather than the left, as is clearly seen in Table 2.5.

With the exception of Finland, the data shows that it is in conservative parties that the nobility are most prominently represented, followed by other party

TABLE 2.5. *Party representation of the nobility (mean percentages)*

Country	Cons.	CD (Prot.)	CD (Cath.)	Right Lib.	Left Lib.	Socialist/Soc. Dem.	Overall
Finland	1	—	—	8	3	0.03	2
France	16	—	6	7	2	0.2	6
Germany	45(a)	3(b)	20	9	5(a)	1	14
Italy	32(c)	—	2	10(d)	2	1	12
Netherlands	42(e)	36	12	11	3	1	15
UK	20	—	—	—	8	1	13

Source: DATACUBE data-set.

Notes: (a) 1848–1933; (b) 1949–98; (c) 1861–1909; (d) 1919–2001; (e) 1849–84. These dates refer to noble representation in particular periods or party families in the period shown; where no dates are shown, the figures relate to the whole period covered by the DATACUBE.

TABLE 2.6. *Party representation of the nobility in the nineteenth and early twentieth centuries (mean percentages)*

Country	Cons.	CD (Prot.)	CD (Cath.)	Right Lib.	Left Lib.	Socialist/ Soc. Dem.	Overall
Finland (1907–13)	5	—	—	21	4	0.2	3
France (1848–1914)	35	—	11	5	3	0.2	10
Germany (1848–1912)	64	—	35	13	6	2	31
Italy (1861–1913)	36(a)	—	—	19	11(b)	2(c)	24
Netherlands (1848–1913)	42(d)	61	18	14	4	0	25
UK (1868–1910)	34	—	—	—	16	0	23

Source: DATACUBE data-set.

Notes: (a) 1861–1909; (b) 1880–1913; (c) 1892–1913; (d) 1849–84. These dates refer to noble representation in particular periods or party families in the period shown; where no dates are shown, the figures relate to the whole period covered by the DATACUBE.

families to the right of centre. In the case of Finland, the nobility were concentrated more in the Swedish People's Party, representing the Swedish minority. In contrast, parties to the left of centre have many fewer members of the nobility and socialist and social democratic parties virtually none. This pattern is also found in Portugal, where the aristocracy was strongly represented in the two monarchic parties, the conservative *Partido Regenerador* and the liberal *Partido Progressista* (Magone 2000: 342–7). Similarly, in Spain—in 1879, 25.4 per cent of Conservatives came from the nobility compared with 7.5 per cent of Liberals, and 17 per cent and 8 per cent respectively between 1910 and 1914 (Linz, Gangas, and Jerez Mir 2000: 377–8, 396). It should also be noted that in a number of cases noble representation was associated with particular parties or party families in particular periods, such as the Conservatives in Germany between 1848 and 1933, in Italy between 1861 and 1909, and the Netherlands between 1848 and 1884, as shown in the notes to Tables 2.5 and 2.6. This contrast between right and left becomes more marked if it is placed in an historical perspective

As Table 2.6 shows, the nobility predictably had much higher levels of representation in the nineteenth and early twentieth centuries, but the association with right of centre parties is much more pronounced, although significant minorities are found in all party families except those of the socialists and communists. However, these were not the parties of the nobility so much as parties in which the nobility were ideologically comfortable. Even in the case of the Tory and Whig parties in the UK, non-aristocratic elements played a key part in their formation and subsequent development. Only in Prussia did the nobility seek to form its own party: shortly after the 1848 revolution, the nobility and other conservative elements declared their intention of forming 'a powerful Conservative party' and invited supporters to buy shares in the *Neue Preussische Zeitung*, which under the title of *Kreuzzeitung*, became 'for many decades the mouthpiece of the Prussian Conservatives and noblemen' (Carsten 1989: 101). Then, in 1861, the Junkers formed the Prussian *Volksverein* (People's Association), which had deeply conservative objectives, seeking a union of German princes under the Prussian monarchy and rejecting parliamentarianism and any idea of ministerial responsibility (Carsten 1989: 116) and in 1876 founded the German Conservative Party, replacing a moribund predecessor. Similarly, in 1893 the German nobility were closely involved in the formation of the *Bund der Landwirte* (Agrarian League), founded to defend agricultural interests, which were allied to the German Conservative Party, prominent in the Prussian Diet, though less so in the Reichstag (Carsten 1989: 134–5).

Even so, the nobility did not entirely lack representation in the centre or left of the political spectrum. Noble representation in socialist or social democratic parties tended to be limited to particular individuals whose sympathies lay in that direction, notwithstanding their noble origin. However, liberal parties also attracted support from the nobility. For example, they were a key element of the Whig faction of the British Liberal Party, although many of them joined the Conservatives after 1886, when the Liberals split over Home Rule for Ireland. In Hungary, radical elements in the nobility had supported the 1848 revolution, but subsequently lost ground to more conservative members of the aristocracy (Ilonszki 2000: 200–1). Similarly, in the united Diet of 1847, the majority of east Prussian noble deputies inclined to a more or less liberal view (Carsten 1989: 100), but the majority of the Junkers were deeply conservative. In contrast, the nobility of southern Germany was more liberal and closely associated with the Catholic Centre Party (Carsten 1989: 195; Lieven 1992: 210–11). Of greater importance was the fact that the nobility were prominent among the leaders of right of centre parties, often holding ministerial office and therefore in a position of significant power and influence.

Nevertheless, the widening of the franchise and the concomitant widening of the party spectrum left the nobility an increasingly small minority within the parties ideologically closest to them, but noble representation was also undermined in a number of cases by regime discontinuity. In addition, extending opportunity structures opened the way for the recruitment of a wider range of occupations and social groups, further challenging representation of the nobility. On the other hand, much of the fluctuation in noble representation can be linked to the fortunes of parties—when parties of the right performed well electorally noble representation tended to rise, as happened, for example, in Germany in 1877, 1878, and 1884, the UK in 1886, 1900, and the two elections of 1910, and a number of elections in Italy and the Netherlands. A marked increase in noble representation also occurred in France at the height of the Boulangist movement in 1889.

2.3.2. *Noble Representation and Regime Discontinuity*

The general pattern of the decline of representation of the nobility is common to all the countries studied (Norway excepted, of course), but regime discontinuity tended to undermine the position of the nobility yet further. It is true that in

some cases, changes to a more conservative regime slowed the decline down—
in France and Spain, for example, but served only to delay the inevitable. In
other cases it had little or no effect on the representation of the nobility, since
it had already declined to very low levels. Thus, in Finland, where it was never
very high in any case, noble representation did not rise above 2.5 per cent after
1919, was 0.5 per cent in 1945 and 1948 and has been zero since. Post-1949
Germany illustrates the same point: averaging only 4 per cent during the Weimar
Republic (1919–33), the highest proportion in the Bundestag has been 3.3 per
cent in 1972. Italy after the Second World War, and Portugal and Spain, following
the restoration of democracy in 1975 and 1977 respectively experienced such long
periods without democracy that, by the time of its restoration, noble representation
had gone beyond the point of no return. Italy also illustrates the importance of
democratization in that, in 1919, three years before Mussolini came to power,
aristocratic representation was 8.6 per cent, half the pre-war figure and stayed at
that level in the early years of the fascist regime. It is Germany, however, that
provides the clearest example of the impact of regime discontinuity, with a fall
from 14.3 per cent in 1912, to 2.2 per cent in 1919, although noble representation
was already in significant decline, having fallen below 20 per cent in 1903 from
its zenith of 43.5 in 1868. A limited rise occurred during the Weimar Republic,
reaching 5.6 per cent in 1924, and 5.5 per cent in 1933. France presents a more
complex picture: the creation of the Napoleonic aristocracy, the restoration of the
monarchy and the further regime changes of the nineteenth century all had their
impact on noble representation. Two years before the 1848 revolution, the nobility
constituted 33 per cent of the Chamber of Deputies, but then fell to 15 per cent
in the Constituent Assembly of the Second Republic, although the sheer size of
the assembly (no fewer than 900 members) meant that numerically the fall was
limited—156 in 1846 compared with 135 in 1848 (Best and Gaxie 2000: 102).
Thereafter, while the proportion reached 18.9 per cent in 1871, the trend was
firmly downwards, falling below 10 per cent in 1893 and declining to 4.3 per cent
in 1914. As one commentator remarked, the nobility 'ultimately rallied to every
regime' between 1800 and 1870 (Higgs 1987: 152).

    While regime discontinuity undoubtedly played a major part in countries like
Germany and Italy, it was within the context of a general decline of noble representation and it is likely that the major socio-economic shifts and attitudinal
changes already underway in the early years of the twentieth century, almost
certainly accelerated by the First World War, had as much, if not a greater effect.
Certainly, this can be seen in countries like the Netherlands and the UK, even
though the one was not directly involved in the war and the other was. In the
Netherlands noble representation fell from 21.0 per cent in 1909 to 10.0 per
cent in 1918 and in the UK from 17.7 per cent in 1910 to 12.9 per cent in
1918. Indeed, counterfactual analysis would suggest that, in the absence of the
First World War and its aftermath countries such as Germany, Italy, and Hungary
would have followed the same path of the continuing but slow decline of noble

TABLE 2.7. *Levels of noble representation in five European countries before and after the First World War (%)*

Country	Before the First World War (% and year)	After the First World War (% and year)
Germany	14.3 (1912)	2.2 (1919)
Hungary	15.7 (1910)	—
Italy	17.1 (1913)	8.6 (1919)
Netherlands	16.0 (1913)	10.0 (1918)
UK	17.7 (1910)	12.9 (1918)

Source: DATACUBE data-set, and Ilonszki (2000: 203).

representation experienced by France, the Netherlands, and the UK. The levels of such representation in five of the countries under study were remarkably similar immediately before the First World War, as Table 2.7 shows.

These data also suggest that, while all countries showed a decline in noble representation, the war had a variable and disproportionate impact, most marked in Germany and to a lesser extent Italy. The cases of Finland and France support this view: both had low levels of noble representation before the war—Finland 3.0 per cent (1913) and France 4.8 per cent (1914), but little different afterwards—Finland 2.5 per cent (1919) (although it had fallen to 1.0% in 1917) and France 4.3 per cent (1919) (DATACUBE data-set).

2.3.3. *Alternatives Sources of Noble Power and Influence*

Historically, membership of the legislature has not been the most important source of noble power and influence in Europe. Of course, as democratization progressed and the formation and continued existence of governments came to depend on retaining majority support in elected legislative chambers, so membership of the latter became more important. However, increasingly it was parties that became the vehicles for securing legislative membership, rather than individuals or particular socio-economic sectors of society. Both before and after democratization, legislative membership was therefore neither the only nor the most important means of exercising power and influence. Of course, many legislatures provided exclusive or near-exclusive means of influence through second chambers, but in general other positions in the state offered the nobility greater power and influence. These were involvement in lower levels of government, in the administration of justice, positions in the state bureaucracy, the holding of military rank and, by no means least, serving as ministers.

Second chambers grew out of estates parliaments in Europe, but in most cases were *reinvented* as countries adopted new constitutions under the pressure of democratization. The old estates parliaments, by definition, usually included representatives of the nobility and second chambers were invariably entirely or substantially aristocratic in membership. The British House of Lords is the prime example, of course, being almost exclusively hereditary and surviving more or less intact until 1999.[3] A second chamber survived in Poland from 1493 until the partitions of the eighteenth century and an upper chamber also survived in Hungary, but had become moribund. However, in most other European countries second chambers were set up in the nineteenth century, usually to act as conservative counterweights to more liberal, popularly elected lower chambers. France actually established a *Conseil des Anciens* in 1795 to counterbalance the lower house and continued to have a second chamber, other than during the Second Republic between 1848 and 1852. With the adoption of a monarchical constitution in the Netherlands in 1815, a second chamber (actually called the First Chamber) was set up. Similarly, the creation of a constitutional monarchy in Piedmont in 1848 resulted in a bicameral parliament, which became the model for the Italian Parliament in 1861. In Spain, the Constitution of 1812 provided for a unicameral parliament, but those of 1834 and 1876 set up second chambers and, in Portugal, the 1826 Constitutional Charter provided for a Chamber of Peers, which apart from two short periods (1828–34 and 1838–42) survived until the 1910 revolution. The 1848 Frankfurt Parliament (Germany's first national parliament) was unicameral, but it proposed a federal constitution with a second chamber representing the German states. The national parliament collapsed in 1849, but in the meantime a new Prussian Constitution had been promulgated late in 1848 and was adopted in 1850. It was conspicuously liberal, with a lower chamber elected by universal male suffrage, but the king, Frederick William IV, insisted on a second chamber, the *Herrenhaus*, dominated by the nobility. This was typical of second chambers established during the nineteenth century (counterweights to popularly) elected lower chambers, and what more obvious counterweight than the nobility?

The only exceptions among the countries studied were the unicameral Finland and Norway, which had, in any case, abolished its nobility in 1821 and which developed a form of internal second chamber by dividing the lower chamber. Denmark, whose second chamber, the *Landsting*, was undoubtedly a conservative counterweight, but it was dominated by the wealthy rather than Denmark's small nobility and was abolished in 1953.

What, then, was the impact of these second chambers? The UK's House of Lords was overwhelmingly aristocratic and its members continued to exercise considerable power and influence in British politics, particularly through the holding of ministerial office, but when, in 1909–11 the Lords directly challenged the Commons, its powers were curbed under the threat of being swamped by new members nominated by the Liberal government. In France, between 1814 and 1848, the Chamber of Peers consisted of some 300 members nominated by the king, but its influence declined under the impact of scandals during the 1840s and it was abolished in 1848. Napoleon III created a senate in 1852 in which more than half the members were nobles (Higgs 1987: 133–5). From 1848 until its reform in 1885, the Hungarian upper house consisted of all male members of the aristocracy, defined as high-ranking families (Ilonszki 2000: 203), but its impact was limited. The Prussian *Herrenhaus* comprised the heads of noble families whose titles pre-dated 1805, life peers nominated by the king, and representatives of estates selected by the higher and wealthier nobility, which 'guaranteed the continuation of the influence of the old Junker families' (Carsten 1989: 112). However, when Bismarck, as Prussian Chancellor, encountered serious opposition in the *Herrenhaus*, he had twenty five new members created to overcome it (Carsten 1989: 120). In Piedmont, nobles constituted a majority of the senate and saw the upper chamber as a means of defending their power, influence, and privileges (Cardosa 1997: 56, 58). However, they were less successful than the Prussian Junkers in extending this beyond national unification. Whereas the Prussian nobility dominated the Bundesrat,[4] the second chamber of the newly created Reich after 1871, the Piedmontese nobility proved unable to dominate the Italian Senate, which, in any case, soon became less important than the Chamber of Deputies. In Piedmont after 1848, the upper chamber was seen as 'a potentially important bulwark of the old ruling class and monarchical authority against the more liberal Chamber of Deputies' (Cardosa 1997: 58–9). As for the second chambers in Portugal and Spain, neither proved especially effective in defending noble power and influence: the Portuguese Chamber of Peers came 'increasingly under the influence of the executive ... [and by] ... the turn of the century had lost credibility' (Magone 2000: 343); the Spanish Senate varied in composition and, although after 1876 it 'had an important aristocratic contingent' (Linz, Gangas, and Jerez Mir 2000: 375, 395), like other political institutions in Spain, it suffered from the frequent political turmoil. In Portugal almost 70 per cent of the members of the Chamber of Peers between 1834 and 1851 had noble titles, but between 1851 and 1890 it was little more than half this proportion—38 per cent (Tavares de Almeida 1995, 129–30). Second chambers exclusively or largely aristocratic in membership also had an impact on recruitment of the nobility to elected chambers. Aristocratic representation in second chambers was in many cases limited to the higher status nobility or similarly limited by monarchical nomination. Consequently, other, usually lesser members of the nobility, were excluded and were available for and sought membership of the elected chamber. For example, this was particularly true of the eldest sons of peers in the UK *before* they inherited their peerages, of the younger sons of peers, and of those with hereditary knighthoods or baronetcies.

With the important exceptions of the UK and, to a lesser extent, Germany before 1918, second chambers were much less important than other sources of noble power and influence. In the pre-democratic age, however, the nobility exercised considerable control over lower levels of government, often extending to the administration of justice, but were also prominent in other spheres at the national level, a situation that continued well into the nineteenth century and in some cases beyond.

In most European countries the power and influence of the nobility stemmed largely from their ownership and control of land and, although many of the privileges attached to membership of the nobility were removed, much of their local power and influence remained intact. In Britain, for example, local government and the administration of justice in rural areas were largely in the hands of the local aristocracy and gentry (Cannadine 1992: ch. 4). Even in may towns patrician mayors were common (Cannadine 1992: Appendix E; Lieven 1992: 204–5, 206). Moreover, ownership and control of land facilitated aristocratic influence in elections, both in securing the election of sympathetic candidates in general and to varying degrees members of the nobility in particular—a factor in a number of European countries. Until 1872, Prussian landowners selected local mayors and could veto decisions made by local assemblies and, as already noted, it was only by the creation of additional members that Bismarck was able overcome opposition to reform in this area in the *Herrenhaus* (Lieven 1992: 214). The nobility also attended the local and provincial assemblies and as late as 1914 no fewer than 56 per cent of those holding the key local government office of *Landrat* were nobles (Lieven 1992: 216). Although in Italy the number of aristocrats holding office declined generally in the late nineteenth century, this 'obscures the extent to which prominence in public affairs at least on the local level continued to be associated with inherited titles and the lineal qualifications of the nobility to community leadership' (Cardosa 1997: 77). Regime discontinuity makes the picture more mixed in France: 'Noble participation in municipal government during the changing conditions of the nineteenth century was not constant. However, it always far exceeded the place of nobles in the national population at large, even during the purges carried out by the July Monarchy and the Second Republic' (Higgs 1987: 144). In general, it was only gradually that the grip of the nobility on local government was loosened on most European countries.

Less mundane and more prestigious was holding important positions in the bureaucracy, especially the diplomatic service, and in the military. Here a largely consistent pattern emerges. Especially before the introduction of open competition in 1870 (a process that took some time have a marked effect), a significant proportion of senior posts in the UK civil service were occupied by members of the nobility (Cannadine 1992: 239–44). However, it was in the diplomatic service that the aristocracy really dominated:

Between 1873 and 1945, eleven men held the post of Permanent Under-Secretary [in the Foreign Office—the most senior civil service position]: nine were peers, close relatives of peers, or bona fide landed gentry; only two came from the middle class.... And the career diplomats who spent their lives overseas were even more aristocratic.

(Cannadine 1992: 280–1, Appendix C)

A similar situation prevailed in Prussia:

In the high Prussian bureaucracy the nobility preserved its predominant influence. At the beginning of the twentieth century the noble proportions of administrative posts was still about 20 per cent.... In 1911 38 per cent of the Prussian senior administrators came from the nobility... [and in]... higher posts of the diplomatic service the percentage of commoners was less than ten.

(Carsten 1989: 144–5)

Among the higher-ranking members of the Piedmontese diplomatic service in the mid-nineteenth century, more than four out of five were nobles and between 1870 and 1900 30 per cent of the ambassadorial posts in the Italian diplomatic corps were held by members of the Piedmontese nobility (Cardosa 1997: 62, 73). In Hungary after 1848, large numbers of nobles who had lost their land or were unable to make a living from it 'began to occupy positions in the bureaucracy' (Ilonszki 2000: 200n) and, earlier in the nineteenth century, many Finnish nobles who had lost their positions as members of the military, following the suppression of the Finnish army, became public officials (Ruostetsaari 2000: 54). France again presents a mixed picture, but under all regimes the nobility was over-represented in the bureaucracy and the diplomatic service.

If the nobility was over-represented in the bureaucracy, then it was even more the case in the military. In 1870, 50 per cent of British army officers were members of the nobility and it was still as high as 35 per cent in 1913, and 22 per cent in 1939 (Cannadine 1992: 273, 264–80). However, it was in Germany that presence of the nobility was strongest in the military, especially the Prussian nobility: in 1900 61 per cent of the generals and colonels and 61 per cent of the general staff were drawn from the nobility; by 1913 it was still as high 52 per cent and 50 per cent respectively; even 25 per cent of the lowly rank of lieutenant were nobles (Carsten 1989: 145). Indeed, under the Weimar Republic 'the nobility retained its domineering position in the Reichswehr', with nobles outnumbering commoners in the ranks of general and colonel (Carsten 1989: 161). In Italy, although the Piedmontese nobility constituted only 5 per cent of the officer corps, two-thirds of the senior generals, a third of the lieutenant-generals, and more than a quarter of the major-generals in the mid-1880s were nobles (Cardosa 1997: 72).

Historically, the nobility also played a part in the European nation and state-building process. In the nineteenth century it was closely involved in the unification of Italy and Germany and were also prominent administratively and militarily in empire-building, especially in the British, German, and Italian cases.

The nobility was also prominent in the holding of ministerial office. Excluding the short *caretaker* government headed by the Duke of Wellington in November–December 1834, of the seven Prime Ministers between 1832 and 1868, only one, Sir Robert Peel, could be described as a commoner (although he was, in fact, the second holder of a hereditary baronetcy or knighthood). In contrast, of the seven Prime Ministers between 1868 and 1914, three were members of the aristocracy and four were commoners. Among Cabinet ministers generally between 1880 and 1914, the proportion of who were members of the nobility was 51 per cent, 56 per cent in Conservative Cabinets and 47 per cent in Liberal ones, but within these means there was a decline from 69 per cent in the Conservative Cabinet of 1886 to 47 per cent in the Cabinet of 1902, and of 60 per cent in the Liberal Cabinet of 1886 to 37 per cent in that of 1908 (Cook and Keith 1975: 28–47; Cannadine 1992: Appendix B; and Butler and Butler 2000a, 2000b: 1–5). A similar situation can be found in the German Cabinet, with 64.5 per cent of the posts during the Kaiserreich, compared with 11.5 per cent during the Weimar Republic. Indeed, under Hitler aristocratic representation actually rose to 27.3 per cent, but brought no significant benefits to the aristocracy (Knight 1952: 33). In the Kingdom of Sardinia between 1848 and 1861, only one of the eight Prime Ministers was not an aristocrat and 55 per cent of the members of the Cabinet were members of the nobility (Cardosa 1997: 5; Cotta and Verzichelli 2003: Table 4). Thereafter, the proportion of the nobility among ministers declined: 1861–76—38 per cent, 1876–1913—28 per cent, and 1913–22—14 per cent (Cotta and Verzichelli 2003: Table 4). During the constitutional monarchy period in Spain (1874–1923), 18.2 per cent of ministers came from the aristocracy—evenly balanced between the *old* (8.7%) and the *new nobility* (9.5%), but 'the aristocracy made its largest contribution within the transitional government of Admiral Aznar [February–April 1931]; however, all but one of these aristocratic ministers were members of the "new" aristocracy' (Linz, Jerez Mir, and Corza 2003: 101). Aristocratic representation in the Portuguese Cabinet, however, was lower: 'between 1851 and 1910, only about 14 per cent of all Cabinet ministers were nobles, and... since 1870, no Prime Minister has been drawn from the older Portuguese aristocratic families' (Tavares de Almeida and Costa Pinto 2003: 6).

The nobility thus continued to exercise power and influence through a variety of positions and institutions—through second chambers, local government, the bureaucracy and diplomatic service, the military, and ministerial office; in short, the state continued to be '... a source of aristocratic opportunity' (Powis 1984: 69). However, it was a declining source, though often more important than the opportunities offered by elected legislative chambers. Why, then, did the nobility continue to seek elective representation? The short answer is because the opportunity existed; it would have seemed foolish not to take advantage of yet another avenue of influence, even power in countries where ministerial office was linked to membership of the legislature. The more complex answer is that membership of elected legislature chambers was one of a number of ways in which the nobility could seek to maintain its influence in the state, not exclusively but as one of a range of opportunities to resist and slow down its decline as an economic, social, and political force in society.

2.4. CONCLUSION

The decline of the nobility in Europe was inexorable and ultimately inevitable. There were variations in the extent and pace of that decline. At one extreme were the Scandinavian countries, particularly Norway and at the other Britain and Germany, with others (France, Hungary, Italy, the Netherlands, Portugal, and Spain) somewhere in-between. There were also similarities and differences—historically low sizes of nobility in Norway, Denmark, and Finland, much higher levels elsewhere, but it was in the intermediate sizes (the Britain, Germany, and Italy) that the nobility were most successful in resisting and slowing decline. The much greater dominance of the Prussian nobility in the unified Germany compared with the Piedmontese nobility in the unified Italy is notable, but the greatest contrast is between Britain and Germany in terms of adaptability:

...the English aristocracy developed parliamentary institutions which proved extremely effective at securing consensus and effective government in a modern society, far more than the efforts of absolute monarchs and their bureaucracies to mediate between conflicting groups and classes as complex industrial societies developed in continental Europe... the English aristocracy adapted itself earlier and more successfully than any other to the many requirements of the modern age. ....

(Lieven 1992: 246)

Contrast this with the reaction of the Prussian nobility:

The tenacity with which the Junkers defended their interests and their influence remained one of their principal characteristics. That they did so successfully was due to the weakness of German liberalism, especially in Prussia. ... In spite of the rapid industrialisation the socially leading role of the nobility remained unshaken until the defeat of 1918. Its heavy weight in social and political life slowed down then growth of a strong and determined middle class and the country's political development in general.

(Carsten 1989: 195)

And somewhere in-between lie countries such as France and Italy. In France,

...under successive regimes from 1800 to 1870, with the possible exception of the Second Republic, nobles were over-represented... in all political assemblies and many bureaucratic and official posts. Similarly, nobles profited by neoseigneurial and patronage politics in the countryside... this place in the sun resulted... from their landed wealth, political allies, adaptability and continuing monopoly of the forms of social distinction.

(Higgs 1987: 152)

Italy was little different:

While nobles lost their corporative privileges and domination of high office with the introduction of civil equality and parliamentary government after 1848, they were still able to take advantage of the deeply embedded social patterns and cultural values to redefine older political roles and carve out new ones in the second half of the [nineteenth] century.

(Cardosa 1997: 87)

In 1795, six years after the outbreak of the French Revolution, the French general, Charles Dumouriez, who served the *ancien régime* and the revolution, famously said that the courtiers of Louis XVIII had 'forgotten nothing and learnt nothing' (*Concise Oxford Dictionary of Quotations*, 118). Faced with the forces of social and political change, this was doubtless true of a significant proportion of the European nobility, but an equally significant proportion learned a great deal and put it to good practice in responding and adapting to their social and political decline. In this regard legislative representation was no exception and conforms to the general pattern of the decline of the nobility, but the importance of legislatures varied considerably in the Europe of the nineteenth and early twentieth centuries. In some cases they were important sources of power and authority, in others more peripheral but not without influence. Yet aristocratic power and influence also depended upon economic factors and maintaining a strong presence in cabinets, the bureaucracy, the military, and local government. For those who adapted, Dumouriez' aphorism could be turned on its head—these members of the nobility had remembered much and learnt a great deal.

ENDNOTES

1   *A note on defining the nobility*: The concept of the nobility or aristocracy is not a precise one and definitions vary from one society and country to another. As Dominic Lieven writes in *The Aristocracy of Europe, 1815–1914*, 'Everyone knows what aristocracy means until they have to write ... about it' (Lieven 1992: ch. 13). Historically, socially, and politically the aristocracy or nobility is normally associated with wealth, privilege, and power based on heredity. Of course, most aristocracies involved the recruitment of newcomers by the creation of new positions and titles, but once created these were hereditary. There are, however, complications caused by regime changes resulting in *new* nobilities being established, by the association of noble rank with particular offices, and, in some societies, by the continued use and informal recognition of titles after their formal abolition, and by the illegitimate assumption of titles. The basic definition used, however, is that of *hereditary rank or status, which was extant at or before the time of first election to the legislature.* Cases in which there was any doubt were decided by country specialists. It should also be noted that the data on legislative representation of the nobility is confined to the elected chamber of bicameral legislatures in the countries concerned, although, where appropriate aristocratic membership of upper or second chambers is discussed.

2   In 1873 it was lowered to 21 but raised again to 25 in 1891.

3   In 1999 the House of Lords Act removed all but ninety-two of the hereditary peers (the remaining members being life peers, serving bishops of the church of England, and senior members of the judiciary). In 2003, the rejection by the House of Commons of various options (ranging from 100% appointed to 100% elected, with other options involving a mixture of the two) for changing the composition of the House of Lords preserved its post-1999 composition. In its 2005 election manifesto, the Labour Party proposed the removal of the remaining ninety-two hereditary peers and allowing a free vote on the future composition of the upper house.

4   It is important to note, however, that the Bundesrat, then as now, consisted of ministers from the Land governments and was and is unique among second chambers.

3

From Servants of the State to Elected Representatives: Public Sector Background among Members of Parliament

Maurizio Cotta and Pedro Tavares de Almeida

3.1. PRELIMINARY REMARKS

Elected parliaments were introduced in Europe for the fundamental purpose of checking and controlling the absolutist (or semi-absolutist) monarchies which in the previous period had greatly expanded their powers thanks to the development of the large and pervasive bureaucracies of the modern state (Tilly 1975; Bendix 1964; Poggi 1978). In this way, even when the king was not (or could not be) directly challenged, his government and his administrative *longa manus* could be scrutinized, controlled, kept within limits. Parliaments and elected representatives were thus primarily conceived as the counterweight of society vis-à-vis the non-responsible power of non-elected bureaucrats.

Given the political reasons behind the introduction of parliaments, it would seem more than natural to see these institutions filled with representatives of civil society rather than with servants of the state. However, as most of our cases show, the picture of parliamentary representation is less clear cut than one would expect from this presentation of the historical plot. When we analyse the background of parliamentarians, it is easy to discover that some form of state service has been for long periods one of the most significant experiences shared by MPs before their first election. On average in the countries discussed here no less than a quarter of the MPs have come from such a background, and the maximum peak has reached approximately 40 per cent (Figure. 3.1).[1]

We later discuss and try to explain the highly significant variations that can be read both across countries and across time in this data. For the time being, it is enough to underline the importance of the phenomenon and the problems it raises for a dominant theme of contemporary democracy, that of the relationship between state and society and of the dualism between public and private.

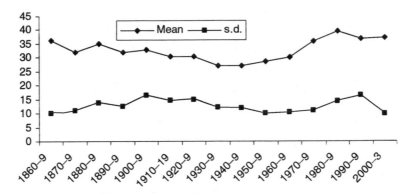

FIGURE 3.1. General public sector background among members of parliament (mean of all countries and standard deviation) (%)

The idea of civil society, which developed in European countries during the eighteenth and nineteenth centuries and became one of the crucial concepts on which contemporary theories of political representation were forged, but also an important instrument of political battles, is based on the distinction between the state and 'something else' which is not the state but pertains to the sphere of economic and social life. It was indeed the development of the new and distinctive reality of the modern absolutist and bureaucratic state which, by opposition, stimulated the rest of society to define itself at first negatively (civil society becomes then essentially 'what is not the state'), but increasingly also in a more positive way (in the liberal perspective civil society is the source and repository of positive values) (see for instance Ferguson 1767; Constant 1819; Tocqueville 1835–40; and now Putnam 1993). Reacting to these positions, *étatiste* perspectives offered an opposite hierarchy of values and expounded the state as the embodiment of universalistic values against society conceived as the expression of private, particularistic interests. Hegel (1821) was probably the best and most influential representative of this position.

But is the clear-cut separation between state and civil society which underlies such opposed political theories an empirically accurate description of reality or rather a simplified ideological representation of what reality should be? Our data suggests that the latter is more the case than the former. A less dichotomous view is in fact well confirmed by broader studies about the development of Western societies and polities in the last three centuries (Poggi 1978). If we want to adopt an empirical perspective we have to accept that the relationship between state and society is more complicated than the one presented in those ideological schemes (Andeweg 2000). And this is true from both sides. The state was never a body fully separated from society: this can easily be seen from the important influences that society with its specific configurations and cultural features has had upon the organizational models of the state apparatus, the recruitment of its personnel, and the values shared by it (Peters 1989). On the other side, society was always far from being completely independent of state influences: on the contrary, its structure and values have been deeply transformed as a result of the development of a rationalized and large-scale administrative system which has come to regulate many strategic aspects of social life (Weber 1921).

Our analysis of parliamentary representation provides some further significant elements suggesting that the border line between state and society has been less clear than expected. Among the 'representatives of society' there has often been a significant number of people who looked very much like 'representatives of the state'. Parliaments and elections have proven to be not only the crucial instrument of expression for those sectors of society who wanted to assert their interests and keep under control the arrogance of state power, but also a convenient avenue for those who had a different goal in mind and thought that the state, or in any case those who had made a career in its offices, should have their voice heard in the law-making institutions. The '*étatiste* establishment', provided that it had not been politically disqualified through a revolutionary upheaval, was generally in the position to exert its influence, defend its interests, and promote its positions using the new institutional instrument of elected parliaments. At the same time, the superior knowledge of the internal mechanisms of the state shared by those who had worked in the public bureaucracies must often have been considered an important resource to be tapped by recruiting former (or present) civil servants into the halls of parliament.

3.2. TWO PERSPECTIVES FOR UNDERSTANDING THE WEIGHT OF THE *ÉTATISTE* BACKGROUND AMONG PARLIAMENTARY ELITES

In order to understand this situation, we can adopt two different perspectives. To put it in a somewhat simplified way, we might call the first perspective a *sociological* one, the second a *political* one.

The first perspective views parliamentary representation essentially as the instrument through which society and its variable configurations are reflected into political life. If we adopt the classical dualistic scheme which sets society against the state, representation is the instrument by which society asserts itself against the state and eventually manages to conquer the latter. On this basis one should expect that the main components of society (and their interests) will be represented in the parliamentary elite and that state officials will not be part of it. It immediately becomes clear that the dualistic view does not square with the data we have seen. A conception of reality and the state–society relationship less simplistic than the dualistic one should take into account the fact that the building of the modern bureaucratic state has also affected society transforming it to a large extent into 'a state society', a society deeply pervaded and structured by *étatiste* elements. It is not incorrect to say that the modern state is not something which is 'completely other' from society, but on the contrary has become in many important respects a highly relevant part of society. To be more specific: those working (at different levels) for the state machine have come to play important roles also within society. The top ranks of the state administration have become a very significant component of the higher strata of society, often mixing with them in a way that makes distinctions not easy to draw.[2] And a not too dissimilar phenomenon would apply also for the middle and lower ranks. It should not come therefore as a surprise that the opening of channels of representation would offer an opportunity also to the *étatiste* components of society to take advantage of this possibility. They should be represented in parliament as any other component of society.

If such a perspective was correct, one would have expected a clear correlation between the importance of the state component within society at large and the share of MPs with a 'state background'. Our data suggests that this is not exactly the case. As we shall see, variations across countries and across time do not correspond fully with this interpretation: comparing countries, we find that not all those with a strong state have a stronger representation of state servants, and analysing temporal trends we do not find a linear growth of this background among parliamentarians in spite of the linear growth of the weight of the state in European societies. These findings confirm once more that political representation is not simply a mirroring process.

The second perspective takes into account the political dynamics of the profound transformation set in motion by the process of parliamentarization of absolutist monarchies. The acceptance of parliamentary representation did not generally mean an immediate and complete abdication by the monarchy and its traditional entourage (both aristocratic and bureaucratic) of their governing role. And the principle of popular sovereignty did not easily prevail over the notion of the sovereignty and supremacy of the state. The stage was thus set for a more or less intense political competition between old and new, between the traditional state establishment and its challengers. The defence of the monarchy and of the absolutist interpretation of the state as the centre and embodiment of political authority could be pursued not only by directly fighting against parliament and trying to limit its powers, as was done recurrently by European monarchies during the nineteenth century,[3] but also through the creation of 'conservative' or 'reactionary' parties which from within the parliament itself would provide support for the monarchy and compete more or less poignantly against 'democratic' currents. These parties would draw their personnel from the traditional establishment and thus also from the high ranks of the state.

This picture must however be nuanced a little. State bureaucracy did not stand only for the defence of monarchical authority, it reflected also the principles of rationalization and administrative progress typical of the modern state (Weber 1922) which had little to do with the traditional bases of monarchical legitimacy. This could lead to the fact that important components of the state bureaucracy were (and were perceived as) modernizing elements and could therefore associate themselves with the progressive liberal wings of political life more than with the conservative ones. The role of civil servants could therefore be significant also in some liberal, 'old left' parties of the nineteenth century.

There are thus both 'sociological' reasons (the representation of important strata of an *étatiste* society) and 'political' reasons (defending the old power system against the new challengers, or promoting the modernization of the country) for expecting a significant presence of parliamentarians with a 'state' background in the early stages of parliamentarization.

On the basis of these two broad sociological and political factors, we can also expect significant variations across countries. Variations in the weight of an *étatiste* background should be due on the one hand to the different impact of the state upon society: in some of the European countries the bureaucratic state has gained a greater domination over society than in others. In these countries, we should therefore expect a larger presence of representatives with a bureaucratic background than in countries, where society has been able to preserve a greater independence vis-à-vis the state.

On the other hand the political resistance against parliamentarization may have been more or less strong and persistent over time. In those countries where it has been stronger and more persistent over time we should expect to find a larger share of parliamentarians coming from the ranks of the state administration; this category should conversely be smaller where the parliamentarization of politics has been accepted more easily. However, at an extreme pole of the spectrum the opposition to parliamentarization may have been so strong to backfire and disqualify the possibility of a significant *étatiste* representation in parliament when this opposition was overcome.

If we now adopt a diachronic look, we have to take into account the working of contradictory factors. On one side, the success of political liberalism (often coupled with economic liberalism) should have made civil society less dependent on the state and should have thus increasingly empowered its less *étatiste* components. With the consolidation of parliamentary representation we should therefore expect to see a phase characterized by a greater number of representatives with a background in the free professions, in entrepreneurial jobs and the like, to the detriment of state officials. Later on, the progress of democratization, with the extension of suffrage, the consolidation of mass parties and of the growth of political professionalism, should have brought within the ranks of parliamentarians a larger number of individuals skilled in the organization and mobilization of societal consent and possibly coming from the lower strata of the population. This should have further weakened the weight of an *étatiste* background and should in particular apply to those political groups which represented in parliament the excluded classes.

On the other side, however, we must remember that in the end democratization has not turned out to be a factor working against but rather in favour of the growth

TABLE 3.1. *Long-term growth of public employment in Europe, c.1890–c.1970**

Public employees as percentage of the labour force

Year	France	Germany	Italy	UK
Mid-19th century	5.0	7.2	2.2	2.4
Pre-1914	7.1	10.6	4.7	7.1
Pre-1939	8.9	12.9	7.8	10.8
1951	17.4	13.4	10.4	26.4
1960	23.3	16.4	12.7	24.0
1980	27.3	25.8	22.3	28.3

* Figures include personnel of the state at all levels of government.
Source: Rose (1985).

of the size of the state. During the twentieth century and particularly after the Second World War the development of large-scale interventions of the state in the economy, the ever broader welfare policies (Flora and Heidenheimer 1981), and the great expansion of state bureaucracies that this has entailed (see for instance the data of Table 3.1) have produced a new situation that could be considered as a favourable factor for a renewed growth in the number of civil servants among the ranks of parliamentary representatives. During this period public employees of different categories have become an increasingly important component of society: their sheer number and the specific interests they carry are elements on the basis of which we should expect an increasing number of persons coming from state offices to be amenable to play a representative role.

The availability of civil servants for parliamentary roles should also be increased by the fact that while pursuing a political career they can generally enjoy much greater job security than people working in the private sector.

3.3. THE VARIABLES AND DATA IN THE DATACUBE

Five are the variables of our data-set that are relevant for this analysis. Var31 provides a summary of the weight of the public sector: all the occupations that are paid by the state and its various articulations are included here.[4] As far as can be determined, this variable includes also people working in state-owned companies (a category of people somewhat different from the rest and which became more relevant after the crisis of the 1930s when state ownership of private companies increased in many European countries). Other variables tap more specific subcategories of public servants. Var30 covers the high ranks of the civil administrative hierarchy, Var32 the military branch of the bureaucracy, Var35 the members of the judiciary, Var27 teachers of different levels and university professors. Particularly when using the summary variable, one should be aware of the fact that the public sector is a broad category with important internal distinctions: even if all its members are paid by public authorities a university professor is in a rather different position from a military officer, just as a judge is different from a prefect, or a director general.[5]

3.4. AN HISTORICAL TREND

In our previous work, the general picture had already been already presented and discussed: the importance of a background in the public sector among parliamentary representatives throughout the whole period of history covered by our data-set appeared undeniable (Cotta and Best 2000: 509 ff.). Parliamentary representation was very clearly not just the preserve of the 'private sector' fighting against the state. Quite the contrary: a substantial proportion of MPs had served the state in some capacity by working in its administrative ranks. When using a non-weighted mean for the countries in the data-set, this group of parliamentarians oscillated between 25 and 40 per cent of the total (see Cotta and Best 2000: Fig. 13.10). It is also clear, when adopting a long-term perspective, that the weight of the public sector has been subject over time to significant changes. Our data shows a fairly distinctive 'U-shaped' curve: the relatively high levels (with means around 35%) which characterized most of the countries in the first decades of the period covered by our analysis were followed later on by a rather substantial decline (Figure 3.1). At the beginning of the twentieth century, this proportion stabilizes around an average of more or less 25 per cent and this level will not change very much until the end of the 1940s. This is still a substantial share but obviously a far less impressive one than that of the previous stage. After another step upward in the 1950s, a new steep and constant rise of this group of parliamentarians begins in the 1960s, at the end of which the original levels of the past have been regained or even passed. In the 1980s, the mean level for the countries of our study is around the 40 per cent mark. Then the very final period of our research (the 1990s) shows again some change: the trend seems to level off and perhaps even to suggest a slight downturn.

The general trend we can observe seems thus to provide some empirical support for the broad hypotheses advanced above and enables us to assess the weight of the explanatory factors discussed. The great importance of this type of background during the first phase of parliamentary representation indicates that the parliamentarization of political systems did not produce in general an immediate and clear-cut break with the traditions of the bureaucratic state and with its patterns of authority. Previous experience in the (high) state ranks was an important resource for a political career also in the new institutional environment. Either because of their social or their political influence, state servants became easily eligible as contenders in electoral competitions and managed quite successfully to get elected. The fact that with the passing of time their importance slowly but continuously declined until the 1940s indicates that a purely 'sociological' interpretation of this phenomenon is not enough. The weight of the public sector in the total labour force never declined during that period: on the contrary, it increased in all the countries analysed here. In order to explain the trend for this type of parliamentary background, we have therefore to introduce other variables, and political factors seem particularly appropriate. The growing consolidation of the institutions of liberalism and democracy provided the political opportunities whereby other types of contenders could gain a comparative advantage vis-à-vis state officials in the recruitment process and in electoral competition. The decline of public servants suggests also that the resistance of the old establishment to outsiders increasingly weakened. This should come as no surprise given the fact that during this period the politics of representation underwent a very significant change. One aspect of this was the growing role of parties in elections, parliament, and the making of governments: for old-style high state officials accustomed to the culture of the 'unity' and 'superiority' of the state it was probably difficult to adapt to the increasingly partisan and antagonistic style of politics.

But this declining trend at some point was stopped and, after a period of stagnation, a new growth began. The steady increase in the percentage of state servants among parliamentarians during the period following the Second World War and especially from the 1960s through to the 1980s is a phenomenon deserving special attention. Its causal background is probably to be found in the impressive growth of the state sector that occurred during this period (Rose 1985; Flora 1987) which in its turn can be further traced to the great political changes in the representation process during the twentieth century, and to its results. Almost inevitably perhaps, the great increase in the number of people working for the state in its different central and local branches in the age of universalistic and intensive welfare systems (see Table 3.1) had to be reflected also in the recruitment of democratic representatives. But again, the simple mirroring interpretation is probably not enough to explain this phenomenon. We have also to consider some more political aspects. The fact that in most of our countries nearly all the parties (also those that had been previously confined to opposition roles and which initially condemned the state as an instrument of evil powers) gained during this period legitimacy as governing parties (*Regierungsfähigkeit*), and thereby the ability to exert an influence over the state administration, is probably a factor of some relevance. Almost all components of the political elite have thus come to accept the state and have in a sense become part of it. Only extremist minorities refuse it or have been left at its margin. As a consequence, the interpenetration between careers in the state and in representation has become far less problematic. Finally, public employment, by guaranteeing in most of the countries the permanence of job positions, offers particularly favourable conditions for embarking on a political career without risking one's job. From a different but not unrelated point of view, that is that of parties, similar arguments have been raised by the theorists of the cartel party when they have stressed the growing dependence of political parties on the state (Katz and Mair 1995).

As with most social phenomena, in this case too a large quantitative growth means also a significant qualitative change. The public bureaucracies of the second half of the twentieth century and the meaning itself of public service in the age of the welfare state and mass democracy have indeed become quite different from those of the nineteenth and early twentieth centuries. The border lines between state and society, public and private, have become in many ways much less evident. To an extent, this factor, combined with others, must have facilitated a larger recruitment of politicians from the public sector.

These interpretations still have a rather conjectural nature. In order to find some firmer ground for evaluating these trends, we have to look a bit more into the details of this variable. One way is to break it down into its different components, the other is to analyse cross-country variations and the third is to look at intra-country variations. The analysis of the different sub-components of the public sector should enable us to interpret more precisely the meaning of this type of occupational background. Cross-country and cross-party (and intra-country) comparisons should help to explore alternative explanations of the importance of this type of background.

3.5. COMPONENTS OF THE PUBLIC SERVICE

So far we have used public employment as a general and encompassing category. There are justifications for this: the main one is probably that being on the public payroll protects the individuals from the risks of the market and therefore to some extent sets them apart from the rest of the population; another one is the presence of elements of a common cultural identity which distinguish state employees from those active in the private sector. Having said this, we should not forget that this category remains a very broad one and one that is internally highly differentiated: a prefect is not the same as a university professor, a judge is not the same as a ministerial bureaucrat even if in the end they are all paid by the state. In order to understand better the meaning of this broad category, it is necessary to assess the importance of different subcategories. Those in our data are: senior civil servants, military officers, judges, schoolteachers, and university professors. By subtraction we can then calculate a residual group including everyone that does not fall into the above categories. The first three subgroups (senior civil servants, military officers, and judges) are those most directly and clearly linked to the state as the traditional centre of authority. But among these judges have typically enjoyed a much greater (though not total) autonomy vis-à-vis the executive power.[6] The fourth category is, in general, the most peripheral.[7]

A more analytical examination of the background of parliamentarians shows indeed some important changes in the balance between the different sub-components of the public sector over time (Figure 3.2). The higher levels of the public service show a trend that is not too different from that of the general category. Their importance declines until the middle of the twentieth century, then begins to rise again and finally in the last decades of the twentieth century shows a new downturn. Rather different is the case of two other categories. Military

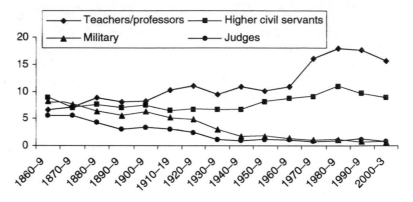

FIGURE 3.2. Sub-components of the public sector (%)

officers and judges, who at the beginning of the period under examination here had a significant importance, show a very clear decline which continues until the end. Their trend is rather similar to the decline of nobility and landed interests. We can probably consider them as a component of the traditional establishment which saw social authority intimately linked with certain expressions of state power.

As for the most peripheral section, school and university teachers, our data tells an interesting story. More or less until the First World War, this group is a fairly small one. It is small in a general sense (less than 8% among all MPs) and its weight within the broader group of public servants is also far from dominant (between a fifth and a fourth of the total). But later and especially after the Second World War its growth will be very strong, making teachers and professors one of the largest categories among parliamentarians. Only in the last years does the trend stop and even change its direction.

We can reasonably say that until the First World War a public employment background among parliamentarians meant fundamentally an involvement in the state as an authority structure. In the second period, that which covers more or less the first half of the twentieth century and which sees a stabilization of the public sector at its lowest levels (around the 25% line), the professorial element oscillates between 40 and 50 per cent of the whole group. And more or less the same proportion will continue to be maintained during the high growth phase of the 1960s, 1970s, and early 1980s when the public sector background moves from a 30 to 40 per cent level. This component shadows again the trend of the broader category in the 1990s, when both begin to decline. The importance of this group suggests a number of considerations: in the first half of the twentieth century, a period when ideology dominated the representative game, it probably indicated the increased relevance of 'discourse skills', but later on it might have reflected also the role of some specific expertises (in the field of economics, the social sciences, medicine, etc.) and more in general the great availability of the teaching class for political positions given the favourable conditions offered by this job.

This exploration of the public sector by subcategories suggests, as might be expected, that we have to distinguish carefully the phases of our long-term story and that the overall meaning of this component for the understanding of parliamentary recruitment changes substantially with time.

3.6. VARIATIONS ACROSS COUNTRIES

To what extent does the general trend we have described indicate a common line of development for the countries we are studying? And with regard to the variations across countries that we will find, can we explain them with the help of factors that have a general validity across countries? Or do they have to do with idiosyncratic developments that escape a common explanation? These are the points we must now address by looking into cross-country variations.

A cross-country comparison indicates that in this field variations across the countries of our study are significant but probably smaller than for other variables (such as the legal profession or local politics background). The standard deviation is in fact one of the lowest among the DATACUBE variables (Cotta and Best 2000). The next point to be stressed is that the same 'U-shaped' curve we have found for the European mean is more or less common to most of the countries examined. This indicates an important element of commonality in the long-term transformation of European countries. A relatively similar phenomenon must be at work behind this long-term trend. Having said this we can notice also that the depth of the 'U' is not always the same and that differences among countries vary in size in different parts of the curve (Figure 3.3).

A more analytical look prompts a number of observations. For three countries (Denmark, France, and Portugal), the curve in the period under examination is somewhat different from that of the other ones. In Denmark, the very high initial levels of this variable show only a minimum decline in the last years of the nineteenth century and then a first peak of growth in the 1920s followed by a decline which extends until the 1950s, when a new sustained phase of growth begins. In France, from the starting point (which was the lowest among all our countries) onward, no decline takes place; there will be only a slow growth until the Second World War and then a more rapid rise. In Portugal, the initial decline (from rather high levels) is soon interrupted by an exceptional growth of state officials in the last decade of the nineteenth century. Among the other cases the shape of the curve is more similar, albeit with variations in the degree both of the downturn and of the upturn. The decline is stronger in Germany, the Netherlands, Norway, and Hungary (more than 15%), less so in Finland, Italy, and the UK (around 10%). As for the growth from the lowest levels of the twentieth century, it will be particularly impressive in France, Germany, Finland (more than 25%) and somewhat weaker in the other countries.

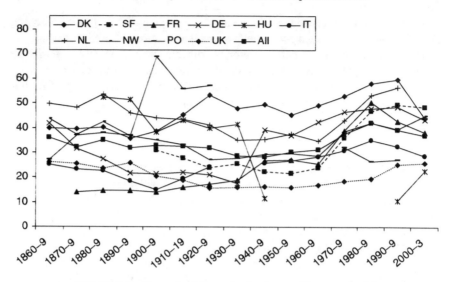

FIGURE 3.3. General public sector background by country (%)

Differences in the shape of the curves are generally more significant in the first phase than in the following periods. If we begin our analysis in the 1860s, the starting point levels for this variable are rather different from country to country. Denmark, Germany, Hungary, the Netherlands, and Norway are characterized by original levels that were much higher than those of France, Italy, and the UK.[8] As for the Iberian countries, our data shows for this variable a contrasting picture: Portugal belongs clearly to the first group (Tavares de Almeida 1995), while Spain seems to fall into the opposite group (Carasa 1997; Cabrera 1998; Linz, Gangas and Mir 2000). Finland, a latecomer in our group of countries, falls somewhat in between the two groups. Such differences between countries raise some interesting questions. The distance between the levels of Germany and the UK could be easily linked to the different weight of the State in one of the initially most *étatiste* and least liberal and in one of the least *étatiste* and most liberal countries of our group. We should also take into account differences in the legal structure of opportunities: 'in Britain civil servants when becoming candidates have to resign from the service and have no right to reintegration: in fact the two careers are incompatible and the choice of a political career means the termination of a career in the civil service' (Allum 1995: 378), a factor which is not altogether unrelated to the former aspects.[9] More surprising, on the contrary, is the lower weight of state background in France (by all accounts one of the most *étatiste* countries in Europe) and in Italy. The explanation we propose is that in the case of France the long initial period of conflicts between the monarchy and parliamentary institutions and the instability of the latter may have provoked a greater reluctance of people with a background in state administration to engage in political life as elected representatives. In the case of Italy the factor that might have initially reduced this presence could possibly be that the bureaucracies of most of the regional states which disappeared with Italian unification were essentially hostile to the new state and to parliamentary life. It would have been strange if members of the new parliament from these regions had been recruited from among officers of the local bureaucracies which initially had little loyalty towards the new Italian state and representative institutions 'exported' from Piedmont.

The generalized decline of parliamentarians with a public sector background in the late nineteenth century and in the first years of the twentieth century produced an increasing convergence among European countries. In the 1920s most countries had fallen under the 30 per cent level and the range of cross-country variations was between 15 and 25 percentage points (the most notable exception being Denmark, where no decline was to be seen, and partially the Netherlands, where the decline was significant but the bottom levels remained rather higher than in the other countries). The influence of the public sector, while still significant, had clearly lost the dominance it had in the past. Political representation in this period moved into the hands of new categories of politicians (for instance, party professionals with a working- or lower-middle-class background).

The great expansion of the post–Second World War period affects more or less in the same way all the countries. The top of the curve is generally reached between the 1970s and the 1980s, when Denmark, France, Germany, the Netherlands, and Norway show levels between 45 and 60 per cent. France has now become more similar to the other countries (it moves up to the 40% and 50% levels). As for Italy, it shows the same trend but without reaching the same levels as the other countries (the top level is around 35%).

For two of the countries that make a delayed return to democracy (Portugal and Hungary) the levels they display for this variable are among the lowest. This result might have to do with the past penetration of the state by the non-democratic regime and its hegemonic party which discouraged recruitment into this pool by the new democratic parties. This result is, however, contradicted by that of Spain where (possibly because of a very continuous model of transition) the weight of the public sector is much higher (over the 40% level in the 1980s and 1990s).

This data suggests that, in the first period, variations in the explanatory factors (be they social or political) should be greater than in the later stages, when a more homogeneous common factor must be at work cross-nationally. Patterns of state-building, nationally specific aspects of the liberalization and democratization processes, and the peculiar political conflicts and alignments among actors of that period should provide some crucial elements for an explanation of cross-country variations. These factors tend to lose their importance with the passing of time and the advent of mass politics; the building of highly developed political organizations, such as mass parties, will then provide new channels of recruitment and new types of politicians will gain an advantage over state bureaucrats. But after the Second World War, the success of mass parties in reshaping in a fundamental way the state itself and its policies probably explains why the public sector, now deeply transformed from the past and 'democratized', can become again a major recruiting 'pool' for political professionals.

A more accurate interpretation of the variations across countries and of their developments should be reached by looking also at the internal components of the broad category we have adopted. We must see whether the different levels in the broader category also entail internal variations in its composition. As we have already stressed, not all public sector occupations have the same meaning. For the sake of simplicity we break down the analysis into three periods: the nineteenth century, the twentieth century until the Second World War, and the second half of the century.

In the first period, in spite of the significant differences existing among countries in the relative levels of the public sector, the internal profile of this background character is, comparatively speaking, not too variable. The component (schoolteachers and professors) which we have considered to be the most peripheral in the public sector is rather weak in most of the countries under examination. The public sector is made up almost entirely of the military, judges, and the higher levels of state administration. This picture is fundamentally true both for the countries that show very high levels of the main variable (Germany, the Netherlands, Norway, and Portugal) and for countries, such as France, Italy, and the UK, that show much lower levels. Among these countries, Portugal stands out for the extraordinary weight gained by the military at the turn of the century. A partial exception to this picture is Denmark, where the schoolteachers and university professors group is rather more significant than in other countries, while the other components (military, judges, and senior civil servants) are relatively weaker (Figures 3.4–3.8).

The data examined during this period indicate that a public sector background among parliamentarians had more or less the same meaning across the countries: it reflected fundamentally, in the representative process, the weight of the state as the source of authority. A position of some relevance in this hierarchy was a significant resource in the representation game: people holding such a position were available to be recruited and able to use it as a stepping stone for a successful political career. What varied across countries was the relative weight of this compared to other types of background.

If we move now to the next period, we can observe a clear and generalized decline of the military. With the inter-war period officers practically disappeared from our parliaments: the (relative) exceptions are Finland, Hungary, and the UK, where until the Second World War more than 5 per cent of the MPs had a military background. If in the first two countries this data fits with the right authoritarian turn of their democracy during that period, in the third it is probably due to the strong links of a military career with those social milieus (aristocracy and landowners) that still provided an important recruiting pool for the Conservative party. Rather similar is the case of a background in the judiciary: even in the countries where it had been relatively more significant

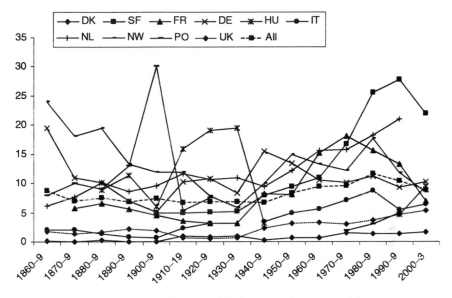

FIGURE 3.4. Higher level civil servants by country (%)

(Germany and the Netherlands) it shrinks now to levels of irrelevance. Somewhat less clear is the picture for the group of the higher-ranking civil servants. The decline from very high percentages is clear in Norway and Germany (but with the Weimar Republic there is a new growth), and albeit from lower levels in France

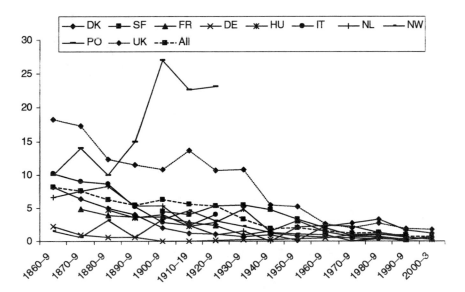

FIGURE 3.5. Military by country (%)

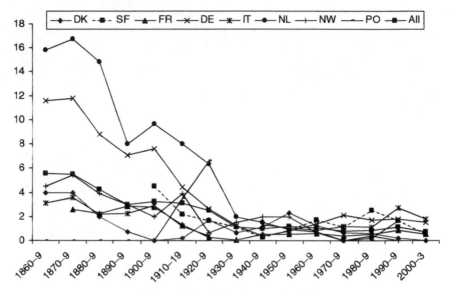

FIGURE 3.6. Judges by country (%)

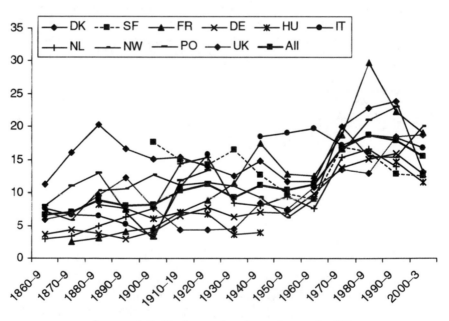

FIGURE 3.7. Teachers and professors by country (%)

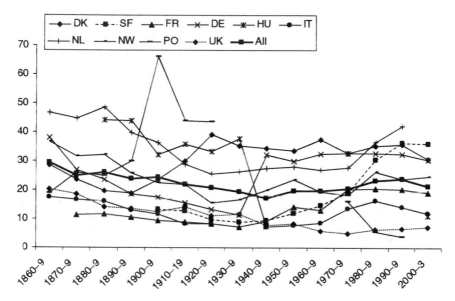

FIGURE 3.8. Public sector background minus teachers and professors by country (%)

(until the 1930s) and the UK, but not in Finland, Hungary, the Netherlands, nor Italy.

With regard to teachers and professors the picture is somewhat different. In most of the countries (France, Hungary, the Netherlands, Norway, and the UK), their number had started to increase during the last part of the nineteenth century and only in Denmark (after the 1870s), Germany, and Italy there had been a decline. But after that a period of decline begins with the second decade of the new century (Denmark, Hungary, the Netherlands, Norway, the UK) or somewhat later (Finland and France) (Figure. 3.7). Germany and Italy are an exception: in both cases, before the rise of the dictatorship, this type of background was growing. The trend of the nineteenth century sets apart this component of public employment from the other ones; but in the inter-war period this category too cannot escape (with only rare exceptions) from the generalized decline of state influence on recruitment.

We come finally to the post–Second World War period, characterized by the generalized growth of the public sector. The only exception is provided by representatives with a military and judiciary background; their decline continues until they practically disappear. Differences among countries are almost irrelevant here: but not surprisingly, the first years of the French Fifth Republic produce a short-term upsurge of MPs with a military background, and in the very last years there is in some countries a limited return of the judicial background. The growth of the public sector is obviously due to other components. For the high ranks of the civil service a moderate (Denmark and the UK) or a strong (Finland, France, Italy, the

Netherlands, Norway, and Portugal) upsurge is to be seen in most of the countries, the main exceptions being Germany, where the fairly high percentage of the first years after the Second World War is followed by a slow decline, and Hungary. We may notice also that in the final years of the twentieth century this component begins in many countries (France, Finland, Italy, and Norway) to decline. Even more clear is the rise of the teaching background: a strong growth is to be seen in most of the countries (Denmark, France, Finland, Germany, the Netherlands, Norway, and the UK), while a high stable level is to be seen in Italy and Portugal. However, for this subcategory too the last elections indicate in many countries (Denmark, Norway, the Netherlands, Germany, France, and Finland) some signs of a decline. What if we look at the public sector as a whole but without teachers and professors? We immediately see that in the second half of the twentieth century it is a rather large component: within a range between 25 and 45 per cent we find Denmark, Finland, Germany, Norway, and the Netherlands, and a little below, France and Italy (Figure 3.8). The size of this component (which is generally stable or on the rise) indicates the increasing internal differentiation of the public sector background.

It is time to summarize these results. The comparative analysis across countries of the different components of the public sector confirms the interpretation proposed on the basis of the global data on the public sector. The extremely significant weight of a public sector background among parliamentary members of all countries after the Second World War no longer reflects the image of the state as the locus of authority, but rather that of the state as the provider of services (among which education is one of the most significant, though not the only one). Why are people with such a background recruited in so high numbers? Because they are for practical reasons more available than other people (public employment enables them to keep their job position while serving in parliament)? Because they possess skills that are in high demand? Because they are asked to represent the interests of a very important sector of society? Possibly for a combination of all these reasons. One could also add to this the plain fact that parties have all become much more interconnected with the state through their role in policymaking and government (Katz and Mair 1995) and are therefore much readier than before to recruit people with a background in that world.

3.7. VARIATIONS ACROSS PARTIES

The next step in the analysis is to discuss the relationship between this variable and the different party families. We want to know to what extent a public sector background can be linked to the political cleavages expressed by parties or to their peculiar organizational features. The more this is so the more we should expect the profile of each party family to be different from the others, while conversely the profile of parties belonging to the same party family would tend to be similar across countries. If this is not the case, it will mean that general factors affecting all the parties in a similar way are at work and explain the levels of this variable. In a long-term perspective we are also interested in seeing whether the degree of specificity of the party families increases or decreases over time.

The figures presented here provide some preliminary answers to these questions. On the basis of our previous analysis we should expect significant variations for the different periods examined. In particular we should expect greater differences across party families in the first period, when a public sector background was more closely linked to the state as a centre of authority (with roots pre-dating the democratization and parliamentarization of political authority). In that age differences between the 'state-builders' and the 'challengers' (to use a Rokkanian terminology) should be more pronounced (Rokkan 1970*a*, 1970*b*). The former should recruit more heavily from among state elites than the latter. The progressive acceptance of the parliamentary system and the extension of suffrage should produce at the turn of the century and in the first decades of the new one a growing homogenization 'to the bottom' of party families. The voice of the state will then be heard less directly in parliament. However, this will not erase differences completely between the old parties, which will continue to recruit (even if less than in the past) from the public sector and the new ones (especially socialists), who will still be unable to open this door. After the Second World War, on the contrary, in the age of wide state intervention, of the universalisation of the welfare state and with the incorporation of opposition parties into the governing establishment of most European democracies (the age of the social-democratic consensus), all parties should become more similar. But this time the homogenezation of party families should take place at the highest levels of presence of public servants. This tendency should be strengthened also by transformations of the parties along the cartel party model.

It is pretty clear from our figures that, at least until the 1920s, the conservative party family with averages between 40 and 30 per cent was the one which drew the largest percentages of its parliamentarians from the public sector (Figure 3.9). If we move from right to left across the party families (from the Conservatives to the Right Liberals, to the Left Liberals, to the Socialists) the mean weight of this background declines accordingly during this period (Figures 3.10–12). The political-ideological proximity to (or distance from) the old *étatiste* establishment appears therefore to be a significant explanatory factor. Only the Christian Democratic (CD) family does not seem to fit into this picture: in the first decades the levels are even higher than those of the conservatives (Figure 3.13). This data, however, has to be taken with caution: since in this period there are only two countries (Germany and the Netherlands) where this family is significant the mean is heavily influenced by just one case—the Dutch one—where the CD parties show an exceptionally high level of this background.

In a developmental perspective it must however be underlined that the original divergence among party families gives way to a growing convergence: by the 1920s, as a result of the decline of this component among conservatives

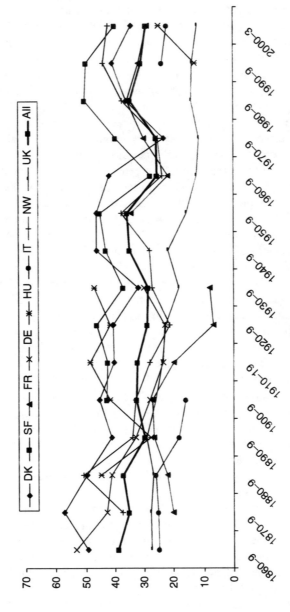

FIGURE 3.9. General public sector background of Conservative parties' MPs (%)

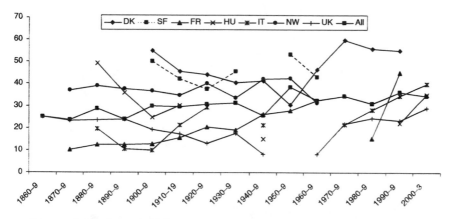

FIGURE 3.10. General public sector background of Left Liberal parties' MPs (%)

(and also Christian Democrats), of a limited growth among Left Liberals and a more sustained one for Socialists, differences in the mean levels across the five families have practically disappeared. The inter-war period is a period of limited decline for Conservatives, Right Liberals, and also Socialists and of limited growth for Left Liberals and Christian Democrats. From the 1940s to the 1980s, a very sustained growth of this variable characterizes Socialists, Christian Democrats, and also Right Liberals; only Conservatives and Left Liberals are an exception to this trend. By the end of this period the Socialist party family has become (with nearly 50%) the one relying to the highest degree upon the public sector for the recruitment of its parliamentary elite. This is not surprising: through

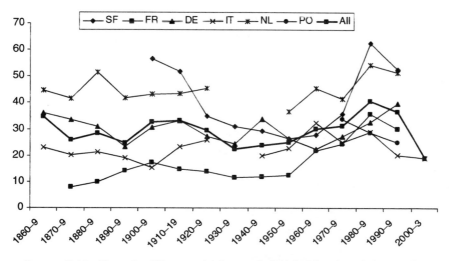

FIGURE 3.11. General public sector background of Right Liberal parties' MPs (%)

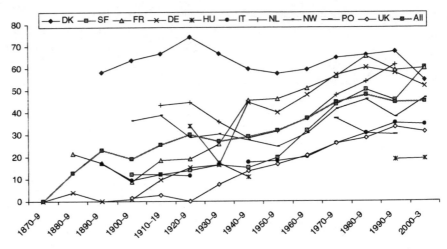

FIGURE 3.12. General public sector background of Socialist parties' MPs (%)

a long process of adaptation and thanks to their increasing ability to have access to governing positions and to shape public policies, these parties have transformed themselves from challengers of the 'old' state to the champions of the 'new' interventionist state, a position which is to some extent shared by almost every other party family but which sees them at the very forefront. With the 1990s and (where the data is available) the first years of the new century, a limited downward trend shared by all party families (with the limited exception of the Left Liberals) begins and seems to suggest that the long *étatiste* trend of the post–Second World War period has reached its peak. New factors (the return of market values and the

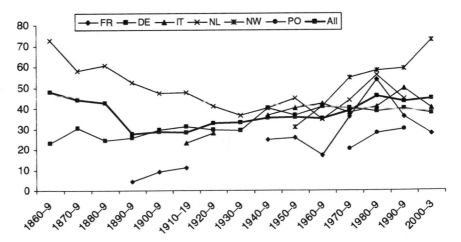

FIGURE 3.13. General public sector background of Christian Democratic parties'
MPs (%)

demand for a greater role of civil society) are probably affecting the representation game and stimulating the selection of representatives with a different background.

In order to complete our exploration, we must now move from the cross-national averages to the country-specific landscapes. In this way, we can analyse to what extent this variable is a significant component in the competition among parties of different families within each political system. Where the differences in the weight of the public sector background between two or more parties or party families are larger, we can assume that also the conflict between political forces over the role of the state in the life of the polity has been greater. As we will see, the degree of polarization is in fact stronger in some countries and weaker in others.

In Germany at the beginning of our period of observation this variable sets dramatically apart Conservatives (and to a lesser extent Right Liberals), who qualify as the party of the state, from Socialists but also Christian Democrats, as the excluded forces. By the 1920s the range of variation has greatly diminished, but the Socialists still trail behind. In Denmark a very clear divide on this variable separates the more state-oriented Conservatives from the Agrarians; but interestingly enough, in this case the latecomer parties such as the Left Liberals and the Socialists will fish in the public sector more effectively than the Agrarians. In Finland in the first years of the twentieth century the Socialist party has only an extremely limited access to this recruitment pool which is, on the contrary, extremely important for all bourgeois parties. In the Netherlands at first the difference between the two main party families (Christian Democrats and Right Liberals) is also quite strong but in a context where both have large access to this resource. However, the advantage of the Christian Democrats in the public sector progressively disappears and the Socialists, when they appear on the scene, show a surprising similarity to the other parties.

In the other countries the overall differences are not so strong. In France the Conservatives are somewhat more *étatiste* than Right and especially Left Liberals, but interestingly enough the Socialists, when they appear, seem closer to the Conservatives than to the Liberals. In Norway the Conservatives are at first more *étatiste* than the Left Liberals but will be soon overtaken by the latter. The division is also not very strong in the UK, where the Conservatives are only slightly more *étatiste* than the Liberals and it is even weaker in Italy between the *Destra storica* and the *Sinistra storica*, the two opposing forces of nineteenth-century politics. However, if we look at specific subcategories of the public sector some differences re-emerge in most of these countries. In Norway the Conservatives draw more clearly from the upper levels of the public sector, while the Left Liberals from schoolteachers and university professors. In the UK the Conservatives count much more upon the military and the Liberals again upon teachers and professors. In France the Conservatives recruit more heavily from the high levels of the public sector and from military ranks; by contrast the Socialists recruit essentially from the teaching sector.

These findings suggest that in most of the countries examined during the last part of the nineteenth century and during the first years of the twentieth century parliamentary representation reflected a competition between 'champions of state authority' and 'challengers'. The intensity of this competition was however variable. It could be extreme, as in Germany where the Socialists were until the 1910s almost totally excluded from such a type of recruitment. In other cases, it meant a significant difference between 'establishment parties' and 'challengers' in the frequency of parliamentarians with a public sector background, but no complete exclusion of the latter. But even where the overall difference seemed hardly relevant a more detailed analysis has shown that significant differences could be found in the internal composition of this type of background.

During the period between the two world wars differences between the establishment and the challenger parties generally decreased, and in some cases the relative positions even changed. In Denmark, the Socialist party became in this period the party with the strongest public sector profile; the same holds true in France, albeit at much lower levels, and in Norway for the Left Liberals. We can say then that a linkage with the authority of the state (and its defence) was increasingly losing its role as a politically divisive factor among parties.

Finally, the period from the end of the Second World War to the 1980s indicates the existence of a common growth factor that cuts across the party families. With possibly only the exception of the British Conservatives, for which there is a decline in MPs with a public sector background, almost all party families show a sustained growth. Particularly, striking is the case of Italy, where the Communist party, moving from a position of almost complete exclusion from this background (around the 10% level in the first three elections), is able to extend its recruitment, at first gradually, but much more substantially with the 1970s when its increasing incorporation in the political system coincides also with a new recruitment pattern (passing the 30% threshold for the public sector background). The generalized growth of this background does not mean that differences across party families are now irrelevant—typically the Socialist family has reached higher levels than Conservatives, and Right and Left Liberals but not of Christian Democrats. Yet it would be difficult to interpret these differences as showing the existence of a serious cleavage between state supporters and state challengers. It seems more a difference between party families that have become more dependent on this type of recruitment and other party families that while making large use of it can have an easier access also to other types of experiences in the private sector.

3.8. CONCLUDING REMARKS

At the end of this analysis, we can summarize the main findings that have emerged from the data we have presented and discussed:

1. The main variable examined in this chapter (the weight of a public sector background among parliamentarians) shows fundamentally a similar cycle

across most of the countries considered here during their long-term process of democratization. Contrary to other variables, this type of background, which has indeed proven to be among the most important characteristics of representative elites, has not shown a linear developmental trend. From its originally rather high levels it generally underwent during the first decades of the twentieth century a significant decline; but later a strong upturn appeared, bringing it back to particularly high peaks. We must therefore look for a common factor or a set of common factors to explain this peculiar 'U-shaped' trend that we have found.

2. The changing relationship between the state (and the social strata linked to it) and the processes and protagonists of democratic representation offers a key to an explanation. The persistent political and social weight of the pre-democratic state and its resistance to the challenges to its pre-eminence originating from within the process of parliamentarization seem the best explanation for the original importance of this background among parliamentarians. The success of the challengers and their model of representation largely based upon the new structures of interest intermediation (such as organized parties and societal interests groups) contributes to explaining the diminished importance of a public sector background in the first part of the new century. However, the success itself of this challenge coming from civil society was bound to produce a new reversal of the trend: the growing importance of the redistributive state in the age of the mature welfare state and the interpenetration between parties and the public sector that has developed, once the challengers have made their way into the political establishment, contribute to explaining the 'return to the state' in the recruitment of parliamentarians which characterizes the second part of the twentieth century.

3. The broad similarity of the long-term trends should not however hide the existence of some important differences in the levels of this variable. The weight of the public sector has not been the same in all countries. Some of them show, in fact, distinctively lower levels. Differences were particularly strong in the first historical phase of the whole process; this is probably attributable to the fact that the political conflict between state and democracy was not equally intense or that it took different forms. On the contrary, the effects of the development of the welfare state after the Second World War have been more homogeneous.

4. A more detailed analysis of the 'composition' of the main variable shows that the meaning of a public sector background changes very significantly with the passing of time. Specific categories of public servants which were more important in the first period (such as high level state functionaries, judges, and military officers) decline significantly with time. Their place will be taken at later stages by teachers and professors or by other categories of public employees. Significant differences in the composition of the public sector exist also across countries. A combined analysis of the quantitative and qualitative aspects of this dimension of the profile of parliamentarians thus seems the best way to evaluate its meaning.

5. Differences between party families are rather important, particularly in the first period of our history, typically pitting parties of the old establishment against the new challengers, with the former possessing a greater number of public servants than the latter. This contrast wanes with time and in fact some of the original challengers—such as the socialist parties—become later the most state-oriented in their recruitment patterns.

6. Finally, the most recent elections seem to suggest that the long growth phase of this component of the background of MPs may have reached its peak and that the new 'privatization' trends may have had some impact also on parliamentary recruitment.

ENDNOTES

1   The countries that could be analysed systematically here were: Denmark, Finland, France, Germany, Hungary, Italy, the Netherlands, Norway, the UK, for which the data-set is more complete. For Portugal and Spain the data available are less complete and they have been introduced only when possible.

2   Throughout the nineteenth century and largely into the twentieth century high-ranking military officers, judges, senior civil servants, such as prefects and ministerial directors, often mingle with the nobility and the high bourgeoisie, sharing elements of their lifestyle, intermarrying, etc. An extreme case of this commixture was that of Russia, where state service at the high levels automatically produced noble status (Labatut 1978; Lieven 1989).

3   As in 1820 and 1874 in Spain, in 1823 and 1828 in Portugal, in 1851 in France, in 1867 in the Netherlands, in 1848 in most of the Italian states and again in 1898 in unified Italy, or in Prussia and then in the German Empire more or less until the First World War (von Beyme 1970).

4   By 'state' we here mean not just the central government but all the branches of public employment which include also local government.

5   The classification of some of these components as part of state employment may in some countries be debatable; this is the case for instance with teachers and university professors in the UK. However, in this book we follow the advice of Rose (1985), who includes them in public employment.

6   In this field things have changed significantly with time. In the last couple of decades the deference of the judiciary vis-à-vis the executive has markedly decreased in most countries (Guarnieri and Pederzoli 1997).

7   Teachers, especially at the university level, tend to consider themselves as part of a special community, that of learning. At the same time it must not be forgotten that they have often played a very crucial role in the nation building process orchestrated by modern states and in propagating the culture of the state. Everybody knows, for instance, the importance of French elementary schoolteachers in the diffusion of the '*esprit républicain*'.

8   In the UK the data is based only on the sum of (retired) military, (retired) high level civil servants, and teachers and professors.

9   When discussing legal structures of opportunities one should bear in mind that they are not exogenous factors unrelated to our explanatory scheme. On the contrary, they typically reflect choices concerning the relationship between representation and the state. It is no accident that where parliament had established for a long time its predominance over the bureaucratic state, as in the UK, such rules would limit more severely the access of civil servants to parliament than in countries where the opposite was true.

4

Why So Few and Why So Slow? Women as Parliamentary Representatives in Europe from a Longitudinal Perspective

Verona Christmas-Best and Ulrik Kjær

4.1. INTRODUCTION

In the push towards gender equality that characterized much of the social development in Europe during the twentieth century, and in spite of women making significant gains in areas such as education and employment, the realm of political representation, especially at national level, has proved particularly resistant to change. So much so that despite increased success in some Scandinavian countries it has been labelled as 'the last bastion of masculinity', with women's level of political representation best described as 'stagnation' (Janova and Sineau 1992: 118). This latter point is certainly supported when long-term trends in the percentage of women in national legislatures across Europe are examined. Despite the granting of female suffrage and eligibility in the majority of European countries during the first half of the twentieth century, in most legislatures women did not break through the 10 per cent barrier until the last quarter of the century, and in some countries, such as Hungary and France, the share of women in the respective legislatures still hovers around this mark. Even in Finland—the first country in Europe to introduce suffrage for women on an equal basis to men (in 1906)—it was not until 1983 that the share of women exceeded the 30 per cent[1] recommended by the United Nations Commission on the Status of Women in 1990 as the acceptable minimum, and which is seen as the threshold for women to have an impact on politics (Inter-Parliamentary Union 2003a). Even today, the average percentage of women in national legislatures across Europe is just 19.2 per cent [2] (Inter-Parliamentary Union 2007). In other words, the optimism of some of the early pioneers of female suffrage that gender parity in national legislatures would follow universal suffrage 'quickly and automatically' was not well founded (Lovenduski 1986). Certainly an overview of women's inclusion in the political elites of Europe appears to support the conclusion drawn

TABLE 4.1. *The level of female parliamentarians in twelve European parliaments by per cent*

Country	Year of election	% of women in parliament at present	% of women in parliament one term previous	% of women in parliament two terms previous
Denmark	2001	38.3	37.7	33.7
Finland	2003	37.5	37.0	33.5
Netherlands	2003	36.7	34.0	36.0
Norway	2001	36.4	36.4	35.8
Austria	2002	33.9	26.8	21.9
Germany	2002	32.2	30.7	26.3
Spain	2000	28.3	21.6	15.7
Portugal	2002	19.1	19.1	10.4
UK	2001	17.9	18.1	8.8
France	2002	12.3	10.9	6.0
Italy	2001	11.6	11.1	15.1
Hungary	2002	9.8	8.5	11.1
Average		26.2	24.3	21.2

by Robert Putnam (1976) that 'an iron law of andrarchy' has been working in the area of political elites and that, as Table 4.1 shows, it still seems to hold good at the beginning of the twenty-first century, at least as a tendency if not as a law.[3]

4.2. THE CONCEPT OF GENDER PARITY

Despite the successes of the early pioneers of women's suffrage, gender parity in the parliaments of Europe did not automatically follow suffrage as expected. In fact, although Duverger's seminal work Duverger 1955) can be said to have paved the way, it was not until the second wave of the women's movement in the late 1960s and 1970s that concerns about gender (and racial) under-representation in political elites became a more prominent feature of empirical research. One of the leading scholars in the field of political recruitment studies, and some one who has paid particular attention to the question of women's share of seats in legislative bodies, is Pippa Norris (e.g. Norris 1985; Norris and Lovenduski 1995; Lovenduski and Norris 1996). Writing about the proportion of women representatives in the European Parliament, she recently commented that 'Based on trends since the first direct elections, we can estimate that women will achieve parity in the European Parliament in the year 2044' (Norris 1999*a*, 1999*b*: 98). This comment presupposes three important facts that characterize much of the extant literature on women in political elites: First, based on the tenet of democratic government as a wholly inclusive and representative system, the concept of gender equality in legislatures is seen as a natural and desirable goal (Paxton 1997; Dahl 1989; Caul 2001). This also raises the question of legitimacy which holds that the composition of a parliament should 'mirror' the electorate (Kjær 2000: 31ff.) in this case, by showing an equal gender balance.

Second, while suggesting that gender parity in a representative legislature is the ideal, the comment also suggests that it is not expected immediately. This is in line with many other commentators who also seem resigned to a long wait before seeing a proportion of women in most parliaments that would come anywhere near parity. For example, in 1999, Reynolds found it striking that 'despite the advances women have made in representation, for the last fifteen years the numbers have plateaued at approximately 12 percent' (Reynolds 1999: 558). Further, although recent figures for the countries[4] in our study show that the level of female representatives in several has passed the 30 per cent atypicality barrier, no country has yet achieved parity.[5] Indeed, the figures even suggest recent declines or possible signs of plateauing in some countries.

A third feature of the Norris quote is the concept that future states can be forecast as a simple extrapolation of the past. In this case, Norris's motive is almost certainly not to estimate the exact time when parity could be expected but rather to use it as a way of illustrating the long-windedness of the increase in female representation in the European Parliament. However, a simple extrapolation can indeed be found in the debate of the gender composition of legislative bodies, even though this way of predicting the future may be dubious.

4.3. RESEARCH FINDINGS FROM THE LITERATURE

In terms of empirical investigations into the lack of gender parity, reasons for women's poor showing in the field of political elites generally fall into three broad areas of influence—cultural/historical, socio-economic, and institutional (Matland 1998a).

4.3.1. *Cultural/Historical Influences*

It is widely accepted that, on average, women do not have the same social or economic status as men (Kaplan 1992). Such differences can be seen to stem from beliefs rooted in antiquity[6] regarding men and women's biologically determined roles in society which, over time, have become embodied in cultural tradition as socially accepted norms. Central to this debate is the concept of patriarchy: this has been defined as 'a set of social relations which has a material base and in which there are hierarchical relations between men and solidarity among them which enable them in turn to dominate women' (Hartmann 1981: 14) and one enduring manifestation of patriarchy has been male domination of legislative power in the majority of cultures. In 1955, in his treatise on women in politics based on reports from four European countries, Duverger wrote, 'In our society, all forms of political activity were until recently, and to a large extent still are, the exclusive privilege of men' (Duverger 1955: 192). Some fifty years later, in his work on the gender gap in legislative representatives in one of the world's biggest democracies (the USA), Kevin Arceneaux was still able to write that 'voters and/or elites have been socialized to view politics as a man's world' (Arceneaux 2001: 144). As Arceneaux also explains, such gendered beliefs may have several consequences for the political activity of women: Women may not become involved in politics because they see it as 'not appropriate'; they may not be recruited by political parties for the same reason; and those who do run for office may face unsympathetic voters.

Diamond (1977) also suggested that a culture which adheres to traditional beliefs, especially concerning hierarchies and elites, will be less supportive of women's participation in politics than a more egalitarian, moralistic culture. The latter is likely to be more accommodating to women in politics because 'Politics in moralistic states focuses on honesty, integrity, and public welfare—ideals that female candidates may more credibly project' (Arceneaux 2001 citing Huddy and Terkildsen 1993). This also suggests that countries demonstrating higher levels of societal modernization, for example, through welfare provision, may be more 'female friendly' (Perkin 1996). Here the second wave of feminism that occurred across Europe in the late 1960s and 1970s is relevant. This sought to remove legal inequalities based on gender and to actualize gender equality (initially linked to access to employment, equal pay, and equal employment rights) and has been associated with the simultaneous rise of women as parliamentary representatives evident in some countries (Kaplan 1992).

Seen from a historical or time perspective, it has also been posited that the earlier a society recognized its female members as full citizens by granting them franchise, the more women are likely to be active in parliament today (Rule 1987; Reynolds 1999; Siaroff 2000). The theoretical base for this eligibility hypothesis is that it takes time to integrate a hitherto unrepresented socio-demographic group into the established parliamentary elite. One explanation for a delay in attaining gender parity, therefore, could be that it takes time to reverse or moderate the initial power structure, that is, gaining the right to stand for election is not likely to have an immediate effect on the inter-gender power balance.

Finally, from a cultural perspective, some literature suggest that predominantly Roman Catholic[7] countries are likely to have fewer women in parliament than countries whose confession is predominantly Protestant, so that not having Roman Catholicism as dominant religion is taken to be a positive factor for women entering a political elite (Rule 2000; see also Kotler-Berkowitz 2001). The role of religion, however, has been disputed by Kaplan (1992) who, although partly basing her argument on the false assumption that Denmark is strongly Catholic, does cite the UK as primarily a Protestant country but which nevertheless has a paucity of female political representatives, even after the efforts of the Blair governments. In addition, some researchers have noted that increasing secularization towards the end of twentieth century may have loosened the hold of religion on women's attitudes towards their social role, even in predominantly

Roman Catholic countries (Inglehart and Norris 2000: 446). However, this might underestimate the enduring effect of culturally embedded social values based on former higher levels of religiosity.

4.3.2. *Socio-economic Explanations*

As was shown in Best and Cotta (2000), although social and educational background of parliamentary elites varies over time and by country, both play a highly significant role in the background of those who become legislative representatives. Even where there are no formal eligibility requirements in terms of education, occupation, etc., it would seem that 'political competences' supporting the selection, election, and success of representatives are better achieved in some parts of the educational system and in certain occupations than in others. Historically, eligibility and/or 'qualifications' to run, such as high levels of wealth and education in the old elites, disadvantaged women because they were typically under-represented or even absent in these groups.

Taking the role of education first: increased access to education since the Second World War is seen as having been one of the most significant and long-reaching influences on the social status of women of the twentieth century (Eccles 1994; Jacobs 1996). As education is an essential qualification for public service, as well as a useful one for entry into political assemblies, this rise in educational level has assisted women in making inroads into areas that were formerly 'off limits', such as engaging in the political affray (Perkin 1996: 11–13). It could be expected, therefore, that countries where women achieve a high standard of education will have a higher percentage of women legislators than countries where women are less well educated. Certainly, higher level of education has been linked to women's entering male-dominated occupational areas (Christmas 2002) of which politics is an example.

With regard to employment,[8] research has shown that long-term structural trends in post-industrial societies[9] have resulted in an increasing convergence of gender roles that have been particularly manifested in a structural revolution in the paid labour force, as well as in changes to the traditional family unit (Inglehart and Norris 2000). Some research, therefore, has suggested a link between women's level of integration into the labour market (full-time work and a high presence in high-status positions) and a country's share of female legislators (Rule 1987; Oakes and Almquist 1993). However, occupations are 'gendered' (Reskin and Roos 1990) and often viewed as the traditional domain of either males or females, although some can be classed as gender-neutral (Hakim 1993*b*; Anker 1998; Christmas 2002). The important factor, therefore, is not whether women in a society work but where they work. For example, where the occupational group serving as the main area of political recruitment is male dominated (such as the military, law, or business leaders), there is likely to be a spillover effect to the process of political recruitment leading to a corresponding under-representation of women in political electoral bodies. Where recruitment is from a gender-neutral (such as public service) or female-dominated (such as teaching) occupational group, then women's entry into the political arena may be enhanced.

One consequence of women's increasing engagement in paid employment outside the home seems to be that, over time, women have gradually realigned their political orientation—whereas women in the past were considered more politically right and conservative than men (Duverger 1955), trends have been towards a more liberal, or leftist orientation (Lovenduski 1986). This 'lean to the left' has resulted in a somewhat symbiotic relationship whereby women have increasingly associated with parties demonstrating a greater compatibility between party preferences and their areas of immediate interest, so that in turn, these parties look more favourably on women's active participation—the culmination of which is that women have greater chance of selection therein. The rise and success of parties related to environmental issues (mirroring increased social concerns) have also acted as a vehicle for women's increased political activities.

4.3.3. *Institutional Explanations*

Even when there is no formal discrimination against women in electoral law, there can be circumstances with regard to the electoral rules that de facto work as an indirect barrier to their election to parliament. In order to be elected, one has to stand for election and, while independent candidates are not unknown, the vast majority of candidates stand as a member of a political party. In all political systems in Europe, political parties represent different political ideologies or standpoints by which they align their membership, and upon which they base their appeal to the electorate. As noted earlier, a link has been proposed between the position of a party and the number of women selected as candidates for election. Generally, left-wing parties support more women candidates and have more women as legislators, and there is typically a positive relationship between the reformist, feminist ideals of the women's movement, and the principles of left-leaning parties. Likewise, parties who do not overly recruit women candidates may not do so because the issues women tend to promote—support for working women, abortion rights, etc.—are not issues supported by the party in general (Arceneaux 2001). For example, in the UK, Conservative policy has been away from public spending on provision for full-time childcare so that only women who are atypical in this regard may be recruited.

In terms of a connection between the proportion of women party members and the number of women selected as candidates or successfully elected, however, no correlation has been found (Hoecker 1998). This is demonstrated by the Conservative Party in the UK and the Gaullist Party in France, where both have high percentages of women members (49% and 50% respectively in the early 1990s) but no corresponding level of women MPs in their national legislatures. On the contrary, these two countries have some of the lowest levels of women representatives, not just in Europe, but in the world. Taking the early 1990s again as an example, in the election of 1992 in the UK just 5 per cent of the Conservative MPs returned to parliament were female (overall percentage of female MPs = 8.8%) and in the 1993 French elections just 6.8 per cent Gaulist MPs were female (6% overall; Bird 2000).

In an attempt to determine what barriers and benefits (socio-economic and political) explain women's level of parliamentary and cabinet representation, Rule (2000) examined the extent of women's legislative representation in sixty-eight developing and established democracies and concluded that the electoral system is the single most important predictor of women's recruitment to parliament. Further, her findings indicate that women fare better under systems of PR, do slightly less well under mixed systems, and come off worst under straight majoritarian, that is first past the post (FPTP) systems (see also Paxton 1997; Matland 1998*b*; Reynolds 1999). Further, multi-member districts seem to be advantageous to women while single-member districts are not.

The way in which parliaments are organized and the characteristics of its members can also influence the proportion of women elected to serve there (Norris 1985; Paxton 1997; Matland 1998*b*; Reynolds 1999; Siaroff 2000; Arceneaux 2001; Studlar and McAllister 2002). For example, findings from a number of studies propose that a low turnover is disadvantageous to women—incumbents tend to be male, with larger margins, and greater access to resources so that women are placed in the position of 'challengers' with little support. Therefore, as Niven reported, 'the single most daunting obstacle to the election of women is simply the inertia built into the system which [can be called] incumbency advantage' (Niven 1998: 22). Indeed, incumbent politicians are likely to be returned to office at a significantly higher ratio than candidates running without office as their starting point. Hence the phenomenon known as 'the victorious incumbent' (Somit, Wildenmann, and Boll 1994) and the seemingly 'catch 22' situation whereby the best position from which to run a campaign for political office is ... political office.

In particular, a low turnover can delay the impact of a possible change in the recruitment habits of selectors and electors in terms of the politician's gender: 'Since women are much less likely than men to be incumbents ... it will take decades for them to achieve equality in office in most nations if the normal advantages of incumbency continue to operate' (Clark 1991: 74). In sum, even if the formal pathways to parliament are open to women, features of elite circulation, such as high incumbency rates, can be a barrier to the election of women (Andersen and Thorson 1984: 144).

The importance given to turnover rates is partly based on the theory of critical mass which posits that once a group reaches a certain size, 'there will be a qualitative change in the nature of group interactions, as the minority starts to assert itself and thereby transform the institutional culture, norms and values' (Norris and Lovenduski 2001). In other words, the more women representatives there are in a parliament, the more it becomes an accepted social norm for women to be active in a political setting, the easier selection and election will be for other women. One way of 'bump starting' the seemingly natural process underlying critical mass theory has been the employment of gender quotas (Dahlerup 1998*b*; Sgier 2003). These may be voluntary (as in the case of Germany) or enforced through legislation (as in the case of France) or even ideologically imposed, as in the states of the former communist bloc. However, while the use of quota systems has been held directly responsible for a dramatic increase in the percentage of women representatives in some countries—for example, in the UK in 1997 when the percentage of women in the UK Parliament doubled[10]—in other countries, such as France in 2002,[11] it has been less successful. Here one could also include post-communist states, such as Hungary, in that the enforced equality of representation during communist times seems to have created a backlash against female inclusion in the political elite following a return to free democratic elections.

4.4. HYPOTHESES AND METHODS

From this short foray into the literature it is evident that several factors can be identified with the level of women's inclusion in a country's political elite. Based on this evidence, ten hypotheses on the level of female legislators can be proposed.

4.4.1. *Hypotheses*

Cultural

1. The eligibility hypothesis—the longer the time span since women were enfranchised and granted eligibility, the higher the current level of female representation.
2. The non-Catholic hypothesis—where the majority religion within the country is not Roman Catholic or Orthodox, the level of female representation is positively affected.
3. The 'politics as a male domain' hypothesis—where the dominant cultural perception of the social role of women and their expected level of active citizenship, is accepting of equal active citizenship the level of female representation is positively affected.

Socio-economic

4. The occupation hypothesis—the level of female representation is affected positively if the prime recruiting base is not a male-dominated occupation.
5. The labour-force hypothesis—where women have a high presence in the labour force (especially in higher status positions), they will also be more present in the political elite.

6. The education hypothesis—the more well-educated women are within a society, the greater their chances of entering parliament.

Institutional

7. The inertia hypothesis—high personnel turnover is a necessary condition for women as newcomers to enter the political elite.
8. The electoral system hypothesis—countries with proportional electoral systems will have higher levels of female representation than those with majoritarian or mixed systems.
9. The quota hypothesis—quota systems facilitate a higher level of female representation (although the effect can be expected to be greater where this is voluntary).
10. The Left party hypothesis—where a left-oriented party is successful, more women are successful as legislative representative.

4.4.2. *Methods*

As Walby comments, 'In order to address contemporary patterns of gendered change in a globalising world we need concepts which do not retreat to even smaller units, but which are able to make reference to a wider horizon of events' (Walby 2000: 525). In this respect, the EurElite database (see introductory Chapter for a full description) is helpful in that it not only offers the possibility to look at the question of female parliamentarians from a longitudinal and comparative perspective[12] but that each election can be examined at the party level,[13] and each party by the constituent characteristics of its members. Such detailed, longitudinal data are particularly important when seeking to test the influence of factors such as those derived from the literature and especially when endeavouring to monitor and compare trends over time. Even though some comparative studies on female parliamentary representation have been making use of longitudinal data (see for instance Studlar and McAllister 2002; Caul 1999) given the scope of the data at our disposal, that is, encompassing the entire period that women have been present in twelve European parliaments, we are able to do this from a much broader perspective. Further, although the EurElite database does not include every European country, it is representative in that it includes countries amongst those with the highest proportion of female representatives in the world (Norway and Finland) as well as countries from among those with the lowest (France and Hungary).

From the EurElite database we will utilize data covering party composition and background variables of representatives of national legislatures for all countries[14] starting from the first election following the granting of full female suffrage, i.e. on an equal basis with the male population[15] to the present day. However, in cases such as Hungary, where free democratic elections were not held for a considerable period (i.e. during the communist era), only data following the reinstatement of a

free parliament is used. This means that the scope of the data varies by country so
that not all countries can be included in all analyses. Where this is the case, the
reduced *n* is noted.

4.5. DATA ANALYSIS

In the empirical part of this chapter, we do not attempt to cover all the hypotheses
put forward earlier but concentrate on those where the advantages of a longitudinal approach is greatest— namely:

1. the eligibility hypothesis;
2. the inertia hypothesis; and
3. the 'Left party' association hypothesis.

First, however, given the potential of the data-set and in order to form a basis from
which to test the hypotheses, we will examine and compare the data to determine
the nature of developments in the level of female politicians across the included
parliamentarian elites and across time.

4.5.1. *Developmental Patterns and Trends*

An examination of the data shows immediately that developments have not followed a linear progression in any country (see Figure 4.1) and that increases in the
percentage of female representatives seem to pass through a sequence of distinct
phases.

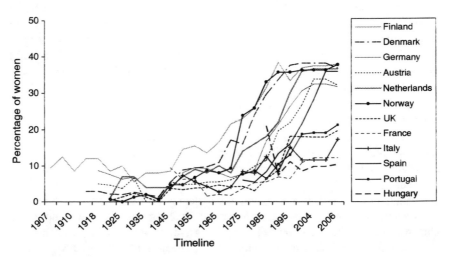

FIGURE 4.1. Trends in percentage of female representatives across time
in twelve European countries

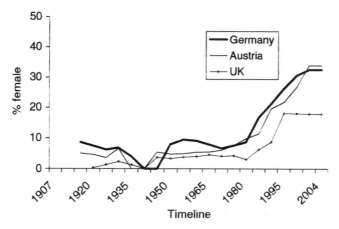

FIGURE 4.2. The percentage of female MPs from 1900 until the first election of the new millennium in Germany, Austria, and the UK

The first phase observed we refer to as the *start-up phase*. This encompasses the time leading to and including the granting of female eligibility (in many cases accompanying female suffrage). To exemplify this we can use the German case: Here this phase culminated in the 1919 elections, when the newly introduced female eligibility led to 8.7 per cent women in the first Reichstag of the Weimar Republic. Following the first entry of women into parliament, as can be seen by Figure 4.2, it seems that the general trend is for there to be a phase where the initial level of female MP's is only momentarily and marginally surpassed, and where little significant movement is seen. We call this the *lethargy phase*.

In the German case, it is seen to be quite lengthy: In the 1980 election, the percentage of women returned to the Bundestag was 8.7 per cent, exactly the same as it had been sixty-one years earlier. In the intervening period, there were only minor fluctuations and the percentage of women never exceeded 10 per cent. However, the data also show that at some point in time most countries experienced a sudden growth in the percentage of women in parliament that marks the starting point of a sustained and notable increase (and whereby the level of female representatives never falls below this take-off point)—we denote this the *take-off phase*. In the German case, this can be seen to be the general election of 1972.

Since the level of female parliamentarians cannot increase indefinitely, we can also include a fourth phase, the *stabilization phase*. There are already indications that some countries are entering this phase (e.g. Norway, Finland, Denmark, and the Netherlands—see Figure 4.3) and that, having exceeded the 30 per cent atypicality barrier, they may nevertheless be plateauing at a level below 50 per cent— something that has been described as 'saturation without parity' (Kjær 1999).

When looking at trends in the percentage of female parliamentarians over time, some similarities in the pattern of phased development can be seen between

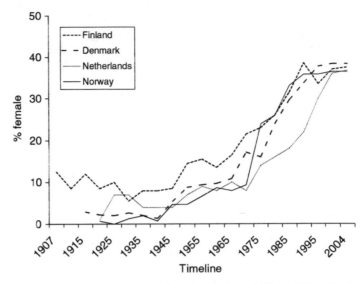

FIGURE 4.3. The percentage of female MPs from 1900 until first election of the new millennium in the Netherlands, Norway, Finland, and Denmark

countries. One group, Germany, Austria, and the UK (see Figure 4.2) have a particularly long *lethargy phase*. Although all granted eligibility to women prior to the Second World War, the take-off phase did not happen before the late 70s and early 80s. Another group, Finland, Denmark, Norway, and the Netherlands (see Figure 4.3) also granted eligibility to women prior to the Second World War but in this group the *take-off phase* comes much more quickly, some twenty to thirty years earlier than the former group.

In the four countries in this group, it is even possible to split the *take-off phase* in two. From the end of the Second World War until the early 1970s, increases were stable but modest. This is followed by a period of more extreme growth from the early 1970s onwards. As mentioned earlier, the data also suggests that these four countries might be entering a *stabilization phase*, and certainly Finland and Norway have experienced some stagnation in the level of female MPs during the 1990s.

In another group, France and Italy (see Figure 4.4) appear to have a similar pattern of development. Neither grants women eligibility until after the Second World War and both hardly meet the criteria for entering a *take-off phase*. By 1995, France only just exceeds its start up level of 1945 (10.9% and 9.4% respectively) and following the election of 2002 has made very little progress with just 12.2 per cent women in the Assemblée Nationale. Italy could technically be said to be in the *take-off phase* because from 1975 the percentage of women in the Camera dei Deputati does not drop below 8.4 per cent but its erratic progress after this time means it is not yet clear whether this will be a sustained progress.

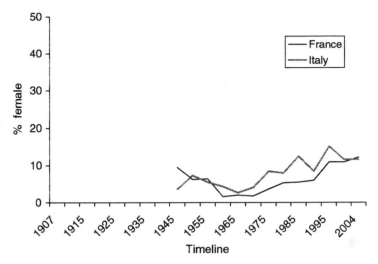

FIGURE 4.4. The percentage of female MPs from 1900 until the first election
of the new millennium in France and Italy

For example, in 1992 the level of female Deputies has fallen back to 8.4 per cent
and by the election of 2001, women only account for 11.6 per cent of Deputies,
having previously achieved 15.1 per cent in 1994.

At first glance Spain, Portugal, and Hungary (see Figure 4.5) also form a group
in that all three present no data for female representatives before the final quarter

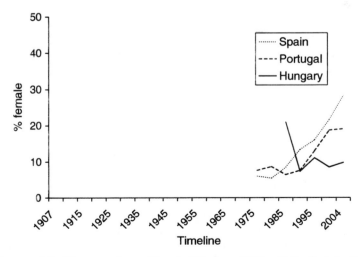

FIGURE 4.5. The percentage of female MPs from 1900 until the first election
of the new millennium in Spain, Portugal, and Hungary

of the twentieth century and whereby they all experienced a return to free democracy following the fall of an oppressive regime. However, Spain and Portugal
present a very different profile to that of Hungary. First, both counties have a very
short *lethargy phase* and have *take-off phases* marked by very rapid increases in
the percentage of female representatives. Hungary, on the other hand, (following
Communist governance with its enforced quotas of female representatives) started
with a comparatively high percentage of women elected to parliament (21% in
1985) but subsequent elections saw the virtual demise of women in the political
elite with no real signs of recovery as yet (9.8% in 2002).

4.5.2. *The Eligibility Hypothesis*

Looking at the level of female representation in the parliaments of the early
21st century and combining these figures with the amount of years that have
elapsed since women gained eligibility in the respective countries, the eligibility
hypothesis seems to be supported. The seven countries that awarded women
eligibility before 1920 have an average share of female MP's today above 33 per
cent [16] while France and Italy, where eligibility was given later, that is 1944 and
1945 respectively, only have 12.2 and 11.6 per cent respectively. If time since the
introduction of women eligibility is regressed on the present share of female MP's,
this single variable can explain no less than 89 per cent of the variation.[17]

In more general terms, a very rigid and deterministic interpretation of this eligibility hypothesis would mean that the percentage of female MPs in a given country
at a given point of time is to be explained exclusively by the time elapsed since
women gained eligibility and not by cultural, socio-economic, or political factors
specific to the country in question. According to a deterministic explanation of
the eligibility hypothesis, the claim would be that increases in female MP's follow
a universal pattern where neither country nor era influence the trend.

One way of supporting such a rigid interpretation would be to show that the lag
observed in Italy and France is due to their late awarding of eligibility to women,
and that their current level of female MP's is proportionate to the length of time
since eligibility was granted. And indeed, as can be seen in Table 4.2, which gives
a comparison of the percentage of women in other European parliaments fifty-
eight years after women obtained eligibility, Italy and France indeed do not fare
worse than the other European countries when the length of time following female
eligibility is taken into account.

However, while these figures suggest that gender parity of a parliamentary elite
is a process that takes time, the question of why the percentages of women in these
two legislatures are lower today compared to other parliaments in our sample is
still not answered. Even more so when developments over time in other countries,
such as Spain and Portugal are considered, where much less time has elapsed since
(admittedly a return to) eligibility and where there is currently a much greater
percentage of women in the political elites of both countries than in either Italy or

TABLE 4.2. *The percentage of women in selected European parliaments fifty-eight years after women obtained eligibility*

Country	% of women in parliament fifty-eight years after women gained eligibility
Norway	15.6
Denmark	15.4
Netherlands	14.0
Finland	13.5
France	12.2
Italy	11.6
Austria	7.7
Germany	7.6
UK	4.3

Source: EurElite data-set.

France. In sum, Table 4.2 shows that, while time may play a role, it alone cannot explain the variation shown in Figure 4.1 and Table 4.2.

4.5.3. *The Inertia Hypothesis*

A more direct explanation as to why the feminization of parliamentary elites appears to be protracted is the effect of high incumbency rates and the correspondingly low turnover rates, whereby low personnel circulation can be said to delay elite transformation that is otherwise under way. We will denote this the inertia hypothesis (inspired by Niven 1998: 22) and note that it is somewhat related to the eligibility hypothesis, since the inertia explanation can be one reason why the lapse of time since women gained eligibility can influence the present level of female parliamentarians.

To test the inertia hypothesis we will use those countries in our data-set where we have longitudinal data since the Second World War or earlier (i.e. nine countries, excluding Spain, Portugal, and Hungary). By looking at the raw incumbency rates, it would seem that an incumbent does indeed have a substantial comparative electoral advantage—on average, two-thirds of the elected MPs in the twentieth century have been incumbents. We can claim, therefore, that the necessary conditions exist for the incumbency-based inertia to function, at least to a certain extent.

The most simple way to test the inertia hypothesis is to examine whether the countries where the parliamentary turnover has been relatively high are the same as those where we find the highest levels of female MPs and vice versa. As can be seen from Table 4.3, which gives the average turnover for each of the nine countries, this initial examination of the data seems not to confirm the inertia hypothesis. The highest level of turnover, an average of 40.7 per cent, is found in Italy, where the level of women in the parliament, according to Table 4.1, is the lowest among the included countries. Alternatively, in Denmark,

TABLE 4.3. *Percentage change in women parliamentarians correlated with average turnover for each of the selected countries over the phases of development*

| Country | | Phase | | | |
	Lethargy	Take-off I	Take-off II	Stabilization	1848–2002
France					
Mean change	−0.8	1.5	—	—	0.7
Mean turnover	31.7	35.9	—	—	33.4
Correlation	−0.76	0.85	—	—	−0.20
Italy					
Mean change	−0.2	2.0	—	—	0.8
Mean turnover	38.9	34.9	—	—	40.7
Correlation	0.86	0.59	—	—	0.48
UK					
Mean change	0.2	3.0	—	—	0.8
Mean turnover	20.6	21.0	—	—	20.7
Correlation	0.50	0.88	—	—	0.47
Austria					
Mean change	0.0	3.2	—	—	1.5
Mean turnover	32.7	32.1	—	—	32.5
Correlation	−0.25	0.70	—	—	0.02
Germany					
Mean change	−0.2	2.9	—	—	1.3
Mean turnover	36.3	28.0	—	—	34.8
Correlation	0.66	0.07	—	—	0.16
Netherlands					
Mean change	0.1	2.9	—	—	1.5
Mean turnover	22.3	22.7	—	—	22.5
Correlation	−0.20	0.71	—	—	0.26
Denmark					
Mean change	−0.2	1.0	2.1	—	1.1
Mean turnover	19.7	22.2	26.1	—	23.4
Correlation	−0.66	0.62	−0.15	—	0.20
Finland					
Mean change	−0.1	0.9	3.1	−0.3	1.1
Mean turnover	29.3	29.1	33.4	—	30.5
Correlation	0.32	−0.14	0.58	—	0.23
Norway					
Mean change	0.0	1.2	5.3	0.2	1.7
Mean turnover	25.0	29.2	22.5	—	27.7
Correlation	0.01	0.58	0.42	—	0.22

where the level of female MPs is very high, the average level of turnover is just 23.4 per cent, so that Denmark ranks seventh out of the nine countries under scrutiny here.

However, before rejecting this explanation for differences in the level of female representation, we should note that the average numbers included cover quite lengthy spans of time, so that variation, as well as correlation, may therefore have been lost. Consequently, we will try to benefit from the different phases identified earlier. For each country, at least two phases, a *lethargy phase* and a *take-off phase*, have been identified, and according to the inertia hypothesis, we can expect to find that turnover rate is higher in the *take-off* phase than in the preceding *lethargy phase*, in each of the countries. Therefore, in the first columns of Table 4.3, the average turnover rates have been split according to the identified phases and again the figures tend to refute the inertia hypothesis. It is true that in countries like France, UK, the Netherlands, Denmark, and to some extent Finland, the average turnover rate is indeed bigger for the *take-off phase* than for the *lethargy phase*, but not only are the differences in these countries minor, in the rest of the countries the opposite case is found.

As this kind of analysis may seem rather rudimentary and lacking in detail, the correlation between the percentage change in female representation and the turnover rate was calculated for each country with each election included as a data-point. Results (see Table 4.3) show that for all countries, except France, a positive correlation exists between increase in the percentage of female representatives and overall turnover in parliament. If data for all countries are merged (all-time and all-countries), a statistically significant correlation of 0.18 is found between increase in the level of female parliamentarians and overall turnover rate ($p = 0.011$; $n = 192$).

It should be emphasized, though, that these somewhat weak correlations do not provide us with an answer to whether or not an inertia effect has been operating within the reshaping of the parliamentarian elites. A high turnover would seem to be only a necessary and not an exclusive condition for women's entry into the legislatures—a higher percentage of women among newcomers than among re-elected incumbents must also be present (Kjær 1999).

In wanting to test this hypothesis more fully and in order to assess the scale of a potential incumbency-based lag effect, we meet the problem that systematic comparative evidence on the percentage of women among the newcomers to all the selected European parliaments is lacking in our data. However, such data is available for Denmark. Here, in order to assess the dimension of a potential inertia effect, we will assume a turnover rate of 100 per cent (meaning that the level of women among the newcomers at each election, using a strong *ceteris paribus* condition, is extended to the whole parliament). In this case, it can be calculated that the average percentage of women in the Danish *Folketing* in the post-war period would not have been 19 per cent as it was but 23 per cent instead. Further, in the period where the inertia effect has been highest (between 1975 and 1990), the average percentage of women MPs would have been 32 per cent and not 25 per cent (Kjær and Pedersen 2004).

In sum, it can be concluded that the inertia hypothesis cannot help us explain the differences in the level of female representatives observed between the countries included in this chapter. Looking at each country in turn and using the phases introduced at the beginning of this section, we do not find the covariation expected by the inertia hypothesis, although when a more detailed analysis using each election as a data-point was performed, a correlation between increase in female representation and turnover rate was found. In addition, an examination of the Danish case, revealed an, albeit modest, inertia effect. However, more detailed comparative work (including the percentage of women among newcomers to parliament) is required before any generalization can be made.

4.5.4. *The Left Party Association Hypothesis*

In order to test the hypothesis that there is a relationship between the number of women returned to a parliament and the success of left-wing parties,[18] a procedure was undertaken that measured the strength of female representation overall against the strength of women returned via left-wing parties. For this analysis, the level of female MPs in a parliament belonging to left parties was calculated as a percentage of all female MPs in the same parliament. However, there was a need to control for fluctuations in the overall size of the left parties. In order to do this, the percentage of left female MPs in a parliament was divided by the percentage of all left MPs. This produced values within a range of 0–4. Where the value returned is 1, it can be said to represent a balanced ratio between the percentage of women MPs and the overall percentage of left MPs. Where this value is higher than 1, an over representation of women through left parties is indicated. Where the value is less than 1, the hypothesis that women are better represented via left parties can be said not to have been proved. Values were computed for all parliaments in the twelve countries included in our data-set.

To facilitate the interpretation of results, the values for each country were plotted as a line graph, which can be seen in Figure 4.6. The most immediate observation is that over time, following a period of erratic behaviour from the early 1920s to the end of the 1940s, there is consolidation with values typically lying between 1 and 2 for all countries. This latter point is reinforced when the standard deviation is plotted. Overall, a general trend for female MPs being over-represented via left parties would seem to be indicated, although there seems to be a suggestion that this maybe reducing in effect over time.

When results for the individual countries are examined, it is clear that the effect of left party membership has a much greater impact in some countries than in others. For example, in Italy, Finland, and Austria, the ratio never falls below 1, indicating a continuous relationship between level of female MPs and affiliation to left-wing parties. On the other hand, following a low-level of female representation overall, in Norway a significant proportion of female representatives were returned via the Conservative, right-wing party, and in Denmark, women's success can be seen to be only marginally linked to the success of the left. To examine these findings further, differences in the percentage of women returned to a parliament by all parties, in the percentage of all MPs returned by left parties,

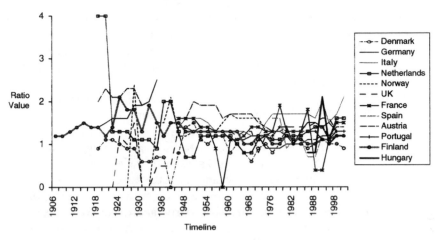

FIGURE 4.6. Ratio of women returned by Left parties and non-Left parties in the parliaments of twelve European countries in the twentieth century

and in the percentage of women returned by left parties over time were correlated. As Table 4.4 shows, a significant positive correlation was found between all three variables. Of particular importance is the significant positive relationship found between differences in the success of left parties over time and differences in the success of women as political representatives over the same time periods.

Having found that the percentage change in level of female representatives correlates highly with the success of left parties, it would be easy to decide that here is the answer to our question. However, this correlation neither explains the process nor can it explain 100 per cent of the variance seen both between and within countries over time. For example, in most countries a substantial feminization of parliament has been taking place over longer periods and has not necessarily coincided with the continuous success of political parties friendly to female legislators. To illustrate this point we can use the Dutch case. As we have seen, the *take-off phase* in the Netherlands started in 1972 and at this time the three party families with the highest percentage of women were the Socialists, the Left Liberals, and the Right Liberals. At that time these party families possessed forty-nine, six, and twenty-two seats in parliament, respectively. After the 2003

TABLE 4.4. *Correlation between percentage differences over time in women in left parties, women in parliament, and all MPs in left parties*

% difference female MPs in left parties	% difference female MPs in all parties	% difference all MPs in left parties
—	0.736**	0.125**
0.736**	—	0.250**
0.125**	0.250**	—

election, the figures were forty-two, six, and twenty-eight seats, which means that the net result for these parties is a loss of one seat. We cannot, therefore, explain the increase from 9.3 to 36.7 per cent in the percentage of female parliamentarians in the Dutch Lower House from 1972 to 2003 solely by changes in the party composition of parliament.

For this reason, we need to look further into the concept of the party as 'prime mover' (Pedersen 2000). Therefore, using political party families as the overall unit of analysis (rather than nation states, as previously), we will examine whether variation in terms of female representation is greater between political parties than between countries. We can also narrow this question further by asking whether the mean level of women in the other party families in the same country, or the mean level of women in the same party family in the other countries, will be most useful to predict the level of women MPs in a given party family at a given time.

As the pattern of party families present in parliament is in no way identical for the included countries, we will focus on just one party family, namely the socialist/social democrats (in the rest of the chapter denoted socialists), since this party family is present in all of the nine parliaments.[19] In Table 4.5, two measures are calculated for each country at the first election of each decade since 1950. The two measures are denoted dC and dE respectively. The first one, dC, is the difference in percentage points between the percentage of women in the party family (the socialists) and the mean percentage of women in the other party groups in the same country. A positive value indicates that the socialists send a group of politicians to the parliament with a higher proportion of women than the other party families on average and vice versa. The second one, dE, is the difference in percentage points between the percentage of women in the party family (the socialists) and the mean percentage of women within the socialist party family in the rest of the included European countries. A positive value indicates that the socialists in this given country send a group of politicians to the parliament with a higher proportion of women than the socialist in the other countries on average and vice versa.

Looking at the dC values in Table 4.5, it is once again demonstrated that the socialists in general are above average when it comes to having women included in their parliamentary groups, but the preponderance of positive values is not huge. However, our main interest in Table 4.5 is that it allows us to assess whether the average of the other party families in the same country or the average among the other European socialist parties is the best predictor of the percentage of women in a socialist party at a certain point in time. The picture is quite blurred, although in some incidences the distance to the mean of the other parties (dC) is smaller than the distance to the other socialist parties in Europe (dE) but vice versa in other cases. However, one weak pattern is found, that is when the time perspective is included. In the first decades the European level of the other socialist parties would have been the best predictor in the majority of the countries, whereas in the later decades this picture is reversed. This means that over time there might have

TABLE 4.5. *Percentage of women within the party family of Socialists/social democrats in nine European countries compared over time to the mean percentage of women in the other party groups in the country (dC) and to the mean percentage of women within the socialist party family in the eight other included countries (dE) (percentage differences)*

	1950	1960	1970	1980	1990	2000
France						
dC	−1	−3	−1	4	−2	1
dE	−7	−10	−10	−7	−20	−21
Italy						
dC	1	−1	−1	−4	14	7
dE	−4	−8	−10	−11	−5	−13
UK						
dC	0	4	−5	4	7	12
dE	−4	−3	−7	−9	−11	−13
Austria						
dC	11	8	6	0	−6	−3
dE	3	1	−3	−5	−3	2
Germany						
dC	8	4	−1	−2	−3	−13
dE	6	2	−4	−5	4	4
Netherlands						
dC	−3	5	6	−6	−4	9
dE	−2	3	1	3	6	15
Denmark						
dC	−7	−5	−2	2	3	−11
dE	0	−1	7	13	13	0
Finland						
dC	4	5	8	9	1	2
dE	10	8	17	20	24	12
Norway						
dC	4	13	10	16	26	15
dE	−3	7	11	22	24	14

Note: For each decade, the first election held in the specific country in that decade is used in the calculations.

been a within-country convergence among the party families and/or a European divergence within the party family. We will take a closer look of each of these suggestions in turn.

The theoretical explanation for convergence is that a mechanism of contagion operates whereby, when a party successfully adopts a new strategy (e.g. including women in their tickets/ parliamentary group) other parties will follow the same strategy and try to equalize this potentially competitive advantage (Duverger 1954; Matland and Studlar 1996). Table 4.6 presents the mean and standard deviation as well as the coefficient of variation among the party families represented at all the included elections and, as can be seen, for most countries a pattern of within-country convergence among the party families concerning level of female representation is found.

Why So Few and Why So Slow?

TABLE 4.6. *Within-country variation in % of women parliamentarians*

	1950	1960	1970	1980	1990	2000
France (n = 6)						
m	3	2	3	4	8	14
s.d.	3	1	3	3	3	4
c.v.	1.0	0.5	1.0	0.8	0.4	0.3
Italy (n = 4)						
m	2	1	2	2	12	11
s.d.	2	2	2	2	6	8
c.v.	1.0	0.5	1.0	1.0	0.5	0.7
UK (n = 3)						
m	3	3	3	5	11	14
s.d.	1	3	2	2	7	8
c.v.	0.3	1.0	0.7	0.4	0.6	0.6
Austria (n = 4)						
m	3	4	5	11	20	31
s.d.	5	5	5	2	6	4
c.v.	1.7	1.3	1.0	0.2	0.3	0.1
Germany (n = 3)						
m	9	7	7	11	22	27
s.d.	3	1	1	3	9	9
c.v.	0.3	0.1	0.1	0.3	0.4	0.3
Netherlands (n = 4)						
m	8	9	11	24	34	40
s.d.	7	8	4	16	10	12
c.v.	0.9	0.9	0.4	0.7	0.3	0.3
Denmark (n = 4)						
m	10	12	17	28	38	40
s.d.	6	7	4	11	10	6
c.v.	0.6	0.6	0.2	0.4	0.3	0.2
Finland (n = 5)						
m	14	12	22	30	33	37
s.d.	5	7	6	11	9	12
c.v.	0.4	0.6	0.3	0.4	0.3	0.3
Norway (n = 5)						
m	3	5	13	22	32	35
s.d.	4	5	10	15	15	22
c.v.	1.3	1.0	0.8	0.7	0.5	0.6

Note: The coefficient of variation (c.v.) among party families is calculated for each decade since 1950, as standard deviation (s.d.) divided by mean (m). For each decade, the first election held in the specific country in that decade is used in the calculations. The mean (m) is calculated as the mean of the percentages of females within each party family.

Table 4.6, however, does not of course allow a formal testing of the contagion hypothesis, since we do not know anything about the motivations in the political parties for nominating women. The evidence is interesting, though, since other studies have concluded that 'there is little support for the diffusion of women's representation across the ideological spectrum' (Caul 1999: 88).

TABLE 4.7. *Within-party family variation in % of women parliamentarians*

	1950	1960	1970	1980	1990	2000
Socialists						
m	8	8	11	18	30	37
s.d.	5	5	9	13	12	10
c.v.	0.6	0.6	0.8	0.7	0.4	0.3
Left Liberals						
m	5	8	16	12	36	19
s.d.	6	9	20	18	36	20
c.v.	1.2	2.1	1.3	1.5	1.0	1.1
Right Liberals						
m	6	5	8	9	21	27
s.d.	7	8	7	7	12	18
c.v.	1.2	1.6	0.9	0.8	0.6	0.7
CD- Protestant						
m	4	5	13	19	27	37
s.d.	4	3	9	8	10	10
c.v.	1.0	0.6	0.7	0.4	0.4	0.3
CD-Catholic						
m	3	4	4	9	11	19
s.d.	2	3	2	4	4	16
c.v.	0.7	0.8	0.5	0.4	0.4	0.8
Conservatives						
m	8	8	14	22	20	25
s.d.	7	7	11	17	17	18
c.v.	0.9	0.9	0.8	0.8	0.9	0.7

Note: The coefficient of variation (c.v.) among the nine countries is calculated for each decade since 1950, as standard deviation (s.d.) divided with mean (m). For each decade the first election held in the specific country in that decade is used in the calculations. N = 9 (Denmark, Germany, Italy, the Netherlands, Norway, the UK, France, Austria, and Finland).

Table 4.6 indicates that within most countries tendencies of convergence among the party families is to be observed and some processes of contagion could be a plausible explanation of this phenomenon.

The concept of European divergence within the party families can be assessed by studying Table 4.7 in which a cross-European mean, standard deviation, and coefficient of variation has been calculated for each decade for each of the six major party families. As can be seen, the picture is more blurred than in the case of within-country variation. However, even though the CD-Catholic party family comes out with a higher coefficient of variation in the first election in the new millennium than in the beginning of the period under scrutiny, the other party families show signs of convergence. Among the Right Liberals and the CD-Protestants the convergence is quite clear whereas among the Socialists and the Left Liberals the convergence is mostly a phenomenon of the most recent times (for the Conservatives only for the most recent election).

TABLE 4.8. *The development in the percentage of women in the parliamentary elites of Europe mean and standard deviation among countries*

	1940–9	1950–9	1960–9	1970–9	1980–9	1990–9	2000–3
M	6.2	7.2	7.3	11.0	16.9	24.8	28.4
s.d.	2.4	3.5	4.0	7.4	10.8	11.2	11.1
c.v. (s.d./m)	0.4	0.5	0.5	0.7	0.6	0.5	0.4

Note: Nine countries are included in the analysis—the mean is taken of the elections held in that decade.

In order to somewhat complete the discussion on convergence/divergence, it should also be noted that convergence/divergence can not only be discussed by comparing different party families within a country or the same party family between countries. It is also possible simply to compare the entire parliament of the different countries and study if some kind of European convergence has been happening. In 1985, Pippa Norris wrote that when it comes to percentage of women in the parliamentary elites 'differences between countries have generally increased since the 1960s' (Norris 1985: 93). As our longitudinal data can show, and as Table 4.8 indicates, divergence was evident before this time. However, Table 4.8 also shows that in the years after Norris's observation the picture has been somewhat altered. The standard deviation has increased but not as pronounced as the mean resulting in a decreasing trend of the coefficient of variation.

Before leaving the area of party divergence or convergence, and theories of contagion, it is useful to examine the concept of critical mass, which has been used when explaining women's political inclusion in parliamentary groups (Dahlerup 1988a, 1988b). Here, critical mass 'refers to a threshold beyond which there is a change of behaviour through acceleration ("chain reaction"), not just incrementalism' (Studlar and McAllister 2002: 238). In other words, as possibly implicated by the 'take-off' phase, and the inertia effect, once the level of female representatives exceeds a certain point (taken as 30% in other studies), the movement towards gender parity will accelerate. As already mentioned, a full investigation of the 'critical mass' hypothesis is beyond the scope of this chapter, but the longitudinal nature of our data enables us to look at changes in the length of time between the levels of female representatives passing important percentage markers (i.e. 10%, 20%, 30%, etc.). If the 'critical mass theory' holds true, one would expect to see that the length of time from women first entering parliament to their reaching the 10 per cent boundary will be longer than that taken for them to move from 10 to 20 per cent, which should also be longer than the time taken to pass the 30 per cent mark. For us to test this, the time taken for women in each country[20] to pass the various percentage markers was calculated and tabulated (see Table 4.9).

As Table 4.9 shows, the average time from suffrage to women passing the 10 per cent level is considerably greater (53.9 years) than time to women

TABLE 4.9. *Time taken for the level of women legislators to pass critical percentage markets*

Country	Year of suffrage	Year passed 10%	No. of years from suff. to 10%	Year passed 20%	No. of years from 10 to 20%	Year passed 30%	No. of years from 20 to 30%
Denmark	1915	1966	53	1979	13	1988	9
Germany	1918	1983	65	1990	7	1998	8
Italy	1945	1994	49	—	—	—	—
Netherlands	1919	1977	58	1989	12	1994	5
Norway	1913	1973	60	1977	4	1985	8
UK	1922	1997	75	—	—	—	—
France	1944	1997	53	—	—	—	—
Spain	1977 (1931)	1989	12	1996	7	—	—
Austria	1919	1986	65	1994	8	2002	8
Portugal	1974 (1931)	1987	13	—	—	—	—
Finland	1906	1948	42	1970	22	1983	13
Average			49.5		10.4		8.5

exceeding 20 per cent (10.4 years) which is greater still than time taken to pass the 30 per cent level. This would seem to suggest that the effect of critical mass may indeed be playing a role in the increases seen in women's level of representation. As suggested by Ramirez, Soysal, and Shanahan (1997), this effect is not just a national phenomenon but also an international one, whereby the struggle for female suffrage and gender parity has always been an international effort and one that has resulted in a more inclusive model of political citizenship. This inclusive model presents a standard that can influence the speed of development in new nation states as well as being a yardstick for other less progressive states.

4.6. CONCLUSION: WHY SO SLOW, AND WHY SO FEW? GENDER PARITY IN THE EUROPEAN PARLIAMENTS

In this chapter, we have investigated why the gender parity envisaged by the early pioneers of female suffrage has not materialized almost a century after suffrage was first granted to women, and we have tried to determine the role played by a variety of factors implicated by other research into the level of female representatives. Taking the stance that gender parity in the parliaments of Europe is a natural goal, the first conclusion that has to be drawn from the various investigations undertaken in this chapter, is that substantial inter-country differences in the level of female representatives still exist across the parliaments of Europe. Indeed, as Figure 4.1 has shown, for a considerable part of the early twentieth century, of the countries in our sample, none had more than 10 per cent female representatives, but by the turn of the century, differences in our sample extend from Hungary with 9.8 per cent to Denmark with 38.3 per cent. Taken at this level, the data seem to speak more for divergence than for convergence in the structures of opportunity for European women to enter the political elite. However, as has also been shown, at the start of the new millennium the data hint at some signs of convergence. At the beginning of the 21st century, of the twelve countries under investigation, six have passed the crucial 30 per cent mark, and one other (Spain) looks set to do so very soon.[21] Nevertheless, the signs of convergence are modest and too recent to use them in an attempt to prophesy future trends in the level of female representatives.

Our work also reveals that, although development across countries can be seen to follow a sequence of phases, there are strong inter-country differences in the time taken to move from one phase to the next, and in the end-state of development. While some countries already seem to be in a *stabilization phase*, others are still in the *lethargy phase* and show little signs of *take-off*. At the same time, an examination of the time taken between the levels of female representatives passing various percentage markers towards the 30 per cent atypicality barrier showed that the time interval between reaching the different percentage markers declined significantly as the percentage of women increased. In other words, in line with critical mass theory, and in support of the inertia hypothesis and the phenomenon of the 'victorious incumbent', it would seem that once the share of women in an elite passes a particular percentage marker, the sooner they are likely to achieve the next. Ramirez, Saysal, and Shanahan's argument (1997) for the influence of a more inclusive world model of political citizenship also appears to be applicable here, in that countries entering the full eligibility 'race' later than other countries seem to play 'catch-up' very rapidly—as in the case of Portugal and Spain. At the first elections after the restoration of democracy in 1975 in Portugal and 1977 in Spain, 8 and 6 per cent women, respectively, were sent to the Assembleia da República and the Congreso de los Diputados (close to the average for the other countries in the sample on start up). Today, Spain is approaching 30 per cent (see n. 21) and Portugal 20 per cent,[22] greater than France, Italy, and the UK where women have been eligible for election for several decades longer. The point to be made is that when democracy was reinstated in the two countries, their parliaments largely followed the lead set by the mean of the rest of the European parliaments with regard to female representation.

Against this conclusion is the case of Hungary. Here too is a country coming late to free democracy and open elections with full eligibility (after the fall of Communism) but the Hungarian Országgyulés has followed a different path from the parliaments of Spain and Portugal. Instead of a rapid and spectacular increase, it has experienced a dramatic decrease in the number of female MPs since the first free elections when 7 per cent of the politicians elected were women—and compared to 21 per cent in the last communist parliament (Ilonszki 2000: 220). In spite of one brief peak of 11 per cent in 1994, in the election of 2002, the percentage was still less than 10 per cent. This phenomenon has been seen in other post-communist states and one explanation may be related to 'Restorative

Tendenzen', that is the desire within a society to return to former ideals and values before beginning to embrace new concepts. However, if Ramirez, Saysal, and Shanahan's theory of developments towards an international model of inclusive political citizenship is correct, then we can expect to see Hungary 'making a move' in the not too distant future. Indeed, amendments to the electoral law concerning affirmative action is already under consideration (Inter-parliamentary Union 2003*a*).

Once again, however, we find countries that stand counter to this suggestion. France and Italy should also be subject to pressure from any such international model of inclusive political citizenship but they appear to resist (at least in the case of France) even the effect of enforced quota systems. One explanation might lie in the different stance taken by feminist groups in the 1960s and 1970s to political engagement, namely either oppositional or collaborative. Feminists taking an oppositional stance rejected any negotiation or collaboration with traditional government, and 'purposely stayed away from the arena of formal power politics for fear of corruption by "the system" and for the belief that true change can only come by directing the protest against the present democratic framework' (Kaplan 1992: 42). The collaborative stance was based on the belief that 'the only way for women to gain any influence is to enter the field of formal politics themselves' (Kaplan 1992: 43). The French feminists took the former stance and it is likely that this has been a contributory factor to the poor showing of women in French politics. When it comes to women in power positions outside of politics, France is statistically one of the leading countries.

Our investigations also supported the hypothesis of a link between the success of Left parties and higher levels of female representatives. Despite some suggestion in our analyses of the EurElite data of a recent decline in this association (perhaps related to Duverger's 'contamination effect'), of the factors tested it remained the strongest predictor of women's level of inclusion in a political elite. We have not been able to examine the broader contextual factors implicated by the literature as influential—factors such as the influence of a country's religious tradition, or the effect of electoral systems, although other research indicates that these are areas that cannot be ignored. In addition, it seems clear that the point in time when women have attempted to enter the political affray is highly significant. Social modernization and the 'contagion effect' suggest that current expectations are towards female inclusion, even if the realization of this is slower in some countries than in others.

In this chapter, we have also demonstrated that assuming there will be a 'natural' closure of the gender gap is an unsafe business. We have pointed to the fact that almost a century after the first women entered a European Parliament less than a fifth of the seats in European parliaments are today held by women. And we have shown that in some countries it seems as if the parliaments have reached a phase of stabilization in terms of female representation. For those who would like to increase the level of female representation a necessary condition is to understand this complex situation. This should also be the first step for those interested in engineering change (Leijenaar 1997; Karam 1998; Squires and Wickham-Jones 2001). We have also tried to analyse what is happening in terms of female representativeness, but like most other commentators, without any definitive conclusions. We have pressed for the inclusion of longitudinal data and data split by party and hope that our own analyses following these lines can be yet another piece in the puzzle of why so few women are included in the political elites of Europe.

As for further research in this area, we have two suggestions: The first suggestion stems from the fact that, where we are able to look at one country in depth (i.e. at a level of data on female representatives not available so far in the EurElite data-set) a great part of the development in the level of female representation can be explained by including one single factor, namely, the level of women among electoral candidates. In an analysis of the Danish case this, 'magnificent' variable was able to explain no less than 95 per cent of the variation in the level of female politicians. Put simply, it would seem that 'when women run, women win ... as often as men do' (Seltzer, Newman, and Leighton 1997: 79). Perhaps, therefore, the metaphorical key to unlocking the question of women's level of inclusion in political elites might be the nomination phase of the recruitment process: it is certainly something to be pursued in future research. As Hazan has commented, 'The level of candidate selection could prove to be the most crucial gatekeeper for getting women into elected office. In light of the prominence this issue has been given in so many countries and parties it is perplexing that candidate selection has not received more attention in the research on legislative recruitment' (Hazan 2002: 117). If the focus was on nomination, it would also entail an examination of the internal procedures of the political parties that would, hopefully, reveal how and perhaps why so few women are being nominated.

The second suggestion is to continue to elaborate the other side of the coin to political recruitment of women, namely the normative discussion of the need for gender representativeness, that is what positive effects will more gender-balanced parliaments have on the functioning of representative democracy. A lot of important and solid theorizing has been done on these questions but still the fund of knowledge is scarce when it comes to empirical works demonstrating the effects of the sex of the politicians. Maybe the best way to convince nominators and voters (not at least the female half of the electorate) about the potential advantages of more gender-balanced polities is to demonstrate the consequences of male-dominated parliaments.

ENDNOTES

1   30% is also the most common cut-off point below which an occupation is classified as gender atypical.
2   Including single Houses and lower Houses in all OSCE-countries.

3   In this and the subsequent analyses, the first election of the new millennium in each of the countries has been used as a cut-off point.
4   Denmark, Germany, Italy, the Netherlands, Norway, UK, France, Spain, Austria, Portugal, Finland, and Hungary.
5   Sweden (not included in our data-set) is the closest European country to achieving parity. Following the 2002 election, women accounted for 45.3% of all members of the Riksdag. For a short overview of the development of women in the political elites in this country see the official Swedish government's site at http://www.riksdagen.se.
6   Explanations couched in theories of natural or biological differences have existed since the days of the Ancient Greeks when women were seen as incomplete or defective males which set them apart from men especially in terms of civil rights (Christmas 2002).
7   Primarily because of the social role set out for women by Roman Catholicism and other orthodox religions, i.e. as bearer and nurturer of children, and playing a supportive role to a male provider.
8   The social role of women may be demonstrated not only through their general acceptance in the paid workforce, but particularly by the level and type of their participation (Hakim 1993*a*; Anker 1998; Rule 2000).
9   Perkin (1996: 8) sees post-industrial society as 'professional', i.e. one where a professional hierarchy has been substituted for class 'as the primary matrix of the social structure . . . [recruiting] to those hierarchies by means of meritocracy, entailing an increase in social mobility from below. It extends to women, thus ensuring their (admittedly limited) emancipation'.
10 Nevertheless, the result was still only 18%—for an excellent discussion of this see 'Blair's Babes' by Norris and Lovenduski (2001).
11 The Parity Law passed on 6 June 2000, and implemented for the first time in national elections in 2002, increased the overall number of women by less than 1%. This would seem to have been because the consequences of breaking the parity law (which are purely financial) were not sufficiently harsh in the face of perceived electoral disadvantages of running female candidates to deter some of the major parties.
12 Most of the previous studies on the question of the percentage of women in a given legislature have been single country studies. However, some studies have been conducted as global statistical analysis including several countries, and often using multivariate analysis (Norris 1985; Rule 1987; Oakes and Almquist 1993; Paxton 1997; Reynolds 1999; Siaroff 2000, etc.). Some of these analyses even use the same set of data, since the Inter-parliamentary Union not only monitors the level of female representation in several countries but has also started to make these data available for the scholarly community (http://www.ipu.org).
13 This is particularly important since political parties, especially in a European context, are thought to be the nexus of political recruitment (Caul 1999).
14 i.e. Denmark, Germany, Italy, the Netherlands, Norway, UK, France, Spain, Austria, Portugal, Finland, and Hungary. In addition, we have included data from other sources for some analyses in order to complete missing data and thus enhance analysis capabilities.
15 i.e. for the UK 1928, for Portugal 1975.
16 Of these seven, only the UK does not have more than 30% female representatives at the beginning of the twenty-first century.
17 Pearsons $R^2 = 0.89$, $n = 9$, $p < 0.001$.
18 Data for parties coded as Communist, New Left, Socialists, and Greens across all twelve countries in the data-set were used.
19 We exclude Spain, Portugal, and Hungary for these analyses as they are latecomers with no data before 1970.
20 Note that Hungary is not included in this analysis due to too many missings and the fact that it only passed the 10% level in one election since 1985 and currently stands below that mark.
21 Following the 2004 election, the percentage of women in the Spanish parliament passed the 30% mark with 126 (36%) of MPs being female.
22 In the 2005 election, this increased to 21.3%.

5

Cultural Capital and Political Selection: Educational Backgrounds of Parliamentarians

Daniel Gaxie and Laurent Godmer

As Émile Durkheim has pointed out in his *Education and Sociology*, education is 'above all, the means by which a society perpetually renews the conditions of its own existence' (Durkheim 1993: 101).

Education indeed allows for the acquisition of a set of elements (knowledge, know-how, behaviours, rules to respect) necessary to the insertion and to the adaptation of individuals within the social world. The latter perpetuates itself to the extent to which the members of society are adequately educated (with regard to the standards of the group(s) they belong to at a certain moment in time). Thus, 'education' can be *informal* (dispensed on a diffuse basis, especially by the family group, neighbours and peer groups, or spontaneous all-life learning) or *formal*, that is dispensed and inculcated by specialized institutions and agents (schools, universities). Thus, in a differentiated society, education prepares to the insertion into the 'general' social world, but also into 'specialized' worlds, for example professional universes as showed by the classical works by Berger and Luckman (1986: 179). Formal education, tertiary education in particular, entails (among other features) a dimension of specialized 'formation' (acquisition of knowledge, know-how, ways of thinking, perceiving, reacting and acting, behavioural norms) allowing for the access to relatively differentiated social worlds (e.g. medical studies for medical professions). However, there are nowadays no or very few specialized education programmes preparing and/or leading to political professions. There are in fact only specialized formal education institutions with programmes more or less adapted to the prerequisites of the political field. Those requisites evolve, and so do the specialized educational institutions preparing for political activities (secondary general education in the past, law schools, literature or medical studies in a more recent past, and administration, law and economics studies in certain states in the contemporary period).

Because of the correspondence between formal education and access to specific universes, and thereby to particular positions in the social world, and given the fact that there is a hierarchy of social worlds and positions, education (both informal and formal education, 'good' education, manners, good taste, good schools, good university titles, esoteric knowledge) also is a social marker and a resource (Bourdieu 1986). In a hierarchical society, positions are marked, characterized and immediately recognizable thanks to symbols (cloths, language, ways of thinking and behaving). In contemporary ('modern') societies, these symbols are more and more the products of formal education (education level, numbers of years passed within the education system, kind of specialization, degree of complexity of knowledge, difficulties of the studies, degree of selectivity and prestige of education institutions). In line with that observation, the sociology of education (see, among others in the major West European languages: Cobalti 1992; Guerrero Serón 1996; Demaine 2001; Otto, Rauschenbach, and Vogel 2002; Cherkaoui 2004) has showed the remaining 'biases' in the recruitment of elite students and the *reproductive logic* of educational systems, while emphasizing the relative 'democratization' that has occurred. Education sociologists have indeed observed that the 'social opening' of tertiary education favoured the emergence of 'new students', who added themselves to the 'heirs' (Ehrlich 1998: 57–8). This led to numerous discussions about the reality of the transformation and about the social meaning and value of the different grades, disciplines, tertiary education institutions (i.e. universities and other superior schools) and even about the comparison between the different education systems. In a context of democratization linked to many reforms (especially in the 1950s and 1960s, Prost 1997: 84), education (actually certain types of degrees) has thus undoubtedly become a manifold *resource*, which is the object of many social, familial and individual strategies, leading sometimes to a 'tyranny of the diploma' (Bauer and Bertin-Mourot 1997). Hence the importance of education in the works of major twentieth-century sociologists such as, for instance, Émile Durkheim, Max Weber. Karl Mannheim (Mannheim and Stewart 1997), or Pierre Bourdieu. Everything happens as if education titles were 'nobility' titles allowing for the access to most of the most leading and prestigious positions, even though the modality of this access varies according to the nature of these leading positions and to their relative location within the system of leading positions. There is an approximate statistical correspondence between the relative situation of a professional position (e.g. the parliamentary position) within the hierarchy of social positions at a given moment and the titles and qualifications of those who come to occupy it. The variation of the relative value of a position combines with the variation of the value of these titles and qualifications. This approximate adjustment is produced within the logic of competitions for the occupation of positions. The more valued a position (to the eyes of the specialized 'public'), the more attractive a position. Besides, the more attractive a position is, the more intense the competition for this position will be. In other words, more resources have to be mobilized, particularly educational titles and qualification so as to be selected to occupy it.

Education thus designates: (*a*) an informal education; (*b*) a level of formal education, for example measured by the duration of the presence in formal education systems providing titles which are more or less 'rare'; (*c*) general (and possibly specialized) learning; (*d*) mastering prerequisites to the access to particular social worlds and to positions more or less high in the social hierarchy of positions; (*e*) acquisition of subjective prerequisite, that is the more or less strong feeling of being entitled (of having both the *right* and the capacity) to access certain positions; (*f*) possibly titles attesting a capacity to occupy determined positions (which are more or less leading positions, prestigious or technical ones). This set of features contributes to a socially recognized 'legitimate feeling of legitimacy', highly visible in attitudes and language. Indeed, since there is a probabilistic correspondence between education titles and social positions, education functions as an *authorization* (or *non-authorization*) process, notably as a *self-authorization* or *self-forbidding* process. Those who hold the adequate education credentials (relative to a determined position) view their intervention as a right, a technical possibility and as a duty. Education is indeed a capital of authority, which socially and subjectively habilitates someone to act, for example in order to seek for the investiture of a political party and to stand for an election. As every kind of 'capital', education is accumulated and used, can be depreciated, developed and transmitted and yields profits. It is a particular form of symbolic capital, which provides diverse forms of symbolic benefits (appropriation of symbolic goods, for instance knowledge, distinction and self-esteem profits). In contemporary societies, access to education (i.e. the access to determined levels of education with all the obligations, rights and privileges attached to them) depends at the same time on 'merit-based' and 'hereditary' mechanisms. The proportion of the access modes to education (for instance access for the first or second generation) depends on diverse factors, especially on the morphological transformations of education systems. Thus, when the access to universities is eased, the number of first generation students grows. Sociological investigations about the success factors indicate that the volume of inherited educational capital at least partly determines the access to the highest levels and titles. The more educated the family milieu of a child, a teenager or a young adult is, the more numerous statistical chances she/hc has to progress in the education systems and to reach the highest echelons. Educational capital helps to increase educational capital. Of course, exceptions to this general 'law' exist, but many of them are only apparent ones. This is the case when the close family members have a low education level, and when the transmission of the educational capital occurs in a less visible way thanks to more distant relatives, neighbours, friends or more or less hazardous encounters.

In line with Durkheim's analyses, education helps to the reproduction and continuation of each society. It entails that within differentiated and hierarchical societies, education (formal and informal) contributes to the reproduction of the hierarchy (in its double meaning of (*a*) reproduction of a hierarchy of positions demanding unequal education levels and occupied by individuals with unequal level and type of education, and (*b*) reproduction of a more or less hereditary access to these positions, mostly transmitted through the family and, indirectly, through the formal education system).

Does education play the same reproduction role in the selection of parliamentary elites? The representative elite seems to be particularly over-educated if compared with the population and to have specific education backgrounds. Such a discrepancy is due to the specificities of the 'political profession', which is based on manipulating symbols and language [the main way of social reproduction as it was observed by sociologists such as Denis Lawton (1998), Basil Bernstein (Bernstein 1975; Atkinson, Davies, and Delamont 1995) or Pierre Bourdieu (1986)], and on network- and coalition-building. What is more, parliamentary selection has become more competitive. Beyond the different social patterns that led to the various systems of education (Archer 1979) which remain, albeit 'Europeanized', autonomous and idiosyncratic, education as a social 'resource' in the political field—or rather as a main element of a 'portfolio of resources' (Godmer 2004)—is often perceived as the most important feature of personal trajectory in political careers, whatever the national context [since it is one of the most common features of recruitment of MPs after the Second World War (Best and Cotta 2000: 517)]. Even though, as Vilfredo Pareto observed, 'aristocracies do not last' (Cohen-Huther 2004: 130), that process seems very slow and ambiguous as far as certain education elites are concerned, particularly within the political field. As a result, the analysis of the levels and types of education of parliamentarians over one and a half century in eleven different countries is a sort of 'laboratory experiment' so as to test this general theory of reproduction.

5.1. HISTORICAL TRANSFORMATIONS OF EDUCATIONAL BACKGROUNDS OF PARLIAMENTARIANS

Such an analysis shows that the evolution of the educational level of deputies is more irregular than the somewhat 'evolutionist' view of a steadily growing relevance of cultural capital in modern societies would lead one to expect.

5.1.1. *Fall and Rise of the Educational Level*

Admittedly, parliamentarians with a primary education—that is to say with only a low level of formal education—are disappearing at the beginning of the twenty-first century (see Figure 5.1). They have almost entirely disappeared in countries like Italy, Norway, Portugal, and the Netherlands. They are presently very few and less and less numerous in Finland, France, and Germany. In Denmark and the UK, they are more numerous, but they account for less than 20 per cent of the whole lower house of parliament and they are on a declining trend.

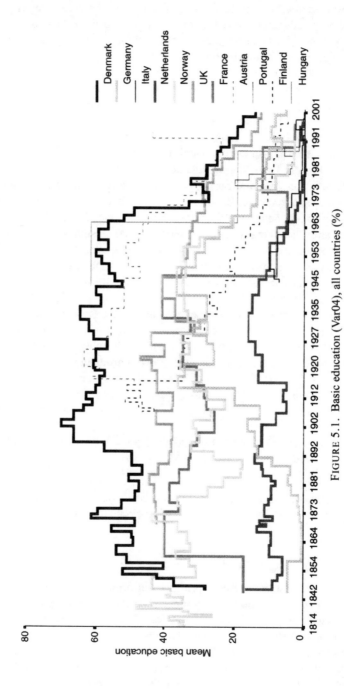

FIGURE 5.1. Basic education (Var04), all countries (%)

In some countries—Italy, the Netherlands, and Portugal—the proportion of elected national parliamentarians with only a basic education has always been low. In many others, the present situation results from a declining presence throughout the twentieth century. Even in the aristocratic and bourgeois parliaments of the nineteenth century, there was a noteworthy minority of deputies with a relatively low degree of education in several countries. They numbered around 40 per cent in France and in the UK in the 1870s or 1880s. Social and political domination was not automatically linked to formal education at that time (see Chapter 2, above, about the nobility in parliaments). In some cases, new political personnel linked to low educated social groups entered parliaments at the beginning of the twentieth century due to the ascent of new political parties, especially Socialist parties. There were about 30–40 per cent of parliamentarians with only a primary education in most European countries, and even around 60 per cent in Denmark and Austria, after the First World War. The declining trend started at the beginning of the twentieth century in Denmark and Finland, in the 1920s in Austria, Germany, and the UK, and in the 1950s in France, Hungary, and Norway. But, when it may be observed, this declining trend follows an ascending period in some countries—Denmark and Germany—or a more irregular evolution elsewhere. Education is one of the domains where the convergence of the characteristics of the representatives in the various European countries is undoubtedly the most striking. With respect to this 'basic education' variable, the features of European parliaments had been very diverse from the mid-nineteenth century to the end of the 1950s, with a percentage of deputies with a basic education varying from almost 0 to 70 per cent. From 1960 onwards, there has been a dramatically fast converging declining tendency. The 'marginalization' of deputies with only a primary education may even be extreme in areas having experienced a post-Communist transition such as Hungary (Matthes 2000: 179) and the former Eastern Germany (Gergs, Hausmann, and Pohlmann 1997: 231), where often less than one tenth of national deputies do not hold university degrees.

Thus, the increase in cultural level and the growing number of deputies with a university education (see Figure 5.2, or less often with an intermediate education (Figure 5.3), are correlated consequences of the fading presence of less educated elected parliamentarians.

In many countries, the proportion of members of European parliaments with a University education has roughly followed a 'U' curve (Figure 5.2). This proportion was high (from around 60 to 80%) during the second half of the nineteenth century. The only two partial exceptions were Denmark (with a high percentage of legislators with only a primary education) and Norway (with a high but declining percentage of parliamentarians with basic education and a growing percentage of holders of intermediate or technical degrees which would be considered as university diplomas in other countries). The proportion of deputies with university education then decreased in many countries (France, Germany, the Netherlands, the UK, and even in Denmark and Norway) or remained stable elsewhere

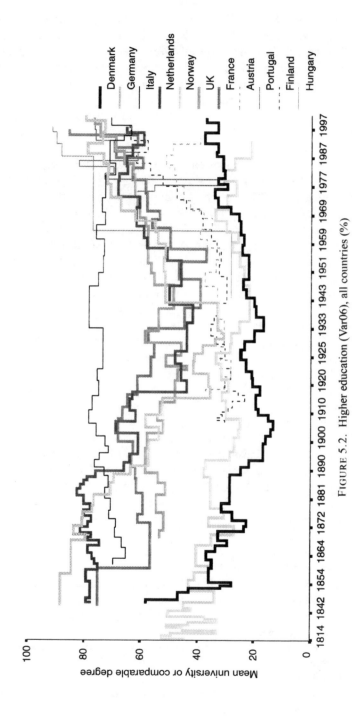

FIGURE 5.2. Higher education (Var06), all countries (%)

Legend:
Denmark
Germany
Italy
Netherlands
Norway
UK
France
Austria
Portugal
Finland
Hungary

Y-axis: Mean university or comparable degree (0, 20, 40, 60, 80, 100)

X-axis: 1814 1842 1854 1864 1872 1881 1890 1900 1910 1920 1925 1933 1943 1951 1959 1969 1977 1987 1997

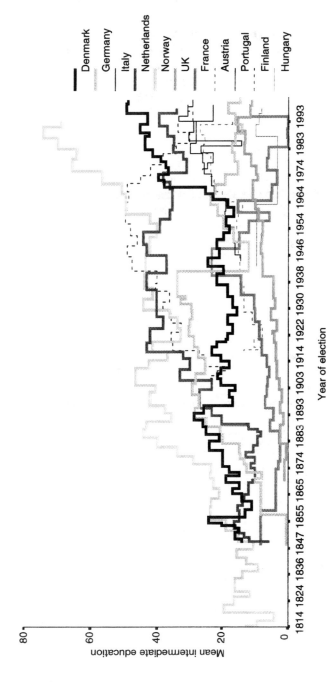

FIGURE 5.3. Intermediate education (Var05), all countries (%)

(Italy and Finland). It reached its lowest level (between 25 and 50%) during the first part of the twentieth century, with the sole exception of Italy. There has then been a quick and strong growth of the proportion of holders of university degrees in the European parliaments during the second part of the twentieth century in almost all countries. That trend was completed in some countries by a parallel increase in the percentage of parliamentarians with an 'intermediate' (but post-secondary) education (Figure 5.3). The growth and the high level of the percentage of deputies with a university degree are other striking convergent characteristics of contemporary European elected national assemblies. However, two parliaments seem to differ from the other ones. The first one is the Italian parliament, where the proportion of highly educated deputies has always been elevated but has been slightly declining for two decades, even if the percentage of legislators with intermediate education has been increasing at the same time (Figures 5.2 and 5.3). But the only true exception is Norway, which has the lowest percentage of deputies with university degree and where a surprising historical downward trend is occurring (Figure 5.2). The explanation of this exception lies in the numerical importance of Norwegian elected parliamentarians with intermediate education (Figure 5.3). Their proportion has strongly increased since the beginning of the nineteenth century. It has reached a surprisingly high level (up to 70%) in the last decades with no other European equivalent. It is as if intermediate education in Norway is regarded as a valuable resource producing the same legitimizing effects as university degrees do in other countries. This is perhaps partly linked to particularities of 'Nordic' education systems, since we also observe a growing proportion of deputies with intermediate education in Denmark (from less than 20% in the early 1960s to almost 50% in the 1990s), and a high proportion (but following a declining trend) in Finland, and in the Netherlands. But these particularities are partly nominal since some post secondary technical degrees are not considered as university degrees in some Scandinavian states, especially in Denmark and Norway. One may also wonder if the lower educational level of Scandinavian deputies is not to a certain extent a consequence of a lesser 'distance' between elected officials and the population and of a smaller value attributed to parliamentary seats within the social system.

In most European parliaments, the proportion of deputies with university education has presently reached a high level (between 65 and 85%), with, again, the exceptions of Denmark and Norway. We may say as well that it has re-reached the high levels of the beginning of the national parliamentary histories. All seems to have happened as if a growing number of deputies with primary, and sometimes technical or secondary education, first partly ousted more educated incumbents, and have been in their turn replaced by more educated newcomers. Nowadays, deputies normally hold a university or comparable degree, as they used to at the beginning of parliamentary history. This evolution is all the more significant that it is accompanied by contradictory invisible factors. One of them is the decline in the role and powers of parliaments. For various reasons, parliamentarians are presently less powerful than they were in the past. Parliamentary seats are less valued and less sought after in upper circles. We know that the higher the powers and status associated with a given social or political position, the stronger the competition to reach it. And the harder social or political competition is, the higher is the amount of resources (among others cultural capital and university titles) that competitors have to invest in the competition. The relative decline in the status of parliaments and parliamentary positions thus has downward effects on social and occupational origins and on the cultural 'level' of parliamentarians. These downward effects remain invisible because of the strength of the various factors favouring an increase in the educational level of MPs. This increase would be even stronger if one could observe it *ceteris paribus*.

The high level of education of parliamentarians is not only a statistical regularity or structure. It has also become an informal political norm and a component of the parliamentarian status. Nowadays, deputies with a low level of education often seem odd to their colleagues or to journalists prone to stress this peculiarity. The lack of formal education is felt to be a handicap by those who are directly concerned or by their peers and partners. Cultural capital has always been one of the conditions of *political authority* but has become more and more significant. That is the reason why political recruitment is, more or less but always, influenced by an iron law of selection, partly based on various social characteristics of the contenders, especially gender, age, social position, and, first of all, cultural capital. Whatever the variations of their quantitative weight, parliamentarians with upper education have always and everywhere been statistically over-represented (if compared with the electorate), even in countries where they are or were less numerous. Deputies with only a basic education have always and everywhere been under-represented (again if compared with the voting population, but even more so if compared with their weight in the active or the overall population), even in the countries where they are or have been relatively more numerous, and even more surprisingly, in political parties (like many Socialist or Communist parties at some stages of their history) which intended to fight the iron law of social selection of political representatives. With regard to elementary education, the homogenization has been extremely visible between the countries of our sample, as it can be easily attested by the decrease of the standard deviation of that variable in the parliaments between 1867 and 2000 (Best 2003: 392).

5.1.2. *An 'Iron Law' of Cultural Selection*

A high level of education has become a tacit condition to begin a political career and to enter a parliament with a legitimate status. This tacit condition seems presently so obvious that, contrary to others like gender or ethnicity, it is rarely stressed and even less rarely combated. It is striking that this condition remains despite the diminishing value and attractiveness of the parliamentary positions due to the diminishing role and sway of the state and the diminishing autonomy of elected national parliamentarians vis-à-vis the executive branch and the leaders of political parties. The iron law of social and cultural selection of politicians and parliamentarians has however been denounced and fought in the past. As mentioned above, many Socialist parties first, then Communist parties, questioned the parliamentary and political hegemony of the ruling class, including the over-representation of intellectual bourgeois within working-class parties in parliaments (see Chapter 11 of this book below). Some Socialist movements or theorists posited that workers' liberation relies on workers themselves. They therefore concluded that Socialist candidates and parliamentarians should be recruited directly *within* the working class. For example, one of the twenty-one conditions to enter the Third International was the 'proletarianization' of the ruling elite of the party, including the parliamentary party. Some Socialist and Communist parties and also some 'multi-classist' and multi organization mass parties like Christian Democrats at certain times, tried to impose what was not then called but which in retrospect looks like 'affirmative action' or 'class quotas'. That is the main reason why the proportion of parliamentarians with only basic education increased in several countries during the first half of the twentieth century. The previously mentioned 'U' curve shows that the iron law of cultural selection of parliamentarians that had so been partly neutralized or weakened during the first half of the twentieth century has been restored in the second half. Strikingly, it has been restored mainly through the transformation of the recruitment processes of political parties, which had tried to fight it for a certain period.

Data shows that the percentage of deputies with university education has increased within almost all countries and political parties since the middle of the twentieth century. But it has to be mentioned that this growth is proportionally more important within political parties, which used to recruit some of their elected officials at various levels among less educated social groups. The German case may be analysed more closely here as an ideal type (see Figure 5.4).

In Germany, as elsewhere, the proportion of deputies with only basic education has always roughly increased as one moves from the right to the left of the political spectrum. The proportion of deputies with the lowest level of education has always been minor within German Conservative and Liberal parties, with only a small rise between 1920 and 1930 (13–18%) for the former, and between 1919 and 1949 (around 12–14%) for the latter. More closely linked to organizations that were representative of various lower or lower-middle social groups (e.g. Catholic workers, clerks, and peasants), the Christian Democratic Party once adopted and developed more atypical modes of recruitment. Figures show a steady growth of the proportion of CD deputies with basic education from the origins to the First World War, then a climax between 1920 and 1949 (with a percentage which varies from around 20 to 34%), and finally a steady regression after the Second World War. It is necessary to notice that the Social Democratic Party of Germany

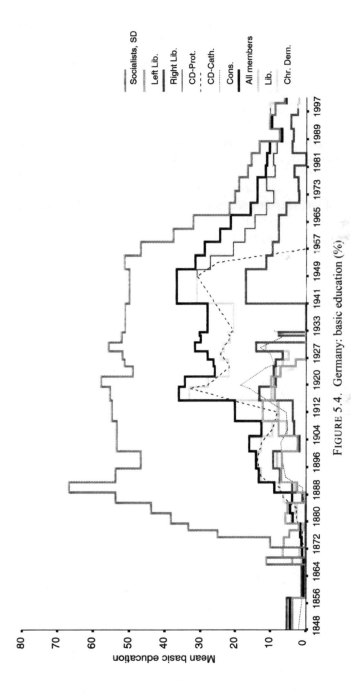

FIGURE 5.4. Germany: basic education (%)

(SPD) has followed a similar evolution at a higher 'level'. Figures again show a steady dramatic growth from its foundation to the First World War, leading to a 'proletarian' style, between 1920 and 1949, with a percentage of deputies with elementary education around 50–58 per cent, and a steady dramatic decrease from around 50 per cent to less than 10 per cent during the last decades.

The greatest part of the increase of the educational level of the Bundestag's members is thus due to the Christian Democratic Party and above all to the Social Democratic Party. It appears as if various atypical parliamentary (and political) recruitments were limited to definite party families at definite periods and/or definite stages of their histories and as if these deviant recruitments were fragile and unable to last. These counter-modes of recruitment seem only at work in nascent and growing parties linked to lower or lower middle 'classes', in the social and historical contexts of the second half of the nineteenth century and of the first half of the twentieth century. Symmetrically, alternative modes of recruitment weakened when these political parties became more established in parliament and in the political field. One may thus conclude that positions in the political field and the parliamentary arena seem a more effective determinant of political and parliamentarian recruitments than organizational and social ties between political parties and plebeian clienteles.

The 'Christian' parties' share of the Bundestag seats rose from 0.7 per cent in 1867, to 18 per cent in 1871, 25 per cent in 1874, and 28 per cent in 1890. The CD parties in parliament stayed at this relatively high level until the First World War. Afterward, during the inter-war period, they faced a regression due to the dramatic ascent of the National Socialist German Workers' Party (NSDAP). After the Second World War and the merger of CD and conservative organizations, the Christian Democratic Union (CDU) has become an established governmental dominant party, oscillating between government and official opposition, with a share of the whole number of seats between 37 per cent (1998) and 53 per cent (1953). It is striking to observe that it was during this last period, when the position of the CDU in the political field changed (i.e. when the party became a fully established pivotal party) that its rather atypical previous mode of recruitment progressively vanished and that the cultural level of its deputies in parliament steadily rose. The resemblance between CD and Socialist parties with respect to the correlation between their dominant position in the political field and the legitimate cultural characteristics of their parliamentarians is close. The growth of the number and the proportion of parliamentary deputies with low educational level in the Socialist party occurred during the nascent and taking-off stages of the history of this party. Its share of the Bundestag seats rose for instance from 0.7 per cent in 1867 to 26 per cent in 1912. The dramatic historical context and the competition with the Communist party (KPD) and with the NSDAP (the elites of which had 'plebeian' aspects), prevented the SPD from becoming a fully established governmental party during the inter-war period, even though it partic-ipated in several governments and even led one of them. The SPD reached this established governmental position after the Second World War, with 32 per cent of the seats and the second largest parliamentary grouping in 1949, the plurality (or 'relative' majority) in the 1972, 1998, and 2002 federal elections, participation in the governmental coalition in 1966, and the direction of the federal government from 1969 to 1982 and from 1998 to at least 2006. Once again, this 'establishing' and changing position period is also marked by a sudden and quick transformation of the parliamentary personnel, notably by a quasi-disappearance of low-educated deputies and a more consolidated quantitative predominance of holders of university degrees. The striking correlations between the changes in the position and status of CD and Socialist German parties and the educational characteristics of their deputies may also be observed with other similar political parties. Figure 5.5 shows for instance that a great part of the increase in the percentage of MPs with a University degree in the House of Commons is due to the Labour Party. There were no deputy with a University degree in the parliamentary Labour Party at the time of its 'establishment' at the beginning of the twentieth century; they were 38 per cent after the Second World War, and more than 70 per cent after the 1997 and 2001 elections. Today, in every European country, the more a party linked to lower or lower middle social groups is established in parliament, the more educated its deputies are, as may be clearly seen in the cases of the CD parties in Denmark, France, Germany, and the Netherlands, as well as with Agrarians parties in Denmark and Finland, with Communist parties in France and Finland, and with the Socialist parties in Denmark, Finland, France, Germany, the Netherlands, and in the UK.

5.1.3. *Changing Specializations: From Law to Economics and Public Administration*

If university education thus seems to be a tacit prerequisite for entering parliament, it is not only due to a 'level' effect, but also because of a 'certification of expertise' effect. One of the most strikingly convergent trends in parliamentary recruitment is the decline of the numerical weight of elected national parliamentarians with law degrees (Figure 5.6).

In all countries of the sample used in this book, a large majority of deputies with University education held a law degree in second half of the nineteenth century. The percentage varied between 50 per cent (Denmark and Norway), 70 per cent (France and Germany) and even 80 per cent or more (Italy and the Netherlands). They are presently a minority among the elected national parliamentarians with university education, their proportion fluctuating between 20 per cent and 40 per cent. Deputies holding a university degree in public administration, economics, sometimes other social sciences, or humanities have replaced these lawyers (see Figure 5.7). Their proportion has steadily increased throughout the second half of the twentieth century. It presently varies from 40 per cent (France, Hungary, Italy, Norway, and Portugal) to 60 per cent

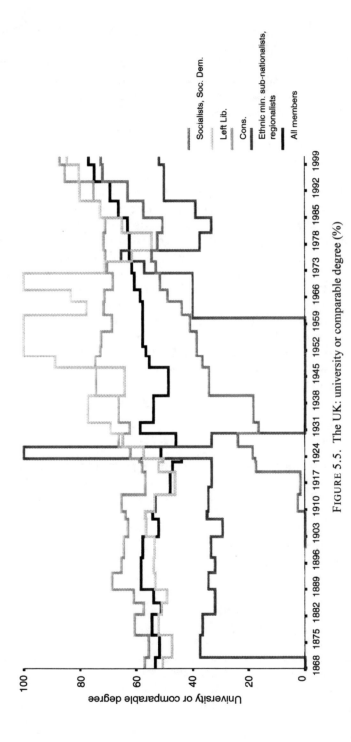

FIGURE 5.5. The UK: university or comparable degree (%)

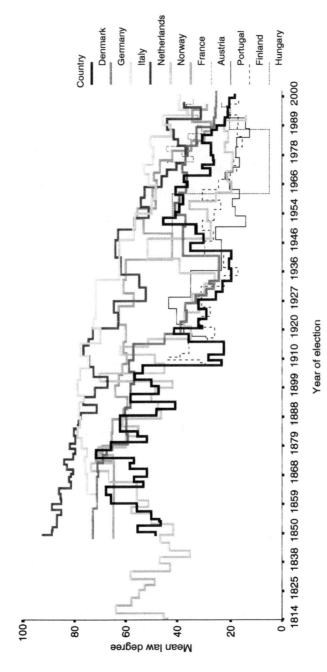

FIGURE 5.6. Legislators with a law degree (Var07), all countries (%)

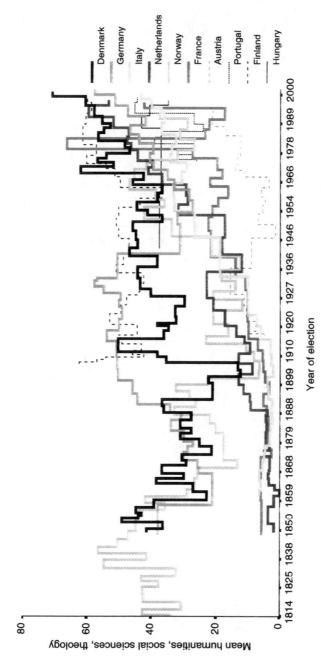

FIGURE 5.7. Legislators with a public administration, economics, humanities, or social sciences degree (Var08), all countries (%)

(Denmark, Finland, Germany, and the Netherlands). The proportion of deputies with Technical, Engineering, Natural Sciences, or Medicine degrees is more irregular, although it follows similar trends in almost all countries. It had increased from 1848 to the mid-1920s, decreased during the thirty next years, increased again until the late 1970s, and is somewhat declining up to now.

These shifts in the academic specializations of parliamentarians are partly a consequence of the transformation of universities' organization. New programmes, degrees, and curricula in government, economics or public administration have been progressively separated from Law faculties and have been dramatically expanded. Formerly, future parliamentarians learnt rudiments of economics, government or public administration throughout their law studies. Their contemporary counterparts enter differentiated departments or faculties when they choose these specialties. They are less likely to hold a law degree.

Another factor lies in the types of state interventions. States have always interfered with civil society' affairs through law. But since the twentieth century, new types of regulations (economic or welfare regulations for instance) and, therefore, new types of skills required to handle them, have been developed.

5.2. THE CAUSES OF THE ELEVATION OF PARLIAMENTARIANS' EDUCATION LEVEL

University-trained politicians have again 'taken over' parliamentary representation. Indeed, the high comparative value of cultural capital within the set of *resources* needed to be (s)elected (Godmer 2002)—as attested by the education level and above all by university degrees, especially rare ones—furthered the prevalence of certain profiles and paths in the selection of parliamentarians. The increase in the attainment rate of tertiary education, or 'academization' process (Apel 1991: 243; Burmeister 1993: 102) has had major consequences on parliamentary life. It is one of the most impressive long-term trends that affected parliamentary selection. It seems tempting to explain it by a macro-social causality system based on the development of mass education. It is more convincing to stress the influence of a set of iron laws that govern political selection.

5.2.1. *The 'Macro-Social', Mechanical Explanatory Hypothesis, and Its Limits*

There is a spontaneous mechanical explanation linked to the long-term development of superior education in the overall population. It is based on the idea that tertiary education is more accessible. This 'societal' explanation is linked to the morphological change that affected educational systems. It is well known that opportunity structures have widened, especially in the second half of the twentieth century. Thus, a fast growing number of would-be parliamentarians or political leaders hold university degrees and can compete within their political party, whereas middle-level origins and statuses (and all the social properties attached to them) would have in previous periods generally prevented them from entering university and/or from claiming parliamentary positions. This 'easier access' to tertiary education may have contributed to a relative diversification of the origins of parliamentarians and to a more open access to party selection, but it may also be a mirage, hiding the limits of the effects of that set of transformations. This 'spillover theory' applied to parliamentary representation brings up explanation difficulties and seems at best to explain only parts of the evolution.

A process of 'quantitative democratization' of education undoubtedly occurred. But the development of a mass education entails manifold processes, which mostly affected the *secondary* education system. In line with industrialization processes and their consequences in terms of public educational policies, compulsory elementary schooling to children was generalized. For example, that process begun in 1870 and 1880 in Britain (then until the age of 10), and led to compulsory schooling until the age of 14 in 1918 (Gal 1979: 108; Cromwell and Rush 2000: 482–3). Formal education is nowadays compulsory by law until ages between 14 and 18 (UNESCO 2002a). The absolute majority of the population aged between 25 and 64 received at least a secondary education in countries such as Germany, Norway, Finland, Austria, or France (Balan, Join-Lambert, and Pape 1994: 1; OSCE 1995). End-of-secondary education diplomas have even tended to become the 'norm' (e.g. the French *baccalauréat*) (Estrade and Minni 1996: 1). There has been an effect of this generalization of compulsory secondary education duration on tertiary education, which has been progressively transformed into a mass education system. Countries such as France and Germany counted, at the beginning of the twenty-first century, more than two millions students in their tertiary education systems (UNESCO 2002b).

5.2.2. *University Graduates: A 'Minority'*

Nonetheless, university graduates remain a *minority* even among young-age cohorts. Although the figures of gross attainment rates are rising, the official percentage of the population of 25–34 years old who attained tertiary education is still relatively low: between 34 and 38 per cent in France, Spain, Sweden, and Finland, 27 per cent in the Netherlands, 22 per cent in Germany, but only 15 per cent in Hungary, 14 per cent in Austria and Portugal, and 12 per cent in Italy (Statistics Norway 2003; *The Economist* 2004). The Organization for Economic Cooperation and Development (OECD) classifies the USA as the first major Western country with approximately more than 27 per cent of 25–64-years-old population being university-degree holders in 2002, whereas this proportion of tertiary-educated population amounted to respectively about 18 per cent in the United Kingdom and 13 per cent in Germany and France (INSEE 1999; Kantrowitz 2003: 52). It is true that such an expansion 'has created a large reservoir of academically trained personnel' (Best, Hausmann, and Schmitt 2000: 175). Thus, there has been a tremendously fast-increasing number of graduates in post-war age cohorts. In France, for example, this process was visible in the 1970s and also in the 1980s (Best and Gaxie 2000: 121). It resulted in a higher proportion of university graduates among the overall adult population, which had been extremely small until the 1950s. During the last quarter of the twentieth century, tertiary enrollment rates continued to increase in countries such as Spain and Portugal, where tertiary education systems had been rendered more accessible (UNECE 2003). The elitist character of an average university title has undoubtedly declined with its relative diffusion. This has had a dual effect: first of all, it may have made it easier for certain political agents coming from middle-class sections of the population to have attained tertiary education and then to have envisaged a transformation of their social and individual resources and competences into a parliamentary career. Second, it has made the possession of a university title a *prerequisite* for such a career, contributing at the same time to a relative 'opening' of the parliamentary profession and to the elimination of militants deprived of such titles. The latter now tend to be part of a logical, functional requirement, in line with the evolution of militant practices, of selection procedures within the political enterprises, and, of course, of the parliamentary work. The so-called 'democratization of education' however is insufficient in explaining the high degree of domination of university-educated agents within parliaments. Indeed, the transformation of the political personnel was extremely rapid. It was not a progressive adaptation to change and in some cases it corresponded to a radical mutation, as it was for instance in the case of the German Social-Democratic party's parliamentarians for whom the brutal 'academization' process lasted barely a decade. The morphological explanation cannot explain why changes in the educational level of parliamentarians mainly affected political parties during the phases of their 'establishment'.

The distance between the active population and parliamentarians has been reduced, but there is a huge gap remaining between their educational levels. Tertiary education undoubtedly developed, but 'prestigious' superior education (especially university and superior schooling) reached wider sections of the population only to a lesser extent. It can be said that in all countries, the social value of the educational titles held by parliamentarians is superior to the average value of university diplomas. There are particular educational tracks leading to parliamentary careers.

5.2.3. *Specific Elitist Paths*

Educational paths of parliamentarians invisibly transformed representatives into a world apart. There are competence effects symbolically attached to certain diplomas that are mobilized to the benefit of leaders and which constitute the distinctive *dominant* expertise-oriented parliamentary *style* (see Bourdieu 1986). In many countries, especially for would-be frontbenchers, the scope of possible tertiary education institutions tends to be relatively limited, as it can be easily observed in the comparatively 'overly elitist' models of France and the UK. Practically, many educational resources remain hard to obtain and have the social status of 'rare' social goods. Even if they are far more complex than their image may reflect, multilevel tertiary educational systems favour the perpetuation of the value of certain studies in parliamentary selection, due to the narrow range of legitimate 'pre-political' student careers. Albeit numerous, the student population (i.e. far more than nine students out of ten) is also excluded from these parallel, elitist systems. In France, only several *grandes écoles* diplomas are especially convertible into the political field, practically giving to their holders a specific status. The *énarques* (former students of the National Administration School (ENA) have a special political status, particularly when they come from the first ranks, access to which is even more socially biased (Eymeri 2001)). In 2002, 15.7 per cent of the deputies were graduates from *grandes écoles* (including ENA) and 14.7 per cent from Institutes for Political Studies (IEPs). This kind of trajectory, which is frequent among the parliamentary population, concerns extremely restricted parts of the population. These institutions are often a *passage obligé* for career politicians who envisage a non-backbencher future, in particular so as to be 'eligible' to a cabinet position. These 'elite' graduates consequently occupy a peculiar place among the almost three-quarters of the deputies who hold an effective, complete tertiary diploma. The British system produces a similar internal differentiation within the tertiary education system: on the one side Oxford and Cambridge (frequently, only certain colleges within the old Oxbridge 'galaxy') and a few elite institutions such as the London School of Economics and Political Science (LSE), and, on the other side, the vast majority of the other universities. It must however be mentioned that this domination is no longer absolute and that 'pre-political student careers' can be diverse even in those very elitist systems. Also, in other countries where superior education systems are less elitist, parliamentarians tend to be alumni of 'good', but often 'regional', universities more than of specific schools (for instance in Italy and Spain). Even in such cases a hierarchy can be observed. Certain student careers may be favoured (notably within economics and law programmes in reputed major regional universities), as well as tracks leading to relatively rare titles. Deputies tend for instance to hold a relatively high number of masters' and doctoral degrees (whereas the *bachelor*, *licence*, *licenciatura* levels were the rule in previous periods, with a predominance of law degrees in particular) and to hold highly valued university titles such as engineering or lawyer 'diplomas' that are statistically rarer among the overall population.

Even in the context of mass education, there has been a social bias weighing on access to university education and degrees, and to 'elite' institutions (Bourdieu 1989). This contributes to the selection of people who grew up in a framework composed of 'educogenic' factors (i.e. numerous contextual elements favouring education, such as a family relation to legitimate cultural 'goods' or foreign languages, the role of certain family relatives or friends, geographic location, access to libraries, and so on, independent the level of education of the parents). Inequalities of access significantly affect who goes to elite schools. To some extent elite schools have become more socially selective than before (Albouy and Wanecq 2003: 29, 35). They accentuate 'reproduction' effects (through the reproduction of differential codes, attitudes, subcultures, etc.), which are visible throughout the entire education system (see the 'classical' Bernstein 1975; Bourdieu and Passeron 1977; Willis 1977), but less and less so regarding access to university first degrees. It is as if there were dynamic homeostatic adaptations operating on that elite subsystem.

In several countries, there is a strong presence of parliamentarians holding *doctoral degrees*, which may be regarded as equivalents of the elitist *'grandes écoles'* and *'Oxbridge'-like institutions*, in terms of structural distinction. This is especially true if one concentrates the analysis on 'frontbenchers' and cabinet members. Parliamentarians holding a Ph.D. degree are numerous, especially in the three main German-speaking states. In Bern, in the National Council (the lower chamber of the Swiss federal parliament), their number was close to one third of the members in the post-war period (Gruner 1970: 140). In Berlin and Vienna, in 2003, these deputies accounted for respectively 15.9 and 19.7 per cent of the total (Deutscher Bundestag 2003; Nationalrat 2003). However, these countries, as well as Nordic states have a more egalitarian university structure (Best, Hausmann, and Schmitt 2000: 175). Thus, attainment of superior education tends to mean attainment of *prestigious* education as embodied in renowned diplomas that can afterwards be converted into 'partisan' capital (i.e. a specific capital provided by activity within the party). The relative territorial concentration may also be observed in many countries, and not only the centralized ones, because Spanish or German deputies frequently come from the major university of their region of origin (in contexts where universities multiplied and were decentralized). Even in other countries, the importance of the title *doctor* obtained in universities should not be neglected. In France, where it is supposed to be devalued by the predominance of *grandes écoles*, it remains very present (14.3 per cent of the deputies elected in 2002 held a doctoral degree).

Reproduction processes are nowadays more based on cultural ground than in the past. In an earlier state of the social structure, members of upper categories used to maintain their social status and position through inheritance of fortune, lands, nobility titles, and family's name and respectability. Higher social status was not always linked to formal education. Aristocrats or 'grand bourgeois' were not always holders of university degrees: they had interrupted their scholarly education at a lower level or they had their own private tutors. The importance of direct inheritance has not disappeared but is certainly declining. The intra-family transmission of social positions, status, and powers is more indirect and relies more on formal education. Children of people occupying high social positions statistically reach high positions in their turn by way of degrees from elite universities. People with a high level of language, culture, and education hand over their cultural capital to their children through day-to-day contacts and informal channels. This 'inherited cultural capital' helps to meet the requirements of schools and universities. Owners of inherited cultural capital are statistically more able to succeed in their school and university career and are therefore more likely to reach high-level occupations. Combined with distinctive and lucrative occupations, high levels of formal education and an elite university diploma are presently core components of a high social status. Consequently, family investments in formal education have risen. In so far as future parliamentarians belong to upper or upper middle social circles, they have strong general social incentives to enter tertiary education institutions and particularly to effectively obtain university degrees.

5.2.4. *The Prevalence of 'Iron Laws' of Political Selection*

Access to parliamentary selection may be viewed above all as dependent on the possession of social titles, which constitute a *portfolio of resources* in which elitist educational background (i.e. a legitimate, recognized educational resource) nowadays occupies a central place. The division between extremely selective institutions and a classical university system favours the quest for the most prestigious diplomas, especially by people for whom education is the only available *distinctive resource*. Partial partisan de-differentiation is visible with regard to education. In every major party, this evolution may be evidenced. It is all the more true that there has been an *establishment* process of political parties, which were previously outsiders, such as left parties in general. Although the effect of this establishment process is not immediate, it is clear that there is a routinization of selecting more 'gifted' candidates supposedly capable of dealing with the responsibilities and the technical tasks faced by an established parliamentary party. Nowadays, only the types of university and specialization may partially differentiate the parties. Education, regarded as the result of 'merit' and of a 'meritocratic system', remains a legitimate selection criterion and thereby a resource that agents may emphasize and publicize in that it is perceived as a socially 'acceptable', unquestioned 'discrimination' tool. Besides, it can be argued that in welfare states, many political 'selectorates' may logically tend to favour parliamentary candidates with some kind of so-called 'technocratic' ability, certified by university degrees, all the more so as technical issues are put on the agenda. As previously mentioned, the evolution towards the legitimization of cultural capital was thus accelerated by the welfare state, which obliges political parties to provide their parliamentary groups with agents 'competent' in different fields. Such a 'technocratization' contributes to explaining the 'teacherization' processes. Furthermore, the cultural capital appears more 'democratic' and more 'meritocratic', albeit being also in a way 'inherited' as has long been demonstrated by sociologists

(Bourdieu and Passeron 1964). The paradoxical force of this reproduction lies in its partial 'inefficiency', that is, in the statistical probability of a minimum failure rate, whereas reproduction was more or less 'automatic' in aristocratic reproduction or in plutocratic reproduction. Thus, since the value of traditional or 'alternative' resources (local 'dynastic' legitimacy, notability, and nobility, or union experience and involvement) has declined, the educational resource has become a central defining feature of party members seeking investiture in the perspective of parliamentary selection. For politicians with a higher educational level, there is an 'implicit legitimacy' to intervene in the parliamentary arena, a specific right to talk, to advise, and to represent. Thereby, as Max Weber observed (1994: 83), education generates new 'estates', no longer based on economic possession.

In addition, the transformation of political parties should be analysed, notably the internal mutation of workers' parties. By becoming government parties, the latter rendered accessible to their leaders highly valued political positions. This is a critical explaining factor of the 'natural' domination of cultural capital as the main selection criterion [i.e. of the 'culturalization' of political selection (Godmer 2002, 2005)]. On the one hand, a party in government has to mobilize agents who are able to head central public authorities, to discuss with top civil servants and to intervene with at least a minimum credibility with regard to technical issues within the media sphere, in parliament, and in international meetings. Political 'enterprises' need leaders with high university education and with an adapted specialization (on selection within parties, see Chapter 6 below). It explains the diversity of the educational background of parliamentarians. They are no longer only lawyers, and they are skilled in various domains of state intervention, often holding humanities and social sciences degrees. On the other hand, the establishment of a party contributes to the increase in the relative value of various positions, such as acquiring the candidate status or local leadership positions. This encourages a highly 'competitive' selection process, in the sense that the volume of resources that an agent needs to obtain in order to have the right to compete and a chance to win, (university titles among others), is undoubtedly increasing. The 'deconstruction' of the working class that has taken place in European societies has also affected the political recruitment centered on former working class background favoured by political parties, which had been previously 'bolshevized', that is 'proletarianized'. In addition, 'new' *outsiders*, more or less marginal parties such as the Greens have somehow 'atypical' parliamentarians, but their difference lies in peculiarities within the space of university titles. In some cases, 'new left' parties (see Chapter 13 below) even favoured the domination of academically trained elected national parliamentarians, as in the Dutch case with D'66 and the Socialists (Daalder and van den Berg 1982: 229; Secker 2000: 292). Later, in several assemblies of Germany (Golsch 1998: 121) and Austria, the success of the *Grünen* was actually an accelerating factor in the academization of parliamentary selection and thereby in elevating the social level of political representatives. 'Rapprochement' processes between representatives and the population, which received different denominations, including 'descriptive' (Pitkin 1984) or 'inclusive' representation (Young 2000), tended indirectly to increase the relative value of 'university' capital in selection procedures or at least to consolidate it. Access of women to the political elite has favoured a slight increase in the educational level of parliamentarians, since they more often come from elite backgrounds, as it is the case with the French women members of the National Assembly and of the European Parliament (MEPs) (Kauppi 1999: 331). The rejuvenation that occurred especially in the German and Nordic assemblies had the same effects. Young militants who entered parliaments were often former student-union leaders and/or active in student-oriented youth branches of political parties. Such 'modernization' processes may partly contribute to the continuous elimination of less educated elected national parliamentarians, a process that was already advanced. They take part in the 'naturalization' of over-representation of university and elite superior schools graduates within European parliaments.

The reconstruction and the development of parliamentary democracy in post-Communist European states in the 1990s and the 2000s did not lead to divergent recruitment processes. On the contrary, very far from the specific pro-working-class bias of the previous regimes, it has to be observed that the parliamentarians of the Eastern European countries that were integrated into the EU in 2004 and 2007 (and those coming from the former Democratic Republic of Germany) have especially high education levels.

Would-be politicians consequently look for highly valued specific diplomas, contributing to the existence of a *cursus honorum* leading to a potential 'eligibility' which is linked to a generally acceptable 'profile'. It is all the more true if one is seeking a parliamentary and/or a cabinet career and '[t]hose who did not reach this educational level are more likely to be outsiders in a parliamentary milieu which may occasionally stigmatize them for that reason' (Best and Gaxie 2000: 121). This 'caste' phenomenon has concrete manifestations, especially throughout pre-war legislatures during which the so-called 'parliamentary eloquence' was the rule. Elected national parliamentarians with upper class and superior education background sometimes used them as a means of exclusion or marginalization in struggles, within the political field (Grèzes-Rueff 1994: 19).

The crux of the issue is that the education of parliamentarians provides a *sapiential authority* (i.e. the right to advise others in an organization) which is 'given to the gifted' and unquestioned. The educational background of most parliamentary representatives has transformed the political profession. Because of the homogeneity that results from the new selection criteria, the parliamentary profession is different from what it was during periods where different sorts of constructed 'merits' (i.e. based on party activity, political loyalty, class backgrounds, union experience, education, birth, and so on) were so to speak 'competing' with each other, especially within Left parties. In short, access to lower houses of national parliaments has become more and more restricted to agents coming from certain socialization canals who combine access to superior, 'politically convertible' education with a high degree of interest in politics.

5.3. CONSEQUENCES: TOWARDS NEW FORMS OF POLITICAL PROFESSIONALIZATION AND NEW CHANNELS OF REPRESENTATION

5.3.1. *A New Type of Professional Politician*

The professionalization of politics and of parliamentary representation has become a general phenomenon. One side effect has been that politics has reached a high degree of differentiation. Parliamentarians are more and more 'Weberian' *Berufspolitiker*, that is, social agents who effectively live from and for politics. But they are also professionalized because they acquire technical skills, knowledge, and know-how. This expertise is attested by education degrees and is also a result of a direct learning process 'on the ground'. Relatively rare educational titles are therefore more and more crucial for them. In this regard, parliamentarians resemble bureaucratic agents (who, according to another definition by Max Weber, possess titles, are recruited through competitive examinations and monitor specific issues). The political professional has now been redefined and has a career, which entails a university education, especially if this means going beyond the *backbencher*, *Hinterbänkler* or *député de base* status (Golsch 1998: 64–6).

As a *broker*, that is acting for local interests in bureaucratic configurations, an elected parliamentarian has also to be aware of territorial issues concerning her or his constituency and region of origin. Because of the complexity and the decentralization of many public policies, this local expertise is another component of the parliamentarians' cultural capital.

5.3.2. *Separation and Autonomization of the Political Field*

Academization tends to be a factor of homogenization of the political field, of increasing social distance between the political field and the general public, and of the lack of 'representativeness' of parliamentarians. Parliamentary representation is commonly perceived as being more and more separate from the population and from the 'real world'. Political selection generates a sphere of its own, less linked to churches, unions, business organizations and leaders, or states than in the past. Hence there is a domination of the political field by a certain 'technical-mindedness' and abstraction. In line with the partial de-differentiation hypothesis, the elite education of deputies is a key variable that may help to explain the homogeneity and the 'parochial' closeness of the political field (Gaxie 2003a). This has an impact also on the public image of parliaments as self-referential, 'esoteric', and technocratic institutions. All in all, 'the aristocracy of intelligence', which had many competitors in the nineteenth century (Phélippeau 1997: 245), and even in the twentieth century, is now in a more oligarchic situation. The political profession undoubtedly 'intellectualized' itself, which increased the gap between it and less educated fractions of the population, the latter tending to perceive politics as a flow of abstract speeches made by 'good-talkers'.

There is indeed an apparent *partisan de-differentiation* process which consists in a unification of selection practices and profiling, in particular with regard to educational resources. Important differences may now be only found in very specific Left parties such as the small present French Communist Party (PCF)'s parliamentary grouping. However, there may remain some *milieu effects*, many left-wing deputies still coming from less elite family and education backgrounds. To sum up, there is undoubtedly a 'parochialization' of the parliamentary sphere which is a 'vicious circle' linked to the routinization of the selection of 'elite' educated parliamentarians, although the relative social value of parliamentary positions may have apparently diminished. The decreasing relative 'power' of representative institutions, combined with the extreme professionalization of politics and the rise of new or renewed forms of 'anti-politics', has contributed to the closing of a sphere in which the dominance of cultural capital is more and more the rule.

5.3.3. *Education and Parliamentarians' Autonomy*

A third consequence of the rising educational level of parliamentarians is their greater autonomy vis-à-vis their political party inside and outside parliament.

On the one hand, almost all deputies belong to a political party and need the various resources (collective political credit, voters' confidence in the party, workforce of activists, money, buildings, labels, programmes, tenets, and so on) that it provides. 'Weberian' independent political entrepreneurs have almost disappeared. Representatives of collective political enterprise have replaced them. Most deputies have been elected as party representatives, although they may also have their own political capital that adds to the party credit among voters and followers. In that respect, deputies have been increasingly dependent on a party throughout parliamentary history. For instance, they more strongly need a party nomination to run successfully than was the case in the past.

On the other hand, a higher formal education gives parliamentarians new opportunities for a greater autonomy. Every elected parliamentarian relies on a portfolio of resources to enter parliament and to play her/his role. Every elected parliamentarian needs money, political credit from voters, political work provided by party activists, friends, relatives, or clients, a place to meet constituents, political analyses, a programme, issue positions, and so on. Some of these resources are *collective* ones, given the fact that they are provided by a collective organization. Others are *individual* resources in that they belong to or are found by the candidate. For example, a campaign may be financed by the candidate's money or by party's money, or both. The candidate may ask for the help of activists and/or friends. She or he may be elected thanks to voters' confidence in the party or thanks to the voters' confidence in her or him, or both, especially in a majority system with single-member constituencies but possibly also with proportional voting system.

Education is an individual political resource for a politician. It helps to acquire authority in the political and parliamentary fields. Some politicians owe their authority mainly to the party they belong to. This was the typical situation of the former 'blue collar', poorly educated working-class party functionaries or deputies. Others hold some individual titles, especially university degrees that empower them to intervene in the political field and in the parliamentary arena. The higher their educational level, the more elected national parliamentarians are able to acquire a personal authority that adds to and may substitute for authority delegated by party. All things being equal, deputies with a higher educational level arc morc able and likely to form their opinion, to take a stand on issues, to deliver statements, and to define a strategy on their own. The more educated the deputies are, the more likely they are also to be recruited through channels at least partly external to a party. Nowadays, career paths through universities and vocational circles are often a prolegomenon to a political career.

The declining proportion of former party functionaries among parliamentarians is a consequence and an indicator of these changing ways of recruiting deputies and of the increasing importance of cultural capital among the various criteria of deputies' selection. Such a decline illustrates a contradictory renewed autonomy in a context of dependence vis-à-vis political parties that characterizes a growing number of deputies. The per cent age of former full-time politicians (who were often party functionaries at the same time) in parliaments had regularly increased since the origins of political parties at the end of the nineteenth century to the early 1960s. It then reached a maximum, varying from 10 to 30 per cent. Germany was the only deviant case with the highest (around 35–40%) and earliest (1920–33) peak. Afterwards, in all countries there has been a declining trend from the early 1960s to the early 1980s and then a stabilization at a lower level.

5.3.4. *A More 'Indirect' Political Representation*

The higher educational level of parliamentarians has also contributed to various changes in the origins of parliamentary personnel, especially among Left parties.

First, the quasi-disappearance of former blue-collar workers among deputies is correlated with the evanescence of parliamentarians with a low level of education. Even if these former blue-collar workers have never been very numerous in most countries, except in Hungary and the UK, their proportion had risen from the origins of working-class political parties, to the early 1950s. It then declined to almost 0 per cent, in a strikingly convergent trend that includes Hungary and the UK.

It seems that teachers and other public sector employees have replaced the former blue-collar workers or full-time politicians with working-class or lower-middle-class backgrounds. As mentioned above in Chapter 3 of this book, there is an increase in the percentage of former teachers and public sector employees in all European parliaments—with the sole Hungarian exception within our sample—especially among Left parties. Teachers are increasingly represented throughout the second half of the twentieth century. They form one of the most over-represented social groups in all European parliaments. The proportion of former public sector employees is presently close to or even greater than 50 per cent in the parliaments of several countries (Denmark, Finland, France, Germany, and the Netherlands).

These changes in the social make-up of parliaments affect political representation of social groups. Societal interests are brought into parliaments through more or less 'indirect' processes. Representation is less indirect when representatives further the interests of groups (either social, occupational, religious, or ideological) they personally belong to. It is more indirect when representatives are professional politicians with specific interests. At the same time, definite backgrounds may lead professional politicians to take care of expectations of groups they come from and with which they are still linked. Even if politicians only allude to social interests, their personal social ties are thus one of the 'mechanisms' through which social demands or expectations are taken into account by the political realm. But this kind of mediated representation is even more indirect when political recruitment and deferential attitudes among voters lead to election of representatives with more 'elitist' features than their constituents. Members of under privileged groups are unlikely to enter a political career and even less likely to enter parliament. They have nevertheless been partly represented in the past by professional politicians coming from their circles. Former blue-collar, working-class party deputies were no longer blue-collar workers, but their blue-collar origins could prompt them to pay attention to working class and lower groups' expectations. As far as their members still participate in elections and cast a vote for left wing parties, politicians of higher social origin presently represent these groups in parliament. The workers' side of the social cleavage, opposing workers and Trades Unions to business and executives' circles, is thus more indirectly, and probably less adequately, represented than it used to be. It is one of the numerous factors that contribute to the widespread political discontent in Europe (Gaxie 2001, 2003*b*). One may even wonder if the traditional socio-economic cleavage still has the same structuring impact on the political realm and if other cleavages, especially oppositions between intellectual and economic bourgeoisies or between public and private sectors, are not becoming predominant (see Chapter 3 below, about public sector backgrounds among parliamentarians).

Even though parliaments remain apparently unchanged, their status, role and position have deeply evolved since the middle of the nineteenth century. Parliamentarians have historically moved from a position of growing supremacy to a more subordinate role. A parliamentary seat is a political position of which the properties and value depend on numerous parameters. The primary parameter is the role of parliament in the institutional setting of the state. This has declined with the strengthening of the executive branch and higher state bureaucracy. A second parameter is the power relationships between parliamentarians and political parties, the transformations of which have been discussed earlier. A third one is the role of the state. After a long period of widening interventions, this role has been declining during the last decades with the devolution of competences to subnational public bodies and to the EU, the sway of a neoliberal mood, deregulations, the weakening of the public sector and the crisis of the nation states' regulatory capacities. The expanding proportion of teachers and public sector employees among parliamentarians is certainly a consequence of the growing importance of cultural capital in political competition. It is perhaps also a consequence of the more limited and parochial role of the state, the decisions of which are less decisive for many social groups than they used to be but retain a greater significance for groups linked to its apparatuses.

6

A Career through the Party: The Recruitment of Party Politicians in Parliament

Stefaan Fiers[1] and Ineke Secker

6.1. INTRODUCTION

With a few exceptions,[2] MPs owe their seats in parliament in the first place to a political party. In some countries, this has been the case since the very beginning of party formation in the mid-nineteenth century. It means that almost all candidates, in their bid for a seat in parliament, have to be 'approved' by a party organization. In this respect the political parties fulfil a vital role in the recruitment and selection of MPs. As gatekeepers, they control both the demand and the supply side of the process of recruitment (Norris 1997a, 1997b). Their gate-keeping role is crucial and cannot be underestimated, since the constitutional and legal requirements to become an MP are kept deliberately easy to meet in almost all countries. They refer to requirements of citizenship, age (although the age barrier has constantly been lowered over the years), and gender (at least until the first half of the twentieth century). Only few parties imposed extra formal requirements for aspirant-MPs in order to be eligible for selection as a candidate (Gallagher 1988: 247; Rahat and Hazan 2001). In this respect, we can conclude that the formal threshold to become an MP is rather low.

But parties do screen candidates on other qualities in order to designate who will compete under their label in the elections. This is not a new phenomenon. Already at the beginning of the twentieth century, Michels (1911) recorded that the road to a party's 'establishment' and a parliamentary seat was closely scrutinized by the party's oligarchy. In fact, in systems of PR, either the central party headquarters or the constituency parties decide not only who will *compete*. They also determine the specific order in which candidates are put on the electoral lists, and in this respect strongly influence the process of electoral choice and thus who will be *elected*. Still, there is a lot of variety both cross-nationally and cross-parties in the recruitment process of MPs (Norris and Lovenduski 1995; Rahat and Hazan 2001). In the framework of this contribution, however, it would lead us too far to go much into details on the specific ways of recruitment. It suffices to say that candidate selection still is one of the most crucial moments in a party's life. Therefore it is often referred to as the 'secret garden of politics' (Gallagher and Marsh 1988).

6.2. PARTIES AND 'PARTY POLITICIANS'

Unlike the presumed lack of information on the course of the recruitment process, we do have undisputed evidence of its outcome: the population of elected MPs. In order to analyse the extent of social representation and the functional aptitude of MPs scholars in the field of parliamentary recruitment are generally interested in two categories of background characteristics (Norris 1997: 6). On the one hand there are the social–cultural background features such as region of origin, educational level, social class, or religious affiliation. They give us detailed information on the extent to which the population of MPs mirrors the distribution of the social classes in a given society and thus respond to a certain degree of descriptive representation. On the other hand, our attention is attracted by more specific, function-oriented elements. These include occupational and political experience of the candidates, which provide us with crucial information on the degree of professionalization of a given assembly.

However, considerable less attention is being given to the direct, occupational ties between the candidates and the political parties, who then act both as an employer and a selector. As a matter of fact having been employed as a party official can be considered to be the first training to the political profession. While second, it introduces a kind of *nepotistic* element in the process: one cannot blame the gatekeepers (selectors) to lay their eyes on candidates in their immediate neighbourhood. These party officials are persons who served the party faithfully in several functions, who are devoted to the party and who are well aware of the party *ins* and *outs*. On top of that, it is quite natural that persons who aspire after a political career are more motivated than others to enter the party organizations in whatsoever function.[3] A record of party service may be seen as facilitating a political career and therefore it is likely to be used as a path to legislative recruitment (Whiteley, Seyd, and Richardson 1994: 117; McAllister 1997).

Hence, we expect to find that a considerable number of MPs started their political career as a 'party politician'. In our analysis, we make a distinction between *party officials* and *party functionaries*. In the first category of *party officials* we consider all leading positions in the political party, taken by politicians, regardless of whether these positions are paid or unpaid. Most, if not all, of these positions are elected positions. In this respect, this category includes positions of national, provincial and local party leaders and secretaries, as well as leading positions in affiliated trade unions, youth's organizations, women's organizations, and other 'officially' recognized organizations of the political party. In our analysis, these two categories have been grouped under one label of *party officials*.

Yet, in this chapter, we also consider two other kinds of candidates, which we have labelled *party functionaries*. First, we have *party employees*, which are non-elective paid positions in the administration of the party. These positions can either be high in ranking (e.g. director of the policy cell, or the operations director), or be located at the lower end of the administrative strata (e.g. clerks from the party headquarters, private assistants to MPs). Second, we include candidates which have not been involved in functions within the political party *sensu stricto*, but who, due to party patronage and their good relationship with the party, have been nominated by the party to other non-elective functions. For instance employees of trade unions, the appointed governors of the provinces in the Netherlands, as well as members of the board of public broadcasting companies and other semi-governmental companies of which the staff is not considered to be a civil servant in the narrow sense of the word (e.g. public transport companies). In all these cases of what we call *party functionaries*, the crux is to what extent the fact of being a party employee or of having direct connections to the party do favour an individual's chance of selection for a parliamentary candidacy. To summarize: a person with a party political background is thus defined as 'a person that has served in (a) an elected leading position in a political party or one of its affiliated organizations, i.e. *the party official*, and/or (b) a non-elective position inside the party administration or patronaged position in another organisation, i.e. *the political functionary*'. When taken together, both categories of party officials and party functionaries are referred to as *party politicians*. They owe or owed their political positions to their respective political parties without the interference of the electorate.

For a correct understanding of this categorization, it is important to point out that patronage functions in the civil service have not been included in this latter category. Nor have we included, second, possible other affiliated jobs, like journalists. Because the DATACUBE data, alas, do not allow for a distinction between journalists in a general and neutral sense and party affiliated journalists. The latter category operated especially at the end of the nineteenth and the beginning of the twentieth century. The figures of Germany are telling in this respect. While in 1871 there were merely twenty journalists and writers in parliament, the SPD-parliamentary party was interspersed with party journalists who became the single most important occupational category by the beginning of the Weimar Republic (Best, Hausmann, and Schmitt 2000: 165–7). It is clear, however, from the start, that the total number of patronaged positions (*party functionaries*) surpasses the number of leading party positions (the so-called *party officials*). However, it remains to be seen if this domination will also be reflected in the number of former party functionaries among the MPs.

Obviously, in dealing with party political background of the MPs, we have to deal with the evolutions in types of parties since the emergence of the first parties in the mid-nineteenth century. According to the seminal work of Duverger (1951), Kirchheimer (1966), and Katz and Mair (1995), we make the distinction between four types of parties. Each of them is covering one period in the history of party formation. In the earliest period of the *cadre* or *elite party* (more or less from 1845 to 1880), we do not expect to find large numbers of party politicians in parliament. The extra-parliamentary party structure was indeed very poorly organized in that time, and the power was in the hands of the party in parliament. The second period runs from 1880 to the 1960s, and is characterized by the emergence and the success of the *mass party*, with its willingness to appeal to the largest possible part of the electorate. According to Katz and Mair (1995: 10) 'these new parties were naturally dominated by those whose principal base was in the party rather than in government', and the parties were imminently linked to predefined groups and pressure groups in society. We expect this to be reflected in a clear increase in the number of party politicians in parliament.

Likewise, we expect the overall image to change after the Second World War, when the *catch-all party* (Kirchheimer 1966) became the dominant party type. It challenged the idea of the political party voicing the ideas of only one part of society. In consequence, 'elections were now seen to revolve around the choice of leaders rather than the choice of policies and programmes' (Katz and Mair 1995: 8). Electoral strategies became more competitive, and the profiles of the electoral candidates became important assets. Finally, with the emergence of the *cartel party* from the 1970s onwards (Katz and Mair 1995), the role of the party in the structure of the state was fundamentally altered. The party became truly a part of the state, and politics became a profession of its own. The open competition between the parties has decreased, as they 'share mutual interests in collective organizational survival' (Katz and Mair 1995: 19–20). At the same time, we notice a blurring of the division between members and non-members of the party. Hence, when this really proofs to be the case, we should expect a drop in our recordings of the MPs's previous party political engagements.

One of the goals of this contribution is particularly to link the data of the individual MPs to the evolutions of the different party types over time. We discuss this in the concluding paragraphs. But let us start with providing descriptive analyses of the evolutions in the share of party officials and party functionaries in several parliaments in Europe.[4] With due regard to the limitations of the number of countries, we then proceed in the second part to the cross-country and cross-parties analyses of the important trends and evolutions.

6.3. RECRUITMENT OF PARTY OFFICIALS

Starting with the analysis of the party officials, we can clearly distinguish between four periods between 1867 and 2002 (see Figure 6.1). The first period runs to the early 1890s and is characterized by a lack of a significant number of representatives with a party background. This is no surprise, since in many European countries political parties only emerged in the second half of the nineteenth century, and extra-parliamentary party formation took even some more decades

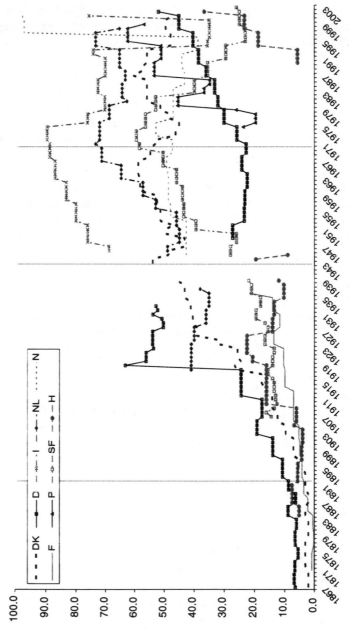

FIGURE 6.1. Share of party officials (1867–2003)

(Lipset and Rokkan 1967). In this period, Denmark, Germany, and Hungary are the only countries with a reported number of party officials among the MPs. Still, their share in the total population of MPs was very moderate and never exceeded the 10 per cent barrier. This stems from the often difficult process of party formation at the end of the 1860s and the early 1870s. Imperial Germany is a case in point, as parties were not allowed to create centralized party organizations until the Law of Association 1899 (Ritter 1990: 27). So long, they were merely regional assemblies of like-minded people, and obviously, this is mirrored in the lack of party officials among the MPs.

The second period, which runs from 1894 until the beginning of the Second World War, is characterized by a permanent rise in the number of party officials. It is a period of extensive party formation and party consolidation, which can be linked to the social agitation at the turn of the century, the reconstruction of democracy after the First World War, and the economic instability of the inter-war period. In the decades before the First World War, the call for universal suffrage, and the introduction of electoral systems with (elements of) PR in a great number of European countries consolidated the pivotal position of the political parties in the democratic decision-making process. It resulted, second, in the breakthrough of the socialist and social-democratic mass parties, which entered parliament in Denmark (1884), France (1885), the Netherlands (1888), Italy (1892), Belgium (1894), and Norway (1903). As we discuss later on, these socialist parties typically were mass parties with a strong, hierarchical structure and strong ties to interest organizations. Third, from this process of party consolidation and institutionalization emerged a new type of politicians: the career politicians. According to Max Weber's well-known typology, these were politicians who considered 'politics as a vocation'. As a result, most socialist delegations in parliament, like in Germany, became largely dominated by career politicians well before 1912 (Ritter 1990: 47; Best, Hausmann, and Schmitt 2000: 167). So generally speaking, until the First World War, we witness a gradual but continuous rise of the number of MPs that previously had been vested with leading party positions. We record 16 per cent in Hungary in 1910, 18 per cent in Denmark in 1915, and 24 per cent in Germany in 1912. Still, in other countries like France (10% in 1914) the share of party officials remained quite moderate.

In the inter-war period, while the general trend is clearly still positive, some countries experienced only mere incremental rises in the number of party officials in parliament. Indeed, in France the number of party officials rose modestly to 14 per cent in 1932. Only the success of the Front Populaire at the general elections of 1936, together with the strong ties of the communist party with the trade unions (Best and Gaxie 2000), caused a rare surge to 21 per cent in the inter-war records. In Denmark and the German Weimar Republic on the other hand, the number of party officials increased dramatically. The share of Danish MPs with a past in a leading party position almost doubled: from an average 25 per cent in 1919 to 46 per cent in 1939. While the highest amount of party officials in the pre-war period was recorded in the German Weimar Republic. At each election until the dramatic elections of 1933, more than half of the MPs had a background in a leading party position. Heinrich Best, Hausmann, and Schmitt (2000: 158) consequently conclude that the contribution of party politicians in the Reichstag between 1890 and 1930 was 'by far more the most important'. This radical development was caused by the introduction of a new electoral system of PR and the strong influence of interest associations in determining the order of candidates on the party lists (Ritter 1990: 47). We also witness strong influences of party experiences in the Netherlands (40%).[5] In Hungary on the contrary, we record a considerable decrease in the number of party officials, with figures dropping from 22 to 12 per cent in 1939.

The post-war period can be divided into two distinct periods. From 1944 until 1972, we witnessed a further consolidation and increase of the share of party officials, and a convergence between the country scores. (West) Germany, however, is a notable exception to this rule: as the newly emerged parties shared low profiles, the share of party officials in parliament consequently remained quite low (around 23%). In all other countries, however, the figures increased spectacularly. In the Netherlands, the share of party officials rose further to 73 per cent in 1971, while Italy (from 68% to 89.5% in 1972) and Finland (from 28% to 59.5% in 1972) recorded similar spectacular rises. The Danish Folketing and the Norwegian Storting, on the other hand, experienced slighter increases, but both institutions ended up with a majority of politicians with previous party offices.

Along with the end of the booming of the welfare state, the share of party officials started to drop in a considerable number of countries at the beginning of the 1970s. Still, the overall image of this fourth period is rather divergent. Germany, Hungary, and Portugal, for instance, experienced a sharp increase in the number of party officials. While at the beginning of the 1970s, less than 30 per cent of the German MPs had a background as leading party official, more than half of them did after the 2002 general elections. The linear rise of the German score in Figure 6.1 is striking, particularly in the late 1980s and throughout the 1990s. It signifies that the German reunification process and the mergers of the various parties did not result in a negative effect, yet on the contrary. Second, and along with the process of party consolidation in the post-communist era, the share of party officials in the Hungarian Parliament grew from a mere 6 per cent in 1990 to nearly 37 per cent in 2002. Similarly, the rise in the Portuguese figures can be attributed to the consolidation process of a young democracy. The share of party officials increases, be it not linearly, from an average 24 per cent at the first post-war democratic elections of 1975 to a high share of 57 per cent at the turn of the century.

Contrary to these three countries, the number of party officials gradually dropped in Italy, Norway, and the Netherlands, to consolidate at a much lower level than before. The Italian case is particularly interesting. Even though the presence of leading party politicians was a little less pronounced in the Italian *partitocrazia* than before, it remained until 1994 virtually impossible to become an MP without having had a previous mandate as party official. Then, following the collapse of the second Italian Republic in 1994, the percentage of MPs with a party background abruptly was halved. Two elections later, however, when the new generation has taken over, the percentage rose to a level comparable to the pre-1994 level. The evolution in Denmark on the contrary is less clear cut, with a further decrease until the end of the 1970s which was followed by a climb until the end of the 1980s, to drop again after 1988. The sharpest decline in number of party officials, however, was recorded in Finland, where at the most recent elections in the data-set (2003) only a quarter (26%) of the MPs had occupied a position in the party leadership. In 1972, the Finnish MPs still recorded 59 per cent of former party officials.

6.4. RECRUITMENT OF PARTY FUNCTIONARIES

The image of the recruitment of party functionaries is somewhat different from the image of the party officials. Notwithstanding the relatively large number of patronaged positions in society, the number of MPs that had enjoyed such a position by the party before they entered parliament is much lower than the number of party officials (cf. Figure 6.2). In fact it has even been extremely low before the start of the twentieth century. Only after the First World War the number increased to a considerable number. Most noteworthy in this respect is the example of the German Weimar Republic. While in Imperial Germany parties were unable to foresee in a lot of patronaged positions, one in three MPs had previously been employed through his party at the first elections of the Weimar Republic in 1919. This share reached a peak of 40 per cent at the 1932 elections. All other countries lagged far behind to this exceptional high number of party functionaries. Yet in the Netherlands, the consolidation of the consociational democracy and the '*verzuiling*' led to a considerable increase of party functionaries, which topped 22 per cent at the last pre-war elections of 1937. It was caused by the numerous checks and balances between the parties, their extensive possibilities for patronage, and the close links with the trade unions, which served as recruitment schools for political talents (van den Berg 1983: 73). Even after the Second World War, the Dutch scores would continue to be among the highest of the countries analysed. In contrast, only a negligible 1 per cent of MPs had occupied similar party-related jobs in pre-war France and on average a mere 5 per cent in Norway and Italy. Recruitment among party functionaries in Denmark (8% on average) and Spain (12%) followed the German pattern of gradual increase, though on a much lower level.[6]

After the Second World War, we first witnessed a period of expansion of the number of party functionaries among the MPs. With the notable exceptions of Spain and Germany, all countries experienced a higher share of party func-tionaries among their MPs than before. In the case of Italy, the large patronage

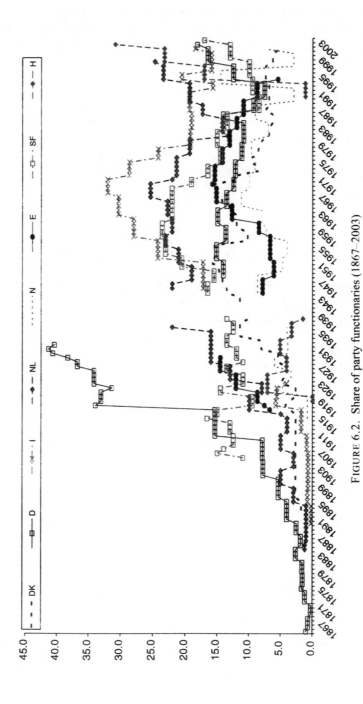

FIGURE 6.2. Share of party functionaries (1867–2003)

possibilities of the *partitocrazia* together with the growth of the party administrations led to a considerable number of over 30 per cent of party functionaries
in the early 1970s. However, all over Europe, the shares dropped from the mid-
1970s onwards. The distribution of positions by the political parties in all kinds
of semi-governmental organizations no longer was considered to be legitimate in
the 1980s. Hence, simultaneously with the decrease in the number of patronaged
positions, the share of party functionaries in parliament started to drop. At the
end of the twentieth century, however, when the parties according to the well-
known typology of Katz and Mair (1995) established themselves as parts of the
state, there was a resurge of the number of party functionaries in parliament in
Germany, Hungary, Finland, and the Netherlands.

6.5. THE ROLE OF THE PARTIES

Up until now, we did not distinguish in our analysis between the patterns of
recruitment of the various parties and party families in each of the countries.
However, we already pointed out that the high share of party officials and party
functionaries in Germany, for instance, could to a large extent be explained by
the electoral successes of the socialist party. The SPD had expanded significantly
with the establishment of the new republican regime in 1919 and for that reason carried much weight in the composition of the Reichstag. In 1924 up to
74 per cent of the 142 German socialist MPs had previously been appointed in
leading positions in the party, while 50 per cent had taken up positions in the
party's administration or in related organizations through their party affiliation and
thanks to party patronage. For the Christian Democrats the figures were 42 and
35 per cent respectively. The high rate of leading party officials in the parliamentary SPD party actually is surprising given the rather loose connections between
the SPD and the *Gewerkschaften* (trade unions), compared to for instance the ties
between the Labour Party and the Unions in the UK.[7]

Yet we found in other countries too that the socialist parties recruited the
highest number of *party officials*, at the beginning of their term in parliament.
In Denmark, about half of the socialist MPs had been recruited from leading
positions in the party, even if their share dropped since the turn of the century. In
Finland, the share was one of three MPs, in France one of four.[8] But unlike their
Finnish colleagues, only few French socialist MPs had been recruited from leading positions in the party organizations, due to the difficult relations between the
trade unions and the socialist party (Williams 1970: 149). Even in countries where
the share of party politicians in parliament was low, the socialist parliamentary
party groups topped the ranking lists. In pre-fascist Italy for instance, the overall
percentage of party functionaries did not exceed 5 per cent, while the Italian
Socialist Party (PSI) recruited 10 to 15 per cent. In the latter party the candidate
selection clearly was in the hands of external organizations, local associations,
union headquarters, and other social organizations (Panebianco 1988: 104). In

TABLE 6.1. *Percentage of party officials (Var011) by party family (1867–2003)*

	Period 1867–93				Period 1894–1940				Period 1943–71				Period 1971–2003			
	Total N	Avg. N per party group	Avg. % party officials	s.d.	Total N	Avg. N per party group	Avg. % party officials	s.d.	Total N	Avg. N per party group	Avg. % party officials	s.d.	Total N	Avg. N per party group	Avg. % party officials	s.d.
Extreme right	106*	11.8	21.8	17.7	1,404	40.1	37.9	32.6	226	28.3	52.7	24.5	508	25.4	83.1	17.2
Conservatives	7,219	104.6	21.0	31.7	9,931	94.6	15.7	11.7	4,233	103.2	52.6	13.0	6,414	106.9	42.8	20.9
Right Lib.	5,725	119.3	31.7	32.4	6,043	86.3	27.6	28.0	1,221	22.6	47.8	17.4	3,051	55.5	52.8	22.0
Chr. Dem.	1,453	30.3	47.5	34.9	2,842	47.4	28.7	21.8	4,835	93.0	46.1	29.8	5,564	64.7	54.2	27.7
Left Lib.	5,939	129.1	14.1	18.3	7,512	67.7	32.6	24.5	828	16.6	57.3	18.7	1,040	18.9	64.1	25.3
Agrarians	756	63.0	2.7	1.2	2,071	28.8	16.4	18.5	1,372	45.7	45.1	13.6	1,022	28.4	52.8	20.6
Socialists	194°	14.9	62.5	29.4	7,630	66.3	34.4	21.4	7,718	110.3	40.8	25.4	12,833	124.6	45.0	26.1
Communists					800†	25.8	43.4	31.9	2,119	48.2	45.4	31.7	2,204	45.0	53.5	22.9

* From 1869 onwards.
° From 1884 onwards.
† From 1914 onwards.

Notes: Missing observations: for the period 1867–93: extreme right (1), conservatives (22), right liberals (10), left liberals (7), and socialists (1); for 1894–1940: extreme right (4), conservatives (35), right liberals (12), christian democrats (5), left liberals (37), socialists (32), and communists (4); for 1943–71: extreme right (1), conservatives (14), right liberals (7), christian democrats (7), left liberals (15), socialists (15), communists (7); and, for 1971–2003: extreme right (1), conservatives (20), right liberals (8), christian democrats (4), left liberals (9), socialists (20), and communists (12).

TABLE 6.2. *Percentage of Var29: party functionaries by party family (1867–2003)*

	Period 1867–93				Period 1894–1940				Period 1943–71				Period 1971–2003			
	Total N	Avg. N per party group	Avg. % party function	s.d.	Total N	Avg. N per party group	Avg. % party function	s.d.	Total N	Avg. N per party group	Avg. % party function	s.d.	Total N	Avg. N per party group	Avg. % party function	s.d.
Extreme right	106*	11.8	0.0	0.0	1,404	40.1	10.6	20.9	226	28.3	5.4	7.0	508	25.4	11.2	10.1
Conservatives	7,219	104.6	0.1	0.3	9,931	94.6	3.0	5.7	4,233	103.2	6.2	9.6	6,414	106.9	6.4	7.2
Right Lib.	5,725	119.3	0.2	0.6	6,043	86.3	3.5	6.7	1,221	22.6	7.1	5.2	3,051	55.5	6.0	8.3
Chr. Dem.	1,453	30.3	0.3	0.7	2,842	47.4	9.1	13.3	4,835	93.0	14.1	15.5	5,564	64.7	9.4	9.2
Left Lib.	5,939	129.1	1.1	2.0	7,512	67.7	2.7	7.3	828	16.6	4.7	10.1	1,020	18.5	5.5	7.0
Agrarians	756	63.0	0.0	0.0	2,100	29.2	3.1	4.1	447	14.9	4.9	6.5	1,918	53.3	8.5	8.6
Socialists	256°	11.6	10.2	12.9	7,630	61.0	21.0	15.4	7,718	110.3	21.5	10.2	12,833	124.6	14.1	9.5
Communists					800†	25.8	29.9	28.7	2,119	48.2	40.5	18.3	2,204	45.0	24.9	19.6

* From 1869 onwards.

° From 1884 onwards.

† From 1914 onwards.

Notes: Missing observations: for the period 1867–93: conservatives (6), and left liberals (3); for 1894–1940: conservatives (15), right liberals (3), left liberals (13), and socialists (10); for 1944–71: extreme right (1), conservatives (14), right liberals (7), christian-democrats (7), left liberals (15), socialists (7), and communists (7); and for 1971–2003: extreme right (1), conservatives (13), right liberals (8), christian-democrats (4), left liberals (5), socialists (12), and communists (9).

the same period the Austrian Parliament counted 15 to 20 per cent of socialist members from a similar background, while in all other parliamentary parties the presence of party politicians was negligible. Only the Dutch socialist party was challenged and eventually outnumbered in terms of recruitment of party officials and party functionaries by the religious parties.[9]

The high scores of the socialist parties in the pre-Second World War period are also illustrated by Tables 6.1 and 6.2 and Figures 6.3 and 6.4. Besides the average size of the parliamentary parties, these depict in respective order the average percentage of leading party officials and of party functionaries by party family for the four periods of our analysis.[10] Even if the aggregated averages are disrespectful of the particular circumstances in which the parliamentary delegations have been elected, they still indicate very clearly two general trends. First, there is a clear increase in the number of leading party officials and a less spectacular rise of the party functionaries over the years. Second, we note an evolution towards convergence until 1971 and again divergence from 1971 onwards for the party officials, and an opposite movement for the party functionaries.

It is not surprising that at the start of the period of investigation the socialist parties came first in number of MPs with a background as party official, as there is a link with the limited size of the parliamentary party groups in that period. We witness a similar pattern for the remaining periods in our research. Each time, the parties with the smallest number of MPs score best in number of party officials in parliament: the communists in the period 1894–1940, the left liberals and extreme right parties in 1943–71, and the extreme right parties again in the 1971–2003 period. For the whole period of 1867–2003 and for all parties, we noticed a negative correlation coefficient between the size of the parliamentary party and the share of party officials of -0.239.[11] In other words: the smaller the parliamentary party group, the greater the possibility of having a considerable number of leading party officials among the elected MPs.

Of course, the extent of the increase after the Second World War varies from one political system to another. In Italy for instance, the strikingly high party political weight of the MPs counted for almost all parties, but with the communist and socialist parties in the first place. In the first two post-war decades, these parliamentary parties of the left were composed for at least 80 per cent out of former party officials. At the same time, they accounted for the highest percentage of party functionaries in the Italian Parliament (varying between 21% and 59%). Notwithstanding its pivotal position in post-war Italian politics and the well-developed party structure, the *Democrazia Cristiana* counted far less party functionaries among its MPs. The figures vary from a mere 7 per cent of party functionaries in 1946 to a 'high' of 18 per cent in 1968. This result is striking, as, in the words of Panebianco (1988) the state was colonized by the DC, which thus looked after the recruitment and promotion of state functionaries who had been loyal to the party, leading to bureaucrats from public institutions behaving as party activists and 'hidden' political professionals.

In most countries, however, the differences between the left and the other parties are less clear cut. The Dutch overall recruitment pattern until the late nineties was equally dominated by the scores of the catholic party.[12] Likewise, in Finland several parties contributed to the high party political weight of parliament, while communist and socialist MPs accounted for the highest amount of party and trade union officials. This pattern of recruitment was dramatically altered from the 1980s onwards. The rise of party functionaries since 1945 was halted, and even turned downwards to a mere 23 per cent at the 1995 elections.

Denmark and Norway are counter-examples to the general rule that left parties allow for more party politicians in their parliamentary parties. In fact, the Danish socialists were surpassed by both the left liberals and the protestant parties. At the same time, the Danish conservatives seemed to be less attached to recruiting previously active party politicians. Quite remarkably, the Norwegian Social Democrats had one of the lowest levels of recruitment of party officials in the whole European context.[13] We come back to this in the concluding remarks to this chapter. In Germany, the only country with a lower share of party politicians in the first post-war decades, the election of party officials had apparently lost its priority to the SPD, while the new multi-denominational Christian Democratic party (CDU) did not focus either on recruiting among these politicians. Still, the SPD outnumbered the CDU in the number of candidates and MPs that were selected *from* and even *by* several interest groups.[14] But in general, the interest of parties in candidates with experience in party offices had dropped until the end of the 1950s, early 1960s.[15]

Finally, with regard to the recruitment of party and trade union employees, the British pattern seems totally different. For a long time, the ideal type of a *cursus honorum* for a Labour MP started with local party membership, to continue via officership in local organizations or trade unions and elected municipal offices (Guttsman 1963). In 1997, Pippa Norris wrote 'still today the steps are well defined. Labour and Conservative politicians commonly rise from constituency party office and local government service to become a parliamentary candidate' (Norris 1997: 4). And even though the selection mechanism of the British Labour Party underwent important changes over time (especially in the 1990s) the impact of the unions remained very strong.[16] Still, this did not lead to a high degree of former party or union employees among Labour MPs. Only one in seven to one in five of the Labour MPs had previously served as an employee of the party or one of its collateral organizations. This can be explained by the fact that the trade unions increasingly replaced former employees by nominal members, whose membership was not related to their occupation.[17] Background data of British MPs after the 1992 elections reveal that nearly all MPs had been active in their local party. A majority served as local councillor, while others served on local public bodies or held office in pressure groups or professional organizations. In all categories, Labour MPs had more political experience than their Conservative colleagues, but they differed most in trade union experience (Norris and Lovenduski 1995: 180).

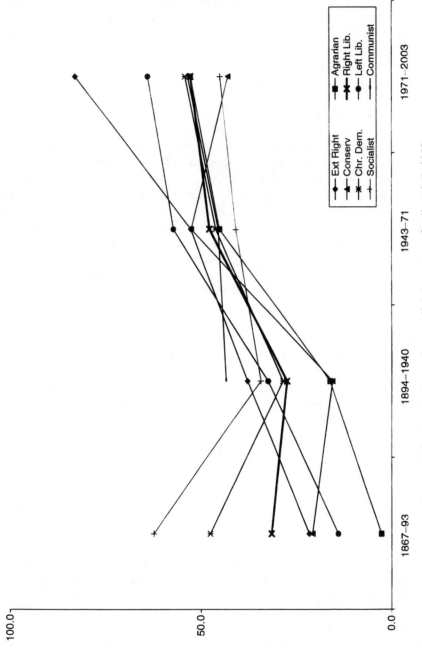

FIGURE 6.3. Average share of party officials per party family (1867–2003)

Legend:
- ◆ Ext Right
- ▲ Conserv
- ✳ Chr. Dem.
- + Socialist
- ■ Agrarian
- ✕ Right Lib.
- ● Left Lib.
- — Communist

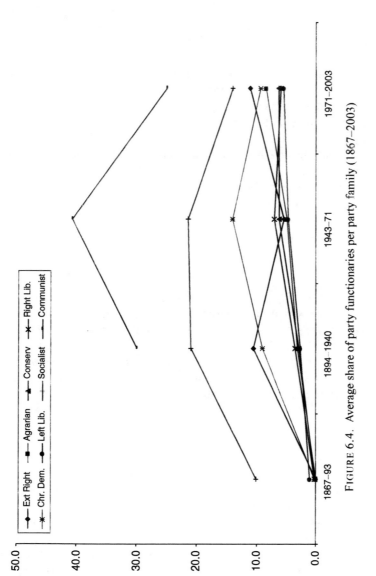

FIGURE 6.4. Average share of party functionaries per party family (1867–2003)

From the analysis of the post-Second World War period, one can draw the following conclusions. First, the pattern of increasing recruitment of former party politicians in parliament is illustrative for the grip of the parties over parliament and the intertwinement of the parties with the state. At the end of the twentieth century, about half of the MPs had previously occupied leading political positions. Second, this increasing trend can be found in all countries (with the exception of Finland since the 1980s). Third, notwithstanding the overall increase in recruitment of party functionaries, experience in party or trade union jobs (our so-called party functionaries) has lost in influence as a factor of importance over the last couple of decades. This is especially the case from the seventies onwards: for half of the parties a mere 10 per cent of the MPs had such a background. And finally, the analysis indicates that when large cohorts of new politicians enter parliament, they temporarily change the traditional recruitment patterns. Denmark in 1973 (Pedersen 1988), Italy in 1994 and 1996 (Verzichelli 1996), and the Netherlands in 2002 are cases in point. Still the results of the Italian election of 2001, and the restoration of most traditional Dutch parties in January 2003, suggest that these developments only have a temporary character. So, in the end, this could well be a mere transitory feature.

6.6. CONCLUDING ANALYSIS AND DISCUSSION

On the basis of our analysis into the evolutions of the recruitment of MPs with a preceding party political career we can draw some conclusions. From the preliminary results of the previous paragraphs, it is clear that we have to take into account at least four elements in explaining the variances cross-nationally and cross-party: specific *national* settings, specific characteristics of the *political parties (or party families)*, the process of *party institutionalization*, and the process of *professionalization* of political functions.

6.6.1. *National Traditions, Electoral Systems, and Constitutional Settings*

First of all, the specific electoral and constitutional national settings not only account for the electoral outcome and the distribution of the seats between the parties, but also influence the profiles of the elected MPs. First and most important in this respect is the electoral system. Until the beginning of the twentieth century several countries applied a majoritarian electoral system, which is known to be particularly less favourable to new recruits, candidates of minorities, and candidates of specific target groups (Farrell 2001; Colomer 2004). These plurality systems lead easily to distorted electoral results too. In the Netherlands, Belgium, and Germany (Best, Hausmann, and Schmitt 2000: 145–6) for instance, the relatively small Liberal parties, with their concentrated electorates, profited from this rule around the turn of the nineteenth and twentieth century at the cost of the religious parties. In Norway the same happened to the left *Venstre* party, some twenty years after its creation in 1885. German socialists on the contrary were for a long time penalized by the particular national and constitutional settings in which they operated. Due to the limitations of the suffrage, the SPD was permanently under-represented during Imperial rule (Albrecht 1960: 316 ff.; Matthews and Valen 1999: 18). It then depends on internal party rules whether special attention is given to the background of the MPs. As has been demonstrated, the system which is applied by the Labour Party was and still is extremely favourable to candidates from specific organized groups. Many safe seats have been occupied by trade union sponsored candidates, who after a long political apprenticeship in local governments had been rewarded a place on the electoral lists (Mellors 1978: 99).

Second, not only the electoral system, but even constitutional elements account as a matter, of course, for varieties in personnel composition of national parliaments. Formal incompatibilities in Spain and Portugal for instance hamper or have hampered the candidacy of trade unionists. Data on recruitment based on party or organizational activities of MPs in these two countries are for that reason not particularly comparable to the situation in other countries and have therefore been excluded from our analysis. Cross-national differences in recruitment are not exclusively due to constitutionally embedded rules. For Norway (Eliassen and Sjøvaag 2000) and the UK (Knapp 1997: 139), corporatism is an important element in explaining the recruitment of trade unionist or affiliated MPs. While in Germany it apparently has become harder to reach a political top function such as Membership of parliament without a previous long political career at local (or regional) level. This was especially the case from the 1980s onwards. This falls in contrast to the image of the party employees, who blamed their low representation in parliament to the practical difficulties in combining their bureaucratic functions with the required amount of campaigning activities.[18] Herzog (1976: 27) summarized the German recruitment pattern thus as 'Parliaments are no meeting places for party functionaries' (our translation). And two and a half decades later, Klaus von Beyme observes that a political career in Germany was not helped along beforehand by activities in party organizations or party administration functions: 'The tendency to prolong one's professional career in the party was limited. Party functionaries have no real chance to climb the ladder in politics. It is even a negative aspect in terms of being recruitment-worthy' (von Beyme 1993: 121, our translation). The British setting on the contrary favours the combination of party political positions and the standing for a parliamentary mandate, thanks to the constituency structure of candidate selecting instruments. Post-war Italy offers an even more outstanding example of the high values set on a party political preparation of a parliamentary career. According to Cotta (1979), the high Italian scores are the result of long-term career within the party, often starting at young age with low-level offices. Similarly, Cotta, Mastropoalo, and Verzichelli (2000) conclude that the increasing substitution of independent social prestige by a party career could be a plausible explanation for the transformations until the 1970s.

Third, foreseeable and unforeseen political events play an important role in the outcome of the elections, and thus in the composition of parliament too. There was the start of the French fifth Republic in 1958, the collapse of the Italian system in 1994, and the murder of Pim Fortuyn in the Netherlands (2002), to name only a few. Mere electoral gains and losses of parties account for the variation in composition too. Particularly in majority electoral systems, a swing of votes leads to new generations of politicians that enter parliament. These 'newcomers' at national level are typically characterized by their lack of long-term party service.

6.6.2. *The Institutionalization of the Political Parties*

A long-term analysis of political parties as recruiting agents cannot be written without taking into account the variations over time of the key characteristics of political parties.[19] Party organizations, most of them dating from the second half of the nineteenth century, evolved and adapted as society modernized. In the beginning, these so-called elite or *cadre parties* were set up as loose meeting places of like-minded people. They were dominated by the parliamentary parties, and in a considerable number of cases even limited thereto, as a formal extra-parliamentary party organization did not exist until the mid-1840s. In consequence, these 'parties' comprised only small numbers of adherents, and the competition among the parties regarded the distribution of privileges on the basis of the ascribed status of their supporters. Suffrage was limited and politics was a favourite pass time for a limited number of financially independent people, who fulfiled their political tasks as a kind of public duty on an honorary basis. Among them were many aristocrats and patricians, but also lawyers and merchants, who after election into parliament continued their professions and business.

By the end of the nineteenth century, we saw the rise of the well-organized mass parties, who acted for predefined social groups. The aim of these groups was to capture control of the state by placing their own representatives in key offices. The party acted as a representative of predefined sectors of society. This party model dominated in the years between 1880 and 1960. Through a process of institutionalization from 1918 onwards, these mass parties became truly a part of the political system and played a pivotal role in all political systems in Western Europe. Some even argue that in the Italian and Belgian partitocracies the state was kept hostage by the parties (Deschouwer, De Winter, and Della Porta 1996). In this new setting, it was crucial for parties to have strong and influential representatives on key positions of the state system. As a result, hardly any non-partisan candidate managed to get elected in the course of the twentieth century.

Moreover, party officials of the mass parties could be considered as the intermediaries of interest groups. This explains why we have found most leading party officials and paid party employees among the socialist MPs. Socialist parties typically were the first ones to build a rigid party organization and to create close links with the newly established autonomous labour movements. The specific ties, however, varied cross-nationally in strength and persistence.[20] With the weakening of social group identities in the second half of the twentieth century, the parties lost their traditional role as an agent of social and political integration (Lijphart 1999). Confronted with the volatility of the voters, political parties became more professional. In a Downsian reasoning (Downs 1957), they were primarily desiring electoral success. According to Otto Kirchheimer's well-known identification (1966) they developed into so-called *catch-all parties* in the 1960s. Parties acted as brokers between the society and the state and built constantly shifting coalitions among the differing interests. These developments implied for instance that ties between the trade unions and social democratic parties became looser. Still, parties kept on being active as a broker, and active members of the party and its 'collateral' organizations were rewarded for rendered services with nomination in offices. Generally speaking, the catch-all party was characterized by more openness to a wider electorate, without requiring the same level of commitment. Regarding nominations in behalf of the party, however, membership still was required. Observing a continuous movement of the parties from the society towards the state from the 1970s, Katz and Mair (1995) defined that in the end, parties became an integral part of the state itself, helped by the allocation of state subsidies. In this typology of the so-called cartel party, politics has become a profession in itself (cf. below).

The DATACUBE data, even though it does not include all observations for all countries, provide us with some indications which fit the description of the four party models rather well. Parliamentarians with experience in leading or administrative party positions appear on the scene in greater numbers as soon as the mass parties developed at the end of the nineteenth century. This development was further strengthened after the First World War, when universal suffrage was introduced in almost all countries and parties became truly institutional-ized. From that period onwards, political parties formed an inherent part of the political institutions and governing bodies. The high percentages of party politicians in the inter-war period in the German and Dutch parliaments, followed by substantial percentages in the Finnish and French parliaments, are illustrative for this development. Parties kept on being the guardians of the interests of special groups in society for a long period, even after 1945. Indeed, as far as we can see the Second World War was not a real caesura with respect to the recruitment of party politicians. The recruitment of MPs did change, however, from the 1970s onwards, with the emergence of the cartel parties. It caused blurring party profiles, as the new strategies entailed the selection of a decreasing number of parliamentary candidates among party employees or functionaries of collateral organizations. In this respect, it no longer automatically served to the benefit of an MP's career to have been investing in long-standing party engagements.

6.6.3. *Party-Family Belonging*

Apart from the development and the position of political parties over time the signature of political parties is supposed to be indicative for the willingness to put party politicians on the electoral lists. There is in this respect however a marked distinction between the two categories of functions understood here as 'party politicians'. Especially in the left parties candidates from leading party positions are expected to have better chances to be selected. Indeed, the highest percentages of party officials in the pre-war parliaments in Germany, the Netherlands, and Finland were found among the socialist parties. In Germany and to a lower degree in the Netherlands, other parties such as the left liberals and the catholic parties likewise contributed to the high number of party politicians in parliament. On the contrary, in Austria, Italy, Norway, and France, neither socialists nor communists valued deeply the representation of party politicians in parliament in the pre-war years. After 1945, the larger number of party officials in the Italian, Dutch, and Finnish parliaments can be attributed in the first place to the recruitment of socialist, communist, and new left parties. In post-war Germany, neither the socialist nor the confessional parties sent many officials to parliament. Germany's new left counted relatively the highest percentage of party political MPs, with over 30 per cent in the 1990s.

The picture of parliamentarians with an experience in other, non-elective functions as party employees or trade union employees is different. They outnumber in all countries the first mentioned political category of party officials. Communists and socialists count for the highest percentage of MPs of this category, again in pre-war Germany. In the other parliamentary parties, this category is also represented rather well. In the Netherlands, these political MPs are primarily found among the Liberal and denominational parties. Socialists from this kind of positions returned in parliament in great numbers only after the Second World War. Until then the party had not been able to participate proportionally in the nomination of candidates in political positions. But properly spoken do party functionaries appear in rather high numbers in all parties in parliament, on the left side as well as on the right. In this respect, the share of these MPs in the Italian partitocracy surpasses those of all other countries. In the post-war period party politicians are found in all parties to the same degree. This underlines a trend across all parties of convergence in the profiles of the MPs.

6.6.4. *Professionalization of the MPs*

The inter-war period saw the rise of another phenomenon, the *professionalization of MPs* which is supposed to have had an effect on the recruitment of MPs. In the twentieth century, most MPs did no longer consider their representative function as purely honorary (Judge 1999). Moreover, throughout the years their tasks as representatives increased to such an extent that it became hardly possible to carry on with any other occupational activity, perhaps with the exception of the free professions. Therefore, MPs in most countries have since long got a salary comparable to the higher civil servants. It is striking that as a matter of fact the phenomenon of paid party politicians as a new occupational category in parliament starts with the emergence of the mass party. In this respect, it is linked to the question of social reform together with the successful struggle for the extension of the suffrage.

The last element regards the possible effects of the professionalization of the political career throughout the twentieth century, and the way in which this affected the place of party politicians in the parliamentary recruitment process. Already in 1911, Robert Michels expressed his fear that professionalization would imply that *Parteiburokraten* would come into power (Michels 1911). As we focused on two elements of party political experience of MPs, and Michels used a somewhat restricted interpretation of political background, we have to split our data into two categories, in order to compare our data with Michels' pronouncement.

We already pointed out that pure party functionaries in Michels' strict interpretation were only marginally present in the total population of MPs. And this was the case in all parliamentary parties and in all countries involved. But their share among MPs did gradually increase from less than 10 per cent around 1900 to a considerable 20 to 25 per cent in the 1970s. Generally spoken the highest percentages were to be found among left parties. The party political character of both the christian democratic and social democratic parliamentary parties in the Bundestag, obviously was a ground for Michels' above-mentioned fear. Since the 1970s however fewer party employees and people with patronaged positions returned to parliament. Their share fell under 20 per cent on average. Only at the very end of the twentieth century, and under the labels of Green or New Left the number of these representatives slightly increased. Regarding Germany the answer on the question above must be differentiated. Although the professionalization of political careers has become very visible, German investigators have demonstrated that at least since the Second World War party functionaries were not part of this process. Indeed, they had rather bad chances to survive in the political arena (von Beyme 1993: 121). Since the 1980s the percentage of SPD-politicians who started their careers as an employee in a trade union for instance is declining. Although a respectable percentage of the most prominent politicians in the 1970s had their roots in the trade unions, the impact of these organizations on political recruitment in general was of minor importance (von Beyme 1993: 128).

Likewise, we found the other category of party politicians, the party functionaries which were nominated in non-elective positions inside and outside the party, in all parliamentary parties considerably less represented. Christian Democrats and Conservatives had a slight edge over the other parties in this respect, at least in the years between 1945 and 1970. Since then party functionaries kept being recruited for parliament in almost the same numbers, but there is no evidence of a still growing professionalization in this respect. The rise of new parties in several West European countries, like Italy, Austria, and the Netherlands, may lead temporarily to deviating recruitment patterns. As to the role of party politicians in this process, however, it is not to be expected that this will be subject to lasting major changes.

The recruitment of party politicians therefore has to be seen in the context of these evolutions of parties, electoral settings, and the process of professionalization of the political career. According to Panebianco (1988: 221), a political professional is he 'who dedicates most, if not all of his work activity to politics and finds there his main source of sustenance'.[21] This process of professionalization of politics is considered to have been culminating after the Second World War, the more so from the 1970s. As a consequence politicians from the various parties resemble each other more and more (van den Berg 1989: 208; Herzog et al. 1993: 44; von Beyme 1993: 121). They developed towards 'a political class *sui generis*, freed from the compulsions of other professions, practised in making use of formal or informal behaviour in the pursuit of a political career, adroit in the arts of manipulation, subject only to the "rules" of struggle for position and interchangeable among different offices rather in the way that the procurators of ancient Rome were rotated from province to province' (Wildenmann 1986: 15). And for most of them, the party served as an instrumental vehicle to become part of this political class.

ENDNOTES

1 The author wishes to express his gratitude to Maurizio Cotta and Luca Verzichelli of the CIRCaP (University of Siena) for their support and help in the final stages of the research.

2 See for instance the few Independent MPs in the British House of Commons. In Finland, a new Electoral Act (1975) gave individuals the right to propose candidates for the *Eduskunta* (Helander 1997: 58).

3 Herzog calls this a 'consolidation of career patterns... Insofar a political party facilitates long-standing career opportunities, those persons interested in a political career will take bearings on them' (Herzog 1976: 27, our translation).

4 We had to rely on indirect sources, and therefore were at the mercy of data and the interpretation furnished by the authors of national case studies. In this case, an overall picture of the recruitment of MPs from a party political background in Europe is restricted to a few countries. Long-term empirical data of this kind were only available for Germany, the Netherlands, and Finland. For France, Italy, and Norway the data on the party political background of the MPs cover shorter periods, while the Austrian and British data exclusively regard functions in political parties or collateral organizations.

5 The DATACUBE data-set contains extra data on the Dutch MPs for the period from 1867 onwards, indicating that 60 to 70% of the Dutch MPs in the nineteenth century would have been 'party officials', in a period when the parties had not really been established. Because of our doubts on the exact coding, we decided not to include the Dutch data of the pre-1918 era in our analysis.

6 The British Lower House consisted of a similar percentage of former party employees after the 1935 election. Other data regarding the recruitment of party political British MPs are not available.

7 See for instance the totally different development of the British Labour Party and the German SPD and their relations with the trade unions (Panebianco 1988: 70 ff.). Hence, von Beyme concludes that there is no comparison between the impact of British or Scandinavian trade unions and German trade unions on the selection of candidates for parliament (von Beyme 1993: 112).

8 This was a higher contribution to the political character of the parliament than that of former party functionaries. Regarding this latter aspect the Finnish socialist MPs were surpassed by an even higher percentage of Left Liberals and members of the Agrarian Party. These parties, however, had fewer seats in parliament.

9 Although there was a difference between the catholic parties, which used to recruit more often among party officials and political functionaries, and the protestant parties, which recruited considerably less party politicians. The highest difference was recorded at the level of the political functionaries: over 30% of the catholic MPs had served as a party functionary in 1937, while the Protestant share was a negligible 4%.

10 The total N per party family in Table 6.1 sometimes slightly differs from the total N per party family in Table 6.2, due to missing values in the country records of some of the variables in the DATACUBE.

11 Significant at the 0.01 level.

12 Other, left MPs, such as the communists, even surpassed all other parliamentary parties in this respect, but were not a decisive factor due to their restricted numerical weight.

13 It is common knowledge that there has always been a cordial relationship between the Labour Party (established in 1887) and the Norwegian Federation of Trade Unions (LO). This is due to the fact that the Labour Party served both as a party and as a trade union for over twenty years. Until the 1930s, a similar development has existed between the Norwegian Agrarian Party and the main Farmers' Association.

14 The CDU owed part of its income to these interest groups (Panebianco 1988: 119). For the figures on the SPD, see Herzog (1975: 104). His research regarded interviews in 1968 with politicians of several levels, and was not restricted to MPs.

15 Dietrich Herzog (1968) even concluded that this occupational category had little chance to be selected for elective mandates, due to the fact that they were in no position to develop local political activities necessary for a nomination.

16 The latter tended to support the candidature of loyal party adherents, who had devoted long service to the organized labour movement as union officials and who often had local government experience (Norris and Lovenduski 1995: 152). The percentage of sponsored MPs between 1945 and 1979 was over 40% (Shaw 1990: 88). At nine elections since 1918 more than half of the Labour MPs were directly sponsored by a Trade Union (Butler and Butler 2000*a*, 2000*b*).

17 Although Labour officially abandoned TU sponsored candidates in 1995, in practice little has changed. Information on Labour sponsoring of TU candidates was provided by Michael Rush on 25 September 2003.

18 See Herzog's remarks, referenced earlier in this chapter.

19 This paragraph is largely borrowed from Katz and Mair (1995 *passim*) and Dalton and Wattenberg (2000: 129).

20 See n. 6.

21 This interpretation of political professionals is shared by many other political scientists, even though Eliassen and Pedersen made a distinction between political professionalization or the parliamentarization of party bureaucrats on the one hand and intellectual professionalization or the parliamentarization of the experts on the other hand (K. A. Eliassen and M. N. Pedersen 1978, quoted by Panebianco 1988: 221–2). Herzog titles the party official as the outstanding example of the political professional, the man who lives from politics (Herzog 1975: 139).

The Geographical Dimension of Parliamentary Recruitment—among Native Sons and Parachutists

Mogens N. Pedersen, Ulrik Kjær, and Kjell A. Eliassen

7.1. GEOGRAPHY AND RECRUITMENT

Geography is often considered the primeval dimension of political representation.[1] When representative democracies were established, the 'territorial interests constituted a basic element in the concept of representation' (Valen et al. 2000: 107). This is not to say that geographic representation has not been contested. Actually, a most serious attack on the idea that politicians are sent to parliament to represent the interests of their locality was made as early as 1774 by Edmund Burke in his speech to the electors of Bristol. For Burke, the national interest should prevail over the territorial interest. As summarized by Hannah Pitkin: 'The duty of each member is to reason and judge about the good of the whole; the selfish wishes of parts of the nation, the wills of individual voters have nothing to do with it' (Pitkin 1967: 170–1).

Geography as the nexus of political representation has been challenged several times, by stressing dimensions such as, for instance, class, race, and gender. Most serious, though, has been the challenge from the political parties. Today parties constitute the pivot of political representation (Holmberg 1989; Manin 1997). However, without questioning the political parties as the major focus of modern political representation, other dimensions are still important. So is, and should be, the classical dimension of geography.

In this chapter, we do not deal with the most general question of the exact role of geographical concerns in parliamentary politics, nor will we pursue the normative discussion of geography as the nexus of political representation. We will claim that today we find in many countries, what could be labelled a poly-focused base of political representation. Geography still forms part of this.

Our (much narrower) focus will be on the role of geography in the process of political recruitment. Again we see that political parties play a central role.

They are the dominating 'gatekeepers' par excellence in all Western political systems. However, geography still plays an important role. The geographical dimension of the recruitment process is most noticeable in majoritarian systems, but it is striking that even under PR systems all but a very few countries have kept geographically defined constituencies as the basis for the electoral system. To put it another way, the institutional arrangements, that is the electoral laws, in almost all Western democracies are built on, and take into account, a geographical dimension. Therefore, we are also somewhat puzzled by the relatively little amount of scholarly attention paid to this dimension of political recruitment. When it comes to characterizing the background of the MPs, most studies have focused exclusively on the composition along dimensions such as class, race, education, and especially gender (see, e.g. Norris and Lovenduski 1995; Norris 1997*a*, 1997*b*).

In the following, we study the territorial relationship between MPs and their constituency. We intend to discuss several aspects of this relationship. The first relationship is the one created by birth. Does the politician have special bonds to his constituency, because he was born there, eventually was brought up there, indeed still lives there? Are there any differences to be found across countries and across time? To what extent is the increased social and geographical mobility in all European societies reflected in the collective profiles of European parliaments? These are questions worth pursuing, not only in their own right, but also because answers may provide us with a deeper understanding of, for example the evolution of national party systems. We shall give some thoughts to these questions, even if we find another relationship of greater importance, theoretically as well as in practical politics.

The relationship in question, and the relationship that will form the main focus of this chapter, is what could be termed the residential connection. This relationship has several dimensions. Sometimes they are even given special names. The French have coined the term *parachutage* for one of the relationships, that is when a politician, coming from the outside, often from Paris, is nominated and eventually elected in a provincial constituency. Seen from the perspective of the party a *parachutist* may be a younger, promising, candidate, who is dispatched into new territory, where the party's chances may look promising. But it may also be a newly appointed minister or secretary of state, who needs to find a constituency and a parliamentary basis. Several other types of *parachutists* have been identified (cf. Thiébault 1988: 83–5; Dolez and Hastings 2003).

The term is French, but the underlying concept is of a universal nature. This is reflected in terminology and usage. In the post-Civil War American language *carpetbagger* is the not-so-nice word for a phenomenon related to *parachutage*— the ambitious politician, who is prepared to travel in order to reach his goal: political office. In American politics, we also find a related term, the *native son*, denoting a politician, who is running for office from his home state or region. Jean Petaux (2003) has studied the terminology used across Europe. He found, that

France is the only country in which a military connotation is used, but that terms for the same concept can be found in most countries. One example: Spaniards speak about *toreros paracaidistas*, but we are also told that they use the term *Cunero*—a foundling, derived from 'cuna' (cradle)—for this phenomenon. A *Cunero* is also the term used about a bull that belongs to an unknown stock of cattle (*Ganaderia*).

A closer scrutiny of usages would probably reveal that words exist, which denotes two polar phenomena: the 'local' candidate and the 'foreign' candidate. According to Ranney (1981: 100), the terms for the 'foreign' aspirant tend to be a pejorative one. The opposite of the *parachutist* is the *local member* or *resident*, a candidate, who is living in the constituency, when he is nominated and elected, and who has thus a special affiliation with the constituency, a quality which is often, but not always, considered valuable. He may even have a closer relationship by being born in the area. These are the real *native sons*.

These geographical recruitment linkages appear in different forms across nations. But even if terminologies and appearances differ, we nevertheless find a set of related phenomena almost everywhere. In a few non-European nations residence is required for nomination, but in most countries no such legal require- ments are stipulated. This does, however, not mean that the 'balance' between, for example, *residents* and *parachutists* is the same across political systems.

Our main objective in this chapter is to gain a better understanding of this geographical phenomenon, in a comparative as well as in a longitudinal per- spective. When approaching the literature, much to our surprise we found that very little has been written about the special phenomenon of *parachutage*. Michel Hastings (2003:12) even speaks about '*une Internationale du silence et de oubli*'. A few older studies deal (in passing) with the phenomenon (e.g. Wheare 1963; Loewenberg and Patterson 1979; Bogdanor 1985; Gallagher 1988). Even more interesting is it that several recent configurative case studies which deal with career opportunities and with the influence of supply and demand in the recruit- ment situation, do not treat the geographical linkage between candidates/elected and constituencies. Social class, gender, age, education, etc. are analysed at length, but the geographical factor is missing (e.g. Norris 1997a, 1997b).

Given this situation, we have decided to proceed cautiously. We will approach the geographical *problematique* from five different angles. At the end of the chapter, we draw together whatever suggestions and hunches collected en route. Before we enter the empirical studies, we devote some pages to a proposal for a conceptual framework (Section 7.2). We also sketch a speculative discussion of the demand—supply side of political recruitment (Section 7.3). Our three empirical studies consist of a descriptive and qualitative tour of Europe (Section 7.4), followed by a longitudinal analysis of available quantitative data from the DATACUBE data-set (Section 7.5). We also present a two-country, in-depth case study of Denmark and Norway, two societies that differ considerably on the geographical dimension (Section 7.6).

7.2. A CONCEPTUAL FRAMEWORK

In representative democracies, the constitution and the electoral laws establish and regulate a relationship between constituencies, which are geographically delimited, and the elected representatives. Constituencies may be single-member constituencies, or they may return several candidates. Constituencies may be geographically extended, or they may be rather small in extension and in terms of population base. Constituencies may even form hierarchical systems, when the electoral system belongs to the two-tier variation of PR (Lijphart 1994)—in Austria we even find a three-tier electoral system. Thus the institutional context of the geographical linkage will differ widely across nations.

For all the differences that we find, there are also at least two similarities to note. First, nomination and election (with the exception of the Netherlands) take place in some kind of constituency; and, second, the local constituency, its voters and its party organization(s) are among the principals of the representative, in many cases even his or her most important principal (Narud et al. 2002). Representation thus links a territorial space with certain social and political characteristics to one or several individuals, also carrying certain social and political traits, including important qualities such as geographical mobility, local familiarity, local networks, etc. In this section, we present a very simple conceptual framework, which, hopefully, provides a basis for the following discussion and presentation of empirical findings.

7.2.1. *Focus on the Residential Relationship*

Looking first at the residential relationship, three nodes are considered:

1. The location of the parliament, typically the Capital city of the country;
2. The location of the constituency, in which the individual seeks election; and
3. The residential location of the elected candidate.

In most countries the relationship between constituency and candidate can be modelled in terms of the three nodes.

The three locations define a spatial triangle for each member of the parliament, and the sides of the triangle sum up to a measure of geographical proximity to the location of the parliament. This measure can be interpreted as a rough measure of the geographical distances, which a member will have to travel in order to sustain and pursue his legislative career (and thus also as a rough measure of some of the costs involved in such a career). According to this kind of recruitment (modelling in terms of rational considerations), one should expect considerable inequality with regard to access to political careers. In particular, it is to be expected that 'localism' (the tendency to nominate and elect individuals, who live in the constituency or its neighbourhood) will prevail (cf. Pedersen 1975).

Another way in which one may describe these categories uses dimensional notation:

1. One-dimensional relationship:
   — Residence and constituency and location of parliament coincide.
2. Two-dimensional relationship:
   — Residence coincides with location of parliament, but differs from location of constituency; or
   — Residence and constituency coincide, but are different from location of parliament; or
   — Location of parliament coincides with constituency, but differs from residence.
3. Three-dimensional relationship:
   — Residence, constituency as well as location of parliament differ from each other.

These logical categories can be rephrased in a more 'real-life' terms. We may choose to consider five categories of members:

1. *Metropolitan Locals*: Members who live in the Metropolis and are elected in a Metropolitan constituency;
2. *Metropolitan Parachutists*: Metropolitan dwellers who are nominated in and elected from a provincial constituency;
3. *Provincial Locals*: Members who are elected from their home constituency in the provincial regions;
4. *Centripetal Parachutists*: Members, who are living in the provincial parts of the country, but who are elected in a Metropolitan constituency; and
5. *Provincial Movers*: Members from the provincial parts who are elected from a provincial constituency away from their home, and who are thus also *parachutists*.

This conceptual scheme is, in principle, applicable in all countries, or, at least, in all countries in which the electoral system is based upon constituencies, that is excluding the Netherlands and Israel. The scheme is also applicable across time. Electoral systems may have changed considerably, for example from a first-past-the-post system to a PR system, but we should ideally be able to compare geographical representation across such divides. It is also applicable before as well as after the emergence of party systems.

By means of these categories, it is also possible to investigate variations in career patterns due to competition for scarce seats. Young and ambitious candidates may have to seek nomination, first and foremost, and they may thus have initially to run for election in constituencies that are not only 'hopeless' in terms of election chances, but even also suboptimal in the sense that they are located far away from the home of the candidate. The candidate may pursue his career by moving to 'safer' constituencies; he may also move closer to home and/or closer to the site of parliament. Party leaders (when they become leaders) may have more freedom to choose (and/or be chosen by) an appropriate and convenient constituency, while the young may have to look for nomination first, later on election from a 'winnable' constituency (Ranney 1965). All these movements can be traced by means of the five categories.

A few modifying comments have to be made. The first is that the 'residential' typology presupposes the existence of one and only one national centre, which also happens to be the location of the parliament. In cases, where the parliament is located in a city, which is not the major Metropolis (e.g. in former times West German Bonn), the conceptual framework may need modification. It can also be argued that countries exist, in which one finds more than one urban and political centre (Italy may be an example of this situation). One also has to admit that (in real life) *parachutage* may take the form of movements from a regional stronghold for a given party to other parts of the country. A surplus of candidates from this stronghold may fill candidacies in constituencies, where the party is weaker. These are problems, which will have to be dealt with, if the typology is used for comparative purposes and more detailed analyses, but in the larger picture they are details.

7.2.2. *Focus on Geographical Mobility*

Leaving aside for a while the 'location-of-parliament-node', we will turn to another triangular relationship that can be discerned, when we make a distinction between place of election, place of residence, and place of birth. Again this relationship can be described as one-dimensional, two-dimensional, and three-dimensional. A simple taxonomy results from combining the logical possibilities. Let B stand for birthplace, R for place of residence, and C for the constituency, in which the politician was elected, we get the following five categories:

I. $B = R = C$
II. $B \neq R = C$
III. $B = C \neq R$
IV. $B = R \neq C$
V. $B \neq R \neq C \neq B$

We will give some of these categories names. As analytical entities or *types* they will figure in the following analyses, see Section 7.5:

    I: *Native son*
    II: *Resident*
    III: *Homecoming son*
IV + V: *Parachutist*

Before we leave this conceptual exercise, it should be added that the two tax-onomies that have been presented might be linked together. A politician may have relations to any constituency everywhere, be it near the political centre or in the political and/or geographical periphery. Even in the Capital, or where the seat of parliament is, we will thus be able to find residents, native sons, homecoming sons, and *parachutists*.

7.3. A MICRO APPROACH

The use of demand-supply models for understanding the recruitment markets has been around at least since Barber's seminal work on lawmakers (Barber 1965: 2), but have within recent years become a dominant approach (e.g. Norris and Lovenduski 1995; Norris 1997*a*, 1997*b*). Individual career opportunities are created and controlled in a constant interplay of a supply of ambitious candidates and the demands of party organizations and other gatekeepers. The various factors that influence this market-like exchange have been analyzed at length; but no one has as yet included the geographical mobility dimension. Before we turn to the empirical parts, we will model the geographical linkage problem in another way. Some would say that what we present is a primitive 'rational choice'-approach. We will not argue against such a label.

'Running for office' is an individual decision. Ambitious young activists may openly pursue a political career. In many parties, it is, however, not considered proper behaviour to demonstrate overzealousness. Modesty is called for. One is 'asked to serve' and 'obliges' to do so. But even if such norms exist, the individual will have to make his or her own decision. Our contention is that aspirants decide to accept/run, because they want to succeed. Among candidates in 'hopeless' constituencies we may, eventually, find a few, who enter candidacy for other purposes, but these individuals only seldom end up in parliament. For the ambitious, the choice then is between constituencies that are more or less 'winnable', list positions that are more or less 'hopeless', and constituencies close to or away from one's home turf. Risks, costs, and possibilities enter the psychological equation, but how they affect the decision of the individual is not well understood.

Turning to the 'demand' side, similar considerations can be made. In all coun-tries, party organizations play a vital role as nominating agencies. But the role differs considerably across countries and across time. We shall (mostly) leave aside the important discussion about the internal relationship between the central and the local party, both of whom may play important roles in the nominating process (Narud et al. 2002). We also leave aside the relationship between local leadership and the rank-and-file members: The latter may (or may not) influence the nomination process by means of referenda and other procedural instruments. We shall assume that the local—constituency—leadership is in charge of the final decision about nomination and/or list composition.

	Resident	Parachutist
Demand side		
Focus on recruitment	Demonstration of local autonomy	Support to national party by recruiting nominee
	Signal to local activists that efforts are rewarded	Candidate may be 'neutral' in local conflict
	Familiarity with local situation and problems	Familiarity with national politics
	Local patriotism	Political vision
Focus on representation	Residency means affiliation and loyalty to local party	Possibly higher political success rate
	Better service to the constituency	Adds glory and lends lustre to local meetings
Supply side		
Focus on recruitment	Familiarity	Training and getting campaign experience
	Power base	Demonstration of loyalty to party leadership
	Local rivalries	Maybe only nomination possibility
Focus on representation	Effective service to local interests	Relatively high costs
	Cumulation of local political offices/power	Demonstration of national leadership potential

FIGURE 7.1. Demand and supply: arguments for choosing parachutists, resp. residents, and arguments *pro-et-contra* parachuting

The important question is the following: Which candidate will (or should) the local leadership prefer: the local resident/native son or the candidate from outside, the *parachutist?* Note the terminology: we do not in this context discuss, what actually happens, but what could happen, if the local discussion is carried out by way of using typical arguments. The conclusion that will be drawn at the end of the day by the local leadership is not our concern, only the arguments. The first observation is that it is difficult to think of more than two strategic goals to be pursued by the leadership. Local leaders will wish to find a candidate, who will attract voters to the party, and they wish to find a candidate with—at least— some chance to get elected, and who will subsequently be able to carry out the representative function in parliament. We shall not pursue the questions about, why these are the goals, only make the point that both goals are important—and obvious.

What kinds of arguments are brought to bear during the nomination process? We propose the following list of *pro-et-contra* arguments that are relevant for the actors, see Figure 7.1.

As said, we are not able to predict the outcome of the interplay of these arguments in the specific situations. Much will here depend on the institutional context. We expect that the character of the electoral system (Majority, PR, etc.) will influence the situation. So will the numerical size of the constituency. So will, in PR systems, the character of the list system. The format of the party system (two-party or multiparty, etc.), and the amount of competitiveness, should also be expected to create different supply-and-demand mechanisms. The interplay of demand and supply, mediated by different institutional and cultural contexts, results in a specific aggregate profile for a given country at a given time. A main contention in the following is that cross-national variations as well as longitudinal variations are created by differences and changes in the institutional contexts. Since the study of aggregate profile variations across Europe is our main task in this chapter, we have only sketched the underlying demand-supply model as a backdrop for the following discussion.

7.4. A QUICK TOUR OF WESTERN EUROPE

What little we know about the comparative aspect, our topic was summarized by Michael Gallagher years ago, when he noted that possession of local roots is the first and most important personal characteristic of nominees in most countries, and that to be seen as a 'foreigner', and especially as a favourite of the party's central office 'can amount to a kiss of death' (Gallagher 1988: 245). But Gallagher could easily have found case stories that contradicted this generalization. One just has to mention the names of Tony Blair, Margaret Thatcher, and in an earlier era, Winston Churchill as prominent examples of politicians, who were elected far away from their home turf. According to Roy Jenkins (2001: ch. XVII) 'many of the most famous figures (in British politics) have been elected in the course of their careers from a bewildering geographical spread.' More than forty years ago, K. C. Wheare made the observation that 'the "carpet–bagger" is a familiar figure in British politics in all parties' (Wheare 1963: 44). The same observation can be made in several other European countries. But still, Gallagher probably was right in stressing the importance of local roots, be it by residence, by birth, or by upbringing. The following remarks come from scattered sources and do not claim exhaustiveness, even if the search has been tiresome. Main findings with regard to the occurrence of *parachutage* are summarized in Table 7.1.

We will begin our tour in the northern part of Europe. In none of the Nordic countries legal residency requirements are in force nowadays, but they have been, and this sets some of these countries apart from the rest of Europe. As we discuss more in details later (see Section 7.6), a residency requirement was on the law books in *Norway* between 1814 and 1952, and Norway still is the country in which the overwhelming majority of MPs are recruited and elected from their residential constituency. *Parachutage* is considered almost impossible by political aspirants as well as by gatekeeping parties. But it happens.

TABLE 7.1. *The geographical dimension of parliamentary representation—basic facts and an estimate of the present level of parachutage*

Country	District magnitude*	Electoral system	No. of tiers	Openness of lists?	Effective no. of parties	Percentage parachutists**
Austria	20.5	PR (list)	three tier	semi-closed	3.5	<10%
Belgium	7.1	PR (list)	two tier	semi-closed	9.8	10–15%
Denmark	10.5	PR (list)	two tier	open	4.8	30–35%
Finland	13.3	PR	one tier	open	5.9	<5%
France	1.0	two ballot	one tier	no choice	7.1	<2%
Germany	2.0	mixed	two tier	no choice	3.8	5%
Iceland	7.0	PR	two tier	semi-closed	4.2	<1%
Ireland	4.0	PR (STV)	one tier	open	3.9	<5%
Italy	19.7	mixed	two tier	no choice	7.1	15–20%
Netherlands	150.0	PR (list)	one tier	semi-closed	5.7	not appl.
Norway	8.3	PR (list)	two tier	semi-closed	4.7	<1%
Portugal	11.5	PR (list)	one tier	no choice	2.9	—
Spain	5.8	PR	one tier	no choice	3.3	—
Sweden	12.0	PR (list)	two tier	open	4.1	<5%
Switzerland	7.7	PR (list)	one tier	open	7.4	<1%
UK	1.0	plurality	one tier	no choice	3.0	35–40%

Sources: The primary sources consulted for information about electoral systems: Lane et al. (1997), Gallagher et al. (2001), Caramani (2000), Norris (2004), and Colomer (2004). Information on parachutage comes from many sources: DATACUBE, Frognier and Mateo-Diaz (2003), Peteaux (2003), information from chapter authors and other 'informants'. We wish in this connection to thank Pedro Tavares de Almeida, Peter Esaiasson, Daniel Gaxie, Svanur Kristjansson, Hans Peter Kriesi, Jan-Erik Lane, Wolf Linder, Wolfgang C. Müller, Michael Rush, Luca Verzichelli, and Liam Weeks. Responsibility for the final estimate for each country is ours, and our informants should not be blamed.

Notes: *Calculated by authors, following Rae (1967: 20) as the average number of seats to be filled from each constituency/district. **Parachutage is here defined as non-residence in constituency at election time.

Residency requirements were never part of *Icelandic* politics. But the small size of the country, the deep split between the relatively big capital, Reykjavik, and the countryside, and the local character of the nominations have always favoured *native sons*. In 1959, a reform of the electoral districts brought their number down from twenty-eight to only eight, a change, which probably made it easier for candidates to maintain local ties. Local residency may not be mandatory since 'local family roots can be substituted for living in the district' (Kristjánson 2002: 130). *Parachutage*, in the special form of imposition of an outsider by the national party leadership, does, however, hardly exist. Before 1959, a few young candidates might improve their career opportunities with the party leadership by running for far-away marginal seats, but such *carpet-bagging* does no longer exist.

Nor did *Denmark* ever practise residency requirements. As we see below (Section 7.5), *parachutage* has always been quite common. Even if a majority of legislators will have some linkage to the constituency, by birth, residency, or both, the 'local' candidate often will have to fight intruders, and he or she does not always win. In several constituencies, it is seen as desirable to be represented in parliament by a high-flying young politician, not to speak about a political leader. Only in one other country (UK) do we find the same high level of *parachutage*.

Sweden upheld a residency requirement until 1969 for its Second Chamber. In the First Chamber, one could find quite a few of the so-called 'National members' (*Rikskandidater*), that is members who, when elected, lived outside their constituency. The proportion of 'National members' was a fairly constant 25–30 per cent before 1920, but then dwindled over the following decades to less than 10 per cent during the 1950s (Nyman 1966: 179–80). Most of these Swedish *parachutists* were high-level civil servants from Stockholm. Members of the unicameral *Riksdag* since 1975 do not have to meet a residency requirement, but as is the case with Norway, most candidates are still recruited from within the constituency. Local affiliations are considered very important resources for prospective candidates (Johansson 1999).

Finnish eligibility rules do not contain residence requirements of any kind. During most of the twentieth century, the relative number of parachutists amounted to approximately 20 per cent. The parachutists were mostly residing in the capital, Helsinki, and in many cases they had some kind of link to the provincial constituency by birth, former residence, or education. *Parachutage* is reported to be decreasing over the last decades and is today relatively rare. This tendency is probably partially linked to a change of the Electoral Act in 1969. At that point in time, it was prohibited to stand as a candidate in more than one constituency—an opportunity which in earlier times had made it possible for prominent politicians to 'show their face' in several regions (Noponen 1968: 84–6; Kuitunen 2002: 82).

Germany is belonging to a group of countries, in which local and regional considerations seem to play a crucial role. The 'mixed electoral system' and the decentralized nature of the nomination processes give preference to local candidates at the lowest level of the *Kreis*. Most candidates do, however, also try to safeguard their career opportunities by making efforts to receive a simultaneous nomination on the party list in the *Land*. The existence of this higher level should make it possible 'to correct tendencies towards an "over-provincial" Bundestag' (Roberts 1988: 114). To what extent this happens is not known. At the higher *Land*-level a complicated bargaining process takes place, and local considerations are often counterbalanced by other considerations (gender, social background, affiliation with party factions, etc.). Studies of recruitment have ascertained that a clear majority of *Bundestag* members have followed a local politics track, the so-called *Ochsentour*. Most of these candidates as well as elected members will have close local connections (by residence and/or birth) to their *Kreis*, and they will have to invest considerable amounts of time and energy doing 'constituency work' (Patzelt 1997). A much smaller number of candidates have received their political training in various party organizations at a higher level. These candidates may bypass a local career. 'This, however, seems to be more the exception than the rule', according to the most recent summary of the complicated German situation (Borchert and Golsch 2003: 152).

To some extent the situation in *Austria* can be compared to that of Germany. Since 1994 Austria practises a very complicated three-tier electoral system (Müller 2005). Some candidates are elected from one of the forty-three multi-member districts, others via regional or national lists. Most of those elected have been listed as candidates at more than one level, thus maximizing their election chances. To speak about *parachuting* is only really meaningful in connection with the lowest tier (and not at all at the national tier). But, like in Germany, even those who are elected at the higher levels may have strong local connections derived from residence and/or birth and therefore will act as representatives for their home district. To live in the constituency is seen as a crucial condition for personal contact with the voters. It is even considered an unwritten norm, a *moral duty*. The data available indicate that *parachutage* must be rare. Nine out of ten members lived in their electoral district, and only 6 per cent did say that they did not live in the district—exceptions were mainly found in the larger cities like Vienna, and among those who were nominated at the national level (Müller et al. 2001: 110–17).

The Netherlands may look like a special case. Regional forces always played an important role. Even if a residence rule never existed, the Dutch politicians during the nineteenth century tended to be locally recruited, mostly even born in the constituency. Even if the traditional concept of constituency has, nowadays, lost most of its meaning, since the country for most practical consequences is administered as one big constituency, and even if the country is small, mostly urban, and densely populated, regional considerations are still present and operating during the recruitment process. Candidates may campaign in their *own* region and attract preferential votes. Parties are also aware of the need of retaining specific links with specific strongholds, and they do so by carefully 'balancing the national lists' (Daalder and van den Berg 1982: 218; Koole and Leijenaar 1988; Leijenaar and Niemöller 2003).

In the *Belgian* PR-based system, *parachuting* is reported to be, if not rare, then at least not typical. According to the latest study, 12 per cent of all members (in 1999) were *parachutists* (Frognier and Matéo-Diaz 2003). Most Belgian MPs have strong local ties and have lived in the constituency most of their life (De Winter 1988, 1997). In the career of Belgian MPs, the *cumul local* always played an important role (De Winter and Brans 2003).

In neighbouring *France*, local ties and especially local office has always been considered an important recruitment asset in most parties. Cumulation of offices (local, regional, and national) has served as a stabilizing force in the otherwise fragile French party system, but it also tended to make the representative more of a local ambassador, and less nationally oriented (Ehrman 1983: 153). There is also agreement in the literature that it is much safer to begin the national career in municipal or regional politics, build up a local base, thus avoiding the risks of high-volatility elections. A well-established local connection is also an important condition for obtaining important local campaign funds (Kreuzer and

Stepan 2003: 132–3). As the international terminology indicates, *parachutage* has a long history and has been used in many French parties, not least by the Gaullists. Interestingly enough, the periodical use of PR apparently made this phenomenon more frequent at the same time as geographical balancing of the lists became more important (Thiébault 1988). Even if it is only recently that the phenomenon has been given focused and systematic attention (Dolez and Hastings 2003), it has always played a role. Its pros and cons have been discussed, and several types of *parachutists* have been identified (Petaux 2003: 68ff.). Apparently, the phenomenon of *parachutage* is considered quite sophisticated and not really amenable to operational definition, not to speak about measurement. One reason for this is that the payment of a local tax in a town within the constituency is mandatory for running, and consequently 'foreign' aspirants will have to take up a local rental, however fake. Some French experts would even argue that the best approximation to a valid measure is the percentage of *députés*, who were not born in the constituency. Paradoxically, *parachutage* may not be quite that frequent nowadays, even if it is easy to find prominent examples. The most recent study, covering three parties (RPR, UDF, and PS) in the 1988 (and 1993) elections, applied a very complex definition of the concept of *parachutist*: 'Acteur politique n'ayant pas un mandat local (municipal, cantonal, régional) dans la circonscription sur laquelle il se porte candidat, n'exerçant pas une activité professionnelle à temps plein dans cet espace local, n'y résidant pas en permanence, mais pouvant y être né ou y ayant eu et y ayant encore des attaches familiales.' Using this definition the author counted approximately thirty-three cases of parachuting candidates per election, and less than half of these were in fact elected. Not an impressive number for a parliament with 555 *députés* (Petaux 2003: 62ff.). Had we, instead, defined the concept as linked to place of birth, we would have ended with a much higher number, indeed ten times as high. The estimate given in Table 7.1 below has to be seen as a first approximation.

On the *Iberian Peninsula parachutage* has existed since long. No information is available for the present Spanish and Portuguese regimes, but some historical evidence exists, suggesting that *native sons, residents*, and *parachutists* are familiar concepts. In Spain, most of the MPs during the Restoration regime (1875–1923) had some link to the constituency-family roots, birth, or residency (Ortega 2001). It has been estimated that about 60 per cent of the MPs elected between 1914 and 1923 represented the province, in which they were born (Cabrera 1998). In Portugal, during the Constitutional Monarchy, available evidence suggests that the majority of the MPs possessed local roots in their constituencies, more so in single-member constituencies than in multi-member constituencies (Sobral and Tavaras de Almeida 1982; Tavaras de Almeida 1991). Pedro Tavares de Almeida also has examined data from the First Republic (1910–26). He found that approximately at most one-third of the members were *outsiders*, the remaining having some kind of links to their constituency by birth, residency, or professional affiliation (Tavaras de Almeida, Fernandes and Santos 2006).

The National Council of *Switzerland* is based on electoral districts corresponding to the Cantons. Thus the numerical size of constituencies varies from one member to thirty-four members, and accordingly relationships between members and constituencies will vary as well. But the federal structure strikes through in nomination practices: the territorial principle is very strong. Swiss experts have counted no more than a good dozen non-residents over the last eighty years, and at present only one member of the *Nationalrat* satisfies the definition used in Table 7.1, that is lives in a Canton different from the one, from which he is elected.

The *Italian* electoral system has changed considerably in recent times (as has its party system). Older information about the residential linkage cannot automatically be taken for valid, like when, for example, Richard S. Katz (1980: 96–7) found that almost 90 per cent of the Italian candidates in his three-country study lived within the constituency, an observation, which suggests a relatively modest practice of *parachutage*. His observations may, however, not be far off the mark. The present electoral system, introduced in 1993, belongs to the same family as the German. It is a 'mixed' system with two tiers. Seventy-five per cent of the 630 members of the Chamber of Deputies are elected by plurality in single-member districts. The remaining members are elected in local multi-member districts but according to the national score obtained by each party on the basis of a vote, which is cast separately but concurrently with the single-member district vote. These seats are filled by means of the traditional party-list PR method (Gambetta and Warner 2004: 239). How this system works out, and how it is perceived by voters and by candidates, has not yet been studied intensively. There is no obligation to reside in the constituency/region, but, just like in France, a *local* address, not least a *domicilio fiscale* (address for correspondence with regard to campaign funds), is important, and one would accordingly expect to find similar problems of measurement. According to Luca Verzichelli (2002), a considerable proportion of elected members will run for election in a new constituency at their second election or third election, thus suggesting a higher amount of *parachutage* than found by Richard Katz. The same author has provided us with an estimate for the 2001 election; using the rough indicator of Table 7.1, his estimate is fifteen–twenty *parachutists* in the Italian case.

Moving to the British Isles, our first stop is *Ireland*. The Irish STV list system makes the parties attempt to create geographically balanced lists. The concept of a 'safe seat' does not have a clear meaning in a personalized PR system. Candidates compete with each other within and between parties, and, consequently, the parties as well as candidates will have to take precautions in order to fight possible electoral risks. Thus candidates on the party's list should preferably, between them, cover the constituency in geographical terms. This is probably the predominant consideration for the nominating agencies as well as for the party members who select candidates. In addition, the national executive of the party is able to bring its 'own' candidates on to the list without overruling or eliminating the locally preferred. The highly personalized and competitive character of the STV system makes it possible to do so (Gallagher 1988:129). But such interference in local matters has to be handled carefully, if counterproductive sentiments are to be avoided. It is no wonder that local roots, and, preferably, a track record of local political activities are essential requirements for initiating a political career in the *Dail*. In the 1957 election, only 10 per cent of the candidates were living outside the constituency, they were contesting, and of these about half were 'ministers, former ministers, or national heroes' (Chubb 1970: 152). In the 1970s, residents and native sons amounted to approximately 90 per cent, and the remaining were mostly Dublin dwellers, who stood for election in wider Dublin (Katz 1980: 97). Another indicator of the importance of the local power base is that *cumul des mandats* is widespread; members of the *Dail* tend to retain their seats in local authorities (Gallagher 2003: 194–5).

The British single-member constituencies create special conditions. Selection is decided on the local level, and the central party organization rarely uses its formal right of veto. The recruitment process is heavily conditioned by the 'winnability' of the seat. Local connections and considerations play a considerable role in all parties. Local roots are regarded as an advantage in the longer run, even if many politicians at their first time nomination tend to be 'outsiders'. Austin Ranney stressed that local connections, even if important in all parties, were not considered equally important in all localities. More specifically he found that the preference for local candidates was most pronounced in the biggest provincial cities, not in the rural constituencies (Ranney 1965: 277). Data from the 1970s indicated that almost three-fourth of all candidates did not live in the constituency (Katz 1980: 97). A few years later, Ivor Crewe admitted that reliable data on residence did not exist, and he did not provide an estimate (Crewe 1985: 52). In a more recent summary of British practices, David Denver did make the observation that the amount of 'carpet-bagging' has been exaggerated and that 'preference for a local candidate—broadly defined—is a powerful force in British selections' (Denver 1988: 67). Data made available by Michael Rush for this chapter indicate that members without any known local connections are common, at least in the Conservative Party, in which they often amount to half of all MPs. In Labour, they were also rather common until the early 1980s. At the latest election (2001) their share was 11 per cent. In the smaller parties they are almost absent. If we add those members, who did not live in the constituency, but who happened to have some connections within the wider region, we arrive at a 37 per cent overall share of *parachutists* in the English case, the highest percentage found in any of the West European countries.

From available studies we have by now been given the impression that the geographical dimension does not play the same role across countries in Western Europe. Are there systematic variations to be found? Earlier studies suggested that the local focus would be strongest in countries with single-member constituencies (Loewenberg and Patterson 1979). Michael Steed (1985: 284) argued that multi-member constituencies make for more localist representation, and that *parachuting* is a characteristic of uninominal countries. But the picture is not that clear. European-wide most MPs have local roots. In some countries almost all are elected in the home constituency. But *parachutage* in one or another form can be found in most countries. In some countries (like UK) the electoral system is organized in such a way that local-constituency interests and conflicts should be expected to prevail, but in UK the frequency of *parachutage* has been quite high. But the same is true in multi-member districts Denmark, while the frequency in France nowadays is quite low. In most systems candidates are presented to the voters in wider geographical districts, even regionally or nationwide, using multi-member lists. In such situations, the geographical dimension tend to work out in subtle ways, depending probably on the size of the constituency, the number of parties competing, and the character of the lists used. In countries with two- or three-tier electoral systems, candidates may simultaneously compete in a constituency and in a wider regional district, thus blurring the simple residential *problématique*. In Table 7.1, we have summarized what little information is available about the present situation in Western Europe. The reader should be aware that most of the figures in the *parachutist* column are estimates. They are either culled from available literature or provided by national experts.

Most intriguing finding emanating from this table is, that no clear connections apparently exist between, on one hand, the amount of *parachutage*, and, on the other hand, the character of the electoral system, the list system, and the party system, factors that have been suspected to influence the geographical linkage. Does this *non-finding* indicate that no relationship exists? Or is the indication rather that the institutional context plays a more complex role? Could it be the case, that national traditions for considering *parachutage* legitimate, respective illegitimate *overrule* other institutional factors? Some of these questions will be discussed in the following parts, especially Section 7.6.

7.5. THE LONGITUDINAL PERSPECTIVE

The DATACUBE data-set contains information about the relationship between the politician and his constituency, as this relationship has changed over time. Information has been gathered about the residential linkage as well as on local political experience as a background variable. Since either type of information is available in the aggregate, the latter variable can only be used as a secondary indicator of the importance of the geographical factor in recruitment.

The data ideally should make it possible to investigate geographical mobility patterns across Europe, and across time, and do so even in a wider sense, because the information about the place of birth is also included in the data-set. When moving from the conceptual discussion to empirical analysis, a caveat is necessary.

First, the information available may be of varying quality. It has been collected at various points in time and space. Data are of the 'process-generated' kind, meaning that it was originally collected for other, mostly official purposes. Some data are reliable, while other may reflect that the 'informants' (often the legislators themselves) may have biased the information right from the beginning. In our case, we have no reason to doubt the reliability of information about birth-place and constituency affiliation. But the information about the residence of the representative, sometimes, may be biased: it is well known (but hard to document) that ambitious *parachuting* candidates may take up residence in the constituency for a while.

Second, even if the conceptual framework is precise and unambiguous, the real world may be more complicated. The linkage between politician and constituency is not always straightforward. Are you, for example, *parachuting,* if you reside within the boundaries of a neighbouring constituency? Are you *parachuting,* if you have lived in the constituency before, or if you own property there? There are many possible physical linkages, which may create special bonds between a candidate and a constituency. Unfortunately, the recorded facts are not detailed enough to provide a full picture. Some of the biases may have the effect of overestimating *parachutage,* others may work in the opposite direction. To the best of our knowledge, the only data-set which provides such detailed information is the one created by Michael Rush (unpublished data). His calculations of various types of local connections indicate that there is, indeed, a considerable 'grey zone' between the 'pure' *parachutist* and the 'pure' *resident.*

A final caveat, and a most important one, has to do with the concept of the con-stituency, as it is understood in the following survey. Sometimes 'constituency' means the geographical unit in which the candidate is nominated. Sometimes it means the broader region in which voters are able to vote for the candidate (e.g. Denmark). But it may also refer to an even broader geographical unit, a province, or a region (e.g. Norway and Germany).

In Figure 7.2–7.6, we present longitudinal data on the relationship between the parliamentarians and the geographical area, where they are elected when entering the parliament for the first time. Systematically collected data are available from the DATACUBE data-set for five European countries only, namely Denmark, Germany, the Netherlands, Norway, and Finland and each of the figures illus-trates the geographic dimension of recruitment in one of these countries. The distribution among the parliamentarians on their geographical relationship to their constituencies is made up according to the typology created in Section 7.2.2.

With data from only five parliaments, and with time series of varying length the comments have to be cautious. Among the five patterns the Norwegian stands out. The fairly constant high percentage of purely local representatives, mostly genuine *native sons,* springs to the eye. The Norwegian *Storting* definitely (among all parliaments) is the one with the closest representational links between con-stituencies and MP's. The pattern (and it is at the same time simple and complex 'explanation') will be discussed in Section 7.6 of the chapter. The other four patterns are all different. Studying the *parachutists* a vague 'U-shape' appears

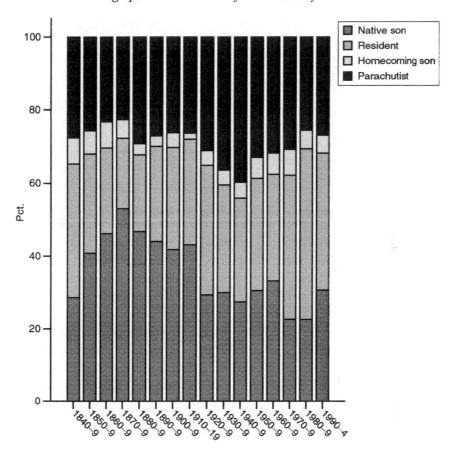

FIGURE 7.2. Longitudinal pattern of constituency linkages. (Denmark)

Note: Native sons, homecoming sons, residents, and parachutists are defined as in Section 7.2.2.

in the Danish case. The situation starts out with a relatively high percentage of locally based representatives; the local element is declining over the late nineteenth century and well into the twentieth, at the same time as the party systems developed and matured. But apparently the local base became more important after the Second World War. Denmark stands out with a (relatively) high number of *parachutists* throughout the 150 years of democratic government. The Danish case is also discussed in Section 7.6 of the chapter.

In the Dutch case, a change of the electoral law in 1918 abolished the electoral constituencies and made the Netherlands one big constituency. Even if local connections still plays a considerable role in the recruitment process, and local political experience is an important recruitment resource, we are not able to follow this lead, since the time series is not extended beyond 1918. After that time, it

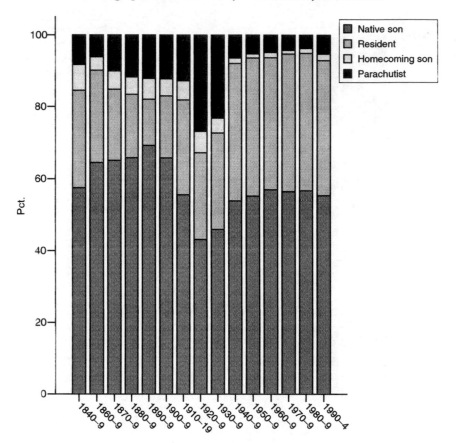

FIGURE 7.3. Longitudinal pattern of constituency linkages (Germany)

Note: Native sons, homecoming sons, residents, and parachutists are defined as in Section 7.2.2.

has not been considered relevant or worthwhile to examine connections between electoral districts and parliamentary candidates and representatives (Secker 2000: 295). But apparently the Dutch parties were quite keen on nominating (and electing) candidates from outside the constituency already in the nineteenth century.

In comparative perspective, relatively many members of the Finnish *Eduskunta* (beginning soon after Finnish independence in 1917) have had an experience in local politics before their first election (Ruostetsaari 2000: 60). Figure 7.6 indicates that this goes hand-in-hand with a high and increasing tendency to 'real' localism. In Section 7.4 of the chapter, we hypothesized that the ban against multiple candidacies might help us to understand the decreasing *parachutage* in Finnish politics. It does, however, not help us to understand the high level of *localism* in a modern nation at the end of the twentieth century, considering that residency requirements were never practised. The German pattern is characterized

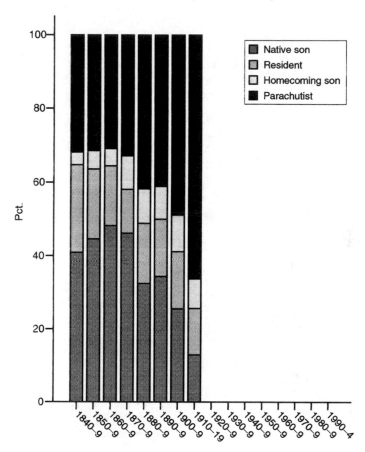

FIGURE 7.4. Longitudinal pattern of constituency linkages (The Netherlands)

Note: Native sons, homecoming sons, residents, and parachutists are defined as in Section 7.2.2.

by fairly high, if varying, localism across the various periods. This tendency apparently correlates with variations in the amount of experiences in local politics (Best et al. 2000: 153).

What we see in Figure 7.2–7.6 is quite bewildering. An interplay of changing electoral systems, changing nomination procedures, and changing legal regulations of nomination requirements creates quite different patterns of geographical linkages. There exists neither one uniform European pattern, nor a uniform diachronic pattern. This is as far as the present data situation will allow us to go. If we are to understand the geographical situation better than we do it today, we will have to move one step down from the aggregate data at the national level to the level of the individual MPs and/or to the level of constituencies. Ideally

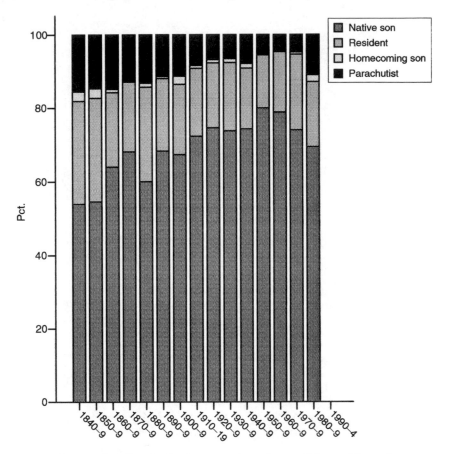

FIGURE 7.5. Longitudinal pattern of constituency linkages (Norway)

Note: Native sons, homecoming sons, residents, and parachutists are defined as in Section 7.2.2.

this could probably be done for quite a few European countries, but not without considerable efforts. We will suffice with a limited case study.

7.6. A TWO-COUNTRY EXPLORATION: DENMARK AND NORWAY

In the preceding sections, we have attacked the geographical aspect of the relationship between the legislator and his constituency from various angles. In this section, we explore two literatures and two data-sets: neither of these is perfect for our purposes, but they are the best available. A double case study will be conducted in the context of Norwegian and Danish politics. The approach should be characterized as a hypothesis-generating case study (Lijphart 1971), or a heuristic case study (Eckstein 1975). Denmark and Norway stood out in Figures 7.2

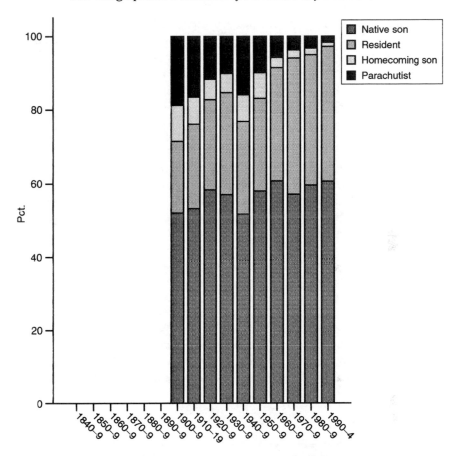

FIGURE 7.6. Longitudinal pattern of constituency linkages (Finland)

Note: Native sons, homecoming sons, residents, and parachutists are defined as in Section 7.2.2.

and 7.5 as very different. It may look surprising that Denmark and Norway, despite a great many similarities with regard to their politics in general, and party systems in particular, differ with regard to the geographical dimension. It should be possible to learn something of general interest from a comparison of these two cases.

In Norway it is still so, that candidates (and legislators) overwhelmingly are elected in the county (*fylke*), where they live, and mostly also were born. This is an intriguing fact, considering that a constitutional residence requirement was abolished more than fifty years ago. Henry Valen has described the situation in precise terms: 'In 1985 only twenty-three out of some 1400 candidates did not live in the constituency in which they were nominated. Even these "alien" candidates tended to belong to their constituencies through work or kinship and were temporarily absent, with the notable exception of a handful of real "aliens" in Oslo and Akershus' (Valen 1988: 224). Again and again the decentralized character of the Norwegian nomination process and the electoral system have been stressed (e.g. Matthews and Valen 1999; Valen et al. 2000; Rommetvedt 2003; Sørensen 2003). The Norwegian electoral system returns to the *Storting* members with very strong links to the constituencies. As a result the Capital, Oslo, is under-represented in parliament, not only because the electoral law allocates too few seats to the Oslo area, but also because Oslo candidates apparently are not able to *parachute* to the provinces.

In Denmark, in contrast, approximately 25 per cent of the members of the *Folketing*, and sometimes even more are elected from constituencies, in which they do not live (Kjær and Pedersen 2004). Some parties in some constituencies apparently even tend to prefer candidates of national standing and have done so for extended periods. It has always been like that, ever since the first days of democratic politics in Denmark.

This introduction brings us to the three questions with which we will deal in the following. First of all, why do Norway and Denmark differ so much with regard to the geographical dimension of representation? Second, why do politicians tend to choose nomination in a constituency removed from their own home base? (and if they do so, how do they move?). And third, what is the impact of *parachutage* on the collective profile of the parliament? By pursuing these questions in an in-depth case study, we may gain better general understanding of the phenomenon, and, eventually, become able to formulate hypotheses for further study.

7.6.1. Why a Difference?

Our argument will be that present differences should be interpreted as unintended and unanticipated consequences of early constitutional choices, decisions made in the nineteenth century. Norwegian and Danish constitutional fathers chose two different institutional solutions, and these choices are still dominating thinking as well as recruitment behaviour in the two countries.

In Denmark, there have never existed geographical restrictions whatsoever with regard to eligibility to the *Folketing*. It was thus always possible to obtain nomination irrespective of residence. The *free-for-all* system was introduced as early as 1848 for the election of the Constituent Assembly. The constitutions from 1849 and onwards have stipulated that eligibility should be identical to the suffrage requirements. This principle has never been questioned in connection with later constitutional discussions and reforms. Thus, from the very first day of the democratic era, a counterposition of *residents/native sons* and *parachutists* would be possible (and could be observed). Conflicts between *local people* and *intruders* have been, since then, if not frequent, then at least sometimes quite spectacular. However, more often than not there is no conflict, and in some constituency organizations there has even existed a tradition for choosing a candidate from outside the constituency, and especially to prefer a prominent candidate, a party leader or another party dignitary (Kjær and Pedersen 2004: 47).

The Norwegian story is different. The Norwegian political system right from 1814 operated a set of complicated legal rules, the effect of which was strengthen the influence of local elites and to sustain a cleavage, that between town and countryside. One of the rules, and probably the most vividly contested, was the 'Farmer's Clause' (*Bondeparagraffen*), which stipulated that the ratio between representatives from cities and rural districts should be 1:2. Another important rule was the so-called *Bostadsbånd*, according to which residency in the constituency, be it a city district or a rural district, was a requirement for nomination, and hence election (Kaartvedt 1964: 69). This rule was, throughout the nineteenth century, contested by a few, who thought that it worked in the direction of creating a less than optimal representation. The rules survived well into the twentieth century. The 'Farmers' Clause' and the residence requirement were abolished as late as in 1952.

From 1952 the legal requirements have been, if not identical, then very much alike in the two countries. Any voter may stand for nomination and election everywhere in the country. But old constitutional rules may live on, far beyond their cancellation. They may live on as unwritten political norms. When we used data from the DATACUBE data-set, we were able to draw two national time series with information about the balance between the various types of geographical representation (see Figures 7.2 and 7.5).These curves should puzzle, but only as long as we are not aware of their proveniences and weaknesses. While the Danish figures probably are as *true* as data ever will be, because they are based upon a strict comparison of residency and constituency, using the wider constituency as unit of measurement, the Norwegian data-set is defined differently. It is based upon a registration of the place of work, and furthermore a simple division of Norway in six regions has been applied (Rokkan and Valen 1964; Eliassen and Brosveet 1977). A critical analysis of the data has also suggested that there is a certain misfit between the traditional regionalization and the much more complicated map of constituencies, especially in older times, when there was a distinction between 'city constituencies' and 'rural constituencies'.

In order to correct for these inadequacies separate analyses were made of the Norwegian data for the period after 1952. We used for this purpose again the Norwegian data archive on *Storting* members, but in a more recent version (Eliassen and Ågotnes 1987). To our astonishment we found only fourteen cases of newcomers to the *Storting*, qualifying as genuine *parachutists*. We shall return to these fourteen members in Section 7.6.2. In relative terms, they represent 1.7 per cent of all newcomers to the Norwegian Parliament between 1954 and 2001.

Even considering the reported data inadequacies, which tend to deflate Norwegian *localism*, we have thus found a marked difference between the two countries. In the European context, they are polar cases, and Norway, in particular, stands out among the European political systems.

7.6.2. *Why Parachutage? Why Localism?*

We might have stopped here. We have observed that legal regulations over many decades were different. In Norway they prohibited *parachutage*. In Denmark, the phenomenon was, if not recommended, then at least allowed. But we wish to dig a bit deeper in the problem, by asking, why we find the peculiar curvelinear pattern of recruitment in Denmark, and why we do not find an 'adjustment' to the normal European pattern in Norway after the opening up of the recruitment market in 1952?

It is tempting to interpret the Norwegian–Danish differences as being (primarily) results of geographical differences between the two countries. The two *geographies* create differential motivations in the market for recruitment, on the supply side as well as the demand side. Let us comment briefly on this aspect. Although Denmark and Norway are similar in many recruitment-relevant characteristics, they do differ in terms of their physical and their political geography—and, in particular, the development hereof. The two different levels of 'localism' that we have observed thus (or maybe) can be understood as an effect of a purely geographical fact plus, of course, for the older period the already mentioned effect of a strict legal rule.

Denmark is a small country in terms of geographical extension. In 2003, it is possible to travel from the Capital to any point in Denmark (and vice versa) in a few hours. The travelling time was, however, until a few decades ago considerable. In the middle of the nineteenth century, when the railways were in their infancy, it would require several days to reach from peripheral Denmark (western and northern parts of Jutland) to Copenhagen, not least because of insecurity related to the passages by ship between the provinces. Travelling time between parts of Denmark made it impossible for most politicians to reach their home or their constituency from Copenhagen on a regular basis. The conditions of work thus have changed considerably over the long period.

In contrast, the Norwegian geography is characterized by the *oblong* shape of the country and the very long distances between the seat of parliament in Oslo and the peripheral parts of the country. Even today it takes considerable time to reach the smaller towns and villages in Northern Norway. In earlier times, especially when most of the travelling had to be done by ships navigating the route along the Norwegian coast, travelling time between Christiania (now: Oslo) and the north could amount to weeks.

What do these differences mean for political recruitment? What are their implications for the commencement, the continuation, and the termination of political careers? What does it mean for the attitudes of the nominating agencies—and the voters as well? Does geography also structure ambitions and opportunities in the various parties? Little is known about this aspect of parliamentary politics. We may, however, suggest that the curves in Figures 7.2 and 7.5 fit our 'geographical' interpretation quite well. Preference for a *native son* can be seen as a result of nominating agencies preferring a candidate, who knows the constituency well, and who lives there part of the year at least. In older times, when the annual legislative service was of shorter duration, but also required that the member was living away from his home base, it was much better to be represented by 'one of our own' than by a candidate from far away, may be even the Capital, the 'Centre'. This was probably the dominant view in Denmark during the first many decades of democratic representation. In Norway it was a legal requirement, not to be tampered with.

With the formation and later institutionalization of the parties as the nominating agencies, the need for local affiliation may have weakened a bit, for party and adherence and loyalty to the party became more important. Seen from the perspective of the ambitious candidate costs were, however, also involved in *parachuting* into a far-away constituency from, say, Copenhagen. Even if daily life was easier for the Metropolitan dweller, he still had to keep his contacts to the constituency and its party organization. Minimizing travel costs (in the widest sense) seems to be rational. It was, however, a cost, which had to be carried, if nomination was not possible nearby. Recruitment patterns in Denmark have been modelled in these terms (Pedersen 1975).

With the revolution of domestic transportation towards the end of the twentieth century, these considerations were, however, made less important. It became easier to parachute and to keep up communication with the constituency. But at the same time, it also became much easier to communicate for the *native son*. The *locals* and the *parachutists* were, so to speak, put on more equal terms. This is, we are well aware, a disputable interpretation of the curvelinear pattern found in Denmark. It does, however, also go some way in understanding the much more stable preference for local candidates in Norway. The fact that the same diachronic pattern can be observed in all major Danish political parties also adds support to the interpretation.

We will, however, have to add a few remarks about another relevant explanatory factor, the electoral system. The Norwegian electoral system with its strict list system does not favour an intruding *parachutist*. He will probably find it very difficult to get a top position on the party list. For the voters, there is no effective way to show a preference for the *parachutist*. For the party organization, there are few incentives to add him to the list. The opposite situation has developed in Denmark over the last thirty years (Pedersen 1966, 2002). With a complicated electoral system, which preserves the traditional electoral districts (*opstillingskredse*) but allows voters all over the much larger constituency (*amtskreds*) to influence the fates of candidates in the election by an effective preferential vote, a new 'market situation' has developed within the constituency. It may even be advantageous to put up as candidate a high-flying *parachutist* in one of the districts, since such a candidate will attract additional votes to the party. The 'trick' for the *parachutist* consists in running for election in a smaller district, but collecting votes from the wider constituency. The 'trick' for the local party organization

TABLE 7.2. *Region of residency and region of election at first entrance into the Danish Folketing*

	Region of residency					
	I	II	III	IV	V	Total
Region of election*						
Copenhagen (I)	11	1	0	0	0	12
Metropolitan region (II)	4	9	1	0	0	14
Islands (III)	5	2	17	0	1	25
Eastern Jutland (IV)	2	1	1	14	1	19
Periphery (V)	2	2	1	2	23	30
Total	24	15	20	16	25	100

Note: All members (1849–2001) (%).

* The five regions are defined as follows: Copenhagen—Søndre, Østre, and Vestre storkredse; metropolitan region—København, Frederiksborg, and Roskilde amtskredse; Islands—Vestsjælland, Storstrøm, and Fyn amtskredse; Eastern Jutland—Vejle and Århus amtskredse; Periphery—Bornholm, Sønderjylland, Ribe. Ringkøbing, Viborg, and Nordjylland amtskredse. (n = 2.104).

may be the chance to obtain a seat in (and a link to) the *Folketing* at the expense of other electoral districts. The nomination and election of a fair number of Danish 'TV-personalities' bears witness to a new trend in the market for candidates (Pedersen 2004).

7.6.3. How do Parachutists Move?

The next step will consist in mapping the movements within the individual country. In the case of Norway, only the data from the post-1952 period will be studied, whereas the Danish situation permits a more comprehensive study. Using a rough measure and dividing Denmark into five regions (see Table 7.2), our first observation is that *localism* is more frequent in Copenhagen than in the rest of Denmark. No less than 92 per cent of those candidates, who are elected from a constituency in Copenhagen, lived there at the time of their first election compared to 64 per cent in the wider Metropolitan region, 68 per cent on the islands, 74 per cent in Eastern Jutland, and 77 per cent in the Periphery.

The distribution is also quite skewed. Politicians with residency in the Copenhagen area seek and win elections all over Denmark, while the opposite movement is much less frequent. Thus it has never happened that a politician with residency in Peripheral Denmark has won an election in Copenhagen. When Danish politicians take the *parachute*, they move away from Copenhagen much more than they move towards Copenhagen. This is, furthermore, a very stable pattern, visible from the very beginning of representative democracy. The pattern fits quite well with the suggestions made in Section 7.6.2. With a sharp competition for the Metropolitan seats, many ambitious politicians have always had to seek election in the provinces, preferably nearby, but eventually as far away as Jutland.

Turning next to Norway, we have to repeat the observation that nothing much has changed over the last half-century since 1952. A total of 2,032 electoral events have occurred in the 19 constituencies, and in only 33 of these we observe a deviation from the pattern of former times. Only fourteen newcomers to parliament (out of 842) were *parachutists* in the formal sense. Of these fourteen members six were living in Akershus and elected in neighbouring Oslo, or vice versa, a movement, which hardly qualify. Three were living in Oslo, but elected from a constituency in the southern part of norway. Another three Oslo residents were elected from the northern part of the country. Only two provincial residents have ever won an election in the Capital. The numbers are small, but the tendency is the same as found in Denmark: *Parachutage*, to the extent it exists at all, mainly consists in Metropolitan dwellers seeking election in a provincial constituency.

7.6.4. *The Effects?*

Our final 'cut' brings us to an important question: Do *parachutists* differ from 'local sons and daughters'? Does the lack of residence requirements open up avenues to the parliament for special categories of ambitious individuals? Even a cursory inspection of the Danish scene, but also scattered information from other European countries, suggests that the *parachutage* option probably benefits younger and well-educated politicians, especially 'high-fliers' with academic credentials. We also expect these politicians to be not as well linked to local politics as the real *locals*, who will often have started their political career in municipal politics. Three indicators will be used to tap differences and similarities: the age at which the politician entered parliament, his or her educational background, and local political experience. See Table 7.3.

The expected pattern comes out clearly in the Danish data. *Parachutists* are on the average a bit younger, when they make their appearance in the *Folketing*. Their group also contains more candidates with an academic background. The *locals* do have more experience from local politics. These patterns are clear and consistent over time. For Norway, the two periods, for which we have data, provide us with puzzling results. Since 'N' for the *parachutists* is so small, we should not comment too much. The Norwegian *Storting* apparently is on the way to become a chamber populated by locally elected and connected politicians with an academic background.

7.7. PROPOSITIONS FOR FUTURE RESEARCH

In this chapter, we have argued that the geographical aspects of political recruitment deserve more attention than given to them so far. Although it has been argued, and still can be argued, that the geographical connections between MPs and their voters are important, in normative terms as well as empirically, our search in the existing literature has revealed that considerable lacunae exist. In

TABLE 7.3. *Age, academic background, and local political experience among new-comers to the Danish Folketing and the Norwegian Storting (residents and parachutists)*

Denmark	1849–1918	1920–53	1953–68	1971–2001
Residents				
Mean age	43.5	46.3	46.1	43.7
Academic background (%)	23.7	17.5	18.8	25.0
From local politics (%)	57.7	55.1	53.1	39.3
Parachutists				
Mean age	42.9	44.5	45.5	41.0
Academic background (%)	42.2	28.3	31.7	42.0
From local politics (%)	30.5	36.1	34.1	22.5
Norway			1954–65	1969–2001
Residents				
Mean age			51.4	43.9
Academic background (%)			31.3	61.3
From local politics (%)			90.6	90.7
Parachutists				
Mean age			51.8	44.1
Academic background (%)			75.0	60.0
From local politics (%)			100.0	50.0

Notes: Residents are MPs who at their first election resided in the constituency in which they were elected, while parachutists resided in a constituency different from the one they were elected from. For Denmark, the amtskredse has been used except for the three amtskredse covering metropolitan Copenhagen, which has been treated as one constituency. For Norway, the Fylke has been used as unit. n = 1.416 (residents) and n = 708 (parachutists) for Denmark and n = 828 (residents) and n = 14 (parachutists) for Norway.

particular, what we have named the residential linkage is not sufficiently studied, considering the variations that can be found with regard to this variable, cf. Section 7.3 above.

This lack of scholarly attention is even more surprising in the light of the modest exploratory studies contained in this chapter. We have discovered that a substantial part of parliamentarians all over Western Europe do indeed have a geographical connection (either by birth or by residence) to the constituencies from which they are elected to parliament. This fact apparently is considered a natural order, bordering on banality. In those few countries, where time series data are available, our analyses have revealed considerable continuity with regard to the residential linkage. The percentages of *parachutists*, residents, native sons, etc. are not much different today from what they were at the beginning of the democratic era.

This, we argue, is not a political banality, but a remarkable and surprising phenomenon. Why stability in this respect, when most other aspects of the representational linkage have changed considerably? If it is true, that all our societies are undergoing a process of 'modernization', such 'modernization' should also manifest itself in de-territorialization (Kjær and Pedersen, 2004). Where you live, where you come from, and where you are born, are supposed to play a minor role for 'modern man'. Modernization is often associated with a weakening, even break-up, of traditional bonds to geographical locations. From this point of view, we should have expected to find a changing relationship between politicians' residences, birthplaces, and the *locus* of representation, the constituency. The expectation has not been borne out. In this respect, 'modernity' apparently has not yet hit parliamentary representation.

The longitudinal findings are also surprising, when they are seen in the light of institutional changes. All across the countries (with few exceptions) electoral systems have changed; party organizations have undergone considerable change, and so have national systems of communication and transport; reforms have introduced financial and other support for legislators, and their electoral campaigns have changed from local encounters in the town's marketplace to highly sophisticated events, based on the newest electronic developments. Legislators have been given all sorts of support, which should make them able to serve in an international environment and survive globalization. But still they mostly tend to be locally recruited, and those who are not 'native sons', will often be 'homecoming sons', or, at the very least, will have to take up residence somewhere and somehow in the constituency. The local linkage is surviving all over Western Europe. Even in a modern country like Norway, where a legal residential requirement was cancelled more than fifty years ago, it is almost impossible to find species of the *parachutist*.

Our exploratory study, conducted across European countries, as well as over time, has not resulted in clear generalizations, not even in clear-cut propositions for future research. We have confirmed earlier findings about the importance for recruitment of local affiliations and roots. But we have also observed the existence of widespread *parachutage*, open as well as in various disguised forms. The occurrence of this phenomenon is apparently not linked to electoral system properties or other institutional factors, neither cross-nationally, nor in a longitudinal perspective. We are left with a puzzle looking for solutions!

The puzzle can be summarized in (at least) nine questions:

1. What make the gatekeepers in the nominating organizations, that is the local branches of the political party choose the 'local' or the 'foreign' candidate in specific situations and contexts? Are cost-benefit considerations dominating, or are the gatekeepers under the spell of tradition?
2. How do the formal and, in particular, the informal power structure in the party, the balance between the central and the local level of the party organization, operate in the recruitment process? Do decentralized nomination processes (always) favour the *native son*?
3. How do the voters evaluate, and to what extent are they allowed to influence, the geographical dimension—is the high percentage of candidates and

representatives with local affiliation due to the voters' preferences or is it mainly a spillover from the nomination phase?

4. To what extent, if at all, do different electoral systems, constituency size, distribution formulae, openness or closedness of lists, and other institutional factors influence the geographical distributions?

5. Is the occurrence of *parachutage* related to party or party type, or is it, when it occurs, a universal phenomenon?

6. Is it true, that *parachutage* normally works to the advantage of candidates from the Metropolitan area or from other political centres, that is, meaning that candidates residing in London, Paris, Copenhagen, etc. have better nomination— and election chances than other candidates?

7. Which candidates will benefit from modernization processes (improved travel and communication situations, *nationalization* of the electoral campaign, etc.)—the residents of the Capital or candidates coming from other parts of the country?

8. What are the consequences for the socio-political characteristics of the various types of candidates? Is it so, that *parachutists* tend to be younger and better educated? Do *residents*, and in particular *native sons*, have more local political experience?

9. To what extent is *parachutage* real? How often do the parachutists retreat, when the operation is completed—when the seat is captured? Do they, for example, try to exploit the incumbency advantage and move to a more secure or a more centrally located constituency?

We invite the reader—and, hopefully, future scholars—to consider these questions, which all deal with the geographical linkage, and which all need (and deserve) to be answered.

ENDNOTE

1   The authors wish to thank the Danish *Magtudredning* and Norwegian *NSD* for financial support and other kinds of help. Section 7.6 is a revised and very much condensed version of an article published in the Norwegian *Tidsskrift for Samfunnsforskning* (Pedersen et al. 2004).

Part II

Variations across Party Families

8

The Changing Nature and Role of European Conservative Parties in Parliamentary Institutions from 1848 to the Twenty-first Century

Valerie Cromwell and Luca Verzichelli

8.1. QUESTIONS, EXPECTATIONS, AND RATIONALE OF THE CHAPTER

The present chapter focuses on a party family, that of *conservative parties*, whose distinctiveness is today particularly hard to define within the European context. Nevertheless, a long-term analysis of European parliamentary elites transformation cannot avoid, for two good reasons, a close look to this party family. First, the criterion of the 'persistent relevancy' of such a party family is an important reason. Although the overall 'weight' of parties, which define themselves as *conservatives* has been declining over time, a group of European centre-right parties, relatively autonomous from the core values of other families, and relatively consistent with the definition of a *conservative party* has never disappeared, and has been perceived by comparative analysts as an important and sufficiently spread model of party. In the third edition of their textbook Michael Gallagher, Michael Laver, and Peter Mair even argue that the performance of this party family has recently improved, since 'they have begun to poll an even bigger share of votes than Christian Democracy parties' (2006: 217). Second, the historical evolution of this group of parties within parliamentary institutions indicates several important features about the whole evolution of representative elites in Europe. According to a classical view, the 'conservatives' have represented, in a large part of the continent, the party of the 'old establishment', which had to face the 'dilemma' of democratization, having on one side to defend (at least partly) the pre-democratic institutional arrangements and interests, and on the other to participate in the emergence of the new democratic environment where, with the expansion of democratic rights, certain social groups and interests were by definition becoming increasingly minoritarian. An analysis of the original features of conservative MPs in the different European parliamentary institutions is therefore an important test evaluating how the 'incumbents' responded to this political dilemma and which common or country-specific peculiarities of the political elites were the result of this challenge during the crucial phases of democratization.

Within the common confines of the basic dilemma of moderate right party elites—how to accept on going change in the world of representation without abandoning the basic values of the 'traditional' establishment—there have been however important variations. The specific objects of conservatives' concerns were not everywhere the same. In Britain, the traditional establishment had long been 'parliamentarised', in other countries it was however markedly characterized by the ideas of an absolutist or semi-absolutist monarchy. Moreover, the links with other ideologies and 'political discourses' varied greatly from one country to another. The willingness to come to terms with liberalism, within a new 'parliamentary view', for instance, took different forms in Europe. According to the literature, this has determined three main 'types' of conservatism.

The first type is the 'liberal conservatism', a category developed on the specific example of the traditional moderate right in the UK. The second type is the 'Nordic conservatism'[1], which combines the typical socio-economic claim of conservatism with an emphasis on the defence of the 'urban upper-middle class' and the state establishment (Rokkan 1970a, 1970b).[2] A third possible model is that of 'authoritative conservatism', a more composite (and younger) group of parties which would have developed in the countries where the 'centre right' could offer an alternative to the left or to the liberal parties centred on a charismatic leadership, a renovated claim for national unity and pride and, when necessary, a populist style. The Gaullist party, formed at the beginning of the Fifth Republic, should be, together with the Irish *Fianna Fáil,* a prototype of this subgroup.

A further theme (inevitably connected to the previous one) which makes the question of 'conservative representation' an interesting puzzle is that of the relationship with the state and the private sectors. Did conservatives represent the party of defence of the private sector or of the state and its authority against revolutionary challenges? Of course, the question should be rephrased today, as the relationship between political representation and public sector has been deeply changed under the long-term effects of the state bureaucratization and, on the other side, by the party cartelization (Cotta and Tavares de Almeida in this volume). However, the delicate relationship with the public sector (and, in particular, with the higher civil service elites) has been, under the claims of a neoliberal message (Magnette 2003), a critical theme also for the new or renewed conservative parties from the 1970s onwards. Taking some of the concepts developed in the study of party organizational change, one should propose a number of possible distinctions: from the classic conservative catch-all party to the transformation in a form of 'cartel' party, and then to the emergence of some centre-right parties dominated by new 'notables' if not by 'alternative elites', including an increasing number of leaders coming from the economic elite and the media.

These considerations lead us to stress the need to combine, in our analysis, a comprehensive diachronic account of the parliamentary elite transformations *within* this party family, together with an accurate look to the degree of 'distinctiveness' of the conservative party family as a whole, vis-à-vis other clusters of European parties also found in the centre-right side of the political spectrum. This research framework is not new, since the cross-party family comparison has been a typical concern in many studies of centre-right and moderate parties in Europe (Kirchner 1988; Wilson 1998). Moreover, in doing this we adopt a method quite consistent and coherent with the analyses provided in the other 'party-family' related chapters in this volume.[3]

We hope to shed light on the difference/similarities among the profiles of the original conservative parties and the liberal (particularly the right-liberal) ones. It is to be expected that, during the early times of democratization, the two groups of representatives could have shown a clear difference in their parliamentary recruitment, corresponding to their different 'social targets' and political agenda. However, some of these differences might have been expected to be somehow reduced or changed in the first decades of the twentieth century, when the socialist threat became real and the relationship between conservatives and liberal turned generally from competition to cooperation, or at least to be transformed into a competition 'to represent strongly similar interests' and to reach the same strata of more complex (and complete) electoral bodies.

The evolution of European party systems in the second half of the twentieth century requires also a broader comparison: in fact, the typical puzzle for analysts of centre-right parties in the age of 'consolidated' democracies has been the 'survival' of traditional conservatism under the pressure of a number of new competitors: new parties (in same cases the heirs to the older conservative parties), which have tried to approach the moderate voters by adding to their appeal elements of 'other' political messages, including liberalism, national culture, and confessional identity. The dilemma has not been completely solved. However, there is a great deal of agreement among scholars on a general interpretation. Depending on a mix of variables, including the cultural tradition, the degree of secularization and the extent of the 'challenge' from the other mass parties (namely the socialist and social democratic parties), the moderate centre-right vote in Europe has been characterized either by a difficult 'competition' among a few parties sharing some of the values of traditional conservatism, or by the disappearance of the traditional conservatives, in those countries where a new 'catch-all' party could attract the totality or at least a large part of the moderate voters. In both cases, there is a difficulty. Where a conservative party survives, its 'weight' can make the difference: smaller conservative formations operating in a multidimensional party system together with other centre-right formations tend to have a different political and social target by comparison with a 'big' conservative party monopolizing this side of the political spectrum (a situation empirically observable only in the significant British case). This is, of course, expected to produce effects on the representative profile of conservative parliamentarians, which could vary from the representation of a small social niche to that of a broader part of society. In other cases, it is necessary to understand to what extent the new 'winners', normally classified as *Right Liberals* or *Christian Democrats,* are still able to take the semblance (and incorporate corresponding values) of a neoconservative party.[4]

Therefore, it is important to look closely at the convergences/divergences among the three *spiritual families*—Conservatives, Christian Democrats, and Right liberals—populating the moderate camp after 1950, in order to produce a systematic comparison in the degree of internal cohesion which one can observe in the structure of their parliamentary elites.

Given this mainly descriptive but somewhat complex framework of questions and expectations, the chapter is organized as follows. First, the long-term parliamentary impact of the parties here coded as *conservatives* is described. Second, a general description of the 'original' profiles of parliamentary recruitment of conservative MPs is given. Third, a broad interpretation of the main cross-national variations among conservative parliamentary parties in the course of the twentieth century is attempted followed by a broader comparison taking in consideration the other party families mentioned above. Finally, we shall present the main implications drawn from this diachronic and cross-national analysis.

8.2. THE FORTUNES OF CONSERVATIVE PARTIES WITHIN EUROPEAN PARLIAMENTS

Table 8.1 provides a detailed list of those parties, which have been coded as 'conservative' by our national experts, providing names, acronyms, and a short note on the timing of parliamentary presence. It should be noted that, the coding scheme used in this project only partially fits with the several (and often contradictory) classifications proposed in earlier literature. However, the selective and differentiated comparison presented (sometimes considering even other parties which have been coded differently and therefore are not listed in the table) will be broad enough to cope with this definitional problem.

In defining the object of the analysis, it is important to check whether the data available are sufficient to study the long-term transformation of parliamentary recruitment in this group of parties. Table 8.1 in its last column shows that the information is reasonably complete (although not fully homogeneous) and the parties included in the table can be considered sufficiently representative of both the group of traditional conservatives[5] and also of a good number of *liberal-conservative* or *neoconservative* parties[6] (Girvin 1988; Raniolo 2000).

Figure 8.1 shows the effective relevance (in terms of parliamentary seats) achieved by conservative parties between 1870 and 1950. The difference between

TABLE 8.1. *Parties coded as belonging to the 'conservative' party family*

Country	Acronym-original name (translation)	Parliamentary presence	Covered in the DATACUBE
Denmark	Nationalliberale (Liberal National party), H, Højre (Right party) KF, Det Konservative Folkeparti (Conservative party) Bondepartiet, Uafhængige, Dansk Folkeparti, Fremskridtspartiet (Progress people's party)	1916–...	Yes
Finland	KoK, Kansallinen Kokoomus (National Coalition party)	1907–...	Yes
France	(Several Monarchist, Bonapartist, and Boulangiste formations)	Third Republic (1871–14)	Yes
	Indépendants (independents) Indépendants et Paysans (national independents)	Third Republic (1919–39)	Yes
	UNR, Union pour la Nouvelle République UDR, Union pour la Défense de la République RPR, Rassemblement pour la République UMP, Union pour une Majorité Populaire	Fifth Republic (1958–...)	Some data
Germany	Café Milan, Panser Hof	1848–49	Yes
	Konservative Partei (Conservative party)	1867–1918	
	Deutsche Konservative Partei (German conservative party)	1867–1918	
	Deutsche Nationale Volkspartei DNVP (German National People's party)	1918–33	
Hungary	(various movements)	1884–1939	Yes
	MDF (Hungarian Democratic Forum)	From 1990	Yes
	Fidesz/MPSZ	From 1998	
Italy	Destra Storica (Conservative fraction of the *liberal elite*)	—	Almost complete
Netherlands	Conservatieven (Conservatives)	1849–88	Yes
Norway	H, Hoyre (the Right)	1884–...	Yes
Portugal	Partido Regenerador (Monarchists)	1834–1910	Some data
	Others (Republican Evolutionist, Republican Liberal party, Republican Nationalist party)	1910–23	
Spain	Conservative Party (Conservative party)	1876–1923	Some data
	UCD, Union Centro-democratica (Democratic Centre Union)	1977–89	Almost
	AP-PP, Alianza Popular–Partido Popular (Popular party)	1977 –...	complete
UK	Conservative party	1848–...	Almost complete

the historical impact of conservatism in UK, in comparison to the rest of Europe, is clear. The figure, indeed, also clearly indicates the parliamentary consolidation and stability of the British conservative party, only temporarily endangered by the electoral defeats of the post-Churchill era. In contrast, in the other

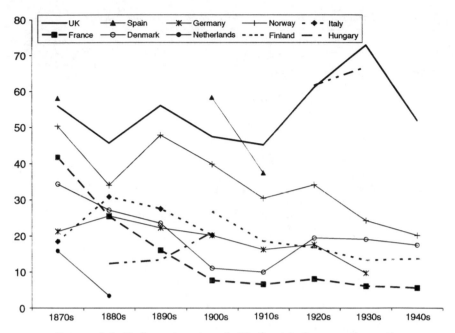

FIGURE 8.1. Parliamentary strength (% of seats) of conservative parties

Note: Decade means (1870–1950).

European countries in the first part of the period considered in this study, the initial conservative position was soon followed by a significant decline leading them in the end to a more stabilized but minority position. In two cases at least, the breakdown of parliamentary parties belonging to this family is seen: the Dutch Conservatives disappeared before the turn of the twentieth century and the early 'pure' conservative-liberal party group in Italy was a few years later absorbed by a more clearly 'liberal' concentration of pro-governmental politicians (*ministeriali*) during the Giolittian age.[7]

In the second half of the twentieth century and the first years of the twenty-first century, a different trend can be seen (Figure 8.2). Here, three phenomena are remarkable, the resurgence of many parties of the conservative family in the years of crisis and retrenchment of the welfare states, the recent decline (paradoxically enough, if one considers other classical conservatives and the past successes) of the British *conservatives*,[8] and the emergence of new parties, in some cases defined as with a clearly majoritarian and governmental orientation in Spain and Italy.[9]

8.3. THE ORIGINAL PROFILE OF CONSERVATIVE PARLIAMENTARY RECRUITMENT

The first key questions which must be considered are the following: which were the main features in the parliamentary elite of the 'original' conservative

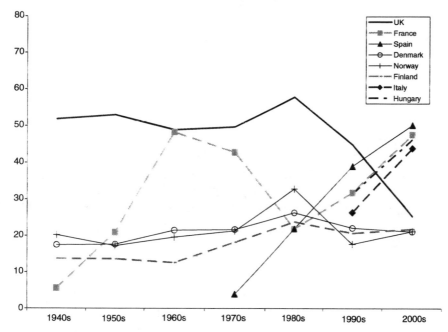

FIGURE 8.2. Parliamentary strength (% of seats) of conservative parties

Note: Decade means (1940–2005).

parties? What was their degree of homogeneity across countries? The graphs built on the bases of decade means answers the first question, as it is relatively easy to recognize some specific characteristics at work in the early practices of parliamentary recruitment among these parties. For instance, the relevance of nobility, of a high level of education and the limited impact of lawyers can be seen (Figures 8.3, 8.4, and 8.5).

The weight of a university education shows some interesting deviations. The Norwegian Conservatives are characterized by the lowest levels; it must be said however that by including at least 40 per cent of members with a higher degree or equivalent, this party group shows a quite remarkable profile in a country where the level of higher education in the parliament is generally low compared to other European countries (Best and Cotta 2000). In terms of education, the Conservative party in the UK has remained, until the 1980s, much more elitist by comparison with the Scandinavian countries and Hungary after 1989. Overall, in more recent years a picture of a narrowing spread of educational recruitment patterns in Conservative parties emerges. Originally, in the early part of the period under consideration, the European gentry, who provided the backbone of Conservative parties, were less likely to have had a university education, but these parties gradually became more middle-class oriented and consequently better educated.

The distribution of the percentages of lawyers on a country by country basis is also somewhat heterogeneous. However, with the exception of the two early

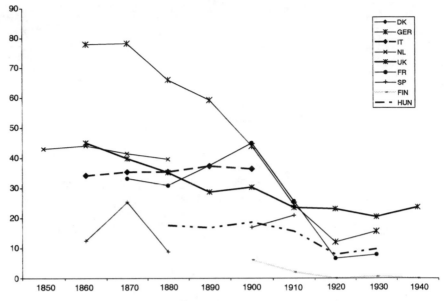

FIGURE 8.3. Nobility among conservative MPs (%)

Note: Decade means (1850–1950).

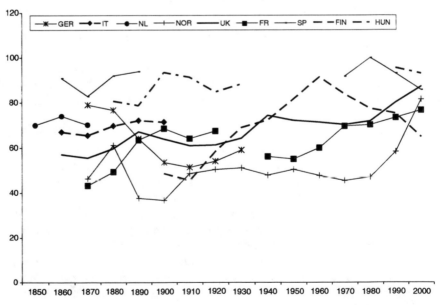

FIGURE 8.4. University background among conservative MPs (%)

Note: Decade means (1850–2005).

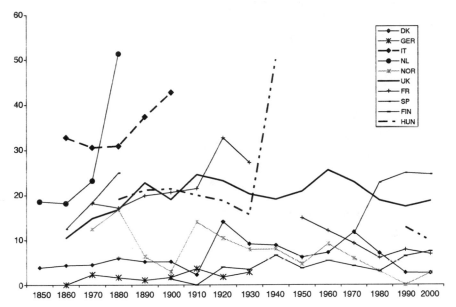

FIGURE 8.5. Lawyers among conservative MPs (%)

Note: Decade means (1850–2005).

short-lived 'conservative parliamentary parties' of the Netherlands and Italy, the impact of lawyers in this group since the very early phase of democratization is relatively weak, with the partial exception of the British conservative MPs (and of the French parties before the Second World War), where the legal profession background always concern about 20 per cent of parliamentarians.

Another interesting, and somehow surprising, variation among the original profiles of conservative MPs concerns their links with the primary sector (a most likely indicator of the typical social stratum of the *rentiers*) (Figure 8.6). The surprise lies in the fact that among British conservatives the weight of this background declines much earlier by comparison with the trends in other countries, where the primary sector had not been considered a significant social basis of party support. This is the case with the conservatives in Nordic countries, which in the first decades analysed showed a limited primary sector background.

Figure 8.7, which focuses on the representation of higher civil servants, shows another general feature of this party family, but also a clear variability among its members. The general trend is that of a decline of this background during the phase of full democratization, with many of the European conservative parties declining after the First World War to levels of only about 10 per cent of 'high public officers' among their parliamentary ranks.[10] In the overall picture there is a strong hiatus between two groups of countries: on one side the German and the Norwegian conservatives which, in the last decades of the nineteenth

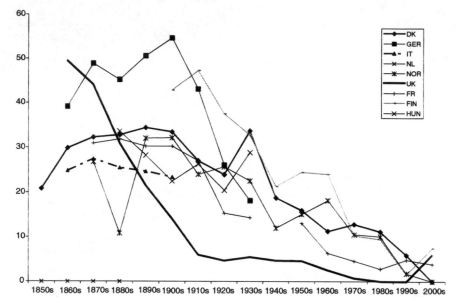

FIGURE 8.6. Conservative MPs with a primary sector background (%)

Note: Decade means (1850–2005).

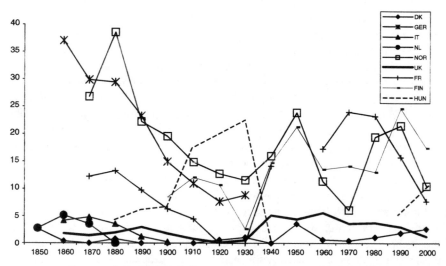

FIGURE 8.7. Higher civil servants among conservative MPs (%)

Note: Decade means (1850–2005).

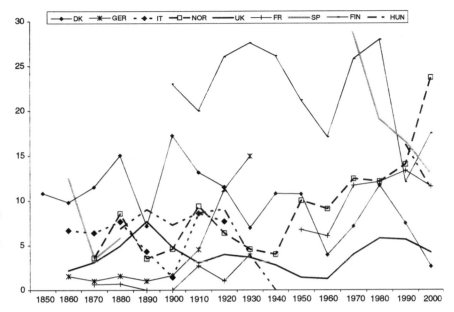

FIGURE 8.8. Teacher/professors among conservative MPs (%)

Note: Decade means (1850–2005).

century, *strongly* represented the bureaucratic elite; on the other side the British and Danish conservatives clearly embodied an opposite model of a conservative party, the model of the 'private sector' defender, promoted by primary sector elites and by entrepreneurs. By the 1920s as a result of the strong downward trend of this indicator in Germany and Norway differences diminished significantly, but without completely disappearing.

Finally, in the early decades of this party family the proportion of *teachers* and *professors* (Figure 8.8) does not seem a typical characteristic with the exception of the Finnish conservatives. In the UK, this indicator has been declining since the 1880s until the late twentieth century, making this party, for a long time, as less tending to recruit MPs with such an occupational background.

On the contrary, Figure 8.9 demonstrates that the business and managerial background, although initially limited in its overall weight, has played an increasing role in the development of conservative elites. In particular, one notices in the UK the increasing numbers and predominance of conservative MPs with business interests. A similar trend is present in Norway until the Second World War). It is important to add that the relevance of businessmen in the UK Conservative party has persisted from the last third of the nineteenth century to the present, unlike other parties, where the tendency seems to have been for them to cut the more direct links with business. In the UK, the tendency in the nineteenth century was for landed families to take up business interests and this was reflected in

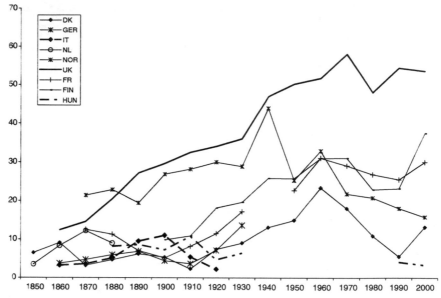

FIGURE 8.9. Conservative MPs with manager/business occupational background (%)

Note: Decade means (1850–2005).

the composition of the Conservative party. In 1879, about 20 per cent of Dutch conservative parliamentarians were businessmen and in Norway in 1880 the level was similar (28.6%), while in the UK in 1880 there were only 12.8 per cent businessmen and those linked to the primary sector were much more numerous (47.3%) than in the Netherlands and Norway. By 1906, the percentages for the UK were being steadily reversed: 29 per cent were businessmen and 14.8 per cent were primary sector. And this trend has persisted: in 1935, 38.9 per cent were businessmen and 5.7 per cent in the primary sector; in 1970, 56 per cent and 1.2 per cent, and in 1997, 56 per cent vis-à-vis no representatives from the primary sector. Among French conservatives the role of the primary sector, quite relevant at the beginning, declines, while that of businessmen and managers increases, although slowly, thus confirming what has been argued by Jean Garrigues (1997) about the importance of businessmen in late nineteenth century (and also during the twentieth century) French politics.

All in all, a number of characteristics shared by the first European conservative parties have emerged, demonstrating their orientation to 'protect' a quite well defined 'social target' and their readiness to *resist* the challenges raised by the new prototypical mass party organizations. However, with the passing of time the evolution of each of these parties towards a new organizational format, somehow 'forced' by the emergence of mass politics and by the effects of the enfranchisement of larger sections of the population, has also determined somewhat different patterns of parliamentary recruitment. The British party and perhaps the Danish conservatives seem to represent, from this point of view, a clearly different 'machine': many of its characteristics are quite different from those of the fellow members of the conservative party family on the continent. Originally, the differences have to be linked to the historical legacy of the parliamentary fraction originally labelled 'Tory party' in the late seventeenth century.[11] However, against the background of the great extension of the franchise and at the same time of the massive economic and social change, the British Conservative party demonstrated great vitality.

With the extension of the franchise came the steady growth of extra-parliamentary party organization at constituency level in all British political parties, and the peculiar adaptation of a 'traditionalist' elite to the model of 'mass politics' under the *first past the post* electoral system, which becomes an exception in Europe after 1918. These factors can explain the persistence of some peculiarities in the British segment of European conservatives.

The data do not contradict what S. M. Lipset and S. Rokkan had argued many years ago, about the transversal effect of the internal social and economic cleavages, leading to the development of parties with similar attitudes to government and to the emergence of what can be seen as a party family. But they also support the argument (stressed originally by Duverger and in other more recent works) of the need to specify what specific 'mission' had characterized each conservative party in its interaction with a given political system.

But a second interesting implication, consistent with the neo-institutional theory about the impact of the 'opportunity structure' in the process of party recruitment (Norris 1997a, 1997b), is that the phenomenon of parliamentary elite transformation cannot be studied without keeping under consideration a number of variables which are exogenous and cannot be controlled by the 'elite selector' in each party or party family. The different size of the British conservative party, together with the specific 'rules of the game' of that political system, can therefore explain some of the features of parliamentary recruitment in this party, when compared to the other centre-right parties of Europe. This point is again considered in Section 8.4 devoted to the parliamentary recruitment of 'modern conservatives'.

8.4. CONSERVATIVE POLITICIANS IN THE AGE OF 'CATCH-ALL PARTIES': TOWARDS A 'CENTRE-RIGHT' PATTERN OF RECRUITMENT?

After the Second World War, the party family of European conservatives has seen its overall weight decline (Figure 8.2), but it has maintained its presence in many party systems. Among the countries covered by our study, the British conservatives have continued to be one of the two most important parties in their political system, alternating in government with the Labour party. Three other country's conservative parties, Norway, Denmark, and Finland, have maintained a quite significant rate of votes/seats and a relevant role within their respective party systems.

To these parties, one must add the important experience of the French conservatives. The formation of a new party of the centre-right dated 1958, when the 'Union for the New Republic', was formed to support the new regime and its leader General de Gaulle, led to the gathering together of various conservative, nationalist, right liberal, and technocratic forces. This party won a relative majority of seats in the National Assembly from 1958 to 1981, 1986 to 1988, and from 1993 to 1997. In 1997, the number of seats held by the conservatives dropped from 257 to 140. Recent years have seen greater party fragmentation. It is however clear that, though the major French parties are still weaker than their British and German equivalents, they are currently much stronger than in the past. In 2002, President Chirac's centre-right party, now known as the *Union for the Presidential Majority*, emerged as a significant victor over the left alliance. This has also been classified as a conservative party.

It is important on the one hand, to seek for evidence and factors explaining the lines of similarity among the recruitment processes developed by these conservative formations. On the other hand, the aim is to combine a necessarily synthetic diachronic analysis of 'traditional' conservative parties with a more accurate look to the process of 'contamination', taking place during the second half of the twentieth century, among the different 'souls' of the European centre-right.

From the point of view of the 'time factor', a certain degree of change must be expected during the long term or, at least, some hints of the reactions and responses shown by the parliamentary elites of conservative parties to the challenges which emerged during the phase of the cold war (Layton-Henry 1982; von Beyme 1985). These challenges determined, in fact, a deep crisis of consensus for conservative and centre-right parties, linked to the rise of the social-democratic and left-liberal consensus. The crisis was particularly evident in UK, and it [change to was to be overcome only during the 1980s, with the phase of the 'resurgence of conservative discourse' (Girvin 1988).

At the end of this decade, the conservative parties might have become much more 'integrated' into the galaxy of the European centre-right: in fact, during the nineties, many of these parties would transmigrate into the European Peoples Party (at least, in the eyes of observers of the European Parliament), and there might be signs of a real 'convergence' between the two party families.[12] Gallagher, Laver, and Mair (2001: 218) argue that the conservative category of parties tends to become an alternative to CD parties, and it is weak or inexistent where the secular conservatism is not strong enough to justify the persistence of such a claim. On the other hand, if the data about party polarization is considered—for instance the comparative assessment provided by Reuven Hazan (1997) for his research on 'central' parties—it is easy to discover that in many cases the 'ratios' of conservative and neoconservative parties are closer to the

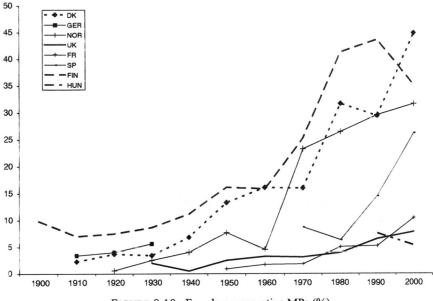

FIGURE 8.10. Female conservative MPs (%)

Note: Decade means (1900–2005).

Right Liberal parties (called by some Liberal-conservatives) in the 'moderate right' sector of the left-right scale, while Christian Democracies tend to occupy the 'central sector'.[13]

This complex evolution justifies the choice to abandon the logic of the country by country comparison within a fixed number of cases previously considered as 'conservative', and to take into consideration a selected set of parties from a broader universe (see below Section 8.5).

Let's start with the diachronic evolution of these parties. Returning to the figures already discussed for the early decades of the period, it is clear that the core group of European conservative parties has tended to remain quite 'homogeneous' in its different national delegations: the Figures 8.4 (university background), 8.5 (lawyers), 8.6 (primary sector), and 8.7 (higher civil servants) show rather stable trends in all the countries, and when a transformation over the period 1950–2000 is clear as in the case of the decline of primary sector background, it is almost perfectly replicated among the different cases.

The thesis of a quite homogeneous transformation in the pattern of parliamentary recruitment is also confirmed—apart from the different evolution of the Nordic parties as is clearly shown in Figure 8.10—by the analysis of two indicators not included in the previous set of figures, because linked to the elite profile in the age of mature democracy. The first one is the inclusion of female representatives, and the second the percentage of full paid party or trade union

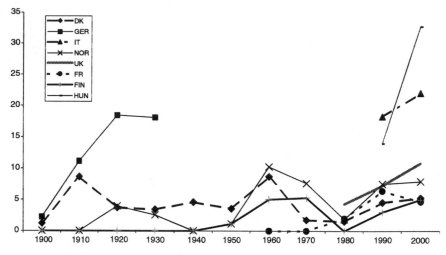

FIGURE 8.11. Full paid politicians among conservative MPs (%)

Note: Decade means (1900–2005).

officers. In comparison with the classic British and French conservatives, Hungary seems to follow the pattern of the Nordic countries, as does Spain which, under the modernization of the *Partido popular* after the breakdown of UDC, has moved speedily towards Nordic levels. Thus, the country-specific effects (including phenomena of 'contagion' from the left to the right parties), can determine some evident variation in the profile of specific cases. With regard to the participation of female legislators in current Conservative parties, there has been a growing gap between two groups, on the one hand Finland, Denmark, and Norway, and, on the other, France, Hungary, Italy, and the UK. Since the late 1970s until the late 1990s, Finland has stood out well above the average of the other countries.

As for what concerns the weight of professional politicians in parliament, a much more homogeneous trend (Figure 8.11) is found. The two major deviations in recent years come, significantly, from two newcomers in the conservative family (*Alleanza Nazionale* in Italy and the Hungarian conservatives), which originated from previous and nationally specific experiences, and therefore show quite a different party organization from the typically 'light' structure of more traditional European conservatives.

As already discussed at the beginning of this section, the degree of homogeneity among historical European conservatives in the second half of the twentieth century was a largely expected phenomenon, and, in the end, it is also a relatively interesting one, being related to a limited number of parties which had already lost, with the only remarkable exception of the British party, their 'predominance' on the centre-right of the political spectrum. In order to understand to what extent conservatives are *still* different it is important to consider a broader political area, the whole sector of the European 'centre-right parties', comparing the overall

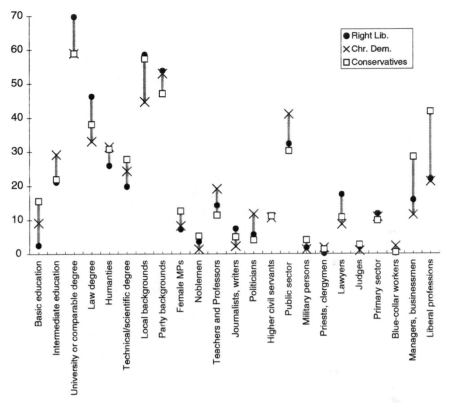

FIGURE 8.12. Characteristics of three families of European MPs

Note: Weighted average values (1950–89).

means of the three party families,—Conservatives, Right liberals, and Christian democrats—which belong to this area, for a series of variables included in the DATACUBE data-set. The results for this study, concerning the period 1950–90, are graphically reported in Figure 8.12.

The first immediate result from this broad array of data suggests rather clearly that there are three *very close* profiles of parliamentary recruitment. The distance between the three families is rather limited on all the indicators, and lower than ten percentage points for most of them. Two indicators, however, show a more evident difference between the profile of conservative parliamentarians and that of the two other groups. One is the relative tendency of the conservative parties to attribute less weight to higher education as a relevant factor of parliamentary recruitment. The second deviant element is the clear tendency among conservatives to select a large number of MPs from the world of the 'private sector', namely businessmen and managers and free professionals, above all in fields different from the law, since the recruitment of lawyers is still more typical among the liberals.

It is clear that until 1945 conservative parties were the ones with a more evident inclination to select from the social and occupational groups of the 'traditional establishment' (i.e. noblemen, military officers, judges). However, these categories are less and less represented in all the European parliaments and, in any case, the distance from the other parties of the centre-right seems on the way to become insignificant during the second half of the twentieth century.

It should be noted that conservative party organizations seem to be 'weaker' than the other centre-right formations, if one looks to the classic indicators of political professionalism. Indeed, if the local elective backgrounds are more typical of these parties in comparison to Right liberals and Christian democrats,[14] the indicators of previous party experience and of the numbers of full-time political officials are both lower among conservatives than in the two other party families.

8.5. THE RECENT 'NEOCONSERVATIVE' ELITE

Thus far, the trend of historical evolution of a relatively homogeneous group of parties, including the historical conservative parties and some 'neoconservatism' political parties which appeared after 1950, namely the French Gaullists, has been observed. If all the possible deviations are placed aside, explaining them in the light of different country-specific factors, the main finding which remains on the table is that conservatives have become more and more similar, from the point of view of the parliamentary profile, to the other centre-right political actors, and in particular to the parties defined, in the DATACUBE grid as *right-liberals*. This supports the thesis of a progressive convergence of the political strategies and, somehow, of the electoral targets in all the parties from the centre-right wing (Wilson 1998). It also makes it possible to conceive an organizational change due to a *contagion effect*: this time not a 'contagion from the left', as that occurring according to Duverger during the early twentieth century, but a more specific process of amalgamation between the organizations of the moderate parties.

Such evidence for the period 1950–90 leads to other questions concerning the last fifteen years. Does the process of 'evolution' within the European centre-right elites continue? Does it move in the same direction, after the 'revolutionary' changes during the last decade of the twentieth century, in particular the end of the cold war, economic globalization and the beginning of a new phase in the process of European integration, entailing some degree of *Europeanization* for national political actors? In reaction to these challenges, the political discourse of the right wing has changed significantly and the competition in this area has increased very much entailing, among other things, the success of new extreme right parties and the transformation of some old liberal parties into neo-populist or xenophobic parties (Ignazi 2003).[15]

Is it possible hence to expect that these important events could have also transformed the representative elites of 'moderate parties' in Europe? In this respect, two hypotheses can be advanced. On the one hand, it is possible to hypothesize that the recent period could have determined the '*return*' of strong country-specific effects, evidencing the different 'sensibility' of each party in front of the new challenges. On the other hand, we could look for a new common pattern among some parties or among all of them, a new *fil rouge*, which would reveal the re-establishment of a 'centre-right' (or neoconservative) model of parliamentary recruitment. Among the possible components of this renewed homogeneity, one could indicate a number of elements such as the relative decrease of party professionals and the return of a 'neo-notable' personnel at the end of the cycle of the mass party, a stronger link with the local territory, and the increase in the representation of the upper-middle classes and of social groups from the 'private sector'.

To shed light on the problems raised here, we must leave the strict logic of the DATACUBE definition of 'conservative party' and to select a number of specific parties that, in the last couple of decades, have marked the evolution of the European centre-right, or simply right when the centre is empty politics, distinguishing themselves from any form of anti-system feelings and political extremisms, and defining themselves as 'governing parties'. This criterion is satisfied by several parties; among them the cases fall into three subgroups: (*a*) the 'classic' conservative parties—namely, the British Conservatives, the Norwegian H, the Finnish KoK, and the Danish Kf—already analysed since their beginnings; (*b*) the liberal-conservative parties—namely, the French post-Gaullist MPM, the Hungarian MDF and Fidesz/MPP, and the Spanish PP—already coded as 'conservative parties' in the DATACUBE; (*c*) two Italian parties from the centre-right alliance, as Forza Italia and An (see footnote 9 above) and another important governmental party—the Portuguese PDS—which, despite its name *Social Democratic Party*, is unambiguously positioned in the centre-right.

The first data examined, the indicators about the persistence and the circulation of the representative elites in these parties during the last fifteen years (Table 8.2), immediately suggest a certain degree of caution, since they show a great deal of variability among the different national parties. As a matter of

TABLE 8.2. *Indicators of turnover and persistence of conservative parties (1990–2005)*

	Mean age (years)	Mean age of newcomers (years)	Tenure (parliam. terms)	Newcomers (%)
H (Nor)	47.6	45.9	2.5	33.2
CONS (UK)	48.7	40.3	NA	17.4
Kf (Dk)	47.2	43.6	2.3	32.7
KoK (Fin)	47.3	43.7	2.5	33.5
UMP (Fr)	52.8	49.6	2.8	37.5
MDF-MPSZ (Hun)	43.9	42.4	1.6	55.8
PDS (Por)	42.8	40.7	1.9	41.9
PP (Sp)	46.8	42.5	2.3	40.4
AN (It)	50.0	46.1	2.5	33.3
FI (It)	49.2	49.0	1.6	63.7

fact, such variability was inevitable, since the panel of parties chosen includes old and consolidated formations, relatively young parties (Pds and PP) and even new born parties like the Hungarian centre-right movements and Forza Italia. On the other hand, the degree of renewal is quite evident also in the most established parties, since the rate of newcomers is always higher than 30 per cent with the only exception of the British Conservatives, whose turnover has been frustrated by the decline of 1992, by the landslide defeat of 1997, and by the disappointing result of 2002. The mean age, as well as the rate of seniority, is consequently decreasing. However, quite a difference exists between some parties which seem to opt rather drastically for newcomers of a younger generation (the British conservatives lead the group, followed by the Nordic and the Iberian parties) and the Italian and the French centre-right parties which on the contrary tend to select new MPs but at a relatively older age.[16]

Looking at the distribution of the different political and occupational backgrounds in the conservative MPs elected in the last fifteen years, we can see a high degree of fuzziness emerging from the data. Each party seems to follow its own 'path' and, even in such a short time span, rather evident fluctuations are present in many trends. Once more, this result should hardly come as a surprise if one remembers the presence of 'new born' parties, the impact of political crises often precipitated by major national issues and/or transformations in other formations, from the conservatives in Britain to the UMP in France. However, two interesting findings should be noted. First of all, there is a relative degree of homogeneity among the traditional Scandinavian conservative parties, which seem to distance themselves from some of the typical transformations of the 'liberal-conservative' parties, and to keep their own pattern of parliamentary recruitment. Second, British conservatives have maintained in some respects a more 'traditionalist' outlook as, for instance, in the limited inclusion of female representatives, but are also more inclined to follow the road of other centre-right parties in Europe. This appears for instance in the tendency to increase the weight of MPs with professional or business backgrounds.

Two figures, showing the differences between the profile of each single party during the last fifteen years and the overall measures of this group of parties, perfectly depict this variation. Figure 8.13 reports differences between the percentage of female MPs in each conservative party and the mean of all conservative parties in the period 1990–2005. It is easy to see that the 'old parties' of the centre-right, for instance the British Conservatives and the French 'Gaullists', are in this respect still very similar, and confirm the gap of female representation which typically characterizes this sector of the political spectrum. By contrast, the three parties of the 'Nordic Conservative' group are today much more oriented to fill the 'gender gap', and they show a percentage of women elected in parliament which is very close to the mean reached by the left parties of the same countries, during the period under analysis. This clearly shows that a fully 'country (or region-) specific' factor is at work.

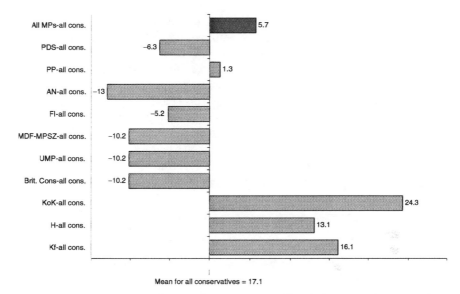

FIGURE 8.13. Differences between the percentage of female MPs in each conservative parties and the mean of all conservative parties (1990–2005)

The following graph (Figure 8.14) shows public sector representation in the conservative parties. A roughly similar picture emerges, but in this case even the behaviour of the Nordic conservatives is conservative, in the sense that they tend to maintain a rather high percentage of state officials among their MPs. Another

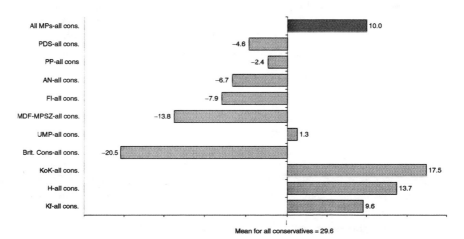

FIGURE 8.14. Differences between the percentage of MPs with a public sector occupational background in each conservative parties and the mean of all conservative parties (1990–2005)

noticeable element is the fact that the under-representation of the public sector unifies most of the conservative parties, both those from the 'first generation' and those formed in the second half of the twentieth century.

In a graph showing percentages of MPs from the 'private sector' the image would be totally reversed. But this does not mean that there is a clear 'pattern' of parliamentary recruitment, since some parties—the British Conservatives, the French Ump, and Forza Italia—are more committed to the selection of business-men and managers, while some are more oriented to the classic 'pool' of the lawyers (the Italian An, the Spanish Pp, and the Portuguese Pds), and finally some others recruit a relatively high percentage of non-legal professionals (the Hungarian conservatives, Ump, but also Forza Italia and Pds).

8.6. CONCLUSIONS

It has here been argued that the parliamentary recruitment of traditional conser-vative parties had a fundamental specificity in the nineteenth and early twentieth centuries. However, such specificity progressively declined. This group of parties, which were significantly strengthened by the arrival of two younger 'generations' of parties, gradually became much more heterogeneous in the second half of the twentieth century. In the recent period, further changes under political pressure have characterized the group of parties currently included in the category of European conservatism. If, in terms of their role within the political system and of their 'policy goals', many of these parties have progressively become more similar to the 'Christian Democratic' image, in many other respects including that of their parliamentary profile, they look more and more like the *Liberal* image or at least, the image of the most rightist of the Liberal parties. This, in a sense, is the end of an historical cycle, since the prototypical notion of Conservatism, that of the party in Britain, emerged in opposition to 'liberalism'.

It is necessary to be cautious in expressing a 'final' evaluation of the legacy of European conservatism. We have indeed seen how many country- and party-specific national and social factors are still at work behind the parliamentary profile of these parties, and that they can explain much more than 'general' trends.

The empirical evidence does not indicate that in the shaping the representative elites of Europe the 'role' of the conservative parties is over. On the contrary, it appears that a number of specific 'peculiarities' shown by conservative elites in their recruitment processes will continue to play a role, although it is difficult to define a strong and self evident 'common pattern'. For instance, new strong governmental parties of the right have emerged in Portugal and in Spain. To these countries Italy can be add: in this case *Forza Italia* is included rather than *Alleanza Nazionale* in the family of conservatism. It has much in common with the current profile of the British Conservatives; probably much more than it has in common with Christian democracies. And this possibly explains the 'good feelings' that seem to reign among these parties which share their style of leadership and a number of policy orientations.[17]

Therefore, the specificity of conservative parties, with their mix of new and old, local and global factors can come back as an important variable in explaining the present and future transformation of representative elites in Europe. This calls for a new set of more precise questions about the perspectives of new centre-right parties and their ability to organize themselves and deal with a changing social and political environment.

ENDNOTES

1 In Girvin's analysis (1988), this is just a subcategory of the former type. According to him, indeed, the historical forms of conservatism are the 'liberal', the 'authoritative', and the 'Christian-democratic' conservatism, which is here individuated as an alternative, although in some respects very close, family (see below).

2 The names of the historical Nordic conservative parties, simply 'Right' or 'National Coalition' recall this different vision. Broad descriptions of the evolution of these parties can be found in Berglund and Lindström (1982); Faurby and Kristensen (1982); Kristiansen and Svåsand (1982).

3 We want to refer in particular, to the analyses provided in this book by Ruostetsaari on Liberal parties and Verzichelli on Christian Democrats.

4 On this point, there is a certain disagreement among scholars involved in the classification of centre-right parties. We have taken this notion of 'neoconservatism' by an excellent research published in Italian by Francesco Raniolo (2000). According to him, should be classified as *neoconservatives* many parties from the centre-right liberalism (Austrian FPØ, German FDP, the Dutch VVD, and others) which in the Cube are coded as 'Right Liberals'.

5 Among the historical conservative parties, only the Swedish MSP (*Moderate Samlingspartiet*) is missing. It is the heir of an old conservative tradition started with the Yeoman's Party at the end of the nineteenth century. In 1935, the Yeoman's and Burgher's party merged with the National party to form the Conservative party, *Riksdaghögern*. Until then the Conservatives received about 25% of the votes in each of the four parliamentary elections after the introduction of universal suffrage. Since the 1936 election, their average proportion of the vote has hovered around 15%. After 1945, the party moved to the right and persisted in opposing welfare reforms. After three consecutive electoral losses, the party changed its name to the Moderate Coalition party and moved more to the centre (Berglund and Lindström 1982).

6 Some parties usually associated to the *neoconservative* stream cannot be analysed here (or in other chapters of this volume) because the CUBEDATA has until now failed in including their countries: this applies to the Austrian FPÖ (*Freiheitliche Partei Österreichs*), the PRL/PVV (*Parti Réformateur Liberal/Partij voor Vrijheid end Vooruitgang*) in Belgium, and ND (*Nea Demokratia*) in Greece.

7 It is worthwhile to remember that, according to many historians, the a pure centre-right parliamentary party disappeared with *trasformismo* (a phenomenon by which the government managed to promote a large conglomeration of different and previously opposed parliamentary streams of the centre and centre-right to support the government and to oppose the new emerging left) during the second decade of the unitary state. In any case, our country experts have coded the presence of a 'conservative group' in the Italian Parliament during the whole period (1861–1909) in which the original data collected by Paolo Farneti distinguishes a group of centre-right MPs (*destra storica*) opposed to the other 'liberals' (1971).

8 One should remember that this decline comes after two decades of extraordinary majorities (53% in 1979, 58% in 1987, and 52% in 1992) which ended with the massive Labour election victory in 1997. The Conservative strength in the Commons then fell to 25% at both the 1997 and 2001 elections: in 2005, however, it slightly increased to 30.6%.

9   The figures concerning Italy after 1990 in the graph is including both the two elections after the transformation of the old extreme right *Movimento Sociale Italiano* in *Alleanza Nazionale* (1996 and 2001) and *Forza Italia* (1994, 1996, and 2001). This is not consistent with our original coding (Forza Italia was considered a Right Liberal Party), but many recent studies have associated Silvio Berlusconi's party to the family of conservatives (for instance, Raniolo 2000; Gallagher, Laver, and Mair 2003).

10   This is also confirmed by the overall rate of MPs with a public sector occupation background. In this case, the average rate among conservative MPs in the first decade of the twentieth century is about 20%, ten points lower than the average of the whole parliaments in Europe. Moreover, this figure is calculated without counting the British conservatives, which would probably determine a further decrease.

11   The 'Tory' title was first used for those who opposed the exclusion of King James II from the Crown. The party has existed in varying forms since the emergence of identifiable parliamentary parties in the years following the arrival of William III in England in 1688 and 'The Glorious Revolution'. For virtually the whole of the eighteenth century, the party was in opposition to Whig parties, which formed administrations for most of the century till the 1780s. In that period with a very limited parliamentary franchise it was difficult to distinguish much difference in the social and economic background of MPs in the different party groupings.

12   The literature on this theme is quite large, particularly concerning the parties within the European Parliament and the European People's Party. See Del Wit (2003) for a recent analysis.

13   However, even this is not a universal 'law'. In Germany, at least during the nineties, the liberal FDP has been positioned in a 'central' placement while the CDU-CSU on the moderate-right side.

14   But this is a clearly an effect due to two parties in particular: the Norwegian and the Finnish conservatives, which (together with the French Gaullists) show a very pronounced rate of local elective experience.

15   The effects of these transformations on the parliamentary elites will be not analysed here. Cfr. Chapter 12.

16   In the case of AN this was quite expectable, since the party shows a rather 'old' political elite tracing its roots in the experience of the traditional neo-fascist Msi. The example of Forza Italia is, on the other hand, more interesting, because it shows the alternative selection in this party, which recruits either among the 'professional' and 'economic elite' strata of the population or among politicians with a long experience in the second ranks of different centrist parties from the 'first republic'.

17   For instance, the position on Europe determines a certain distance from many Conservative parties and many CD parties. While we were concluding the writing of this chapter, the British Conservatives were discussing the proposal to detach themselves from the European People's Party group in the European Parliament. This would mean a clear inversion in the path of convergence between the two party families, started with the early 1990s.

9

Restructuring of the European Political Centre: Withering Liberal and Persisting Agrarian Party Families

Ilkka Ruostetsaari

In general one can distinguish between two approaches to party ideologies. The difference between them lies in the assumed responsiveness of parties to the opinions of voters; while the first approach is focused on the competitiveness of parties, the second pursues an institutional approach. The first approach which owes much to the ideas of Anthony Downs is associated with authors who relate party ideology to spatial competition between parties. In his *Economic Theory of Democracy* (1957), Downs makes use of the idea of the political spectrum where there is a left-wing and a right-wing position on political issues and intermediate positions between them (Ware 2001: 18). Even if this approach conforms with our everyday notions of 'left' and 'right' in politics, there are, nonetheless, reasons for arguing that it fails to capture subtle but important differences between parties which are thus in danger of being lumped together within one 'party family'. One major problem with this approach is that party programmes embrace only certain aspects of party ideologies. In other words, a programme is a party's 'public face'; it is what the party says it wants to do (ibid. 20).

The second approach to party ideologies does not deny that they can be understood in terms of left and right on the political spectrum. However, this approach does not see parties merely as institutions which respond to the opinions of voters but as institutions which may be also governed by much older beliefs and values originating from the founding period of the party. In view of this, we should not analyse party positions on the basis of a present spatial dimension but according to the origins of different parties. That most European parties can be seen as part of an identifiable 'family' is a result of the circumstances at the time of their founding. Such circumstances included the claim to defend particular kinds of interest which were not restricted to one country. The political scientist who has most prominently influenced this tradition is Klaus von Beyme. Focusing his analysis on the European liberal democracies von Beyme (1985) identifies nine major party groups—or *familles spirituelles*—as he calls them—under which most of the parties can be classified (ibid. 22).[1] Although no two political parties are quite the same in different countries, the parties in particular groups share considerable family resemblances. According to Gallagher et al. (1995: 181), three characteristics can be used to define different party families in Europe.

First, parties can be grouped according to some shared 'genetic' origin—parties which were mobilized in similar historical circumstances or with the intention of representing a similar interest can be treated as having a distinct resemblance to each other. On these grounds, for example, all agrarian parties can be considered to belong to the same family. The second set of family resemblances is defined by the parties themselves in terms of the way in which they forge links across national borders. Such links may take the form of transnational federations such as that established by various liberal parties. The liberal and the agrarian parties belong to the same party group in the European Parliament (Group of European Liberal, Democrat and Reform Party, ELDR) and most of them are also members of the Liberal International. The third way in which party families can be identified has to do with the extent to which the policies pursued by one party in a country are similar to those pursued by another party in another country (ibid.).

All these criteria seem to have been fulfilled fairly well by the European liberal and agrarian parties. One must nonetheless ask whether these party families have enough to do with each other to be amenable to study in the same context. The answer is positive. First of all, they have the same location between the right and the left in the political spectrum in most European countries. In other words, the strongest agrarian parties have emerged in systems where liberalism is weak or non-existent, whereas the strongest liberal parties tend to be found in countries where there are no agrarian parties (Gallagher et al. 1995: 200).

The agrarians and the liberals have common historical roots in many countries. For instance, in Sweden several leading figures of the Agrarian Party had a liberal background, and in the early 1970s there were advanced plans for the Centre Party to merge with the Liberal Party. The failure of the merger was in fact a crucial turning point: thereafter the Centre Party's share of the vote declined almost continuously (Widfeldt 2001: 4–8, 11). A small Finnish Liberal Party was merged with the Centre Party in 1982, mainly for financial reasons. Ideologically, the merger was not a success and it was revoked as early as 1986.

The purpose of this chapter is to inquire, first, whether the three 'centrist' party families, that is the right liberals, the left liberals, and the agrarians, have a distinctive identity across national borders compared to the other parties as far as recruitment of MPs is concerned. Moreover, to what extent has the distinctiveness of a party family, if any, been maintained or has declined over time? We may start, however, by analysing the origin and the ideology of these party families. Second, we study the popular support of these parties in different European countries as reflected in the DATACUBE data. A major part of the study concerns social background factors such as the education, profession, political experience, and sex of liberal and agrarian MPs. Finally, we explain the distinctiveness of the party families as well as changes in the recruitment patterns of MPs representing them.

9.1. THE LIBERAL PARTY FAMILY

The term 'liberal' has been used since the fourteenth century but has had a wide variety of meanings. The Latin *liber* referred to a class of free men that is men who were neither serfs nor slaves. However, the term 'liberalism' denoting a political allegiance was not used until the early part of the nineteenth century. Even if liberalism may not have existed as a systematic political creed before the nineteenth century, it was nonetheless based upon ideas and theories which had evolved during the previous 300 years (Heywood 1998: 24). Speaking of liberalism, however, it is useful to differentiate the extensive and prolonged liberal tradition of thinking from the *liberal party ideology* which more or less firmly governs the viewpoints and political action of the liberal political parties in different countries (Borg 1979: 1–2).

The first established political parties were groupings of the bourgeoisie who looked to political organization to secure their interests against the landowners who controlled the state. These parties emerged in the nineteenth century, and towards the end of that century liberals were an influential political factor in many of the emerging liberal democracies. They aspired to remove state restrictions, some of them dating from the medieval era, on the production and trading of goods and they preferred a strict separation of state and society. In order to secure influence liberals required both access to the state and protection from arbitrary action by the powerful landed classes who had controlled the European states during the era of commercialization. Due to this, key elements in the liberal creed were legal and political rights for citizens, although many nineteenth-century liberals believed that citizenship entailed having 'a stake' in society, that is having property or education (Ware 2001: 29).

Even if liberal parties are often seen to represent a centre group in Western European politics, in practice they represent a diverse range of ideological concerns. Historically, liberal parties have been associated with the impulse to extend the franchise, promote individual rights, and resist clerical influences in politics. Liberal parties thus constituted the pre-socialist democratic opposition to conservatism and the right. Some of these characteristics have survived and are more or less common to all European liberal parties—an emphasis on individual rights and anticlericalism. However, over time other liberal concerns have emerged, and two clear facets of European liberalism can now be identified (Gallagher et al. 1995: 197).

In its broadest sense, liberalism was a philosophy which gave primacy to individual freedom, the freedom of the individual as the supreme social right unrestricted by intervention from the state, other individuals or society, freedom from the 'tyranny of the majority' (Schwarzmantel 1998: 68). Within the first element of European liberalism, the emphasis on individual rights has led to a concern for fiscal rectitude and opposition to all but minimal state intervention in the economy. This right-wing element of liberalism has been prominent in Austria, Belgium, Germany, Italy, Luxemburg, the Netherlands, and Switzerland—however, the rejection of state intervention does not fit for all countries and for all periods: in Italy for instance during the nineteenth century the idea of minimal state intervention was not typical of liberalism. It has tended to emerge in countries which are also characterized by strong CD parties and hence where the anti-clerical component of liberalism was once important (Gallagher et al. 1995: 197).

The second element in European liberalism reflects a more centrist, if not left-leaning, position in which a concern for individual rights and progressive politics has engendered an emphasis on social justice and egalitarianism. In fact, many liberal parties are today supportive of permissive social policies (Ware 2001: 30). This aspect has tended to emerge in countries where the main right-wing group is a secular conservative party which has taken over the more anti-interventionist liberal tendency and where the anticlerical element in liberalism has proved less relevant. This element can be found in Denmark, Finland, Norway, Sweden, and Britain, and is also represented by the Democrats '66 in the Netherlands as well as by the Italian Republicans (Gallagher et al. 1995: 197–8).

The presence of two major elements in liberal ideology and the diversity of liberal party strategies suggest that any overall characterization of liberal party policy concerns may be misleading. While the left-leaning British, Norwegian, and Swedish liberals all put a major emphasis on the need for a controlled economy, this emphasis is absent from programmes of the Austrian, German, Dutch, and Italian liberals (ibid. 198). In fact, we may ask whether the differences between these two liberal subgroups are so important that they should not be included a single party family? Some commentators have, in fact, argued that liberalism is an incoherent ideology, embracing contradictory beliefs, especially regarding the appropriate role of the state. In common with all political ideologies, liberalism has been subject to change, as its basic principles have been applied to changing historical circumstances. 'No political ideology is rigid or monolithic; all encompass a range of views and even rival traditions' (Heywood 1998: 26).

According to Budge and Keman,

(w)hat they have in common, at least in the minds of activists and supporters, outweighs what separates them. And what they share is a concern with individual freedom—which has then branched out, in the one case, into a concern to remove as many external constraints as possible on individual choice and action and in the other, into a concern to give the individual a social basis for actually using his civil freedoms. The concern with freedom should give liberal parties characteristic policies ... which differ from those of Conservatives, Christians, and Socialists, none of whom are averse to massive state interference and regulation of the individual to secure their particular ends

(Budge and Keman 1993: 95).

Moreover, all liberal parties emphasize a commitment to welfarism, and in common with the left and agrarian parties, they also stress the need for some environmental protection (Gallagher et al. 1995: 198).

Thus, in the present study the liberal political tradition is divided into two party families, that is the right liberals and the left liberals. The difference between these subgroups, evaluated by country experts, is that the right liberals are ideologically closer to the political right whereas the left liberals are more centrist or even leftist-oriented.

All in all, characteristic of all liberal parties is an emphasis on freedom, democracy, decentralization, and equality of opportunities, reflecting a continuing and pervasive concern for individual rights and freedom, as well as reluctance to tolerate more authoritarian styles of governing. These liberal parties now reflect a set of political appeals which echo elements of both the new left and the traditional right. This may stem from the shared contemporary orientation of all three groups towards the growing middle-class electoral constituency (ibid.).

Judging from the DATACUBE data, the liberal political tradition has persisted in parliament from the mid-nineteenth century to the present in France, Germany, Italy, the Netherlands, and the UK. In Norway, the tradition was broken at the beginning of the 1980s. Furthermore, in Hungary the liberal parliamentary representation which had emerged before socialism was conspicuously revived after the collapse of the Eastern Bloc. However, support for the Hungarian liberals declined rapidly in the 1990s (Ilonszki 2000). In Portugal, liberal parliamentary representation emerged in 1975 after the Carnation revolution, while in Denmark and Finland liberal representation emerged in parliament in 1906 and 1907 and has since then persisted.[2]

The left liberals were represented in European parliaments in: Germany in the period 1848–1933 (i.e. Freedom Party, German Democratic Party), France 1848–1968 (e.g. Democratic and Socialist Union of the Resistance, Rally of the Republican Lefts), the UK since 1868 (Liberal Party, Social Democratic Party, Liberal Democratic Party), Norway 1877–1981 (Liberal Party), the Netherlands 1879–84, 1891–1937, 1967–94 (e.g. Democrats 66), Italy since 1880 (Radicals/Republicans, Republican Party, Italian Renewal), Denmark since 1906 (*Radikale Venstre*), Finland 1906–79 (Liberal Party), and Hungary since 1990 (Alliance of Free Democrats) (Figure 9.1).[3]

The right liberal tradition has been represented in France (Moderates, the National Centre of Independents and Peasants) and Germany since 1848 (Casino Party, National Liberal Party), the Netherlands since 1849 (Liberal Union, Union of Free Liberals, Liberal State party, Union for Freedom and Democracy), Italy since 1861 (the so-called Historical Left—*Sinistra Storica*—the Liberal Party, Forza Italia), Finland since 1907 (the Swedish People's Party), Portugal since 1975 (The Social Democratic Party), and Hungary 1990–4 (The Alliance of Young Democrats) (see Best and Gaxie 2000; Best, Hausmann, and Schmitt 2000; Cotta,

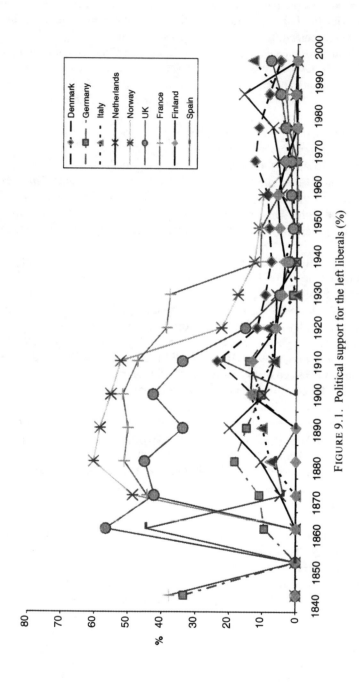

FIGURE 9.1. Political support for the left liberals (%)

Mastropaolo and Verzichelli 2000; Eliassen and Sjovaag 2000; Ilonszki 2000; Magone 2000; Pedersen 2000; Ruostetsaari 2000; Rush and Cromwell 2000; Secker 2000) (Figure 9.2).

During the second half of the nineteenth century, the electoral challenge has pressed the liberals to adapt their ideology so that it could continue to attract middle-class voters. At the beginning of twentieth century liberal parties had lost a considerable part of their access to working-class voters with the rise of socialist parties. Furthermore, the vast increase in the size of commercial and industrial firms, which transformed economies previously based on small entrepreneurs, together with the declining salience of religious cleavages, have also eroded the original middle-class base for liberals. 'But just as liberals have had to adapt, so other parties have "stolen some of the liberals" clothes'—for example, social democrat and ecology parties today usually have just as "liberal" an approach to social permissiveness as liberals' (Ware 2001: 31).

As far as political support for the right liberals is concerned, their heyday can be placed in the era prior to the First World War. After the war their support decreased dramatically to less than 15 per cent in most European countries. A turn occurred in the 1970s and support for this grouping started to increase steadily. The trend among the left liberals is identical in the sense that the heyday of this party family can also be seen to fall in the era prior to the First World War. However, voter support for them was less than that for the right liberals and the negative turn in support after the First World War was milder. However, the new upward turn for the right liberals never extended the left liberals.

9.2. THE AGRARIAN PARTY FAMILY

As their name suggests, agrarian parties were primarily special-interest parties. They were initially mobilized in the late nineteenth and early twentieth centuries to represent the specific concerns of farmers and the agricultural sectors. Although agrarian parties emerged from Ireland to Estonia and Bulgaria, they are essentially a Scandinavian phenomenon, with a strong presence in Denmark, Finland, Iceland, Norway, and Sweden. Outside the Nordic area, an agrarian party persists only in Switzerland. Outside Western Europe agrarian parties re-emerged in some post-communist democracies (Gallagher et al. 1995: 199).

Many of the first 'green wave' parties became victims of the collapse of democracy and the rise of rightist authoritarianism in the 1930s and their subsequent re-emergence a decade later was suppressed by the tightening grip of Communist rule. By contrast, the Nordic agrarian parties operated in stable democracies only briefly disrupted (outside Finland and Sweden) by the Second World War (Arter 2001a: 163). It was not so much the emergence of farmers' parties—agrarian parties were formed in several countries before and after the First World War—or their subsequent electoral strength which was a distinctive

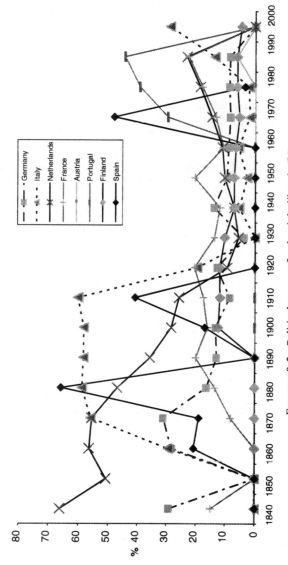

FIGURE 9.2. Political support for the right liberals (%)

Nordic phenomenon. Rather, it was their persistence until the late 1950s and 1960s. The peculiarity of the agrarian parties of Finland, Norway, and Sweden lay in their durability and their survival in predominantly industrialized societies (ibid. 162).

The conditions for the emergence of a strong agrarian party were set out by Lipset and Rokkan (1967) in *Party Systems and Voter Alignments*. According to them, strong agrarian parties emerged when the following four conditions were met:

1. The cities and industrial centres were still numerically weak at the time of the decisive extensions of the suffrage.
2. The bulk of the agricultural population was active in family-scale farming and either owned farms or comprised legally protected leaseholders largely independent of socially superior landowners.
3. There were important cultural barriers between rural and urban areas and much resistance to the incorporation of farm production into the capitalist economy of the cities.
4. The Catholic Church was without significant influence (Arter 2001a: 163–4).

These conditions were well met in Scandinavia. The Scandinavian countries at the time of the emergence of the agrarian parties were characterized by numerically significant primary sectors employing between about a third (Denmark), two-fifths (Norway, Sweden, and Iceland), and four-fifths (Finland) of the economically active population. Furthermore, the agricultural population comprised predominantly independent farmers rather than crofters and agricultural labourers. In Scandinavia, there was a sizeable core class of medium-sized farm owners and this was what largely provided the basis of agrarian party mobilization. Throughout the Nordic region, moreover, the emergence of class-based farmers' parties was also facilitated by the absence of other major social cleavages such as religion (Scandinavia is principally a Protestant region) or language (Arter 2001b: 63–5, 2001a: 164–5).

The Finnish Agrarian League, the most powerful agrarian party in Europe, was, alongside the Norwegian and Swedish parties, a by-product of the superimposition at a stroke of mass democracy—universal suffrage and a proportional electoral system (PR) on a predominantly rural society under Russian rule. The Finnish, Swedish, and Norwegian agrarian parties all emerged as mass membership parties. In the Finnish and Swedish cases (differing from the Norwegian sister party), this involved direct membership and there were no formal ties to interest organizations. They antedated the emergence of agricultural producers' organizations (Arter 2001a: 165–6). Despite lacking formal ties, however, the memberships of the agrarian party and the agricultural producers' organization overlapped.

9.3. TRANSFORMATION OF THE AGRARIAN PARTIES INTO CENTRE PARTIES

As the economic structure of the Scandinavian countries changed, the agrarian parties were confronted with new challenges. Modernization involved responding to the twin processes of industrialization and urbanization by taking steps—a new name, programme, or electoral strategy—designed to move the party in a catch-all direction. In particular, there was a concern to penetrate the increasingly urban electorate. The three Nordic agrarian parties with a capital 'A' changed their names to Centre parties, in Sweden in 1958, Norway in 1959, and Finland in 1965. Despite a prolonged decline in its support there was no debate in the Danish agrarian party about a fundamentally new approach. In fact, in 1963 it emphasized its traditional liberal credentials by adding the suffix 'Denmark's Liberal Party'. Prior to the pursuit of strategies designed to facilitate the adaptation of the parties to an increasingly urbanized electorate, the Finnish, Norwegian, and Swedish Agrarians consolidated their class base by overhauling their organizations and promoting their positions as mass membership parties (Arter 2001*b*: 173–6). The Danish *Venstre* is the deviant case among the Nordic farmers' parties. It has never changed it name, it is not called a Centre Party and, it is not a centre party. Although *Venstre* in Danish means 'left', it is much further to the right on the ideological continuum than its Nordic sister parties. In fact, the Danish party can be seen as a half-sister to the Nordic agrarian parties (Andersen and Jensen 2001: 96).

One result of the process of adaptation is a curious amalgam of agrarian party policy concerns. Despite their move away from a distinctively rural base, the agrarian parties continue to stress the interests of agriculture and farmers and are the only party family to do so. Two other emphases also reflect their particular heritage: one on decentralization, which harks back to their peripheral roots, and the other on environmental protection which, in its anti-industrial bias, is also characteristic of these parties. At the same time, however, agrarian parties emphasize welfare provision, social justice, and the need for a controlled economy, which suggests a leftist orientation. On the other hand, they favour both private enterprise and the maintenance of traditional moral values, which would indicate a distinctly conservative impulse. Although this mix of policy concerns allows agrarians to appeal to both right and left, their earlier positions in the Scandinavian party systems suggest a fairly close alignment with the Social Democrats (Gallagher et al. 1995: 199–200). Ideologically, the centre parties, at least in Finland and Sweden, have been particularly reluctant to refer to themselves as bourgeois parties, a term frequently used by the Liberals and the Conservatives. Instead, they prefer to call themselves 'non-socialist' (Windfelt 2001: 18).

In spite of a concern to expand from being class parties, the Swedish and Norwegian parties have appeared at various times to be single-issue parties, closely identified in the public view with an unequivocal stance on controversial questions such as opposition to nuclear energy in Sweden and opposition to the EU in Norway. This has been their greatest strength and their greatest weakness, achieving short-term electoral growth, but a growth which proved ephemeral. In contrast, the Finnish practice of governmental cooperation 'across', that is involving right-wing and left-wing parties, has militated towards pragmatic policy stances and a concern to avoid marginalization through single-issue attachment. All in all, the Finnish Centre Party has not been linked to a single issue in the same way (Hokkanen 1996; Arter 2001*b*: 80–1). Thus, as there is no longer any single issue common to all agrarian or centre parties they cannot be termed as a 'single-issue party family' (see Budge and Keman 1993: 91).

It seems evident that after the Second World War the proportion of farmers among voters for the agrarian party was still greater in Finland than in the other Nordic countries. However, the share of farmer votes in Finland has decreased rapidly and in the late 1990s was smaller than it most other Nordic countries. No more than 10 per cent of the supporters of the Finnish Centre Party are any longer farmers, while the proportion is smaller only in the case of the Danish party, 7 per cent in 1998. In fact, the Centre Party possesses the most heterogeneous support base of all the Finnish parties (Arter 2001*b*: 92; Andersen and Jensen 2001: 117).

In the countries covered by the DATACUBE, the agrarian political tradition has persisted only in Denmark (since 1849), Finland (since 1907), and Norway (since 1919). In Hungary, smallholder-agricultural parties existed as early as the beginning of the twentieth century. There were also agrarian parties under the communist regime until 1989, but their position was not independent vis-à-vis the hegemonic party. After the collapse of state socialism, representation of independent smallholders revived. Moreover, the agrarians had marginal parliamentary representation in Germany (1918–33) and in the Netherlands (1918–33 the Union of countrymen/rural residents and 1963–77 the Farmers' Party), and Austria (1920–30) (Best, Hausmann, and Schmitt 2000; Eliassen and Sjovaag 2000; Ilonszki 2000; Pedersen 2000; Ruostetsaari 2000; Secker 2000) (Figure 9.3).

9.4. HYPOTHESES

On the grounds of the social origins and the ideological dispositions of the three party families, four hypotheses about their legislative recruitment patterns are proposed. The hypotheses are based on the understanding that education and political experience have been seen in previous elite studies as key factors which account for recruitment of elites (Best and Cotta 2000). It has been also established that the recruitment of elites from public sector's professions and female representation are connected to the introduction and expansion of the welfare state (e.g. Ruostetsaari 1997).

First, by reason of the agricultural and rural background of the agrarian parties, MPs representing them should be less well educated than their liberal colleagues. Liberal MPs are expected to be recruited to a larger extent than their Agrarian

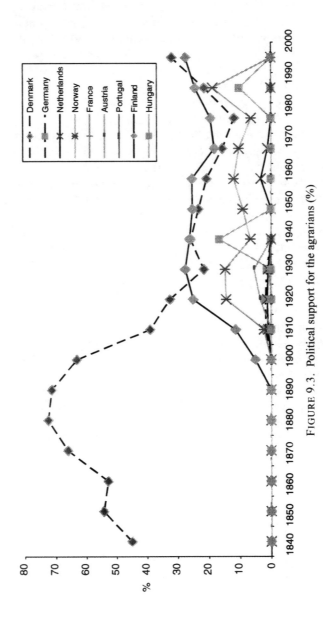

FIGURE 9.3. Political support for the agrarians (%)

colleagues from middle classes and urban areas, where economic and even geographical opportunities for education are better than for those coming from lower classes and rural areas. Moreover, the cultural capital of the upper and middle classes should have favoured higher formal education.

Second, as the following of the agrarian parties was composed mainly of independent farmers, that is entrepreneurs, MPs representing these parties are expected to be mainly recruited from private sector professions. By contrast, Liberal MPs from a middle-class background are expected to have a stronger bases in the public sector, because today most liberal parties are supportive of permissive social policies implemented by the public sector (Ware 2001: 30). Even if the differences between the right and the left liberals have decreased as far as attitudes to state intervention are concerned, the former have traditionally supported minimal state intervention while the latter have supported more egalitarian positions and the welfare state. We may thus hypothesize that MPs representing the right liberals are recruited more from the private sector than their left liberal colleagues, who, by contrast, are supposedly recruited more from the public sector professions than their right liberal colleagues.

Third, despite the absence of formal ties (except in Norway) to interest groups, membership in the agrarian parties and the agricultural producers' organizations should overlap. Similar links between the liberal parties and white-collar interest groups are less likely because of their ideological heterogeneity. Thus we may hypothesize that, compared to their liberal colleagues, agrarian MPs should be politically more experienced in elective offices and party or interest group organizations before recruitment to parliament. As the middle class is numerically weak in rural areas and small municipalities, local councils, and boards are manned much more with Agrarians than Liberals. In fact, political experience can be seen as a political resource which may compensate for lacking formal education (Yrjölä 1973).

According to the fourth hypothesis, female representation is expected to be greater in the liberal party families than in the agrarian party family. This hypothesis is based on a patriarchal tradition which agriculture has traditionally reflected even if women have played an important role in the households of independent farmers (e.g. Saarinen 1992). On the other hand, the liberal political tradition has laid more stress on egalitarianism and social justice.

Finally, we expect to observe convergence over time between the agrarians, the right liberals, and the left liberals. In other words, the differences between these party families should have decreased as a result of social changes and ideological rapprochement.

9.5. EDUCATION

We may start the analysis of agrarian and liberal party families with education, which is one of the most important preconditions for recruitment to most elites (e.g. Ruostetsaari 2004). As far as the education of MPs representing the three party families is concerned, before recruitment it is highest among the right liberals and lowest among the agrarians (Figure 9.4).[4] In accordance with the hypothesis both liberal party families are above the European mean while the agrarians are below it. Until the 1930s, the proportion of MPs who had received no more than basic education was much larger among the agrarians than in either of the liberal party families. Compared to the European political parties there are significant, even if decreasing differences between both liberal and agrarian party families in respect of university education. In the late nineteenth century about three-fourths of right liberals, three-fifths of left liberals but only a fifth of agrarians (i.e. of the Danish party) had taken a university degree (Figure 9.5). The share of university degrees among all European party families started to increase in the 1930s. However, in the case of the right liberals the change occurred not before the 1950s and in the case of the left liberals a decade later. Among the agrarians, the proportion of university degrees has increased since the 1970s. The right liberals were overtaken by their left-wing counterparts in the 1980s. The slight decrease of university education among the right liberals since the 1980s may be accounted by the fact that they were recruited more generally from free professions, managers, and party and union officials at the expense of public sector professions.

As far as education is concerned there are, however, marked differences between national parties within the three party families. Especially, there are significant differences in the case of the left liberal party family. Danish and—until the 1960s—Norwegian left liberals have received a university degree less frequently than their German, Dutch, Finnish, French, Hungarian, Italian, and British (from the 1930s to the 1970s) colleagues. In the case of the right liberal party family, among Finnish and French MPs academic education is less frequent than on average, while, from the beginning of twentieth century to the early 1980s, Italian right liberal MPs have received a better education than right liberals MPs on average. In the case of Danish agrarians university degrees are less frequent, while especially in Hungary but also in Norway and Finland (after the Second World War) their colleagues are better educated than agrarian MPs at large.

The differences between party families do not only concern the level of edu cation but also the field of academic education. A law degree has been more common among both liberal groups, especially the right liberals, than among European MPs at large. By contrast, there have always been few agrarian MPs who have taken law degrees. Degrees in the humanities, social sciences, or theology are much more characteristic of the agrarians. However, these degrees are also held more often by the liberals, especially the left liberals, than agrarian MPs. By contrast, MPs representing all three party families have more often taken university degrees in technology, engineering, natural sciences, and medicine than European MPs on average. In this case, too, both liberal groups are better educated than the agrarians even if these disciplines have connections to agricultural professions.

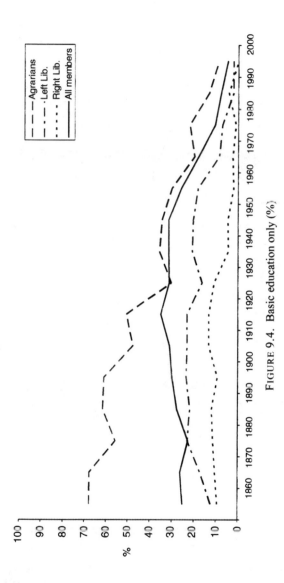

FIGURE 9.4. Basic education only (%)

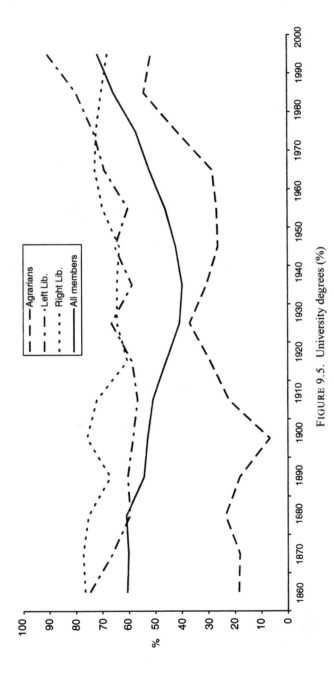

FIGURE 9.5. University degrees (%)

The Danish and Hungarian agrarians have always held law degrees more frequently, while their Finnish and Norwegian colleagues have training in jurisprudence much more rarely than European agrarians at large. As far as the left liberal party family is concerned, a law degree is a more typical academic education for Dutch, French, Hungarian, and Italian MPs but less typical for Danish, Finnish, and Norwegian MPs than for European left liberals at large. The pattern is almost the same in the case of the right liberals; especially the Finnish right liberals have rarely taken law degrees (the difference from the right liberals at large during twentieth century has been of 20–30 per cent).

An academic education in technology, engineering, natural sciences, or medicine has been more typical than the mean for the Norwegian agrarians and left liberals and the French right liberals. By contrast, these disciplines have been more rarely the choice of agrarians in Denmark, Finland, Hungary, and Norway but also among Finnish right liberals and Hungarian left liberals. Furthermore, degrees education in the humanities, social sciences, or theology were taken more frequently than in the party families at large by Danish agrarians (since the 1970s), German left liberals (until the 1930s), and German right liberals. More infrequently these disciplines were taken by the Finnish and Norwegian agrarians as well as by the left liberals in France and Italy and the right liberals in France.

However, even if there are differences in respect of education within countries, the variations seem to be more significant between party families. In other words, the differences between parties representing most countries go in the same direction as the party families at large. Although the educational differences between the three party families decreased for a long time they started to grow again in the 1980s with regard to university education. This may be due to changes in the occupational structure, in particular to the declining proportion of public sector professions, such as teachers, which require an academic degree.

9.6. OCCUPATION

In the first half of the nineteenth century about a third of MPs were recruited from the public service. The share decreased in the early twentieth century but started to grow again with the introduction of the welfare state. A new incipient decline was seen in the 1990s, since when the share of MPs recruited from the public sector has decreased, reflecting the decreased size of the public sector (e.g. Ruostetsaari 2000: 83). This trend was also evident in the three party families studied, the only exception being the left liberals which saw an increase of the share of public sector professions in the 1990s. The pattern of differences between the three party families was clear in the twentieth century. The left liberals were recruited more frequently than the right liberals and especially the agrarians from public sector professions. The differences between party families have decreased, however, since the 1980s. The differences between the party families regarding recruitment from the public sector are in accordance with the hypothesis (Figure 9.6).

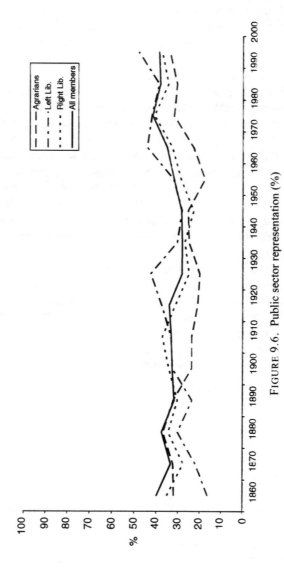

FIGURE 9.6. Public sector representation (%)

National variations within party families are recognizable, but not significant. Whereas the Danish and Finnish left liberals and the Dutch right liberals were always recruited more often from public sector professions than their party families at large, the reverse applies to the left liberals in France, Italy, and the UK (until the 1930s) as well as to the right liberals in France (especially until the 1940s), Germany, and Italy.

This public sector representation has not, however, meant extensive representation of senior civil servants. Since the mid-nineteenth century the proportion of senior civil servants has been less than 10 per cent among European MPs at large. The lowest level was reached in the 1920s, whereafter it increased slightly until the 1990s, when it turned to a decline. Among the agrarians the share of senior civil servants, except in the 1990s, has always been smaller than the European mean. By contrast, among both liberal party families the share was mainly above the mean in the twentieth century. However, contrary to the hypothesis, left liberals are recruited in general less frequently from the higher ranks of the civil service than right liberals.

The representation of teachers and professors has been somewhat higher among European MPs that that of senior civil servants (see Figure 9.7). The same pattern recurs in the case of the party families studied. Both liberal groups are above the European mean. In accordance with the hypothesis, the left liberals have been a favoured political home for members of the searching professions. The proportion of school and university teachers has varied markedly among right liberal MPs. Contrary to the hypothesis, it was above the European mean during the first half of the twentieth century. The representation in the agrarians, however, differs significantly from the liberal pattern. From the mid-nineteenth century to the 1930s, the share of teachers among the agrarians was much above the European mean. This was predominantly attributable solely to the Danish agrarian representation which contained a high contingent of teachers. However, over representation of teachers in agrarian parliamentary parties ended in the 1940s when the share of teachers and professors dropped below the European mean. This can be partly explained by the emergence of agrarian representation in Finland and Norway, where fewer agrarian MPs were recruited from schools, but it was predominantly due to a sharp overall increase of teachers' representation since the 1970s.

The legal profession has been traditionally seen in many countries as a useful, even the most important springboard for the MP's career (Matthews 1954: 30–1; Dogan 1961: 69). However, the agrarian groupings are again not the political home of lawyers. The proportion of agrarian MPs recruited from the legal profession has always been lower than the European mean, while by contrast, among both liberal groups the share has been clearly higher on average. Especially, the right liberals can be seen as a party family of lawyers. As law can be seen as a traditional private sector profession, the pattern is in accordance with the hypothesis that the agrarian MPs are more frequently recruited from private sector professions than their liberal colleagues. The same general patterns in the

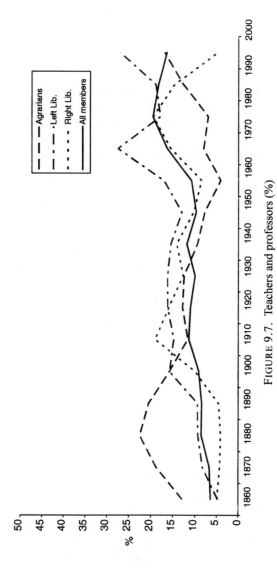

FIGURE 9.7. Teachers and professors (%)

three party families also concern the profession of judges and prosecutors. It is remarkable, however, that the number of MPs recruited from legal profession has decreased in both liberal party families since the 1950s, because the establishment and expansion of welfare state policies and state intervention entails increased legal regulation and conflict. Differences between the three party families have decreased since the 1990s as far as recruitment of MPs from the legal profession is concerned (Figure 9.8).

The representation of political party and trade union functionaries emerged in European parliaments in the last decade of the nineteenth century. In fact, as far as the professionalization of politics is concerned this is particularly important in that MPs with this background were political professionals *before* recruitment to parliament. The proportion of these political professionals increased until the 1940s, whereafter it turned into a decline. In the 1990s, the average representation of professionals was no more than 10 per cent. However, the representation of political professionals among the three party families has been clearly below the European mean. This pattern can be attributed to the fact that the parliamentary representation of political professionals has been principally channelled through the left-wing parties. However, in contrast to the situation existing among the liberals, the share of party and pressure groups officials among the agrarians has increased since the 1940s, which indicates links between the agrarian parties and the agrarian interest groups. This change is in accordance with the third hypothesis. Since 1990, however, a reversal of trends among both liberal parties families becomes apparent with a sharp increase of MPs being recruited from pressure group organizations and party apparatuses, indicating a turn to professionalism in both party families (Figure 9.9).

It is not unexpected that the representation of the primary sector among agrarians parties has exceeded the European mean since their beginnings. The representation of farmers among agrarian MPs increased up to the Second World War, when it began to decline. In the 1990s, only a fifth of agrarian MPs were recruited from the primary sector. One might easily assume that the representation of the primary sector has been a monopoly for the agrarian parties. This, however, is not the case. The agrarian parties are characteristically a Nordic phenomenon and in other countries farmers are represented mostly by Conservative or Christian Democratic parties. On the other hand, although most farmers have voted for Agrarian or Centre parties where such parties have existed, they have never been totally alone in defending the interests of farmers and rural economy (e.g. Christensen 2001: 50). It is true that a much smaller proportion of liberal MPs have been recruited from the primary sector than their agrarian colleagues, but a significant share, more than the European mean, of left liberals (from the 1910s to the 1960s) and right liberals (from the 1930s to the 2000s) was nonetheless recruited from primary sector professions. In fact, we may refer here to an increasing convergence: the differences between the agrarians and both liberal party families have diminished significantly since the 1970s (Figure 9.10).

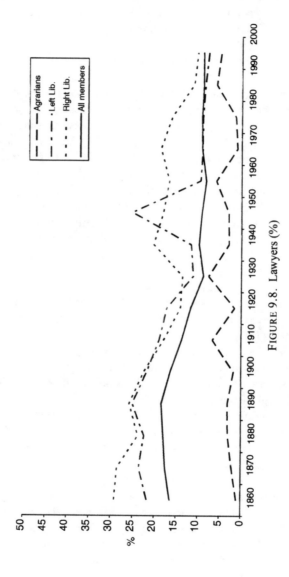

Figure 9.8. Lawyers (%)

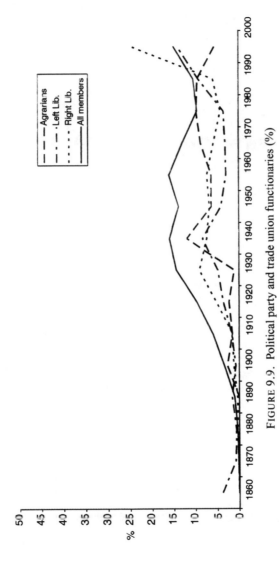

FIGURE 9.9. Political party and trade union functionaries (%)

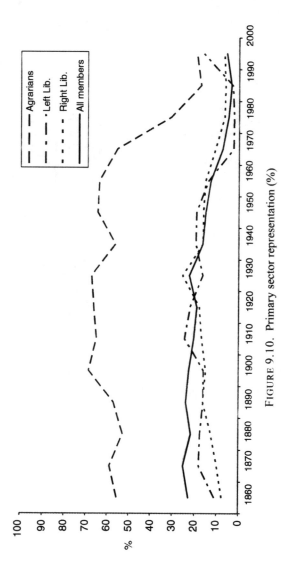

FIGURE 9.10. Primary sector representation (%)

Even if the primary sector is a natural source for recruitment of agrarian MPs there are important national differences within the party family. While Finnish and Dutch agrarians are predominantly recruited from primary sector professions, their Danish, Hungarian, and (since the 1960s) Norwegian colleagues are recruited more rarely than the average agrarian MPs from this background. By contrast, the Danish and especially Norwegian left liberals are frequently recruited from the primary sector, while their colleagues in Finland, France, Germany, Hungary, Italy, and the UK are recruited less rarely than European left liberals at large. The right liberals also recruit infrequently from an agrarian background. However, there are exceptions like the MPs of the Swedish People's Party, which were much more frequently recruited from the primary sector than the other right liberal parties.

In view of their primary sector background, it is understandable that the agrarians are to a lesser extent a party of business. By contrast, the share of entrepreneurs and managers among both liberal party families has exceeded the European mean since the nineteenth century. In accordance with the second hypothesis, their proportion has been higher in the parliamentary groups of the right liberals than in those of the left liberals. In this respect, the difference between the liberal party families has increased: the proportion of managers has risen among the right liberals but declined among their left liberal colleagues. The representation of small businesses as well as blue-collar workers, soldiers, and clergy has always been marginal among the parliamentary factions of the three party families studied.

As a whole, occupational differences between the three party families are rather volatile and more significant within party families than within countries. An important exception, however, is the primary sector, where differences are significant between party families within the same countries, especially in Finland but also in Denmark, Hungary, the Netherlands, and Norway. Moreover, regarding the private/public sector dimension after the Second World War the right liberals were recruited more and more from the private sector while the left liberals came more frequently from public sector.

9.7. POLITICAL EXPERIENCE

Politicians' competence and professionalization are affected not only by formal education, but also by their experience as elected or appointed representatives in other bodies previous to recruitment to parliament. Active participation in party activities furthers upward mobility in two ways: by virtue of the education and training offered and by the relations which it creates (Dogan 1961: 82). In fact, insufficient formal education can be compensated by political activities (Yrjölä 1973: 76; see also Ruostetsaari 2003).

Until the 1930s more than half of European representatives had a local political background, that is they have been elected to a municipal or regional council or government prior to their parliamentary career. Subsequently the share decreased, but started again to grow in the 1970s. In accordance with the hypothesis that the agrarian MPs are politically more experienced than their liberal colleagues the agrarians had a higher share of MPs with a background in local offices while, for most of the period covered, all three party families analysed in this chapter were locally more entrenched than their colleagues in general, the left liberals until the 1980s, the right liberals a decade longer. The differences between the party families increased since the 1940s but turned to decline in the 1990s (Figure 9.11).

The professionalization of European MPs, measured in terms of party positions, that is as chairman or vice-chairman of party organization on national, regional or local level, increased from the end of the nineteenth century until the 1960s. All three party families exceeded the European mean, although the agrarians did so only after the Second World War. Throughout the whole period MPs of both liberal party families had a higher share of leading party office holders in their ranks than the agrarians. These results indicate a different weight of the 'assets' involved in the recruitment process. In the case of agrarian MPs it was rather local offices which counted, in the case of liberal MPs it was their position in party hierarchies. In general, with regards to party positions the three party families have converged in the twentieth century (Figure 9.12.).

The degree of pre-recruitment experience in political offices is much lower if it is measured in terms of membership in a regional party office or national party council, or by holding governmental positions before recruitment to parliament. The share of MPs with other political experiences is also much smaller than that of MPs holding local elective positions or leading party positions. However, it is important to note that both the liberal and the agrarian party families have always exceeded the European mean, that is they are more experienced at the highest level of party organization than their colleagues. Convergence between the three party families occurred until the 1970s while thereafter the proportion of the agrarians with other parliamentary experiences surpasses clearly that of the liberal party families until the beginning of twenty-first century (Figure 9.13). The general European pattern is that few MPs, clearly less than 10 per cent, have functioned as a cabinet minister before recruitment to parliament. This also holds true in the case of the three party families studied.

The accumulation of political experience, that is the numbers of MPs with three or more types of political offices, is presented in Figure 9.14. This group of representatives, who can literally be called political professionals, has always been very small in Europe, no more than 11 per cent. Professionalization started to increase slowly in the 1910s and the upswing lasted, excluding the break caused by the Second World War, until the 1970s, when it turned into a decline. A new raise commenced in the 2000s. This trend indicates the growth of a new type of politician—the expert representative. This is a highly educated professional, more frequently female, who works in the public sector as a civil servant. Such expert representatives have seldom served as functionaries in either political parties or

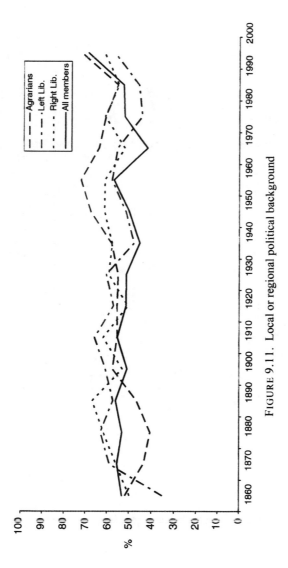

FIGURE 9.11. Local or regional political background

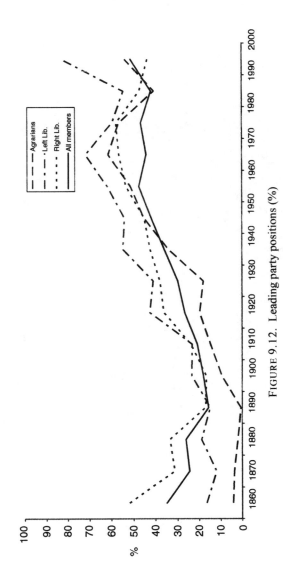

FIGURE 9.12. Leading party positions (%)

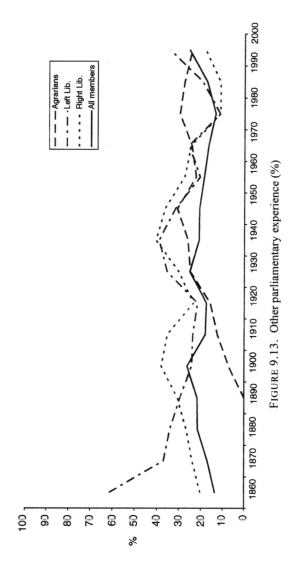

FIGURE 9.13. Other parliamentary experience (%)

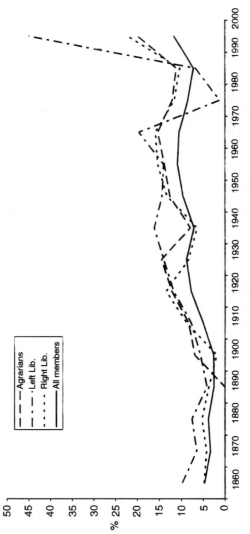

FIGURE 9.14. Three or more types of political professionalization (%)

labour unions or held a leading party position, or had any other parliamentary experience. This trend fits well with the debate on image politics and the growing role of the mass media in politics; electoral success requires publicity and prominence in the public arena based, for example, on professional merit more than active and prolonged activity in a party organization (Ruostetsaari 2000: 84).

MPs representing the three party families studied have been more professionalized than European MPs in general. Partly, this high degree of professionalization might be accounted for by the fact that electoral support for the European liberal parties was fairly weak in the twentieth century and the size of their parliamentary groups was small. In this situation it is likely that a high proportion of MPs will be party leaders. This explanation, however, does not fit the agrarian parties, which were, especially in Finland and Denmark, major cabinet parties. In these bigger parties, party leaders constitute a smaller part of the parliamentary group. Due to their power these parties may have attracted ambitious individuals who have aspired to a political career, which may thus explain the marked professionalization in the agrarian parties.

However, as far as the mean number of elections per MP and the share of newcomers in parliament are concerned, the development does not unequivocally support the increasing trend towards professionalization. In other words, the mean number of elections of MPs representing the three party families is not systematically higher than the overall mean. Moreover, the proportion of newcomers is not systematically smaller for liberals and agrarians than for all European MPs. Both of these trends are inconsistent. The hypothesis was based on the assumption that the agrarians are politically more experienced, that is professionalized, than the liberals because they have close links to, or at least overlapping membership in the agricultural producers' organizations while, the liberals coming from the middle class do not have similar supporting groups. As the differences between party families are not straightforward the hypothesis is not verified.

As a whole, with regard to various forms of political experience acquired before recruitment to parliament, there are significant differences, even greater than in the cases of education and profession, within party families. Concerning local or regional political background, for instance, the Danish agrarians are clearly less experienced than their Dutch, Finnish, and Norwegian colleagues, who are much more experienced than the party family at large. In the case of the left liberals, the Danish, Dutch, Italian, and Hungarian MPs are less, but their colleagues in Finland, France, and Norway are more, experienced than the average left liberal MP. Moreover, the right liberals in Germany, Hungary, and Italy are less experienced while their Finnish and French colleagues are more experienced than the party family at large. On the other hand, the differences within countries are minor; for instance, in Finland MPs belonging to the three party families are clearly more politically experienced than is the case in these party families at large.

In fact, if we examine the accumulation of political experiences (three or more types), differences between the three parties are minor in any single country whereas within the party families they are more significant. In other words, the Finnish and German (from the 1910s to 1930s) agrarians have always been politically less experienced while their Danish and Dutch colleagues have been more experienced than agrarian party family representatives at large. The left liberals in Finland, France (since the 1940s), Germany, and Hungary have been less experienced, but their colleagues in Denmark, Italy, the Netherlands, and Norway (until the 1990s) more experienced, than is the case in the party family at large. Regarding the right liberals Italian and Dutch MPs have been less experienced but their Finnish colleagues more experienced than in the party overall. Until the 1930s, German right liberals were more experienced but since then less experienced than their average colleagues. In France the trend was to the contrary; until the 1930s right liberals were less experienced but since then more experienced. All in all, the differences within the three party families have increased since 1920s as far as accumulation of political experience is concerned.

9.8. FEMALE REPRESENTATION

Female representation has not been a phenomenon typical of agrarian parties. In accordance with the hypothesis the proportion of women among agrarian MPs was smaller than that among European MPs in general. Since the 1970s it has, however, exceeded the mean. Among the left liberals female representation was higher, even if it did not exceed the mean every decade. In the case of the right liberals the trend is somewhat different. Female representation exceeded the mean only on to the 1920s and again in the 2000s. The differences between the agrarian and the liberal party families concerning female representation have increased since the 1996s when the female representation started to grow generally in European parliaments (Table 9.1).

9.9. CONCLUSIONS

Our study concerning the agrarian, the right liberal, and the left liberal party families was based on four hypotheses and guided by the additional assumption that, as a result of social changes, a convergence between party families has occurred. The first hypothesis suggested that, in view of the agricultural and rural background of the agrarian parties, MPs representing these parties should be less educated than their liberal colleagues. This hypothesis was verified. MPs representing both the right and the left liberals are more highly educated than their agrarian colleagues. However, the differences between the party families are decreasing, although the difference still prevails as far as academic education is concerned.

TABLE 9.1. *Average female representation by decades (%)*

	Agrarians	Left Lib.	Right Lib.	All members
1860	0	0	0	0
1870	0	0	0	0
1880	0	0	0	0
1890	0	0	0	0
1900	4	1	2	1
1910	2	1	2	1
1920	1	6	5	3
1930	1	5	3	3
1940	2	8	5	6
1950	4	5	6	7
1960	4	8	5	7
1970	10	16	7	10
1980	21	12	7	15
1990	25	33	20	21
2000	38	14	26	26

The second hypothesis was based on the fact that the constituencies of agrarian parties were composed mainly of independent farmers. Especially in Nordic countries agriculture was based on small-scale independent farming which means that MPs representing these parties were mainly recruited from private sector professions. Even if the differences between the right and left liberals have decreased as far as attitudes to state intervention are concerned, traditionally the former have supported minimal state intervention while the latter have supported more egalitarianism and the welfare state. Thus, we could hypothesize that MPs representing the right liberals would be recruited to a larger degree from the private sector than their left liberal counterparts.

Recruitment of European MPs from the public sector professions has increased since the beginning of the twentieth century. The growth accelerated in the 1960s but declined in the 1980s. This trend can be explained by the consolidation of the welfare state in the 1960s and the criticism of state intervention voiced by neoliberal ideology and the doctrine of New Public Management in the 1980s. For instance, in Finland the proportion of MPs recruited from the public sector, the total number of public sector personnel and the public total expenditures in the GNP increased identically after the 1960s (Ruostetsaari 1997: 45).

As far as the party families studied are concerned the hypothesis regarding public sector recruitment as a whole was verified. The differences between the party families started to grow in the 1960s but turned into a decline in the 1980s. However, if we look at individual professions there are certain trends which deviate from the hypothesis: the left liberals are recruited less from the higher ranks of the civil service than the right liberals; many teachers and professors were elected as right liberal MPs in the first half of the twentieth century.

Despite an absence of formal ties to interest groups, membership in agrarian parties and in agricultural producers' organizations overlap. Similar links between the liberal parties and white-collar interest groups are less likely. Thus, according to the third hypothesis, agrarian MPs are assumed to have had more experience than their liberal colleagues in elective offices in public bodies and party organizations before recruitment to parliament. The professionalization of politics, measured by the degree of political experience, increased steadily from the beginning of the twentieth century, excluding the break caused by the Second World War and the 1980s and 1990s. The hypothesis, however, was not verified. The share of MPs with some type of political experience is largest among the agrarian party families. Moreover, fewer agrarian MPs had accumulated several types of political experience than their liberal colleagues.

According to the fourth hypothesis, female representation is greater in the liberal party families than in the agrarian party family. This conception was based on a patriarchal tradition which the agriculture has traditionally reflected even if women have played an important role in the households of independent farmers, especially in Scandinavia. On the other hand, the liberal political tradition laid more stress on egalitarianism and social justice. The hypothesis was supported in the sense that the proportion of female MPs was lower in the agrarian party family than in both liberal party families from the 1920s to the 1960s. However, in the early twentieth century it was higher, and in the 1970s and 1990s the proportion of female MPs was higher in the agrarian party family than in the right liberals. It is likely that this was due more to a country and region effect: agrarian parties are strong in the Scandinavian area where openness to female recruitment has become greater than in the rest of Europe.

It seems evident, however, that the political professionalization of the liberals and the agrarians cannot be explained by the same factors. It is likely that the high degree of political professionalization of the left and right liberals can be accounted for by the educational and occupational resources of members of these political groups. Here what is involved is the accumulation of cultural, political, and social capital. By contrast, as the educational resources and abilities acquired in working life—which can be utilized in politics—are scarcer among the agrarians, they may have compensated for these meagre resources by active political and interest group participation.

As far as education, profession and especially political experience before recruitment to Parliament from the three party families are concerned, the differences are more important within party families than between parties in different party families representing the same country: the agrarians, the left liberals, and the right liberals coming from a single country have been fairly similar and differences have run in the same direction; for instance, the Finnish agrarians, left liberals, and right liberals have had more local political experience since the early twentieth century than their respective party families at large. Furthermore, the national recruitment patterns have been fairly stable, and the changes with regard to a political party in one county since the early nineteenth century have been modest.

It is evident that in the long term the differences between the right liberal, the left liberal, and the agrarian party families have decreased with regard to occupational and educational background but increased in terms of political experience and female representation. The hypothesized convergence between the three families is seen most strikingly in the representation of the primary sector. For instance, in the 1930s about 70 per cent of European agrarian MPs were recruited from primary sector professions, in the 1990s less than a fifth. At the same time the share of right liberal MPs recruited from the primary sector dropped from a quarter to 5 per cent. In the 1910s, one in four left liberal MPs were recruited from the primary sector, in the 1990s less than 1 pre cent. This indicates that in terms of their professional background, the cluster of political groups recurring to the agrarian tradition can no longer legitimately be called an agrarian party family but rather a party family of the political centre.

This is not to deny that many agrarian parties have long functioned as class parties representing principally one social class (*classe gardée*) (see Arter 2001*b*). Hence, they have had close, at least informal relationships with agricultural interest groups. In fact, they have operated in many countries in a more or less cohesive and closed 'agricultural triangle' composed of representatives of public administration (the Ministry of Agriculture), interest groups (agricultural producers' association), and a political party (the Agrarian Party) (Christensen and Egeberg 1979; Richardson and Jordan 1979; Helander 1981; Ruostetsaari 1985). The symbiotic interest intermediation between an interest group and government via a powerful political party has been termed a *parentela* relationship (La Palombara 1964). Although the agrarian party families have clearly transformed from class to catch-all parties, this traditional pattern of political coalition-building still persists. As a result of the European integration, however, coalition-building is a more complicated task and the 'agricultural triangles' are looser than, for instance, two decades ago. Likewise the Social Democrats have their most loyal cooperation partners in the labour unions, although most of their voters nowadays come from the middle class. Hence we may conclude that the party families' basic patterns of coalition-building are 'frozen': they are fairly independent of structural changes in society, from industrialization to postmodernization.

This trend concerns especially the agrarian party family, while the *classe gardée* of the right and left liberals has always been much wider and more heterogeneous. However, lack of 'natural' coalition partners from the third sector, instead of opening them an access to an increasingly 'destructured' and 'individualized' constituency, has contributed to the electoral decline of the liberals. On the grounds of their respective class background it is surprising that the liberals, once a major political tradition in the nineteenth century, have withered and the agrarians, once an interest group representing one profession, have persisted (even increasing their support in Denmark and Finland) also in the context of postmodernism and the information society.

This means that, even if differences between party families have decreased, the agrarian party family continues to evince distinctive characteristics. Nowadays the agrarian parties do not so much represent agriculture, but more peripheral regions vis-à-vis the centre. In fact, Lane and Ersson (1995: 105) have preferred the term rural party to agrarian in their classification of European agrarian groups. This strategy of leaning on regions may also be successful in the future, as the EU has focused more attention on the principle of subsidiary, that is the role of regions in EU decision-making. On the other hand, this strategy may be risky for electoral success, as populations are everywhere in Europe concentrating into larger cities and peripheral regions are consequently losing inhabitants, that is voters. Not only the agrarians but also the liberals are faced with a dilemma. The dilemma of the two liberal party families is that even if the middle class, their natural recruitment source, is growing everywhere, they are in danger of being overwhelmed by the major European parties, that is the Social Democrats and the Conservatives or the Christian Democrats, which are also targeting this expanding part of the electorate.

The electoral problem for liberalism during the twentieth century was the need to adapt its ideology so as to continue to attract middle-class voters. Very early in the century, the liberal parties lost a considerable part of their access to the working-class vote with the rise of the socialist parties. The vast increase in the size of commercial and industrial firms, which transformed economies previously based on small entrepreneurs, together with the declining salience of religious cleavages, have also eroded the original middle-class base for the liberals. But as just the liberals have had to adapt, so other parties have 'stolen some of the liberals' clothes'. For example, the Social Democrats and Green parties today usually adopt just as 'liberal' an approach to social permissiveness as the liberals (Ware 2001: 31): Both the left and right liberal party families have also lost part of their distinctive identity in respect of the recruitment patterns of MPs.

ENDNOTES

1   According to von Beyme (1985), in European politics the *familles spirituelles* are in order of emergence Liberal and Radical parties, Conservative parties, Socialist and Social Democratic parties, Christian Democratic parties, Communist parties, Agrarian parties, Regional and ethnic parties, Right-wing extremist parties, and the Ecology movement.

2   Sweden is not included in the DATACUBE data.

3   Figures in this chapter are based on the means of elections per decade.

4   The all-members line in the figures of this chapter represents all countries included in the DATACUBE, not only the countries where the three party families under study exist.

Christian Democratic Parliamentarians: From a Century of Multifaceted Recruitment to the Convergence within a 'Larger Family'?

Luca Verzichelli[1]

10.1. INTRODUCTION: RESEARCH QUESTIONS AND STRUCTURE OF THE CHAPTER

This chapter deals with one of the largest and well-established party families of the European political landscape. There is no need, therefore, to justify the inclusion of an analysis of *Christian Democratic parties* in this section of the volume, which is devoted to parliamentary elite transformations across the main families of political parties in Europe.

Very much has been written on the ideological and/or pragmatic nature of this 'spiritual family' of parties, its historical origin and its evolution towards the catch-all model of party format (Pridham 1977). On the contrary the comparative analysis of the elite structure of CD parties does not seem sufficiently developed. The degree to which the ruling elites of the different national components of one of the broadest families of parties in Europe (and in Latin America) show a similarity in their composition and patterns of recruitment is still largely unexplored by empirical research. Interesting descriptions of the elite structures are available within monographic works devoted to some important CD parties,[2] but very few works have attempted a comparative analysis, and these have limited the attention given to the transformation of political elites.

As a matter of fact, an analysis of the historical and cross-country variations within the CD parliamentary elites could provide interesting empirical evidences and a number of arguments for supporting or rejecting some of the theses proposed by historians and social scientists in their long-term explanations of the Christian democratic phenomenon. I will therefore concentrate my analysis on the arguments and evidences which are more directly connected with the cognitive questions raised by the editors of this volume in the introductory chapter of the present volume. I will in particular try to answer the basic questions which lie at the heart of all the chapters in this book dealing with a specific family of parties: are such families characterized, for what concerns parliamentary recruitment and models of representation, by peculiar transnational lines of convergence? Or, on the contrary, do they represent rather irregular clusters of historical experiences, which are to be explained only in the light of country or party-specific factors?

In Section 10.2 I start by looking at the main theories about the formation of CD parties, during the first part of the twentieth century. This will allow me to define a set of expectations on the degree of homogeneity—across countries and in a long-term perspective—of the parliamentary elites elected by these parties. Such an analysis can contribute to solve an 'old' question concerning the existence of fundamental differences between parties born from the 'catholic reaction' and other forms of confessional or multi-confessional parties (von Beyme 1985; Kalyvas 1996).

Second, I will investigate some specific country factors impacting on recruitment patterns and candidate profiles of different CD parties. This exercise is particularly helpful in order to test the hypotheses based on the different organizational and cultural features which would have denoted some peculiar experiences, for instance the Italian Christian democracy (Leonardi and Wertman 1989). In order to achieve this goal, I propose, in the central section of the chapter, a diachronic analysis of the long-term transformations of CD parliamentary elites in three countries: Germany, the Netherlands, and Italy. This selection of cases is determined by the data availability, since we do not have complete and comparable long-term series for other relevant cases such as Austria and Belgium. The sample seems in any case satisfactory, since it covers three crucial party experiences that have followed, in their respective domestic political systems, different pathways in reaction to the challenges of the nineties.[3]

This last argument brings us to the final point addressed by the chapter: the destiny of the parliamentary elites of this ideological family after the recent party transformations due to the turbulent environment of the post–cold-war period. As some comparative assessments have pointed out (Hanley 1994; Pelinka 2004), there is a paradoxical situation in the recent evolution of the CD party family: soon after 'celebrating the victory', at the end of the cold war, most of the parties included in the federations of the European People's party and of the Christian-democratic International (today the largest transnational party in Europe and the most populated assemblage of national parties over the world[4]) are facing a serious identity crisis. Such a crisis has entailed the decline of some 'historical' CD parties, but also the partial shift of their political vocation and/or the rise of a new generation of parties, which are formally attached to the CD supranational organizations but also relatively autonomous from the ideological strands typical of the past (Gallagher, Laver and Mair, 2001). A recent research on this party family in Europe (Van Hecke and Gerard 2004) describes the factors which lead to changing the nature and political message of the CD experiences. Among them are to be mentioned, the acceleration of the European integration process with the establishment of the Economic and Monetary Union, the trend towards a bipolarization in the European context, the growing importance of European leadership for national government leaders, the need to answer a number of questions raised by different sectors of the centre and of the far-right wing (from the problem of immigration to the safeguard of traditional values vis-à-vis the new proposals of experts and scientists and bioethics challenges, from the neoliberal challenge to the recurrent law and order demands, etc.).

As previously mentioned, this chapter does not intend to provide a full-fledged explanation of the evolution of several 'variants' currently included in this party family. Instead of this, it will illustrate the main lines of diachronic and cross-country variation, aiming, at first, to describe the degree of internal coherence noticeable among the parliamentary elites of the 'traditional' CD parties. It will then compare these patterns with those of some new main parties of the family (in particular the Spanish *Partido Popular* and the Italian *Forza Italia*), which represent the 'natural' terms of comparison, since they occupy the same political space of the old CD parties and, last but not least, have become today the most relevant actors within the European People's party.

10.2. THE EMERGENCE OF A CHRISTIAN DEMOCRATIC PARLIAMENTARY ELITE: WHEN AND HOW?

The appearance of several CD parties in Europe, during the first part of the twentieth century, has been illustrated by comprehensive comparative analyses (Duverger 1951; von Beyme 1985), as well as by specialized studies on this party family (Fogarty 1957; Irving 1979; Caciagli 1992; Kalyvas 1996). Many authors have stressed the different ability of these parties to win a significant electoral consensus, thus obtaining a relevant portion of parliamentary seats, and to consolidate themselves as 'nationwide parties'. Curiously enough, however, not a single work, in the literature, measures in details the different patterns of parliamentary penetration of CD parties. A simple time-line graph with the transformation of the parliamentary strength of some selected CD European parties during the period 1850–1940 (Figure 10.1) clearly evidences the different timing and success of the appearance of these elites. This confirms the argument raised by Klaus von Beyme (1985) on the multifaceted political missions of CD parties in Europe.

The figures about the parliamentary presence of CD parties can be connected to the qualitative differences among these historical parties which specialist studies have stressed. Starting with the largest historical CD parties the earliest and most successful case of parliamentarization (and, subsequently, of access to the executive threshold) of a confessional party is the Catholic party in Belgium (*Katholijke Partij/Parti catholique*, then *Christelijke Volkspartij/Parti Social Chrétien*). This party used to play the role of the 'main challenger' for the liberal elite, being

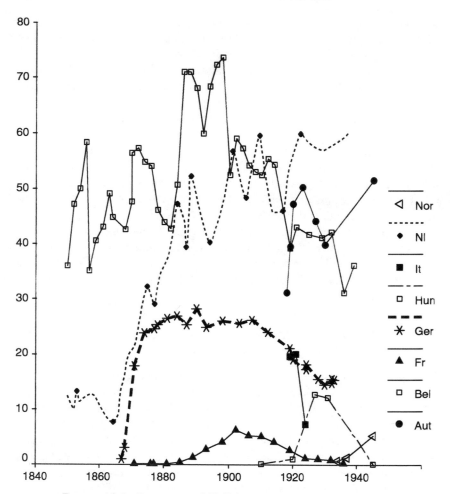

FIGURE 10.1. Percentage of Christian Democratic seats in selected
European countries (1848–1945)

in more than one moment the dominant political actor of the country. Over
a 'majoritarian' threshold of 40 per cent we find, also, the Dutch Christian
democrats and, later, the Austrian CD party (*Katholische Volkspartei*, 1907–34).
Here we have to introduce a first distinction between the unitary confessional
parties expressed by the 'catholic-reaction' (the Belgian and the Austrian CDs)
and the multiple and competitive parties typical of a 'multi-denominational state',
like the Dutch CDs.[5]

In a second 'class' of parliamentary strength we should consider both the
German *Zentrumpartei* and the Italian *Partito Popolare*, both important actors in
their respective parliamentary scene, but with a share of seats limited to about

20 per cent. The two parties had a strong common feature in their catholic imprinting, but were born at different times (the *Zentrum* already in the 1870s and the PPI only in 1919) and under different circumstances. The *Zentrum* represented the expression of a confessional minority (with no counterpart in the Protestant majority of the population); on the other hand, the Italian PPI was the final answer to the old problem of the 'catholic isolation' vis-à-vis the dominance of the secular liberals, but also a tool to respond to the menace of other mass party organizations, in particular the socialist one.

The other CD experiences during the period 1850–1950 had a more minoritarian character. In particular, one should mention the French case, which is usually considered to be a failure (during the third republic) but was then (during the fourth republic) a relative though short-lived success. One should also analyse other minor CD actors, like the Scandinavian protestant parties, which, according to Lipset and Rokkan (1967) and von Beyme (1985), would represent a further sub-family of confessional parties.

On the other hand, the Figure 10.2 reveals the different performances of CD parties after 1945, in correspondence with the crystallization of the main European party systems. Here one can roughly distinguish two types of CD parliamentary impact, reflecting in some way the distinction between forms of 'catchallism' (van Kesbergen 1994) and a sort of 'minority' mission. In the first group we find the new German inter-confessional Christian democracy (*Christlich-Demokratische Union*, strictly connected with the Catholic Bavarian *Christlich-Soziale Union*), the Dutch and Belgium parties, and finally the Italian *Democrazia Cristiana* and the Austrian *Österreichische Volkspartei*—two parties formed after the authoritarian interruptions but strongly grounded on the previous confessional party experiences. In the other group we find the French and Scandinavian CD formations, the first (the *Mouvement républicain populaire*) being a successful Catholic-based formation at the beginning of the Fourth Republic,[6] the latter embodying a group of clearly minoritarian 'defenders' of the orthodox protestant values in their respective countries.

In order to complete the picture, a third type could be considered here, which embraces the recent evolution, during the last fifteen years, of CD or 'quasi CD' parties, in a broader number of Southern and Central-Eastern European democracies. The clearly decreasing trend of traditional CD parties in the 'old' Western democracies is partially balanced by the small increase during the last couple of decades of the Nordic protestant parties (Gallagher, Laver, and Mair 2001) and by the success of new CD parties in the Central-Eastern Europe (Poland, Romania, but also Hungary, Czech Republic, and others). Moreover, we have to note in this period the success in Southern Europe of a number of parties, formally linked to the European People's party (*Partido Popular* in Spain, *Forza Italia* in Italy, *Nea Dimokratia* in Greece...) even if not explicitly Christian Democratic, which represent the 'new face' of this political area.

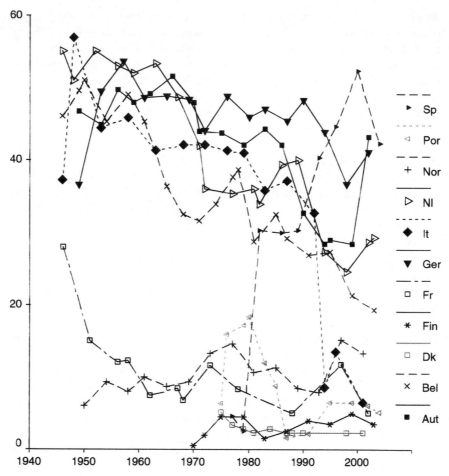

FIGURE 10.2. Percentage of Christian Democratic seats in selected
European parliaments (1950–2005)

As mentioned before, I will not cover the latter topics: our research design is
in fact limited to long-term transformations in Western Europe (and the data on
Central-Eastern European countries will be discussed in another volume related
the *Eurolite project*). However, I will briefly discuss the problem of 'compatibility' among parliamentary elites from 'old and new' CD parties, in Section 10.5 of
the chapter.

The starting point of the analysis is therefore a simple question: what point(s)
in time can be identified as the consolidation of an effective CD parliamentary
elite in Europe? To answer this question I will have to consider the stabilization
of a *critical mass* of MPs from confessional parties in a significant number
of European parliaments and the existence of some distinctive features in their

process of recruitment. The data presented in the previous figures already tell us that the control of the first condition appears rather problematic, if one compares the historical situation of CD parliamentary elite with the representation of other party families: in fact, the emergence of a significant body of CD MPs has to be placed in a broad time span between 1860 and the second decade of the twentieth century (without considering the late emergence of protestant parties from the Scandinavian countries). This evidence offers some support to the criticisms moved to a mechanical definition of the CD 'party family' simply based on the sociological cleavage theory: both the criticism based on the substantive negation of the historical autonomy of such a party family[7] and the recent theory developed by Stathis N. Kalyvas suggest that the formation of confessional parties, at the dawn of the twentieth century, has to be interpreted as the result of strategic decisions made by a number of political actors which change from one country to another and across the time.

In order to control the differences among the parliamentary profiles of confessional parties, at the moment of their effective breakthrough, I will have to propose an asynchronic comparison, selecting the average values of the measurements of some important dependent variables (social and political features of CD MPs) during periods (those corresponding to the parliamentary consolidation of our parties) which are partially different from one country to the other.

Once I will have isolated some elements of distinctiveness of the CD parliamentary elite, I will face a more complex interpretative problem: to understand if these original features were connected to some 'national peculiarity', expressing specific party patterns in each domestic reality, or, on the contrary, might have somehow 'crossed the national borders' forming, since the very origin of European CD parties, a sufficiently homogeneous recruitment pattern within the whole party family. Again, the literature on the historical formation of these parties suggests different alternative hypotheses on this point. Many scholars agree on the occurrence of a common pattern of elites configuration among the main European CD parties. For instance, the idea of a rather similar pattern in the elite development of the German *Zentrum* and the Italian *Partito Popolare* is consistent both with the theories based on a relatively strong 'homogeneity' of the Christian Democratic Party family (i.e. Duverger 1951; von Beyme 1985), but also with the interpretation developed by Kalyvas. One can also assume, using the same argument, that the Catholic elite in the Netherlands would have been more similar to the MPs of the former two parties, while the protestant representatives would have shown other characteristics, which perhaps could be compared to the profile of the 'Nordic protestant' MPs.

Table 10.1 includes the average values concerning the measurements of some characteristics of CD MPs in a few European countries during the phases of historical consolidation of their movements/parties. I have considered, when necessary, more than one line for a single country, thus marking the historical evolution of different parties. For instance, we see here the phase of consolidation of the

TABLE 10.1. *Characteristics of Christian Democratic MPs: average values during selected periods*

Party	Period	Public sector background	Liberal professions	Military persons	Priests, clergymen	Primary sector	University degree	Mean age (years)	Noblemen legislators	Local/regional political background	Leading party position
Germany-Zen.	1871–7	30.1	5.8	0.0	15.1	32.7	83.7	50.6	43.8	35.6	5.0
Netherlands-ARP	1884–7	74.5	6.3	20.9	3.1	4.9	77.4	48.8	69.6	33.8	48.2
Netherlands-RKSP	1884–7	49.9	39.3	5.4	0.0	0.0	91.1	52.2	5.4	39.3	80.4
France-CDs	1893–1902	6.3	37.5	1.6	3.9	31.4	59.5	43.7	18.6	80.6	3.8
Netherlands-KVP	1905–13	49.3	22.7	4.0	0.0	4.0	60.0	49.2	29.3	52.0	54.7
Netherlands-ARP-CHU	1909–17	45.4	12.4	4.1	0.0	1.0	58.7	53.7	23.7	40.6	49.2
Italy-PPI	1919–24	26.4	45.8	2.9	0.0	6.8	79.5	43.7	12.6	—	—
Hungary-CDS	1927–31	29.5	27.6	1.2	20.9	11.7	86.8	49.1	13.2	42.8	24.6
Italy-DC	1946–53	37.1	49.5	0.5	0.0	3.6	81.9	47.1	0.0	43.7	71.8
France-MRP	1946–56	27.1	20.7	1.6	1.0	16.7	41.2	46.6	5.2	—	—
Germany-CDU/CSU	1949–57	37.8	10.4	0.3	0.47	11.5	59.3	52.1	2.8	44.4	18.2
Norway-KRF	1950–8	31.7	5.1	0.0	0.0	32.7	22.9	58.4	—	84.7	52.4
Finland-KD	1972–9	42.6	—	12.0	0.0	12.0	70.7	48.3	0.0	62.1	69.5
Denmark-KRF	1973–7	100	0.0	0.0	17.7	0.0	45.8	50.3	—	—	78.6
Portugal-CDS	1975–9	20.3	39.30	0.0	0.0	0.0	89.0	42.6	—	4.7	31.3

German *Zentrumpartei*, but also the post-Second World War consolidation of the inter-confessional CDU-CSU; the two Italian Catholic party experiences (the Popular Party before Fascism and Christian Democracy after 1945); the emergence of a CD parliamentary group in the French Third republic and the (ephemeral) emergence of the MRP between 1946 and 1956. In the case of the Netherlands I have decided to include four experiences: the first phase of consolidation of a group of catholic parliamentarians and of the protestant ARP (around 1880), the phase of the parliamentary institutionalization of the catholic KVP (after 1904) and, in the same period, the formation of a double protestant parliamentary party (the persistent ARP and the CHU). Finally, the table reports some analogous information about four minor parties which emerged more recently and belong (in a broader definition) to the CD family: the Hungarian CDS during the intra-war periods, the Norwegian KRF, the Finnish KD, the Danish KRF, and the Portuguese CDS.

What are the most important findings to be drawn from this table? At a first glance, a rather assorted cluster of profiles emerges. If we take two classic indicators of long-term parliamentary transformation like nobility and primary sector background, we clearly see that, according with the overall trends of all European countries (Best and Cotta 2000), the weight of both indicators declines over the time. At the same time, we can see that the penetration of nobility and landowners among the parliamentary groups of confessional parties is rather irregular from one case to another: in the Netherlands, the profile of the Anti-revolutionary party is much more characterized by these social groups than its Catholic counterpart in the second part of the nineteenth century. At the same time, the parliamentary group of the German *Zentrum* is also pictured here as an elite of nobles and landowners, which contrasts with the catholic representative elites emerging in the same period in the Netherlands and in Italy.

All in all, it would seem more fruitful here to look for outliers with regards to each single variable, rather than attempting to define possible 'benchmarks' of what could be considered a normal distribution in this group of parties. For instance, in the Netherlands the already mentioned ARP was clearly representing the interests of some 'traditional social groups', and gave voice to the military elite, to high state servants, and to the nobility. This seems consistent with the historical role of the Calvinist party as the opponent of liberal and modernist instances. The Catholic party, on the other side, was in fact more characterized by semi-professional 'political entrepreneurs.[8]

Another peculiar feature can be found in the German catholic *Zentrum*: the profile of its parliamentary group is dominated by the representation of the primary sector and also, at least at the beginning of its parliamentary experience, by a considerable presence of clergymen among its ranks. Again, this small hint can be significant if one compares it to the absence of clergymen within the PPI, the first catholic party in Italy, due to the tensions with the Roman Catholic Church on the opportunity to override its policy of refusal of any participation in the liberal and secular state (the so called *non-expedit*).

The CD parties born in the mid-twentieth century, in times of mature democracy, seem to acquire a more convergent pattern of recruitment. Nonetheless, some national peculiarities persist: the MPs of the French MRP were, for instance, more oriented to represent the primary sector, thus reproducing a typical concern of moderate parties. The same applies (although to a lesser extent) to the German CDU-CSU and, of course, to the Nordic parties, which basically challenged the old conservative and agrarian parties. This does not apply however to the Italian Christian democracy, whose parliamentary personnel was marked since the very beginning by the ambivalence of a composite party (see below). It represents in fact, within its ranks, together with some traditional social groups also some public sector middle-high functionaries and party professionals.

An effective instrument for a more precise assessment of the configuration of the CD parliamentary elite, during the period of its formation, can be offered by a systematic comparison between its overall profile and the profiles of other large party families. In particular, one can compare, for a set of crucial indicators, the average values describing the profile of CD parliamentarians to those of two potentially 'competing' types of party. In order to locate the position of the CD elite in a comparative frame, we have to take into account two possible terms for this comparison: a party family from the traditional centre-right and another family of 'mass parties' of the twentieth century. Of course, the second choice is relatively easy, because the Socialist-Social democratic family represents, all over Europe, the prototype of the 'mass party' opposed to the centre-right actors since the beginning of the century. The other comparison is more problematic, as different party families of our data-set could be considered as a possible comparative term in the 'most similar' logic of selection. Here I propose the Right Liberal family. This is essentially because of its wider distribution (in comparison with the conservative family) among the countries included in the data-set.

For this purpose, I have calculated the means for the CD, Right Liberal, and Socialist MPs in the historical time span between 1900 and 1975.[9] The interest of the analysis is twofold, as we can evaluate both the overall position of the CD family vis-à-vis the other groups, and its degree of internal variance.

For what concerns the first dimension, it is clear that the CD MPs prove to be an ideal 'midpoint' among the profiles of the Right Liberal and the Socialist representatives. Figure 10.3 displays the variables where the overall mean for the period analysed brings the CD MPs to an intermediate position between the other two groups. As one can see, the majority of the dependent variables used in the data-set are included in this analysis and clearly show the 'intermediate' nature of the CD elite vis-à-vis the other two families. In most of the cases, the position of the CD MPs is closer to the Right Liberals, but there are also significant indicators showing a more marked closeness to the socialists. This is the case, for instance, of the figures concerning the type of university background and the

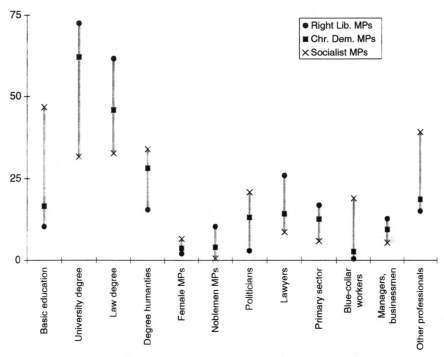

FIGURE 10.3. Characteristics of three families of European MPs:
average values (1900–76) (%)

percentage of fully paid politicians. These figures would therefore clearly show a more pronounced role of 'party professionalization' in the CD parliamentary recruitment in comparison with the other party families of the centre-right.

It would be worthwhile to add here some information, concerning the variables not included in the graph (those where the CD overall mean does not fall between the Right Liberal and the Socialist figures). Among them, we find some subcategories of the 'public service' occupational background (such as judges, higher civil servants, and teachers), which clearly constitute a set of preferential features within CD recruitment. In the case of teachers and university professors, in particular, the overall mean is significantly high, being close to the value of 15 per cent. This supports the image of a pattern of parliamentary recruitment where we can see a number of different components at work: the persistence of some traditional forces normally present in the recruitment of centre-right or conservative MPs (for instance the primary sector) is balanced by the presence of new social groups, such as professionalized politicians, teachers/university professors, public officers. A substantial confirmation of the above findings comes when we develop the comparison between CD elites and those of other moderate parties (see the chapter on conservatives) and also if we compare the CD average values to a wider centre-right cluster of families including both the Right Liberals and the Conservatives. In fact, this additional test would only slightly change the results of the set of variables of Figure 10.3; the CD MPs would again be in a median position between the centre-right and the socialist clusters.

I have pointed out the 'intermediate position' of the CD representative elite, vis-à-vis the other two party families, but to what extent is such a position to be explained in terms of a stable, distinctive pattern of recruitment? Or is it, on the contrary, the result of a particularly irregular distribution across countries? Of course, in order to provide a satisfactory answer to these questions, we would need deeper and more qualitative information on the role of country and/or party-specific factors, which are not available in our extensive and aggregate data-set. With the available data we can however start reflecting on the bases of the descriptive statistics derived from the distributions of the three series considered above. According to this point of view, we can undoubtedly argue that the figures concerning the CD party family have to be considered as the result of a rather scattered distribution trend: in fact, the measures of the standard deviation of the overall mean are, for all the variables used in Figure 10.3, systematically higher than those concerning the Right-Liberal MPs. Moreover, the analysis of the standard error of the mean—another descriptive tool measuring how much the value of the mean may vary from one sample to another—indicates that the variance across countries of the means related to the parties of the CD family is, on the whole, higher than what observed within the socialist family.

In the end, this exploration of aggregate data and of variance indexes enable us to argue that the peculiarities one can note in the long-term transformation of CD parliamentary elite are more evidently connected to 'local factors'—that is to the specific conditions for the emergence of parties with strong anti-liberal or anti-conservative (and then anti-socialist and anti-communist) claims—than to a robust common pattern of parliamentary recruitment. This does not mean that the representatives from this party family *have no distinctive features at all*. If one looks carefully at these first data and compares them with similar elaborations concerning socialist or conservative and liberal parties (as analysed in other chapters of this volume) it is then possible to understand that, for instance, they are since the beginning of their parliamentary experience characterized by a 'mass party' profile. That is to say, they represent a wide range of social groups and ground their political personnel on a rather high degree of political professionalism. At the same time, they normally represent (although with a non-irrelevant degree of internal variance) a high percentage of liberal professionals and a rather highly educated political elite, thus marking a clear sign of distinctiveness from the other 'mass party' model emerging all over Europe, that of the Socialist party. However, these features seem to be, at least in the childhood phase of this parliamentary elite, more oriented to mark a negative distinctiveness than a positive one. In other words, CD parties tended initially to produce a representative elite, which looked more dissimilar to that of their historical challengers than similar to their homologues from the other countries.

10.3. PARLIAMENTARY RECRUITMENT OF THE EUROPEAN CHRISTIAN DEMOCRATIC PARTIES: LONG-TERM TRENDS

It is now time to have a closer look at the evolution of CD parliamentary profiles during the whole twentieth century. Two basic hypotheses can be derived from the party organization literature: the first one emphasizes the relative diversity marking the origins and, to some extent, the persistence of the parliamentary parties included in this family. The second hypothesis points, on the other hand, to the convergence which should have characterized the elite of these parties in the final part of the twentieth century, due to the *cartelization* of their political organization.

We can start from the first argument. The selection of representatives from the CD parties in Europe, during their long-term evolution, has been strongly affected by several country and party specific factors which would have determined different patterns of transformation, particularly in those realities where the confessional parties have played a pivotal role within the political system (Germany, the Netherlands, Italy, but also Austria and Belgium). In particular, one can refer here to the cases of the Italian DC as a 'governing catch-all party', typically dominated by a high level of factionalism, an evident inter-class claim and rather different degrees of territorial penetration from one region to another. The literature on the historical pathways of transformation of the Italian parliamentary elites has depicted Christian Democracy as a modern mass (and then catch-all) party which was able to adapt its system of political recruitment to the different cultural areas of the country and over time. Cotta's analysis of parliamentary recruitment in the first thirty years of republican democracy (1979, 1982) clearly defines such a process as the building of a modern (that means fundamentally different from all the experiences of the past, including the pre-fascist popular party) clientele-mass party recruitment system. The degree of political professionalism of this elite soon became very high (sometimes higher than some centre-left and left parties), but until 1992 the typical recruitment pattern of Italian CD MPs was characterized by the combination of strong features of political and party socialization with significant societal resources and territorial links which proved particularly important in determining the internal ranking of preferences[10] and the effective success of candidates from the DC lists.

According to the classical analysis of the Dutch political system provided by Lijphart (1968*a*, 1968*b*), one should not expect to have a very dissimilar evolution from the CD parliamentary elite in the Netherlands. Here, it is true, the presence until the 1960s of separate confessional parties, should have encouraged the persistence of some historical differences in the profiles of Catholic and Protestant representatives. On the other hand, we know that the process of convergence had begun a long time before (the phase of the *accommodation*) and the reduction of the electoral space for confessional parties had become another factor increasing their homogeneity. Nonetheless, one should expect that, within a very composite party as the CDA, the opportunity for some sort of 'mixed recruitment' system, including traditional and innovative features, would be larger than in other more cohesively structured parties.

For what concerns the German inter-confessional parties born after the Second World War, the literature usually stresses the fact that within these parties the weight of the religious cleavage declined rapidly (Schmitt 1990). After a few electoral rounds the Union twin parties appeared solidly grounded on a 'social pact', which determined very distinctive profiles of their parliamentarians cutting, to a large extent, across the two confessional components of the CSU and CDU[11] and surely different from the shape of the SPD and FDP representatives (Best, Hausmann, and Schmitt 2000).

All in all, what we expect from the historical evolution of the parliamentary elite transformation in these three European experiences (which will be the object of our next empirical test), is a certain degree of variance, which should somehow confirm two impressions already surfacing in the previous paragraph. First, the greater 'flexibility' in the recruitment system of all the CD parties, due to their wide socio-political claim and, in the end, to the original ambivalence of a 'modern' party which is at the same time linked to traditional societal strata. Indeed, this would apply particularly to Italian and Dutch CD MPs. Second, the idea that, in specific CD parties, a stable-mixed recruitment system could be established over the years, enabling the presence, within the ranks of their representatives, of a wider range of social categories.

The second hypothesis, on the other hand, contemplates a process of progressive convergence among the parliamentary elites of the different CD parties. In fact, even if the original elements of variance depicted above are unquestionable, there is a convergence towards some forms of political recruitment which would characterize the 'mature model' of the European People's party, as a pivotal party naturally oriented after the Second World War towards some governmental role. The basic argument here lies in the idea that the family of the European CD parties could have represented the typical party organization moving in the direction of the 'cartel party' model (Katz and Mair 1995). Without recalling the details of this model, its periodization and its implications in terms of parliamentary elite transformations (see Chapter 6 in this volume), I will simply argue that the organizational transformations occurred to these central governing parties from the 1970s onwards should have brought significant innovations in terms of parliamentary recruitment. While the nature of CD representatives as 'professionalized agent of the state' has been reinforced, some traditional practice of the conservative or liberal-like recruitment have instead been abandoned.

In order to provide empirical support to the above arguments, I will now examine the long-term evolution of the parliamentary elites of the most significant CD parties. I will use a standardized descriptive measure of the dependent variables selected from the DATACUBE archive: the diachronic evolution of the average values for ten years periods concerning a number of social and political backgrounds of CD MPs.

Starting with the university background, a social indicator frequently used by the recent literature, the 'U curve' noted by Cotta and Best in their transnational comparison (2000: 497) and discussed by Gaxie and Godmer in this volume is confirmed in all the most significant CD parties (Figure 10.4). There is a partial exception with the Italian case, where the authoritarian experience (1924–43) probably interrupted a process of evolution in the recruitment of the pre-fascist PPI which consequently determined an apparent degree of continuity in this variable between the MPs from this party and those from the *Democrazia Cristiana* elected after the return of democracy.

Another clear indicator of homogeneity among the three CD national delegations is the decrease of two elements such as the weight of law degrees among MPs with a university background (an indicator of the type of education) and the percentage of lawyers in parliament (an indicator of occupational background) (Figures 10.5 and 10.6). The only partial deviant trend here is represented by the limited original relevance of these factors in the German delegation during the period of the Reichstag. This was indeed dominated, for what concerns the CD representation, by a party—the Catholic *Zentrum*—more linked to other social strata (in particular, the primary sector).

Another interesting minor deviation is represented by the Italian figure for the most recent election (2001) which finds an explanation in the coding strategy which was used for this legislature: here I have only considered the parliamentary group from the UDC (the small post-Christian Democratic party joining the centre-right coalition) as pure 'CD MPs'. However, the parliamentary group of this party represents only a minority of the former CD politicians currently seating in parliament. We can find many others of them among the MPs of the *Margherita* (the Liberal Democratic list, coded as liberal-left)[12] but also within the other parties of the right side, such as *Forza Italia* and *Alleanza Nazionale*.[13] In any case, the predominance of lawyers within the 2001 UDC parliamentary group reflects an old feature of the Italian parliamentary elite, its geographical segmentation; in fact, many parliamentarians of the UDC come from the south (particularly from Sicily) where the social position of the lawyer always played an important role in the political recruitment of moderate parties.

Significantly enough, the non-political variable showing the lowest degree of homogeneity is the percentage of female MPs Even in this case we can confirm some conclusions reached from the specialist analyses (cfr. Kjaer and Christmas in this volume for an in-depth analysis): although this indicator reflects

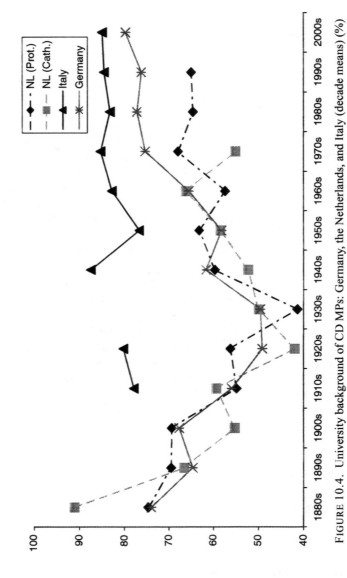

FIGURE 10.4. University background of CD MPs: Germany, the Netherlands, and Italy (decade means) (%)

Note: After the reunification in 1980 of three parties (the catholic KVP, the protestant CHU, and ARP) the MPs elected in the new inter-confessional Christian Democratic Appeal (CDA) have been here indicated as *protestant*.

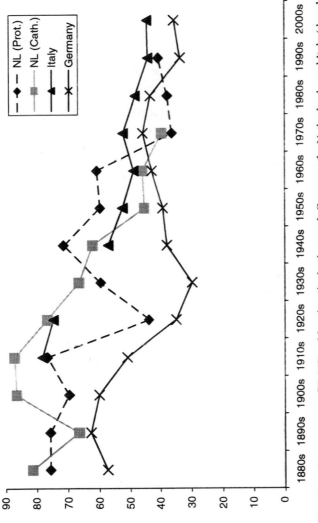

FIGURE 10.5. Law degrees among CD MPs with university background: Germany, the Netherlands, and Italy (decade means) (%)

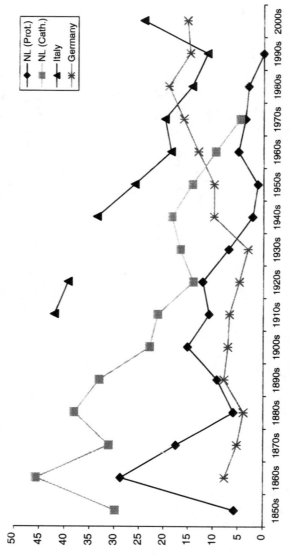

FIGURE 10.6. Lawyers among CD MPs with university background: Germany, the Netherlands, and Italy (decade means) (%)

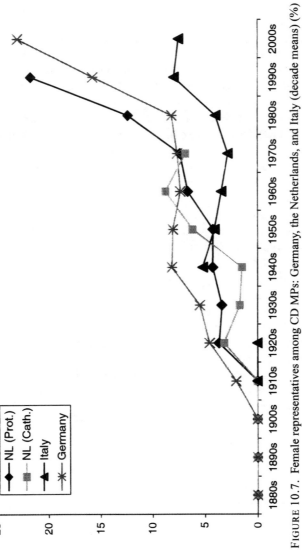

FIGURE 10.7. Female representatives among CD MPs: Germany, the Netherlands, and Italy (decade means) (%)

also variations across party families (being particularly higher, for instance among the new left and greens political formations) the long-term analysis of CD parliamentarians evidences that female representation is more strongly subordinated to a country logic.

The decrease of some traditional social features is balanced by the emergence of other political characters. It would be particularly interesting to stress the presence, already from the early twentieth century, of professional politicians which became later an important feature of the CD parliamentary elite (Figure 10.8). Nonetheless, two partial deviations from this picture must be underlined. The first is the historical discontinuity between German CD representatives before and after the Second World War which is at odds with the expected trend, since the parliamentary group of the late Catholic *Zentrum* was characterized a lot more than the CDU/CSU groups by party professionals. The second deviation is not a diachronic but a cross-country one, since the Dutch CD MPs (both protestant and catholic) show, in comparison to their German and Italian colleagues, a marked increase over the decades of their rate of political professionalism.

The growth of a component of professional politicians among the European CD MPs does not necessarily mean that a career in party offices should also be increasing as a typical background of the parliamentary elite. In fact, the rate of MPs with a party office background (Figure 10.9) has, with the exception of the German case, declined during the last decades. The bizarre aspect of the Italian line, particularly the peak for 2006, should not surprise and probably hides a trend in line with the others countries, since it has to do with specific short-term episodes or with the changing definition of our sample.[14]

On the other hand, observing the trends of the local elective backgrounds of MPs (Figure 10.10) one can discover that the political professionalization of CD representatives, particularly with regard to their 'political training' in the subnational political environment, is still very high. This accentuates the impression of a highly professionalized recruitment, based on a variety 'political resources' more than on a 'strictly party curriculum'. Among these political resources we also have to add those professional backgrounds which used to be more typical of mass-party organizations than of 'liberal parties'. For instance, the presence of academics, intellectuals, and higher civil servants (all these categories seem to grow or at least remain significant in all the CD subgroups here considered). Together with the other findings I have described above, this would mean that, on the whole, the long-term transformation of the classic Christian democratic recruitment seems to correspond rather well to a 'cartelization' of these organizations. Other tests, not fully reproduced here for reasons of space, confirm the same evolution, with the increase of the local political experiences and the persistence of the political background also among the MPs elected in other—less statistically significant—CD parties.

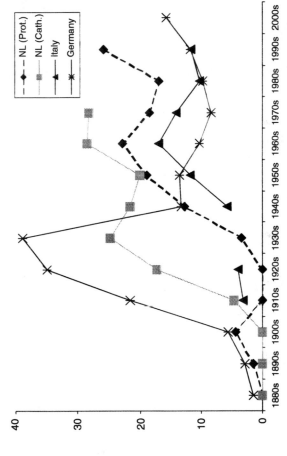

FIGURE 10.8. Full paid politicians/trade unionists among CD MPs: Germany, the Netherlands, and Italy (decade means) (%)

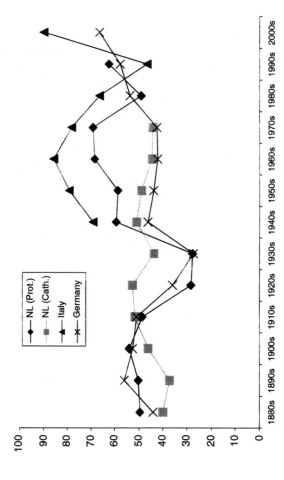

FIGURE 10.9. Party office background among CD MPs: Germany, the Netherlands, and Italy (decade means) (%)

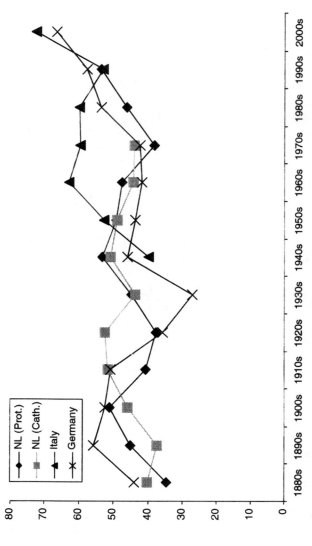

FIGURE 10.10. Local political background among CD MPs: Germany, the Netherlands, and Italy (decade means) (%)

10.4. RECENT DEVELOPMENTS: NEW TYPES OF CHRISTIAN DEMOCRATIC REPRESENTATION?

As mentioned in the introductory remarks, the question of the current transformation of the CD party format in Europe is not under discussion in this chapter. Nonetheless, the long-term series from the DATACUBE archive provide useful instruments to test some first exploratory hypotheses about the real impact of the changes occurred within the CD area during the last thirty years. This important party family has been challenged in its 'classic' foundations but seems, nevertheless, to have more than one possibility to recover and to play an important part in a new phase of European history, at the dawn of the twenty-first century.

It is useful to remember the most recent steps of the long trajectory of the CD parties in Europe: first of all, during the 1980s, we have the first signs of decline of some traditional central parties in Europe. Among them, the Dutch CDA, whose votes fall below the 30 per cent threshold in 1982 and decrease in an even more evident way during the nineties. Both Belgian CD parties were also declining in the same period, while the Italian *Democrazia Cristiana*, after a slow electoral decline during the 1980s, suddenly collapsed in the turmoil of the political scandals of *Tangentopoli* (1992–4). The exception is represented by the German CDU/CSU, whose consensus remained unaltered during the long Helmut Kohl's 'monarchy' (the percentage of CD vote being constantly higher than 40 per cent between 1976 and 1994). However, notwithstanding the fact that the party has always remained in this decade the 'natural' alternative to the SPD for the chancellorship, the defeat in 1998 and the difficult internal crisis during the following four years represented also for the CDU/CSU the materialization of the new challenges suffered by the whole of Christian democracy in Europe (Hanley 1994). These challenges do not seem completely overcome, even after the 'quasi-victory' of the 2005 elections. In spite of the return to the first position among Bundestag's parliamentary groups and the important pay-off of the chancellorship, the real CD consensus remains quite far from the times of Helmuth Kohl.

If many 'old' CD parties have seemed to suffer the 'de-freezing' of the European party systems, other new or renovated formations have entered the 'central' sphere of the political spectrum, gaining strong electoral support and claiming some of the typical CD principles. They have joined (at least as observers, but in most of the cases as full members) the European People's Party in the course of the nineties, contributing to reinforce the nature of the EPP group within the European Parliament, as an alternative to the left (in particular, to the Party of the European Socialism). The first example of this 'new generation' of centre/centre-right parties was the Spanish *Partido Popular*, which joined the EPP in 1991 (the same year of the affiliation of the Austrian ÖVP and of the Swedish KDS). Other Nordic conservative parties were admitted to the EPP as observers, and in 1992 the era of the convergence between the EPP and the British Conservative party started when the members of European Parliament (MEPs) elected in the lists of the latter decided to join the EPP group in the European Parliament, thus forming the new EPP-ED (European democrats). Later on, the new party of *Forza Italia*, founded by Silvio Berlusconi in 1994, was also admitted as member of the EPP (1999), and the French *Union pour un Mouvement Populaire* followed in 2001. Finally, a number of parties from the Central-Eastern Europe joined in the recent years the CD supranational party.

Many implications, concerning the transformation of parliamentary representation, can be derived from this important historical phase, marking the evolution from a 'pure' CD family to the current composite nature of the EPP federation. A first hypothesis will concern the consistency and homogeneity of patterns of political recruitment in a renovated and enlarged CD party family: the entrance of neoliberal, conservative and 'secularized' parties should have brought some important innovations, particularly in the social composition and in the pattern of circulation of the political elite. More specifically, the new parties should show a more evident similarity with the features of other traditional rightist conservative families: a greater importance of private-managerial occupations in their social backgrounds and a reduced impact of the party-based pathway in the political career should for instance emerge.

On the other hand, a partially deviant hypothesis could be grounded on country-specific features characterizing some parties which would resemble to some traditional aspects of CD political recruitment but not other ones. According to this line of reasoning, one should expect the recruitment of the parliamentarians of *Forza Italia* to be somehow similar to that observed in the Italian *Democrazia Cristiana*, although with a more secular outlook; in the same way the post-Gaullists of the UMP should not be expected to differ dramatically from their 'fathers'.

Finally, and this is another partially alternative hypothesis, one can think that *all parties* belonging to the central-EPP area are nowadays more or less affected by a process of transformation, leading the whole party family towards a 'post-CD' model where old and new features are mixed. We can assume here again that the traditional 'catch-allism' of the moderate-confessional mass parties is evolving towards another model, coherent with the definition of *cartel party* and with an organizational format which resembles an 'electoral machinery control party' (Katz 2002). From the point of view of parliamentary recruitment, we notice in fact a general decrease of some traditional features of the CD parliamentary elite, for instance, the solid party and local elective backgrounds of their backbenchers. On the other hand we also notice that all the parties from this area would in any case show some difference with the other classical patterns of recruitment which had characterized conservative and liberal parties in the past, for instance, the declining impact of the liberal professions and the increase of the 'higher public service' as typical social backgrounds of the representatives.

These hypotheses delineate an intriguing puzzle which would deserve to be explored in greater depth with a more specific and intensive research based also on a number of variables which are not in the DATACUBE. For this purpose the influence of religious associations in parliamentary recruitment and the commitments of MPs to specific legislative issues such as support to religious education, limitation to divorce, abortion, etc. would be relevant. I will provide nothing more than a first comparative assessment of the recent variations within the group of EPP parties for what concerns some characters of parliamentary recruitment. My benchmarks will be the 'classic' CD formations from the countries covered by the DATACUBE (namely, the CD parties from the three countries analysed above) and the two largest parties from the last generation: the Spanish PP and *Forza Italia*.[15]

A first test has to be conducted on the persistence today of a 'critical mass' of truly CD parliamentarians. Table 10.2 gives the number of cases (where each case is a group of MPs from the lower chamber elected in a given country/year)

TABLE 10.2. *Parliamentary strength of selected CD parties after 1990*

Country	Year of election	Party	Number of MPs (lower chamber)	% (lower chamber)
Denmark	1990	Kd	4	2.3
	1998	Kd	4	2.3
	2001	Kd	4	2.3
Germany	1990	Cdu/Csu	319	48.2
	1994	Cdu/Csu	294	43.8
	1998	Cdu/Csu	245	36.6
	2002	Cdu/Csu	248	41.1
	2005	Cdu/Csu	226	36.8
Italy	1992	Dc	206	32.7
	1994	Ppi, Ccd	54	8.6
	1996	Ppi, Ccd/Cdu	85	13.5
	2001	Udc	40	6.5
Netherlands	1994	Cda	34	22.7
	1998	Cda	28	18.7
	2002	Cda	43	28.6
	2003	Cda	44	29.3
Norway	1993	Krf	13	7.9
	1997	Krf	25	15.2
	2001	Krf	22	13.3
	2005	Krf	11	6.5
Finland	1991	Kd	8	4.0
	1995	Kd	7	3.5
	1999	Kd	10	5.0
	2003	Kd	7	3.5
Hungary	1990	Kdnp	20	5.2
	1994	Kdnp	23	6.0
	1998	Kdnp	0	—

Source: DATACUBE archive, integrated when necessary with the data published on the internet archive: *parties and elections in Europe*. http://www.parties-and-elections.de/

included in our archive and concerning parties coded by our country experts as CD. As one can see, we still have a significant number of parties but their weight in terms of parliamentary personnel is clearly declining. Only the size of the CD German delegation remains typical of a 'major party'. The Dutch CDA has been severely reduced (and its weight remains lower than 30% after the two most recent elections), and the same applies to the Italian post-DC formations. The Norwegian protestant party, the only one which has improved during the nineties, gets more than 10 per cent of MPs, while all the other cases, including Hungarians, Danish, and Finnish have to be considered minor parliamentary actors.

I will not comment all the elements of divergence which still characterize this composite party family, as some of the graphs already discussed show. On the other hand, it must be stressed that the decrease in the size of these parties seems to have favoured a historical trend of convergence among their parliamentary profiles. This assertion can be supported by a simple measure of statistical variance: the standard deviation's coefficients among the DATACUBE entries concerning CD parties in the nineties are significantly lower than those calculated during the previous periods.

On the other hand, we can take the most significant among the cases described in Table 10.2 (the CD representatives in Germany, the Netherlands, Italy, and Norway) and compare them with the profiles of *Forza Italia* and *Partido Popular*. This comparison shows a clear distance between the two subgroups, indicating thus some interesting peculiarities of the 'old CD' parties vis à vis the new central parties. The most striking divergence lies in the fact that the new parties are a lot more connected with the 'private sector', and especially with professional and managerial social strata, thus exploiting a typical asset of liberal and conservative parliamentary elites. Figure 10.11 illustrates the extent of the difference in the weight of these social groups in the parliamentary personnel of PP and FI, in comparison with the other current EPP parties.

On the other hand, the typical features of catch-all organizations tend to disappear in the new central parties, while they keep being relevant among the old CD parties. Another 'radar graph' including some political backgrounds and occupational backgrounds normally associated with high degrees of political careerism, is very illuminating (Figure 10.12): while political backgrounds seem to go together, in the old CD parties, with a solid parliamentary presence of teachers, other groups from the 'public sector', and with professional politicians (the stereotype seems to be in this respect the Norwegian KRF), in FI and in the PP all these characters are less important. The relative differences between these last two actors (with a more professionalized parliamentary elite in the PP) can be explained in the duvergerian terms of a genetic theory of party, the birth of the PP being much more 'internal' and rooted in the traditional organization of other previous party experiences, in comparison with the political group founded by Silvio Berlusconi.

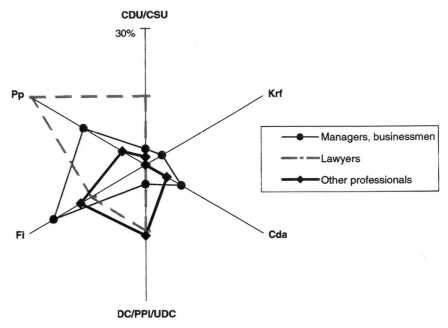

FIGURE 10.11. Liberal professions background of national MPs
(mean percentages) in some EPP parties (1990–2005)

One could also provide an explanation based on the 'lifespan approach'. After only a decade of parliamentary experience, *Forza Italia* can still be considered as a 'beginner parliamentary party' and its MPs could probably be integrated/substituted by other more 'skilled' representatives as time passes by. On the other hand however, the MPs elected in the *Partido Popular* during the last decade come from a longer parliamentary experience. This would suggest that by now their features should have acquired a higher degree of stability.

10.5. CONCLUSION: FROM THE MULTIFACETED RECRUITMENT PATTERNS OF AN HISTORICAL PARTY FAMILY TO CONVERGING BUT 'LESS CHRISTIAN DEMOCRATIC' ELITES

In this chapter I have discussed a series of data with a clear, although modest, purpose: to understand if the political formations belonging to the historical party family of the European Christian Democracy have been recruiting parliamentary elites which are more similar among themselves or closer to some country-by-country patterns which affect parties from different traditions. Answering this question has allowed me to develop some arguments concerning both the specific explanations of the different origins of CD representative elites in different countries of Europe, and the longitudinal interpretations of their transformations.

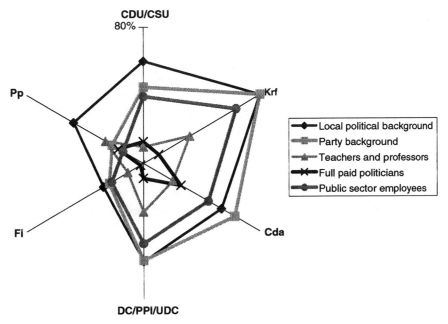

FIGURE 10.12. Political and occupational backgrounds of national MPs
(mean percentages) in some EPP parties (1990–2002)

All in all, the broad answer is that the representative elite of the CD party family was, and to some extent remains, very differentiated in its internal components. In Section 10.1 of the chapter I have argued that the impact of some of the original features of each CD party in Europe is particularly evident when one examines the system of recruitment of parliamentary representatives. If we consider the subfamilies of catholic and protestant (or inter-confessional) parties we notice a clear division line over the decades. On the other hand, the intensive analysis presented in the central section of the chapter, which is centred on three important CD parties (the Italian, the German, and the Dutch one), shows that, under the 'parliamentary recruitment' point of view, these different examples of Christian democracies were somehow characterized by a similar destiny, which I have connected to the process of party cartelization. I therefore support the argument that, if some of the original features of the different CD 'models' are still at work, a process of convergence among CD elites has been evident in the course of the late twentieth century, along the line of the 'post-mass party model' transformation.

This last argument has led to a discussion about the current degree of homogeneity between 'old' CD parties and other experiences occupying the centre of the political spectrum in some European political systems. This discussion, which has been approached in the final section of the chapter, would need a more systematic empirical evidence to be developed in a fully interpretative key. In fact, I have simply matched some results of my study concerning the traditional CD MPs with the representatives of some new party actors recently affiliated to the European People's Party. I have in particular considered the MPs elected in the *Partido Popular* and *Forza Italia*, two parties occupying the 'space' of the traditional Christian democracy in two catholic countries during the recent decades. The main descriptive finding is that, at the beginning of the twenty-first century, there is a clear divide between old and new parties belonging to this broad area. We are, however, also living in an uncertain situation which could possibly lead to some forms of convergence: the challenge now is to discover whether such a convergence will imply the dissolution of the basic features of such a glorious 'party family' in the European parliaments. The analysis of the parliamentary elite will be crucial (together with other dimensions such as that of political discourse and of policy platforms) in order to understand the real extent of this change.

ENDNOTES

1 I am grateful to Karl Schmitt of the University of Jena, who has commented an earlier version of the chapter, providing generous and illuminating suggestions.

2 See for instance Pridham (1977) on the German Christian Democracy; Zuckerman (1979) and Leonardi and Wertman (1987) on Italy; De Winter (1992), Lucardie and ten Napel (1994), and De Winter (1992) on the Netherlands and Belgium.

3 For a comparative analysis of the different policy orientations of CD parties in these countries see van Kesbergen (1999).

4 A broad description, although a bit dated, of the supranational CD organization can be found in Papini (1997).

5 As it is well known, in the Netherlands the first organization directly inspired by a religious ideology, in order to oppose the liberal elites' dominance was the Calvinist party founded in 1878 by Abraham de Kuyper (*Anti-Revolutionaire Partij—ARP*). The catholic counterpart was organized a few years later (*Rooms-Katholieke Staatspartij—RKSP* until 1939, then renamed *Katholieke Volkspartij—KVP* until 1980). A third party, the protestant (but more liberal oriented) *Christelijk-Historische Unie* (*CHU*) was created in 1908. Given this framework, which persisted until 1980 when the 'Christian Democratic Appeal' was created, the Netherlands has been for a long time the only case where two religious subcultures (Calvinist and Catholic) were organized within the party system.

6 One should at least remember that, after the disappearance of MRP, a small CD group (*Centre démocrate, Centre des démocrates sociaux*) was active all the same at the parliamentary level within the *UDF*. Unfortunately we have no possibility to distinguish this group using the aggregate data, and therefore an analysis of the parliamentary profile of these deputies of the Fifth Republic is impossible.

7 The extreme argument here, usually attributed to Maurice Duverger, is that CD parties would very often have been '. . . conservative parties which changed their name'.

8 Translation from the Italian *Organizzatore politico*, a term employed in the first years of the twentieth century indicating those party activists (from the Socialist and then the Popular party) at the local level who used to spend most of their life in political business. Perhaps this definition does not fully coincide with the weberian 'living off politics', but it surely entails some pronounced degree of political professionalism.

9   The definition of the time span responds to two basic requirements: (*a*) to consider the *phase of formation* of all the most important CD parties present in the countries included in the data-set; (*b*) to have a sufficient number of cases in order to limit the distorting effect of the outliers.

10   This ranking was important to weight the relevance (and consequently the parliamentary presence) of the different 'factions', but the final say about who had to get the sit was to the voters. Thanks to the multiple preference vote system, the competition among individual candidates or small groups of candidates connected by the same ideological values or by a political 'sponsor' was extremely evident until 1992, the last election won by the DC. That of 1992 was also the last election run under the PR system but, significantly, the first one without the multiple preference vote (which had been abrogated by a referendum in 1991).

11   We have no data to distinguish the profile of Bavarian Christian Democrats from the one of their colleagues of the CDU. We could probably infer some of their peculiarities from the social structure of their *Land* (starting with the importance of social and occupational groups related to the primary sector). But the fact that these representatives have been considered in the literature and are entirely integrated with the other German CD MPs is in itself an indicator of the cohesiveness of such an elite.

12   The most important component of the *Margherita* was in fact the new *Partito Popolare Italiano*, whose elected MPs are counted as CD, together with their centre-right colleagues, in the CUBE entries relative to 1994 and 1996.

13   The percentage of MPs with a past activity within the old *Democrazia Cristiana* was higher than 30% in 2001, that means roughly the same electoral strength of the 'real' last DC in the late 1980s (Verzichelli 2002).

14   In the 1990s, this curve touches its minimum value because of the disruptive effect of the Christian democratic breakdown, (which entails the election in 1994 and 1996 of a number of outsiders in all the parties included in this definition of the CD family). The only figure included in the following decade (2001) is biased by the lower number of deputies included here (the sole centre-right CD troops of UDC), many of them 'recycled' from the old ranks of Christian Democracy.

15   The data on the PP have been kindly provided by Miguel Jerez Mir. In the DATACUBE version of the original file on the Spanish parliamentary elite, currently in progress, the PP has been coded as a *Conservative party*. Forza Italia, whose aggregate data are in our comparative data-set, has been coded until now (elections of 1994–2001) as a right liberal party.

Socialist and Communist Members of Parliament: Distinctiveness, Convergence, and Variance[1]

Gabriella Ilonszki

11.1. FRAMEWORK AND HYPOTHESES

This chapter examines the parliamentary representatives of the socialist and communist parties. The analysis of these two party families is a particularly challenging task because their transformation throughout more than a century offers an insight into how the often turbulent political history of these parties had an impact on the representative bodies. As both party groups were latecomers (initially outsiders or even challengers to the existing regimes), one can assume that also their representatives were different from those of more established groups. We can also assume that as the socialist parties—in some cases even the communists—got more established, their representatives became increasingly similar to other parties' elites. In what steps has this happened, with regard to which characteristics of the parliamentary group is it the most obvious? Has it been a one-sided process through which the socialists (and, probably, much less so the communists) adapted or a more complex phenomenon by which the other parties' representatives have been acquiring features that formerly 'belonged to' the socialists? Have the communist representatives also gone through a 'similarization' process or have they maintained their distinctiveness vis-à-vis the other parliamentary party groups? What has been the stronger tendency in these party families: the strength of the family pulling their representatives in the same direction or the strength of the concrete country environment as a source of variation and diversity? Has the significance of these two dimensions (party and country) changed over time? The answers to these questions on similarity, distinctiveness, and variation are built around the following hypotheses.

The first hypothesis is that in the first phase of their 'parliamentary career' socialist MPs were dissimilar from the other MPs. When in the nineteenth century the formation of the socialist and social democratic parties took place, from their organizational attributes, political agenda, and marginal position, we would expect that their representatives would have been highly *different* from the representatives of the other parties. The 'old' parties by then had been established mainly as cadre parties, created by the status elite, and originated within parliament (Duverger 1955). By contrast, the socialists were the first mass parties (Duverger 1955; La Palombara and Weiner 1966). Thus to illustrate the political 'difference' (rooted in the party's organizational difference) some direct political characteristics of the MPs will be selected from the EurElite database: the share of professional politicians (those who live on politics and have some party and trade union function), the share of party leaders (those who have a leadership position in the party at any level), and the share of local politicians. These will be called politicians, party leaders, and local politicians in turn. These variables express the significance of the modern mass party in the evolution of MPs' distinguishable features. In addition, the marginal position of the party both politically and in its social composition makes it opportune to choose some other variables from the database for analysis. Political marginality can be illustrated by the share of newcomers, that is, those who are elected to parliament for the first time. The changing proportion of newcomers will remain a good indicator of the level of stability or embeddedness that the parties achieved throughout the entire period. Social marginality of the MPs will be connected to the (low) level of education and/or occupational background. Of course, other variables might also be illuminating regarding the 'difference, similarity and variance' thesis but probably these are the ones that would reveal most clearly how the changing political place of the parties transforms some fundamental (social and political) attributes of their elite within a wider process in which convergence but also variations prevail.[2]

The socialists' political place developed together with the development of mass democracy. They depended on the opportunity structures of the regimes and paradoxically they fought to broaden their opportunities while frequently challenging them. Although pressures and resistance from the ruling classes against them reached different levels in different countries, in no country was this process unproblematic. As has been demonstrated elsewhere, ruling-class responses varied from direct oppression through institutional obstacles to control via parliamentary and electoral means (Bartolini 2000*a*, 2000*b*: 313ff.). To become fully accepted members of contemporary democracy, the socialists had to overcome the four Rokkanian thresholds of legitimization, incorporation, representation, and executive power. This required that their right to organize and to participate actively in political life be recognized, suffrage extended to the working classes, electoral systems changed to lower the barriers of entry into parliament and that finally, their partaking in responsible party government be accepted (Rokkan 1970*a*, 1970*b*). By crossing these thresholds, the socialists' distinctiveness has weakened and a similarization process has taken place.

On this basis, the *second hypothesis* is that in this process the socialist parliamentarians have been getting closer and have become increasingly similar to the other parties' MPs. The reasons for this lie in organizational, ideological, political, and social developments. Organizationally, the social democrats ceased to be the only mass parties because most of the other parties also moved substantially in this direction. As a result, similar career patterns emerged in the other parties as well: for example, party officials must have appeared in large numbers. Ideologically and politically, they lost their anti-system character. Consequently—following the general economic and social transformations of capitalism—the social composition of the party family changed: low-status groups were increasingly replaced by the more educated and those in non-manual professions. Although *similarization* has occurred with varying speed and intensity in the different countries examined in this chapter, we can rightly assume that the consolidation of the socialist party family supported the trend of their MPs' similarization to a great extent. The same variables that will be applied to demonstrate the first hypothesis (newcomer status, political career background, and social background) can be used to show the consolidation/similarization process.

Table 11.1 summarizes some major political steps that describe the socialists' widening political opportunities, such as the timing of party formation, major franchise extensions, and the first appearance of socialist MPs, in parliaments and then in governments, by country. For the first appearance of socialist MPs two numbers are indicated: the first is the 'accepted' date in academic literature (e.g. Przeworski and Sprague 1986, or Mackie and Rose1991) and the second is the figure in the EurElite database.

Socialist and social democratic parties were formed well before manhood suffrage was introduced in Austria, Norway, Italy, the Netherlands, Finland, Hungary, Portugal, and Spain, while in Germany, Denmark, and France the Left party formation followed male enfranchisement, which had taken place comparatively earlier than in the other countries (indeed, in Germany the two ran in parallel). Although the connection between enfranchisement and the proportion of the left vote, and thus the appearance of party representatives in parliaments is not direct, the socialist party family entered parliament fairly soon after enfranchisement.

In a handful of countries, socialist parties entered the government for the first time after the First World War. Under more normal conditions, the first socialist cabinet was created somewhat later: in the UK, Denmark, Finland, then in Norway in 1935, and in the Netherlands in 1939. In Spain, the first socialist ministers formally joined the government in 1931 in the period of the Republic. In the second half of the twentieth century, socialist cabinets were indeed common. For example, in Norway, the Labour Party was in government for more than forty years. These developments provide a sound basis for the assumption that differences not only between the socialists and other parties but also between these parties' representatives diminished.

While the socialists became increasingly embedded in the parliamentary and political history of liberal democracies, most communist parties failed to become an influential political group, although in some countries they had impressive success. The communist parties were all founded as split-away groups from the socialists during and immediately after the First World War and the two

TABLE 11.1. *Stepping stones in the development of socialist parties*

Country	Party organizationally consolidated	Party MPs first in parliament	Party MPs first in parliament in the database	Male universal suffrage	Party first in government	Party recurrently in government (after year)
Austria	1889	1897	1918	1907	1919	1945
Denmark	1878	1884	1884	1848	1918	1924
Finland	1899	1907	1907	1907	1926	1937
France	1905	1893	1848	1848	1936	1945
Germany	1875	1871	1867	1871	1919	1919
Hungary	1890	—	1905	1945/1989	1944	1994
Italy	1892	1895	1892	1913	1945	1963
Netherlands	1894	1888	1888	1918	1939	1945
Norway	1887	1903	1903	1900	1928	1935
Portugal	1911	1911	1975	1878/1969	1919	1976
Spain	1910	1910	1977	1930/1976	1931	1982
UK	1906	1892	1900	1918	1924	1929

Sources: Rose and Mackie 1991; Przeworski and Sprague 1986: 36; Bartolini 2000: 251, 360.

parties remained antagonistic and politically different. Among communist parties a radical orientation prevailed and most of these parties maintained their original organizational and political attributes. For example, on the basis of their more rigid party organization, it can be assumed that there should be more party leaders and more professional politicians in their parliamentary ranks. Their constant reference to working-class (or low-status) groups might hint at the prevalence of working-class MPs in their ranks. Thus *the third hypothesis* will be that communists remained *distinct* from the socialists and, consequently, did not go through a process of homogenization with the other parties. Understandably, the same variables can be applied here as in the case of the socialists.

Lastly, this chapter targets the issue of *variation*. The existence of variations within the left party family is a widely accepted thesis and can be demonstrated throughout all the periods (Bartolini 2000*a*, 2000*b*). We can assume that variations prevail in the composition of their parliamentary elite as well. Differences are rooted in diverse electoral fortunes, the continuous or disrupted nature of the political history of the country they operate in, the party's organizational strength and type (in terms of membership and trade union connection, which are indicators of mobilization potentials), and their place in the political system, including the share and distribution of socialists and communists. Thus, the *fourth hypothesis* is that in the background of the similarization process country *variations* are maintained. But do variations become more explicit over time? What explains them best—size, organization, political history, or some other more nationally (and not party) rooted phenomena? Although we cannot test variation on all variables, those will be applied that reveal the career patterns and are also connected to organizational and political historical attributes, namely the 'politician' and *local politician* background. We can also hypothesize that when a dominant theme prevails in the party family, the extent of variation is smaller, while in more relaxed periods there is more room for diversity, which is reflected in the parliamentary elite composition as well.

11.2. THE BEGINNING—HOW TO BE DISTINCTIVE

According to the first assumption, at the beginning of their parliamentary existence socialist MPs were highly different from the other parties' members. As Figure 11.1 indicates, the number of socialist MPs only slowly increased. It is only well into the first decade of the last century that the proportion of socialist MPs reached the 5–10 per cent level in a handful of countries. Low numbers themselves might be an indication of 'difference'.

Table 11.2 shows in a more explicit way the strength of these parties before the First World War. Eight countries had a couple of elections before 1917 on the basis of extended franchise. While on average the share of socialist MPs in parliaments is not high, electoral performance in some countries is impressive. Low percentage figures do not necessarily hide low 'performance', however. For

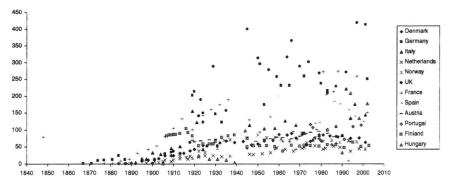

FIGURE 11.1. Socialist parties in parliament

example, the German average proportion is only 7.8 per cent in this period, but this covers fifteen elections—the first two couple of which, necessarily, were not yet fully contested. By the first decade of the last century, German proportions are well above 10 per cent, that is 20.1 per cent in 1903 and 13 per cent in 1907. Similarly, in Denmark in 1906 21.2 per cent, and in France in 1906 12.2 per cent of the MPs belonged to the socialist parties. These proportions reveal that by that time in the countries where enfranchisement was well advanced, its impact was visible in the increasing presence of socialist party representatives in parliament. Denmark, the Netherlands, and Norway stand out for their electoral stability: the socialists' share exceeded 10 per cent on average before 1918 throughout a fairly high number of elections. Finland represents an exception because—still under Russian dominance—the social democrats managed to appeal to the lower classes (including the agrarian population) to an unprecedented degree.

TABLE 11.2. *Average parliamentary strength of socialist parties before the First World War (number of elections in brackets)*

Country	Mean % before 1917
Austria	—
Denmark	13.3(13)
Finland	44.5(8)
France	7.5(11)
Germany	7.8(15)
Hungary	0.2(1)
Italy	5.5(7)
Netherlands	8.0(6)
Norway	11.3(5)
Portugal	—
Spain	—
UK	3.9(4)

TABLE 11.3. *Differences between socialist and 'other parties' MPs in % (unweighted means)*[a]

Variable/period	1890–9		1900–9		1910–19	
	Socialists	All others[†]	Socialists	All others[†]	Socialists	All others[†]
Newcomers	55.1	30.3	52.9	30.6	43.0	40.1
Basic education	45.7	25.2	46.6	23.6	54.3	25.0
Party leaders	54.7	14.2	29.7	20.6	36.2	28.8
'Politicians'	8.0	0.7	12.4	1.0	15.6	3.2
Local politicians	23.5	53.4	40.2	51.6	53.6	51.9

[†] All others means all MPs minus Socialist MPs.
[a] As clarified above, party leaders are those who have held a party position, and politicians are the party and trade union functionaries for whom politics is a profession.

In addition to party formation and franchise extension (see Table 11.1), the *degree of mobilization* and the *electoral system* also explain the extent of the socialists' parliamentary presence. For example, in Germany the share of votes cast for working class parties can be explained not only by the early enfranchisement of all males but also by strongly contested elections and a high degree of mobilization in this period (Best, Hausmann, and Schmitt 2000: 143). By contrast, in the UK the majority electoral system and the dominance of the two major parties (together with the attempt of the liberals to incorporate some of the Labour agenda) inhibited the appearance of Labour MPs in parliament (Rush and Cromwell 2000).

The lack of *financial compensation* to parliamentarians also limited the opportunities for the socialists. With the sole exception of the Netherlands—where financial compensation was introduced as early as 1798 (Secker 2000), financial rewards to parliamentarians were not provided, on the assumption that high social status and financial independence were 'normal' assets for a parliamentarian. In fact, the Bismarckian constitution extended the ban on all direct payments to Reichstag members to protect amateurs from professionalization (Best, Hausmann, and Schmitt 2000: 167). Then, in the pre–First World War years or some time later, an honorarium was introduced everywhere, thus increasing the opportunities of lower-class candidates. In Germany, financial rewards were introduced in 1906, in Britain in 1911, in Italy in 1912, in Spain a per diem was granted in 1922.

All in all, the belated creation and the marginal social and political position of the socialists had an impact on the first groups of their representatives. Table 11.3 shows the differences regarding some important attributes (variables) that have been selected as the main dimensions of analysis.

In this 'initial period', the weak establishment of the socialist parties and their MPs is reflected in all the selected variables. The consolidated character of the other parties' MPs is reflected in the low percentage of newcomers (around 30%).

By contrast, the above 50 per cent share of newcomers in the socialist elite in the first two decades demonstrates the novelty of the parties. In the 1910s, the two groups began to draw closer to each other.

As the left advocated the interests of the lower classes, and a low level of education regularly expresses marginal position, among the socialist MPs the less educated appear in higher proportions than among the old parties' representatives. Even the upwardly mobile, literate, dynamic groups in the left elite lacked formal education because of their low social status. In this respect, the differences prevailed and even increased in this period: the share of those with only basic education increased from 45 per cent to 54 per cent in the socialist's ranks while it remained around one-fourth among the other parties' MPs. As is demonstrated later (see Figure 11.8), marginality as reflected by the educational level of socialist was not necessarily complemented by manual professional background—many with a low educational level served as party and trade union officials or party journalists; they were, so to speak, working-class party intellectuals.

In the age of liberal parliamentarism, when mainly members of the upper and upper-middle classes served as representatives, the socialists were the first modern politicians. This is reflected in the 'politicians' and 'party leaders' variables. The share of 'politicians' among the socialists was initially 8 per cent while in the other party groups on average it was 1 per cent. Not surprisingly, in both groups this proportion grew throughout the period, expressing the tendency by which politics as a profession became increasingly widespread in those decades (Weber 2004, 1919). Nevertheless, the share of 'politicians' among the socialists was still five times higher than among MPs in the other parties even in the last decade of this period. Being the representatives of the first mass parties, they were different in this respect from the other mainly cadre-party representatives. In the case of socialist candidates, who were paid by the party as journalists, party officials, or trade union officials, party salary was a way to circumvent the problem of their coming from lower social strata than the MPs of other parties.

The proportion of 'party leaders' evolved somewhat differently. Their majority position among socialist MPs in the first decade diminished later because, understandably, among a larger number of MPs the share of party leaders automatically dropped. An opposite trend evolved in the other parties: they transformed their party organization and adopted a modern mass party structure, and thus party leaders appeared in much larger proportions among their parliamentarians. Differences in local political background spectacularly disappeared during the first period indicating that socialists became increasingly embedded in liberal democracies.

After this examination of the first period we can conclude that—as assumed—there were significant, although, decreasing differences between the socialists and the 'other' representatives. Franchise limitations, mobilization needs, the type of the first group of politicians these parties needed to be able to mobilize, and the newcomer or outsider status both of the party family and of its leaders provided

TABLE 11.4. *Average parliamentary strength of socialist parties (number of elections within brackets) (%)*

Country	1918–44	1945–69	1970–2001
Austria	37.9(6)	44.8(7)	47.5(8)
Denmark	38.6(11)	42.9(10)	43.9(13)
Finland	34.8(9)	25.4(7)	27.1(10)
France	23.9(5)	16.2(8)	31.5(8)
Germany	29.4(9)	37.7(9)	40.8(9)
Hungary	7.9(6)	16.7(1)	35.9(4)
Italy	20.6(3)	17.3(6)	20.1(9)
Netherlands	22.7(6)	27.7(7)	31.9(9)
Norway	32.1(7)	50.7(7)	40.4(8)
Portugal	—	—	36.0(10)
Spain	—	—	43.8(8)
UK	24.5(7)	50.7(7)	46.4(9)

Source: Own calculations from the Eurelite database.

the background for this distinctiveness. Probably, there will be no other period again in which intra-party family similarity is as strong and important as in this one. Interestingly enough, political consolidation and political convergence with the other families after this initial period was quicker and more pronounced (see the political career variables) than social convergence (as reflected by basic education).

11.3. SOCIALISTS, COMMUNISTS, AND THE OTHERS

11.3.1. *Socialists and Communists in Context*

The distinctiveness of the socialist parliamentary elite began to fade away after the First World War. In the inter-war decades—with the exception of countries where democracy was disrupted (Austria, Germany, and Italy), they became a fully accepted political force, and after the Second World War they became indisputably a mainstream party everywhere. The effect of their belated arrival lost its importance: they became embedded in the political system of their respective countries.

Their electoral increase was in itself a source of similarization. As Table 11.4 demonstrates, between 1918 and 1944, the share of socialist MPs was above one-third of all parliamentarians in Denmark, Norway, Austria, and Finland; and France, the Netherlands, and the UK show somewhat lower but still high proportions (about one-fourth). The disrupted Italian and German cases differ from each other because the length of the democratic experience was longer and the number of elections was higher in Germany than in Italy. After the Second World War the socialists' average electoral strength further increased; although Italy, France, and Finland show lower figures, all of them having huge rival communist parties and France even a less consolidated party system. Finally, the picture has been most homogeneous since 1970: the proportion of socialist MPs is high, stable, and similar between countries—with the exception of Italy where the communist–socialist divide and communist dominance prevailed until the end of the 1980s.

Political integration went in parallel with socio-economic changes (see Chapter 15 in this volume). The transformation of the social composition of socialist MPs and their similarization to those of other parties is no surprise in view of the changing composition of these societies. Workers never were a majority in any European society (Przeworski and Sprague 1988: 33) and the economic transformation increased educational levels while the demand for the manual workforce decreased. The growth of the middle class and the new social stratification challenged the old notions of class dichotomy according to which socialists and social democrats naturally belonged to one side of the cleavage. These changes had political and ideological implications. The need to attract more support—external to the working class—further contributed to the similarization of the socialist MPs to the entire parliament. 'The quest for electoral allies forced socialist parties to de-emphasize that unique appeal, that particular vision of society, which made them the political expression of workers as a class, an instrument of historical necessity' (Przeworski and Sprague 1988: 50). A new type of socialist parliamentary representative was in high demand. This change began in the middle of the last century and intensified in the 1970s. While 'most Social Democrats moved to the left from the 1940s to the 1960s...almost all European Social Democrats moved to the right in the 1970s, in the 1980s and further...in the 1990s' (Volkens 2004: 28).

Party type and organization also had an impact on the composition of the parliamentary elite. First, the transformation of the other parties in the direction of the mass-party model was a major source of convergence between the socialists and the other parties (e.g. party people began to dominate the 'old' parties'parliamentary groups as well), then the catch-all party structural and political attributes of both the socialists and the other parties explain why MPs with similar societal and political features would be selected on both sides. On all these grounds, we can expect similarization tendencies between socialists and others. In the following pages, I will examine, with the same variables as above, how the socialist parties got embedded into (parliamentary) politics and how their MPs became similar to those of other parties.

Before doing so, however, let us also put the communist parties in context. The relationship between the socialist and communist parties is complex. Although they were born with the same political–deological agenda, that is to eliminate capitalist exploitation, their initial—seemingly tactical—differences developed into fundamental divisions. As was noted above, the communist parties were created as split-away groups from the socialists and social democrats, which make the question of how their political–ideological differences were reflected in the composition of their respective parliamentary groups even more interesting. Communists had a more varied history than the socialists, and they went through more disruptions and discontinuities. Post-First World War radicalization was

FIGURE 11.2. Proportion of communist MPs in the parliament

most obvious in Germany, Italy, Finland, and Austria, the countries where—with the exception of Austria—the impact of the Communist party was later the most pronounced. The organizational fragmentation of the left was apparent in Finland, Germany (after the Second World War here the communists were banned), Italy, and France.

Nevertheless, behind the radical anti-system surface, communist parties have also gone through some transformation. In addition to mere tactical changes that we cannot consider here (e.g. we cannot assume that a turnaround from anti-system radicalism to popular front tactics in the inter-war years was directly reflected in parliamentary composition within a short period), more fundamental changes also occurred. For example, the Euro-communist turn of the Italian communists in the 1970s or the unavoidable consequences of the economic and social transformation might be reflected in their parliamentary groups' composition. Despite variations, with few and rare exceptions communist parties have maintained their class-based ideology and have not developed into catch-all parties. Thus, on several grounds, we can assume that convergence between the socialist and communist parliamentary elite did not become a major trend and the communists maintained their distinctiveness both from the socialist and the other parties' MPs.

The electoral fortunes of the communists never reached the level of the socialists on average (See Figure 11.2 and Table 11.5), although occasionally they represented substantial proportions: this happened in Germany after 1930, in Finland at the beginning of the 1960s, in France from 1946 to 1956, and in Italy

TABLE 11.5. *Average share of communist MPs (number of elections within brackets) (%)*

Country/period	1918–44	1945–69	1970–2001
Austria	—	2.4(3)	—
Denmark	1.6(3)	6.1(6)	3.8(3)
Finland	22.2(4)	13.8(7)	16.0(10)
France	14.3(5)	8.3(7)	9.0(8)
Germany	10.4(6)	3.8(1)	—
Hungary	25.6(1)	16.5(1)	—
Italy	3.2(2)	24.0(6)	30.9(5)
Netherlands	2.5(6)	5.0(7)	2.8(5)
Norway	2.3(2)	3.3(3)	0.6(1)
Portugal	—	—	12.6(10)
Spain	—	—	10.4(8)
UK	—	—	—
Altogether	10.9	10.4	9.4

Source: Own calculations from the Eurelite database.

in the entire post-Second World War period. Nevertheless, in all these cases they were at the centre of political conflicts: in Germany, the rivalry between the social democrats and the communists contributed to the crisis of the Weimar Republic: in Finland and in France, they strongly supported the Moscovite agenda; and in Italy, they were regarded as an anti-system party and thus were not allowed to join government ranks. By contrast, in Norway, Denmark, the Netherlands, and the UK the role of the communists remained minor (indeed in the UK they never reached parliament benches). Among the latecomer cases communists were influential in Spain and Portugal while in Hungary—although they had gathered strength after WWII due to the international circumstances—they did not return into parliament after 1990.[3]

The communist parties' electoral fortunes showed greater variations (see Table 11.5) than those of the socialists. On average, their electoral fortunes declined throughout the three periods (unlike the socialists, see Table 11.2 and 11.4 again). Only very rarely did they get in any way close to the government benches. It was only at a special historic moment, after the 1945 elections, that they were accepted as coalition partners—although only temporarily—in Austria, France, Finland, and Italy, not to mention Hungary where this was only a prelude to the communist takeover. Special cases are Spain and Portugal, where—under the circumstances of regime transformation—a strong communist alternative to the socialist parties emerged and endured for some time.

After the above examination of the changing party contexts in the following pages the composition of parliamentary elites will be presented in detail. Figures 11.3–11.7 include data about the socialists, the communists, and all the other parties. This provides an opportunity to test both hypotheses: the similarization of the socialists and the prevailing distinctiveness of the communists. Since here the main focus of our interest is the general differences and similarities between

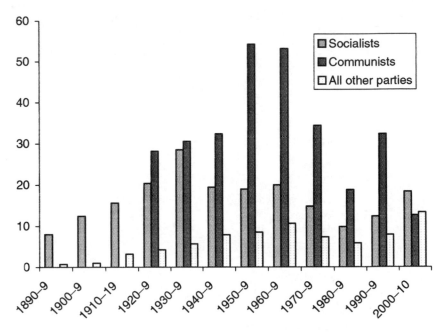

FIGURE 11.3. Politicians in party families

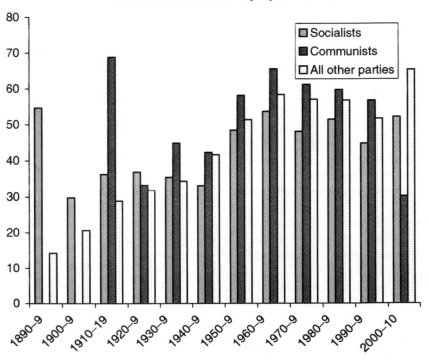

FIGURE 11.4. Party leadership positions in party families

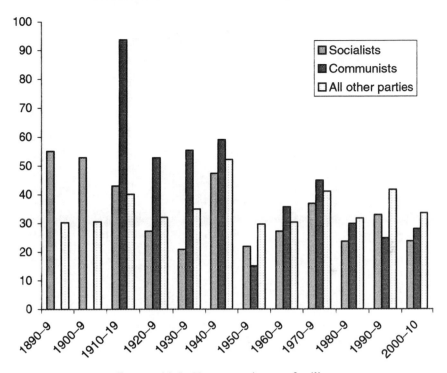

FIGURE 11.5. Newcomers in party families

the three large groupings, Figures 11.3–11.7 are drawn on aggregate data of the party averages in all countries

11.3.2. *Similarities and Differences*

In the first part of this chapter, it has been found that the high proportion of *politicians* within the socialist party family made them clearly different from MPs in the other parties. The presence of professional politicians in the parties, as has been argued above, is connected to how a party is organized and how a modern professional political group replaces the status elite and the amateurs. Understandably, the socialist parties were the first to have sent the highest numbers of party politicians to parliament because the party-centered model of recruitment began in these parties and thus party and party-press people as well as trade union officials were a dominant group at the beginning. As Figure 11.3 shows, the socialists maintained their advantage in this respect throughout the entire more than a century-long period, but the difference between them and the other parties has changed considerably. Initially, the difference was more than tenfold, and in the inter-war decades it was still spectacular because the increase in the

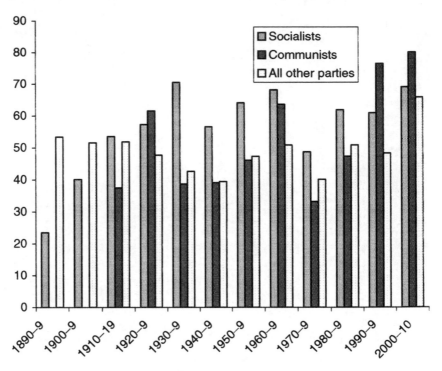

FIGURE 11.6. Local political background in party families

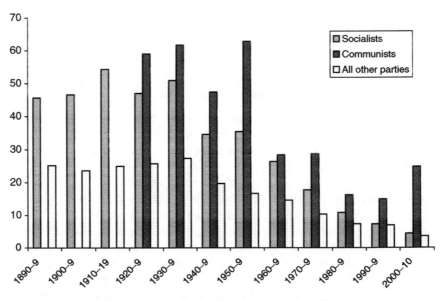

FIGURE 11.7. Basic education in party families

proportion of socialist 'politicians' (they reached 20 to 28 percentage point levels on average at that time) was not fully compensated by a modest increase among the other parties' parliamentarians: nevertheless, the difference between the two groups diminished to 'only' five to sixfold.

One can distinguish three periods: until the end of the 1930s the share of politicians in the socialist and in the other party groups is on the increase, then in the 1940s and 1950s stabilization is the main tendency (although on different levels), and from the 1960s onwards the socialists and the other parties' parliamentary compositions run very much in parallel in this respect, with minor increases and minor decreases probably reflecting electoral variations. In the 1970s, the difference dropped below 10 per cent and as of now it is indeed miniscule. All in all, a decline concerning the socialists and a modest although steady increase concerning the other parties resulted in the convergence of the proportion of politicians.[4]

The communists, without exception, had a much higher proportion of politicians among their ranks than either the socialists or all the other parties. The socialists and the communists even showed opposite trends until the 1960s: the share of politicians among the socialists slowly decreased (from 28.5% in the 1930s to 19.8% in the 1960s), while in the communist party groups they represented 30.5 and 53.1 per cent respectively. The socialists' convergence and similarization to the other parties and the communists' highly disciplined party organization are reflected in these numbers. Afterwards, the share of politicians among the communists also began to decline only to increase again in the 1990s— but their difference from the socialists has been maintained. With respect to the last two decades of the twentieth century, we have to be careful in our analysis because the database includes for the 1980s only four countries with communist MPs: Italy, Finland, Spain, and Portugal. In the latter two, the selection criteria and career pattern of the communist parliamentarians were different from the start, owing to their post-authoritarian experiences, while in both the Finnish and the Italian cases, the transformation of the selection routes, in addition to the evolving crisis of communist ideology and communist regimes, explains why a clear 'politicians' profile began to diminish. Nevertheless, as a general trend, we can conclude that the socialists and other parties have become similar while in the communist parliamentary elites the proportion of 'politicians' began to decrease only belatedly and not convincingly.

The share of party leaders shows different patterns. Politicians, as has been pointed out above, are defined as a group basically living on politics while party leaders occupy leadership posts at different levels of the party (not only the top positions) and they do not necessarily pursue politics as a profession. Substantial similarity between the share of socialists and other parties reveals that party political position is a regular, normal background of MPs in both groups (see Figure 11.4), not surprisingly since party has remained the main selection route for parliamentarians until very recently.

The difference between the socialists and other parties concerning party leadership proportions was high only at the beginning of the period under consideration when the majority of the socialists who got into parliament were party leaders but the other groups' MPs were still non-party amateurs. Then this difference began to diminish. The other parties demonstrate a one-way tendency of continuous increase and the party-leader levels of the two groups cross each other in the 1930s. In numerical terms the two groups were closest to each other in that decade, the share of party leaders being 35 per cent among the socialists' and 31 per cent among the other parties' MPs. After this, the trend changed, that is the share of party leaders became somewhat higher among the other parties than among the socialists, but basically they follow the same direction, with some minor difference in the 1970s.

Party leadership posts among communist parliamentarians—similarly to the figures for 'politicians'—are constantly higher than among either the socialists or the other parties (except for the 1920s, when the socialists had higher proportions of party leaders than the communists).[5] The difference is not that dramatic in this case, however, because the high share of party leaders seems to be a feature of all party groups. Still, the 'politicians' and 'party leaders' dominance in the parliamentary elite of the communists is more pronounced than in either of the other groups. Interestingly, when from the 1970s onwards, the share of politicians began to decrease the share of party leaders remained stable in the Communist party, that is party leadership background took over in the circumstances of electoral underperformance and shrinking parties.

Political consolidation versus political uncertainty can possibly be identified as the main explanatory sources in the background of the above variables with respect to the socialist and the communist parties. This view is strengthened when the share of newcomers in the respective parliamentary elites is observed (see Figure 11.5).

After the First World War, apparently, the socialist parliamentarians were more embedded in parliament than the others: in each single decade since 1930, the share of newcomers has been the lowest among them. Similarly to party leadership proportions, the 1930s are, in this case also, the 'turning decade'. Before that the socialists' and the other parties' elite composition followed opposite trends: a decrease of newcomers in the case of the socialists and an increase in all other parties. From the 1930s they go together, although more ups and downs occur with the socialists. After the decades of consolidation a new peak of newcomers occurred in the 1940s: after the war, with several regimes newly born and even the stable ones responding to new challenges, the share of newcomers understandably increased in all party groups. Interestingly enough, the proportion of newcomers and the proportion of party leaders are inversely related: a more stable, more continuous group tends to cement party leaders into the parliamentary arena, or party leaders tend to maintain their parliamentary position in larger numbers. For example, between 1940 and 1949, the share of newcomers represented 47 per cent among the socialists and 52 per cent among the other parties, while the share of party leaders was 33 and 41 per cent respectively; in the next decade, the share of newcomers was 22 per cent among the socialists and 29 per cent among the other parties, while the share of party leaders was 48 and 51 per cent respectively.

As has been argued above, the electoral chances of the communists and the socialists varied. While the socialists after their consolidation became an embedded group (indeed, the most embedded), the communists on average showed higher turnover rates—with spectacular differences between periods. First of all, they came in one rush: the first communist parliamentary group consisted almost entirely of newcomers. Second, they had a very high proportion of newcomers in all decades until 1950 (well above 50%), which reflected the political uncertainty surrounding these parties. From the 1950s the situation has changed. In the 1950s, the communists showed the lowest turnover rate of all parliaments and of all parliamentary groups, possibly because in that period only the large Italian, French, and Finish communist parties mattered in parliamentary politics and their cemented elites were the expression of the highly institutionalized and disciplined features of the party. Indeed, this low percentage of newcomers tells us more about the communist parties and their elite at that time than about the communist–socialist divide. From the 1960s the share of newcomers began to increase again and exceeded the socialists' and other parties' similar figures (one factor was that in the 1970s two new large parties, the Portuguese and the Spanish entered the picture, and another was that the selection criteria in the huge Italian party were also transformed) only to decline from the 1980s onwards. Overall, in the past two decades the share of newcomers has reached relatively similar levels in the three groupings, at least there have been no significant differences between them. In fact, this runs against one of the assumptions, namely that as a more secretive, centralized, disciplined (Selznick 1960) party, it will produce a lower share of newcomers than the other parties. This assumption was spectacularly confirmed only in the 1950s (not surprisingly); later it seems, the communist parties behaved in a more party-like manner and adjusted to the general parliamentary-political environment. The communists' diminishing political influence from the 1980s is reflected in the small size of their parliamentary groups and, not unrelated to this, in the somewhat lower turnover rate. It is indicative that in the 1970s there are 1100 while in the 1990s only 208 communist parliamentarians in our data-set. Paradoxically, the decline of newcomers in the communist parliamentary group in the past decades is due more to the decline of the party family than to its stabilization.

How are these former trends underlined or challenged with respect to the local politics background of the different elite groups? A local politics background might be connected to different political factors: selection criteria, career pathways as determined by political–cultural traditions, a country's regional-territorial dimensions can be reflected in it, not to mention the fact that it tells us about how a group is rooted in wider, lower, and deeper politics. When we observe the country differences in Section 11.5 of the chapter, these variations among countries will become more spectacular.

Initially, the difference between the socialists and other parties was huge: 23 per cent of the socialists as against 53 per cent of other party MPs had local politics backgrounds. This reflected the lack of municipal, regional, county, etc. positions in the left. The two groups got very close to each other between 1910 and 1920—with a mere two percentage point difference. Similarly as with the other variables, until the 1930s the two groups followed different trends (proportions of socialist MPs with a local politics background increased and those of other parties decreased), then from the 1940s they followed basically the same trends, each decade bringing either a minor growth (the 1960s and 1980s) or a minor decline (the 1970s and 1990s) for both groups, although the socialists regularly maintained higher proportions (see Figure 11.6).

By contrast, with the exception of the 1990s (and the 1920s) in the communist parties MPs with a local politics background were always under-represented in comparison to both the socialists and the other parties. As we have pointed out above, local ties can be regarded as a resource of embeddedness into the regime. Although the communists on average had lower levels of local politics background (regularly around 40%), they show wide variation: the peaks being in the 1920s, then in the 1960, and also in the 1990s. What explains this fluctuation? The answer lies in two factors, which warn us to be more careful with the presentation and analysis of the communist than with the socialist data. First, in different periods different countries are covered by the communist part of the data-set (e.g. in the 1920s we have the German but not the Italian data, to mention just one example), partly because the *life pattern* of the communist parties is not as straightforward as that of the socialist parties. Second, the communist parties often change their basic attributes within one country. It seems that communist parties have been more affected by external influences, political and policy alterations, which might have had an impact on the selection criteria and thus on the composition of their parliamentarians. As a result, both the general trend in the transformation of the parliamentary elite is more linear and the country variations more clear-cut in the case of the socialists, while in case of the communists it is more difficult to identify either a general developmental trend or fundamental country variations. For example, the local politics background of French communists changed from 55 per cent in the 1920s to 75 per cent in the 1990s, while in the Netherlands it changed from 75 per cent in the 1930s to 30 per cent in the 1970s. Of course, exceptions can be found; for example, in the Finnish communist parliamentary group, the share of local politics backgrounds was maintained at a high level throughout the entire eighty or so years, an indication not only of party roots but of country characteristics as well.

As both the socialists and the communists—at least initially—claimed to be the representatives of the lower classes, it is essential to examine the composition of their MPs from this perspective. The share of those with only basic education can

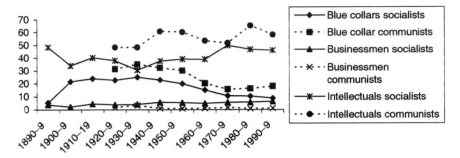

FIGURE 11.8. Occupational categories in socialist and communist parties

illustrate to what degree the MPs were connected to marginal positions in society. It is unquestionable that socialist and communist MPs were historically less educated than other MPs. According to Figure 11.7, the decline in the proportion of those with basic education began in the 1930s in the case of the socialists, in the 1940s in the other parties and in the 1960s among the communists. Nonetheless, the difference between the socialists and the others remained considerable for a long time. Despite the tendency of similarization, only in the 1970s did the difference in the proportion of MPs with basic education between the socialists and the other parties diminish to below 10 per cent (indeed, to 7%). Since then, the difference has further decreased. Interestingly, while in the communist parliamentary elite basic education was always more widespread than among the socialists (not to mention the other parties), the new communist groups in the 1940s and 1950s showed new peaks in the proportion of basic education. This clearly indicates that the newcomers came from marginal status and indirectly suggests that the political history of the communist parties had then fundamentally to 'restart'.

Overall, one cannot neglect the impact of broad societal transformations in the evaluation of this variable: eventually the decline in the proportion of those with only basic education became the main trend in all party families and the impact of party family differences became secondary in comparison to the impact of societal transformation.

The occupational background—as illustrated in Figure 11.8—shows a somewhat different picture. Three groups of occupations have been created from the variables that are at our disposal in the database: business people are a self-evident category, intellectuals contain the liberal professions—journalists, lawyers, and judges, teachers of different kinds—while blue-collar workers include not only the industrial workforce but also those working in the primary sector. At the beginning, the share of intellectuals was high both among socialist and communist MPs, while manual workers represented smaller proportions. To make the mass party work, an educated and enlightened group was badly needed. This dynamic new leadership group, a significant portion of which entered parliament, did not come directly from the lower classes but from those groups of the lower classes that were socially upward mobile (Ruosteetsari 2000: 73).

The share of intellectuals was somewhat lower in the inter-war years, but they were always over-represented as compared to the blue collars in every period in both parties. The share of blue collars shows a decreasing trend in both parties but among the socialists their proportion was always lower than among the communists. Societal changes as well as changing voters' support of the socialist party equally explain why the proportion of blue collars continuously declined after the peak in the 1930s, the high season of the mass party. The share of business people remains notoriously low in both party families. The missing proportions include first of all those with a political occupation (politicians) in addition to civil servants, the military, and priests. It is important to observe that at the European level the lower occupational categories never dominated the parliamentary elite of either of the two left party families—irrespective of the political or policy agenda that they advocated in different periods.

In this section, in harmony with the original hypotheses, it has been confirmed that the socialists became more embedded in parliamentary politics and also increasingly similar to the other parties' MPs while the communists maintained most of their distinctiveness. In addition, we have found several other dimensions in the transformation of the parliamentary elite. For example, the communists were more dissimilar from the other parliamentarians at the beginning than the socialists, and with respect to several variables they maintained their differences from the socialists throughout the entire period under consideration. They also showed large country variations, which depended largely on the level of left fragmentation and on regime disruptions versus continuities. Changing electoral fortunes, political ups and downs, and overall political or even regime changes carry more weight as explanations for the transformation of the communist MPs, while the socialists, being more consolidated and, politically increasingly embedded, follow more straightforward patterns and, with respect to several variables, the transformation of their parliamentary elite runs in parallel with other parties, the 1930s being an important turning point.

11.3.3. *Parliamentary Elite Composition—Is It Politically Relevant?*

In all the above dimensions, we were able to identify basic differences between party families. But can we find more direct connections between parliamentary elite features and concrete political developments? To what degree can the characteristics of the representative elite explain political events, and how do certain political changes explain the characteristics of the representative elite? Although this connection is possibly more indirect, several other and more fundamental dimensions have to be explored if we are to understand political change or elite characteristics. This section examines how far the parliamentary elite is a reflection and/or an indicator of the political situation. One example will be drawn

TABLE 11.6. *Characteristics of German and all other European socialist and communist MPs in the 1920s (%)*

	Socialists		Communists		Other parties	
	In Europe	In Germany	In Europe	In Germany	In Europe	In Germany
Newcomers	27.3	23.8	52.8	67.1	32.0	31.8
'Politicians'	20.3	48.8	28.1	63.4	4.2	17.9
Party leaders	36.8	70.2	33.0	68.4	31.6	49.1
Local politicians	57.3	50.7	61.5	39.4	47.7	37.0

from the interwar years and the others from the Southern and the Central European democratization processes.

1. The intense rivalry between the two left parties in the Weimar Republic and the eventual regime disruption raise the obvious question as to whether the composition of the parliamentary elite was to some degree responsible for the ferocious atmosphere there, or at least a connection can be drawn between the two. The German social democrats were forerunners in the development of the socialist party family, and so too were the communists on the extreme left. The parties' electoral fortunes initially varied but the gap became tighter. The communists began with an electoral support of approximately 10 per cent and their peak was 15.9 per cent in 1932, while the socialists' strength diminished from 40 per cent in 1920 to 21 per cent in 1932, and then to 19 per cent in 1933. During the entire period, the share of *politicians* remained constantly higher among the communists than among the socialists but party leaders dominated the socialists more. It is obvious at first glance (see Table 11.6) that both political groups were highly politicized in comparison not only to the other German MPs but to communists and socialists in Europe as a whole at that time. The intensity of the political atmosphere and party antagonism is well reflected in these figures. The data indicates the political fever of the Weimar regime: the figures show that the parliamentary elite not only reflected the controversies but also contributed to them. From a broader perspective this picture strengthens former arguments, namely that the rigid distinctiveness of the communists was more obvious when the left was highly fragmented and amid troubled political circumstances.

2. The Spanish and Portuguese post-authoritarian experiences are peculiar from a different perspective. When in the middle of the 1970s these two Southern European countries went through democratization (despite the differences in their regime change scenarios), both their communist and socialist left were strong. The communist electoral proportions were on average more modest in Spain (approximately 5%) than in Portugal (15%), yet also in Portugal a downward trend in communist strength can be observed in the 1990s (6–7%). Thus, in the first place it might be worth considering in what ways under post-authoritarian circumstances the two left parties representatives are similar to and different from

TABLE 11.7. *Communist parliamentary elites in Portugal and four other countries (%)*

Variable/country	Portugal	Finland, France, Italy, and the Netherlands
Basic education	32.4	19.6
Local politics	21.2	59.7
Party leaders	31.9	65.0
'Politicians'	13.5	25.7
Newcomers	46.7	34.7

other parties of the same families in Europe: what happens when parties are reborn or return to the political surface after a long period of repression: do they adjust to the new circumstances abruptly or do they return to an old (former) newcomer pattern?

To explore the communists, I have chosen as the focus of comparison the four communist parties that were a stable political force in the same period in Italy, France, Finland, and the Netherlands. Unfortunately, we have comparable data only for one election between 1970 and 1989 in Spain, and I, therefore, had to limit the comparison to Portugal on the one hand and to the four established cases on the other. As for the post-authoritarian communist parliamentary elite, it seems highly likely that they will be of more marginal origin (social status and political position) because of their difficult past in the authoritarian period. We can also hypothesize that because of the long authoritarian legacy—and despite the Moscovite orientation of the party and the revolutionary environment of the transition—a shortage of party cadres should have prevailed in the Portuguese case. Indeed, both hypotheses are confirmed by the data. As to the first, the level of newcomers is higher, the share of those with only basic education is higher, and local political background is lower than in the four established communist parties. These data all express lack of embeddedness and marginal status. As to the second, a much lower level of *politicians* and party leaders is observed, which makes Portuguese communist parliamentarians differ from the others. Portugal was different from *the four* but it was also different, in this respect, from the first group of communists who appeared after the First World War. Adaptation and more established conditions might explain these features. We must also consider that the other four communist parties, as established groups, had already gone through some significant transformation in terms of basic education, local politics background and parliamentary experience. Thus, a combination of old and new phenomena explain the features but certainly the Portuguese communists showed a much less party elite-centered and less politicized character than the first group of communists (see Table 11.7) in Europe.

3. Southern European socialist parties attracted large electoral support from the beginning of the regime transformation. In Spain, the socialist vote fluctuated

between one-third and a half of the electorate (the peak being in the 1980s) and in Portugal between one-quarter and a half with larger figures at the beginning and at the end of the twenty-five-year long cycle. We can rightly hypothesize that no substantial differences will be found between them and other parties of the socialist party family because these parties were not organized in a vacuum, but were under the influence of their European brothers, who strongly supported them. In the 1970s, the socialists were already highly consolidated and had adopted a mainstream political orientation in Europe, and this is what the Southern European socialist parties experienced from the start.

This hypothesis was only partially confirmed. In Table 11.8, the first Portuguese and Spanish socialist parliamentary groups are compared to all the European socialists in the 1970s. First of all, a big difference emerges between the Spanish and Portuguese socialists concerning the share of party leaders and of politicians. Apparently, not only the communists (as has been demonstrated above) but also the socialists had in Portugal a lower degree of partyness.

As to the European average figures, the difference is most impressive with respect to the low level of local political embeddedness and, of course, the share of newcomers. Table 11.8 includes the share of the main occupational backgrounds among the parliamentarians (in the way that it has already been applied, see Figure 11.8). The differences between the Southern European and the other European cases are not substantial, which is in a way surprising considering the fact that these societies and economies were much less developed than the Western European countries in the sample. It seems that the parliamentary elite's occupational composition does not reflect directly the level of societal develop-ment but is rather a feature of the party status. It is striking that during the two decades between the 1970s and the 1990s both countries' socialist parliamentary elites reached and even exceeded the European average figures in terms of local political background and party leaders' proportions.

4. Another theme of interest could be how the post-totalitarian Hungarian case is comparable to the Southern European experiences in terms of the parliamentary elite background. Of course, differences have to be borne in mind. While the Spanish and Portuguese socialists can be regarded as genuine members of the socialist party family, the birth certificate of the Hungarian socialists had to be proved: with political statements and policies they had to demonstrate that they were a *legitimate child* in the family. Despite the differences in the conditions of their creation (not to mention here the time-span between the two democrati-zation processes), my hypothesis is that the Hungarian socialists would not be significantly different from either the Southern European cases or the general European pattern. One reason is that the reformist orientation in the Hungarian socialist party was very strong from the start and they had strong incentives to adjust and prepare a modernizing and democratic agenda. Unfortunately, owing to missing data only the first parliamentary group and the parliamentary group

TABLE 11.8. *Characteristics of socialist MPs in Spain, Portugal, Hungary, and 'all Europe' in different periods (%)*[+]

	Spain, first election	Portugal, first election	Hungary, first election	Spain, last two elections	Portugal, last two elections	Hungary, last two elections	Europe, 1970s average	Europe, 1990s average
Basic education	22.6	21.2	0.0	0.4	0.4	0.0	17.4	7.4
Local politician	4.0	9.6	18.2	80.0	65.0	51.3	60.8	60.9
Party leader	45.2	15.2	24.2	64.3	58.6	27.1	48.0	44.7
'Politician'	22.1	0.0	8.4	15.9	0.0	28.7	15.6	12.3
Newcomer	100	68.2	81.8	40.8	57.5	30.6	26.8	32.9
Blue collar	14.5	—	6.3	0.0	1.6	3.1	11.7	8.8
Businessmen	5.0	7.9	2.1	11.6	1.2	5.2	5.5	6.3
Intellectual	51.4	39.7	67.3	63.8	67.1	54.0	64.0	45.9

[+]The parliaments included are 1995 and 1999 for Portugal, 1996 and 2000 for Spain, and 1998 and 2002 for Hungary (the first being 1976, 1978, and 1990, respectively).

of the last two elections in the three countries will be presented—in addition to the European average figures for the 1970s and the 1990s (see Table 11.8). This provides an opportunity to see the similarities and differences between the countries in addition to the entire European party family, as well as their evolution and possible convergence.

The Hungarian socialist group was between the Spanish and Portuguese groups in terms of the share of party leaders and politicians but the over-representation of Hungarian MPs with a local political background indicates that they are a successor party: some of their old political connections prevailed. The Hungarian socialists were latecomers but they successfully adapted (or over-adapted) to the European patterns. By the 1990s, the higher level of politicians and the lower level of newcomers among them than in Southern Europe is a clear indication that they became a professional political group owing also probably to their inherited legacy. These proportions are also higher or are at the same level than the European averages. The reason for this lies in the fact—and this is the real difference between the Southern European and the Hungarian socialist MPs— that the Hungarian socialists are the successors of the communist party. Their parliamentary elite initially and to some degree even nowadays could use the career routes of the old party: they have been selected via the party first of all.

The brief illustrations above demonstrated that the composition of the parliamentary elite might be a good indicator of political processes: for example, party political fever was reflected in the German left, or the need to quickly adapt to European patterns became apparent in the Southern and Central European latecomer cases. The analysis of parliamentary representatives is highly relevant in enriching our knowledge about the parties' status and even about the country's political context.

11.4. VARIATIONS WITHIN THE PARTY FAMILY

The analysis conducted in the previous sections has shown that in the case of the socialist party family a growing similarity with the parliamentarians of other party families can be demonstrated, while, on the contrary, communist MPs largely maintained their distinctiveness from other parliamentary groups. Already at that stage, however, variations have been observed—particularly with respect to the communist parliamentary groups. Their more vulnerable political fortunes, weaker embeddedness in the political system of the respective countries, and a far lower level of political consolidation have been offered as explanations, which are also connected to the communist parties' political goals and slogans.

In the case of the socialist party family, we can also observe variations. Within the main trend of convergence with other parties country differences are apparent. From among the variables that have been formerly analysed some are particularly illustrative in this respect. While the changing proportion of newcomers can be explained by electoral fortunes and the declining proportion of those with only

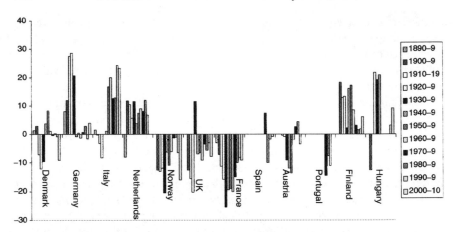

FIGURE 11.9. Proportion of politicians in socialist parties

basic education depends on broad societal changes more than on anything else, the variables that are connected to the MPs' career routes are probably rooted more deeply in country characteristics. Thus two main party organizational dimensions have been selected to illustrate variation: the share of *politicians* and the share of *local politicians*.

As has been already mentioned, the increasing partyness of the parliamentary groups was an early and clear tendency in Germany, Italy, the Netherlands, and Finland. For example, in Germany in 1912, 74 per cent of the social democrats were functionaries or party journalists—the latter also paid by the party, of course (Best, Hausmann, and Schmitt 2000: 168). In Italy, at the beginning of the twentieth century, journalists constituted about one-third of the socialist parliamentary group (Cotta, Mastropaolo and Verzichelli 2000: 244). Germany had the highest ever proportions of politicians in the inter-war years, but after the Second World War the share of politicians substantially decreased. In the Netherlands, recruitment from party political organizations sank to its lowest in the inter-war decades (Secker 2000: 300) and the tendency changed only after the 1950s. By contrast, in France the dominance of party officials was more spectacular among communist party representatives (some 70% after 1936) than among the socialists. France was different in other respects as well: the first 'typical groups' (Best and Gaxie 2000) of socialist MPs (small businessmen and journalists) were replaced by party officials (one-fifth to one-third) only in the 1920s and 1930s. Overall, the socialists did not become substantially more homogeneous with respect to the share of politicians, as is demonstrated in Figure 11.9. Is there a clear-cut pattern behind the changes?

Germany, Italy, Finland, Hungary, and at a more modest but consistent level the Netherlands stand out as countries where the share of politicians was above the average of 'all European' socialists. In Germany, however, a decline can be observed: the extreme politician character of their MPs (which is connected to the high level of politicization and partyness of the selection process) and the dominance of the party hierarchy decreased. As a contrast, in the case of Italy the dominance of politicians began only in the 1940s (owing to the relatively late start and then the early repression of mass politics there) and was maintained until the 1990s. The high level of politicians is spectacular in the case of Hungary—the only and single column of under-representation is misleading because it covers only one MP before enfranchisement.

On the other hand, Norway, the UK, France, and Portugal fall into the opposite category: they are constantly under the European socialist average in the proportion of politicians. An explanation for this may be the strength of local politics (which in the case of Norway and France is well known) or the trade union connection in the British case, while the latecomer Portugal's data might originate in the authoritarian tradition in that country and the type of systemic change when politicians were in shortage and were even deselected. Three countries do not show a constant pattern: Denmark and Austria had lower than average shares before the Second World War, after which we can observe a modest increase, while in Spain, after the negotiated transition, first over-representation and then decrease can be observed.

What about the local politics background? This might reflect regional differences in recruitment patterns (certain parties are more embedded in a region than others) or direct local political posts. A local politics background is connected to the organizational features of parties, to the selection process, and to local policy preferences; thus it has been more typical in some countries than in others. It has been most typical and on the highest level in Norway where it has become an important channel of recruitment. The Norwegian Labour Party had the highest proportion of MPs with a local politics background in the first part of the last century but then the share of local politics background for all parties was above 80 per cent there. Local ties in Norwegian politics complemented some regional cleavage dimension since the socialists historically tended to recruit more MPs from the more remote parts of the country (Eliassen, and Marino 2000). High levels of local politics background were typical also in France, Finland, and UK in the first part of the last century.

We can, however, observe a changing historical scene in this respect. Local political background remained at a high level in Finland, remained low and decreased continuously in the Netherlands, increased in Germany in the post-Second World War era, and fluctuated in Italy. All in all, the local politics background of MPs shows changing country patterns (see Figure 11.10).

Apparently (although not exclusively), country variations in local politics background follow an opposite trend from country variations in the proportion of politicians. Germany, the Netherlands, Portugal, and Hungary are below the average; Norway, France, and Finland are above, while Denmark, Italy, the UK, and Spain fluctuate around the average. In some countries, a party political and a

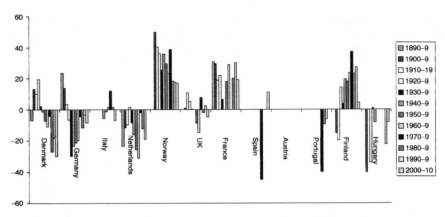

FIGURE 11.10. Local political background in socialist parties

local political career (and possibly selection route) are complementary (this is the case with Germany, the Netherlands, and Hungary), although in the German case we have to note the smoothing down of the peaks and large waves. Finland shows above-average proportions in both fields, and Portugal below average.

Having seen the variations and the richness of differences that still prevail within the socialist party family, an obvious question emerges: what has been the major factor explaining them? Is it the party family or is it the country? Does the local politics or 'politician' background of MPs correlate more with the fact that they are part of the socialist family or that they belong to a particular country? Local ties seem to be very strongly related to country characteristics. But the 'country or party' question would depend on the variable itself. Then the period would change and bring forth different country patterns reflecting some political transformation within the country.

On the one hand, we can observe similarization with other party families, while on the other hand, we can find differences which are more country-based. We now examine this question for the variables that have been most widely used in this chapter: basic education, newcomer position, politician's status, and local politics background. For different periods, I have measured the strength of the relationship between two nominal variables, for example between party and local politics background, or between country and local politics background by period. (see Table 11.9).

Before the First World War, differences between countries were greater with respect to local politics background, level of basic education and the share of newcomers than differences between parties. In other words, on the one hand the development of opportunity structures largely determined how the socialist elite appeared in these respects. The connection between these variables and *party* as such was insignificant. By contrast, the share of politicians was significantly determined by party differences. That is, the nature of the party family (as has

TABLE 11.9. *Strength of the relationship between country and party and selected variables in different periods (Cramer's V)*

Variable/period	-1917		1918–44		1945–69		1970–	
	Country	Party	Country	Party	Country	Party	Country	Party
Local politics	0.864*	0.751	0.798*	0.716	0.847*	0.743*	0.83*	0.698
Basic education	0.786*	0.703	0.786*	0.725	0.794*	0.689*	0.683*	0.57
'Politicians'	0.417	0.441*	0.702*	0.619	0.801*	0.704	0.728*	0.655
Newcomer	0.814*	0.717	0.79*	0.722	0.819	0.751	0.77*	0.701

* Significant at the 0.01 level.

been demonstrated above) had a large impact on the share of politicians among the parliamentary elite.

Between the two wars, with respect to all variables, we can find significant country variations but insignificant party variations. This is in harmony with the fact that regime continuities versus disruption determined the fate of the left-wing parties in those decades. The connection, however, was somewhat weaker in the inter-war years than before the First World War. Above, we have found the 1930s as the 'turning point', that is, the period when convergence and similarization between the socialist and non-socialist party families began. Still, according to the measurement this was significantly connected to the country (political regime). After the Second World War both party and country differences were significant with respect to local politics background and basic education—with the impact of the countries being stronger than the impact of party. On the other hand, in terms of the politician's career and the proportion of newcomers, the party impact was insignificant. Indeed, after the war the changing opportunities (as reflected in the share of newcomers) were again country-dependent and the politician's career became a stable pattern in non-socialist parties as well. After 1970, as expected, country differences proved stronger than party differences: country was in a strong and significant correlation with all the four variables while party did not have a significant correlation with the variables.

All in all, we can conclude that after the stabilization of the socialist party family the country has gained increasing importance in determining the variables that we have selected, that is, those we have identified as the most revealing about the political embeddedness of a political group.

11.5. CONCLUSIONS

The main question in understanding the socialists' parliamentary elite transformation was the road they had to cover from the margins to the centre and to become politically similar to other political groups. This process of political integration was the factor that most determined the features of the socialist parliamentary groups. It has been found that with respect to several variables the socialists and the other parties converged in the 1930s—as the thresholds of mass democracy were successively crossed. Of course, this is only true in general terms because in the countries where democratization was interrupted this tendency was also blocked and continued only after the Second World War.

It also became clear from the above analysis that the parties' parliamentary elite developments are very closely related—indeed rooted—in the political history of the parties themselves. As we have seen, the transformation of socialist MPs originated in a diversity of factors. (*a*) It was due to party-based convergence, as the other parties too changed their attributes and acquired the organizational and structural features of the socialists. (*b*) It was due to political factors because as the socialists became an accepted political force the characterizing features of their MPs became necessarily similar to those of the other parties—for example, the share of newcomers began to decrease. (*c*) It was due to societal factors, as revealed by the diminishing share of those with only basic education, and finally (*d*) the country legacy mattered—for example, when the local political embeddedness of the parliamentarians gathered strength.

Within these general trends, however, it remained obvious throughout the analysis that (particularly) the socialist parliamentary elite developments occurred under a double determination: that of the party family, and that of the respective country. When formulating the hypotheses at the beginning of this chapter we left this as the most open issue. Which factor exerts a stronger pull, the party family or the country? Eventually, it is an interesting finding that after several changes in this respect, more recently country variations seem to determine the (selected) characteristics of the MPs the most. This suggests that after convergence occurred in the fundamental political and societal dimensions, country variations gain significance. However, in contrast to the first period of our analysis, that is before the First World War, in which country variations were also important and were rooted in fundamental differences in political opportunity structures, nowadays country variations are based on more 'modest' differences (which we can also call strong national traditions) such as the importance of local politics.

Our knowledge about representation has been broadened when we have found to what a large degree representatives reflect the political and social environment they work in. Perhaps, these are not the most widely used concepts of representation, yet nevertheless it was instructive to observe how the feverish state of a political regime is reflected in the over-politicized nature of the socialist (and communist) MPs, or how a political mechanism like recruitment patterns is reflected in the career routes and thus potentially in the representation background of MPs.

One observation, at least, is in order regarding our findings with respect to the communist MPs. By the 'end' of the period under consideration with few exceptions they disappeared from the analysis. While the fate of the traditional communist parties is the result of complex political and international developments, obviously the long prevailing distinctiveness of their parliamentary groups is a strong indication that they followed different organizational, recruitment and representation patterns.

From academic literature it is known that leadership effects have always been more pronounced in the socialist party family because these parties have been built on 'invented identities'. As Kitschelt argues, 'the future of social democracy to a large extent lies in the hands of party leaders and activists' (1994: 4ff.) because the class appeal has become increasingly blurred and class arguments more challenged. This is a paradox given the fact that the stabilization of the left parliamentary elite has been taking place amid rising volatility of the electorate and decreasing party membership figures (Dalton 2002). Thus a further question remains: how have the public and elite connections and the representation agenda been affected by the transformation of the socialist parliamentary groups?

ENDNOTES

1 I would like to thank András Schwarcz for his devoted help in processing and analysing the data that have been used in this chapter.

2 Some variables which are not discussed here for reasons of space are dealt with in other chapters (e.g. the role of women politicians on the left in Chapter 4) or are analysed from a different perspective (e.g. the role of professional politician MPs in general in Chapter 6).

3 This chapter deals with the communist parties, while the post-communists are excluded (neither the German PDS nor the Italian *Rifondazione Comunuista* are covered).

4 The first decade of the twenty-first century, not yet completed, is left out of this analysis.

5 We shall leave out of the analysis, as before, the incomplete 2000–10 decade.

12

The Extreme Right[1]

Juan J. Linz, Miguel Jerez Mir, and Carmen Ortega

12.1. INTRODUCTION: EXTREMISMS ON THE RIGHT

An analysis of the extreme right must discuss whether the object we are dealing with is really an 'extreme right' or a variety of 'anti-system' opposition
parties (depending on the period and the system), protest parties, conservative
authoritarian parties, truly fascist parties in the interwar years, and finally, so-
called 'neo-fascist' and 'anti-immigrant' (more or less racist) parties in recent
years. The enumeration already tells us that this is a heterogeneous category of very doubtful validity for a collective characterization across time and
countries.[2]

While the other 'political families' analysed in this book are defined by an
ideological heritage—certainly evolving over time—and a certain continuity, the
'extreme right' is, in most cases, basically defined in positional terms. It is
therefore more heterogeneous. The most defining elements are the 'anti-system'
dimension (which in case of victory means a regime change) and the perception by
the society and other parties of being on the right rather than on the left. Since 'the
system' changes, the hostility focuses on different dimensions over time and much
of the same happens with the being on the right. It is possible that an 'extreme'
and 'anti-system' party unable or without hope to gain power, tunes down its
hostility, adapts to the system, and even aspires to participate in it and gain a
share in power. This was the case with most of the 'extreme left' and was also the
evolution of some of the 'extreme right' parties. It is today difficult to define the
Italian *Alleanza Nazionale*, incorporating the old MSI, as an anti-system party.[3]

Certainly, there has been some continuity between legitimist monarchic authoritarianism of the right and the conservative authoritarianism and revolutionaries
(Payne 1995) of the twentieth century, but even so Carlists and Alfonsine anti-
democrats in Spain, for example, had different roots. The Fascist movements
of the twentieth century in the inter-war years did not link with the nineteenth
century anti-liberal and anti-democratic tradition, but would be new politics.
There are some, but often ambiguous links between the post—Second World War

segments of the extreme right and the fascist legacy. Overall however discontinuity outweighs continuity.[4]

During the early twentieth century, a cluster of new rightist and conservative authoritarian forces emerged also in European politics. They rejected moderate conservatism and old-fashioned reaction in favour of a more modern, technically proficient authoritarian system distinctive from both leftist revolution and fascist radicalism. These forces of the new right may in turn be divided into elements of the radical right and a more conservative authoritarian right (Payne 1995, table I.2 for examples; Rogger and Weber (eds). 1965; Nolte 1966; Blinkhorn 1990; Linz 2000).

In the constitutional monarchies dominant in nineteenth-century Europe the anti-system opposition on the extreme right could not articulate itself as a party. Throne and altar could continue to cooperate. Even in Italy, where the *non-expedit* of the pope against the 'usurping' Savoy monarchy could have been the basis of an opposition on the right, protest opted rather for principled abstention. However, in two countries the conflict between absolutism, traditionalism, and liberalism led to a dynastic conflict and civil war. In Spain with the Carlists against *Cristinos* and *Isabelinos* (and up to the new democratic monarchy in 1977–8), and in Portugal between the partisans of Don Miguel and Doña Gloria. In France, the conflict between Legitimists and Orleanist and later of these two monarchical factions and the bonapartists with the Republic (after 1848 and 1875) also created the basis for an anti-system right. The dynastic conflicts reflected ideological and social conflicts which in turn were reinforced by the loyalty to the different pretenders. We find here the origin of an extreme and anti-system right articulating an ideological programme, absent in the stable liberal-constitutional monarchies slowly evolving towards more democratic rule. Those grouped as extreme right had in comparison little in common over time and in different countries. Only the fascists, *stricto sensu*, had an affinity, though some of them and a number of scholars would even question the identification as fascists of both the PNF and the NSDAP. We feel that fascism is however a 'family of parties' but we would question its identification with nineteenth-century anti-liberal and anti-democratic parties and with some of the more recent populist or xenophobic parties.

There are many differences between fascists on one side and the conservatives and even the conservative radical right on the other, but the absence of links with religious organizations and the non-religious, anticlerical and even anti-religious positions is a significant feature of the former. This might not be true for the Romanian Iron Guard and the Croat *Ustacha*, where nationalism links with a religious identity, and initially for the Belgian Rex that emerged out of the Christian Democratic party but soon encountered the opposition of the Church.

The data on the social characteristics of the representatives of 'extreme right' parties, particularly for the very small parties, may not be very revealing. Those parties often are flash parties, or when important, a response to a historical situation, rather than representing well-defined social groups: social classes, status groups like the nobility, occupational groups like farmers, or the religious segment of society. They are, in some cases, as we shall see, expressions of a generational revolt (as data on age of fascists will confirm), responses to a particular crisis. These elements—for example, veteran experience of the First World War, border nationalism, the impact of recent immigrations to Europe, etc.—since they are not always applicable to other parties, have not been coded in the DATACUBE. The normal variables of sociological elite analysis are on the contrary, less apt to distinguish them from other bourgeois or conservative parties. The great differences in political career, office holding, etc. can be considered as defining them, but it could be argued that they reflect the position of the parties in the system—excluded therefore from some positions—rather than characteristics of the individual members before entering politics.

In contrast to the parties of the extreme right in the nineteenth century, that did not reject the left-right continuum and their own placement, the fascists generally rejected the left–right dichotomy, in their effort to provide a synthesis between left and right and to represent the whole nation. In some cases, the fascist parties, or some wings of them, wanted to occupy a place on the left, congruent with their anti-liberal, anti-conservative, anticlerical, economic interventionist anti-capitalist (or at least anti-'big' or international capital) programmatic positions. However, they never managed to be accepted as part of the left by the left, from where they often borrowed their symbols, names, and rhetoric. Our inclusion of the fascists in the extreme right in the DATACUBE and in this chapter, in no way ignores the left component and even—occasional—appeal of fascist ideology and parties. As latecomers on the political horizon, fascists found practically everywhere the space on the left occupied by socialists, communists, anarchists, and syndicalists. There was no room for a 'national left', national-socialism, national-syndicalism, a national revolutionary party (Linz 1980).

The study of parliaments does not provide us with much information on fascist movements, except in Italy and Germany. If they were really successful, there would not be any free elections, and if they were not, their representation would be very small and dwindling, since most democratic parties would combine efforts to defeat them (and, in a few cases, outlaw them).

It should be kept in mind that a number of the top leaders and founders of fascist movements were never elected to parliament. In Spain, José Antonio Primo de Rivera was elected only once but not on a fascist electoral list; Ramiro Ledesma Ramos and Onésimo Redondo were never elected. The same is true for Rolão Preto in Portugal. In France two leaders, Déat and Doriot, had been parliamentarians of the socialist and communist parties.

Few of the studies of fascist movements devote attention to the composition of the leadership, the candidates they present for office, the MPs, compared to the growing scholarship on the electoral ecology of the fascist vote and some work on party members. The interpretation of the data on the party elites, however, can only be made by comparing them to those of other parties and movements (Linz 1976).

The importance and weight of the extreme right in European politics (with the exception of Italy and Weimar Germany) has not been its parliamentary representation but its presence in the streets, its capacity for violence, and its ideological influence. The fascists used their parliamentary presence for its black-mail potential, its disruption of the parliamentary process, but not so much in the hope to obtain access to power. Only the failure of the democrats to form stable governments in Italy, and the negative majority of national-socialists and communists in Germany, made them *Koalitionsfähig*.

In most countries, the fascist parties had only minority or even small minority representation, and for a short period, and therefore the collective biography of the parliamentary group is not too useful for an understanding of those parties. In addition to the leadership principle in their organization further reduced the significance of the MPs. Paradoxically, the number of Fascists (strictly defined) elected freely into European parliaments, with the exceptions of Italy, Germany, Romania, and Hungary, was extremely small, while the number of those some-times considered 'neo-fascists' has been significant. No one would assign the same significance and role to them and to the fascist movements in the inter-war years.

Counting the successful fascist parties in Romania—66 deputies in 1932 (Heinen 1986)—and Hungary (10 in 1935, 31 Arrow Cross, and 7 others in 1939), and the one-time success of Rex in Belgium (21 elected in 1936) the total parliamentary representation in Europe outside of Italy and Germany would not be much over 100 and this not at the same time. One more argument against the characterization of the inter-war years as the 'age of fascism'.

Adding the information on all the fascists in the interwar parliaments would still basically result in a universe constituted by the PNF members in Montecitorio and NSDAP members of the Reichstag, since the party representation of both is so large. In the quantitative analysis we will therefore focus on these parties.

In the case of parties gaining few legislative seats, it is more revealing to focus on the membership—when there are data—and on the districts in which they obtained a significant electoral support as social, cultural, and economic contexts. This has been the approach of most of the monographs and the comparative analyses on fascist parties—outside of Italy and Germany (Laqueur 1978; Linz 1978, 1980, 1998; Larsen, Hagtvet, and Myklebust ed. 1980; Merkel 1980; Griffin 1991; Payne 1995; Paxton 2004). The basic sociological variables, rather than detailed biographies, tell us very little.

In a sense, fascist parties from their inception were the model of 'catch-all parties' since their conception of the nation, their rejection of the internal class conflict, even their hostility to the clerical/anticlerical conflict, their conception of the *Voksgemeinschaft*, meant to appeal to the 'whole nation'. This was to be reflected in a systematic selection of candidates of diverse targeted groups. They did not think like the communists that they should represent a class—the industrial workers (at least before the Popular Fronts and the Second World War)—or like the Conservatives, that the better classes, businessmen, higher civil servants, successful professionals, and the nobility were specially qualified to be representatives. Only the Christian Democrats early on wanted to represent the whole *popolo cristiano*, from the trade union leaders to the aristocrats. Unfortunately, the size of the parliamentary groups does not allow to test this early catch-all image of fascist parties in contrast to other parties.

Our analysis of the representation of the fascists is limited because it does not include Romania nor the Baltic Countries. Particularly, regrettable is the non-inclusion of Romania, where the Iron Guard was in terms of electoral success the third most voted fascist party in Europe. Among the countries included, the UK, the Netherlands, Denmark, Norway, Austria, and Spain have only marginally significant parties, and even in France the electoral cycle led to an infra-representation of its different fascist parties. In Portugal, the fascist party was founded already under the *Estado Novo* and therefore for the Republic we are dealing only with parties of the Authoritarian Right (Costa-Pinto 2000).

It is difficult, once the Marxist interpretation of fascism has been proven largely wanting, to see the extreme right in terms of a socially well-defined constituency. The right (but not only the right) is nationalistic but the extreme right is ultra- or radically nationalist, a nationalism often linked to irredentism, expansionism-imperialism, anti-internationalism (today critical of the EU, NATO, and UN), xenophobia, and frequently anti-semitism. Those positions characterized fascism but not only fascism. Today hostility towards immigrants and asylum seekers has been one of the main themes and attractions to voters of the new European right. The extreme nationalism is related often to the borderland origin (and areas of voting strength), to experiences abroad that shaped the view of the world, to mixed ethnic background leading to a heightened awareness of the nation of choice, and very often to war experiences or a military background. The detailed biographies of leaders support these patterns. A number of leaders of nationalism can be linked to their birth or living abroad (Rosenberg, Darre, Hess, Röhm, Albiñana in Spain), their frontier background (Hitler was an Austrian born in Branau on the German border), or their marginal ethnic background (in the case of the leaders of Hungarian National-Socialism, and of Codreanu, the leader of the Romanian Iron Guard).

The extreme right—both fascist and non-fascist (particularly the latter)—has often a strong 'intellectual' component: journalists, editors of magazines, publicists, that we are less likely to find among moderate conservatives. The extreme right is born in a particular subculture which is important since it represents an ideological programme rather than specific interests of business or farmers like the moderate right.

Religion and religiosity have been important in European politics since the Reformation and in modern politics since the French Revolution. The traditional extreme right has been religious and clerical—although not necessarily following the hierarchy when it made its peace with the liberal state. However, the modern extreme right breaks with that continuum: it is often not only anticlerical— certainly critical of the Vatican—but often a-religious and even atheist or pagan. In some cases, we find also those who identify with non-orthodox positions in the Church.

The presence of a strong Christian Democratic party reduces the political space for both a secular Conservative and an Extreme Right party, in part because the Christian Democrats appeal to conservative voters, and stand against the Marxist left like the conservatives and the extreme right. This, nevertheless, should not obscure the fundamental differences. The presence of the *Zentrum* in Catholic Germany was a significant barrier to the DNVP and the NSDAP, the *Popolari* in Italy to the progress of the PNF (Linz 1978), the ÖVP in Austria to the pan-Germans and the NSDAP, the religious parties in the Netherlands to the national-socialists, and in Belgium to the Rex. Even the CEDA in Spain, which was less CD than those other parties, limited the space available to the two extreme right monarchist parties (*Renovación* and the *Tradicionalistas*), and its somewhat 'fascisticized' youth organization (JAP) competed successfully with the Falangists.

Extremist parties have a limited chance to come to power. First, with very few exceptions, they are not able to rally a large number of votes and fewer parliamentary seats. Their access to power depends on the fragmentation, disunity, and incapacity to cooperate with the moderate parties which leads to a stalemate and/or loss of power of the democrats. The cooperation of a semi-loyal opposition is often decisive in gaining access to governmental power, forming coalition governments.

The PNF and NSDAP, and probably the fascists (as well as the communists), represent in European parliaments a classic example of the Paretian circulation of elites: the displacement of an ageing and stable political elite by outsiders, young newcomers, rejecting the consensus building and negotiable representation of interests by the readiness to use violence in order to gain power on the basis of loyalty to a leader and ideological commitment. In contrast to most other parties, they are not part of a process of more or less continuous elite renewal, but often represent the sudden massive entry of total newcomers.

The activism of extremist parties, the constant effort to mobilize their militias, members and voters, makes politics a full-time occupation. This means that young fascists (and communists) often interrupted their studies and did not gain or hold on to stable employment, which has led to their characterization as 'declassés', downward mobile. However, their status is a reflection of a deliberate decision to devote themselves to politics. If successful, the reward would be power. Leaders of other parties are not likely to experience the same discrimination in public employment and they are likely to be functionaries of trade unions, business or agricultural interest groups, or they would practice their professions. The data on full-time party occupation we have for NSDAP parliamentarians are congruent with this analysis (Döring 2001: 399–412; see also Hubert 1992; Schumacher 1994).

Fascist parties experienced a significant programmatic—rather than ideological—change in their effort to conquer power, and from 'movement' to 'regime'. In other parties, one would expect such changes to be reflected in the composition of the parliamentary elite. This is not likely among the fascists, given the bond between followers and a charismatic leader and the discipline he imposes. Besides, we do not have records of parliamentary representation of such parties under democratic conditions for any length of time.[5]

Table 12.1 shows which parties were coded as extreme right—as decided by each national team—from the late nineteenth century to the end of the twentieth century. All those parties which gained at least once seats in the lower or unique chamber are presented in the table as long as data were available in the DATACUBE format. As it can be observed, we have extreme right parliamentary representatives in most European countries (Austria, Belgium, Finland, France, Germany, Hungary, Italy, Norway, the Netherlands, and Spain), but their presence is limited to a low number of elections (sixty-three processes).[6]

The rise of extreme right parties in Europe comes in waves (von Beyme 1988; Epstein 1996). According to Epstein, since the late nineteenth century, Europe has experienced several waves in which extreme right groups have surged and have been reactivated in most countries: (*a*) the anti-Jewish wave at the end of the nineteenth century as a precursor of the contemporary fascism; (*b*) the fascist wave in the 1920s and 1930s; (*c*) the phase between 1945 and 1984 where the extreme right was practically non-existent in most European countries; and (*d*) the wave of the new radical right starting in 1984.

12.2. FROM THE LATE NINETEENTH CENTURY TO THE SECOND WORLD WAR

12.2.1. *Spain: A Traditional Anti-Liberal Right, a Modern Radical Right, and a Weak Fascism*

In contrast to more advanced European countries, in Spain the extreme right protest against the aristocratic-bourgeois conservatism that had accepted the liberal-constitutional state had its roots in the nineteenth century. The entrenched system of the dynastic parties was questioned by the minority of ageing *Tradicionalistas*. Neutrality in the First World War (although coinciding with a social and political crisis) prevented the emergence of a veterans movement, the tensions generated by the Moroccan War contributed to the crisis in the army, but not to a civilian nationalist movement, and the monarchy was still not questioned except by the left and regional nationalists. Even so, the followers of Antonio Maura, particularly the *maurista* Youth, questioned the *canovista* system from

TABLE 12.1. *Representatives of extreme right parties in national parliaments in Europe*

Country	Year of election	Party label	English party label	Number of representatives	Date of foundation
Germany	1919				
	1924(1)	Nationalsozialistische Freiheitspartei (NSFP)	National Socialist Liberty Party	32	1924
	1924(2)	NSFP	National Socialist Liberty Party	13	
	1928	Nationalsozialistische Deutsche Arbeiterpartei (NSDAP)	German National Socialist Workers Party	13	1920
	1930	NSDAP	German National Socialist Workers Party	110	
	1932(1)	NSDAP	German National Socialist Workers Party	232	
	1932(2)	NSDAP	German National Socialist Workers Party	201	
	1933	NSDAP	German National Socialist Workers Party	288	
Italy	1921	Partito Nazionale Fascista (PNF)	National Fascist Party	35	1919
	1924	PNF	National Fascist Party	280	
	1946	Uomo Qualunque (UQ)	Common Man	32	1945
	1948	Movimento Sociale Italiano (MSI)	Italian Social Movement (MSI)	7	1946
		Partito Nazionale Monarchico (PNM)	National Monarchic Party	14	1946
	1953	MSI	Italian Social Movement (MSI)	29	
		PNM	National Monarchic Party	39	
	1958	MSI	Italian Social Movement (MSI)	24	
		PNM	National Monarchic Party	11	
		Partito Monarchico Popolare (PMP)	Popular Monarchic Party	15	1954
	1963	MSI	Italian Social Movement (MSI)	27	
	1968	Partito Democratico di Unità Monarchica (PDIUM)	Democratic party for Monarchic Unity	8	1961
		MSI	Italian Social Movement (MSI)	24	
		PDIUM	Democratic party for Monarchic Unity	6	
	1972	MSI	Italian Social Movement (MSI)	56	
	1976	MSI	Italian Social Movement (MSI)	34	
	1979	MSI	Italian Social Movement (MSI)	31	
	1983	MSI	Italian Social Movement (MSI)	42	

(cont.)

TABLE 12.1. *(continued)*

Country	Year of election	Party label	English party label	Number of representatives	Date of foundation
	1987	MSI	Italian Social Movement (MSI)	35	
	1992	MSI	Italian Social Movement (MSI)	34	
	1994	Alleanza Nazionale (AN)	National Alliance	105	1993
	1936	Parti Social Français	Social French Party	7	
	1956	Union pour la Défense des Commerçants et Artisans (UDCA)	Union for the Defence of Merchants and Craftsmen	44	1953
	1986	Front National (FN)	National Front	35	1972
Hungary	1884	Országos Antiszemita Párt (OAP)	National Antisemite Party	17	1883
	1887	OAP	National Antisemite Party	8	
	1927	Fajvédő Párt	Race Protection Party	4	1923
	1931	Nemzeti Szocialista Párt (NSzP)	National Socialist Party	5	1928
	1935	NSZP	National Socialist Party	6	
	1935	Magyar Nemzeti Szocialista Párt (MNSzP)	Hungarian National Socialist Party	1	1933
	1935	Népakarat Pártja	Party of National Will	1	1935
	1939	Népakarat Pártja	Party of National Will	1	
	1939	Nyilaskeresztes Párt	Arrow Cross Party	28	1939
	1939	Magyar Nemzeti Szocialista Párt	Hungarian National Socialist Party	3	1937
	1998	Magyar Igazság és Élet Pártja (MIEP)	Justice and Life Party	14	1993
Netherlands	1933	Nationaal Socialistische Beweging (NSB)	National Socialist Movement	1	1931
	1937	NSB	National Socialist Movement	4	
	1982	Centrum Partij (CP)	Centre Party	1	1980
	1989	Centrumdemocraten (CD)	Centre Democrats	1	1984
	1994	CD	Centre Democrats	3	

Country	Year	Party	Party	Seats	Founded
Norway	1933	Nasjonal Samling	National Union Party	1	1933
	1936	Nasjonal Samling	National Union Party	1	
	1973	Anders Lange Partiet	Anders Lange Party	4	1973
	1981	Fremskrittspartiet (FrPa)	Progress Party	4	1981
	1989	FrPa	Progress Party	22	
	1993	FrPa	Progress Party	10	
Finland	1933	Isänmaallinen Kansanliike (IKL)	People's Patriotic Movement	14	1932
	1936	IKL	People's Patriotic Movement	14	
	1939	IKL	People's Patriotic Movement	8	
	1975	Perustuslaillinen Oikeistopuolue (POP)	Constitutional Party of Finland	1	1973
	1983	POP	Constitutional Party of Finland	1	
Spain	1931	Tradicionalistas	Traditionalists	4	1860s
	1933	Renovación Española (RE)	Spanish Renovation	15	1933
		Tradicionalistas	Traditionalists	21	
		Partido Nacional Español (PNF)	Spanish National Party	1	1931
		Falange Española (FE)	Spanish Phalange	1	1933
	1936	Renovación Española	Spanish Renovation	13	
		Tradicionalistas	Traditionalists	9	
	1979	Fuerza Nueva (FN)	New Force	1	1976
Belgium	1936	Rex	Rex	21	1936
		Vlaamschasch National Verbond (VNV)	VNV	16	1933
	1939	Rex	Rex	4	
		VNV	VNV	17	

'regenerationist' anti-parliamentarian and Catholic corporativist perspectives, increasingly influenced by the *Action Française* (Tussel and Avilés 1994). In that milieu new political elites started emerging, but the Primo de Rivera dictatorship co-opted some, others tried to articulate a Christian-democratic-social party (the PSP), while others, after the fall of Primo de Rivera, opposed the restoration of the liberal-conservative constitutionalism, forming small monarchist authoritarian groups. Although Maura and his supporters were not an extreme right, it was among the *Mauristas* and the civilian supporters of the Primo de Rivera dictatorship, where the founders of the Alphonsine monarchist right —*Renovación Española*—and its intellectual milieu—the journal *Acción Española*—initiated their political career. Without much success they would oppose the Republic, democracy and the left, to end becoming among the main supporters, and office holders, of Franco.

This new generation of conservatives of the extreme right would not fight for the restoration of the monarchy of 1876, but for the instauration of an authoritarian monarchy. This idea, articulated by Calvo Sotelo, a minister of Primo de Rivera, would become the institutional programme of Franco. The extreme right, together with the revival of Carlism, would pre-empt some of the space occupied in other countries by the fascists. While they looked with some sympathy towards the *Falange*, they ultimately did not support it. The non-fascist extreme right, while gaining little electoral support, with a small membership— except the Traditionalists—became an important ideological competitor of the more moderate right, and contributed to the polarization that led to the civil war.

The Spanish extreme right was not that different from the French *Action Française*, the right wing of the DNVP or the *Stahlhelm*, or sectors of the Hungarian right, except perhaps that it had less support of business (except in the Basque Country) and the agrarian supporters of *Renovación Española* did not control votes like the DNVP. It was like its European counterparts, a generational revolt of aristocrats, upper bourgeois, some higher civil servants, and intellectuals, against the system of democratic liberal-constitutionalism. Their ally against the democratic republic and the threat of the left radicalism would not be a mass fascist movement but a segment of the army.

The extreme right opposed to the restored monarchy was represented by the supporters of the Carlist dynasty and a splinter of them—the *Integristas*—that supported a reactionary Catholicism, against liberalism, and the traditional laws of the different regions (the *Fueros*). Their position made them ineligible for official positions like cabinet membership. *Integristas* constituted a small parliamentary minority elected mainly in Navarre, the Basque Country, and sometimes in Catalonia, where in 1902 they joined the *Solidaridad* Coalition with Regionalists and Republicans. The total number of seats held between 1903 and 1923 was occupied by thirty-four persons. The *Comunión Tradicionalista* (another name for the party) would be represented in the Republican Cortes by twenty-four deputies holding four seats in 1931, twenty-one in 1933, and nine in 1936. They supported the 1936 uprising with their militias and would be fused by Franco with the *Falange* to form the *Falange Española Tradicionalista y de las J.O.N.S.*, the single party of the regime.

If we turn to their biographical data, except for the districts they represented, they are not different in their occupations and education from other deputies, they are not disproportionately from the nobility, but obviously as anti-system politicians had no *cursus honorum* in the administration and never were cabinet members (with the exception of the Franco regime). They did not represent a particular social stratum or social elite, but an ideology and the electorate in some regions and some districts where the population had identified strongly with the Carlist cause in the nineteenth century civil wars (Blinkhorn 1975).

In contrast to other European democracies, the space of the extreme right in parliament during the Spanish Republic (1931–6) is not occupied by the fascist party—*Falange Españolay de las Juntas de Ofensiva Nacionalsindicalista*—but by the members of *Renovación Española* and *Tradicionalistas*. *Renovación*. founded in 1933 and led by José Calvo Sotelo, represented authoritarian monarchism supporting the return of Alfonso XIII. It was represented by nineteenth deputies holding fifteen seats in 1933 and thirteen in 1936 (Gil Pecharromán 1994).

The deputies of the extreme right—*Renovación Española* and *Tradicionalistas*—were mostly lawyers: 47.4 per cent in 1933 and 50 per cent in 1936, more than the average of the Chamber. In the *Renovación* parliamentary group, university professors, journalists and writers, are 19.9 per cent in 1933, 7.7 per cent in 1936, and elite civil servants 13.3 per cent and 15.4 per cent. In 1936 landowners, with 9.1 per cent in 1936, are more represented than in the Chamber as a whole, but are probably fewer than in the extreme right in some other countries. The number of businessmen and bankers is a bit larger than in the Chamber. Both *Renovación* and the *Tradicionalistas* are represented by upper-class persons, mainly professionals including engineers, a high status profession, but certainly with no populist lower-middle class component.

In the three democratic elections of the Republic—1931, 1933, and 1936—only one fascist entered the legislature (and for that on a conservative list)—José Antonio Primo de Rivera, the son of the general who was dictator from 1923 to 1930 (Payne 1999). Professionally an educated lawyer, he had inherited a nobility title, and was young, 30 years old when elected in 1933. Since the falangists did not gain parliamentary representation—in contrast to the PNF and the NSDAP—the previous parliamentary experience of Franco cabinet members would be as MPs of the *Bloque Nacional*, that is *Renovación Española* and the *Tradicionalistas*, and one CEDA' leader, Serrano Suñer, brother in law of Franco.

12.2.2. *Italy: Extreme Nationalism and Fascism*

At the turn of the century, in the aftermath of the African defeat at *Adua* in 1896, a new rightist intellectual climate, critical of the constitutional liberal state of the Risorgimento, was being articulated in literary and political magazines by a number of brilliant writers and journalists (Gentile 1973, 1989, 2003; Musiedlak 2003). They were hostile to parliamentarism and the parties, concerned about massive emigration to the Americas, which they wanted to be channelled into imperial acquisitions, irredentist in the Trentino and the Adriatic, but also antisocialist. They felt that the class conflict should not be in the nation but between the 'proletarian nation'—an expression of the poet Pascoli popularized by Corradini—and the plutocratic nations. They established links with the syndicalist movement. Their hatred would be directed against the Liberal Prime Minister Giolitti. In 1910, they founded the *Asociazione Nazionalista Italiana* (ANI) which would later, as a party, participate in elections obtaining sixteen seats in 1913, and eleven in 1921 (Ballini 1988), and create a party militia—the *Sempre Pronti*. Both would fuse with the fascists in 1923. The party was active in bringing about Italian intervention in the First World War. It remained however an elitist and royalist authoritarian party rather than a mass party with a left component like early fascism. It played an important role in facilitating the coming to power of Mussolini and the appointment of ANI leaders to the ministries of interior and justice helped the Duce to weather the Matteotti murder crisis. However, in the thirties its leaders would be marginalized. As an authoritarian nationalist party it had some affinity with *Action Française*. Some of the Nationalists, that fused with the PNF in February 1923 and appeared on the *Listone* (the coalition list for the elections of 1924), played important roles in the institutionalization of the regime in the 1920s (De Grand 1978).

There is no question of the decisive role that the First World War and its consequences—interventionism that divided the parties, including the left, war service, and problems of reintegration in civil society—played in the birth of Fascism. The data on age of PNF deputies in a sense stand in for that generational experience. We have information on the war experience of deputies of different parties (Musiedlak 2003: 124, table 3.2). The veterans (*ex-combattenti*) that, in the 1921 legislature, were 23.7 per cent, reached 89 per cent among the Nationalists, and 77 per cent among the Fascists, compared to 17.3 per cent of the Socialists, 17 per cent of the *Popolari*, and 15.4 per cent of the Reformist Socialists. In the ranks of the *Democratici liberali*, they were 15.2 per cent.

The fascists gained for the first time 36 parliamentary seats among 535 in the 1921 election (Ballini 1988). This was the only parliamentary election in which the Italian fascists participated before the March on Rome. With the exception of two districts, they ran on the *Blocchi Nazionali* lists, a conglomerate of parties and candidates, formed after complex negotiations. Of twenty-three constituency lists, they were in ten cases at the top of the list, in five in the second, in eight in the third, and in six in the fourth place. In two cases, where there was no agreement on a coalition, they presented their own list gaining one seat in each (Petersen 1975). The election was accompanied by considerable violence. Of some eighty fascist candidates, thirty-five were elected—taking into account that Mussolini was elected twice. Also taking into account some changes of party

TABLE 12.2. *Selected indicators for extreme right MPs in Germany and Italy during the inter-war period*

	Year of election	Number of mandates	Mean age (%)	Newcomers (%)	Mean age of newcomers (years)	Basic education (%)	University degree (%)
Germany							
	1924(1)	32	42.4	93.7	42.4	6.2	43.7
	1924(2)	13	43.6	23.1	44.1	7.7	53.8
	1928	13	42.1	61.5	38.4	23.1	61.5
	1930	110	38.4	87.3	37.5	22.7	37.3
	1932(1)	232	38.7	57.8	37.5	19.0	32.8
	1932(2)	201	39.5	7.0	42.3	18.4	33.3
	1933	288	40.1	27.1	39.7	18.4	32.6
Italy	1921	35	37.7	94.3	37.2		68.6
	1924	280	38.9	76.8	37.6		69.6

after the election, the parliamentary group can be characterized by the following data.

It was a young group, the mean age being 37 years (see Table 12.2). Four were between 25 and 29, that is below the age to be eligible but consolidated their election a year later (three of the four were among the most prominent leaders of the movement and the regime: Bottai, Farinacci, Grandi); fourteen between 30 and 34, eight between 35 and 39, eighteen between 40 and 45, and four between 47 and 56. Two-thirds had a university degree. Occupationally, there were sixteen lawyers—which means that almost half of them had that condition—three journalists, three industrialists, two navy officers, two university professors, two railroad employees, one merchant, one rural trade unionist, one farmer, one doctor in agrarian sciences, one doctor in commercial sciences, a technical manager, one physician, and one retired general (Petersen 1975). Clearly, a middle-class group—except for five noblemen—with a larger number of professionals than businessmen and with a significant agrarian component, but not too many white-collar employees (see Table 12.3).

One of the most interesting characteristics of the Fascists elected in 1921 is the areas where they were elected. None in the islands, only one in the South (Puglie). They came mainly from the Centre, particularly Emilia and Tuscany (14 of 106 elected there) and the north (8 of 186). Most significant is that in the new border district, with a Slavic minority, Venezia Giulia, four of sixteen elected belonged to the PNF, a reflection of the border nationalism so characteristic of some fascist parties. Significantly, of the eleven seats of the *Nazionalisti* (2.1% of the vote) only two were elected in the north, none in the Centre, but three in Lazio and the remainder in the South and Sicily. They also gained one seat in Venezia Giulia, which therefore stands out as the most fascist-nationalist region. The territorial distribution of seats gained by the PNF and the ANI suggests that

TABLE 12.3. *Social profile and professional occupation of extreme right MPs in Germany and Italy during the inter-war period* (%)

Year of election	Number of representatives	Noblemen legislators	Teachers and professors	Journalists, writers	Politicians	Higher civil servants	Military persons	Priests, clergymen	Lawyers	Judges	Primary sector	Blue-collar workers	Managers, businessmen	Public sector employees
Germany
1924(1)	32	9.4	15.6	15.6	18.7	6.2	3.1	0.0	3.1	0.0	3.1	9.4	9.4	31.2
1924(2)	13	15.4	7.7	7.7	15.4	0.0	7.7	0.0	7.7	0.0	7.7	0.0	15.4	23.1
1928	13	15.4	0.0	15.4	38.5	0.0	0.0	0.0	0.0	0.0	7.9	7.7	7.7	7.7
1930	110	5.5	6.4	10.9	37.3	8.2	0.0	0.0	3.6	1.8	11.8	10.9	4.5	19.1
1932(1)	232	6.0	2.6	7.3	36.2	6.5	0.4	0.0	2.2	0.4	21.5	12.9	6.0	12.5
1932(2)	201	6.5	3.0	7.5	38.3	6.0	1.5	0.0	2.5	0.5	18.9	10.9	7.0	14.4
1933	288	8.0	2.1	6.2	35.8	8.0	1.0	0.0	2.1	0.3	20.5	11.8	5.9	14.9
Italy
1921	35	14.3	20.6	2.9	0.0	0.0	14.7	0.0	38.2	0.0	2.9	2.9	5.9	35.3
1924	280	7.1	12.5	8.6	4.6	2.9	8.2	0.0	34.6	1.0	3.6	1.0	8.2	25.4

they were different in their social base and at the same time complementary. To some extent a similar North–South divide will persist after the Second World War within the extreme-right and in the MSI between the more radical and the more pragmatic wings.

In the April 1924 election[7] the 'national' list—the *Listone*—gave the Mussolini government 64.9 per cent of the vote and 356 seats.[8] In four districts the PNF, in order to reduce the representation of the minority, presented additional lists, and obtained eighteen extra seats. In total, the fascist lists gained 374 seats, of which 260 were truly fascists and 114 democratic liberals and Clerico-Fascists, with one of the remaining seats going to a dissident fascist. Obviously, the 375 deputies of the fascist list are representative of the 'regime', not of the 'movement'—to use De Felice's distinction. Even the 260 more strictly fascists would not be representative of the original nucleus of the party in the same way as the 36 elected in 1921.

In the 1924 election, Mussolini made strategic use of the geographical spread of Clerico-Fascist support, assigning fourteen places on the *Listone* to Catholic candidates: one from the *Unione Nazionale* and the remainder former *Popolari* deputies (Pollard 1990: 36). It would also make little sense to include in an analysis of fascist parliamentarians politicians like Orlando and Salandra, part of the old liberal elite, but elected on the *Listone*. The *Listone* represented a clear option for the Mussolini government although non-fascist party members were among the candidates. The opposition, on the other hand, was divided among many parties as a result of the fractionalization that had taken place over the years (Farneti 1978).

The Fascists elected in 1924 are *homines novi*. Of 220 only 39 (17.7%) had been previously elected to parliament. Even more noteworthy, they were young: their average age was 37.2 years compared to 48.4 of the non-fascists on the lists. Among the 140 not PNF deputies of the *Listone* 87, that is 62.1 per cent, had prior parliamentary experience (Petersen 1975: 650).

A detailed analysis of the parliamentarians elected on the *Listone* tells us more about the fascist takeover of power and its consolidation than about the movement. The different components of the government majority—Fascists, Nationalists, 'Clerico-Fascists', and conservative Liberal politicians—had a role in enabling Mussolini to institutionalize the regime. The non-fascist and non-nationalists in the *Blocchi* and the *Listone* pose an interesting problem for comparative-quantitative analysis. Certainly the Liberals, Clericals, and Conservatives on these lists were not 'extreme right', but they contributed decisively to the legitimation of fascism, and in 1924 to the consolidation of Mussolini in power. Their views were on the right, but did their cooperation with the fascists mean that they identified with the long-range plans, ideology, and hostility to liberal-democratic parliamentarianism of the latter? A large number of them, formed in the political culture of *trasformismo* probably were thinking of the PNF as another party to be co-opted in the system to reinforce the 'right' and break with the Giolittian period.

They would deserve separate systematic comparative study and comparison with the other 'Liberals'.

12.2.3. *Germany*

In the case of Germany, we are bound by the decision to consider only the NSDAP as the extreme right, though from many points of view the DNVP in the early days of the Weimar Republic, and particularly since Hugenberg took control of the party and entered the Hitler cabinet, should be considered part of the extreme right rather than a *normal* conservative party. Perhaps sociologically it continued largely being part of the conservative lineage but ideologically and functionally it was 'extreme right' even when not fascist (Eley 1990).

It is not the purpose of this section to provide an analysis of Nazism, covered by an extensive and excellent scholarly literature. Here we limit ourselves to a collective portrait of the parliamentary representation of an anti-parliamentary party, to use the characterization and study by Heinrich Best (1997).

One of the most distinctive characteristics of the NSDAP MPs is their young age compared to the parties of the Weimar coalition and the DNVP, whose average age in five legislatures—1928 to 1933—ranged between 49.2 (SPD in 1932 II) and 52.8 years (*Zentrum*/BVP in 1928). The NSDAP mean in contrast ranged between 38.4 years in 1930 (when the representation grew to 110 MPs from the only 13 of 1928) and 42.1 in 1928 (Best 1997) (see Table 12.2). These data are fully congruent with one of the characteristics of fascist founders and elites: that they represent a generational revolt (one fascist programme wanted to exclude from public office anyone over 30), a revolt closely related to the war experience. This means that the formative experience in the adolescence was either the war or the immediate post-war. What is striking is that the KPD parliamentarians have an almost identical generational experience that differentiates them from the SPD deputies, whose average age is 10 or 11 years older.

The number of participants in the First World War among the parliamentarians was 23 of 34, or 67.6 per cent in the 1924 Reichstag, 9 of 15 in 1924–8, 8 of 12 in 1928–30, 90 of 114, or 78.9 per cent in 1930–2, 165 of 232, or 71.1 per cent in 1932–3 and 221 of 302, or 73 per cent in 1933 (Döring 2001: 415, table 8).

The NSDAP with its sudden success was a party of newcomers to parliament, 61.3 per cent of the 13 MPs elected in 1928 and fully 87.3 per cent of the 110 elected in 1930. None of the established parties had a comparable number of newcomers, and the KPD (a post-war party experiencing a serious internal crisis) in 1928 had 54.5 per cent of new elected among its fifty-five deputies, and after the electoral success in 1930, 52.5 per cent of eighty. The renewal rate for the SPD in 1928 was of 19.6 per cent and less than 5 per cent in the last two elections, for the *Zentrum* of 26.7 per cent in 1930, and it reached 28.4 per cent in 1928 for the Liberals in crisis. It is noteworthy that the radicalization of the DNVP was accompanied by both a loss in the number of mandates and a renewal rate of 43.5 per cent of its parliamentary group (Best 1998).

Fewer Nazi than bourgeois parliamentarians had a university education—around one-third compared to about 50 per cent for the Zentrum/BVP and a higher proportion for the Liberals and the DNVP. Even so, the number of university graduates was twice that of the SPD *Fraktion* and much greater than the 10 per cent of the KPD. The educational differences are related to the proportion of workers which was 7.7 per cent in 1928, 10.9 per cent in 1930, 12.9 per cent in 1932 (1), 10.9 per cent in 1932 (2), and 11.8 per cent in 1933, higher than on the benches of the SPD and of the bourgeois parties, but considerably lower than in those of the KPD. Extremist parties do not recruit their leadership among the higher civil servants and governments often do not allow civil servants to be members of such parties or discriminate against them. It is therefore not surprising that few NSDAP parliamentarians were public servants at the time of the election—compared to the larger numbers of the Z/BVP, Liberals, and DNVP. Even the SPD had a few more public employees in its ranks. However, the NSDAP had more than the other extremist party, the KPD.

The literature on Nazism has emphasized the importance of the rural electorate in Protestant Germany for the breakthrough in 1928, the shift of voters from regional and farmers' parties to the NSDAP and the ruralist-romantic-*völkisch* ideology (especially of Darre). It is not surprising therefore that farmers (and farm-workers) should be disproportionately represented in the parliamentary group, particularly in 1932 and 1933 (see Table 12.3), in contrast to the Liberals and in proportions not too different from the Z/BVP, that obtained the votes of the Catholic peasantry.

Nazi lawmakers were generally newcomers but, if they had been members of the Reichstag, it was of smaller extreme right groups or the DNVP and none came from the left. This was not the case in some other countries: let us remember the Labour party leader Mosley in Britain, the PCF leader Doriot, the socialist Déat in France, and foremost the left socialist Mussolini in Italy.

The absence of women in the parliamentary Nazi party is not a reflection of their absence from the movement, but the result of a formal decision of the leadership against the demands of *völkisch* women's groups.

The NSDAP parliamentarians were not like those of other parties. They marched into the Reichstag in formation and party uniform, devoted their efforts to obstruction, demagogic proposals, and boycott of sessions. In the thirties, they generally joined with the DNVP and Agrarian party deputies, and quite often with the KPD in voting against the government. At the same time they claimed their rights to parliamentary office (like the presidency for Goering), invoking 'the legality of the way but not of the goal' as Goebbels had put it in 1931.

Of the NSDAP and affiliated parliamentarians in office before 1945 only one would return to the Bundestag and three to different *Länder* parliaments (Döring 2001: 464). After the Second World War, the Constitution allowed the outlawing of extremist parties to prevent neo-Nazism. This rule was applied in a few cases. The different parties of the extreme right, due to the threshold for representation gained seats in local and *Länder* elections, but their largest vote in a federal election was 4.3 per cent for the *Nationaldemokratische Partei Deutschlands* (NDP) in 1969 (Kailitz 2004: 55).

12.2.4. *France: Birthplace of Modern Extreme Right Ideologies and Movements but Fewer Extreme Right Parliamentarians*

Since 1789 France was the country of liberal and democratic revolution but also of counter-revolution, legitimism, and Napoleonic plebiscitarian authoritarianism. After the defeat of 1870, new forms of populist extremism—movements representing new forms of nationalist radicalism, seen as proto-fascist if not as fascist (Sternhell 1989)—had under the Third Republic considerable success. It was also the birthplace of authoritarian conservative-monarchical-revolutionary thought: *Action Française*. The Dreyfus affair was a catalyst of the anti-republican and anti-semitic right.

The weight in the political culture of Europe and Latin America of *Action Française* is not measured by its representation in the *Chambre des Députés* or in city councils, nor even by its membership, but by the impact of the writings of its intellectuals—particularly Charles Maurras—and its newspaper *Action Française*. *Action Française* candidates ran for parliament only once in 1919.

We are not going to tell the story of the several rightist *Ligues*, that attacked the politicians of the Third Republic (while fighting among themselves), but were unable to create a large movement and a party able to gain parliamentary seats. Parliamentarians, ex-parliamentarians, and future MPs were linked to them, but despite all the rhetoric (many of the leaders were intellectuals and journalists), the *Ligues* did not endanger the parliamentary regime. They were not strictly speaking fascists, and when fascist movements or parties appeared on the scene— like *Valois's Fascieau* and later the PPF of Doriot—they opposed them. The *Croix de Feu*, growing out of a veterans movement, when the Popular Front in 1936 outlawed the Leagues, became a party—the *Parti Social Français* (PSF)—and elected eight deputies which basically acted like conservative politicians (Rudaux 1967; Passmore 1995). The PSF initially supported Pétain and Vichy but in contrast to the 'true' fascists its leaders did not become collaborationists with the Germans.

France had a flourishing fascist or crypto-fascist intellectual climate, a multitude of attempts to generate a fascist party. The *Parti Populaire Français* (PPF), founded by the communist mayor of the Parisian working-class suburb Saint-Denis, is probably the most authentic French fascist party. Doriot had been since the early twenties a deputy of the communist party and held on to his seat after the expulsion of the PCF for dissenting on the party line towards the socialists. So the PPF had been represented in parliament by someone elected as a communist, who only resigned his seat after losing the support of his constituency. In 1937, his anti-communism had allied him in a *Front de la Liberté* with a number of leaders of the conservative extreme right. We do not have to deal with the *Rassemblement National Populaire* founded by Marcel Déat in 1941 since it never participated in an election. Déat however had been a socialist deputy and even a cabinet member in the 1930s, before he turned fascist via a 'neo-socialism' and became a collaborationist with the Germans (Burrin 1996).

In the 1930s, as Philippe Burrin has shown, men of the left, like Bergery, Déat, and Doriot, evolved politically to end being fascists. It is their participation in the politics of the Third Republic and their frustrations with their parties that through complex paths ultimately led them to fascism. The impact of the success of fascism in Italy and Germany in contrast with the weakness of France and the failures of the democratic politicians, together with a pacifism (partly reflection of the bloody experience of the First World War led them to search for peace with Germany.

The parliamentary presence of the fascists and the extreme right, alone, cannot though capture its importance in the cultural and political scene.[9] Certainly, nothing comparable could be said about the post—Second World War neo-fascist, neo-Nazi groups and intellectuals or the groupings of the extreme left. The age of the extremes was the first half of the past 'short century'.[10]

12.2.5. *Hungary: Authoritarian Rule and Fascist Opposition*

Hungary in the inter-war years presents us with a complex and paradoxical situation of a conservative authoritarian regime which allows partly competitive elections. The fascists (in our sense) are tolerated as the opposition, but sometimes subject to repression and do not gain power until the end of the war when they do it with German support.

In Hungary, we can compare a traditional non-democratic oligarchic elite, the supporters of Count Bethlen, and a radical authoritarian right (with fascist strains in its programme, ideology, and policies) led by Julius Gömbos (1932–6) and Bela Imrédy (1938–9), with fascist parties. Among them the Arrow Cross led by Ferenc Szálasi and other parties close to it made the Hungarian fascist one of the four electorally most successful fascist movements in Europe.

The liberal-constitutional traditions were strong enough to permit the survival of an institutional framework with elections, that were manipulated to assure the victory of the government party—mainly with limited suffrage and the open ballot in country districts and small towns—but were competitive in the cities, assuring a multiparty system. The communists were outlawed. In that context of rule by the right, an extreme right opposition of fascist groups in opposition and sometimes persecuted could emerge. Among these groups the Arrow Cross had a dominant role (Lacko 1959).

Margit Szöllösi-Janze (1989) provides us with data on the parliamentary representation elected in 1939 and compares the 26 Arrow Cross (NYKP) deputies and others associated with the extreme right, adding to 49 MPs, with the 178 members of the government party and the 295 MPs.

On the government party benches forty-five deputies (25.3%) were landowners, many of large holdings, compared to only four (8.2%) of the forty-nine of the extreme right. The next largest group among the right was civil servants, thirty-seven (20.8%), compared to one (2.1%) of the extreme right, something related to the 1938 legislation barring radicals from the service. The presence of the military among the extreme right is given by retired officers with eight deputies (16.3%) among them the leader Szálasi himself. University professors were represented among the government party MPs (8 or 4.3%), but absent among those of the Arrow Cross, while three (6.1%) teachers sat for them, compared to one (0.6%) among the former. Businessmen and managers were under-represented in parliament (only 2.4%) but not in the government party (12.8%), and were absent from the Arrow Cross benches. The free professions constituted a significant segment of parliament (23.1%), slightly less for the government party (19.7%), but a larger number—seventeen or 34.7 per cent—in the Arrow Cross. Lawyers were respectively forty (13.6%), twenty-one (11.8%), and nine (18.4%) respectively. Among the professionals, medicine, an occupation of low prestige and a channel of upward mobility, was over-represented (8.2%) among the Arrow Cross compared to Parliament (3.4%) and the government party (2.8%). Employees were relatively few in parliament (7.5%) and even fewer on the government side (6.7%), but larger numbers among the Arrow Cross (16.4%), half of them engineers. Artisans and merchants, the old middle classes, were practically absent from parliament (1.7%), as manual workers, though two of them were elected for the Arrow Cross compared to one for the government party. The Arrow Cross certainly recruited its elite predominantly from outsiders to the conservative establishment of landlords and civil servants.

Another indicator of the 'marginality' of the Arrow Cross is the much larger number of bourgeois members, thirty-four of fifty, that is 68 per cent compared to 43per cent of the government party (1921–132) and 54.5 per cent (1932–44). The aristocracy was represented by only two members, 4 per cent compared to 8.9 per cent of the government party deputies in both periods, and the gentry by twelve members, or 24 per cent, compared to 43.9 per cent (1921–32) and 32.2 per cent (1932–44) of the government party MPs.

The age structure in 1939 was also congruent with what we know of other fascist movements: 38 per cent were under 41 years, compared to the 15.8 per cent of the government party (even fewer in 1931, 7.9%), 60 per cent between 41 and 60, compared to 73.5 per cent among the conservatives, and respectively 2 per cent and 16.7 per cent, respectively over 61. The Arrow Cross included a substantial number of those born after 1900, who were not part of the original Szeged clique or who could not be absorbed by the Gombös machine during the crisis years (Janos 1989), that is, the conservative counter-revolutionaries and the radical conservatives, but of the new generations.

12.2.6. *Belgium: Extreme Nationalism and an Extreme Right Drifting Towards Fascism*

In the inter-war years a number of extreme right parties appear and gain votes and few seats but the three main democratic parties limit their success. In fact *Rex*, the most successful, gained 11.5 per cent of the vote in 1936 and 21 seats, but when its leader Leon Degrelle, having forced a by-election in April 1937, confronted in Brussels a candidate supported by all major parties and the Archbishop of Malines, obtained only 19 per cent of the vote compared to Van Zeelands 75.8 per cent. In the subsequent national election in 1939, *Rex* saw its vote reduced to 4.4 per cent and its representation to only 4 deputies of 202. The party, originally inspired by *Action Française* and attracted by the Italian model during the war identified closely with the Germans.

Among the twenty-one Rex deputies, seven were lawyers, five businessmen, four journalists, one industrialist, one metal worker, and the mayor of a town; a composition not that different from other bourgeois parties. Degrelle was not a candidate in 1936. Born in a small town in 1906, his father, a brewer, was an active member of the Catholic party. He studied law in Louvain but never took a degree. He was active in the Catholic Youth movement, assumed the direction of a publishing department and launched into many publishing ventures, and after breaking with the Catholic party, initiated his new political life (Etienne 1968; Wallef 1980).

Hostility to political parties and parliament, advocacy of corporatism and of a strong executive, anti-communism, hostility to big business and labour unions, and an appeal to the middle classes characterized many different movements. Some had a limited appeal through their magazines and newspapers, some organized a larger support, and a few created militias. The main appeal of the more successful ones was their demagogic attack on the corruption of politicians and by implication of the system, symbolized by the 'broom' of the *Rex* and the rethoric of their leaders. They differed in their location on the divide between Flemish and French speakers and the conception of the Belgian state. *Verdinaso* the League of the Dutch-speaking partisans of national solidarity, led by Van Severen (1894–1944) a war veteran, for example, started advocating *Dietschland*, a union of the Dutch speakers, evolving to advocate a larger *Dietsche Rijk* incorporating Luxembourg and reconstructing the historic Burgundy. Others were 'Belgian' nationalists claiming Luxembourg and Limburg. *Rex* was successful in the French-speaking areas, mainly in rural and small town districts, and therefore at some point sought an alliance with the Flemish nationalists, *Vlaamsch National Verbond* (VNV). Except for the nationalist basis of the VNV, they did not have the support of organized sectors of society: business, farmers, trade unions, or the church, but sometimes of enthusiastic youth, students, a few intellectuals, journalists, veterans, and army officers. This weakness explains the 'flash' and limited electoral success (Stengers 1966).

The Flemish nationalists gained four seats in 1921, six in 1925, eleven in 1929, nine in 1932, sixteen in 1936, and seventeen in 1939. In 1933, the VNV was founded to unite the various nationalist organizations under the chairmanship of Staf De Clerq (1884–1942) a former schoolmaster and nationalist deputy (1919–32). In competition with *Verdinaso*, it adopted (in contrast with previous Flemish nationalists), an authoritarian, anti-party, 'solidarist' position in favour of a reunification of the *Dietsche* people. In its pageantry and the leadership principle it turned to fascism. In 1936 it elected sixteen deputies, in 1939, seventeen. It received money from Germany and would collaborate with the German *Militärverwaltung*, although many left the party.

12.2.7. *Finland: A Defeated Extreme Right Movement Becomes a Small Party*

In Finland, *Lapua*, a movement with some characteristics of a fascist organization, once its 'subversive' attempt had been defeated by the defence of legality by the conservative President Svinhufvud and was outlawed, changed into the *Isänmallinen Kansaliike*, the People's Patriotic Movement, in 1932. It gained fourteen seats in 1933 cooperating for two years with the conservatives before radicalizing into a more fascist party, gaining in 1936 8.3 per cent of the vote and maintaining the same number of seats (Karvonen 1998). It never improved that result: in 1939 it obtained 6.6 per cent of the vote and only eight deputies. Isolated on the political scene, the Isänmaallinen Kansanliike (IKL) was more successful than fascist parties in Scandinavian countries, but much less than in the Baltic republics (Rintala 2000; Kasekamp 1965).

The educational and social profile of the Patriotic Movement legislators greatly differs from the one typical of the Finnish parliament in the 1930s—a man 48 years old, with basic or intermediate education and working in the primary sector, a previous political experience at the local level although no leading party positions. The Patriotic Movement in parliament was mainly composed of much younger and well-educated men: more than 80 per cent held a university degree, mainly in humanities and social sciences. Concerning occupational background, both in 1933 and 1936, half of them were teachers and professors; the second largest group was military persons (over 30%) and the third one the primary sector (25%). Following the 1939 elections the weight of these occupational groups varied: the one of teachers and military persons was lower and the one of primary sector was higher. In any of the legislatures three quarters of the IKL deputies were public sector employees. In all of them, half of the IKL MPs had previous political experience at local level and party leading positions. In 1933 most (85.7%) were newcomers. That proportion was severely reduced in 1936 when the party maintained the same number of deputies (35.7% of newcomers), and more moderately after loosing almost half of them in 1939 (25%).

12.3. POST-WAR EXTREMISTS AND NEO-FASCISTS

Roger Griffin (1993) and numerous other authors have written extensively on the wide range of post-Second World War extremists groups and parties, publications, intellectual circles, and ideologists that show different degrees of affinity with fascist heritage (Hainsworth 1992; Ignazi 1994; Kitschelt 1995). This is a complex world, but we do not have to deal with it here since most of these organizations did not participate in elections, or gained only few votes. Three however have won significant and continuous parliamentary representation (but only three cabinet memberships in coalition governments). After the Second World War and the fall of most of the dictatorships in Europe, there was considerable fear of a survival or revival of fascism, particularly given the number of those displaced from their positions in the old regimes and of refugees. Constitutions in Germany and Italy outlawed anti-democratic parties, a legislation that was enforced in Germany. Many of the rightist votes in Germany went to the *Bund der Heimatvertrieben und Entrechteten* (BHE) which Adenauer co-opted into democratic politics by offering it a cabinet seat and which, with prosperity, disappeared. In Spain, the transition by *reforma pactada/ruptura pactada* and the presence of *Alianza Popular* on the right, not rejecting the Franco period but supporting the democratization, left a potential extreme right without an electorate. *Fuerza Nueva* thus gained only once one seat.

There are different perspectives on the 'neo-fascism' today:

1. One stresses the limited appeal of *groupuscules*, survivals of the past, disturbing but without political significance.
2. Another sees them as groupings that, without a chance of electoral success, develop new forms of activity and organization which allow them to have a broad impact on public opinion and thereby indirectly on 'mainstream' parties.
3. Others see them as groups that cannot be ignored since they may become important in a crisis of democracy.

Without ignoring the second interpretation we tend to share the first perspective, and in Europe at least we see the third as a quite remote possibility. When we look at the table in Ignazi (1994: 244) on the vote in legislative elections in eight European countries between 1981 and 1993, in a total of forty-six elections in which they presented candidates, only in one did they gain more than 15 per cent of the vote (the Austrian Fpö in 1990, 16.6%) and only in seventeen over 5 per cent. Their success was sporadic with one significant exception: the MSI that continuously had between 6.8 and 5.4 per cent of the vote. The different extreme right parties—some of them clearly neo-Nazi—in Germany after the Second World War are not included in our analysis because they did not gain representation in the Bundestag, despite some temporary successes in *Landtag* elections. Their limited and temporary appeal, the outlawing by decisions of the Constitutional Court and the threshold of 5 per cent in the electoral law that excluded them from gaining representation, account for their absence from the Bundestag.

Another set of parties can be described as anti-party protest movements with a populist appeal. The *Uomo Qualunque* (UQ) in Italy and the Poujadists in France probably fit that characterization. Neither their ideology, or rather programmatic statements, nor their organization or style would allow us to consider them fascist or neo-fascist. To the extent they appealed to the 'little man', marginal old middle classes, shopkeepers, and artisans, they fitted some of the Marxist inspired conceptions of fascism and some commentators tried to fit them under the label fascist.

The more parties can be seen by their ideology and style to link with the fascist past or tradition the smaller their appeal. Their dilemma is to attract support on a broad range of concrete issues or themes adding supporters who would be alienated by fascism. The only post-Second World War party of any significance that links with the past but is probably on the way of becoming part—as AN—of the party system of democracy is MSI. It early formulated its position in the formula: '*non rinnegare e non restaurare*' (Ignazi 1994: 17).

12.3.1. *Italy*

One of the particular features of Italian politics is related to the fact that only this country has a long-term continuity of extreme right MPs (Table 12.4). This 'party family' was represented at the national parliament by the UQ in 1946, by different monarchist parties from 1948 to 1968, by the MSI from 1948 to 1992, and AN since 1994. In 1993, the MSI changed its name to *Alleanza Nazionale* (AN) in order to establish a distance with regards to the Mussolini's heritage and its neo-fascist legacy and thus exploit the opportunity offered by the crisis of the Christian Democracy. AN, in fact, secured a considerable electoral success in the 1994 parliamentary election and in the following ones. Its evolution towards the conservative-right wing was approved in the national party congress of 1995. Since then, the National Alliance cannot be classified as an extreme right group but more as a nationalist-conservative party (Wal 2000).

The Front of the *Uomo Qualunque* was founded in 1945 by Guglielmo Giannini. It was conceived as a party against all parties (Setta 1975). This extreme right party gained a moderate success in the 1946 election, obtaining thirty-two seats. Its parliamentary group was mainly composed of well-educated people with a university degree. Concerning their occupational background, most of them were lawyers, public sector employees, managers/businessmen, and teachers/professors. Most of them had neither previous political experience at regional or local level (74%) nor party positions before their recruitment to parliament (72%).

Soon after the 1946 election, the appeal of the UQ drastically declined as the monarchists appeared and the MSI force became consolidated. The MSI was

TABLE 12.4. *Gender, age, and newcomers among extreme right MPs during the period following the Second World War*

	Year of election	Number of representatives	Female legislators	Newcomers	Mean age	Mean age of newcomers
Italy	1946 (UQ)	32	2.9	94.1	50.3	49.9
	1948 (MSI)	7	0	68.2	42.7	42.6
	1948 (Mon)	14	0	78.6	45.6	45.3
	1948 (All)	21	0	75.1	44.6	44.4
	1953 (MSI)	29	0	77.8	45.3	45.8
	1953 (Mon)	39	4.8	61.9	49.9	49.5
	1953 (All)	68	2.8	68.7	47.9	47.9
	1958 (MSI)	24	0	48	45.1	41.4
	1958 (Mon)	26	0	12.5	54	41.3
	1958 (All)	50	0	29.5	49.7	41.3
	1963 (MSI)	27	3.7	25.9	46.9	37.3
	1963 (Mon)	8	0	12.5	57	40
	1963 (All)	35	2.8	22.8	49.2	37.9
	1968 (MSI)	24	0	21.7	47.6	41.4
	1968 (Mon)	6	0	16.7	56.6	61
	1968 (All)	24	0	20.7	49.4	45.3
	1972 (MSI)	56	0	44.4	50	45.8
	1976 (MSI)	34	2.8	11.4	54.1	55.7
	1979 (MSI)	31	0	32.3	53.0	44.8
	1983 (MSI)	42	4.5	30.2	51.9	46.7
	1987 (MSI)	35	2.6	10.8	55.1	50.7
	1992 (MSI)	34	6.1	34.4	50.8	44.5
	1994 (MSI-AN)	105	5.7	73.3	50.8	49.9
Netherlands	1994	3	33.3	66.6	49.4	45
	1982	1	0	100	47.9	47.9
	1989	1	0	0	54.9	0
Norway	1989	22	4.5	0	42.9	41.7
	1973	4	0	100	52.7	52.7
	1981	1	0	100	47	47
	1993	10	10	0	46.2	29
France	1956	44	0	100	45	45
	1986	35	2.9	82.4	49.5	46.5
Finland	1983	1	0	0	57	0
	1975	1	0	0	49	49
Hungary	1998	14	7.1	64.3	52.9	50.2

founded in 1946 (Ignazi 1989: 29). In its initial stages, the MSI had clear links to the pre-war fascist movement.[11]

The high educational level of extreme right legislators (see Table 12.5), higher than the average until the middle 1980s (see Figure 12.1), is just one indicator of their relatively high social status. During the whole period, their parliamentary group was basically composed of five occupational groups: lawyers, public sector employees, managers and businessmen, teachers and professors, and professional politicians (see Table 12.6). Within the extreme right it is possible to notice

TABLE 12.5. *Educational level of extreme right MPs during the period following the Second World War*

	Year of election	Number of representatives	Basic education	Intermediate education	University or comparable degree
Italy					
	1946 (UQ)	32	6.1	12.1	71.9
	1948 (MSI)	7	0	16.7	83.3
	1948 (Mon)	14	0	7.7	92.3
	1948 (All)	21	0	10.3	89.3
	1953 (MSI)	29	0	13	87
	1953 (Mon)	39	0	10.5	89.5
	1953 (All)	68	0	11.6	88.4
	1958 (MSI)	24	0	26.1	83.9
	1958 (Mon)	26	0	16.7	83.3
	1958 (All)	50	0	21.2	83.6
	1963 (MSI)	27	0	19.2	80.7
	1963 (Mon)	8	0	25	75
	1963 (All)	35	0	20.5	79.4
	1968 (MSI)	24	0	17.4	82.5
	1968 (Mon)	6	0	33.3	66.6
	1968 (All)	24	0	20.6	79.3
	1972 (MSI)	56	0	20.8	79.2
	1976 (MSI)	34	0	11.1	88.9
	1979 (MSI)	31	0	22.6	77.5
	1983 (MSI)	42	0	27.9	72.1
	1987 (MSI)	35	0	27.0	73
	1992 (MSI)	34	0	34.4	65.6
	1994 (MSI-AN)	105	0	33.3	66.6
Netherlands					
	1994	3	33.3	33.3	33.3
	1982	1	0	0	100
	1989	1	0	0	100
Norway					
	1989	22	0	72.7	27.3
	1973	4	0	25.0	75.0
	1981	1	0	0	100
	1993	10	10	40	50
France					
	1956	44	0	0	9.6
	1986	35	0	0	50
Finland					
	1983	1	0	0	100
	1975	1	0	0	100
Hungary					
	1998	14	0	7.1	92.9

some significant differences between monarchists and neo-fascists particularly in the first two legislatures. The neo-fascists, with more full-time politicians and journalists, show a profile characterized by a greater degree of political professionalism and, with the weaker weight of public sector employees, reveal also

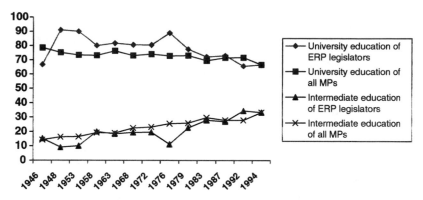

FIGURE 12.1. Educational level of Italian extreme right MPs (1948–94)

a greater marginality vis-à-vis the new democratic state. The monarchists, with more managers, businessmen, and landowners, correspond much more to a profile of *notabili*; moreover the greater numbers of public sector employees and teachers indicate a greater degree of integration. The decline of the monarchists from the 1960s onwards will make the profile of the extreme right more influenced by that of the MSI. It will be in the 1980s that the profile of MSI deputies (and thus of the extreme right) will loose some of its peculiarities and will become more similar to the average of all members. This is very clear for instance from the steady growth of public sector employees (and also from the decline of businessmen and managers) (Lotti 1963).

Concerning the political background of extreme right representatives, the most important development has been the steady growth in the proportion of members with political experience at local or regional levels before their recruitment to parliament. Since 1979 the proportion of MSI members with national or regional political background increased over time while that of the average member tended to decline. For the whole period a large majority of MSI deputies also hold leading party positions, national, or local (see Figure 12.2).

These data do not reflect huge variations with the average profile of the Italian deputies, although since the late 1970s the MSI representatives show a tendency to have more political and party experience than the typical deputy: roughly 90 per cent of them had at least a political function before obtaining a seat in parliament, the proportion for all members being 77 per cent.

In its first two legislatures the percentages of newcomers both for monarchists and MSI representatives were particularly high. Since then the proportion of newcomers dropped significantly to levels that are fairly similar to those of the rest of the parliament (see Table 12.4).

As the MSI turned into MSI-*Alleanza Nazionale* in 1993 and later simply AN, we found some elements of continuity as well as some others of change regarding the social and political profile of its deputies. Most AN representatives

TABLE 12.6. *Occupational background of extreme right MPs during the period following the Second World War*

Year of election	Number of mandates	Journalists, writers	Politicians	Lawyers	Primary sector	Blue-collar workers	Managers, businessmen	Teachers and professors	Higher civil servants	Military persons	Judges	Public sector employees
Italy												
1946 (UQ)	32	3	0	30.3	6.1	0	18.2	12.1	6.1	6.1	3	27.3
1948 (MSI)	7	14.3	28.6	28.6	0	0	14.3	0	14.3	0	0	0
1948 (Mon)	14	7.1	0	21.4	7.1	0	28.6	7.1	0	0	0	31.3
1948 (All)	21	9.5	9.5	23.8	4.7	0	23.8	4.7	4.8	0	0	22.7
1953 (MSI)	29	14.8	36.3	37.0	0	0	3.7	3.7	7.4	0	0	11.1
1953 (Mon)	39	2.4	0	14.3	19.0	0	26.2	14.3	7.1	7.1	2.4	31.8
1953 (All)	68	7.7	15.5	24.0	10.9	0	16.6	9.8	7.2	4.1	1.4	23.9
1958 (MSI)	24	4.0	32.0	28.0	0	0	12.0	16.0	4.0	0	0	20.0
1958 (Mon)	26	0	0	25.0	8.3	0	33.3	16.7	4.2	0	0	33.3
1958 (All)	50	1.9	15.4	26.4	4.3	0	23.1	16.4	4.1	0	0	26.9
1963 (MSI)	27	3.7	25.9	33.3	0	0	11.1	14.8	3.7	3.7	0	18.5
1963 (Mon)	8	12.5	0	25.0	12.5	0	37.5	12.5	0	0	0	33.3
1963 (All)	35	5.7	20.0	31.4	2.8	0	17.1	14.3	2.8	0	0	22.2
1968 (MSI)	24	0	21.7	43.3	0	0	21.7	4.3	0	4.3	0	8.6
1968 (Mon)	6	0	0	16.7	16.7	0	16.7	16.7	16.6	0	0	33.3
1968 (All)	24	0	17.4	37.9	3.3	0	20.7	6.8	3.3	3.3	0	13.3
1972 (MSI)	56	5.6	14.8	37.0	0	0	18.5	11.2	1.9	2.3	0	16.7
1976	36	8.3	19.4	41.7	0	0	11.1	8.3	2.8	2.8	0	13.9
1979	32	16.7	16.7	36.7	0	0	3.3	3.3	3.3	3.3	0	12.9
1983	42	14.0	14.0	34.9	0	0	4.7	9.3	2.3	2.3	0	18.6
1987	35	10.8	13.5	37.8	0	0	8.1	8.1	2.7	0	0	13.5
1992	34	12.1	15.2	27.3	0	6.1	6.1	3.0	3.0	0	3.0	21.2
1994	105	2.9	24.8	22.9	1.0	0	3.8	9.5	1.0	1.0	1.0	20.0

Netherlands											
1994	3	0	33.3	0	0	0	33.3	0	0	0	0
1982	1	0	0	0	0	0	0	100	0	0	100.0
1989	1	0	0	0	0	0	0	100	0	0	100.0
Norway											
1989	22	9.1	0	0	0	9.1	18.2	9.1	9.1	0	31.8
1973	40	25.0	0	25.0	0	0	0	25.0	25.0	0	50.0
1981	1	0	0	0	0	0	0	0	100.0	0	100.0
1993	100	0	20.0	0	0	0	0	20.0	10.0	0	50.0
France											
1956	44	0	0	2.3	3.8	0	19.2	2.3	0	0	1.9
1986	35	8.6	0	17.1	2.9	0	25.7	8.6	5.7	0	14.3
Finland											
1983	1	0	0	100.0	0	0	0	0	0	0	0
1975	1	0	0	100.0	0	0	0	0	0	0	0
Hungary											
1998	14	0	21.4	7.1	0	0	0	21.4	0	0	0

Note: The 'Public sector employees' column includes all the other categories of state servants (judges, military officers, high civil servants, teachers, and professors).

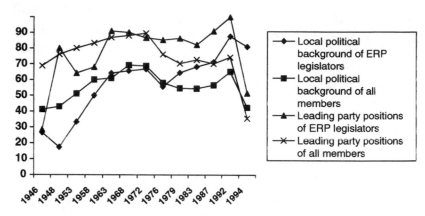

FIGURE 12.2. Local political background and leading party positions of
Italian extreme right MPs (1946–94)

had university training and a profession usually linked to high social status. In
addition, most of them had political experience at local or regional level preceding their MPs status. The most important developments were the downfall
of representatives with political background and party experience before their
recruitment to parliament and the rise of full-time politicians. The turnover
rate rose significantly in 1994, thanks to the great electoral success of the
reformed party: of the 105 members 73 per cent (among them more than one
coming from the ranks of the collapsed Christian Democracy) were newcomers
(see Tables 12. 4).

The MSI is the only successful party which, after the Second World War, links
explicitly with the pre-war fascism. To an extent, the tension between the PNF as
a movement and the PNF as a regime, between the original left-leaning ideology
and the practice of the regime, articulated after 1943 in the *Carta di Verona* of the
Republica Sociale Italiana (RSI) in the north, was reflected in the party. Also the
memory of fascism in the south, liberated early by the Allies, and in the north,
where the RSI fought a long civil war with the partisan Liberation Movement,
were very different as was the popular reaction to the MSI. The two tendencies
would be represented in the leadership of the party.

12.3.2. *France: From Poujade to the Front National*

It would be difficult to characterize Poujade's *Union de Défense des Commerçants
et Artisans* (UDCA) and the party he created, that gained forty-four seats in
parliament in 1956, as neo-fascist. The *Front National* on the basis of some of
its ideological positions is closer to fascism, but not if we consider a linkage with
the pre-Second World War fascist parties a criterion. It is more than a protest
movement, a populist upsurge, but not a party like the others on the right. The

Front National is probably the extreme right party of significance least integrated into the democratic political system, and one generating strong opposition, particularly when its leader, Le Pen—who founded it in 1972—made a bid to the presidency. Its presence at the local level is significant but as a result of electoral laws its parliamentary role has been limited. It is certainly the most important extreme right party in Europe and is different from the parties of the right in its positions, implicit ideology, style of politics, and social bases. Its presence, competitive offering, has an effect on other parties; in tight elections with single-member districts and run-off its coalition or blackmail potential are not to be ignored (Birenbaum 1992).

The profile of Poujadist representatives greatly differs from the average of the legislature inaugurated in 1956, particularly concerning educational level: among its representatives, only 10 per cent had university training (more than 50% for all members). On the other hand, its group in parliament was mainly composed of managers and businessmen (presumably small size business). One characteristic feature of Poujadist representatives is that more than 90 per cent did not hold any political function before their recruitment to parliament. This high proportion contrasts with the average of 32 per cent for all members. In addition, all of them were newcomers whereas the overall proportion of newcomers in the French parliament was at the time around 30 per cent. The average age of Poujadist legislators was 45 years, which made them the youngest members in the 1956 French parliament. While the proportion of women was very low in that legislature, there were none in the Poujadist group (see Tables 12.4–12.6)

As for the *Front National*, the biography of Jean Marie Le Pen gives us many elements to understand the party that he created and controls. Born 1928 in provincial France where his father owned a fishing boat and a mother from a farmer's family, graduating from a Jesuit school, at 19 he enrolled in the Law School in Paris, where he became involved in right-wing student politics, later linked with J. Isorni, the lawyer of Pétain, and the leader of the National Union of Independent Republicans (UNIR), that in 1951 elected four deputies. In 1953, without having completed his studies, he enlisted in the Foreign Legion and went to Indo-China. The French humiliation there contributed to decide his political engagement which led him to Poujade rather than to a fascist group. The UDCA had burst on the scene after the retirement of De Gaulle from active politics and in 1956 the *Groupe d'Union et de Fraternité Française* managed to gain 2.6 million votes and 53 seats of the National Assembly. Le Pen was among them, the youngest member in the legislature. In the biography of a number of deputies of the Front National, a significant experience is their service in the Algerian War, a connection of some of them with the OAS, and consequently rejection of De Gaulle as *abandoniste*. It is also congruent with support of *pied-noir* electorates. The biographies also highlight intentionally—probably to dispel the 'fascist' label of the FN—the Resistance record of some FN leaders. Otherwise the representatives are—as deducted from the data mentioned above—a mixture of upper middle and middle class, with workers absent (although workers are an important component of their electorate). Curiously, there are candidates with a distinguished sports record. A sprinkling of diplomats and higher civil servants presumably adds to the respectability of the party. Of the twelve *Rassemblement* not FN members elected in 1986, several had previously been elected or held office in parties of the moderate right, but none of the left. As to links with the past, there are some links to Vichy and a reaffirmation of the traditional symbols of the French extreme right (but not of fascism) like the celebration of Jeanne d'Arc and with traditionalist Catholicism—like the schismatic Msgr. Lefebvre.

The initial cadres of the *Front National* beside *poujadistes*—as Le Pen who had been previously elected in the 1956 National Assembly under that label—include neo-fascists, intellectuals, anti-Gaullists, and those nostalgic of the Vichy regime, some of them direct collaborators with the Germans (Mayer and Sineau 2002: 44).

Although the National Front is one of the strongest extreme right parties of this period, it only gained a significant parliamentary representation in 1986 thanks to a change in the French electoral system.[12] Since then, the party has never achieved more than one seat in the national parliament.[13]

Previous work on the NF (Ysmal 1996) shows that the profile of its political elites differs from the typical one of a conservative party. According to our data half of the NF legislators elected in 1986 held a university degree. Concerning occupational background, we found five main groups among them: managers/businessmen (25.7%), lawyers (17.1%), public sector employees (14.3%), and journalists/writers, and teachers/professors (8.6% each group). Blue collars or military were completely absent. Among NF representatives there was a larger proportion of lawyers and—with the exception of right liberals—businessmen than in any other group in parliament. Conversely, public sector employees and teachers were under-represented. However, noblemen were over-represented, accounting for 12 per cent of the NF group (see Table 12.6).

Women were poorly represented in the National Front group—only one sitting female representative of thirty-five legislators—although that was not certainly a particularity (5% for the whole National Assembly). In 1988, Yann Piat, the only female National Assembly deputy of the NF was also the only woman in the twenty-member Political Bureau (Declair 1999: 145). The mean age of the NF legislators was 49 years, only two points below the average.

The most striking fact about the NF parliamentarians is the relative large number of men with no political function before being recruited for parliament: the few French legislators with no political experience before their coming to parliament (13%) contrasts with the fact that half of the NF representatives had not previously held any political office. As expected most of them (82%) were newcomers.

This is not the place to decide if the FN is or not 'neo-fascist', but there seems to be no simple answer. It clearly links with an extreme right tradition, among other things in its anti-Semitism, it has affinities in terms of its extreme nationalism, critique of parliamentarianism, and the type of generational experience (Indo-China and Algiers) with the fascist syndrome, but in its style it is different from fascism. Griffin (1993: 161) is probably right in writing: it is 'reformist rather than revolutionary, criteria which disqualify Le Pen's NF, though they may well accommodate neo-fascist elements in both policies and support'. Ignazi (1994: 234) concludes: 'The FN is the prototype of the post-industrial extreme right, disidentified of the myths of historical fascism, responsive to the new demands and challenges of contemporary society and its new conflicts.'

12.3.3. *Norway: The Fremskrittspartiet*

The extreme right is represented in the Norwegian parliament by the Anders Lange Party, later renamed Progress Party (FrPa). Originally named after its leader, it was founded in 1973. Lange had previously been a member of the Norwegian conservatives and, in his younger days, of the right-wing Patriots League of the 1930s (Svasand 1998: 77–8). Soon after its foundation, the party gained parliamentary representation in the elections held in 1973. Lange was one of the four party representatives, but died a few months later. His party was taken over by Carl I. Hagen who renamed it Progress Party before the 1981 general elections. Before his recruitment by the Anders Lange Party, he had no previous political experience.

Since its foundation the party has managed to achieve parliamentary representation in all parliamentary elections. In the legislature inaugurating the twenty-first century, it was the second largest party in parliament with 26 seats of 165. This party, like the Danish *Fremskrittspartiet*, with which it shares many characteristics, is difficult to define. Neither of them has links with the fascist parties before the Second World War and it makes little sense to characterize them as neo-fascists. They are certainly distinct from the conservatives in their countries and reject the party system *in toto* and have been generally isolated by the other parties. They have no specific class appeal, and in a sense are populist parties. They started as the political vehicle of a particular leader controlling the organization, but later, after leadership crises, became more institutionalized. In their platforms, they advocated a radical economic liberalism, lower taxes, and less government intervention, but without challenging the welfare state. In a sense they express a protest against the establishment—the dominant parties and institutions—but without articulating alternative institutions. A protest that has something in common with the earlier Poujadism, the Dutch extreme right, the Austrian Fpö, and even the French *Front Nationale*.

In its initial stages, the picture of the educational background of FrPa deputies greatly differed from the typical profile of a Norwegian MP. During the first three electoral terms, its group in parliament was mainly composed of well-educated people with university training, whereas the large majority of Norwegian legislators had an intermediate education. Following the 2001 parliamentary election, 46 per cent of the party representatives have university training, 42 per cent intermediate education, and only 12 per cent basic education. The occupational profile changes greatly across elections. The main group among them are public sector employees but their weight, as was the case for other occupational groups, varies from one election to another. Some features of their occupational background differentiate them from the other Norwegian MPs: first, the under-representation of professional politician (there was no full-time politician among extreme right representatives until the 1993 legislature when two of ten had that condition); and second, the absence of primary sector workers among them.

With regard to political background, MPs of the Norwegian FrPa had either limited or no political experience in local government in 1973, when they reached parliament for the first time under Anders Lange label. Since then, the Progress Party has increased the proportion of MPs with local political experience. The variable 'leading party positions' shows that since the first electoral term the Progress party placed most of its leaders in the parliamentary arena. After the 2001 parliamentary election, all Progress Party representatives have both local and party experience before their recruitment to parliament. In this regard, the Progress Party is characterized by accumulation of political functions among its representatives: since 1981 more than 60 per cent of its representatives held two political functions. Today, the normal practice for Progress Party representatives (77%) is to hold two political functions.

In its first electoral term, all four FrPa representatives were newcomers. During its second legislature, three out of its four representatives had that condition. Since then, the proportion of newcomers varies greatly across elections, according to party strength. Today, only seven of twenty-six party representatives are newcomers.

12.4. CONCLUSIONS

Our analysis of parliamentarians of the extreme right covering different periods of the twentieth century and including both fascist and non-fascist parties has confirmed the difficulties we had from the start anticipated in providing any simplified image of such a heterogeneous party family. The limited size of many parliamentary expressions of this political area and often the short lasting, 'flash' character of their successes have added further obstacles to a quantitative analysis.

With all these caveats, the analysis of the profiles of the parliamentarians of the extreme right has contributed to shed some further light upon a number of interesting features of these political groups and also to better detect its internal articulations.

Our data has confirmed in particular that, from the point of view of the political elites they have expressed, the fascist experiences of the *entre deux guerres* years are significantly different from previous cases of extreme right groups of authoritarian monarchist orientation but also from the parties that after the Second World War have tried to revive a fascist experience (as the Italian MSI) and even more from those that more recently have elaborated populist and semi-racist answers to the problems of immigration and globalization. From the analysis of parliamentarians emerges with absolute clarity the age dimension and the outsider character of the original fascist parties: with them a new and much younger political personnel, that had little to do with the existing political establishment and that capitalized on very special experiences (such as that of the war and of internal violence) made a rather sudden appearance. Fascism, in its different manifestations, represented a revolt against bourgeois liberal society, not by the old conservative-aristocratic elites, but a new generation of power seeking men. For them *politique d'abord*, the 'nation' against 'class', implied a rejection of the representation of interests of society in parliament or the aspiration to the hegemony of the working class of socialist-revolutionary leaders. Fascism would co-opt with more or less success members of the establishment-business, professional particularly technocratic, and the *ex-classe dirigente*, but ultimately subordinate them to the party activists that conquered power.

The age aspect will be conspicuously absent both from the older and the more recent extreme right experiences. Even those more strongly connected with the history of fascism as the Italian MSI will have from the beginning significantly different traits. Partly because more than at the future (as their model had done when it stepped on the political scene) they will look at the past. Partly because they will become institutionalized as minority excluded forces within a democratic regime sufficiently consolidated to keep them at bay. However, by being marginalized by the other political forces the new parliamentary representatives of the extreme right will show a number of features that set them somewhat apart from the parliamentarians of the other parties.

ENDNOTES

1   The authors would like to thank Luca Verzichelli for the generous help provided in the elaboration of the data and the preparation of tables and figures.
2   Although the term 'extreme right' has been accepted in Europe as referring to a particular party family (see von Beyme 1985), there is no agreement on its meaning and authors have defined it in a great variety of ways.
3   It seems as if the Italian polity would have a special capacity to 'domesticate' and integrate originally 'anti-system' parties.
4   Blinkhorn (1990: 1–13) provides us with a useful overview of the relationship between conservatism and fascism and the emergence of an extremist authoritarian conservatism, though perhaps underestimating the distinctive totalitarian tendency and more or less explicit anti-conservatism of fascism.
5   When defining parties as extremist, as anti-system, non-democratic (since we are dealing with parliamentary democracies), disloyal, we encounter a difficult question: parties that are part of a political family, that in terms of practice and ideology normally would not be considered anti-system but that in certain moments could be considered semi-loyal (Linz 1978 and 1980), are

to be classified as extremist for a particular period? Such parties are ready to cooperate or be tolerant with extremists. In some cases faction within such parties fits our description. We are thinking of the followers of Salandra among Italian liberal-conservatives, the DNVP under the leadership of Hugenberg, and the CEDA, to give some examples. The answer in this study has been that without ignoring these lapses, for the purposes of a sociological analysis, they should not be taken out of their respective political families.

6 The real number is higher considering that some legislatures are missing either because there was not enough data (particularly in the case of Spain: roughly two dozens of them before 1924) or they were not yet available in the DATACUBE format.

7 The fascist electoral reform of 1923 gave two-thirds of the seats to the list which would achieve the relative majority in all of Italy, as long as it obtained 25% of the vote.

8 By 1924, it is not easy to distinguish the real-fascists on the *Listone*. This explains the discrepancy between the 227 given by Petersen and the 280 so classified in the DATACUBE database.

9 The reading of Sternhell (1986) should make this clear.

10 For a bibliography of the French extreme right and Fascism we can refer to Paxton (2004: 241–4).

11 In 1948, five of its seven representatives in the Italian parliament had held some minor leadership positions in the pre-war fascist movement. In 1986 the plurality two ballots system was replaced by a proportional system, which allowed the National Front to win thirty-five seats. Two years later, in 1988, France returned to a plurality system, which deprived the party of most of its parliamentary seats.

12 Yann Piat was elected in 1988 but she resigned soon after the election; Marie-France Stirbois was elected in a by-election in 1989, and Jean Marie Le Chevalier was elected in 1997

13 His election was invalidated by the French Constitutional Council two months later. Finally, the NF won no seat in the 2001 parliamentary election.

13

Parliamentary Elites of New European Party Families: Unsuccessful Challenges or Chaotic Signs of Change?

Filippo Tronconi and Luca Verzichelli[1]

13.1. ANARCHISTS, ALTERNATIVES, BEGINNERS? 'NEW POLITICS' REPRESENTATIVE ELITES AFTER 1970

In the logic of a long-term comparative analysis of parliamentary elite transformations in Europe, the study of political and sociological profiles of green, 'new left/alternative left', and ethno-regionalist MPs could be considered as a 'residual' exercise, given the limited size of such political elites and their relatively short historical impact.

Differences between these party families, and particularly between the first two and the third one, are fairly clear, and hardly need to be recalled here. But some interesting similarities may also be stressed. The first one is that they all represent a challenge, in a broad sense, to the established parties of their respective party systems. In different ways, they have more or less successfully tried to aggregate new interests and give a voice to issues that traditional parties usually neglected. The second similarity is a consequence of the first one and refers to the timing of the emergence of these parties. It has often been underscored that a slow process of de-freezing of traditional party alignments started in the seventies in many European countries, along with a new materialist post-materialist cleavage (Inglehart 1984; Franklin 1992). The rise of Green and New Left parties is usually interpreted as a result of this trend. An interesting, and not always emphasized, thing is that the birth (or at least the re-emergence) of ethno-regionalism takes place in the same years and, in a number of cases, it can be explained along the same lines as a consequence of party dealignment, the rise of post-materialist issues (Melucci and Diani 1992), and the failure of traditional parties to keep strong linkages with civil society[2] (Lawson and Merkl 1988). The ethno-regionalist party family is, strictly speaking, not a new one but many of its members have experienced a 'second birth' in the 1970s, both with a sudden electoral success, and with a sharp redefinition of goals and ideological references. This justifies their inclusion in this work. It is not by chance, after all, that most ethno-regionalist parties sit in Strasbourg in a common parliamentary group—the Greens/European Free Alliance group—with the Greens (De Winter and Gomez-Reino 2002).

At the same time, these party families remain, after some thirty years from their emergence (or re-emergence) on the political scene of many European democracies, a relatively 'obscure object', which can be approached starting from several points of view, and studied in the light of rather different interpretative theories.

In a sense, to observe the emergence of new parliamentary elites, oriented towards some kind of radicalism or 'minoritarian' ideological discourse, can mean also to reflect upon a new form of political representation. The representatives who are inspired by post-materialist and libertarian principles are, in fact, often depicted as alternative political actors: minor but significant 'challengers' for the well consolidated and relatively homogeneous political elites produced by the old *weberian* and *duvergerian* mass parties. The theory of the post-materialist challenge (Inglehart 1984) has been evoked, by many observers, as the first significant sign of the end of party control over the process of political recruitment. A mechanical (but not always evident) consequence of such a challenge should have been the transformation of the political elite: the leadership originated by the new parties would have taken the semblances of an 'anarchist elite' (Dalton 1996). More similar to some specific social groups than to a broad class-based universe (Offe 1985), the new left elites would have brought a remarkable renewal not only in the physical composition of political elites, but even in the criteria of recruitment and circulation. It is less clear if this 'anarchist' pattern of change could apply to ethno-regionalist parties too. Some of them share with Greens and New Left parties a post-materialist attitude that could be reflected in the composition of their parliamentary elites, but others clearly do not.

In a different perspective (which does not concern the very nature of political elites but focuses on the consequences of party system change) one can interpret the new *red-and-green* political elites, as well as the ethnic minorities elites, as the ultimate challengers to the traditionally *frozen* party alignments of the twentieth century (von Beyme 1984; Kitschelt and Hellemans 1990). Several authors, mainly in an implicit way, indicate the emergence of these minor *party families* as the conclusion of the long-term transformation of party systems in Europe. In this perspective, the *new left* family should be considered as a sort of redefinition of those values which had been once 'submerged' by other party families. In particular, in this family we would find today the heirs of some radical Socialist parties and many of the old Communist parties that between 1945 and 1990 populated large areas of Western Europe (Bell 1993). On the other hand, the Greens should have occupied the space (already evident in the 1970s) created during the post-materialistic *revolution* and not completely 'occupied' by the radical parties originated within the liberal and the socialist wings. On the other hand, the 'ethnic revival' (Smith 1981) and the resurgence of peripheries, after a long wave of centralization of political functions, have created (or recreated) in many European regions a political space favourable to the success of ethno-regionalist parties. In some cases, the typical goals of ethno-regionalism (protection of minority languages, rediscovery of local cultural traditions, and claim for autonomy from the centre of the state) have gone alongside with a clear positioning also on non-ethnic issues, towards left libertarian stances (this is the case, for example of the Welsh *Plaid Cymru* or the Spanish *Bloque Nacionalista Galego*), or more traditional social democratic positions (the Scottish National Party), or even towards neo-populism (the *Lega Nord* and the *Vlaams Blok*). In these cases, the challenge to traditional parties is more direct: ethno-regionalist parties explicitly contend votes to left and social democratic parties or to moderate right or CD parties.

A third possible approach could also be used in the study of new political party elites—an approach developed in some analyses about the consequences of the entrance of post-materialist values in the European *high politics*.[3] The basic idea, here, is that these elites could be studied as *new born political elites:* their role during the period 1975–2000 should be conceived, following a *party lifespan approach* (Pedersen 1982), as a phase of socialization within the institutional arena, corresponding to the *childhood* of their parties. In fact, parliamentary elites from small alternative, protest or single issue parties seem to have gone through a long process of *adaptation* to the institutional side of politics (Della Porta and Diani 1999). In some cases (but it actually applies essentially to the green family and to a few ethno-regionalist parties), they have crossed the desert of their *instinctive opposition mode* and transformed themselves into governmental elites, thus reaching the fourth and final *threshold of relevance* which characterizes the maturation of a small party, according to a rokkanian long-term perspective (Müller-Rommel 2002: 3).

The subtitle of the chapter synthesizes the complex theoretical puzzle we have here briefly sketched out, and raises an explicit question. In fact, we are going to illustrate the meaning of parliamentary elites' transformations in three *party families* of the European scenario, starting from two alternative working hypotheses: the first one explores the possibility that MPs expressed by these parties symbolize the *new challenges* to the overall profile of political representatives. The second hypothesis argues that the transformations in the parliamentary profiles within these parties indicate clear signs of instability within the whole democratic political class: the representatives of the new parties would be, in other words, less oriented to follow the paths of historical convergence which have until now characterized the evolution of many 'traditional' party elites during the twentieth century (Cotta and Best 2000). However (and here the *lifespan approach* comes again), this peculiar tendency to produce an overall more various elite profile could be linked either to an initial phase of party institutionalization, or on the contrary to a more structural feature of a given party family.

The few data available and the reduced dimensions of the elite groups included in these ideological families will not probably enable us to reach robust and statistically significant findings. We hope, however, to be able to clarify matters by discarding one of these two broad hypotheses and concentrating on the other one, or on the contrary by reaching the conclusion that we have to keep both of them. In the next paragraph (para. 2), we will clarify what kind of impact we can expect from the parliamentary presence of the 'new party families' in Europe. Then, after some clarifications about the problems found when analysing small parliamentary parties (para. 3), we will move to the presentation of some 'working hypotheses', that will lead to the exploration of the parliamentary profiles of the three party families (para. 4). Finally, we will make an attempt to provide some comparative interpretations of our findings (para. 5).

13.2. THE IMPACT OF THREE 'NEW' PARTY FAMILIES WITHIN PARLIAMENTARY REPRESENTATION IN EUROPEAN COUNTRIES

Green politics and *New Left politics* have became significant issues, in the Western democratic context, starting with the decade following the 'post-materialist revolution' and, even more evidently, after 1990, when the decline of international communism helped the replacement of many *revolutionary movements* with alternative-ecologist parties (Bell 1993; Müller-Rommel 2002). In the same period, several ethno-regionalist parties gained representation in national parliaments for the first time, or increased it significantly. Politicians who can be classified as representatives of these parties are today active in many European legislatures. Since 1989, both a Green/European Free Alliance group and a European Alternative Left group have been created in the European Parliament of Strasbourg, representing, respectively, the fourth and the fifth largest trans-European formations, after the Popular/Conservative group, the Party of the European Socialists and the Liberal democratic federation.

Nonetheless, if new left, green politics, and ethno-regionalism have become typical key concepts indicating new challenges to the traditional European party systems (Mair 1993; Ware 1996), to say that *green, new left*, and *ethno-regionalist* parliamentary representatives could be conceived today as three strong and coherent realities in the current European parliamentary elites is far from being a shared conclusion. A rough illustration of this impression is given by recent comparative assessments (Lane and Ersson 1995; Gallagher et al. 2001), representing the evolution of the overall electoral force of the most important party families in Europe. According to most of the observers, the *post-materialistic challenge* (Dalton 1996) to the European party systems has produced just one interesting (but feeble) result: the emergence of a 'green' party family able to pervade a number of European party systems yet without crossing a low threshold of about 5 per cent of the voters. According to Ferdinand Müller-Rommel (2002), behind the overall figure we should be able to read at least two different situations: the first where we find a *strong green performer*, which has created the conditions for high and stable electoral results and parliamentary strength (Germany and Belgium, at least up to 2003 elections) and the second, that of a *weak green performer,* where electoral results are modest and parliamentary representation is absent or very small.

Ethno-regionalist parties have consolidated their presence in European political systems during the seventies, but clearly their presence is limited to areas where some kind of ethnic distinctiveness, however defined, exists. Although present in most countries, sometimes as parties, sometimes within less clearly defined organizations, ethno-regionalist representatives have gained access to national parliaments in five countries, Belgium, Finland, Italy, Spain, and the UK.

Concerning the *new left* parties, Lane and Ersson (1995) do not even recognize the 'identity' of such a family, and assign the parties we consider (following Gallagher et al. 2001) under this label to their primary 'spiritual' families, namely the socialist and communist families—in case of 'class' or 'marxist-oriented' libertarian parties—or even the liberal family—in case of radical or 'civil rights-oriented' protest parties (see Kitschelt 1988 for these definitions). In any case, we are talking about a family of parties which would be present in a very limited number of democratic legislatures, reaching less than 2 per cent of the average votes in Europe (Gallagher et al. 2001: 230).[4]

In this chapter, we are not going to contribute to the debate about the very nature of the new European party families. What we want to do, in line with the research design of the present volume, is to understand what real challenges have been brought to the historical patterns of parliamentary recruitment and career and, if this is the case, what explanations (in terms of new party models or, on the contrary, in terms of country specific factors) can be provided. In this perspective, we will keep the original categories provided by the coding instructions of the *Cube-Eurelite project,* even if, in the context of the analysis of the different variables, we will refer to the green and the ethno-regionalist parties in terms of European *party families,* while we will produce mainly *country-specific* explanatory discussions when talking about new left parties.

We can start discussing the reasons leading us to propose a specific analysis of parliamentary elites shaped within the three party families. The first possible objection concerns, of course, the relative size of these minor parties. Our answer to this question is rather simple: green, ethno-regionalist, and new left/libertarian elites (even if the latter are less present and recognizable) reflect minor but *consolidated* electoral areas. The extent of voters oriented towards these parties has grown, during the last two decades, in a large number of European democracies. This assertion is easy to be verified if one looks at the relative success of some green parties in the last two decades.[5] The electoral performance of ethno-regionalist parties has followed in many (but not all) cases a cyclical pattern,[6] which is reflected in the overall European average, reaching its peaks in the 1970s and the 1990s. As for the new left parties, we can still consider this group of political forces as a significant one only if we take the broadest definition of such a party family, including not only the libertarian radicals and socialists already active during the Cold War, but also the heirs of the former communist parties (both from the western and the central-eastern side of Europe) transformed in left-socialist forces not aligned with the *Party of the European Socialists*. For the reason we will explain later, in this chapter, we will consider some post-communist parties under this label.

With these clarifications in mind, we can assert that new politics issues started having a parliamentary representation of some relevance during the 1970s, and experienced more significant developments in the following 25 years. That is to say, new left representation is, to a large extent, the effect of the students and workers mobilizations. It was developed in the age of the oil shocks and after the first echoes of the 'planetary' contaminations. Thus, the political impact to be connected to these new (and small) parliamentary forces has to be measured mainly in terms of the degrees of innovation they were able to produce vis-à-vis the organizational and political continuity of the elites from other formations, particularly, the traditional families of the Communists, the Socialists, and the Liberals.

The second element marking the peculiarity of these party families is their attitude to represent 'minority vocations'. Since the very beginning of their institutional history, all the parties included in these families were conceived as the creation of (small) sectors of political and/or intellectual elites who wanted to stress a specific set of demands (from civil rights, to environment protection, to the recognition of a minority language group) without a real or realistic capability to penetrate the largest part of the public opinion. These demands, in fact, have been usually considered 'incompatible' or at least 'isolated' from the traditional cleavage structure developed during the twentieth century and still perceived as the most important 'predictor' of party alignments. In other words, the historical transformations and the recent crises both of 'middle-class' and of 'working-class' parties could not change a rather largely shared view, according to which *new politics parties* keep being perceived as 'different' from the traditional ones, but are still less appealing than these.

13.3. HOW TO DEAL WITH DATA ON NEW PARTIES: THE SMALL 'N' PROBLEM AND THE SIGNIFICANCE OF 'CHALLENGERS' MPs

Scholars involved in electoral analyses can avoid to impose severe cut-off points, in order to select the parties to be analysed, when they seem to be anyway relevant in the functioning of a given party system (Sartori 1976); actually, the small size of some parties can sometimes be the crucial variable in the selection of specific case studies (Müller-Rommel and Pridham 1991). Even those who want to study governmental behaviour are often attracted by the role of *small pivotal* parties. On the other hand, when we have to study legislative elites, the minute dimension of some parliamentary groups can produce a number of problems in terms of data reliability and comparability.

As one can see, the dilemma we face in this chapter is as much intellectually stimulating as empirically frustrating. In order to propose a realistic research design, we have decided to state a first cognitive problem which constitutes the puzzle of this chapter: does the belonging to an ideological or spiritual party family of the 'new politics', give rise to the same strong distinctiveness that we have noted in most of the European party experiences of the twentieth century (Cotta and Best 2000; Borchert 2003)? This general problem entails an immediate question about the existence of a real divide between the old parties elites' configurations and the 'new world'. In terms of political homogeneity, the question is particularly important if we look at the family of the *new left*. What is new left politics? How many parties and which ones can be definitively considered in this category? As mentioned above, these questions still need to be answered by the experts of party politics, who deeply disagree on the existence of an autonomous 'spiritual family' like this.

In the context of a comparative analysis of the 'party by party' dimension of the long-term variations of twentieth century's parliamentary elites, a very important task would be to provide a comprehensive account about the impact of the *new politics* on the parliamentary elite configuration over the last twenty-five years. Operatively, it means that we should try to achieve the following goals:

1. We should produce a systematic overview about the presence of ethno-regionalist, new left, and green parliamentary elites in Europe over the last historical period. This would already be an original contribution, since most of the researches on new party families have preferred other levels of analysis, namely party organization, relationships with social groups, or the question of the 'reliability of new parties in coalition governance and electoral strategies' (Müller-Rommel 2002). Moreover, studies on European ethno-regionalism have often focused, starting from the 1970s, on the risks of violent conflicts among groups and the best ways to avoid them, or, more recently, on the growing powers regions are acquiring in many European countries. Specific studies on ethno-regionalist parliamentary representatives are, as a matter of fact, lacking at all.
2. We should individuate, within and outside the group of countries included in our data-set, some hints revealing the impact of these new groups of representatives in the recent transformation of parliamentary elites.
3. We should then extract the most relevant cases in point, to be discussed in depth. Namely, those examples of 'new politics' parliamentary representation

which would indicate a possible turning point or even an evidence of the discontinuity between the old and the new politics at the level of parliamentary elites.

In order to reach these goals, we will consider the period 1975–2003 which, following a party lifespan approach (Pedersen 1982), can be viewed on the whole as the *adolescence* of a number of our parties. Here the diachronic approach, otherwise dominating the Eurelite research project, is therefore to be substituted by a synchronic one. At the same time, the descriptive-quantitative analysis is only useful to extract relevant cases to be discussed in a more interpretative perspective by means of a qualitative in-depth analysis. Considering such an investigative framework, we propose to avoid, at this stage, sophisticated statistical and logical tools. Instead of this, we will try to understand what the data say, using the simplest descriptive indicator we have: the average values of the variables included in the DATACUBE. More exactly, we will try to find which are the series of average values, marking the most remarkable distances/similarities between the party families covered here and the general trends.

A final remark to be raised here concerns the different meanings we can attribute (and in fact we do attribute) to the impact of the different party families at the level of parliamentary elite transformations. As we will explain better in the conclusive section, in this approach, we argue that parties belonging to the same ideological stream should show similar features in their elite's socio-political profile and clear differences when compared to the profile of other 'competitor' parties. On the contrary, when the lines of distinction appeared only at the initial moment of the parliamentary representation of a given party, and when they are not followed by a coherent cross-country consolidation of this peculiarity, we cannot speak of a real family of parliamentary representatives, and we will be forced to discuss eventually interesting data at the disaggregated 'national party level'.

13.4. WORKING HYPOTHESES AND DATA EXPLORATION

Because of what we have illustrated above, this chapter will not provide full explanations of evident patterns of party elite transformations within the European parliaments. We will rather try to provide some tentative interpretations concerning the evolution of new left, green, and ethno-regionalist parliamentary elites at the turn of the twenty-first century. The basic rationale for the chapter can therefore be simplified in a single, ambitious but still underdeveloped, question: do the new (minoritarian) elites linked to 'alternative' party families who appeared at the heart of European political landscape only after 1975, present significant signs of diversity vis-à-vis the traditional elites?

To answer this question, we have at first to come back to the definition of party family itself: looking at the empirical data, can we really speak of three

autonomous families of parliamentary representation? After having possibly measured some degree of distinctiveness in the profile of these elite groups, can we
look for one (or more) pattern of parliamentary recruitment in order to interpret
these signs of change?

The small dimension of the elite groups representing these new political actors
and the short time span suggest avoiding, at the moment, more ambitious explanatory theories. It is better to think in terms of 'working hypotheses' which can
be used to guide a wide set of empirical explorations. In this perspective, the
main issue related to the transformation of the new 'families' of parliamentary
elites is the degree of dissimilarity from the consolidated patterns of traditional
parliamentary parties. Here, we should discover, at first, if the characters of the
slices of parliamentary elite included in these party families can be presented as
the profile of 'outstanding minorities', resulting from the partial process of de-
freezing of European party systems, or as the examples of possible alternative
patterns of elite transformation, potentially pursued by other 'post-materialist'
parties, from the liberal galaxy to the new socialist one.

Starting from a 'rokkanian assumption' implying the consolidation of party
systems and the long-term continuity of the interests represented, we can develop
here a first working proposition which sounds as follows:

Proposition 1: party system changes occurring after the seventies are basically the consequence of a challenge to the 'old system of elite convergence' and, to a large extent, mark
the end of the standardization which had characterized the pre-existing party elites.

In other words, in the old politics, party elites used to conflict among themselves
over policy preferences and cultural values, but they had become increasingly
characterized by rather similar processes of recruitment and political career
(Pedersen 1976; Cotta 1979). Conversely, 'new politics' elites are the fruit
of a new demand of 'diversity' and they express, therefore, such a diversity
through their own processes of recruitment and circulation. It must be clear
that this general argument about the attempt to reach a new 'equilibrium' in
the configuration of the representative elite does not necessarily mean that
big changes should actually occur in the elite configuration. Given the limited
dimension of the new party families, we will probably find just small hints of
change.

A rather frequent argument in the scientific debate about the persistence of class
voting and the weakness of 'single issue orientations' stresses the 'too limited'
appeal of green (and libertarian) political discourse (Dobson 2001). According to
this view, the more the elites expressed from the new parties will try to embody
specific and innovative characters (low degree of political professionalism, orientation to represent new and/or disregarded social groups) the less they will
find a large 'consensus' from the traditional blocs of voters. Interestingly enough,
some analyses of the Western European political elites in the age of the crisis
of the party rule (von Beyme 1993; Mastropaolo 1993) also stress the possible

'convergence' of both right and left (protest or anti-establishment) parties towards a figure of 'non-political politician'. Following this line of reasoning, we can then argue that:

Proposition 1a: the consolidation of green, new left, and ethno-regionalist parties has brought remarkable signs of change within parliamentary elites. But these signs are essentially 'negative' (what new elites try to mark is the difference from the old ones). At the end of the day, the distinguishing elements in these elites are some striking but isolated features (rapid circulation and mortality, close links with ONGs and associations, strong female representation, high level of education, and typically in the social sciences) with no real establishment of a common 'strong pattern' of political recruitment and socialization.

On the contrary, one can follow the argument of the 'libertarian' attitude of most of the green and new left movements (Kitschelt 1988), and some of the ethno-regionalist ones, emphasizing the 'alternative' message without taking into account the rise of a possible alternative ruling class. With this reasoning, we would probably reach the conclusion that:

Proposition 2: the emergence of 'new politics' party families has to be conceived on the whole as a challenge to the classical 'rationalism' of the organization of political recruitment and political elites, that characterized all the 'mass party' experiences. Therefore, the empirical findings we have to search for are indicators of 'chaos' more than indicators of a specific elite configuration. Finding this kind of evidence would, in other words, confirm that new politics parties (or some of them) do not have any interest in consolidating specific models of political representation.

In this vision, the main argument is that green, new leftist, and ethno-regionalist elites do not represent a clearly defined *direction* of change (although they bring evident signs of a *chaotic* change) simply because they aim at challenging the relationship between elites and public, rather than modifying the 'genetic structure' itself of the elites.

Of course, we will have to contemplate the possibility that the three supposed party families could have different impacts and, therefore, the test of the two working propositions could bring different results when speaking of green, new left, and ethno-regionalist MPs. We must not forget that, while in many European democracies the first family has already gained access to the core institutions,[7] the second and especially the third one are composed by very assorted forces, many of which are still at the borders of the European political systems. It is therefore conceivable that, for the parties included in the two latter families, the *lifespan effect* could be rather different in comparison with the green parties.

On the basis of these considerations, we will present, in the following pages, the descriptive data about the profiles of the three party families' MPs in some European parliaments between 1975 and 2003.[8] The three series of data will be analysed separately and compared with the average figures for all MPs in the same parliaments, during the same time span. We will start with the green family, to continue with the other two party families in the next paragraphs.

13.4.1. *First Exploration: The Profile of Green Representatives (1980–2003)*

The DATACUBE data-set currently available includes twenty-two cases coded under the category of *Greens*, coming from five countries: Germany, Austria, Finland, Italy, and France. The size of these groups of elected representatives is never larger than fifty-five MPs (the size of the German *Grünen Fraktion* in the Bundestag of 2002). In terms of seat percentages, the size of the green group is normally smaller than 10 per cent. In addition to these data, we can also analyse some figures referring to the MEPs belonging to the green group between 1989 and 1999.

The social and political profiles of green MPs are significantly deviant when compared with other groups of parliamentarians. Generally speaking, the comparison with the whole body of representatives (considering only the countries where green MPs are present) gives good reasons to those who define the environmentalist parliamentarians (in a somehow derogatory sense) *middle-class radicals*. They are in fact well educated and clearly attached to particular social or intellectual elite groups. Their typical feature, that of representing the public sector more than the private occupational groups (Dalton 1996) is confirmed by our data: in Germany, Italy, and France the percentage of green representatives with such an occupational origin is greater than 50 per cent. But even in Finland and Austria this figure is higher than in the whole parliament. Furthermore, this public sector orientation looks quite different from what we have observed in several European mass parties during the second half of the twentieth century: in fact, among public sector MPs of the green family we often find academics (very often with a hard science background), teachers, and top-administrative officers in a higher proportion than in other parliamentary groups.

Coming to the degree of pre-electoral political socialization, the picture is not very different from what we have seen looking at the old twentieth-century 'class parties'. But we can argue that two peculiar factors concur to determine this relatively high level of political professionalization. First of all, we are dealing with small parties scattered over the whole national territory and organized on a national basis. It is extremely probable, therefore, that being the few positions potentially available in parliament naturally 'reserved' for the national party leadership, the competition for parliamentary recruitment could be in these parties virtually non-existing.[9]

A second peculiarity in the political socialization of this group of representatives resides in its 'discontinuity'. Differently from the career path of many parliamentarians elected for the traditional mass parties (especially socialists and communists), the representatives from the green groups show a significant degree of 'mobility': in fact they are very often recruited directly from the galaxy of social movements, and sometimes they have been experienced in other political formations. Unfortunately, we do not have systematic comparative data on this point, but a quick look at the profiles of green parliamentarians belonging to the new born *European Greens* party confirms the impression that, generally speaking, their career pattern is rather different from that of other left parties (Dalton 1996: ch. 5).[10]

Some DATACUBE variables enable us to define where exactly green politicians are different. Studies produced in the past stressed in particular the specific intellectual and technical competences of this elite group, due to the relevant role played by the *environmental associationism* in the recruitment of green politicians and, above all, to the fast circulation of MPs (Kitschelt and Hellemans 1990). Data about green MPs individuate at least three interesting elements marking the peculiar profile of this party family: the predominance of scientific/environmental expertise, the orientation towards equal social/gender representation, and the limited weight of seniority in structuring their political careers.

The first character can easily be confirmed, if one looks at Figures 13.1 and 13.2. Environmentalist representatives tend to be, on average, more erudite than their colleagues. Even in a highly *non-professionalized* legislature as the European Parliament, where many seats are left to personalities coming from the scientific community and the *civil society,* the Greens maintain a small advantage in this particular ranking. According to our expectations, the greater extent of the academic background is to be totally ascribed to specific scientific competences (Figure 13.2): in fact, environmentalist parties bring in the parliament a significant degree of expertise in the technical and natural science fields.

The second point to be stressed concerns the orientation of this new party family to overcome the traditional gender inequality in political representation (Chapter 4 in this volume). Data about women representation in the European parliaments are unquestionable (Figure 13.3): in all the assemblies, the presence of female green MPs is much higher, in some cases twice as high, than the overall figures. The phenomenon is even more striking in a diachronic perspective. The most recently elected parliaments are, in fact, characterized by a stabilization of female representation rates, while the growth of women among green parliamentarians is still underway in Germany (52.2% in 2002), Italy (37.5% in 2001), and Finland (78.6% in 2003).

The third point we were mentioning above, the low level of seniority, draws our attention immediately to a question debated since the beginning of the green parliamentary experience, when a systematic rotation of representatives was put into practice by the German *fundamentalists*, and the 'refusal' of the notion itself of a political career used to be a typical catch-word of the protest movements.

If we look at our data about MPs circulation, we can see that during the nineties green parties have gradually brought their parliamentary turnover rate to a more 'normal' measure. It is true that on average (Figure 13.4) their renewal rate is still higher than in other parties, but differences are less remarkable and in any

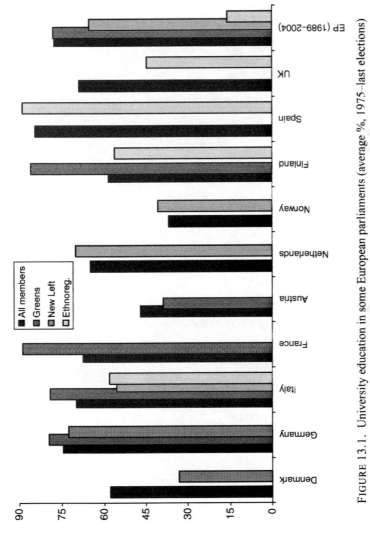

FIGURE 13.1. University education in some European parliaments (average %, 1975–last elections)

Note: Values weighted by number of MPs of each group in each legislature.

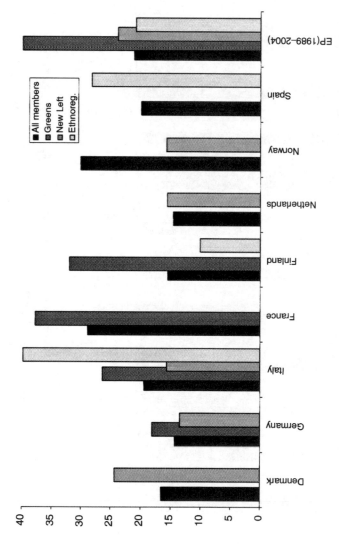

FIGURE 13.2. Technical/scientific type of university degree among European MPs (average % of MPs with a university degree, 1975–last elections)

Note: Values weighted by number of MPs of each group in each legislature.

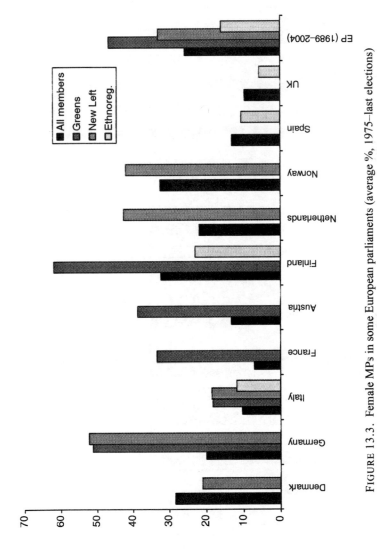

FIGURE 13.3. Female MPs in some European parliaments (average %, 1975–last elections)

Note: Values weighted by number of MPs of each group in each legislature.

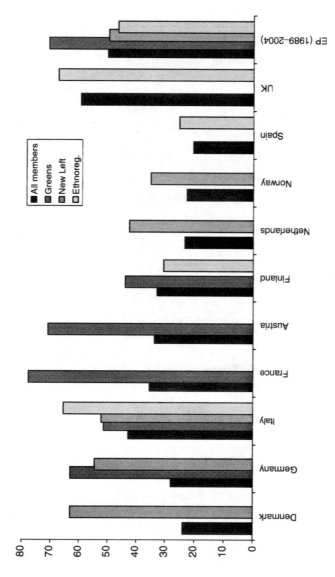

FIGURE 13.4. Newcomers in some European parliaments (average %, 1975–last elections)

Note: Values weighted by number of MPs of each group in each legislature.

case increasingly lower.[11] We can therefore assume that the transition to a 'small but established' governmental party (Müller-Rommel 2002) implied, among other things, the consolidation of a more lasting parliamentary elite. This does not mean that green parties cannot still be characterized today by a rather different model of parliamentary recruitment. In fact, the mean age of newcomer MPs is still significantly lower than in other political groups: green representatives at their first election are at least 2 years younger than their colleagues, as all the country cases (but the figure for the French Greens is not really reliable, as it includes only nine MPs) as well as the EP data shown in Figure 13.5 confirm.

But the most evident examples of the difference between the profile of green MPs and the other parliamentarians concerns the occupational background, namely the specific category 'teachers and professors' and the aggregate category 'public sector background'. The first is one of the most frequent features in the whole population of MPs, whose range oscillates between 10 per cent and 25 per cent. However, among green MPs the rate is at least 10 per cent higher in each national group, and the increase is also visible in the European Parliament where the overall figure is 23 per cent and the green rate is 33 per cent. As far as the public sector background is concerned, the distances are much less evident, but the inclination of Green parties to increase the representation of civil servants is confirmed in all the cases analyzed here (Figure 13.6 and 13.7).

13.4.2. *Second Exploration: The Profile of New Left Representatives*

If we move now to the New Left party family the existing data we can exploit, using the DATACUBE file and some data on MEPs, cannot help us much: overall, only thirty-nine cases of our CUBE data-set have been coded as 'new left' groupings of elected MPs. These groups come from five countries (Denmark, Germany, Italy, Netherlands, and Norway) and, notwithstanding the fact that they are all placed after the end of the Second World War, their historical and ideological context is rather different from one case to the other. In Norway and the Netherlands, we have traditional alternative left parties crossing the whole period after the war.[12] In Italy, the new left appears with the crisis of the 1970s (which also determined an increase of the new left representation in the two countries mentioned above) and originates different parties, respectively characterized by a 'liberal radical' and by a 'marxist libertarian' origin. In Germany, we have coded as 'new left' the former Communist Party of the DDR, after its readaptation to the competitive system. In Italy again, at the end of the twentieth century, we find *Rifondazione Comunista* (Communist Refoundation), a new openly communist formation which was born from the fusion of the former 'Stalinist' faction of the PCI with some extreme groups of the new left. Finally, the Danish *Faelles Kurs* (Ordinary way), a recent radical-populist movement, which has been able to maintain a handful of seats since its first appearance in 1987, but changing its ideological and strategic orientation in the party spectrum.

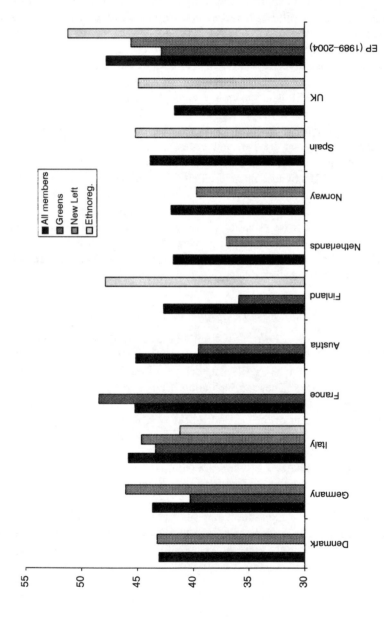

FIGURE 13.5. Mean age of newcomers in some European parliaments (average %, 1975–last elections)

Note: Values weighted by number of MPs of each group in each legislature.

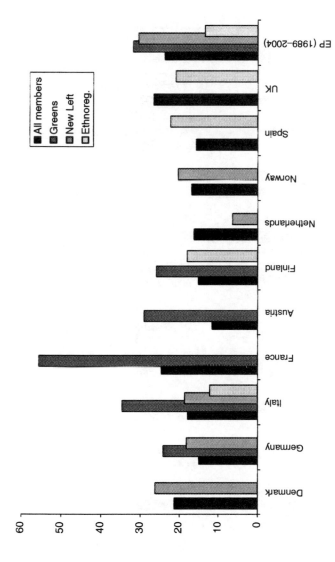

FIGURE 13.6. Teachers and professors in some European parliaments (average %, 1975–last elections)

Note: Values weighted by number of MPs of each group in each legislature.

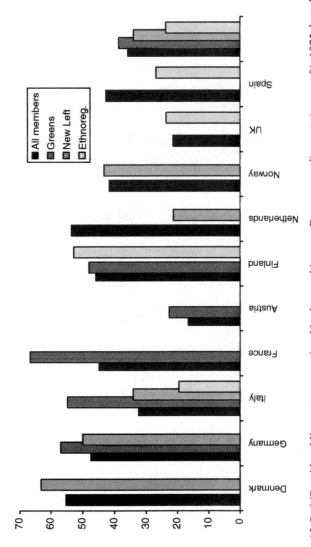

FIGURE 13.7. MPs with public sector occupational background in some European parliaments (average %, 1975–last elections)

Note: Values weighted by number of MPs of each group in each legislature.

According to what has been said before, we have added to these figures the representation of the *post-communist* and *other left* groups in the European Parliament, after the fall of international communism: following the 1994 elections, the *European Unity Left* included MEPs from five EU countries: the Danish SF (Left Socialists), the French PCF, the Spanish *Izquierda Unida,* the Italian *Rifondazione Comunista,* and the Portuguese PCP. This new formation could therefore be considered still a 'traditional' communist elite, being formed for the most part by representatives of the three communist parties (the French one, the Portuguese, and the Greek) which had refused in 1989 to follow the Italian PDS in its slow approach to the socialist supranational party. Nonetheless, under the label of *Unity left,* the three *irreducible* communist parties could live under the same roof with a less 'orthodox' Communist Party (the Spanish one) and, after the 1995 accession, with the red-green representatives from the Finnish Left Alliance and the Swedish *Vansterpartiet.*[13] The process of transformation of this group, from a pure communist nature is even more evident after the 1999 elections: now, the EUL-NGL group is formed by MEPs coming from ten EU member states, which are planning to open the road to a more formalized *European federation* where marxist, libertarian, and left-environmentalist values could live together.[14] In addition to the parties already mentioned, the Dutch Left socialists, and some representatives of minor alternative left parties from Greece and France (particularly, *Lutte Ouvrière* and the trotzkists) are also part of this group, which reached a noticeable performance at the 1999 European elections.

Speaking from a parliamentary point of view, this family thus represents a significant area in Europe, but it's easy to note that *statistically speaking,* the average number of individual MPs falling in each DATACUBE entry is very small, obviously determining a problem of data reliability. Using the same technique adopted for the other family analysed above, we can still build a synchronic analysis based on the parliamentary mandates covered during the interval 1975–2003. For what concerns the European Parliament, we will take into consideration only the fully *post communist* group of the last two legislatures (1994 and 1999).

Looking at the general distribution of average values, the first impression is that in this family national party delegations are much less similar to each other, being more affected by country-specific determinants. Variability among countries (or better, among different party organizations) is always noticeable. However, some variables where a common trend is visible can be identified.

For instance, differently from the Greens, New Left MPs show a generally lower level of university education, although the difference with the overall population of MPs is not so remarkable (Figure 13.1). The salience of a law degree as the main field of education is lower than in the overall parliamentary population (and this is a feature shared with the Greens), but in this case such a decrease is equally balanced by humanities and natural sciences backgrounds. Significantly enough, all the New Left parliamentary groups considered in these data display a small salience of local elective backgrounds (Figure 13.8), but, on the contrary, political professionalism is well rooted among their representatives, as Figures 13.9 and 13.10, about party offices and percentage of party and trade union officials, tell.

This last information seems particularly interesting when drawing a tentative portrait of New Left representatives. They belong to very different party organizations, having a very different ideological legacy. But, differently from other liberal or environmental radicals, they seem strongly subordinated to such organizations under the profile of parliamentary recruitment. Party organization and party career still seem to matter, in this case, determining the structure of opportunity for a parliamentary election: the low percentage of party offices in the German PDS delegation (Figure 13.9) is probably to be explained by the fact that only offices from the new party (and not from the communist organization in the previous regime) have been coded. Looking at the following figure, the percentage of full paid politicians, we can see how MPs from PDS and from *Rifondazione Comunista* show a high degree of political professionalism. But, also the Norwegian Left socialists and the Dutch pacifists seem to indicate an interesting process of 're-professionalization' of these party elites, which should be explained by the ideological legacy of traditional Marxist organizations.

As a consequence, parliamentary selection seems to be much more connected with a (relatively) long period of party socialization: the mean age of newcomers indicator shows in fact very different values in comparison with the green family (Figure 13.5). In some particular cases where the new parliamentary elite is, in fact, the transposition of some old party elites from the communist era (take the case of the German PDS) this evidence is obvious. But even the other parties represented in this family show a mean age of parliamentary selection which is very close to the average, and very similar to the figures for conservative or right-wing parties. More controversial inferences can be drawn when one looks at the percentage of newcomers (Figure 13.4): in all the groups analysed here, the difference with the overall rate of turnover is larger than 10 per cent. In this case, however, we should be able to distinguish if such a phenomenon has to be connected with the volatility of a given parliamentary elite (it can be the case of a not really consolidated party like the Danish *Faelles Kurs*) or, on the contrary, the decisive factor is the external party organization, which in some cases prefers (and is able) to impose a frequent renewal of the parliamentary delegation. This is a typical feature of the marxist party model, which still seems to be present in organizations like the German PDS or the new Italian Communist parties (*Rifondazione Comunista* and *Partito dei Comunisti Italiani*).

In general, social and occupational backgrounds of these groups of MPs are not very different from the traditional configuration of Socialist parliamentary fractions. The representation of the public sector is normally higher than the average but not so deviant, with the exception of the Dutch case (Figure 13.7). On the other hand, New Left party groups tend to stress some particular features of their modernity: for instance, they show a considerable number of personalities

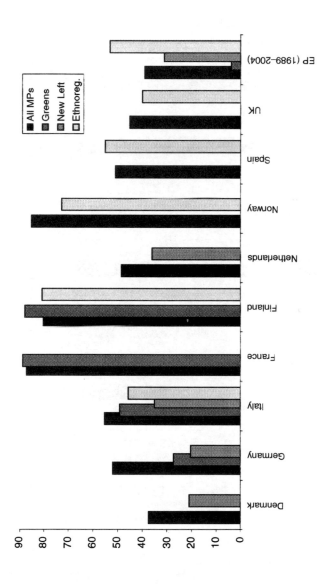

FIGURE 13.8. MPs with local elective background in some European parliaments (average %, 1975–last elections)

Note: Values weighted by number of MPs of each group in each legislature.

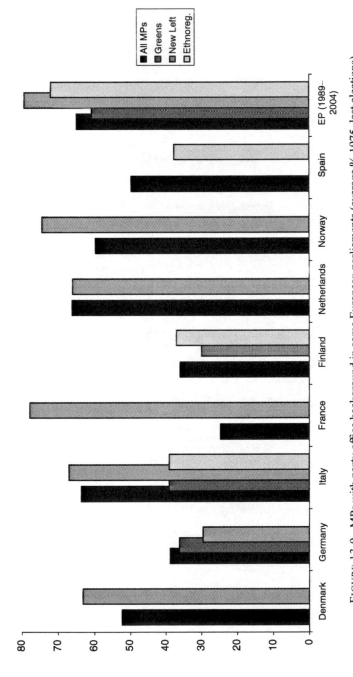

FIGURE 13.9. MPs with party office background in some European parliaments (average %, 1975–last elections)

Note: Values weighted by number of MPs of each group in each legislature.

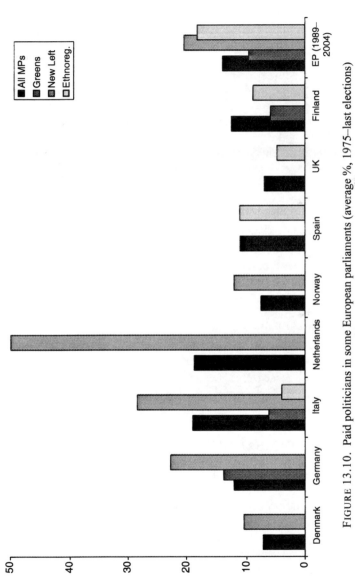

FIGURE 13.10. Paid politicians in some European parliaments (average %, 1975–last elections)

Note: Values weighted by number of MPs of each group in each legislature.

recruited from the media and from the intellectual milieu, as well as a remarkable number of women, even if this figure remains smaller than in the green subgroup.[15]

13.4.3. *Third Exploration: The Profile of Ethno-Regionalist Representatives*

As already stated, ethno-regionalist, parties do not have an easy access to national parliaments. Their political vocation is, by definition, 'minoritarian' and local. Furthermore, electoral formulas and the geographical cutting of electoral constituencies can have a strong impact on the capacity of these parties to gain representation, and have been historically used to either allow or to hamper their access to legislative bodies.

For the present research, data from four countries are available (Finland, Italy, Spain, and The UK), to which we can add the European Parliament. In two cases, Finland and Italy, data refer to one single party, the *Svenska Folkpartiet* and the *Lega Nord* respectively, while in the other two countries and in the EP, data cover several parties. In the Spanish case in 2000 (the last electoral year covered), eight parties sent their representative(s) to Madrid. Among them, the two biggest parties (the Catalan *Convergencia i Unió* with fifteen MPs, and the Basque *Partido Nacionalista Vasco* with seven MPs) represent two-thirds of the whole ethno-regionalist representation, the remaining six parties adding up to eleven MPs.[16] British figures cover the *Scottish National Party* and the Welsh *Plaid Cymru*, as well as Northern Ireland parties, both unionist and nationalist.[17] The numerical impact of these parties in their parliaments is rather limited in UK (2.5 to 4.3%) and Finland (from the 6.5% of 1987 the *Svenska Folkpartiet* has decreased to 4.5% in the legislature of 2003), while more important in Spain (normally around 8%) and Italy. In this last case, it is worth recalling the exceptional weight of the *Lega Nord* in the 1994–6 legislature. Having obtained a very favourable distribution of candidates in pre-electoral negotiations within the centre–right coalition (Di Virgilio 1995), the *Lega Nord* was, at the beginning of that legislature, the most numerous parliamentary group (117 MPs, 18.6% of seats) with just 8.4 per cent of votes. As far as the European Parliament is concerned, we will take into account members of the European Free Alliance, where many ethno-regionalist MEPs sit.

We have argued in the initial pages of this chapter that ethno-regionalist parties could represent a challenge to the establishment playing, at least in some cases, a role functionally similar to that of new politics parties, even though in possibly different directions. Our aim is now to see if this argument is valid, and to what extent, for parliamentary representatives of this party family. One of the distinctive features of both green and new left parties, as we have seen, is a relatively high circulation of representatives. For ethno-regionalist parties this is true only in the case of the *Lega Nord* (65.5% of newcomers, 23% more than the national average in the same period), while values are closer to the average in Spain and the

UK, and slightly lower in Finland and in the EP (Figure 13.4). The same pattern applies to the age of MPs, another distinctive character of green parties. Here we find again that *Lega Nord* newcomers are on average four years younger than their Italian colleagues, but in Spain, the UK and especially Finland, this value is reversed: ethno-regionalist newcomers are generally older than the average. Even the other typical feature of new politics parties (the strong female representation) is not present within the ethno-regionalist family (Figure 13.3): the *Lega Nord* is close to the national average (11.9% of women, the mean being 10.4%), while in the other three countries (and in the EP) figures are below it (up to 10% less in the Finnish case). How should we interpret these data? Shall we simply abandon our hypothesis that ethno-regionalist parties share some features with the other two party families included in this analysis? There are, in our opinion, two ways of better articulating the hypothesis in order to keep it congruent to data. The first one is to be careful in distinguishing the ethno-regionalist party family in general terms from the parliamentary representatives of these parties. As we have seen, parliamentary representation of this group of parties is heavily constrained by their small size and territorial concentration. This introduces some unavoidable biases: MPs profiles never perfectly reflect party elite profiles, but in our case the distortion is even more evident, since only some of the parties gain representation at national level. The second point, often underlined by observers of this party family (see for instance Urwin 1983; De Winter 1998), is that it includes diverse cases, sharing the common features of territorial concentration and representation of (what is claimed to be) a minority group, but interpreting this representation in substantially different directions. If we look at the parties included in our data, we find indeed a new populist party (the *Lega Nord*) together with a moderate liberal party with a 100 year history (the *Svenska Folkpartiet*, founded in 1906); eight parties in Spain, ranging from the post-materialist left-oriented *Bloque Nacionalista Galego* and *Partido Andalucista*, to the CD *Partido Nacionalista Vasco*; seven parties in UK, from moderate to extremist unionists and nationalists of Northern Ireland to the Scottish and the Welsh party.

In this view, the three figures previously shown look more readable. The profile of the *Lega Nord*, in spite of its opposite ideological orientation, is closer to that of other 'challengers' in terms of elite circulation, seniority, and even female representation. The other parties are older and more contiguous to the political establishment,[18] and this contributes to explaining the more 'traditional' profile of their MPs.

The anti-political establishment character of ethno-regionalist parties emerges again from the occupational background of their representatives. Full-time politicians (Figure 13.10) are under-represented in three countries, being the Spanish figure equivalent to the national average, while they are slightly over-represented in the EP. The *Lega Nord* shows, again, the most outstanding figure with only 4 per cent of full-time politicians, about one-fifth of the national average. The other side of the coin is given by a relatively strong presence of representatives chosen from civil society. Not among intellectuals, as it happens with journalists and writers in the green parties, but rather coming from the world of private enterprises. Managers and businessmen are over-represented, particularly in the British and the Finnish cases (Figure 13.11).

Finally, the territorial aspect of representation obviously gains a particular relevance when considering this party family. Data about local and regional political background are to some extent surprising. One could expect a generalized pattern of political careers beginning in local elective bodies, before reaching the few seats ethno-regionalist parties can wish for at national level. This only seems to be the case in Spain, where the percentage of MPs with a local or regional political background is ten points above the national average. In Finland the two values are equal, while in Italy and the UK we find a reversed situation, ethno-regionalist representatives having less local or regional political experience than their national colleagues (Figure 13.8). A possible interpretation of these data is that local and regional political experiences indicate different aspects from one case to the other: the importance of territoriality emerges in some cases, while in others this variable seems to be a proxy for political seniority and party careers. A different view on links between parties and territory is the place of birth of MPs (Figure 13.12). In this case, the territorial vocation of the ethno-regionalist party family emerges clearly in all parliaments where they are present. Between 80 to 95 per cent of ethno-regional MPs are elected in the same region where they were born, while the average value is about 70 per cent in Italy and the UK, and much lower in the other countries.

13.5. TOWARDS A TENTATIVE INTERPRETATION

To achieve a comprehensive interpretation, in the light of the working hypotheses illustrated above, we would probably have to wait for a few more years: the redefinition of a new and post-communist party family is currently taking place, while a more definitive configuration of the green representatives will be only possible when the threshold of the *maturity age* will be overcome by these parties. As far as ethno-regionalist parties are concerned, both the different parliamentary size and the diverse role played within the party systems seem to have a strong impact on the elite profile of the few examples included in this family. Nonetheless, we can at least provide a first comparative report based on the distribution of some DATACUBE variables (main social and political backgrounds of MPs) during the period 1975–2003. Such an elaboration is useful to come back to the synchronic perspective we have proposed at the beginning of the chapter, and to test the general hypothesis considering these three party elites as potential alternatives to 'traditional' MPs. What is particularly interesting, in this perspective, is the deviation between the profile of the three groups of MPs analysed here and the overall profile of European representatives.

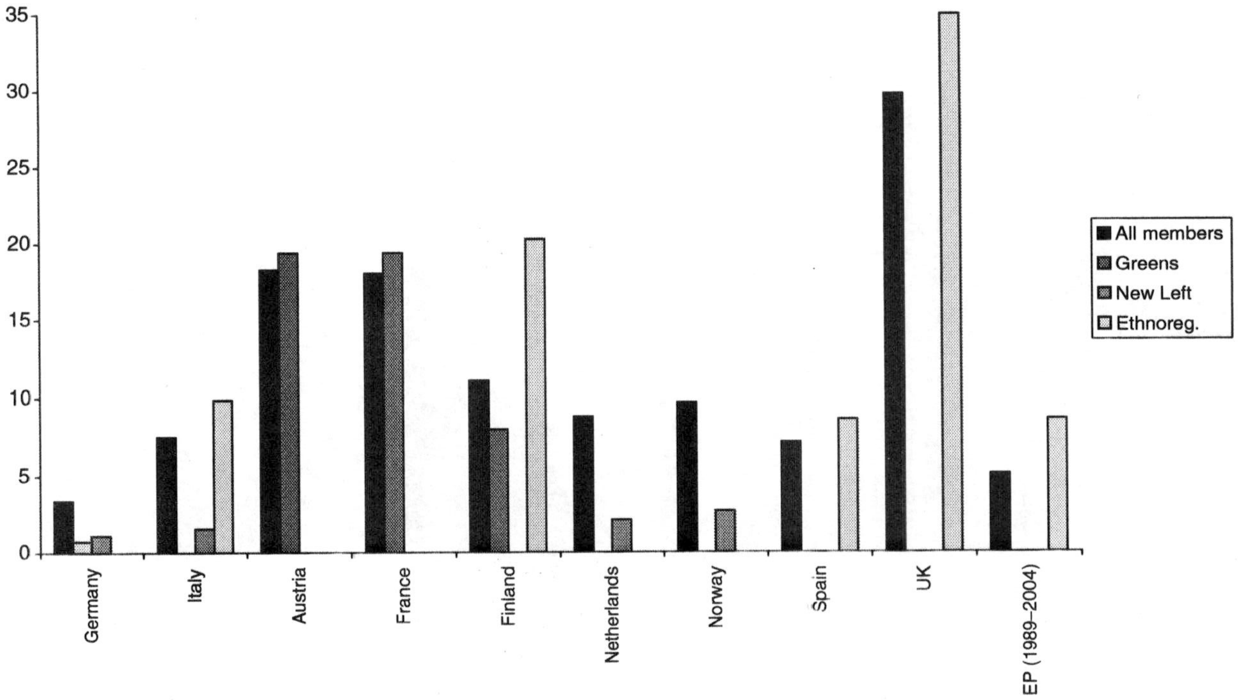
35
30
25
20
15
10
5
0
Germany
Italy
Austria
France
Finland
Netherlands
Norway
Spain
UK
EP (1989–2004)
All members
Greens
New Left
Ethnoreg.

FIGURE 13.11. Businessmen/Managers in some European parliaments (average %, 1975–last elections)

Note: Values weighted by number of MPs of each group in each legislature.

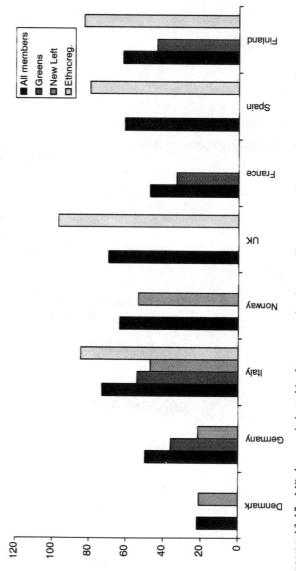

FIGURE 13.12. MPs born and elected in the same region in some European parliaments (average %, 1975–last elections)

Note: Values weighted by number of MPs of each group in each legislature.

In more details, we will now try to extract some evidence emerging from a basic comparison of means, in order to develop a first interpretative model contrasting the profiles of the three families. We will use deviations of the weighted means (concerning some selected social and political variables) of the three party families from the overall means in twelve European parliaments. In this way, we will produce a virtual comparison between the three party families studied here and the general profile of European representatives, in order to detect the degree to which our three groups 'deviate' from the general picture (Figure 13.13).

The picture which emerges from these data is the following: green MPs are characterized by features which can be connected with 'post-modern' demands: a (relatively) high percentage of women among MPs, many non-legal professionals, many teachers and intellectuals, but low percentages of traditional characters of modern parliamentary elites such as 'lawyers in politics', full party and pressure groups officials and former blue-collar workers. Conversely, new left groups mix some of these characters (women, professionals) with more traditional features (full-time politicians, party background). Coherently with our expectations, green MPs are largely recruited within the public sector (in this respect they are very alike the socialists) while new left MPs are equally divided among 'public sector occupations', private occupations and purely political backgrounds, and the ethno-regionalists show a clear predominance of a private sector background (namely lawyers and businessmen).

Finally, the average age of access in parliament of these groups of representatives is different: the Greens show the youngest age (at least three years less than the average of the socialists group), while new left and regionalist MPs do not deviate too much from the overall trend. This evidence can also be read as a trace of the different pattern of political socialization of the typical 'new politics' formations of the green (and partly also of the alternative left) camp.

Of course, the above arguments have to be considered *cum grano salis*. If specific characters like female representation and university background are confirmed in all the national subgroups of Greens, the same cannot be said about the indicators of political professionalization. The comparison between the two most durable green parliamentary groups (the Italian and the German one) shows this point: if the first is characterized by a low rate of full-time politicians, the latter displays a significant percentage of professional politicians and a low percentage of lawyers (the strongest occupational background among Italian green MPs).

This is not surprising if one keeps in mind the original difference between fundamentalist and middle-class factions of the green movement (Müller-Rommel 1989; O'Neill 1997: 17). The small size of groups among new left MPs does not allow the same control by country. But this is another good reason why it is important to carefully consider all kinds of generalizations at this level of analysis.

Our final exercise summarizes the evidence that we have illustrated so far by way of some synthetic indexes. In Figure 13.14 we compare the three party

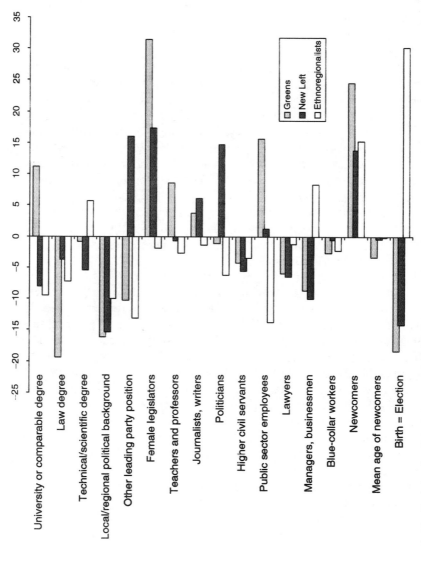

FIGURE 13.13. Social and political background of MPs: Deviations of three party families from overall means in twelve European parliaments (average %, 1975–last elections)

Note: Values weighted by number of MPs of each group in each legislature.

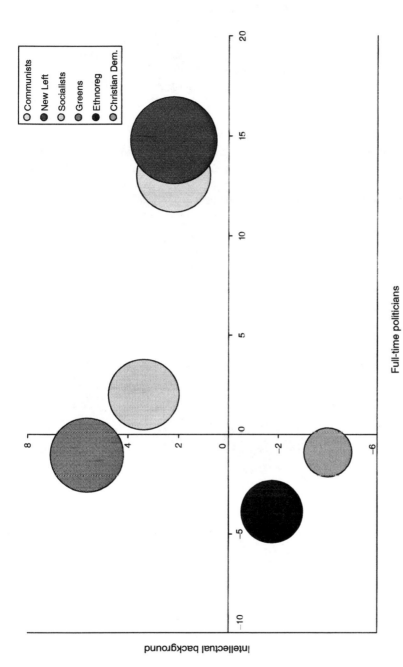

Full-time politicians

FIGURE 13.14. Intellectual and political background of Greens, New Left, and Ethno-regionalist MPs, compared to main party families: Deviations from overall means in twelve European parliaments (average %, 1975–last elections)

families on the basis of (*a*) the average presence of intellectuals among their parliamentary representatives, and (*b*) the average presence of full-time politicians.
The first index is given by the sum of journalists and writers, and teachers and
professors; the second one summarizes the percentages of full-time politicians
and of MPs having covered leading party positions. As in Figure 13.13, the values
are expressed in deviations from the overall mean of European MPs, that is ideally
located at the intersection of the origin of the axes. The diameter of the circle is
proportional to the standard deviation internal to each party family, giving a rough
idea of how heterogeneous they are.

The figure suggests three deeply diverging profiles. As expected, green parties
show a high percentage of intellectual MPs, combined with a low number of full-
time politicians. Ethno-regionalists share this last feature with the Greens, but
intellectual workers are in this case below the overall mean. The New Left family
shows the strongest presence of full-time politicians, and is located somewhere
half way (but well above the mean) in terms of intellectual representatives.

In Figure 13.15 we consider two more aspects. On one dimension we have the
public or private sector background of parliamentary representatives, obtained

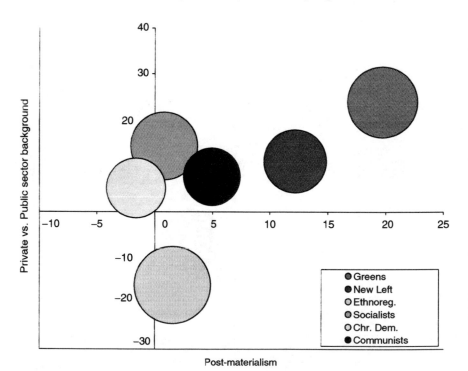

FIGURE 13.15. Public/Private sector background and post-materialist profile of Greens,
New Left, and Ethno-regionalist MPs, compared to main party families. Deviations from
overall means in twelve European parliaments (average %, 1975–last elections)

by subtracting the percentage of managers and businessmen from that of public sector employees. On the other one we have an index of post-materialism of MPs which is built by combining information on female representation, newcomers, and mean age of newcomers, following the assumption that a high number of women and a larger circulation of elites are typical features of new politics organizations.

This time differences emerges more clearly between ethno-regionalists and the other two party families. Green parties show the highest positive deviations from the overall mean on both dimensions, confirming on one side their public sector profile, and on the other, their commitment to a balanced gender representation and their challenge to the 'iron law of oligarchy', that claims long career patterns and slow elite circulation. Also New Left parties show positive figures, both on the post-materialist profile and the prevalence of representatives with a public sector background, even though their score is lower than that of the Greens on both dimensions. On the contrary, the profile of ethno-regionalists MPs is more oriented towards the world of private enterprises and lacks, on average, the characteristics of post-materialist representation.

13.6. FINAL REMARKS

In this chapter, we have tried to develop some general hypotheses about the recent emergence and the following transformation/consolidation of parliamentary elites representing the most recent party families of the European scenario. The basic rationale of the chapter resides in the idea of investigating the effects of the 'original features' of these parties on their parliamentary troops, and the possible adaptation/acquiescence of these elites to the existing parliamentary context (this last hypothesis seems to apply particularly to the green family).

In Section 13.1 we have introduced two arguments: the first of them is summarized by the idea of a persistent challenge to the old parliamentary elite, the second one is reflected by the picture of a number of 'disorderly signs of change'. A change which cannot be ascribed to the emergence of fully alternative models of recruitment and elite circulation, since they can be better explained by a general decline/crisis of some traditional characters *across* different party families. At this stage, we cannot say very much about the 'solidity' of the above arguments. We can nonetheless at least say that the first one can be considered a promising exploratory proposal for further analyses. Looking, particularly, at the green parliamentary elite, we can say that indeed *some kind of challenge has emerged* in this period. A challenge related with the peculiar social and political background of MPs, which has been probably modified during the years, with the passage from an anti-party to a more pragmatic profile (O'Neill 1997).

On the other hand, we can argue that there are some interesting disorderly signs of change, particularly in the area of the new libertarian-left and in some groups of MPs representing ethno-regional parties. These groups are very different from each other, and somehow differ within themselves: features which derive from some cultural heritage (for instance the high degree of political professionalization of MPs from post-communist parties) are balanced by other aspects typically rooted in new libertarian and left-populist parties.

ENDNOTES

1 We want to thank all the friends and colleagues from the *Eurelite Network* who have provided information and references about the political parties covered in the chapter. In particular, we are grateful to Michael Edinger, Mogens Pedersen, and the two editors of this volume. Though the chapter is the fruit of a collective work, Filippo Tronconi is particularly responsible for paragraphs 3 and 4 while Luca Verzichelli for 1, 2, and 5.

2 The same mechanism of linkage failure, though operating in a definitely different direction, can be observed in the 1980s, the years of the so-called 'silent counter-revolution' (Ignazi 1992). Extreme-right parties which appeared in those years are dealt with in another chapter of this book. It is interesting anyway to notice that at least two parties belonging to the ethno-regionalist family—namely the *Lega Nord* and the *Vlaams Blok*—could be included for some aspects in the list of extreme-right parties appearing along with the silent counter-revolution, and share with them a number of features.

3 See some implications discussed by Pogunkte (2002) concluding a research on the experience of Green parties in some European national governments.

4 More exactly, Gallagher et al. (2001) consider, in this family, the Danish SF (which has been coded by the Eurelite country experts under the socialist family), some Icelandic, Swiss, and Irish parties (not analysed here because their countries are not included at the moment in our archive), the Dutch Green-left party and the Norwegian Left socialists.

5 The green parties were recently able to get 9.4% in Austria, 8% in Finland, 5.6% in Belgium (adding the performances of the two ecologist parties), between 5% and 7% in Netherlands (where two elections have been held in 2002 and 2003) and 4.5% in France. Among the 'weak' parties we have to mention the Irish greens (3.8%), the Danish greens (2.4%), and the Italian greens (2.2% of votes reached in 2001 with a list including also a small Social Democratic Party).

6 The Scottish National Party is probably the best example of this cyclical success: from 0.5% in 1966 (that meant 5% of Scottish votes) it rose to 2.9% in 1974 (30.4% in Scotland), then slipped back to 1.1% in 1983 (11.8% in Scotland), and rose again to 2% in 1997 (21.9% in Scotland).

7 Particularly relevant, under this point of view, is the access to the national government, which occurred in Belgium, Finland, Germany, France, and Italy. On this point, see Müller Rommel (2002: 6 ff.) and, more recently, the special issue of the *European Journal of Political Research* (Rihoux and Rüdig 2006).

8 We have used for the following analysis the most recent version of the DATACUBE archive (May 2004) and an archive, currently in progress, about the MEPs elected between 1979 and 1999.

9 However, if we focus on the biggest green group in Europe (the German *Grüne*), several figures suggest that in such a case, given a relatively small national party leadership, many 'non-professionalized politicians' have had the chance to be elected. In fact, the average percentages of German green MPs with a local elective background (27.3), or a party background (36.1) and of full time paid politicians (13.9) are significantly smaller than those recorded for the other party families.

10 Examples of such type of career come from some Italian party leaders (Scalia, Mattioli, and Francescato).

11 The percentage of newcomers among the Bundestag German greens, for example, declines from the 70% of the 1980s to 23.4% in 1998, but rises again somewhat (43.6%) in 2002 (thanks perhaps also to an increase in this year of the seats from forty-seven to fifty-five).

12 The Socialist Left party in Norway (SV) was the heir of the left radicalism already present in the post-war period, but it has been consolidated particularly in 1973, when it led the anti-ECC

protest. A similar origin, which is very much based on intellectuals contributions and links with youth movements, has the pacifist-socialist (PSP) party in the Netherlands, active since the 1960s. The other Dutch party considered in this family is the Radical-left party (PPR), founded in the 1970s.

13 In fact, the adhesion of these parties was followed by the decision (1996) to change the name of the EP group from the simple *European Unity Left* to *European Unity Left—Nordic Green Left.*

14 During the month of January 2004, in Berlin, a meeting of European left parties was held, putting the bases for a common platform before the 2004 elections. During a following meeting in Rome (8 May 2004) the appeal for a party of European Left (EL) indicated the need to make communist, libertarian and environmentalist values live together. A coordination body of the new party federation has been elected, whose president is the leader of the Italian neo-communist party, Fausto Bertinotti. The parties included in this group are the Italian *Rifondazione Comunista*, the French Pcf, the German Pds, the Spanish *Izquierda Unida*, the Austrian Communist party, the Slovak Communists, the *Party of the Democratic Socialism* (Czech Republic), *the* Bohemian *Communist party*, the Greek *Synaspismos*, the *Left party* from Luxemburg, and the *Workers party* from Estonia.

15 The only new left party showing a clear increase of female representation is the German PDS. The other groups are quite close to their national average values.

16 In the 2004 elections (not covered here), these figures have changed significantly. *Convergencia i Unió* has slipped to ten seats, while the left-wing *Esquerra Republicana de Catalunya* has become the second regionalist party of Spain rising from one to eight MPs, thus getting one seat more than the *Partido Nacionalista Vasco*.

17 In this case Northern Ireland parties are prevalent, with fourteen seats of twenty-three after 2001 elections. The Scottish National Party and *Plaid Cymru* have five and four seats, respectively. Among Northern Ireland parties, it must be reminded that *Sinn Fein* elected representatives do not actually take the seats they win, refusing to swear the oath of allegiance. Thus, after 2001 elections, unionists have eleven seats, while nationalists are only represented by the three Social Democratic and Labour Party MPs.

18 The *Svenska Folkpartiet* has participated in most of the governmental coalitions since 1945 and, as a unique case in the European scenario, it has led the Finnish executive for a short period in 1954. In the British and Spanish cases, as we have already noticed, moderate centre–right parties are predominant in terms of parliamentary seats.

Part III

Comprehensive Analyses

14

Cleavage Representation in European Parliamentary History

Heinrich Best

14.1. THE CLEAVAGE CONCEPT AND ELITE THEORY

More than thirty years ago Stein Rokkan set the agenda for the discipline of comparative politics by assigning to it a double task: *the accumulation and evaluation of information* about past and present systems of government and the construction and testing of parsimonious models for the *explanation of variations* in the development, structuring, and performance of such systems (1967; 1999: 95). Today, after one generation of unremitting research efforts following these lines, Rokkan's agenda seems to be as topical as it was in the late 1960s, and political research is still called up to account for the changing patterns of cross-national variations without recourse to teleological self-explanations. Apparently, the 'parsimonious models' requested and envisaged by Rokkan are still in the making, or requiring improvement and revision. This agenda can be extended without restriction to the concept of political cleavages which was a cornerstone of Rokkan's theory of the structuring of competitive mass politics and still is a pivotal element of contemporary political sociology (Lipset 1960; Rae and Taylor 1970; Zuckerman 1975; Inglehart 1979; Knutsen and Scarbrough 1995; Kriesi 1998; Manza and Brooks 1999; Evans 1999; Bartolini 2000a, 2000b).

Empirically and theoretically, the concepts of political cleavages and political representation share a wide stretch of common ground in that they both deal with the problem of to what extent and in which ways social disparities and deprivations are translated into political divisions. Both concepts can be distinguished by the systemic levels of polities and societies on which they are focusing: while the concept of political cleavages emphasizes the enduring attachment of voters to parties resulting from voters' social positions, the concept of political representation examines the symbolic and instrumental links between latent social groups and political elites (Hetherington 2001; Mansbrige 2003). However, both concepts and the related phenomena are mutually connected: To some extent political elites are a 'product' of political cleavages, in that politicians owe their positions to having presented themselves successfully as advocates for the grievances and interests of certain segments of the electorate (Miller 1999; Wessels 1999). On the other hand, political cleavages are to some extent a 'product' of political elites, in that politicians translate social disparities and deprivations into political demands and build up the organizational strength to make them heard in processes of political decision-making (Bartolini and Mair 1990). Neither political elites nor political cleavages are 'givens' of polities but 'products' of highly contingent interactions of individual and collective actors. It seems to be exactly this double contingency in the interactions between political elites and electorates that makes it so difficult to develop 'parsimonious models' accounting for the cross-nation variation in cleavage mobilization and cleavage structures (Lipset and Rokkan 1967; Rokkan 1970a, 1970b).

The present chapter attempts to contribute to this effort by exploring the theoretical and empirical linkages between political cleavages and parliamentary representation. It starts from observations made in past studies of legislative recruitment, showing that until 1933 German parliamentary parties and conflict groups differed markedly in the social and political backgrounds of their representatives and that these differences in recruitment patterns could be systematically related to the make-up of their electoral support markets, to their policy orientations, and to systemic policy outcomes (Best 1990, 1997).

As a first step into the direction of parsimony, we propose a model of cleavage development which focuses on five contexts and categories of investigation (Best 1982; Graph 14.1):

1. the *cleavage-structure*, as an enduring pattern of political conflict, which is anchored in the social-structure and has found its expression in the party system;
2. social and political backgrounds of legislative elites *(elite-structure)*, in which socialization experiences, recruitment and career patterns, incumbency, turnover and the interlockingness with other segments of the elite-system manifest themselves on the individual level;
3. *legislative behaviour* as an expression of issue-orientations, group-connections, and strategic coalition formation of legislative elites;
4. *systemic policy outcomes*, by which we refer to central decisions at state level in which, besides legislative elites, other segments of the elite-system too are involved and which, in particular, concern the regulation of the access to power and the range of exercising of power; and
5. the *organization of political order* in which systemic policy outcomes are codified and operative in the long term.

Between these foci of investigation, the following connections are postulated:

1. an influence of the cleavage-structure on the recruitment of legislative elites in such a manner that caucuses and parties tend to select and support candidates whose social and political backgrounds have a specific symbolic or instrumental bearing on groups they are targeting in the electorate; further, a direct influence of the properties of the electorate on the behaviour of the actors in the legislative process in such a manner that the perceived interests and expectations of the voters effects the decisions of the elected through the anticipation of voting-behaviour;

2. an influence of legislators' social background characteristics and career patterns on their legislative behaviour through acquired values and issue-orientations; these can be mediated via socialization and/or relations of interest;

3. an effect of legislative behaviour on systemic policy outcomes in such a manner that the capability of parliamentary leadership-groups to form coalitions and to arrive at (internal) compromises influences their chance to acquire and expand positions of power in competition with other segments of the elite-system;

4. a repercussion of systemic policy outcomes on legislative behaviour, in particular by establishing the constitutional prerogatives and responsibilities of parliaments; further an effect of systemic policy outcomes on legislative recruitment, in part directly by suffrage and eligibility rules, in part indirectly by allowances and financial compensations for legislators; and finally an effect of systemic policy outcomes on the cleavage-structure, for example, via the granting or denial of possibilities of political articulation and participation for oppositional milieus, or ethnic, religious and other minority-groups.

In this model, two criss-crossing dimensions of investigation are being connected: on the one hand, we can distinguish categories of investigation that characterize the socio-political context for the action and the recruitment of legislative elites (cleavage-structure, systemic policy outcomes) from those that focus on elites at individual level (elite-characteristics, legislative behaviour). On the other hand, the categories of investigation can be classified according to whether they belong primarily to the polity (legislative behaviour, systemic policy outcomes) or whether they are primarily related to the social system (cleavage-structure, elite-characteristics). Therewith this approach can be characterized simultaneously as multilevelled, in the sense of a connection between contextual and individual levels, and as transcending areas, in the sense of an interlocking of social and political analysis.

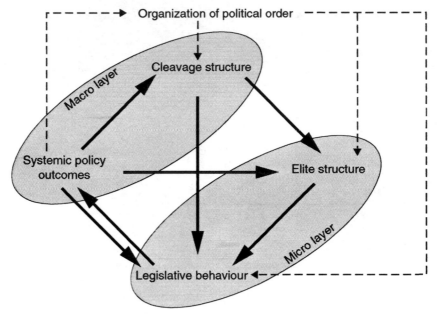

GRAPH 14.1. A non-recursive model connecting political cleavages and legislative elites
Source: Best (1982/1990).

It is obvious that we have here no *explanatory model* informing us of the causes for the emergence of variations between cleavage-structures over space and time, but rather a descriptive grid specifying the plexus of factors interacting in the process of cleavage development and policymaking. To infuse explanatory power into the model, it is necessary to (re)define its connections as causal relationships that link social structure via the social background of legislative elites to the stability and performance of political order (Birnbaum 1978; Best 1990).

A *locus classicus* for such an approach is Otto Hintze's famous article on *Das monarchische Prinzip und die konstitutionelle Verfassung* (1911), where he outlined why parliament in Imperial Germany had not succeeded in gaining the 'ruling influence in the state' as it did in contemporary Britain or France, and as had been hoped by leading German liberals after the foundation of the German Empire. The main reason he gave was that German parliamentary elites were 'completely lacking in the necessary inner unity and solidarity which would, under all conditions, be the prerequisite for a role in political power'. He attributed these divisions to their lack of social homogeneity and their acting as 'agents of special interests of singular social classes, occupational groups, branches of the economy, regions and religious denominations'. He concluded that 'with us parties are, properly speaking, not political but rather socio-economic or religious-confessional formations. This is connected with the fact that it is actually the life of the bourgeois society—as opposed to the actual political operation—which finds expression in our representative bodies. That is, however, a formation of the party system which leads more to a monarchical leadership of the state than to parliamentary influence' (Hintze 1911: 337–8; author's transl.). Although Hintze restricted his argument to Imperial Germany at the turn of the century, we have here a more general theoretical model which links social structure at large, the party system, the social make-up of parliamentary elites, and their ability to establish parliamentary democracy. Elements of this model can be found in modern political theories and explanatory schemes such as the Lipset–Rokkanian cleavage concept (Lipset and Rokkan 1967), Lorwin's concept of 'segmented pluralism' (1971), or Lijphart's Consociational Democracy model (Lijphart 1968*a*,1968*b*, 1977). More recently, Field and Higley (1985) proposed a taxonomy linking states of elite structure with the stability or instability of representative institutions. Both, elite structure and regime stability are connected in a unidirectional and deterministic relationship: 'As a causal variable an elite state always predates the stability or instability of political institutions' (1985: 30). The ability of elites to develop and to maintain a culture of peaceful competitiveness is the prerequisite for a stable representative democracy, whereby high structural integration and value consensus of elites are the bases of their consensual unity, and their consensual unity is the prerequisite of performance and stability of representative democracy. Field and Higley's taxonomy became a widely accepted point of departure and an explanatory tool in elite studies. Research on the processes of democratic consolidation in Southern European and Latin American countries (Higley and Gunther 1992) and, recently, also in the post-communist polities of Central and Eastern Europe (Higley and Lengyel 2000) has drawn on their proposition.

14.2. RESEARCH CONCEPTS AND METHODS

In the following pages, I present and discuss some results of an exploratory investigation into the variations of political and social backgrounds of European legislators. The focus will be mainly on one linkage (although the pivotal one) of the model presented above: the connection between cleavage structure and elite structure. Some additional inferences will be made about the connection between elite structure and the stability of representative democracies (i.e. systemic policy outcomes). For the purpose of this study four large European polities were selected which represent different paths of political and socio-economic development in the nineteenth and twentieth centuries: France, the 'republican' model with an early introduction of universal male suffrage, a weak party system, and a relatively slow industrial development; Germany, the failed democracy of the 1930s, with an early introduction of universal male suffrage, a strong party system and a fast track industrialization; Great Britain, the polity with the steadiest set of political institutions, a gradual extension of suffrage during the nineteenth and twentieth centuries and the status of being the first industrial nation; Italy, another failed democracy with an experience of about twenty years of fascist dictatorship and a latecomer with regard to suffrage extension, industrialization and the development of party organizations (Best and Gaxie 2000; Best, Hausmann, and Schmitt 2000; Cotta, Mastropaolo, and Verzichelli 2000; Rush and Cromwell 2000).

The time span covered extends from the 1870s, that is from the completion of state building in Germany and Italy, until the end of the twentieth century. Within these time–space coordinates, we see an enormous variation of political developments and political systems, ranging from stable (Great Britain) and instable (France) democracy to temporary takeover of totalitarian (Germany) and authoritarian (Italy) regimes. Changes of elite structures will be traced by cross-sectional analyses of the social and political backgrounds of parliamentary parties at five points in time:

1. the 1870s, when there were wide differences between the four polities under investigation with regard to suffrage extension and party formation, whereby Germany and France had implemented full male suffrage (and eligibility) while the development of mass parties was most advanced in Britain and Germany;
2. the last elections before the First World War, when all four polities had introduced male suffrage and eligibility, while party systems in Italy and France had taken shape, now including socialists;
3. the interwar period that was (with the exception of Great Britain) characterized by a further extension of party systems—particularly by the emergence of communist and right wing extremist parties—, by the introduction of female suffrage in Great Britain and Germany and—most importantly—by the Fascist and Nazi takeover of power in Italy and Germany;
4. the post-Second World War period, which is represented by parliaments of the first half of the 1960s—a period of consolidation of polities and party systems at the peak of post-war prosperity and before the political shake ups of the late 1960s; and
5. the last parliaments before the turn of the twentieth century that saw, again with the exception of Great Britain, another extension of party systems by Green and New Left parties and, in the whole of Europe, an end to communism as an international threat.

The following analyses of legislative elite structures are based on contingency tables, breaking down social and political backgrounds of legislators according to party family. While the composition of party families follows standards proposed by Gallagher et al. (2001) and needs no additional clarification except for some early parliaments (such as the ones in Italy) the selection and definition of political and social background variables should be examined in greater depth. The idea was here to select variables that have some bearing on general, social, and political divisions and can therefore serve as 'tracers' connecting party families to political cleavages through the recruitment patterns of their political elites. This should, however, not be misunderstood in the sense of a one-to-one 'mirroring' of social divisions at the level of political elites—although this can sometimes happen, as in the case of religious and ethnic cleavages. In most circumstances, however, legislators and voters of a party family are recruited from different social quarters. A case in point are the traditional working-class parties whose supporters are—in the raw state—disqualified to serve as representatives and who have to go through a career in working-class organizations before becoming eligible (Bourdieu 1981, 2000). This example shows also, however, that, although the electorate and the elite of a given party family differ, elites will differ between party families as well. We assume that these differences between party families in elite recruitment had (and presumably still have) an impact on cleavage mobilization and elite consensus: on cleavage mobilization, because the reinforcement of divisions in the electorate improves career opportunities and career stability for those elites who have strong symbolic ties and instrumental attachments to the social quarters they target in their campaigns and whom they claim to represent; on elite consensus, because elite conflicts are an opportunity to 'dramatize' social divisions in the electorate, while a segmented elite will lack the structural prerequisites for consensus and cooperation.

The link between cleavage structure and elite structure is constituted by the concept of 'powers' involved in the process of political competition. I am drawing here from Pierre Bourdieu's theory of forms of capital that has recently been extended to the political sphere by the concept of the '*capital représentatif*' which signifies '*l'ensemble de resources (sociales, économiques, organisationelles ('capital parti'), intellectuelles, physionomiques . . .), convertibles et converties politiquement, qui caractérisent les représentants, et dont les valeurs respectives sont définies par le marché des positions représentatives, les transactions et les luttes qui s'y jouent*' (Godmer 2002, Vol. 1: 13).

The taxonomy in Table 14.1 is associates resources and (privileged) affiliations to polity and society, incumbents and challengers in the political arena according

TABLE 14.1. '*Powers' involved in the process of political competition*

	Polity		Society
Incumbents	State		Land
		Competence	
Challengers	Party		Capital

to their attribution at the turn from the nineteenth to the twentieth century. 'Competence', which is vaguely identifiable with Bourdieu's 'cultural capital', can be attributed to neither marginal category although it has presumably closer links to 'State' and 'Capital' through the expertise allocated here. By 'Land' I mean landed interests, that is large estates with an associated control over those cultivating them; by 'Party' I mean not only party organizations but also affiliated associations and trade unions (*Vorfeldorganisationen*); by 'Capital' I mean the whole sphere of business with an associated control over the employed labour force; by 'State' I mean the whole public service, including the educational system (Dunleavy 1980). I expect that different party families are associated with different 'powers' and that this association is reflected in the recruitment patterns of 'their' legislative elites. I also expect that by the representatives' affiliations to these 'powers' social divisions and political cleavages are manifested on the parliamentary stage.

To analyse these relations I have used Correspondence Analysis (CA), which is an exploratory statistical technique that displays the rows and columns of a rectangular data matrix as points in a scatter plot, often called a map (Greenacre 1993). Its primary value lies in the visualization of relations within aggregate categorical data although it provides a much more comprehensive set of statistics, as, for example, Principal Component Analysis, to which it is sometimes compared. An examination of CA's graphical displays should consider that it produces a vector space and that Euclidian distances between the column-points and row-points should not be interpreted. Two aspects of the maps are of particular significance for the analysis of cleavage representation and cleavage development at parliamentary level. These are namely the point-distances from the centroid or weighted average of the profile space which indicate the degree to which a profile point deviates from the mean and the direction of spread of profile points around the centroid which indicate the 'correspondences' existing in the data. Like in multidimensional scaling or factor analysis a substantive interpretation of the spacial distribution of profile-points may be given, starting with the principal axes providing the basis for a dimensional style of interpretation. The appropriateness of a map to reproduce a profile space is expressed by its percent share in the 'total inertia'. Percent values attributed to the axes indicate their weight in the reproduction of the profile space. Both measures are important aides in identifying and assessing the structuring factors involved in processes of cleavage representation. Normally, CA is used to analyse a data matrix which contains absolute frequencies but there are applications that suggest the use of relative frequencies as input data (Müller-Schneider 1997). For example, this kind of application is appropriate for the comparison of different studies or different subgroups with different numbers of cases. In this study, party families were introduced as column variables, while social and political background variables were included as rows. Relative frequencies were interpreted as group specific indicators of structures and their changes.[1] The scatter plots or maps used for

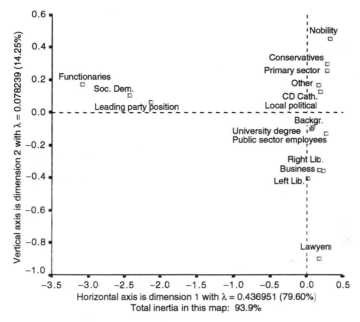

FIGURE 14.1. German parliamentarians, 1874

inter-temporal and international comparisons of cleavage structures based on CA are displayed in Figures 14.1 to 14.21.

14.3. ELITE STRUCTURE AND CLEAVAGE DEVELOPMENT: FRANCE IN COMPARATIVE PERSPECTIVE

To assess the potential of research concepts, data, and methods for comparative analyses of elite structures and structural change, the following presentation of results will start with a longitudinal examination of France (Best and Gaxie 2000). When we look at social and political background variables, the 1876 *Chambre*—the starting configuration of the Third Republic after the passing of its constitutional laws—was dominated by the opposition between 'Land' (represented by nobility and primary sector) and 'Competence' (represented by university degree and lawyers (see Figure 14.17)). A second (although much less significant) polarity is spread out by the polarity between 'State' (represented by public service employees) and 'Capital' (represented by managers and independent entrepreneurs). Political parties (which were in France at the time rather proto-parties and caucuses) are plausibly placed in this space of structural oppositions: On the main axis the Right (Conservatives) corresponds to 'Land', the Right Centre, the Centre Left and the unaffiliated to 'Competence'; on the second coordinate, the Left Centre corresponds to 'Capital' and the No

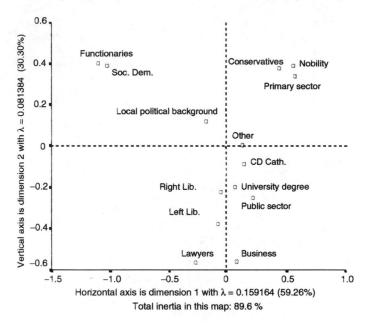

FIGURE 14.2. German parliamentarians, 1912

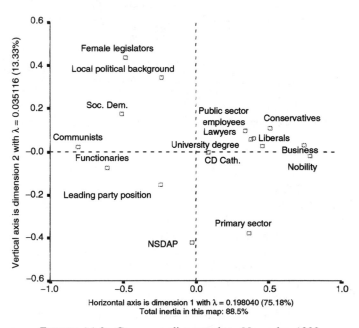

FIGURE 14.3. German parliamentarians, November 1932

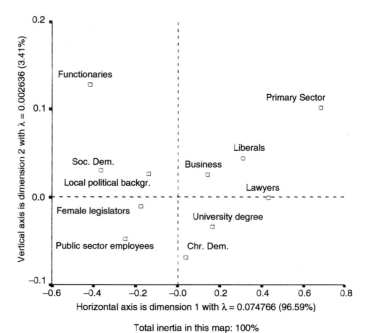

Total inertia in this map: 100%

FIGURE 14.4. German parliamentarians, 1965

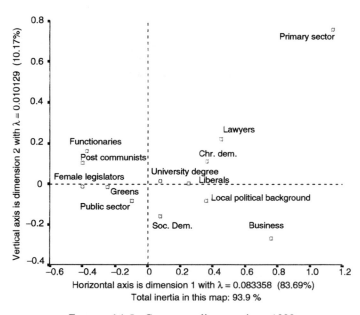

Total inertia in this map: 93.9 %

FIGURE 14.5. German parliamentarians, 1998

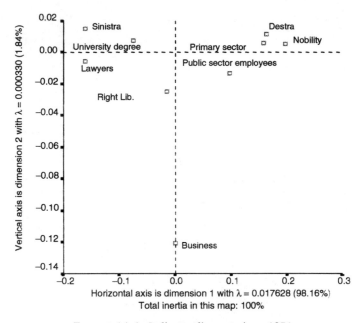

FIGURE 14.6. Italian parliamentarians, 1874

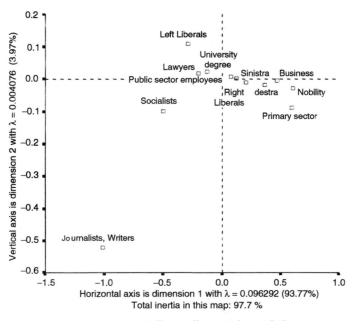

FIGURE 14.7. Italian parliamentarians, 1913

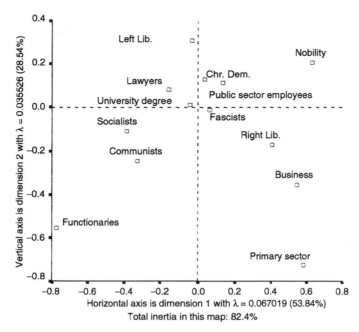

FIGURE 14.8. Italian parliamentarians, 1924

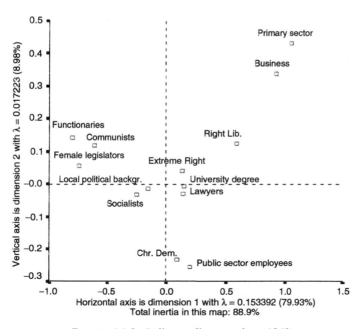

FIGURE 14.9. Italian parliamentarians, 1963

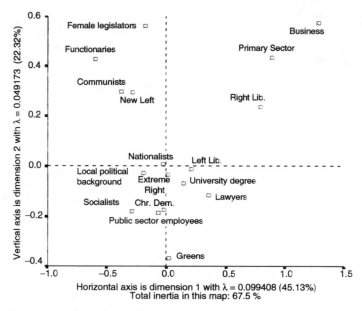

FIGURE 14.10. Italian parliamentarians, 1996: plot 1 (dim. 1 vs. dim. 2)

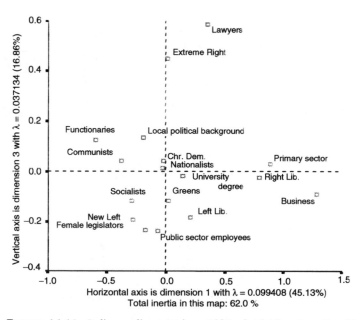

FIGURE 14.11. Italian parliamentarians, 1996: plot 2 (dim. 1 vs. dim. 3)

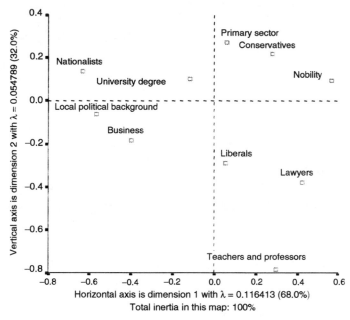

FIGURE 14.12. United Kingdom parliamentarians, 1874

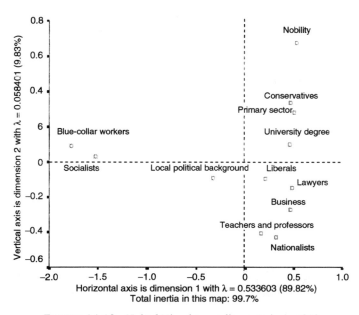

FIGURE 14.13. United Kingdom parliamentarians, 1910

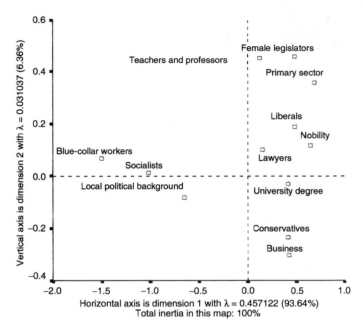

FIGURE 14.14. United Kingdom parliamentarians, 1935

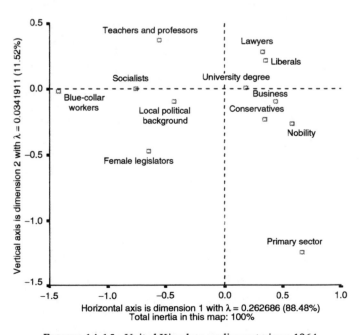

FIGURE 14.15. United Kingdom parliamentarians, 1964

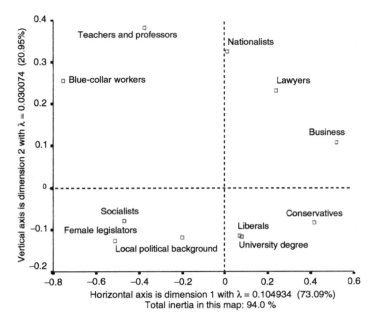

FIGURE 14.16. United Kingdom parliamentarians, 1997

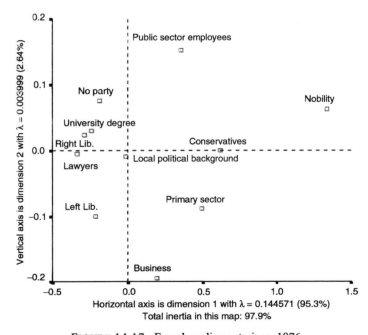

FIGURE 14.17. French parliamentarians, 1876

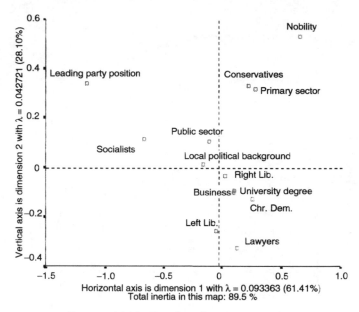

FIGURE 14.18. French parliamentarians, 1914

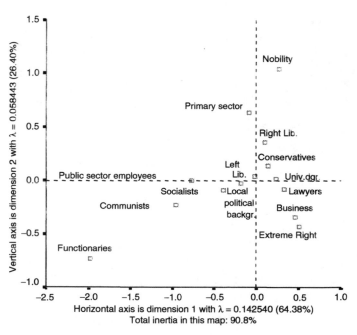

FIGURE 14.19. French parliamentarians, 1936

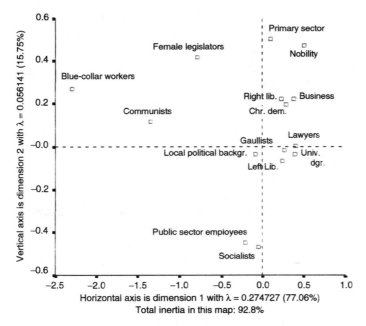

FIGURE 14.20. French parliamentarians, 1962

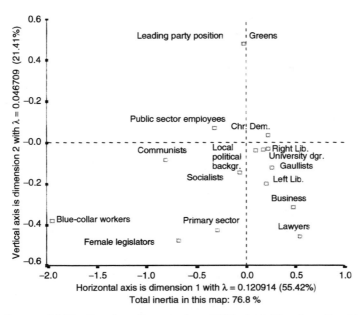

FIGURE 14.21. French parliamentarians, 1997: plot 1 (dim. 1 vs. dim. 2)

Party category to 'State'. Although it would be rash and inappropriate to claim that parties and powers were exclusively and indissolubly linked to each other, we have here an indication that the structural bases of elite competition are reflected in the patterns of elite composition.

Forty years later, in the Chamber of 1914, the polarities between 'Land' and 'Competence', Conservatives and Liberals were still present, although they were now superseded by the dominant opposition between Socialists and 'Party' on the one side, and the other parties and powers on the other (whereby 'State' is now placed close to the centre of the configuration, indicating that there were no exclusive correspondences with any party family) (see Figure 14.18). At this time 'Party' means working-class party and designates the new main challenger in the system of socio-political powers. However, it is interesting to see that the legislative representation of the socialist party family was placed relatively near the centre of the configuration, which means that it shared important structural features with other political groupings. This pattern distinguishes the French Third Republic at the outbreak of the First World War from other polities, such as Germany and Great Britain (see Figures 14.2 and 14.13). We see here the structural prerequisite for the emergence of the *République des camarades* that was portrayed so vividly by Robert de Jouvenel (1913): a structurally integrated elite that manages to overcome ideological divisions on the basis of multiple social links and common experiences. The early inclusion of socialist ministers in French cabinets will have been almost surely supported by this configuration.

In 1936, the halcyon days of the *République des camarades* were over, while France had to prepare for another European war. The basic configuration of Powers and Parties opposing each other looks quite similar to that of 1914, although with Communists and right-wing extremists two new challengers had entered the political arena (see Figure 14.19). Left Liberals and Socialists, Right Liberals and Conservatives (of whom very few were left) were now closely related and paired respectively, indicating that they had very similar recruitment patterns and prefiguring the parliamentary coalitions and oppositions to come. The public sector (now mainly incarnated by teachers and professors) had further migrated to the left. Deputies of the *Parti communiste* as a 'party of a new type' are most closely related to the pole of 'partyness'. The vertical axis of the map is the dividing line between the adversaries and the supporters of the *Front Populaire* with the wavering Left Liberals and Centre-right in the middle of the configuration.

In 1962, the configuration of powers and parties had dramatically changed. Left Liberals, Socialist, and Communists took up clearly distinct positions in the map, with Socialists corresponding to the state sector and Communists being connected to blue-collar workers (who were in fact in most cases *permanents*, i.e. party or trade union officials), while the Centre Left was placed at the same spot as the Gaullists close to the centre of the configuration (see Figure 14.20). In general, we see a centripetal process of structural rapprochement between the parties of the right (now including the Centre Left) and a reverse process of drifting apart among the parties of the left.

Thirty five years later, in the Assembly of 1997, this movement had reversed again, with Communists and Socialists becoming more similar in their legislative recruitment patterns (being particularly connected via their link to the public sector) while parties of the centre and the right are clustered in one quadrant also including 'privileged' social positions in the economy and the professions (see Figure 14.22). The sequence of party families on the main axis fairly well represents the order in which they are conventionally placed on the ideological left–right continuum. This configuration is no coincidence because it recurs in the other polities and periods under investigation, in that either the principal or the secondary axis can be interpreted as the left–right dimension. This is not a trivial result because neither ideology nor policy related indicators were included in the correspondence analyses. What we see here is a left–right differential in recruitment patterns. However, in many situations this differential does not suffice to depict the differentiation in elite structures. Particularly new and challenging parties have peculiarities in their recruitment patterns that distinguish them from established parties. In the given case, this applies to the Greens who are placed exactly at the pole of 'partyness' (two-thirds of them held high party offices against an average of 28% among all French MPs in the 1997 Assembly) thereby resuming the tradition of left parties establishing strong links between their parliamentary representation and national party organizations. However, in the French Assembly of 1997 even a two-dimensional solution is not sufficient to depict the differentiation of the political elite structure (applying the conventional 10% criterion of 'inertia' to be represented by one axis). A third dimension opposes the 'State' to the 'Economy' with the Left Liberals, the Greens and the Socialists being positioned in the 'State' sector of the configuration, and Communists, Gaullists, and Right Liberals being located in the 'Economy' sphere, which is again internally differentiated into labour and capital. What we see here is that after 130 years of eventful political history, changes of the constitution, political professionalization, mediatization, etc. societal 'powers' and political parties are still connected via elite recruitment and the structural bases of political conflict in the social and political backgrounds of legislative elites can still be recognized.

14.4. STRATEGIES AND DYNAMICS OF CLEAVAGE REPRESENTATIONS: A COMPREHENSIVE VIEW

The French case is a variation on a general European theme: The connection of societal 'powers' and party families via legislative recruitment creates a socio-political space in which societal hierarchies and disparities are manifested by political oppositions. In seventeen of nineteen configurations analysed in the present study this socio-political space takes the shape of a two-dimensional pattern (Stokes 1963; Budge 1994). All correspondence analyses have identified a single main line of conflict which can be interpreted with only one exception as an opposition between the 'right' and the 'left' (Laponce 1981; Fuchs and Klingemann 1990). The one exception is the 1874 plot for the UK where the main political opposition was formed by an antagonism between (Irish) Nationalists and Conservatives, and the main social opposition by the distinction between an implantation into the fabric of local politics versus an association to the networks of aristocratic families (see Figure 14.12). Here we have a hybrid structure where the main cleavage had an ethno-cultural basis with class distinctions being closely correlated to it, in that in Ireland ethno-cultural and economic hegemony was simultaneously exerted by the English upper class (Best et al. 2001). The two cases with three-dimensional solutions appear in the most recent cross-section of our analyses. During the 1990s in Italy and France the shake up of party systems with the emergence of New Left and Green parties broke up the pattern of bipolarity which had been 'frozen' during the cold war (see Figures 14.10, 14.11 and 14.21, 14.22). The antagonism between 'old' and 'new' parties corresponds here to a differentiation of the respective recruitment patterns. The German situation during the 1990s is different in that the two new parties which had emerged since the 1980s as successful challengers at national level—the Greens and the post-communist PDS—fit into the established left–right-sheme of legislative recruitment by clearly expressing the typical 'left' pattern of legislative recruitment through functionaries and public servants (see Figure 14.5).

In general—and this includes Italy and France—we see a tendency towards a reduction of complexity in cleavage structures: the main lines of political confrontation between party families tend to coincide with differences in their parliamentary recruitment patterns. The association between elite structure and cleavage structure is constituted by the links between political parties and political 'powers', that is the individual and aggregated resources available to collective and individual actors in the process of political competition. I explain this correspondence with a twofold mechanism of legislative recruitment and self-recruitment: on the one hand, parties want to be recognizable not only by the programmes they offer to their electorates, but also by the personnel they present to them. They gain credibility by matching their campaign pledges with their recruitment practices. On the other hand, applicants for office entering the political arena choose sides according to the political options and the career opportunities parties offer to them. The powerful interaction between these two mechanisms of selection and self-selection creates the clear patterns of Correspondence-Analysis results. Even in modern parliaments, where catch-all strategies of voter mobilization, political professionalization and careerization should have worn away differences between parties, we see distinctive patterns of legislative recruitment. The most recurrent one is the left–right distinction which is—without introducing any indicator for ideological or policy orientations—more or less neatly reproduced in all CA-maps presented here. We assume that selectorates

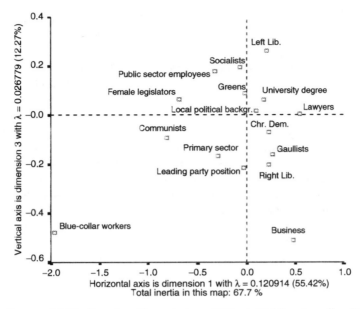

FIGURE 14.22. French parliamentarians, 1997: plot 2 (dim. 1 vs. dim. 3)

on the right and left of the party spectres are recruiting their MPs from different social quarters according to the availability of candidates (the input side) and (on the output side) to their instrumental or symbolic uses in the competition for power, particularly in addressing the electorate (see Figures 14.11, 14.15, 14.16, 14.19–14.22).

However, these relations create no isomorphic one-to-one associations between cleavage-structures and elite-structures but a rather loose and shifting coupling. A case in point is the increasing closeness between parties of the left (first the Socialists and later the Communists) to the 'State', which was the result of systemic policy outcomes (like an opening of public services to applicants with the leftist sympathies, or the expansion of the welfare state). Another example is the loosening of the ties between 'Land' and established parties of the Right, which partly resulted from 'Land' being degraded from an incumbent to a challenger. The German November 1932 Reichstag, which showed the NSDAP in a challenging position towards the other parties and the association of 'Land' with it is a good example for such a realignment (see Figure 14.13). This episode also exemplifies the connection between cleavage-development and the representative process because— since the late 1920s—the NSDAP successfully embraced and partly absorbed the militant and even violent agrarian protest movement of the Weimar Republic. Part of its strategy was to open the ranks of its parliamentary party to members with an agrarian background (including officials of agricultural associations). The benefit of this strategy of cleavage mobilization was that it attracted the agrarian vote, particularly in the protestant East and North of Germany, and thereby formed a cornerstone of the NSDAP's huge electoral successes in the 1930s (Best 1997).

If we, finally, address the question of to what extent and in which ways the links and correspondences between cleavage structures and elite structures affect orientations and behaviour of policymakers we have to consider that the EURELITE database does not provide data on elite behaviour or orientations. Earlier studies have suggested, however, that particular close and mutually exclusive links between cleavage structures and elite structures might affect the ability of legislative elites to compromise, to form coalitions and to conclude those elite 'settlements' that are, according to Higley et al., the prerequisite for achieving stable and consensual democracies (Best 1990). Conversely, the entrenchment of political elites in separated and mutually exclusive 'milieus' can disintegrate the polity and undermine the bases for elite consensus. A comparison between Germany and France from the 1870s until the 1930s supports this view, which was so concisely formulated by Otto Hintze (1911).

On the other hand, and this is an important finding of the EURELITE Project, the structural bases of elite competition vary, not only between polities, but also within one polity over time. We have seen realignments between parties and 'powers' and the ensuing reallocation of both in the maps of the elite structure. These realignments are fostered by long-term social change (like the decline of 'Land' as a significant social power) or by systemic policy outcomes (like the access of formerly ostracized leftist parties to the sinecures of the state, or the growing 'partyness' of political forces in the centre or on the right of the political spectre). Their implementation, however, is in most cases the result (although not always an intended one) of strategic decisions of the elite groups and factions involved. In their entirety, these realignments change alternately the structural bases for elite competition between a state of 'segmented pluralism' (Lorwin 1971), that is a situation of mutual exclusiveness of the structural bases for elite competition, and 'multiple heterogeneity' (Blau 1974), that is a situation where the structural bases for elite competition (and cooperation) are overlapping.

ENDNOTE

1   Data was provided by the EURELITE project—a scientific network sponsored by the European science Foundation and designed to study differences between recruitment and career patterns of European political elites over a period of 150 years (Best and Edinger 2005). A fuller description of the design and purpose of the project is given in the introduction of this volume.

15

Paths of Institutional Development and Elite Transformations

Maurizio Cotta and Luca Verzichelli

15.1. DEMOCRATIZATION AND THE TRANSFORMATION OF PARLIAMENTARY ELITES

The time period covered by the DATACUBE is that during which most of the European countries have accomplished the democratization of their political system. According to the distinction proposed by Robert Dahl (1970), this has meant reaching high levels of liberalization (i.e. freedom of public contestation) and universalizing the electoral inclusion of adult citizens; or, if we prefer to put it in Rokkan's words, overcoming the thresholds of legitimation, incorporation, and of executive power. With the first concept Rokkan refers to the 'effective recognition of the right of petition, criticism, demonstration against the regime . . . regular protection of the rights of assembly, expression and publication . . . ', with the second to the extension of suffrage so that 'potential supporters of rising movements of opposition were given formal rights of participation on a par with the established strata', ending with the inclusion of the entire adult population, and with the third to the ability of legislative institutions to exert pressure on the executive so that 'parliamentary strength could be translated into direct influence on executive decision-making' (1970). To these three thresholds Rokkan added a fourth one, that of representation, when through a change of the traditionally majoritarian electoral systems and their substitution with systems of proportional representation 'the barriers [were] lowered to make it easier to gain seats in the legislature' (Rokkan 1970a, 1970b: 79). With few exceptions (mainly limited to the Anglo-Saxon countries) this too was a normal step in the process of democratization.

We can also add that this process has entailed, at some stage, the building of a developed system of 'party government', that is a situation where policies are formulated primarily by parties, who play also a predominant role in the selection of candidates to representative positions and in the electoral competition, and where governments are normally composed of party affiliates (Katz 1987).

While in the end relatively similar results have been attained by all the countries included in our research,[1] the timing of these results, and the paths through which they have been reached varied significantly. Thus, if we observe retrospectively the European countries at different time points during this historical period, it is easy to discover that they have often shown marked differences in terms of their regime profile.

In a parallel way, we have documented that the profile of the parliamentary personnel has changed significantly during the same period in all European countries and that, while substantial differences could be found across countries, important similarities in the direction of the main trends of change were also apparent (Best and Cotta 2000).

What have been the relations between the transformations of representation, shown by our analysis of the changing profiles of parliamentarians over the past 150 years, and the different developmental paths taken by democratization? This is the main question this chapter proposes to address. The expectation to find a link between the transformations of the political regime (of some of its crucial rules and institutions) and the profiles of the parliamentary personnel seems easy to justify: all the changes mentioned as part of the process of democratization touch directly or indirectly upon elements connected with the representative function and the selection of its main agents, the MPs at the national level.

The liberalization of European political systems, by granting an increasingly full recognition of the rights of political opposition and dissent and by promoting the creation of a pluralistic public sphere, has challenged the old static and ascriptive model of estates representation—centred essentially on representation by peers and delegates—which had previously characterized European history. At the same time liberalization has opened a new space for more dynamic political entrepreneurs capable of interpreting representation in terms of competing opinions and interests rather than in terms of status (and its reproduction).

Extensions of suffrage have obviously expanded and changed in its composition the *demos* to be represented: this has meant not only more voters, but different voters (not just male members of the upper classes but also small shopkeepers, peasants, workers, and finally women of all classes) with new interests, opinions, identities that had to be incorporated in the political discourse of representation. As it is well known with the changing size and nature of the electorate the style also of representation, the way in which the representatives connect with the represented, could not remain unchanged.[2] The new conditions have necessarily required on the side of the representatives rather different skills and resources to reach out for the voters.

It must be considered however that the legal extension of suffrage could produce all its innovative effects only inasmuch as it had been prepared, accompanied or followed by a real political mobilization, which could pull the newly enfranchised strata of the population out of political passivity and push them to make full use of their rights. Organized political parties have typically been a crucial factor in producing this mobilization, playing a key role in giving a new form to the relationship between represented and representatives in a context of mass participation.

Parties have thus become a crucial intermediary in the game of representation, making it possible to establish strong linkages between a mass public and its representatives. At the same time, they have progressively 'captured' the elected representatives transforming them from relatively independent players into the instruments of their political play. Because of the control acquired by parties on parliamentary recruitment, and the establishment of a strong party discipline in the representative assemblies, parliamentarians have, in some sense, become 'party servants' and they have been recruited by parties according to their needs.

The role of parties in the 'production' of representatives must obviously receive a special attention. Their impact has been manifold. On the one hand they have been agents of change: the successive waves of new party creations which have characterized the stages of democratization have generally meant also the selection of at least partially different parliamentarians. On the other hand, the stabilization of party systems has produced also a stabilization of recruitment patterns and the closing of opportunities for representatives that were not in tune with the new party standards (Pedersen 1976).

Transformations in the role of parliament vis-à-vis the executive should have also affected representation and the recruitment of representatives. When parliaments gained ascendance over the executive their members became obviously more influential and at the same time came to be part of a somewhat different game. They were not just called to give voice to the interests of their voters: they were also engaged in producing a government for the country. This has entailed a greater degree of responsibility but has also opened up a new career avenue, that of minister (Blondel and Thiébault 1991).

Finally, the shift from majoritarian to proportional electoral systems has affected in many ways the nature of the representation links. First because it has typically broadened the constituencies thus increasing the distance between representatives and represented, second because, by introducing the vote for a list at the place of the vote for a person, it has enhanced the importance of party mediation in the process of representation.

Most of these steps in the process of democratization and the differences among European countries in their timing and sequences are related to a period in time which typically stretches until the First World War or, in some cases, to the first years following that conflict. Only for what concerns the extension of the franchise to women there are cases where it was further delayed: France and Italy waited until the Second World War, Portugal and Spain until the democratic restoration of the 1970s, to grant this right. But when it comes to another crucial aspect of democratization, the build up of large party organizations and the structuring of a mature party system—and we do not mean simply the organizational build up of socialist parties but also the reactions of bourgeois parties to this development and on the party system level the incorporation of the new mass parties as legitimate players at the parliamentary and executive level—these aspects have taken a good part of the twentieth century to develop.

Finally, if one takes into consideration not only the achievement of the basic elements of democracy but also the consolidation and persistence of this regime, very significant variations occurred among European countries not only during the second half of the nineteenth century but also throughout the twentieth century. Many countries have experienced one or more crises or interruptions in the process of democratization either before or after the achievement of mass democracy (in most of the cases during the first years after this threshold). In such cases, either a step back in the process has taken place and the country has returned to some previous stage of more traditional and less democratic regime (as are the cases of a return to a 'governing monarchy'), or else a new form of non-democratic regime (authoritarian or totalitarian) has been established.

Regime discontinuities, by producing a more or less prolonged interruption of the representation processes, should have affected the typically incremental change in the profile of representatives. The end of democracy entails as its consequence that the largest part of the political personnel (willingly or unwillingly) leaves the political scene while a minority may accept to be co-opted into the authoritarian regime. When democracy is re-established the comeback of the old politicians is, for a number of reasons (passing of time, new interests, disillusion with politics, deaths, involvement in the non-democratic regime, etc.), far from assured. A greater space for new politicians thus opens up.

Summarizing what we have said so far, the process of representation and the recruitment of representatives, which is a crucial component of this process, have had to face, during the period studied in this book, multiple challenges of adaptation to significantly changing institutional conditions (changes that may have been more or less gradual and incremental), and in some cases even the trauma of dramatic (and more or less prolonged) interruptions of regime continuity.

15.2. SEARCHING FOR EXPLANATIONS: SOME PRELIMINARY HYPOTHESES

What is then the relationship between the different paths of democratization and the variations—across countries and over time—we have discovered in the profiles of parliamentary elites? Can we establish meaningful correspondences between them? And, making a further step ahead, can we use the first aspect for explaining the second?

The understanding of the interactions between political development and long term changes in the elite structure was certainly a central concern of political science after the behavioural revolution.[3] In a stock taking book, brilliantly summarizing and evaluating the results of two decades of empirical studies dedicated to political elites, Robert Putnam argued that '...modification in recruitment channels, selectorates, and credentials can influence the composition of political elites independently of changes in socio-economic forces or functions. Mass suffrage and competitive elections, for example, appear often to have a "democratizing effect on the characteristics of elected elites" ' (1976: 170).

More specific questions about the impact of political development on the structure of political elites have been addressed during the seventies by two Scandinavian scholars who were following the Rokkanian lesson: Pedersen, in a *'four variable model'* of explanation of the elite transformation, linked the compositional profile of parliamentarians to the mutual influence between party opportunity structures and political changes (i.e. changes in the distribution of parliamentary seats), occurring in the light of a long-term social transformation (Pedersen 1976). On the same line of explanation, Kjell Eliassen (1978) showed the consequences of social and political innovations of the early twentieth century (namely, the increase of political participation) on the parliamentary elite structure in Norway, explaining the diachronic change of Norwegian elites by means of a two-sided model of transformation of political mobilization and institutional change.

Such promising approach notwithstanding, the research on this specific topic has been limited to a few case studies, stressing the country-specific factors which could have affected the birth and the consolidation of their respective political elites. The possibility to combine the analysis of a wider cross-country aggregate archive on long-term changes of parliamentary elites and some other data related to democratization patterns should enable us to make a further step ahead in the direction of a more systematic exploration of the relationship between the two dimensions and to develop and test more comprehensive explanatory hypotheses. In this chapter, we will start from a wide set of possible explanatory arguments derived from the above mentioned literature, which will then be refined and progressively reduced in the light of the results of data analysis.

The starting point of our research is a very broad and simple hypothesis which can be derived from a preliminary understanding of the process of democratization: *'The institutional democratization of the political regime will produce also a democratization of representative elites.'* The elimination of the old predemocratic power structures and of the barriers to the inclusion of the popular strata in the political process should open the way also to a much larger participation of the new societal strata in the recruitment of the political personnel and reduce the dominance of the traditional upper strata of society. According to this hypothesis we should find a positive correlation between the opening of political regimes and a growing proportion of MPs from the previously excluded or underrepresented groups of the population (men of the lower classes and women of all classes).

The basic assumption behind this hypothesis is that the process of representation is fundamentally a process driven from the 'bottom' and that it hinges on the reflection/reproduction of the traits of the represented. This view, while not completely ungrounded, is however at best partial. It has to be corrected in order to take into account a less simplistic interpretation of the process of representation. The expectation that new voters will necessarily express new representatives rests on the strong assumption that the former will be able to articulate their demands and translate them into representative choices. This might not be fully warranted especially during an initial period. New voters might not immediately generate new demands. This was indeed often the case for peasants deeply immersed in the traditional way of life of the countryside and deferent towards traditional social authorities, and for women, who for a very long time after obtaining voting rights did not articulate a demand for a gender based representation, but accepted the existing class or religious bases of representation. Beside this we have to consider the fact that representation is not only demand driven but is also a function of the supply, which is influenced by the availability of candidates and by the choice of candidates made by the individual and collective actors which have gained control of the selection process (Norris 1997a, 1997b). The supply will be, first of all, determined by the incumbent elite groups, who will strive to survive (and adapt gradually) under the new institutional conditions; then by the new political entrepreneurs entering into the electoral market with a more innovative offer specifically tailored upon the new voters.

The original hypothesis could then be transformed in a somewhat more elaborate one: '*The democratization of representative elites will follow the democratization of the regime with greater or smaller delays depending on the one side on the mobilisation of the new voters and on the other side on the ability of established elites to maintain their hold on the process of representation and of new elites to challenge them.*'

Another aspect deserves some attention. The transition from restricted to mass suffrage enhances significantly the requirements of professionalization and the role of a specific intermediary actor in the process of representation, that is the party, which indeed becomes the focal centre of representation. Voters vote the party more than the candidates; and the party selects the candidates who are typically recruited from its own ranks. The new supply will therefore be affected by these factors.

We will then reformulate the hypothesis as follows '*the process of institutional democratization will promote a democratization of the representatives but also their professionalisation and partisation*'.

In other words the democratization of the elites will develop to the extent that it will be compatible with the requirements of professionalization and the needs of parties. Professionalization will require from parliamentarians the control of skills and resources enabling them to reach a large scale electorate, to communicate with it and, at the same time, to devote a larger amount of time to political activities. Up to a certain point some non-political professions (such as that of journalist or the legal one) and relatively high levels of education will help in this direction. But, increasingly, a paid position in party organizations, or in trade unions and other interests groups, and public employment will provide more effective opportunities of political professionalization. Partizsation means also that representatives will have to pass the scrutiny of party organizations: to have occupied a position of responsibility in the party at any level will obviously enhance the chances of selection. The qualities required to make a career within parties will depend from the nature of these organizations. The more dense these organizations the greater the role of a party bureaucracy with its own internal career: this will therefore become the main qualification for the selection as a parliamentary candidate. A lighter organization will leave more space to external recruitments based, at least partially, on resources generated outside the party (membership of interest groups, technical qualifications, prestige, etc.). Democratization, professionalization, and partization will thus produce only partially convergent effects.

So far our discussion has focused on the possible effects of a dominant trend of transformation affecting all our cases. This trend, however, may be characterized by significant variations in the speed and continuity of the transformations. Our main hypothesis will have to be corrected for taking into account these factors.

We will then say that '*under gradually changing institutional conditions the process of recruitment of parliamentary representatives should be expected to produce changes of an incremental nature in the profiles of legislators*'. The renewal of the parliamentary elite should be due mainly to 'molecular' substitutions (dying or retiring parliamentarians leaving their places to younger ones co-opted into the elite), or to the effects of the changing political fortunes of parties (losses and victories will produce respectively exits and entries into the pool of representatives) (Pedersen 1976). Except in the case of major party breakdowns and landslide victories, continuity should prevail in the overall profile of parliamentarians.

On the contrary, '*significant and abrupt institutional changes should stimulate wider and deeper changes in the elite profile*'. Both because incumbent parliamentarians and existing parties will have to face an institutional environment that is different from the one to which they had become adapted and because a wider space will open for challengers having the resources to exploit the new conditions. Finally, '*regime interruptions should typically foster an even more radical change*' in the composition of the representative elites, since the traditional mechanisms of recruitment will be destroyed and new mechanisms will have to be put in place when democracy is restored.

Before we attempt to test these hypotheses, we will illustrate and discuss our dependent and independent variables. With regard to the former we will analyse different aspects of the profile of parliamentarians and their variations. In particular three basic dimensions will be considered: democratization of recruitment, professionalization and partzation of careers, institutional consolidation of parliamentary elites.

With regard to the independent variables we will complete and translate in a comparable format the information about the processes of democratization in the countries to be examined. In this effort, we can use a number of consolidated data-sets on democratization. In particular, we will combine long-term data concerning suffrage extension and electoral organization (Caramani 2000), with data concerning levels of political mobilization such as those about electoral turnout (Mackie and Rose 1991, 1997), development of class parties vote and organizational density of parties (and particularly of the socialist ones) (Bartolini 2000).

15.3. THE DEPENDENT VARIABLES

The depth of the changes in the profile of elected representatives over the time period covered here has been already documented in a previous work (Best and Cotta 2000) and extensively explored in several chapters of this volume. We can summarize this point by presenting a broad common picture and some of the most significant cross-country variations. The common picture reveals three important dimensions of change in the recruitment of parliamentarians: democratization of recruitment, professionalization and partization of careers, and institutional consolidation of elites. The first dimension has meant the breaking of the monopoly of the upper classes over parliamentary representation and the opening of the pool of eligible candidates to much wider and more varied sections of the population. The second dimension has entailed that the recruitment process has increasingly favoured a personnel with high levels of skills and resources specifically tailored to the process of political representation and to parliamentary work. People without a serious training in the mechanisms of democracy and a long-term engagement in political life have had diminishing chances to succeed. The party has become a crucial instrument in this direction. The third dimension has meant that representatives have attained a high degree of institutional entrenchment: renewal rates have decreased and their tenure in parliament has been generally significant, thus producing a real representative class. These transformations have affected without exceptions all the countries we have studied.

The impact of the first dimension of change is well documented by the fall of aristocratic parliamentarians, which from being initially a very significant component of representative assemblies progressively loose ground and finally disappear (Chapter 2 of this volume), by the decline of MPs with a university degree which goes on until the 1940s (Chapter 5), and of those with a background in the high echelons of public administration (again more or less until the 1930s–40s) (Chapter 3) (Figure 15.1). On the other hand we have seen, during the last decades of the nineteenth century and the first decades of the twentieth, the significant rise of parliamentarians with only the lowest levels of education, of blue-collar workers, and (but only after the Second World War) of women. The less educated, the lower classes, and (later) the weaker gender have thus profited from the opening of recruitment and the breaking of the monopoly on representation of the upper classes and males. It must be noticed however that

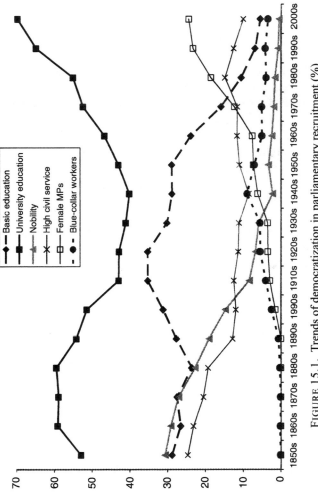

FIGURE 15.1. Trends of democratization in parliamentary recruitment (%)

in the end the democratization of recruitment has not progressed beyond a given point: approximately by the 1940s the weight of MPs coming from the working classes and with lower levels of education has ceased to grow and has then begun to decline. Representation of the lower classes by the lower classes seems to have reached a peak beyond which countervailing factors have been at work. It must be said however that the same does not seem, so far, to apply for women: when, after a long latency, their representation takes off the upward trend keeps developing steadily (Chapter 4).[4]

For a better understanding of democratization of recruitment and the limits of its development we have to pay attention to the other force which can be seen at work, that is the professionalization of the representative career. This force proves at first to be compatible and even favourable to that of democratization but later shows increasingly divergent effects. The developmental trends of different types of occupational backgrounds of MPs provide the relevant evidence of this phenomenon, indicating also that the nature of the political profession has changed with time. The pattern shown by our data is that of 'successive waves', whereby different occupational backgrounds first grow and then decline to leave space to new ones. In an earlier phase—the last decades of the nineteenth century and the first of the twentieth—we see that, in parallel with the decline of the traditional establishment, professions that are more highly compatible with an active political and electoral engagement (such as that of lawyer, journalist, or writer) become more frequent among MPs (Figure 15.2). Later on their growth levels off and even reverses and their place is increasingly taken by pure 'professionals of politics', that is by parliamentarians coming from a paid position in the party organizations or in trade unions and similar organizations. These political jobs, which particularly in the first stages of the organizations of mass mobilization are available also for people from the lower classes, show a constant and significant increase throughout the first half of the twentieth century,[5] but will from then on begin to decline. In the last decades of the twentieth century we will rather see the growth of public servants, teachers and professors, and in general a strong comeback of high levels of education.

Some other aspects require to be mentioned here to complete the picture. The first is that, behind such waves in the types of occupational backgrounds, we can detect the constant importance for parliamentarians of an experience in local politics before moving up to the institutions of national representation. This confirms the strong connections between parliamentary life and local interests (Figure 15.2). The second aspect is the growing importance of a party engagement in the recruitment of parliamentarians. Throughout a great part of the twentieth century the percentage of MPs who, before their first election, had occupied a leading position in the party organization at the local or national level has constantly increased. Finally, the stabilization of political careers is shown by the (slowly) declining levels of turnover at elections (with the obvious exceptions of the periods following institutional discontinuity).

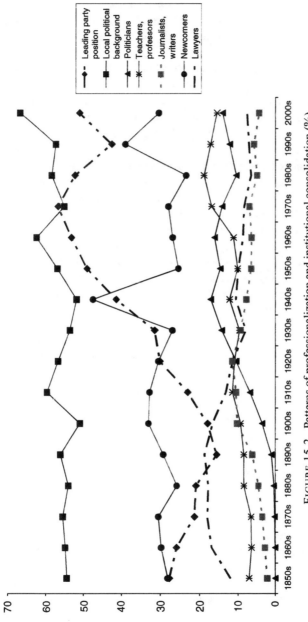

FIGURE 15.2. Patterns of professionalization and institutional consolidation (%)

The extensive political experience which has increasingly come to be required for successfully qualifying as a serious candidate to parliament has probably become an obstacle for a further democratization of recruitment: individuals with a middle-class background have been favoured compared to those from the working classes. It is probably also part of this process of professionalization the fact that, after the Second World War, university education has regained in importance and occupations linked with knowledge have become more frequent (see for instance the growth of teachers and professors). It is also a reasonable conjecture to consider the decline in the weight of lawyers a consequence of a more advanced stage of professionalization of political life. In the earlier stages of the historical period examined here the legal profession had undoubtedly played a role contributing to the proto-professionalization of politics: lawyers had some of the skills that could help them to play the representative role in an age of weak party organizations and the flexibility in their working schedule that made them available when politics was a part-time job (Eulau and Sprague 1984). But the development of a more specific organization of politics and the transformation of the representative job into a full-time engagement has produced a new type of specialists and a much greater demand on the time of politicians; in this situation free professionals such as the lawyers could hardly compete with the organization professionals produced by mass parties and trade unions.

The renewed growth of representatives with a public sector background after the Second World War might be connected with both phenomena. Democratization, by fostering the growth of a 'big state', has possibly stimulated an increased demand of 'representatives of state interests' (i.e. interests of the state bureaucracies); at the same time public employees could probably show some of the features fitting in an age of political professionalization (both in terms of policymaking skills and availability for a full-time job) (see Chapter 3 in this book).

If we now look in a synthetic way to the common trends, we can identify a succession of types of representatives which correspond also to changes in the models of representation (Cotta and Best 2000). Representatives of the traditional establishment (nobles, landowners, high state officials) with their roots in the society and politics of the ancient regime embody what can be called 'deferential or status representation'. The next type is that of the proto-professionals or independent political entrepreneurs (lawyers, and other free professionals, journalists) to which corresponds a 'representation of elite opinions and local clienteles'. The third type is that of the organizers of mass mobilization, the party and trade union functionaries with low levels of education and a lower class background, and of 'cleavage representation'. The fourth type is that of the professional politicians and technocrats (people with long party and electoral careers, high levels of education, mostly with a public service background) to which corresponds a 'representation of mass opinion voters and of organized interests'. Obviously the succession of these types of representation is not neatly defined and the substitution of one type of politician with the following one is only partial. To a certain extent, different types of politician will coexist throughout the process of transformation.

Within these broad trends, our data shows also some important variations across countries. As it can be easily seen, these variations have to do with differences both in the starting points and in the tempos of change. To take only a selective look at some of the most important variables we find, for instance, with regard to the weight of nobility (a clear indicator of the survival of the pre-democratic establishment), differences linked to the starting levels (Germany and the UK having from the beginning much higher levels than France), but also to a different persistence in face of changing conditions—the case of the UK being particularly striking for the survival well into the twentieth century of a significant minority of parliamentarians with an aristocratic family background (Figure 15.3).

At the opposite extreme of the social spectrum the representation of blue-collar workers attains only in the UK important levels and somewhat lower but still significant ones in Finland, Germany, France, and Norway during the central decades of the twentieth century, while it will never really take off in countries such as Denmark, Italy, and the Netherlands (Figure 15.4).

If we consider now the professionalization and partization of politics we can see that with regard to the role, for MPs, of a party career, Germany, Denmark, and the Netherlands have anticipated the developments of the other countries, while France and Finland have clearly lagged behind (Figure 15.6). After the Second World War Italy has joined and even overcome the first ranks. And if we restrict our analysis to the politicians that lived off politics they reached the highest peak in Germany earlier than in any other country and gained a high level of importance in Finland, Italy, and the Netherlands while they played a much weaker role in France, Norway, and the UK (Figure 15.5).

To what extent such differences in the profiles of representative elites both at the beginning of the period considered and in different phases of their development have to do with variations in the paths of democratization or with other factors? This is the main question we will try to address in the following parts of this chapter.

15.4. THE INDEPENDENT VARIABLES

If our explanandum are patterns of representation, defined here on the basis of combinations of features of parliamentary representatives, the independent variables we will employ are the different components of the democratization process (and the indicators used to measure them). Before attempting to test the different hypotheses we have to explore analytically dimensions and steps in the processes of democratization.

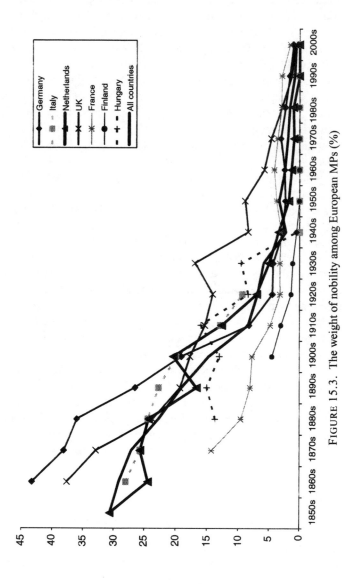

FIGURE 15.3. The weight of nobility among European MPs (%)

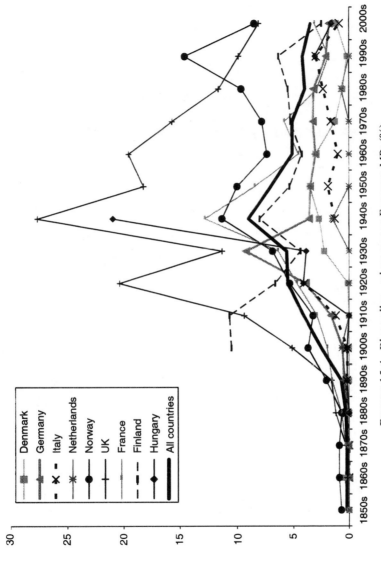

FIGURE 15.4. Blue-collar workers among European MPs (%)

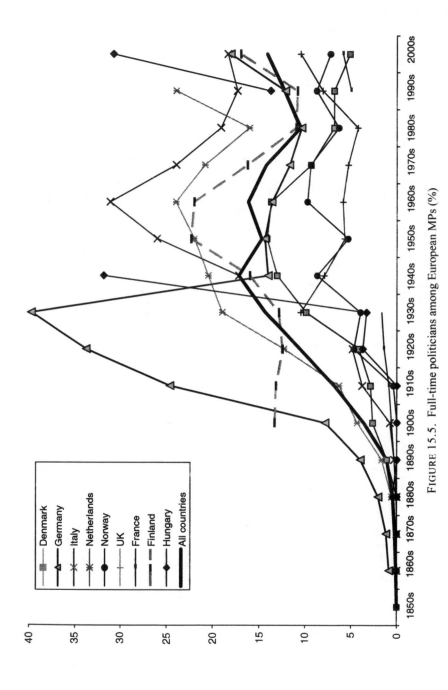

FIGURE 15.5. Full-time politicians among European MPs (%)

Legend:
- Denmark
- Germany
- Italy
- Netherlands
- Norway
- UK
- France
- Finland
- Hungary
- All countries

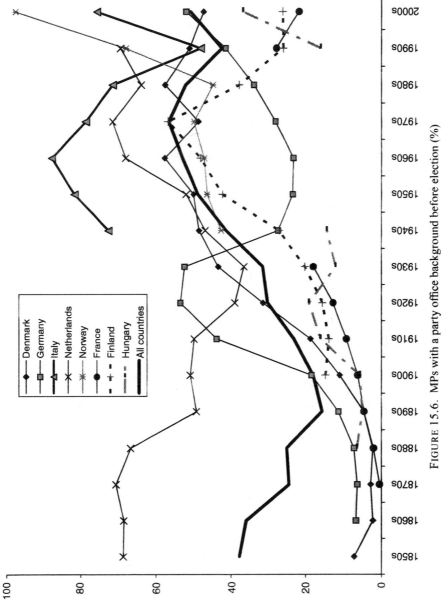

FIGURE 15.6. MPs with a party office background before election (%)

On the basis of the vast literature on democratization the most relevant aspects we can identify are the following ones:

1. *Liberalization*
2. *Extension of suffrage*
3. *Electoral mobilization*
4. *Democratic (parliamentary) control of executive power*
5. *Electoral system change*
6. *Development of organized parties*
7. *Regime interruptions*

Among these dimensions, and assuming that a basic threshold of liberalization had been reached by all the countries considered in our study,[6] we will concentrate on extension of suffrage, electoral mobilization, electoral system change, development of organized parties, and regime interruptions.[7] For the dimensions taken into consideration we will now provide a synthetic appraisal of variations across countries and over time.

1. *Extension of suffrage*. We want to document here the steps that lead to a fully universal franchise. Typically, the process begins from very restrictive conditions whereby only the upper strata of the population are included in the electoral process, and only after a relatively long delay the rest of the adult population is included (Rokkan 1970*a*, 1970*b*). In a few cases, however, a relatively large (male) franchise was granted from the first stages of the representative regime and only more limited extensions were then required to reach universal suffrage.

The relevant question to be asked here concerns the length of the time span it took to reach the final destination and the number of steps that this required (Table 15.1). As it is easy to see, differences in this sphere are very significant in Europe (Figure 15.7). If we set at 20 per cent of the adult population enfranchised before 1880 a conventional threshold that separates 'early comers' and 'late comers', we have on one side Denmark, France, and Germany, while on the other side there are Italy, Norway, Netherlands, and the UK. Finland is among the latecomers (until 1906 the franchise is restricted to a very small proportion of the population), but as it sometimes happens to latecomers the next step brings the country on the forefront of democratic suffrage: in 1906 universal male and female voting rights are granted. By 1910 only Hungary and Italy lag seriously behind the group and by 1920, when all the countries have moved to full inclusion, France, Hungary, and Italy are still behind because of an only male suffrage.[8]

2. *Electoral mobilization*. Since the extension of franchise did not mean automatically that all those granted the right to vote made use of it, the degree of electoral mobilization is a significant intervening variable between the extension of suffrage and its effects. In a simplified way, it could be assumed that the lower the electoral mobilization the lower would be also the impact of suffrage extensions and vice versa, the greater the electoral mobilization the greater also

TABLE 15.1. *Steps of suffrage extension and electoral systems in ten European countries*

	1850s	1860s	1870s	1880s	1890s	1900s	1910s	1920s	1930s	1940s
Denmark	Ext.(1849) *Pl*						Un.Sf.(1918) *Mix. PR*(1918)			
Germany		Un.M.(1867)	*Maj.*(1971)					Un.Sf.(1920) *PR*(1918)	Dem. Break. (1933)	*Mix. PR*(1949)
Italy		Min.(1861) *Maj.*(1861)		Ext.(1882) *Lim. V* (1882)	*Maj.*(1892) Ext.(1897)		Un. M.(1913) *PR*(1919)	Dem. Break. (1924)		Un.Sf.(1946) *PR*(1946)
Netherlands	Min.(1850) *Maj.*(1850)						Un. M.(1917) *PR*(1918)			Un.Sf.(1946)
Norway	Min. *Maj.*(1851)			Ext.(1885)		Un.M.(1900)	Un.Sf.(1915)			
UK	Min. *Pl.*	Ext.(1868)					Lim. F.(1918)	Un.Sf.(1929)		
France			Un. M.(1871) *Maj.*(1871)				*Mix. PR*(1919)			Un.Sf.(1945) *Maj.*(1946)
Portugal	Min.(1852) *Maj.*(1852)						Ext.(1911) *Lim. V.*(1911)	*Maj.*(1928) Un.M.(1918)	*Pl.*(1932)	
Finland					*Lim. V.*(1890)	Un.Sf.(1907) *Pr.*(1907)			Dem. Break. (1926)	
Hungary				Min.(1884) *Maj.*(1884)				Un.M.(1927) *Mix.-Maj.*(1927)		Dem. Break. (1945)

Legends:

steps of suffrage extension:
Min. = less than 25% adult male
Ext. = more than 25% adult male
Un. M. = universal Male suffrage
Lim. F. = Universal male and a limited percentage of female
Un.Sf. = Universal suffrage, only limitations due to immorality or crimes

electoral systems:
Pl. = plurality system
Maj. = majoritarian (run off system)
Lim. V = Limited vote
Mix. M = Mixed system with a prevalent majoritarian effect
Mix. PR = Mixed system with a prevalent PR effect
PR = Proportional list system

Source: Mackie and Rose (1991).

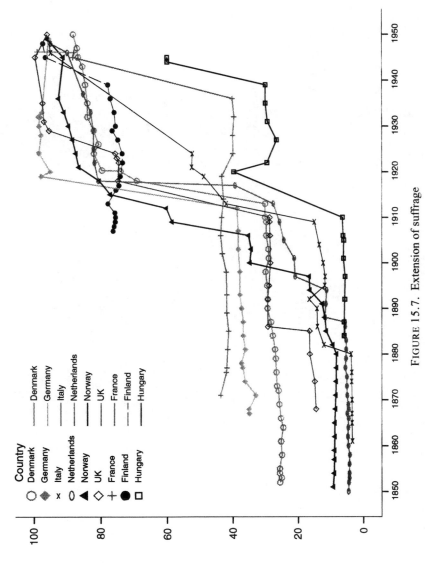

FIGURE 15.7. Extension of suffrage

Source: Electorate as a percent of adult population (older than 20 years). Caramani (2000)

should be the effects of a larger electorate. Electoral mobilization can be measured by turnout percentages (Figure 15.8). A more sophisticated analysis would require to distinguish between turnout of the old and new enfranchised strata, but this is beyond our possibilities here.

If we define a threshold of high mobilization at about 70 per cent of the electors, this level was reached in most of the countries between 1880 and 1890. Oscillations however remained very broad for a longer period and, in particular, we can detect in many countries (Britain, Denmark, Finland, and Norway) a serious although temporary decline of electoral participation during the early decades of the twentieth century. Italy is, among our countries, the one which shows the most delayed increase in turnout: only after the Second World War it will pass the 70 per cent threshold.

3. *Electoral system change*. For our purposes it is enough to document (only) major changes in the electoral system, as the one from a plurality system to a PR system, or, in the case of an already established PR system, changes that affect very significantly the degree of proportionality (see Table. 15.1). On this point, what it is striking is the very high degree of synchronism in the adoption of PR systems: except for UK and France, the end of the First World War is the common point in time for such a change.

4. *Development of organized mass parties*. The rise of modern mass parties with a large and articulated membership organization is a crucial innovation in the political life of democracies and an innovation with particularly important effects on the process of representation. Both the selection and the behaviour of parliamentary representatives will be deeply affected by this new factor. This factor is obviously linked to the extension of suffrage. However it is not totally dependent from it as it is shown by the different degree of development of organized mass parties in countries with the same levels of suffrage: it is therefore meaningful to use it as a further explanatory factor. In order to assess comparatively and diachronically the impact of organized parties we could use as a measure the percentage of parliamentary seats gained by this type of parties. Here, for practical reasons, we will use an even more simplified indicator: the percentage of seats of socialist and (since 1917) communist parties, as they typically were the first and main organized parties in the crucial years of democratic evolution (Figure 15.9).

Developments here are not too dissimilar, but one can find significant lags of about ten years between the countries analysed. The most evident exception is Finland, which in the first period outdistances the whole group of countries with its high levels of around 40 per cent.

5. *Regime crises and democratic interruptions*. Although many of our countries have experienced serious crises during the first phases of democratization, crises linked essentially to disputes about the role of the monarchical head of state and of the parliament in the formation of cabinets, this has produced an autocratic experience with the abolishment of the previous liberal constitution

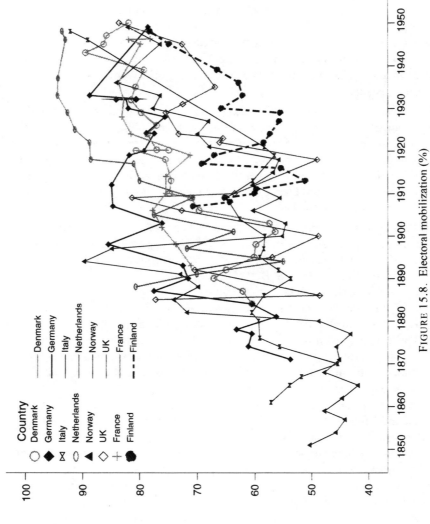

FIGURE 15.8. Electoral mobilization (%)

Source: Caramani (2000).

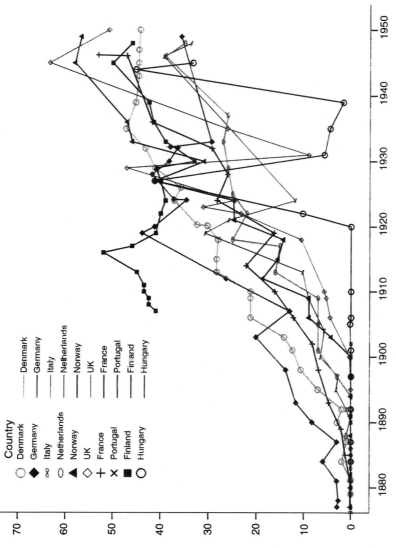

FIGURE 15.9. Parliamentary strength of Socialist and Communist Parties in ten European countries (%)

Source: DATACUBE.

only in the case of France (1850–70), and in Spain (1875).[9] Much more dramatic have been the interruptions in the democratic development which have taken place during the twentieth century. These crises, which have typically exploded in the wake of the process of mass mobilization, have produced new peculiar forms of non-democratic regime which, in some cases, have shown to be able to persist effectively for a significant span of time (Linz 2000). In these regimes competitively elected parliaments have been replaced by assemblies elected or nominated via non-competitive processes and dominated by single or hegemonic parties.

15.5. WHAT EMPIRICAL EVIDENCE FOR OUR HYPOTHESES?

It is now time to discuss our empirical evidence and to see how it fits with our initial hypotheses. The starting point will be the preliminary and broad hypothesis that democratization of the regime should have fostered also the democratization of the parliamentary elite. This hypothesis will be explored through an analysis of the relationships between the components of democratization we have selected and specific features of parliamentary elites.

15.5.1. *Extension of Suffrage and Parliamentary Representation*

We suggest to begin from the extension of suffrage, not because this is necessarily the first step in democratization, but because it is the dimension for which the impact upon elite features would seem more obvious. Our countries provide a good deal of variance in the independent variable: timing, speed, and width of suffrage enlargement display significant differences across countries. The data shows also (Figures 15.3–15.6) that variations across countries in some of the crucial dependent variables are sizable. We have thus material to check our basic hypothesis with the help of observations both within countries and across countries. A simple run of a bivariate analysis among the data covering the period of suffrage extension (1870–1929) shows indeed a series of significant correlations between extension of franchise and indicators of recruitment democratization such as percentage of noble MPs, levels of education, percentage of blue-collar workers (Table 15.2).

This overall finding suggests a more detailed exploration of the relationship: for this purpose we propose to compare the features of parliamentary elites at different stages of suffrage extension within each country, and across countries with similar and dissimilar levels of franchise.

A preliminary exploration of the situation can be done by a synchronic comparison. We will start by examining the decade 1870–9, a period when all our countries had established (sufficiently) free parliamentary elections and which we can therefore consider as a conventional point of departure. At this stage our cases vary from the universal male suffrage of France and Germany, to a wide but not universal franchise in Denmark, to the restricted suffrage of the UK (which had experienced a first limited extension in 1867) and Norway, to the

TABLE 15.2. *Parliamentary profiles, suffrage extension, and mass party mobilization (1870–1929), Pearson correlation coefficients*

	Electorate as a % of adult population (20 years)		Electoral turnout		Percentage of communist and socialist seats		Organizational density of Left parties	
	Pearson correlation	Sig.	Pearson correlation	Sig.	Pearson correlation	Sig.	Pearson correlation	Sig.
Noblemen legislators	−.651**	.000	−.272*	.013	−.680**	.000	−.538**	.000
Female legislators	.644**	.000	.109	.232	.786**	.000	.296**	.000
University degree	−.467**	.000	−.043	.640	−.510**	.000	−.686**	.000
Primary sector	.082	.314	−.336**	.000	.080	.322	.436**	.000
Blue-collar workers	.546**	.000	−.061	.510	.570**	.000	.102	.207
Managers, businessmen	−.052	.521	−.109	.236	−.213**	.008	−.295**	.000
Lawyers	−.433**	.000	−.160	.079	−.422**	.000	−.525**	.000
Liberal professions	.316**	.000	−.080	.412	.480**	.000	.615**	.000
Teachers and professors	.354**	.000	.065	.481	.442**	.000	.571**	.000
Higher civil servants	−.068	.399	.035	.703	−.187*	.021	−.228**	.004
Judges	−.370**	.000	.106	.246	−.327**	.000	−.347**	.000
Military persons	−.258**	.001	−.328**	.000	−.283**	.000	−.370**	.000
Public sector employees	−.209**	.009	.146	.110	−.139	.086	.225**	.005
Journalists, writers	.552**	.000	.318**	.000	.673**	.000	.681**	.000
Politicians	.717**	.000	.280**	.002	.744**	.000	.263**	.001
Local political background	.204*	.011	.112	.221	.147	.068	.209*	.009
Party background	.132	.204	.068	.568	.134	.196	−.048	.644
Mean age	−.238**	.003	.293**	.001	−.346**	.000	.020	.803
Mean number of elections	−.294**	.000	.043	.659	−.139	.104	.077	.365
Newcomers	.159*	.049	−.016	.858	.051	.530	−.051	.528

* Correlation is significant at the 0.05 level (two tailed).

** Correlation is significant at the 0.01 level (two tailed).

extremely restricted suffrage of Italy and the Netherlands. Three variables will be used here as positive indicators of the persistence of the traditional pre-democratic establishment and vice versa as negative indicators of the democratic openness of recruitment: the percentages of MPs with (*a*) a nobility title,[10] (*b*) a university degree, and (*c*) a background in the high ranks of the civil service (including the judiciary and the armed forces).

A first inspection of these variables (Table 15.3) indicates that the relationship with our independent variable is far from being clear. With regard to the weight of nobility, France fits with the expectations (large franchise and low level of nobility), and the same can be said for the UK (low franchise and high level of nobility), but Germany contradicts them blatantly being one of the two countries with the most extended franchise in the 1870s and at the same time the least democratic representation. Italy, with the most restricted electorate, shows levels of aristocratic background which are significantly lower than in the German case. In a similar way when it comes to education our data shows that the correspondence between the frequency of a university degree and restricted suffrage is far

TABLE 15.3. *Average values for selected variables in European parliaments (1870–9)*

	Nobility	Public sector/high level p.s.	University education	Basic education	Working class	Primary sector	Lawyers	Local government	Party office	Mean age (years)	Newcomers	Number of successful re-elections (N)
Denmark	n.d.	39.6/10.4	26.5	55.4	0	50.0	3.5	43.3	2.7	47.4	21.3	3.5
Germany	38.1	31.5/23.7	80.5	1.4	0.1	29.4	9.4	46.1	6.2	50.8	40.8	2.2
Italy	25.8	22.8/14.7	69.9	n.d.	0	19.9	41.0	n.d.	n.d.	47.8	29.3	2.7
Netherlands	25.6	48.3/32.0	79.1	10.1	0	0.2	21.7	58.4	n.d.	53.2	17.2	3.8
Norway	n.d.	38.2/24.1	32.3	35.5	1.1	34.6	8.1	85.6	n.d.	50.2	31.4	3.1
UK	31.0	n.d./18.7	53.2	42.6	0.4	32.7	17.9	9.7	n.d.	48.4	30.7	n.d.
France	14.2	13.9/13.1	59.0	38.1	0.3	18.8	30.8	65.5	0.5	50.8	50.6	1.7
Spain	46.9	12.0/n.d.	89.0	0	0	20.2	20.8	n.d.	n.d.	n.d.	59.2	n.d.
Portugal	19.0	37.5/n.d.	n.d.	n.d.	0	24.0	7.7	n.d.	n.d.	n.d.	n.d.	n.d.

Note: Except where specified data are %; n.d.: non-available data.

from perfect. France and Germany offer, once more, two quite different patterns: Germany has a much higher level of university graduates than France. On its side Norway, still with a very limited suffrage, displays a percentage of MPs with high levels of education that is strikingly low compared to the other countries with a similar franchise. Again, a wider franchise does not seem then to entail necessarily a more democratic character of the representative elite and vice versa. With regard to our third variable, Netherlands and Norway, among the countries with limited suffrage, fit the expected pattern (a high level of top state officials); less so the UK and Italy. Among the countries with extended male suffrage France and Denmark show comparatively low levels on this variable, but Germany is again one of the countries with the highest levels.

The evidence surveyed so far suggests the need to refine the discussion of this relationship in two directions. The first is to move from a static comparison to a more dynamic exploration and to look more carefully into the effects of all the extensions of suffrage. We will therefore measure variations in the dependent variables after all significant expansions of suffrage. In this perspective it should be taken into account that the effects may not be immediate: we will therefore consider not just the first but the three elections following a suffrage extension. Thus, for evaluating changes in the dependent variables, we will compare the mean values of the three elections after the extension with those of the three elections before the extension. The second step will be to check to what extent the democratization of elites takes place even independently from suffrage extensions. For this purpose we will examine what have been the variations in our dependent variables during periods without any change in the extension of the franchise.

With regard to the first check the results are of some interest. In the case of Italy the first extension of suffrage in 1882 has some impact on the presence of noblemen in parliament and no impact whatsoever on the weight of highly educated MPs. In the three elections after the extension the mean rate of noble parliamentarians declined of about 4 percentage points (but in the following elections there will be more or less a return to the previous levels). As for education the percentage of university graduates increases somewhat. The next extension of 1912 (which introduces universal male suffrage) has a stronger impact on the first variable, but none on the second. In both cases the impact on the weight of high state officials is limited (Table 15.4).

In the Dutch case the impact seems clearer. After the extension of 1888 the size of the nobility shows a substantial decline, and the same applies to higher education and high state officials. The next extension (1897) has no impact on the size of nobility and public service, but some impact on the levels of high education. The third extension of 1918 (by which fully universal suffrage is attained) has again very strong consequences: nobility is halved, university education falls significantly, and the top levels of public service face another reduction.

TABLE 15.4. *Suffrage extensions and their impact on selected variables and turnout (%)*

Country and date of suffrage extension	Nob. before extension	Variations nobility	University education before extension	Variations university education	High public servants before extension	Variation high civil servants	Blue-collar workers before extension	Variation blue-collar workers	Variation turnout	Variations turnover
Denmark 1918	—	—	17.7	+2.2	2.0	+2.3	NA	NA	+2.4	+6.8
Italy 1882	25.6	−4.8	70.2	+2.2	13.6	−1.8	0	+0.3	−0.5	+1.2
Italy 1913	19.9	−8.1	75.6	+0.4	6.4	−0.5	0.1	+2.1	−3.5	+14.3
Netherlands 1888	25.6	−6.6	80.2	−11.5	32.2	−7.5	0	—	NA	+13.3
Netherlands 1897	17.7	+1.0	68.7	−5.0	24.7	—	0	+1	+2.4	+0.7
Netherlands 1918	16.3	−7.6	63.0	−17.0	23.7	−4.0	0	—	+12.4	+11.7
Norway 1900	—	—	31.0	−5.0	16.8	+0.5	3.0	+0.7	−25.8	−12.7
Norway 1910	—	—	26.0	+4.0	17.3	+5.9	3.7	−0.1	+0.9	−7.6
Norway 1916	—	—	28.0	+3.0	23.2	−7.3	3.6	—	+6.9	+1.0
UK 1886	27.6	−7.8	52.5	+4.3	15.7	−2.1	0.8	+0.8	−18.5	−12.9
UK 1918	16.5	−3.1	53.2	−7.0	11.4	+1.9	7.2	+9.5	−12.2	−0.4
Hungary 1920	13.5	−7.1	95.4	−20.0	7.1	+0.6	0	+5.6	n.d.	+24.8

Note: All values before extension are the mean of the last three elections. Variations are calculated by comparing these values with the means of the last three elections after the extension (including the first one after the change which is indicated by the date). Data have been calculated to the first decimal digit.

In Denmark we have included no other steps in suffrage extension (as that of 1876) because in spite of some changes in voting rights the size of the electorate over the adult population did not change significantly until 1918. In the Netherlands in 1888 and 1897 the income thresholds were significantly lowered. In 1917 vote was also made compulsory. In Norway the suffrage reform of 1885 based on new income criteria did not produce a significant increase in the size of the electorate; the elections of 1910 saw a larger electorate due to a limited opening for women. For the UK we have not measured the impact of the 1867 reform because our dataset does not include the data for the previous period. The data of 1886 reflect the reform of 1884.

In the UK the first expansion considered here (1886) has no impact on the level of education (in fact the percentage of university educated MPs increases four points), but is followed by a substantial decline of nobility. After universal suffrage is introduced in 1918, university education shows a significant decline and nobility is further trimmed. In both cases the impact on high state officers is weak or nil.

In the case of Norway, where we do not have the nobility variable, the data about university education indicates that the first extension of 1900 is followed by a limited drop, but the following enlargements do not confirm this trend (after 1910 there is a four points and after 1916 a three points rise). But in 1916 there is a significant negative impact on high civil servants. In Denmark the extension to universal suffrage in 1918 has a similar effect: the level of university education increases (and the same happens to civil servants).

We have neither included in this table nor in the following one the data concerning the percentage of blue-collar workers. With the only exception of the British franchise extension of 1918, which produces a significant growth of this indicator (from 7.2% to 16.7%), in all other cases percentages and variations are almost irrelevant.

A synthetic appraisal of the cases examined shows the existence of a variable relationship between enfranchisement and democratization of MP recruitment (Table 15.5). For sixteen cases (a half of the thirty-two cases) we could trace only rather weak or even negative effects. In thirteen cases there was a fairly strong democratization effect and in three others a medium effect. If we consider the first indicator (nobility), in almost all the cases there was a drop in this variable (with the exception of the Netherlands after 1897). The second and third indicator show, on the contrary, a declining strength in the relationship with our independent

TABLE 15.5. *Recruitment democratization after franchise enlargements*

	Nobility indicator	University indicator	High public sector indicator
Strong recruitment democratization (≥ −5%)	Hungary 1920 Italy 1913 Netherlands 1888, 1918 UK 1886	Hungary 1920 Netherlands 1888, 1897, 1918 Norway 1900 UK 1918	Netherlands 1888 Norway 1916
Intermediate recruitment democratization (≥ −2.5%−< −5.0%)	Italy 1882 UK 1918		Netherlands 1918
Weak or negative recruitment democratization (< −2.5%.)	Netherlands 1897	Denmark 1918 Italy 1882, 1913 Norway 1910, 1916, UK 1886	Denmark 1918 Hungary 1920 Italy 1882, 1913 Netherlands 1897 Norway 1900, 1910 UK 1886, 1918

Note: In case of a significant increase in turnover the year is underlined.

variable. Only in the Netherlands there is a clear and consistent association in the direction expected for education (larger enfranchisement, lower levels of university education) and also for public service (again with the exception of 1897). In the other countries the pattern is more ambiguous and in some cases there is even a negative (albeit weak) relation: extensions of suffrage are followed by higher percentages of university education and of top civil servants. Of the countries considered only the Netherlands shows the expected relationship of enfranchisement with all three indicators (except for nobility after 1897), and Hungary with the first two. In Britain and Italy there is a clear relationship only with the first one. In Denmark and Norway, where only the second and third indicator are available, the impact on them is, for the first country, practically nil or against the expectations and only partial for the second.

The data examined suggest that the extension of voting rights may have had effects upon recruitment but also that the relationship between democratization and recruitment is far from deterministic. In a good number of cases an enlargement of the electorate did not produce, at least in the short term, any significant change in the aspects of the profile of parliamentarians that we have selected. Other elements must have been at work to explain a greater or on the contrary a reduced impact of this aspect of democratization. Three other factors could be seen as relevant: the 'size' of each suffrage extension, the rate of turnover in parliamentary recruitment and the level of electoral mobilization (to be measured by turnout rates) that followed this step.

With regard to the first one the evidence is inconclusive: the size of the extension does not seem to have a clear role in determining the importance of the impact. Among the cases with the strongest level of recruitment democratization many are indeed characterized by significant extensions (but we can find also the case of the Netherlands in 1888 which is one of the smallest extensions of suffrage). However, also a good majority of the cases of low recruitment democratization are cases of significant suffrage extension.

As for the second factor it seems reasonable to hypothesize that we should expect a greater impact of the extension of suffrage upon the profile of parliamentary representation in the direction of its democratization when a more accelerated circulation of elites has taken place and the opposite when circulation has remained stable or even decreased. Using as a measure of turnover the percentage of new elected MPs at each election we can check if an extension of suffrage triggered a more intensive renewal in parliamentary representation. If we compare the situation before the extension of suffrage and afterwards, which can be done again by comparing the means of the three elections before and after, variations across countries are indeed significant (Table 15.5). The extension of suffrage is followed in a number of cases (Netherlands 1888, 1918; Italy 1913; Denmark 1918; Hungary 1920) by a noticeable increase in the rates of renewal of parliamentary representatives; in all the other ones (Italy 1882; Netherlands 1897; Norway 1916; UK 1918) the impact is however nil, or (Norway 1900, 1910 and UK 1886) even opposite to what expected. If we now compare changes in turnover rates with our measures of recruitment democratization, we find that in the majority of the cases (eight out of thirteen instances) with a high level of democratization of recruitment there was also a significant increase of turnover (Table 15.5). There are however also some exceptions (three of nine: UK 1886, 1918 and Norway 1916) where democratization of recruitment takes place without an increase of turnover or even in spite of a decrease. Vice versa if we consider the cases where democratization of recruitment was low or negative we find that in a majority of cases (eleven of sixteen instances) turnover showed a low increase or even a decrease. Summing up we can say that our expectations are broadly confirmed: in general extensions of suffrage produce greater effects upon the degree of openness of parliamentary recruitment when they are able to shake the inertia of political elites and to stimulate a faster rate of renewal. Exceptions are however far from rare.

With regard to the third factor, that is variations in turnout, our expectation was that when the extension of suffrage was followed by a significant drop in the level of vote attendance, showing thus a limited mobilization of the new enfranchised strata, democratization of recruitment should be more reduced than when participation remained constant or even increased. Our data however do not support this hypothesis: if we compare the cases where the drop in participation was significant (UK 1886, 1918; Norway 1900; Italy 1913) with those where it remained stable or even increased (Italy 1882; Netherlands 1897, 1918; Norway 1910, 1916; Denmark 1928) the differences in the impact upon our indicators of democratization of recruitment are not significant (Table 15.4).

In order to double-check the relationship between enfranchisement and democratization of recruitment we can look now to the other side of the medal—periods of stable franchise rights—to see whether during such periods the level of 'democraticness' of recruitment remained unchanged or on the contrary it underwent significant variations. In the first case the view that suffrage extensions plays a crucial role in determining the transformation of recruitment would be reinforced; in the second case we would be encouraged to look also to other factors.

We will start from countries and periods with a restricted franchise (Table 15.6). In the case of Italy we can consider two periods of unchanged franchise levels: from 1861 to 1882 and from 1882 to 1913. In the first period there is a very limited decrease of the nobility, stability of the education indicator and a somewhat greater decline of top public servants; during the second the picture does not change much: the decline of nobility increases a bit its speed while that of public servants slows down. Overall, changes during the two periods are extremely gradual. For the Netherlands we have quite a long period of observation before the first extension of suffrage: from 1849 to 1887, over almost 40 years of parliamentary life and elections, our first indicator shows almost no change (but significant oscillations around the mean) and the other two only a limited increase. This is thus a period of great stability in the profile of the representative elite. And

TABLE 15.6. *Changes in selected indicators during periods of unchanged franchise (%)*

Country and periods of unchanged franchise		Nobility	University education	Top public servants	Mean turnover rates
Denmark (35yrs.)	1849–84	n.d.	−29.3 (0.83)	−11.1 (0.32)	25.7%
Denmark (31yrs.)	1884–1915	n.d.	−9.2 (0.29)	−4.1 (0.13)	20.8%
Finland (10yrs.)	1907–17	−4.0 (0.40)	−4.5 (0.45)	−5.0 (0.50)	26.6%
France (43yrs.)	1871–1914	−14.1 (0.33)	+8.3 (0.19)	−10.1 (0.23)	37.1%
Germany (41yrs.)	1871–1912	−26.4 (0.64)	−31.2 (0.76)	−15.9 (0.39)	39.3%
Italy (19yrs.)	1861–80	−3.1 (0.16)	+0.8 (0.24)	−4.6 (0.24)	29.3%
Italy (28yrs.)	1882–1910	−6.3 (0.22)	+5.8 (0.21)	−5.3 (0.19)	26.4%
Netherlands (38yrs.)	1849–87	−0.6 (0.02)	+1.2 (0.03)	+3.4 (0.09)	16.1%
Netherlands (19yrs.)	1897–1917	−4.0 (0.20)	+3.0 (0.15)	+1.0 (0.05)	24.0.%
Norway (35yrs.)	1848–83	n.d.	−9.4 (0.26)	−21.3 (0.61)	31.4%
UK (17yrs.)	1868–85	−17.0 (1.00)	−2.1 (0.12)	−7.8 (0.46)	36.3%
UK (24yrs.)	1886–1910	−3.3 (0.14)	−0.6 (0.03)	−1.4 (0.06)	27.9%
Hungary (36yrs.)	1884–1920	−5.8 (0.16)	−0.7 (0.02)	+11.0 (0.30)	33.5%

Note: For each indicator we provide the total change of the period and within brackets the mean yearly change. The turnover rates have been calculated without counting the first election of the period: this election which has followed a suffrage extension or in some of the cases even a regime change may have had especially high levels.

if we consider the second period of unchanged franchise, which goes from the partial extension of 1897 to the universalization of male suffrage in 1917, we find again an almost complete continuity for all the three indicators.

In the UK, on the contrary, a significant decline of the weight of MPs with an aristocratic background takes place before the extension of suffrage of 1886. A decline which is much steeper than the one in the twenty-four years following the franchise reform of 1886. As for the other indicators we have significant changes only for the size of top public servants in the first of the two periods. Of the two periods the first is, therefore, to be considered one of important transformations, while the second is more one of continuity (but change becomes more significant if we add the indicator of blue-collar workers which shows a sizable growth). For Denmark we have split the long period of substantially unchanged franchise into two sub-periods (from 1849 to 1883 and from 1884 to 1915); the most important changes take place during the first period and concern both indicators available: university education and percentage top levels of the civil service decline substantially. The second period is, on the contrary, one of more limited change which affects mainly university education. In Norway between 1848 and 1883 we have a strong decline of high civil servants and a more limited one for university education.

Let us examine now some of the countries which have reached, at a comparative early stage, a large or universal (male) suffrage, such as France and Germany. To maintain some elements of comparability with the other countries we will examine them only for the period extending until the First World War. We have already noticed how different the two parliaments are since the beginning from the point of view of their social composition, with Germany much more characterized by an aristocratic recruitment and by the weight of university education and high public service. If we now examine what happens with the passing of time, we find some interesting results. In the German case the original paradox (an aristocratic representation with a democratic franchise) weakens with the passing of time: a significant decline takes place both for the nobility and for the university education indicator. Dividing the period between 1871 and the First World War in two sub-periods, initially (187–87) the decline is somewhat slower for nobility, but more intense for university education; later (1887–1912) the speed of change almost doubles for nobility but slows down a little for education. In both sub-periods there is also a more or less constant decline for the third indicator. In the French case the decline of the nobility (from levels which were from the beginning quite lower) develops rather steadily; but it is somewhat stronger at the beginning and slower in the second period. There is also a moderate decline in the weight of high public servants. Contrary to the German case, the impact of time on education is nil or opposite to what expected: the rate of parliamentarians with a university degree keeps rising throughout this period. The interpretation that can be offered to this phenomenon is probably the following: a bourgeois and intellectual recruitment challenges with increasing success the remnants of the old regime, but prevents also the lower classes from making more significant inroads into representative assemblies.

To these two countries we can add Finland. During the shorter period of universal suffrage before the war (1907–17) all three indicators show a fairly significant decline.

Table 15.7 summarizes the main findings of our analysis. As we have seen the results are mixed. Processes of democratization of recruitment have developed even during periods of unchanged franchise: but not in all countries with the same speed and not in all countries with the same effects on the three indicators we have proposed. A clear majority of the cases (twenty-two of thirty-six) fall into the lowest category of change. This confirms the expectations that without an extension of the voting rights the established elites could defend their hold on power with considerable success and that transformations were at best slow. Among our cases Italy is particularly noteworthy for the almost complete resistance of its recruitment patterns to any democratization during both the periods examined. The same applies to the Netherlands until 1887 and again between 1897 and 1917, and to the UK between 1886 and 1910.

There is, however, also a significant number of cases where a sustained (or at least intermediate) pace of change developed even without extensions of franchise. Among the countries that had not reached universal suffrage before the First World War we can count the cases of the UK between 1868 and 1886 (with regards to the first and third indicator), of Denmark in the years 1849–84 (second and third indicator) and 1884–1915 (second indicator), of Norway between 1848 and 1883 (second and third indicator).

TABLE 15.7. *Recruitment democratization during periods of unchanged franchise*

	Nobility indicator	University indicator	High public sector indicator
Strong recruitment democratization ($\geq$ −0.50 per year)	Germany <u>1871–1912</u> UK <u>1868–85</u>	Denmark 1849–84 Germany <u>1871–1912</u>	Finland 1907–17 Norway 1848–83
Intermediate recruitment democratization ($\geq$ −0.25–> −0.50)	Finland 1907–17 France <u>1871–1914</u>	Denmark 1884–1915 Finland 1907–17 Norway 1848–83	Denmark 1849–84 Germany <u>1871–1912</u> UK <u>1868–85</u>

Weak recruitment democratization ($<$ −0.25 per year)	Hungary 1884–1920
	Italy 1861–81,
	   1882–1910
	NL 1849–87,
	   1897–1917
	UK 1886–1910
		France <u>1871–1914</u>
		Hungary 1884–1920
		Italy 1861–81,
		   1882–1910
		NL 1849–87,
		   1897–1917
		UK 1868–85,
		   1886–1910
			Denmark
			1884–1915
			France <u>1871–1914</u>
			Hungary 1884–1920
			Italy 1861–81,
			   1882–1910
			NL 1849–87,
			   1897–1917
			UK 1886–1910

Note: The cases where mean turnover was $\geq$ 35% are underlined.

A different story is that of the three countries—France, Germany and Finland—that had reached 'immediately' universal male suffrage. Here, when considering the period of 'suffrage rights continuity', we are obviously talking of a situation when all possible extensions of (male) suffrage are already behind and electoral democratization has been attained.[11] The first two countries show more or less an opposite 'behaviour'. Germany is at first obviously a laggard with regards to democratization of its parliamentary recruitment, but during this period will reduce significantly the distances through a vigorous process of change. On the contrary France, which was clearly ahead from the beginning on all three indicators will change only rather more slowly (or show, as in the case of the education indicator, even an opposite trend). The two countries probably represent two opposite models of abrupt (electoral) democratization. Germany is a case of democratization from above, whereby the traditional establishment maintains initially a full control of the representative institution and only with time accommodates new political elites. France is on the contrary one of democratization from below with (repeated) breakdowns of the traditional establishment: parliamentary representation is thus from the beginnings less under the imprint of the characters of the past, but as a result change will later be slower. Finland indicates the possibility of a third way: a very limited weight of the traditional establishment from the beginning, but even so a fairly significant pace of democratization.

Combining these findings with the previous ones we can confirm that the linkage between democratization of recruitment (at least as measured by our indicators) and extensions of the right to vote is far from being a mechanical and short-term one. The cases where an expansion of suffrage produced also in a relatively short time a democratization of recruitment are balanced by cases where the effects were very weak or nil. On the other hand, we have ascertained that even if the lack of suffrage extensions normally leaves patterns of recruitment unchanged there are also cases where significant transformations happen during periods of unchanged franchise. To some extent this could be explained as the delayed effects of an extension of suffrage taking place before the beginning of that period. These data confirms in general the significant inertia of recruitment patterns. This inertia is obviously stronger when institutional rules are not changed; but our analysis suggests that at least on the short-term established political elites are often able to maintain a strong degree of control on recruitment even when challenged by institutional changes that open the access to larger strata of the population. The limitations to the (short term) impact of suffrage extensions are confirmed also by the fact that, in a majority of cases, suffrage extensions are not followed by a sizable increase in the rate of renewal of parliamentary representatives. As shown by our data this intervening variable is rather important to explain democratization of recruitment: when the quantitative rate of renewal of parliament is stronger a qualitative change in the direction of a more open recruitment is also more probable.

Having seen the impact of democratization of suffrage upon democratization of recruitment (and its limits) it is time to explore another aspect in the transformation of representation in democratic countries: that of professionalization. The changes the representative game has undergone under the conditions of an enlarged political citizenship and the new requirements its actors have had to face both on the input side—where the ability to connect with wider and more varied strata of voters in the electoral and social arenas was at stake—and on the output side—where it was the capacity to stand a much heavier decision-making work-load in the representative institutions—have produced a demand of skills, knowledge, resources that are not necessarily at the disposal of those who are most 'similar' to the represented. A profile fitting with these new requirements may be produced by certain occupational backgrounds which are particularly compatible with a more intense political activity and by a more intense and prolonged political experience before the first parliamentary election. The percentage of MPs with an occupational background as teachers, professors, journalists and writers, with a party office or multiple political experiences (in local elective offices, in the party organizations, etc.) before entering parliament, and the frequency of full-time politicians are possible indicators of political professionalization. Our data broadly support the view that these types of backgrounds should gain more importance with the process of democratization. Considering the period 1870–1930, the extension of suffrage is positively correlated with the frequency of occupations such as that of teacher and professor, journalist and writer, with a pure political profession and with an extensive political experience before the first election of MPs (Table 15.2). But if we examine in a more detailed way the effects of specific suffrage extensions on these variables we see that they are neither immediate nor automatic.[12]

These results suggest that also for this component of recruitment we have to look for a somewhat more complex model of relationship between institutional transformations and features of the parliamentary elites.

15.5.2. *The Formation of the Twentieth-Century Party Systems and the Incorporation of the New Mass Parties*

The extension of suffrage was from the institutional point of view the crucial transformation in the process of democratization, but on a political level its importance was matched and perhaps even surpassed by the process of formation of new parties and by the consequent transformation of the party systems which eventually led to what Stein Rokkan has called the freezing of party alternatives and to the dominance of fairly stable party alignments throughout a good part of the twentieth century (Lipset and Rokkan 1967; Bartolini and Mair 1990).

The formation of the developed party systems of the twentieth century is obviously a rather complex and multifaceted process. We will not try here to discuss all of its aspects. We will rather concentrate our attention on the most important one: the birth and growth of the class parties of the left. It is difficult to deny that this has been a central factor in the reshaping of the original party systems of the early phase of democratization, and that their full development, together with the accomplishment of their incorporation as legitimate political partners, has contributed to the long-term stabilization of political alignments. The growth of these parties has played a crucial role in the political mobilization of the lower classes and the promotion of their interests, has contributed significantly to the development of new contents and styles of representation and has deeply challenged the power of established elites. With regards to the sphere of political recruitment it has also typically meant a significant inflow not just of new but also of different parliamentarians.

The development of left parties at the electoral and organizational level has been widely analysed by an endless number of case studies and has received a systematic in-depth comparative analysis in the recent work of Bartolini (2000). A significant amount of data concerning this specific component of the modern party systems is therefore available. We will try to make use of it to evaluate the impact of this phenomenon in the field of parliamentary representation, specifying at first what are the reasons for expecting significant transformations in the profiles of elected representatives following the growth of the new socialist (and in some cases communist) parties. We will then formulate some alternative hypotheses.

The first most obvious reason, which can be derived from a 'bottom up', mirroring view of representation, is that these parties reflected a new demand of representation: large strata of the population, which had been previously excluded from political life and which shared interests that until that time had not been taken into account (or at best only partially), found in the socialist parties their channel of representation. This demand could be expressed (also) through representatives that shared the background of the represented or at least were less distant from their social profile. Things however can be seen also from a different and 'top down' perspective. In fact mobilizing and representing the working classes was quite another job than representing the upper and middle classes. It required developing innovative forms of organization, which could turn the newly enfranchised citizens from passive subjects into active participants by compensating for the more limited resources which would have otherwise handicapped them in the field of political action. Organized parties and trade unions have therefore gained a crucial role in representation and it was from within the ranks of these organizations that a large part of the representatives were drawn. The parliamentarians should therefore be 'organization men' more than 'men of the people' (Michels 1911) or rather men of the people inasmuch as they have become involved in the party organizations. Their profile should thus reflect their organizational background.

If the first interpretation applies, the opening of the electoral gates to the working classes and the success of class parties should entail a significant growth of MPs with a working-class background and low levels of education. If the second prevails other features will be more significant: for instance we will find a stronger component of MPs which are fully or partially employees of the party and its organizations.

In order to assess the impact of the development of socialist parties upon political representation we will start from their electoral and parliamentary success and we will try to establish how the composition of parliaments has changed with the progressive growth of their fortunes. But is this enough? Some doubts can be voiced. The electoral (and parliamentary) growth of socialist parties may not be the only relevant variable. Another aspect at least should be considered: their organizational density. As we have said one of the particularly innovative traits of socialist parties has been the new organizational forms that they have adopted contributing to a new model of party. It is well known however that this overall picture hides important differences among socialist parties: their organizational strength shows substantial variations. The ratio of party members to party voters is a simple tool to evaluate these differences. Using this measure it has been shown that the organizational density of socialist parties has varied significantly (Bartolini 2000: 300ff). Given what we have said about the role of organization in parliamentary recruitment we should expect a visible impact of this variable upon the profile of representatives.

We will therefore first check the relationship between parliamentary strength of socialist parties and elite profiles, then add the organizational strength as an intervening variable. If we concentrate our attention on the six decades between 1870 and 1930 which is the crucial period of Socialist growth we find that the electoral and parliamentary weight of Socialist parties are significantly correlated with most of the variables we have used to characterize the profile of parliamentary elites (Table 15.2). The electoral size of left parties is positively correlated with the frequency of low education levels, with the percentage of working-class MPs, of journalists and writers, teachers and professors, of full-time politicians, and with parliamentary seniority and negatively correlated with the weight of nobility and university education, with the percentage of lawyers and age. For what concerns indicators both of democratization and of professionalization of recruitment these results fit therefore with our expectations. If instead of using the electoral success we run the same correlations for the parliamentary size of Socialist parties the results are not too different except for education.

Are the effects similarly strong across countries? We will explore also for this factor its relationship with our dependent variables on a country by country basis. More specifically we will check to what extent a step up in the parliamentary weight of socialist parties has coincided with significant variations in the democraticness and professionalization of recruitment. For this purpose we have defined a sequence of thresholds in the size of the parliamentary groups of this party family and analysed to what extent, in the elections following the overcoming of the thresholds, significant changes in our dependent variables could be detected. Overall the results (see Table 15.8) go in the direction expected. The indicators of democraticness of recruitment (both negative—nobility and university education—and positive—basic education and working-class background) show in general that an increasing opening of recruitment parallels the growth of the socialist parties; but the intensity of change is not the same everywhere. At one extreme of the spectrum we have Germany where three indicators out of four confirm a very strong democratization (only the number of blue-collar workers increases but slowly). Denmark, Norway, the Netherlands, and the UK show a similar, albeit somewhat weaker, trend on two or more indicators (with a particularly strong rise of blue-collar workers in the UK and Norway, and a decline of university education in the Dutch parliament). At the opposite extreme we have France and Italy where the only significant effect concerns the nobility indicator. It is worth mentioning the case of Finland which appears in our data-set only after having passed the highest threshold of Socialist seats. In this case we do not have a trend but just one time point: on all indicators, however, we have among the highest levels of democratization of recruitment.

The impact of Socialist growth is thus significant but uneven across countries. While in some countries there is a clear effect of democratization in the other ones the effect is more limited and does not seem to open very much the access of representation to the lower classes.

If we look now at indicators of professionalization (percentage of journalists and writers, of full-time politicians, and of MPs with a party office before the first election) we find a pattern which is not too different. In all the countries our indicators show with the passing of the subsequent thresholds some growth of

TABLE 15.8. *Left parties growth and indicators of recruitment democratization and professionalization before the Second World War*

Left seats	University education					Basic education					Nobility					Blue-collar workers				
	<10%	>10%	>20%	30%+	40+	<10	10+	20+	30+	40+	<10	10+	20+	30+	40+	<10	10+	20+	30+	40+
Dk	27.4	15.6	15.6	20.9	20.3	48.8	67.5	64.0	59.0	62.5	NA	NA	NA	NA	NA	3.0	3.0	—	—	1.5
Nor	27.0	30.4	32.8	28.5	23.6	27.1	29.6	34.1	32.1	33.8	NA	NA	NA	NA	NA	—	3.0	4.3	6.0	10.3
Fin	n.d.	n.d.	n.d.	n.d.	31.8	n.d.	n.d.	n.d.	n.d.	45.0	37.3	23.7	n.d.	n.d.	4.5	n.d.	n.d.	n.d.	n.d.	10.5
Ger	81.6	57.2	55.0	n.d.	36.0	1.3	13.6	16.2	n.d.	35.2	17.7	12.9	17.5	n.d.	2.9	—	0.5	0.4	n.d.	3.0
UK	54.8	48.2	47.3	43.9	46.0	39.6	42.2	43.9	47.1	44.0	17.7	12.9	13.3	14.1	12.9	5.1	11.8	16.9	21.3	25.9
Neth.	68.7	63.5	46.0	n.d.	n.d.	13.0	5.5	13.0	n.d.	n.d.	17.3	14.0	8.7	n.d.	n.d.	—	—	—	n.d.	n.d.
Fran	60.0	67.3	60.9	n.d.	n.d.	37.5	26.7	31.3	n.d.	n.d.	9.6	6.2	3.9	n.d.	n.d.	0.5	2.5	3.8	n.d.	n.d.
Italy	74.3	77.3	n.d.	75.1	n.d.	NA	NA	NA	NA	NA	25.0	17.1	n.d.	8.6	n.d.	0.1	0.8	n.d.	1.6	n.d.

	Journalists					Politicians					Party position				
	<10	10+	20+	30+	40+	<10	10+	20+	30+	40+	<10	10+	20+	30+	40+
Dk	9.6	14.5	18.6	21.5	15.5	2.6	—	2.7	3.5	8.4	2.6	8.0	13.6	25.6	42.0
Nor	3.3	4.1	6.2	6.6	6.0	NA	0.5	4.5	5.0	4.0	NA	NA	NA	NA	NA
Fin.	n.d.	n.d.	n.d.	n.d.	18.3	n.d.	n.d.	n.d.	n.d.	13.3	n.d.	n.d.	n.d.	n.d.	14.6
Ger.	5.6	9.0	13.1	n.d.	14.0	6.1	4.7	10.3	n.d.	33.3	6.1	12.4	20.4	n.d.	59.7
UK	6.0	5.9	8.2	10.6	8.0	NA	4.0	11.3	11.0	13.0	NA	NA	NA	NA	NA
Neth.	1.3	9.0	9.0	n.d.	n.d.	47.0	4.5	10.3	n.d.	n.d.	47.0	49.5	50.5	54.4	54.5
Fran	5.9	7.8	7.3	n.d.	n.d.	0.9	0.8	1.0	n.d.	n.d.	0.9	7.0	11.3	n.d.	n.d.
Italy	3.0	2.0	n.d.	5.6	n.d.	NA	1.8	n.d.	5.8	n.d.	NA	NA	NA	NA	NA

Note: NA: data unavailable; nd: no data because this level of party vote is not attained.

professionalization. Variations are however not irrelevant. The strongest pattern, with a very substantial increase on all three indicators, can be found again in Germany. The trend is also sufficiently neat for Denmark (for all three indicators) and the Netherlands (for the two available ones). It is visible but weaker in Norway, France, Italy, and the UK. In these cases however the lack of data for a number of indicators weakens our conclusions.

If we add into this picture not just the size of Socialist parliamentary representation but also the organizational density of these parties (as measured by the ratio of members per voters), we find an interesting factor that contributes to explain differences among countries. Denmark, Finland, Germany, and Norway are, in the period covered, the countries with the highest levels of density, while the Netherlands, France, and Italy show the lowest levels (Bartolini 2000: 240 ff). The UK apparently falls in the second group, but mainly because the indirect and collective structure of the Labour party makes the direct individual party membership less relevant; if one were to count trade union members the organizational density would be much greater. We can thus add to our findings that, where the density of party organization is weaker, the impact of the growth of the socialist parties upon democratization and professionalization of recruitment is also more limited.

15.5.3. *A Multivariate Analysis*

At the end of this discussion on the potential causes of the transformations within the parliamentary elite profiles in Europe during the phase of democratization, we have attempted to build a more comprehensive explanatory model. This was done by way of a number of multivariate analyses using as dependent variables the measures of parliamentary elite profiles included in our data-set, and as possible explanatory factors a wider set of political and social variables, including other data collected in the context of our project (an election counter starting with the first universal male suffrage,[13] the type of electoral system,)[14] or by other authors (electoral turnout by Caramani 2000; organizational density of left parties, enfranchisement, literacy by Bartolini 2000).

We have tried to select *the strongest explanatory factors* of the elite profile changes during the crucial phase of democratization (1870–1930), exploring a number of models where the dependent variables are the DATACUBE variables showing, within that period, a clear and significant correlation with a number of indicators of institutional change and emergence of a class-party model. The main findings of our exploration are presented in the Tables 15.9 and 15.10, concerning, respectively, the factors of 'democratization' of MPs profiles and those who clearly indicate a political professionalization of the elites under analysis. The data for the first group of models say that it is quite difficult to find *one only* perceptible factor of the elite transformation: the decline of university background can be explained both with the left party density but also with a societal factor like

TABLE 15.9. *Factors of democratization of parliamentary elites*

	Mod I Dep. Var.: University background			Mod II Dep. Var.: Nobility			Mod III Dep. Var.: Higher civil servants			Mod IV Dep. Var.: Lawyers		
	Beta	T	Sig.	Beta	T	Sig.	Beta	T	Sig.	Beta	T	Sig.
(Constant)		7.834	.000		1.869	.074		.954	.345		15.253	.000
Election counter starting with universal male suffrage	.066	.514	.609	-.067	-.497	.624	-.474	-2.452	.018	-.003	-.024	.981
Organizational density of Left parties	-.575	-5.984	.000	-.262	-2.639	.015	-.280	-1.941	.058	-.074	-.928	.358
Percentage of communist and socialist seats	-.138	-.969	.338	-.246	-1.455	.159	-.460	-2.156	.036	.160	1.358	.181
Percentage of population able to read and write	-.492	-4.681	.000	.330	2.460	.022	-.197	.995	.325	-1.049	12.029	.000
Electorate as percentage of adult population (over 20 years)	.021	.116	.908	-.496	-2.430	.023	.903	2.497	.016	.486	3.245	.002
Type of electoral system (lower chamber)	-.064	-.516	.609	-.059	-.497	.624	-.960	2.636	.011	-.494	-4.803	.000
Turnout (lower chamber elections)	.218	2.107	.040	-.166	-1.373	.183	-.177	-.217	.829	.137	1.595	.117

Mod I: R = .878; R² = .771; Adjusted R² = .738; St. error of estimate = 10.8

Denmark and Norway were excluded because of missing data

Mod II: R = .933; R² = .870; Adjusted R² = .830; St. error of estimate = 5.1

Mod III: R = .695; R² = .484; Adjusted R² = .410; St. error of estimate = 3.9

Mod IV: R = .918; R² = .842; Adjusted R² = .8119; St. error of estimate = 4.3

Note: 1870–1929 Linear regression analyses.

TABLE 15.10. *Factors of 'political professionalization' or parliamentary elites*

	Mod I Dep. Var.: Local political background			Mod II Dep. Var.: Full paid politicians			Mod III Dep. Var.: Journalist/writers			Mod IV Dep. Var.: Teachers/professors		
	Beta	T	Sig.	Beta	T	Sig.	Beta	T	Sig.	Beta	T	Sig.
(Constant)		1.642	.107		−1.768	.083		−1.105	.275		1.294	.202
Election counter starting with universal male suffrage	.453	2.042	.047	−.559	−3.723	.001	−.209	−1.537	.131	.152	.757	.453
Organizational density of Left parties	.172	2.647	.006	.359	3.202	.002	.488	4.808	.000	.522	3.489	.001
Percentage of communist and socialist seats	.378	1.545	.129	.731	4.413	.000	.630	4.195	.000	−.173	−.783	.437
Percentage population able to read and write	.244	1.348	.184	.121	.991	.327	.126	1.138	.261	.052	.321	.750
Electorate as percentage of adult population (over 20 years)	−.192	−.619	.539	.393	1.871	.067	−.381	−2.001	.051	−.462	−1.646	.106
Type of electoral system (lower chamber)	.388	1.818	.075	.145	1.005	.320	.075	.572	.570	.619	3.209	.002
Turnout (lower chamber)	−.297	−1.672	.101	−.014	−.113	.910	.144	1.319	.193	−.113	−.705	.484

$R = .567$
$R^2 = .321$
Adjusted $R^2 = .224$
St. error of estimate = 13.4

Netherlands was excluded because data are not homogeneous

$R = .830$
$R^2 = .688$
Adjusted $R^2 = .644$
St. error of estimate = 5.5

$R = .826$
$R^2 = .744$
Adjusted $R^2 = .707$
St. error of estimate = 3.0

$R = .677$
$R^2 = .445$
Adjusted $R^2 = .366$
St. error of estimate = 4.3

Note: 1870–1929. Linear regression analyses.

degree of literacy (the latter being, surprisingly, also the strongest explanatory factor of the decline of lawyers among MPs). At the same time, the two other declining trends related to the process of elite democratization (presence of higher civil servants and nobility) present a quite mixed and confusing grid of potential explanatory factors.

On the other hand, all the indicators of political professionalization (unfortunately we cannot add the party office background for a series of data inconsistencies) are clearly explained by the emergence of a new type of parliamentary representation, namely, that of the 'class party' of Marxist tradition. As expected, the increase of the parliamentary representation of the left parties (communist and/or socialists) is the most likely factor for the explanation of the increase of full paid politicians in European parliaments, while another factor of party change, the organizational density of left parties, provides a quite robust explanation of the other dependent variables used here (local elective backgrounds of MPs and two occupational backgrounds which are clearly associated to political professionalism, such as that of journalist and teacher/professor).

The control by dummy (country-specific) variables did not provide a significant result for all these models, but from a number of descriptive statistical controls we can anyway argue that the country factor plays a decisive role in most of the variables under analysis, particularly those related the 'elite democratization' process.

This exploration with the help of multivariate analyses cannot of course say a definitive word for the explanation of the parliamentary elite transformation before the Second World War. However, we can argue, with a certain degree of empirical support, that the most important signs of political professionalism have to be linked to the simple but crucial phenomenon of the appearance of the new mass parties (typically the left-class parties), which historically 'followed' the first signs of elite democratization (more or less related to different institutional factors, including of course enfranchisement), but gave the parliamentary elite transformation a decisive push. Or at least, the effect of the mass-party emergence looks much more 'transversal' than those determined by other institutional factors, across the different European countries. These parties have brought with them a largely new and professionalized political elite and have, in the end, determined an evident 'contagion effect' even within the parliamentary groups of the other parties.

15.6. BETWEEN DISCONTINUITY AND ADAPTATION: THE EFFECTS OF REGIME CHANGES ON THE EUROPEAN PARLIAMENTARY ELITES OF THE LATE TWENTIETH CENTURY

So far, we have discussed the linkage between continuous institutional and political change and parliamentary elite profiles during the processes of first democratization and the emergence of a mass-party based democracy in Europe. We will now consider the impact of more discontinuous transformations such as the occurrence of interruptions of the democratic experience or of other changes altering deeply the overall institutional scenario.

Of course, a number of phenomena could be potentially listed here as 'significant intervening variables': constitutional reforms, introduction of new regulations concerning electoral procedures; strong electoral and party system dealignments, and phases of leadership turnover. Among these systemic factors we will concentrate our attention only upon those representing the most critical junctures of democratic history and not upon those responsible only of 'smooth and long-term changes'. The effects of some of these phenomena, in particular the long-term impact of societal changes and of the transformation of party organizations, have been already discussed elsewhere in this volume. For instance, the chapter by Fiers and Secker, analyses the effects of the 'cartelization' of political parties, thus explaining in terms of the evolution of political professionalism a rather general transformation of all parliamentary elites in Europe. On the other hand, some chapters devoted to specific party families have stressed recent widespread phenomena of parliamentary elite transformation,[15] such as the de-ideologization of mass parties, which have been conducive to different patterns of recruitment, and in particular to the broadening of the social and occupational profile of MPs and to its growing variability. In the next pages we will try to see to what extent the effects of democratic interruptions and of 'intra-democratic transformations' upon parliamentary recruitment should be considered alternative or complementary to other 'local' or country-specific explanations.

The first aspect we will consider is the impact produced by democratic discontinuities on the processes of parliamentary recruitment. The assumption here is that countries having to deal with a breakdown of democracy, a non-democratic phase and then a democratic reconstruction, should display some specific differences in the developmental trends of their parliamentary elites as compared to the countries where democratization was a continuous process. In particular we will expect a more incremental and moderate process of change for the latter and greater and more abrupt transformations for the former. To assess these differences we will compare the two groups of countries on a number of different dimensions.

The second aspect we shall consider are differences among discontinuous countries. The original assumption must be refined to take into account the variability—in particular in terms of duration and transformative intensity—of the periods of democratic interruption. We can therefore expect that their impact will not be the same. Two parallel hypotheses will guide us: the first that *the longer the phase of non-democratic regime, the greater will be the discontinuity and change in the overall profile of the new democratic elite compared to the old*. The second that *the greater the depth of the non-democratic experience the greater also will be elite discontinuity*.

We will then analyse political changes occurring in a context of democratic continuity, arguing that even a strong 'intra-democratic transformation' could determine a critical change in the profiles of parliamentary elite. Constitutional changes or robust innovations in the electoral systems are in fact very often accompanied (or caused) by explicit requests to change the 'ruling elite'. The actual impact of such changes in the processes of elite formation and circulation is not sufficiently discussed in the literature on democratic changes and should receive a better attention.

These points suggest a series of theoretical questions which cannot be exhaustively explored in the space of this chapter and with the limited empirical support of our data-set. Our data however enables us to make some steps towards assessing the linkage between democratic crises and parliamentary elite transformations. Figure 15.10 presents the range of variations in terms of regime and institutional change among the countries covered in our research. A first clear divide is to be seen between discontinuous and continuous democracies. Among the countries of the first group, five experienced a democratic breakdown during the *entre-deux-guerres* period.[16] In the case of Hungary, which after a short revolutionary episode, just after its birth as an independent country, had experienced until 1940 a more or less continuous period of 'limited democracy', the short democratic revival at the end of the Second World War was brought to an end in 1948 with the establishment of the communist regime. However, we will not cover here this last case, whose peculiarities for what concerns the comparison between pre-communist and post-communist democracies would require a more specific discussion.

The countries forming the group of 'continuous democracies' in our panel can be treated as a fairly homogeneous core of polities where the democratic model has not been under serious discussion during the last eighty years. This is confirmed also by the fact that they do not present either what we have called 'intra-democratic transformations'. On the contrary, two countries of the first group—France and Italy—have experienced also serious intra-democratic crises/realignments: in France the transition from the Fourth to the Fifth Republic, but also the short lived 'experiment' of the reintroduction (only for the general election of 1986) of a PR system; in Italy the introduction of a mixed-majoritarian electoral system, which has coincided in 1993–4 with a fundamental reorganization of the party system.

The nature of the institutional changes summarized in the figure is varied, but a similar twofold problem emerges with regard to the effects of these phenomena on the long-term transformations of parliamentary elites. First of all, one should ask to what extent a critical event, such as a political transition, can determine 'immediate' effects (for instance, a high rate of parliamentary turnover, or the rise of a specific type of politicians), or more long lasting innovations. We could seek here guidance in the neo-institutional literature, which considers political processes as path dependent and stresses the elements of inertia to be explained with the 'status quo bias' of political institutions (Pierson 2004). In the analysis of representative elites this question has not yet received the attention it deserves. Secondly, one should explore how a democratic interruption, beside creating the

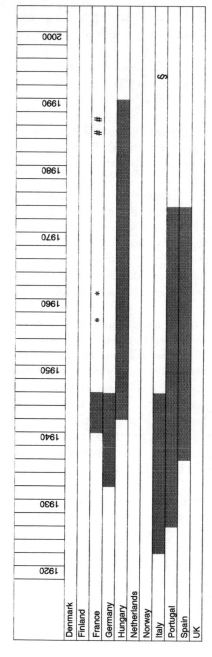

FIGURE 15.10. Regime crises or interruptions in eleven European countries (1920–2005)

Notes:

■ Democratic interruption and abolition of the parliamentary rule;

* Instauration of a new semi-presidential form of government in France (1958–62);

Introduction of PR electoral system in France (1986) and return to plurality system (1988);

§ Introduction of a Mixed-majoritarian electoral system in Italy and party system crisis (1994).

conditions for certain specific characters of the new parliamentary elite, can also influence the process of consolidation of the new parliamentary elite, which may take a more or less prolonged period of time.

15.6.1. *Continuous versus Discontinuous Democracies: What Differences?*

Unfortunately, the available data can only partially help us to answer the above mentioned questions. Indeed, we have to cope both with the lack of extensive control (we cannot count on the same standard information for all the countries) and also with a not fully adequate type of data, since the DATACUBE file has been built having basically in mind indicators for democratic continuity. Nevertheless, some interesting hints about the impact of democratic interruptions on parliamentary recruitment can be discussed.

Does democratic discontinuity make a difference in the long-term transformation of parliamentary profile? This is the first question to be raised. Two variables included in our data-set can tell whether the presence of a democratic crisis becomes a fundamental reason of instability of the parliamentary elites: these variables are turnover (or the percentage of newcomers in a parliamentary term) and seniority (measured as the mean number of elections of the members of a parliament). In all the countries characterized by democratic continuity these indicators are extremely stable between 1920 and 1970, with the mean turnover being lower than 25 per cent and the mean seniority higher than three elections. On the contrary, they become typically unstable in the other group of countries, not only (as perfectly expected) in the first legislatures after a democratic interruption, but also in the following ones. The rate of newcomers in the discontinuous democracies is 57.4 per cent in the three post-authoritarian legislatures and goes to 35.0 in the following ones, while concerning the mean number of re-elections, the measures are respectively of 1.7 and 2.6.

As expected, a regime discontinuity produces also a discontinuity in the parliamentary elites. However, if we make the same exercise not with the variables concerning the institutional entrenchment of parliamentary elites but with variables concerning the social and political profile of MPs, we do not find the same differences between continuous and discontinuous democracies. All the tests we have conducted on three crucial occupational variables—the percentage of parliamentarians coming form the legal profession, with a public sector background, or a full-time political job—gave negative results. The trends observed for the discontinuous democracies after the Second World War are very close to those of the continuous democracies in the same historical phase (with a decline of lawyers and party functionaries and a revitalization of public sector background).

This seems to suggest that, beyond the necessary renewal of political representatives, which, after the longest and/or deepest democratic interruptions which had created a 'generation gap' in the political elites, can take the form of a total turnover, there is not on the middle-term a similarly strong effect at the level of parliamentary profiles. Other reasons, for instance country specific and/or party family specific factors, should therefore be found in order to explain the variability in these aspects.

15.6.2. *Variations among Discontinuous Countries: The Impact of the Duration and Depth of the Authoritarian/Totalitarian Rule*

We will now compare more in details the discontinuous cases in order to assess the impact of the differences in their experience. The breakdown of democracy and the advent of an authoritarian or totalitarian regimes entail first a suspension for a given period of the working of the normal democratic processes (and among them also of the process of parliamentary recruitment) and secondly a period of operation of a different type of regime. This means that we should consider two potential effects of this period: on one side that of the passing of time on the other side that of the impact on social and political life of the regime. Duration and intensity of the non-democratic regime are thus the two dimensions to be considered.

With regard to the two cases of re-democratization at the end of the 1970s in the Iberian countries the specialist literature has stressed the totally new scenario, for the political elites that have emerged from the transition, in comparison with the last 'proto-democratic' elites of the 1920s and 1930s (cf. Linz, Gangas, and Jerez Mir 2000; Magone 2000). We will therefore concentrate our attention upon the three cases—France, Germany, and Italy—where democracy was re-established at the end of the Second World War. More than the pure length of the democratic interruptions it is the nature of the non-democratic regime and maybe other factors that seem to be decisive in determining how deep was the reshaping of parliamentary elites after the interruption. We can argue this on the basis of a simple exercise of comparison on some selected variables (Table 15.11). As one can easily see, when analysing differences between the average values for the three elections before the democratic interruptions and the first three elections after re-democratization, the most evident signs of change occur in Germany. If one compares with Italy, where the non-democratic *intermezzo* was about twice as long, it appears that the duration of the regime was not the crucial factor. The comparison between France and Italy is also interesting. The fact that changes were equally or even more significant in the first country seems to confirm that the length of the interruption (only four years in France as compared to more than twenty in Italy) was not so important. Probably other factors such as the degree of continuity/discontinuity between pre-authoritarian and post-authoritarian party systems should be brought into the explanation.

If we use all the available information on parliamentary profiles, building a simple index of change defined as the sum (in absolute values) for each variable of differences between the means observed before and after the democratic break, we

TABLE 15.11. *Parliamentary elites features before and after democratic interruptions (%)*

	University or comparable degree	Local/ regional political background	Other leading party position	Teachers and professors	Politicians	Public sector employees	Lawyers
Germany							
Before the break	32.4	22.7	52.5	6.4	40.1	17.6	2.4
After the break	51.9	38.8	25.3	6.8	14.5	38.1	7.9
Difference	*+19.4*	*+16.1*	*−27.2*	*+0.5*	*−25.6*	*+20.5*	*+5.5*
Italy							
Before the break	74.7	n.d.	n.d.	16.4	5.7	24.0	37.5
After the break	75.7	45.0	75.0	18.3	19.5	25.8	28.1
Difference	*+1.0*	*−*	*−*	*+1.9*	*+14.4*	*+1.8*	*−9.4*
France							
Before the break	51.2	74.7	17.9	11.4	1.7	18.8	23.6
After the break	39.4	n.d.	n.d.	17.5	n.d.	26.8	15.3
Difference	*−11.8*	*—*	*—*	*+6.0*	*—*	*+8.0*	*−8.3*

Note: Differences in selected indicators (%).

can confirm the relatively weak effect of the length of the authoritarian duration. Germany has indeed an average difference of 16.4 per cent, showing again the strongest degree of change; France follows with 7.2 per cent and Italy with 5.7 per cent. The German case suggests that, more than the duration of the interruption, other factors, such as the intensity of the social and political earthquake produced by the Nazi regime explain the amount of change. To this perhaps should be added the conditions surrounding the end of the democratic interruption, in particular the fact that the re-establishment of democratic rule in Germany was strongly controlled by external forces. In Italy, beside the weaker penetration of the authoritarian regime, one could add the fact that the rebirth of a pluralistic party system during the last years of the war was more autonomous and the role it played during the transition greater; this possibly produced greater elements of continuity with the pre-authoritarian past. The fact that, twenty-two years after the last general elections, the members of the new democratic parliament were to a great extent beginners (Cotta 1982), was somewhat balanced by that element of continuity. On the contrary in France, the passage from the Third to the Fourth Republic was, in spite of the short time elapsed, relatively more dramatic in terms of party system and institutional change.

Another aspect we have to discuss in order to assess the impact of the processes of re-democratization is the ability of the new democratic systems to produce in a relatively short time the reconsolidation of its parliamentary elite. A systematic analysis of this dimension would require additional data about the consolidation of the party system and the persistence of a 'pool of candidates' to the most important national representative office. Some relevant hints emerge however from our comparative data-set. These hints, which can be connected to the classic dimensions of parliamentary elite institutionalization as defined by Nelson Polsby (1968), concern the reduction of elite turnover and the stabilization of the new post-authoritarian generation of representatives.

In order to assess correctly the impact of regime discontinuity we must distinguish it from that of other disruptive events, such as the Second World War, which have affected also continuous democracies. The data on parliamentary turnover in the elections after the Second World War (Table 15.12) confirm the expectation that also such events can have a significant impact upon parliamentary

TABLE 15.12. *Measures of parliamentary elite consolidation after a democratic interruption*

	Year	Mean Age	Tenure	Newcomers (%)
Discontinuous democracies				
France	1945	44.9	1.6	79.8
France	1946	44.9	1.6	23.1
France	1951	48.7	1.5	32.2
Italy	1946	50.2	1.1	84.0
Italy	1948	45.6	1.3	53.1
Italy	1953	47.0	1.9	35.7
Germany	1949	50.6	1.0	95.1
Germany	1952	50.8	1.5	51.8
Germany	1957	51.9	2.0	33.4
Portugal	1975	41.8	1.0	100
Portugal	1976	39.8	1.3	71.5
Portugal	1979	43.1	1.6	46.2
Spain	1977	44.1	1.0	100
Spain	1979	43.1	1.6	40.3
Spain	1982	42.8	1.6	58.9
Hungary	1990	45.8	1.0	96.4
Hungary	1994	46.2	1.4	63.7
Hungary	1998	45.8	1.7	48.7
Continuous democracies				
Denmark	1945	49.5	2.2	36.5
Denmark	1947	50.8	2.5	27.0
Denmark	1950	51.9	2.6	22.2
Finland	1945	49.5	3.1	50.0
Finland	1948	50.1	3.2	25.5
Finland	1951	49.3	3.3	27.5
Netherlands	1946	49.9	2.2	42.0
Netherlands	1948	50.9	2.8	16.0
Netherlands	1952	52.5	3.3	14.0
Norway	1945	51.3	1.9	66.7
Norway	1950	54.0	2.3	27.3
Norway	1954	54.3	2.5	27.3
UK	1945	49.4	—	51.2
UK	1950	49.9	—	27.1
UK	1951	49.7	—	8.5

recruitment. The rate of newcomers in the first post-war election was in fact higher than 50 per cent in the UK, Norway, and Finland, reaching quite remarkable peaks also in Denmark and the Netherlands. It is a fact, however, that in all these countries, the other two indicators of parliamentary renewal—mean age and mean number of re-elections—were not oscillating as in the case of the discontinuous democracies and that in two or three elections also the rate of turnover returned to 'normal' values.

In the discontinuous countries levels of turnover were as expected significantly higher, but also differences among them were substantial. The French case is the one with the lowest level among the three countries, but when one compares Germany and Italy, the first democratic election brings in post-Nazi Germany (1949) 95 per cent of MPs with no previous representative experience at the national level, that is, about ten points more than the percentage of beginners in the Italian Constituent Assembly of 1946. Once more the duration of the democratic interruption is not the only factor at work. Moreover, if one looks at the sequence of the first elections, it is possible to discover that the reconsolidation of a stable parliamentary elite was relatively more uncertain in a country like France, where the rate of newcomers, after declining to 23 per cent in the second post-war elections of 1946, rises again to 32.2 per cent, due to the political uncertainty of the Fourth Republic. On the contrary, the curve of parliamentary turnover in Italy is more linear (although higher in its mean values) and the third elections (1953) are to be considered the achievement of an ordinary level of turnover, having the party system and the party elites already established their roots in the parliamentary scene.

It may be of some interest to bring into the picture a comparison with three more recent democratizations—Portugal, Spain, and Hungary. In all three cases the rate of newcomers in the first democratic elections was maximum. The extremely long interruption of democracy (forty years or more) prevented in these cases any continuity with the past. More interesting is to examine the following elections. The persistence of higher levels of turnover until the third round of elections seems to suggest that the consolidation of the new parliamentary elites has required in the recent democracies a longer period. The greater weakness of parties that seems to have characterized the last part of the twentieth century is a possible explanation of these data.

15.6.3. *The Impact of Intra-Democratic Transformations*

We are left now to consider some cases of 'intra-democratic transformations'. These transformations may concern the constitution, other important institutional rules (such as the electoral ones) or more strictly political aspects (such as the basic features of the party system), involving different degrees of 'critical change'. Among our cases the French crisis of 1958 and the constitution of 1962 represent the highest level of transformation, a full political transition with fundamental changes in the form of government. On the contrary, the reintroduction in the same country of the PR system in 1986 is to be judged a minor change, or even a failed attempt of change, since the new system was applied just one time. The electoral transition of 1994 in Italy was a more significant event since the new electoral rules, coinciding with a deep crisis of the old party system, contributed to open the way to a deep restructuring of Italian political life (D'Alimonte and Bartolini 2002).

Our data document the significant effects of such critical points. The transition between the Fourth and the Fifth Republic in France effectively meant a substantial transformation of the parliamentary elite. Among the most remarkable features, we can note first of all the high level of turnover of 1958 (69% of newcomers), and with regard to the profile of parliamentarians the increased importance of a university degree (particularly of a scientific and technical type) and of occupational backgrounds in the high levels of public administration (including also the military sector) and in managerial positions, the return of a strong relevance of the local elective background (see on this point Kreuzer and Stephan 2003), the decline of lawyers (from an average of about 15% to a measure always lower than 10% in the Fifth Republic), and of the primary sector (from an average of about 12% to figures lower than 5%).

The temporary change of the electoral system in 1986, following another important reform attempt—the new rule limiting the *cumul de mandat* in 1985— did not produce any particular effect on the parliamentary elite profile: the only interesting shift among our indicators of elite persistence concerns parliamentary tenure which declines in 1986 from a mean of 3.5 to 2.4 elections. This is however mainly due to the 'majority shift' between socialists and center-right parties. In fact, all the other measures are rather stable (including the rate of newcomers, which actually declines to 30%) and minor changes in all our dependent variables have to be explained with the different balance among parliamentary parties.[17]

In Italy the period between 1994 and 2001 can be considered an example of middle level impact of institutional changes on the parliamentary elite. The strong immediate effects in terms of parliamentary persistence of the election of 1994 (a rate of turnover of almost 71%, with a strong decline of tenure) was not corroborated by a comparable change in the substantive qualities of parliamentary personnel. The parliamentary party of Forza Italia, founded by Silvio Berlusconi a few months before the 1994 elections, is the only real, though very significant (it has been the largest party since 1994), exception in this respect, because of the remarkable presence of MPs with a 'private sector' or a 'liberal profession' background, and a very limited degree of political experience (Verzichelli 2002). However, this kind of innovations should be controlled in a longer perspective, since they can be partially explainable with the 'childhood phase' of the life-cycle of this party. Two other effects produced by the three first applications of the mixed-majoritarian system seem to be potentially more permanent: the more evident 'territorialization' of the parliamentary selection (proven by the increased importance of local and administrative backgrounds, to the detriment of party background) and the persistence of a higher degree of turnover in comparison with the phase of the PR system (Verzichelli 2002). The percentage of newcomers in 1996 and 2001 remained higher than 40 per cent, a measure never reached between 1953 and 1992.

15.6.4. *Current Challenges: How the Democratic Process is Reshaping the European Parliamentary Elites*

The two cases of 'intra-democratic transformations' briefly sketched above show that even without a full democratic discontinuity parliamentary recruitment can undergo significant shocks. And this is not the end of the story. Current discussions about *post-parliamentary democracy* (Andersen and Burns 1996) and the emergence of an *organic system of governance* (Mény et al. 2000) alert us to the possibility of further changes with a potential to affect the traditional characters of representative elites. For sure, what European democracies are living in these years is a complex phenomenon of adaptation which can influence in several ways the notion itself of representation and, consequently, the features of parliamentary elites. To what extent the *new European governance* could transform the social and political characters of parliamentarians is far from being clear right now. Western political elites are for sure at the centre of a 'quest for reforms' (Borchert 2003), but we can argue, at the moment, that the basic features of parliamentary recruitment are not under discussion. Therefore, the 'direct effects' of institutional changes upon MPs profiles, should be limited to the minor shifts determined by new rules about eligibility, incompatibilities and cumulation of mandates.[18]

Much more interesting is, for our purposes, the emergence of a number of 'indirect effects' of the new governance system on European patterns of parliamentary representation. Namely, the need for a more accountable 'delegation' within the parliament, the need of closer links with the 'public fora' of discussion, the segmentation of deliberative arenas and the emergence of a multilevel institutional setting can determine substantive changes in the profile also of national parliamentarians. The social and occupational composition of our parliaments, for instance, can be somehow influenced by these claims, as the decline of some traditional figures (i.e. lawyers) and the increase of other features (i.e. technocratic and managerial background) seem to confirm.

Even more evidently, the patterns of career and circulation of the European parliamentarians should have significantly changed in this time. We cannot provide original and innovative evidences in order to test this assertion. However, there is a coincidence between some 'hints' which have emerged from the most recent entries in our data-set and other recent pieces of research. For instance, the decline of tenure and the increase of turnover in the last fifteen years[19] could possibly be connected with the evolution of the structure of political careers in Europe both at the supranational and sub-national level. We have to remember that, at the supranational level, the 2004 election of the European Parliament has marked the historical turning point when, thanks to the definitive prohibition of the dual mandate, two formally separated parliamentary mandates have appeared. For this and other reasons, twenty-five years after the introduction of a directly elected assembly at the EU level, we can start discussing about the possibility of an autonomous *filière* of political careers at the supranational level (Verzichelli and Edinger 2005). And for what concerns the relationship between national and sub-national parliamentary mandates, recent studies have shown that the amount of politicians 'moving down' in order to benefit from innovative pathways of political career is growing in some European realities (Stolz 2003), a phenomenon which is clearly connected with the devolution/regionalization processes and with the increasing role of local politics in Europe.

15.7. CONCLUSIONS

In this chapter we have addressed a theme—the influence of the processes of democratization and transformation of democracy upon parliamentary recruitment—which is fascinating as well as complex. After having synthetically described some of the most relevant transformations in the profiles of parliamentary elites in European countries during the last 150 years—the historical period of the long and often difficult process of construction and consolidation of democracy—we have analysed on the basis of some broad working hypotheses their relationship with the crucial institutional and political aspects of this process.

Our empirical explorations have shown that a significant relationship exists between institutional and political change on one side and transformation of patterns of recruitment and career of parliamentary elites on the other. This relationship however cannot be reduced to a simple and linear model of causation. More specifically, the concept itself of democratization, which we commonly use to define in a synthetic way the deep and long-term institutional transformations of European political systems, cannot be transposed *sic et simpliciter* to the recruitment and profiles of parliamentary elites. The 'opening' of the institutional conditions of political life to the influence of the citizenship did indeed produce a progressive dismantling of the original pre-democratic and elitist political establishment and the access to parliamentary institutions of individuals from larger social strata, but could not produce in the end the total elimination of differences between represented and representatives. We must acknowledge that the nature itself of representative democracy is a crucial 'obstacle' to any integral implementation of that meaning of 'democratization'. Because of the process that produces them and the role they have to play, representatives are necessarily different (at least under certain aspects) from the represented. The adaptation of the representative system to the conditions of full democratization on the input (electoral) side has fostered a robust growth of structures and mechanisms of political intermediation (parties and other organizations for the articulation and aggregation of interests and for the steering of the political processes of democracy). From these structures and mechanisms representatives have received an important imprinting, which can be interpreted with the help of the concepts of professionalization and partization. Some of our findings are therefore less surprising. We will briefly recall them.

The opening of the gates of democracy and in particular the extension of suffrage has undoubtedly triggered deep changes in the features of political elites, but this generalization requires a number of qualifications. The impact of change has been on the short term often limited and has in general required a more middle term time span to produce all its effects. These effects have been unequal across countries. The trends of change, observed in many aspects of the social and political profile of parliamentarians, have been linear only if we consider subperiods of the long-term cycle considered in this book. For a number of important aspects (such as education, background in the public service, working-class origin, etc.) an initial trend has subsequently been reversed. In a more general way this can be interpreted to mean that the democratization of representative elites, which to an extent has indeed taken place, has had to face at some point internal and external limitations linked to the previously mentioned paradoxes of representative democracy.

The empirical evidence has shown also that to explain our dependent variables the role of parties as intermediary actors of representation, and especially the emergence of the organized mass party of the 'class' type, plays a central role. Weber's analysis of parties finds in our data full support. This variable, however, does not have in all countries the same impact essentially because the success and the density of this type of party organizations have not been the same everywhere.

We have also found that democratic continuity/discontinuity matters. Countries enjoying a continuous institutional development can experience smoother and more incremental transformations of their parliamentary elites. On the contrary interruptions of the democratic experience entail a significant deal of instability in the elite profiles. The comparative analysis has shown however that also the impact of discontinuity varies across countries and that the crucial factor is probably the quality of discontinuity more than its length. To this should be added also the party variable—degree of consolidation and persistence of party structures and of the party system—related to the periods preceding the democratic breakdown but also to the first phase of re-democratization

ENDNOTES

1   This obviously does not mean that today there are no more differences among the countries we analyse—that is Denmark, Finland, France, Germany, Hungary, Italy, the Netherlands, Norway, Portugal, Spain, and the UK. If one adopts for instance Lijphart's framework (1999), some of these countries are nearer to the model of majoritarian democracy while others more to the consensus model.

2   The point had already been noted by Max Weber (1919) in his analysis of parties; see also Duverger (1951), Sartori (1976), and Manin (1997).

3   We do not aim at producing a complete reference list here. As examples of country studies focusing on the country-specific factors of parliamentary elite transformations we can mention the seminal works of Dogan (1961), Polsby (1968), and Sartori (1963). See also Best and Cotta (2000).

4   This may have to do with the fact that class and gender are qualities of a different kind. From the point of view of availability and of the relationship with professionalization they probably work differently. Lower class occupations conflict more with the requirements of the political profession that the feminine gender (once prejudices and exclusions have been overcome).

5   It should be added that our numbers probably underestimate this phenomenon because of many other positions that are in fact a political job in disguise.

6   In some countries, however, problems of legitimation with regards to some opposition groups (socialists in particular) persisted. In the German case restrictive norms against Catholics and Socialists remained in place until the 1880s; and in Italy repressive actions against Catholics and Socialists were adopted during the last years of the nineteenth century.

7   We will leave aside the dimension of parliamentary control of executive power mainly because it would require a detailed exam of historical events in order to assess with precision the decline of monarchical influence in the selection and guidance of cabinets.

8   France, Hungary, and Italy will grant the suffrage to women after the Second World War. Portugal and Spain only with the return to democracy in the 1970s.

9   There are other cases but concern political units that later disappeared or were deeply changed: such as the pre-unitary states in Italy and their liberal constitutions of 1848, or Germany and its constitution of 1848.

10   As explained in Chapter 2 of this volume in the case of the UK instead of a nobility title, which entailed a seat in the House of Lords and was therefore incompatible with sitting in the House of Commons, we have considered the belonging to a family holding a nobility title.

11   With the exception of women. This limitation, while obviously relevant from the normative point of view, is in view of the variables selected here to evaluate the democratization of recruitment largely irrelevant.

12   In Italy only the extension of 1913 produces a significant growth of teachers (+9.7%), journalists (+2.0%) and full-time politicians (+3.2%); in the Netherlands that of 1897 (+3.4% journalists and +2.7% politicians) and of 1918 (+3.7% teachers and +4.6% politicians); in the UK that of 1886 (+3.4% teachers and +2.0% journalists) and that of 1918 (+2.0% journalists); in Denmark that of 1918 (+9.4% leading party positions, +1.2% politicians); in Norway that of 1900 (+2.1% teachers), of 1910 (+2.0% journalists), and of 1916 (+2.1% politicians). With regards to the other variables and the other extensions the effects are irrelevant. As with the previous variables the effects of suffrage extension are calculated by comparing the means of the three elections before and after the extension.

13   In this variable, all the elections before the universal male suffrage have been coded 0, while all the following ones with a progressive number.

14   This variable has been defined here as a scale from the minimum of proportionalism to a maximum of proportionalism, where 1 codes a plurality system, 2 a majority system, 3 an alternative vote system, 4 a mixed majoritarian system, 5 a limited vote/single transferable system, 6 a mixed PR system, and 7 a pure PR.

15   We refer, above all, to the analyses provided by Ilonszky and Verzichelli on, respectively, Socialist-Communist and Christian Democratic MPs. However, the discussions about the recent evolution of relatively small party groups could be also relevant here. For instance, the theme of the effect of 'post-materialist revolution' on green and new left MPs (Chapter 13 in this volume) can be extended to other party elites.

16   One could also distinguish two further sub-groups: the first, that of discontinuous democracies which saw a democratic restoration after the Second World War—the second wave of Huntington (1991)—that is Germany, Italy, and France; the second, made of those countries which have

experienced a long-term authoritarianism and the re-democratization only during the third wave (Spain and Portugal).

17   In particular, we want to refer to the higher presence of teachers, professors and, generally speaking, of the public sector among centre-left oriented legislatures.

18   The most important change at the normative level should be the introduction of a 'term limit' which has been experimented in local legislatures in USA and debated also at the federal level. But there is no sign of such a discussion in Europe so far.

19   Overall, in our twelve European parliaments, the average turnover has reached a level of 39.9% during the 1990s, successively receding to 31.6% in the first part of the new decade. However, the figures are significantly higher than the average of the 1980s (26.9%) and of the two decades before. For what concerns tenure, the average for the nineties is 2.3 and in the first half of the new century 2.4. In the 1980s it was 2.7.

16

Conclusions

Maurizio Cotta

In this book the long cycle of political representation in European countries has been explored through the observation lens of the crucial actors of this central process of contemporary democracy—the parliamentarians. After a significant 'prehistory' of this concept, and of the political phenomena it describes, dating back to medieval and pre-modern Europe, representation has made—with the liberal and democratic revolutions of the first half of the nineteenth century— its great come back in the political landscape of the continent as the main 'challenger' of absolutist monarchies and has then progressively affirmed itself in the second half of the nineteenth century as the central mechanism of the new constitutional regimes that have displaced the former. Its institutional success has inaugurated a deeply innovative form of political life and has triggered a long-term opening of the political game to an increasingly broad involvement of pre-viously excluded societal strata and political groups. This has led representation to become strictly linked to the concept (and realities) of democracy, to the point of creating an almost indivisible political dyad—representative democracy and democratic representation (Sartori 1987; Manin 1997).

The 'democratization of representation' (which has also meant, we must not forget, a deep reformulation, in a representative sense, of the concept of democ-racy) has been, throughout its developmental history, a contentious process. The political conflicts, originating from requests for the opening of the access of the new voters (and of the political groups representing them) to the representative and governing institutions and from the resistances of the incumbents to this opening, were significant in all countries. In some cases, however, they could be accommodated through a continuous adaptation of the processes and institutions of representation, while in some others they triggered dramatic crises that have lead to a (temporary) disruption of democracy and representation. In the latter cases the process of adaptation was interrupted, for a shorter or longer time period, and could be resumed only after the non-democratic regime showed, on its turn, the failure of governments, not based on a pluralistic representation of the political community, to solve the problems of contemporary societies. The new democratic and representative processes, once they were re-established, had to recover some of the interrupted threads of the past and, at the same time, to face the challenges of a new historical phase. Legacies of the past were thus in some way combined with new developments.

Democratic representation is an elaborate political mechanism and, to be fully comprehended, deserves to be studied from more than one perspective. The study of those who are 'represented'—the voters—and of their behaviour; the study of parties and party systems as the main actors of the competitive game which is the central 'engine' of representation; and the analysis of government- (and coalition-) making and of legislative behaviour have rightly attracted the attentions of scholars who are interested in exploring the functioning of representative processes. The study of the real men (and now increasingly women) who undertake this 'job' (and, as we have seen, this is indeed a job, although not only) is surely not the least relevant perspective. The selection, by the parties and the other political groups who control this process, of the men and women who will then be proposed to the voters and the decisions of the voters to support them or not have maintained throughout the history of representation a crucial role. Not to say of the fact that, within the parliamentary halls, these people will give to representation a concrete life through the law-making process, debates, questions, etc., to which they participate.

When analysing from this point of view the political history of democratic representation which stretches from the mid-nineteenth century to the beginnings of the twenty-first century, what are the crucial ciphers through which we can interpret this *longue durée*? Change and continuity, diversity and similarity are the two dyads that appear immediately relevant.

Over the approximately 150 years of ascendancy and dominance of representative institutions in Europe (and in other parts of the world) change is obviously not to be considered a surprise. And in fact, if we compare without any mediation the starting points and the end destinations of this period, the amount of transformations that the same concept, that of parliamentary representation, covers is impressive. It could be even asked whether, sometimes, the use of the same word is more misleading than illuminating and clarifying. What is there in common between the representation of limited groups of the population which was largely based on organic social linkages, personal interactions and on the amateur politicians of aristocratic or upper-class origin, and the representation of wide masses, based on indirect linkages essentially mediated by large impersonal organizations (such as parties) and increasingly by television and other mass media, where representatives are full-time professionals of this function? The distance is obviously abysmal. The analyses conducted in this book of different features of parliamentarians have documented at length the extent of changes.

To the obvious cipher of change it is not, however, unwarranted to add that of continuity. Representation has meant the creation and development of new political elites which have been generally able to consolidate their power bases in the political processes and institutions of representation. These elites have proven capable of ensuring their persistence and reproduction, and to a significant extent to weather the maelstrom of social change. As it is attested, for instance, by data concerning turnover from one election to the other, the process of substitution of representative elites has been predominantly an incremental one. The incumbents have generally dominated elections. Out of 391 elections covered in our dataset, in 62 per cent of the cases less than a third of the parliamentarians were newcomers and only in 11 per cent of the elections a majority of parliamentarians was new to the institution. We can safely assume that the newcomers have been, to a significant degree, socialized into the institutional culture by experienced representatives and that innovations brought by the new entries have had on the short term a relatively marginal impact. Only on a longer term they have been able to produce more significant changes. The strength of the inertia in the recruitment of parliamentary elites is well documented by analysing how certain traits of the parliamentarians have persisted over time and have been substituted only with difficulty.

On a different axis of analysis our study has documented the significant degree of variations existing across countries. Again something which should not come as a surprise. The different social, economic, and religious configurations of the European countries, the variable political histories and paths through which they have built their representative institutions have necessarily been translated into different results for what concerns the profiles of representative elites. If representatives are faithful to their name and role they will obviously reflect some, at least, of the peculiarities of the country represented. To this should be added that variations derive not only from the demand side of representation but also from the supply side. How the agencies (parties in particular) that select representatives were born, how they were organized, and what was their programmatic profile, all these aspects have significantly contributed in producing different types of representatives.

At the same time, our explorations have documented not only variations across countries; in the picture they have offered significant elements of commonality are also to be found. Certain common trends that go beyond the borders of a country have emerged. The decline of the role played by the nobility in representative institutions, the long-term 'U curve' of public servants and of university graduates—a trend according to which these features, which had originally a significant weight, have during the early part of the twentieth century lost some of their importance, only to regain it in a very strong way in the second part of the century—are good examples of this similarity of developments. On a different level we can recall also the rise of party based professionalism during great part of the past century until a saturation and levelling off seem to have been reached in the last decades. These and other features suggest that similar problems and challenges have been faced in all of our countries by the politics of representation and that not too different responses have been given to them. More difficult is to decide to what

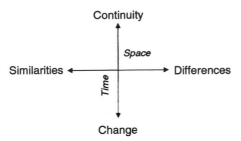

FIGURE 16.1. Parliamentary recruitment in Europe: dimensions of variation

extent these similarities can be explained by similarities in the social conditions of European societies, by the in-built constraints of the mechanisms of parliamentary representation, or by phenomena of influence and imitation across the borders.

The results of the analyses of this book can, therefore, be read along two basic axes of variations—time and space—that define for the profiles of parliamentary representatives the four opposite poles of change, continuity, diversity, and similarity (Fig. 16.1).

This multiform landscape of parliamentary representation has been explored in this book from different but complementary perspectives. In the first part a series of strategically important characteristics of parliamentarians have been analysed in a comparative way to document the long-term change and its different phases. These data, by providing a rich amount of information about the intermediaries of representation, offer at the same time important elements to understand better who has gained access to representation and in what way this has been made possible. Combining an analytic reading of the findings for each variable and a more comprehensive view of their results we can have a more precise evaluation of the transformations of representation in Europe.

The analysis of the presence of nobility, of a background in the state service (particularly in its highest ranks) and of levels of education among parliamentarians has enabled to shed a better light on the first phases of parliamentary representation. The crucial role of the upper classes, characterized by a nobility status, often an important role in the service for the state and high levels of education, in the first steps of the new political mechanism is well documented by our data. Representative institutions show in this way their potential of enabling and legitimizing a partial transfer (and conversion) of elements of the *ancien régime* into the new one. At the same time, the clear decline of these components indicates the role of the new institutional mechanisms in facilitating a progressive retreat of these groups from the political frontline, to make space to new political forces and to different brands of politicians.

These variables contribute also to document the importance of differences in the traditions of European countries. The ability of the *ancien régime* to survive into the new one was variable and the resistances to the emergence of new political elites were not the same everywhere. The data on the composition of parliamentary elites may well complement the analyses, conducted from a more qualitative historical point of view, of the conflicts that have characterized the early days of parliamentary representation.

The contemporary presence, within parliaments, of a different breed of politicians and then its growth is documented not only in a negative way by the same variables, but also in a positive one by other indicators such as the percentages of lawyers and other free professionals, of journalists and writers, and of schoolteachers and university professors (and in some countries even priests). The representation of traditional society and of the established powers has had increasingly to come to terms with a new emerging elite, the members of which, only to a limited extent, stood as representatives of their similar, but were rather acting as representatives of broader components of society, in particular the new enfranchized middle classes. They represented the electorate in a more indirect way, through their specific qualifications which made them able to interpret effectively in the political game the interests of the voters.

For representation to move beyond the confines of an educated middle class has proven in all countries, as it might be expected, particularly problematic. The opening of the electoral gates to the working classes has been translated only with great difficulty and to a limited extent in the representation of the working classes by parliamentarians of the working classes. The access to the seats of parliamentary representatives of individuals with the lowest levels of education and coming from the ranks of the workers has been generally limited and delayed. This means that the new classes of voters have been predominantly represented by people from different social backgrounds. And to the limited extent that their representation has been assured by 'peers', fellow agricultural and industrial workers, this has happened essentially thanks to a mechanism of party professionalization, by which these workers have in fact changed their original condition into that of full-time functionaries of party organizations.

The progressive entrance into an age of advanced political professionalization is clearly documented by many of our variables. In a particularly direct way this is shown by the increasing importance, before the first election to parliament, of a career spent within the party, which entails local or national responsibilities of leadership, and which for, a somewhat more restricted number of MPs, means even a full economic reliance on (and dependence from) the party or parent organizations. This process is also, perhaps more indirectly, attested by the return during the second half of the twentieth century of public employment as the leading occupational background of representative elites. Public service has become often a disguised form of political profession.

These data show that, as the political system was opened to new stakeholders, representation has also opened the way—albeit generally with a temporal lag—to new elites. At the same time it is clear that changes in the profiles of parliamentary elites have not simplistically mirrored the expansion of citizenship. What we see is, in fact, a gradual transformation of the nature and meaning of representation. Under restricted suffrage representation of the upper classes meant essentially a direct and organic link between representatives and represented, who shared not only the same social position but also very thick personal links (the aristocrat sitting in parliament was not just a peer for his represented but was linked by a net of social and family relations with them, or by a patronage relationship to the lower positioned). Later on, under conditions of broader franchise, the representation of the much larger middle classes has been accomplished by individuals who continued to be rather similar in their social origins to the voters but less organically linked to them. The importance of skills acquired through certain professions—the intellectual or the free professions—took over the role of status and its networks. But when it came to the final stages of democratization the distance increased and the relationship between representatives and represented became even more indirect. At this point politics became in itself a true profession with its admission procedures, internal selections, and career steps. Politicians have become a much more self-referential group, the links of which with society and its different components are of a procedural and institutional nature (essentially achieved through the electoral processes), rather than of a personal and social one.

Among the great transformations of representation, the last one from a temporal point of view—that which has opened to women the door of representative institutions—deserves a special mention. As it is well documented in this book, this (long delayed) transformation is particularly apt to show some of the complexities (and the inertia) of representation. The feminine half of society was in Europe the last excluded section of the community to win the right to have access to the representative process. Yet, when this happened, the right to be represented, even if exercised in the voting box, was for a very long time translated only minimally in the access of women to the role of representatives. The representation of women voters has remained firmly in the hands of a professionalized political class, which happened to be predominantly of the male sex. To what extent this has meant also that the interests and demands of women have been neglected is a question that, to be answered empirically, would require a different type of data and cannot be seriously discussed here. It is however clear that, in the last decades, this absence has been increasingly perceived by large parts of public opinion as a serious limitation to a satisfactory working of representation, generating in this case a militant demand of representation by 'peers' (women should be represented by women). The political mobilization of this demand has probably had an impact on this aspect of representation, with women subsequently gaining larger weight (although still with very substantial differences among countries) in many parliaments. It remains however to be better understood whether this has meant different representatives and also a different type of representation, or simply that the political profession has (at least in part) eliminated previous discriminatory practices and now also elected women can become professional politicians as men.

In the second part of the book, the focus has been on parties as the crucial actors, particularly after the take-off of democratization of suffrage, in the process of representation. To reduce the enormous amount of complexity, and following a current practice, individual parties have been regrouped into 'party families'. For the main party families—conservatives, liberals, Christian democrats, socialists, and communists—but also for some smaller but particularly revealing ones— agrarians, extreme right, greens, new left, and regionalist parties—the analysis of the specific profiles of their parliamentary groups has been conducted with the purpose of exploring to what extent, within each party family, the recruitment is internally homogeneous and to what extent it is distinctive compared to other party families. In other words, do the similarities across countries of parties belonging to the same European-wide family outweigh the differences among them or vice versa country specificities make the idea itself of a European party family irrelevant? The picture that comes out of the detailed analyses conducted for each of the party families is surely less 'black and white' than the two alternatives just mentioned. It confirms however that each party family carries a specific 'representational programme' and that this translates to a measurable extent also into a specific profile of its parliamentary representatives.

What are the implications of these analyses in terms of the two axes of varia- tion? With regard to the temporal axis the first implication is that party families are, over time, factors of change: their appearance in successive waves in the representative game and their different rates of growth (and decline) determine the entrance and then a changing balance of parliamentarians with (at least in part) specific profiles. To the extent however that party families become institutionally entrenched they represent also a factor of continuity by perpetuating their own peculiar type of representation. As for the spatial axis, party families can be seen as factors of similarity across countries: the existence of the same party family in different countries determines (to a certain degree) the replication of the common features shared by its parliamentarians. At the same time however the different weight that a party family has in each parliament (or in the extreme case its complete absence) is a factor of dissimilarity across countries.

This picture is further complicated not only by the fact that party families are not totally homogeneous internally because of the weight of country specific fac- tors, but also of other factors that pertain to the 'histories' of party families and to their reciprocal relationship. The analyses of this book have provided interesting empirical evidence that a life-cycle effect matters. Some specificities of a party family may be stronger in its 'young age' when the new party family is a chal- lenger of the existing representative equilibrium, but later fade somewhat away. In part, but not completely, linked to this is the degree of marginality/exclusion of a party in the political system. As it has been shown quite convincingly by the analysis of the socialist party family, its transition from an original situation of exclusion to one of full incorporation in the political systems of many countries has determined important changes in its parliamentary recruitment profile. Also the size of a party family matters. When its size in a country is especially small some features of its parliamentary elites will be distorted.

In the third part of the book, an attempt has been made to develop more comprehensive perspectives of analysis. A first perspective, focusing on the societal bases of representation, has explored, with regard to a limited number of country cases and with the help of correspondence analysis, the relationship between the parliamentary representatives of different party families and social cleavages. A second perspective has attempted to establish in a systematic way the relationship between paths of institutional and political transformation of the representative regimes of Europe and patterns of parliamentary recruitment. Within a broad common evolution in the direction of a fully inclusionary and party based representative democracy, European countries have followed paths of change that differ significantly in terms of their points of departure, of the sequences and tempos of transformations, of their degree of continuity or discontinuity. The repercussions of this common evolution and of its internal variations on the profiles of representative elites have been obviously significant, but in many ways less direct and immediate than it might be expected on the basis of a too simplistic interpretation of democratization as a process of 'opening' of politics to society, by which, via the channel of representation, the former becomes more similar to the latter. The data analysed have shown abundantly that representation, with its mechanisms of production and reproduction of elites, is not only a channel through which society, its interests and identities enter into the space of politics, but also a filter and an intermediary that selects, delays, transforms societal inputs, and institutional changes. Representative elites in consolidated democratic regimes have come increasingly to form a professionalized political class, with its own dynamics and inertia, that cannot therefore be seen as the simple product of social and institutional changes, but operates as a relatively independent factor in political life. The importance of representative elites as an element of continuity must in particular be stressed. Their ability to entrench themselves through the institutional mechanisms of electoral and parliamentary life and through parties and their role in the recruiting process has undoubtedly meant that change could be domesticated and reduced in most of the cases to manageable dimensions.

To sum up, our explorations have confirmed that, on the long term, under the umbrella of one concept, that of representation, very impressive transformations have taken place. The fact that these transformations have been, in most of the cases, the result of limited incremental changes and only rarely of abrupt ruptures, has made them less visible on the short term, yet nonetheless significant.

While it is possible, with the use of some of the data we have analysed, to evaluate the past and to gauge the long-term change, it is more difficult to assess to what extent the concept of representation (and the elaborate knot of analytic elements and normative values it implies) will be able also in the future to provide not only the main descriptive tool but also the fundamental normative support for the political discourse on democracy as it has done throughout the past 150 years. On one side, it can be said without too many hesitations that representative institutions—and concretely the men and women that, over the years, have given life to them—have won a hard fought competition with dangerous and powerful competitors. Proving not only to be a more just and humane system of governance, but also a system more capable than others to solve the excruciating problems of contemporary societies. The diffusion of these types of institutions all over the world is a very concrete manifestation of this success. On the other side, past and present successes do not exclude the existence of present and future problems that may challenge the institutions of representation. To an extent some of these problems derive from the success itself of representative democracy. The fact that this form of political regime has enabled and fostered the development of richer, better educated, more dynamically pluralist societies is probably the main factor that makes so many citizens in democratic polities unsatisfied with representative democracy and its limitations and fuels the demand for alternative or complementary forms of democracy to give more fully voice to their needs and demands. The current paradox of democratic representation is probably the other and connected source of these problems. The fact that more democratization has meant that representatives have increasingly become, via a deep process of professionalization, a true political class separate from society, is inevitably an element that increases their distance from the citizens and potentially opens a space for distrust.

To what extent the answers to these problems will come from new (complementary or alternative) forms of democracy or from changes internal to the representative institutions and inducing new transformations of the profile of parliamentary representatives is a question that as of today remains open. The history of representation, that our book has hopefully contributed at least a bit to enlighten, shows in any case that the potential for adaptation of this political device should not be underestimated.

References

Albouy, V. and Wanecq, T. (2003). 'Les inégalités sociales d'accès aux Grandes Écoles', *Économie et Statistique*, 361: 27–52.

Albrecht, M. (1960). *De invloed van het kiesstelsel op de samenstelling van de volksvertegenwoordiging en op de vorming van de regering.* Amsterdam: de Arbeiderspers.

Allum, P. (1995). *State and Society in Western Europe.* Cambridge: Polity Press.

Almond, G. A., Flanagan, S. C. and Mundt, R. J. (1973). *Crisis, Choice and Change*, Boston, Mass: Little Brown and Co.

Andersen, J. G. and Jensen, J. B. (2001). 'The Danish Venstre: Liberal, Agrarian or Centrist?', in D. Arter (ed.), *From Farmyard to City Square? The Electoral Adaptation of the Nordic Agrarian Parties.* Aldershot, UK: Ashgate, pp. 96–131.

Andersen, K. and Thorson, S. (1984). 'Congressional Turnover and the Election of Women', *Western Political Quarterly*, 37: 143–56.

Andersen, S. and Burns, T. (1996). 'The European Union and the Erosion of Parliamentary Democracy. A Study of Post-Parliamentary Governance', in S. Andersen and K. Eliassen (eds.), *The European Union: How Democratic Is It?* London: Sage, pp. 227–52.

Anderson, C. (1993). 'The Composition of the German Bundestag since 1949. Long-Term Trends and Institutional Effects', *Historical Social Research*, 18(1): 3–25.

Andeweg, R. (2000). 'Party Government, State and Society: Mapping Boundaries and Interrelations', in J. Blondel and M. Cotta (eds.), *The Nature of Party Government: A Comparative European Perspective.* Houndmills, UK: Palgrave.

Anker, R. (1998). *Gender and Jobs: Sex Segregation of Occupations in the World.* Geneva: ILO.

Apel, H. (1991). *Die Deformierte Demokratie. Parteienherrschaft in Deutschland.* Stuttgart: Deutsche Verlags-Anstalt.

Apter, D. (1965), *The Politics of Modernization.* Chicago, Ill.: Chicago University Press.
—— (1973). *Political Change, Collected Essays.* London: Frank Cass.

Arceneaux, K. (2001). 'The "Gender Gap" in State Legislative Representation: New Data to Tackle an Old Question', *Political Research Quarterly*, 54(1): 143–60.

Archer, M. S. (1979). *Social Origins of Educational Systems.* London-Beverly-Hills, CA: Sage.

Arter, D. (2001a). 'Conclusion', in D. Arter (ed.), *From Farmyard to City Square? The Electoral Adaptation of the Nordic Agrarian Parties.* Aldershot, UK: Ashgate, pp. 162–83.
—— (2001b). 'The Finnish Centre Party: A Case of Successful Transformation?', in D. Arter (ed.), *From Farmyard to City Square? The Electoral Adaptation of the Nordic Agrarian Parties.* Aldershot, UK: Ashgate, pp. 59–95.

Atkinson, P., Davies, B., and Delamont, S. (1995). *Discourse and Reproduction: Essays in Honour of Basil Bernstein.* Cresskill, NJ: Hampton Press.

Balan, D., Join-Lambert, É., and Pape, Ch. (1994). 'Les diplômes des Français', *Insee Première*, 305: 1–4.

Ballini, P. L. (1988). *Le elezioni nella storia d'Italia dall'Unità al fascismo, Profilo storico-statistico*. Bologna: Il Mulino.

Barber, J. D. (1965). *The Lawmakers*. New Haven, CT: Yale University Press.

Bartolini, S. (2000). *The Political Mobilization of the European Left, 1860–1980. The Class Cleavage*. Cambridge: Cambridge University Press.

—— and Mair, P. (1990). *Identity, Competition and Electoral Availability. The Stability of European Electorates, 1885–1985*. Cambridge: Cambridge University Press.

Bauer, M. and Bertin-Mourot, B. (1997). 'La tyrannie du diplôme initial et la circulation des élites: la stabilité du système français', in H. Mendras and E. Suleiman (eds.), *Le recrutement des élites en Europe*. Paris: La Découverte, pp. 48–63.

Bell, D. S. (1993). *Western European Communists and the Collapse of Communism*. Oxford: Berg Publishers.

Bendix, R. (1964). *Nation-Building and Citizenship: Studies of Our Changing Social Order*. New York: Wiley.

van den Berg, J. (1983). *De Toegang tot het Binnenhof. De maatschappelijke herkomst van de Tweede-Kamerleden tussen 1849 en 1970*. Weesp: Van Holkema & Warendorf.

—— (1989). 'Het "pre-fab-kamerlid." De gewijzigde recrutering van de Tweede-kamerleden sinds 1971–1972', in J. Th. J. van den Berg a.o (eds.), *Tussen Nieuwspoort & Binnenhof. De jaren 60 als breuklijn in de naoorlogse ontwikkelingen in politiek en journalistiek*. Den Haag.

Berger, P. and Luckmann, T. (1986). *La construction sociale de la réalité*. Paris: Meridiens Klincksieck.

Berglund, S. and Lindström, U. (1982). 'The Conservative Dilemma: Ideology and Vote Maximisation in Sweden', in L.-H. Zig (ed.), *Conservative Politics in Western Europe*. London: Macmillan, pp. 69–82.

Bernstein, B. (1975). *Classes, Codes and Control*. London: Routledge & Kegan Paul.

Best, H. (1982). 'Recruitment, Careers, and Legislative Behaviour of German Parliamentarians, 1848–1953', *Historical Social Research*, 23: 20–55.

—— (1990). 'Elite Structure and Regime (Dis)continuity in Germany 1867–1933: The Case of Parliamentary Leadership Groups', *German History*, 8: 1–27.

—— (1997). ' "Strategien" und Strukturen Parlamentarischer Repräsentation einer Antiparlamentarischen Partei. Die Reichstagsfraktion der NSDAP, 1928–1933', in A. Bäuerkämper et al. (eds.), *Gellschaft ohne Eliten? Führungsgruppen in der DDR*. Metropol.

—— (2003). 'Der langfristige Wandel politischer Eliten in Europa, 1867–2000: Auf dem Weg der Konvergenz', in S. Hradil and P. Imbusch (eds.), *Oberschichten–Eliten–Herrschende Klassen*. Opladen, Germany: Leske & Budrich, pp. 369–99.

—— and Cotta, M. (eds.) (2000). *Parliamentary Representatives in Europe, 1848–2000. Legislative Recruitment and Careers in Eleven European Countries*. Oxford: Oxford University Press, pp. 492–526.

—— and Edinger, M. (2005). 'Converging Representative Elites in Europe? An Introduction to the EurElite Project', *Czech Sociological Review*, 41(3): 499–509.

—— and Gaxie, D. (2000). 'Detours To Modernity: Long-Term Trends of Parliamentary Recruitment in Republican France, 1848–1999', in H. Best and M. Cotta (eds.), *Parliamentary Representatives in Europe, 1848–2000. Legislative Recruitment and Careers in Eleven European Countries*. Oxford: Oxford University Press, pp. 88–137.

—— Cromwell, V., Hausmann C. and M. Rush (2001). 'The Transformation of Legislative Elites: The Cases of Britain and Germany since the 1860s', *Journal of Legislative Studies*, 7: 65–91.

—— Hausmann, C., and Schmitt, K. (2000). 'Challenges, Failures and Final Successes: The Winding Path of German Parliamentary Leadership Groups Towards a Structurally Integrated Elite, 1848–1999', in H. Best and M. Cotta (eds.), *Parliamentary Representatives in Europe, 1848–2000. Legislative Recruitment and Careers in Eleven European Countries*. Oxford: Oxford University Press, pp. 138–95.

von Beyme, K. (1970). *Die parlamentarischen Regierungssysteme in Europa*. Munchen: Piper.

—— (1984). *Parteien in westlichen Demockratien*. München: R. Piper.

—— (1985). *Political Parties in Western Democracies*. Aldershot, UK: Gower.

—— (1988) 'Right-wing Extremism in Post-war Europe', *West European Politics*, 11(2): 1–18.

—— (1993). *Die politische Klasse im Parteienstaat*. Frankfurt: Suhrkamp.

Bird, K. (2000). 'Gender Parity and the Political Representation of Women in France', paper presented at the International Political Science Association World Congress, Quebec City, 1–5 August, 17pp.

Birenbaum, G. (1992). *Le Front National en Politique*. Paris: Éditions Balland.

Birnbaum, P. (1978). 'Institutionalization of Power and Integration of Ruling Elites', *European Journal of Political Research*, 6: 105–15.

Blau, P. M. (1974). 'Parameters of Social Structures', *American Sociological Review*, 615–35.

Blinkhorn, M. (1975). *Carlism and the Crisis in Spain, 1931–1939*. Cambridge: Cambridge University Press.

—— (ed.) (1990). *Fascists and Conservatives, the Radical Right and the Establishment in Twentieth-century Europe*. London: Unwin Hyman.

Blondel, J. (1997). 'Political Progress, Reality or Illusion?', in A. Burgen, P. McLaughlin, and J. Mittelstraß (eds.), *The Idea of Progress*. New York: W. de Gruyter.

—— and Thiébault, J. L. (eds.) (1991). *The Profession of Government Minister in Western Europe*. Houndmills, UK: Macmillan.

Bogdanor, V. (1985). *Representatives of the People?* Aldershot, UK: Gower.

Borchert, J. (2003). 'Professionalised Politicians. Towards a Comparative Perspective', in J. Borchert and J. Zeiss (eds.), *The Political Class in Advanced Democracies*. Oxford: Oxford University Press.

—— and Golsch, L. (2003). 'Germany: From "Guilds of Notables" to Political Class', in J. Borchert and J. Zeiss (eds.), *The Political Class in Advanced Democracies*. Oxford: Oxford University Press, pp. 142–63.

Borg, O. (1979). 'Liberalismi ja poliittiset puolueet', in O. Borg et al. (eds.), *Poliittisia aatteita valistuksesta nykypäivään*. Jyväskylä: Jyväskylän yliopiston historian laitos. Yleisen historian tutkimuksia, 3:1–43.

Bourdieu, P. (1977). *Reproduction: In Education, Society and Culture*. London: Sage.

—— (1981). 'La représentation. Éléments pour une théorie du champ politique', in *Actes de la recherche en science sociale*, 36–7, février–mars: 3–24.

—— (1986). *Distinction: A Social Critique of Judgements of Taste*. London: Routledge & Kegan Paul.

—— (1989). *La Noblesse d'État*. Paris: Minuit.

Bourdieu, P. (2000). *Propos sur le champ politique*. Lyon: Presses universitaires de Lyon.
—— and Passeron, J. C. (1964). *Les Héritiers*. Paris: Éditions de Minuit.
—— —— (1977). *Reproduction, Education, Society, and Culture*. London and Beverly Hills: Sage Publications (1st French edition 1971).
Budge, I. (1994). 'A New Spatial Theory of Party Competition: Uncertainty, Ideology and Political Equilibrium Viewed Comparatively and Temporally', *British Journal of Political Science*, 24: 443–7.
—— and Keman, H. (1993). *Parties and Democracy. Coalition Formation and Government Functioning in Twenty States*. Oxford: Oxford University Press.
Burmeister, K. (1993). *Die Professionalisierung der Politik am Beispiel des Berufspolitikers im parlamentarischen System der Bundesrepublik Deutschland*. Berlin: Ducker & Humblot.
Burrin, P. (1996). *Living with Defeat, France under German Occupation, 1940–1944*. London: Arnold.
Bush, M. L. (1983). *The European Nobility—Vol. I: Noble Privilege*. Manchester, UK: Manchester University Press.
—— (1988). *The European Nobility—Vol. II: Rich Noble, Poor Noble*. Manchester, UK: Manchester University Press.
Butler, D. and Butler, G. (2000*a*). *British Historical Facts, 1900–2000*. London: Macmillan.
—— (2000*b*). *Twentieth-Century British Politics Facts, 1900–2000*. Basingstoke, UK: Macmillan.
Cabrera, M. (1998). *Con luz y taquígrafos. El Parlamento en la restauración, 1913–1923*. Madrid: Taurus.
Caciagli, M. (1992). *Christian Democracy in Europe*. Barcelona: Institut de Ciencias Politiques i Socials.
Cain, B., Dalton, R., and Scarrow, S. (eds.) (2003*)*. *Democracy Transformed ? Expanding Political Opportunities in Advanced Industrial Democracies*. Oxford: Oxford University Press.
Cannadine, D. (revised edn. 1992). *The Decline and Fall of the British Aristocracy*. London: Macmillan.
Caramani, D. (2000). *The Societies of Europe. Elections in Western Europe since 1815*. London: Macmillan.
Carasa, P. (ed), *E'lites Castellanas de la Restauración. Una aproximación al poder poltic en Castilla*, vol. II, Salamanca: Junta de Castilla y León.
Cardosa, A. L. (1997). *Aristocrats in Bourgeois Italy: The Piedmontese Nobility, 1861–1930*. Cambridge: Cambridge University Press.
Carsten, F. L. (1989). *A History of the Prussian Junkers*. Aldershot, UK: Scolar Press.
Caul, M. (1999). 'Women's Representation in Parliament: The Role of Political Parties', *Party Politics*, 5(1): 79–98.
—— (2001). 'Political Parties and the Adoption of Candidate Gender Quotas: A Cross-national Analysis', *Journal of Politics*, 63(4): 1214–29.
Cherkaoui, M. (2004). *Sociologie de l'éducation*, 6th edn. Paris: Presses Universitaires de France.
Christmas, V. (2002). Factors Involved in Women's Atypical Career Choice: A Comparative Study of Women in East and West Germany before and after Reunification, doctoral dissertation, University of London, Senate House Library.

Christmas-Best, V. (2006). 'Left-Right-Left? The March of Female Representatives into European Parliaments and the Role of Leftist Party Affiliations', in F. Engelstad and T. Gulbrandsen (eds.), 'Comparative Studies of Social and Political Elites', *Comparative Social Research*, 23: 3–24.

Christensen, D. A. (2001). 'The Norwegian Agrarian-Centre Party: Class, Rural or Catchall Party?', in D. Arter (ed.), *From Farmyard to City Square? The Electoral Adaptation of the Nordic Agrarian Parties*. Aldershot, UK: Ashgate, pp. 31– 58.

Christensen, T. and Egeberg, M. (1979). 'Organized Groups-Government Relation in Norway: on the Structured Selection of Participants, Problems, Solutions and Choice Opportunities', *Scandinavian Political Studies*, 2(3).

Chubb, B. (1970). *The Government and Politics of Ireland*. Stanford, CA: Stanford University Press.

Clark, J. (1991). 'Getting There: Women in Political Office', *The Annals of the American Academy*, 515: 63–76.

Cobalti, A. (1992). *Sociologia dell'educazione. Teorie e ricerche sul sistema scolastico*. Mila: F. Angeli.

Cohen-Huther, J. (2004). *Sociologie des élites*. Paris: Armand Colin.

Colomer, J. (2004). *Handbook of Electoral System Choice*. London: Palgrave.

Concise Oxford Dictionary of Quotations (2001). Oxford: Oxford University Press.

Constant, B. (1819). *Discours sur la liberté des anciens comparée avec celle des modernes*. Paris.

Cook, C. and Keith, B. (1975). *British Historical Facts, 1830–1900*. London: Macmillan.

Costa-Pinto, A. (2000). *The Blue Shirts, Portuguese Fascists and the New State*. Boulder, CO: Social Science Monographs.

Cotta, M. (1979). *Classe politica e parlamento in Italia*. Bologna: Il Mulino.

——(1982). 'The Italian Political Class in the Twentieth Century: Continuities and Discontinuities', in M. N. Czudnowski (ed.), *International Yearbook for Studies of Leaders and Leadership: Does Who Governs Matters? Elite Circulation in Contemporary Societies*. Dekalb, IL: Northern Illinois University Press, pp. 154–87.

——(2000). 'Conclusion. From the Simple World of Party Government to a More Complex View of Party–Government Relationships', in J. Blondel and M. Cotta (eds.), *The Nature of Party Government*. London: Palgrave, pp. 196–222.

——and Best, H. (2000). 'Between Professionalization and Democratization: Synoptic View on the Making of the European Representative', in H. Best and M. Cotta (eds.), *Parliamentary Representatives in Europe, 1848–2000. Legislative Recruitment and Careers in Eleven European Countries*. Oxford: Oxford University Press. pp. 492–526.

——and Verzichelli, L. (2003). 'Ministers in Italy: Notables, Party Men, Technocrats and Media Men', in P. Tavares de Almeida, A. Costa-Pinto, and N. Bermeo (eds.), *Who Governs Southern Europe? Regime Change and Ministerial Recruitment, 1850–2000*. London: Frank Cass.

Cotta, M., Mastropaolo, A. and Verzichelli, L. (2000). 'Parliamentary Elite Transformations along the Discontinuous Road of Democratisation: Italy, 1861–1999', in H. Best and M. Cotta (eds.), *Parliamentary Representatives in Europe, 1848–2000. Legislative Recruitment and Careers in Eleven European Countries*. Oxford: Oxford University Press, pp. 226–69.

Crewe, I. (1985). 'MPs and their Constituents in Britain: How Strong are the Links?', in Vernon Bogdanor (ed.), *Representatives of the People?* Aldershot, UK: Gower, pp. 44–65.

Cromwell, V. and Rush, M. (2000). 'Continuity and Change: Legislative Recruitment in the United Kingdom, 1868–1999', in H. Best and M. Cotta (eds.), *Parliamentary Representatives in Europe, 1848–2000. Legislative Recruitment and Careers in Eleven European Countries.* Oxford: Oxford University Press, pp. 463–92.

Daalder, H. and van den Berg, J. Th. J. (1982). 'Members of the Dutch Lower House: Pluralism and Democratization, 1848–1967', in M. N. Czudnowski (ed.), *Does Who Governs Matter? Elite Circulation in Contemporary Societies.* Dekalb, IL: Northern Illinois University Press, pp. 214–42.

Dahl, R. A. (1961). *Who Governs?—Democracy and Power in an American City.* New Haven, CT: Yale University Press.

——(1970). *Polyarchy, Participation and Opposition.* New Haven, CT: Yale University Press.

——(1989). *Democracy and its Critics.* New Haven, CT: Yale University Press.

Dahlerup, D. (1988*a*). 'From a Small to a Large Minority: Women in Scandinavian Politics', *Scandinavian Political Studies*,11: 275–98.

——(1998*b*). 'Using Quotas to Increase Women's Political Representation', in A. Karam (ed.), *Women in Parliament: Beyond Numbers.* Stockholm: International Institute for Democracy and Electoral Assistance (IDEA).

D'Alimonte, R. and Bartolini S., (eds.) (2002). *Maggioritario finalmente? La transizione elettorale Italian, 1994–2001.* Bologna: Il Mulino.

Dalton, R. J. (1996). *The Green Rainbow. Environmental Groups in Western Europe.* New Haven, CT: Yale University Press.

——(2002). 'Political Cleavages, Issues, and Electoral Change', in L. LeDuc, R. Niemi, and P. Norris (eds.), *Comparing Democracies 2. New Challenges in the Study of Elections and Voting.* London: Sage, pp. 189–209.

——and Wattenberg, M. P. (eds.) (2000). *Parties without Partisans. Political Change in Advanced and Industrial Democracies.* Oxford: Oxford University Press.

——Flanagan, S. and Beck, P. A. (eds.) (1984), Electoral Change in Advanced Industrial Democracies, Princeton, N.J.: Princeton University Press.

——Cain, B. E., and Scarrow, S. E. (eds.) (2003). 'Democratic Publics and Democratic Institutions', in B. E. Cain, R. J. Dalton, and S. E. Scarrow (eds.), *Democracy Transformed? Expanding Political Opportunities in Advanced Industrial Democracies.* Oxford: Oxford University Press, pp. 250–75.

Declair, E. G. (1999). *Politics on the Fringe: the People, Policies, and Organization of the French National Front.* Durham, NC: Duke University Press.

De Grand, A. J. (1978). *The Italian Nationalist Association and the Rise of Fascism in Italy.* Lincoln, NE: University of Nebraska Press.

Della Porta, D. and Diani, M. (eds.) (1999). *Social Movements: An Introduction.* Oxford: Basil Blackwell.

Del Wit, P. (ed.) (2003). *Democratie Chretienne et Conservativisme en Europe. Une nouvelle convergence?* Bruxelles: Editions de L'Universitè.

——and De Waele, J. M. (eds.) (1999). *Les Partis verts en Europe.* Bruxelles: Ed. Complexes.

Demaine, J. (ed.) (2001). *Sociology of Education Today.* Basingstoke, UK: Palgrave.

Denver, D. (1988). 'Britain: Centralized Parties with Decentralized Selection', in M. Gallagher, and M. Marsh (eds.), *Candidate Selection in Comparative Perspective.* London: Sage, pp. 47–71.

Deschouwer, K., De Winter, L., and Della Porta, D. (1996). 'Comparing Similar Countries: Belgium and Italy', *Res Publica*, 38(2) (special issue).

Deutscher Bundestag (2003). *Alphabetische Liste der Abgeordneten', 'Studienfächer', 'Schulbildung' and 'Hochschulbildung.* Berlin: Deutscher Bundestag (online publishing www.bundestag.de).

De Winter, L. (1988). 'Belgium: Democracy or Oligarchy', in M. Gallagher and M. Marsh (eds.), *Candidate Selection in Comparative Perspective.* London: Sage, pp. 20–46.

—— (1992) 'Christian Democratic Parties in Belgium', in M. Caciagli (ed.), *Christian Democracy in Europe.* Barcelona: Institut de Ciencias Politiques i Socials.

—— (1997). 'Intra- and Extra-Parliamentary Role Attitudes and Behaviour of Belgian MPs', *Journal of Legislative Studies*, 3: 128–54.

—— (1998). 'Conclusion: A Comparative Analysis of the Electoral, Office, and Policy Success of Ethnoregionalist Parties', in L. De Winter and H. Türsan (eds.), *Regionalist Parties in Western Europe.* London & New York: Routledge, pp. 204–47.

—— and Brans, M. (2003). 'Belgium: Political Professionals and the Crisis of the Party State', in J. Borchert and J. Zeiss (eds.), *The Political Class in Advanced Democracies.* Oxford: Oxford University Press, pp. 45–66.

—— and Gomez-Reino, M. (2002). 'European Integration and Ethnoregionalist Parties', *Party Politics*, 8(2): 483–503.

Diamond, I. (1977). *Sex Roles in the State House.* New Haven, CT: Yale University Press

Di Virgilio, A. (1995). 'Dai partiti ai poli: la politica delle alleanze', in S. Bartolini e R. D'Alimonte (eds.), *Maggioritario ma non troppo. Le elezioni politiche del 1994.* Bologna: Il Mulino, pp. 177–232.

Dobson, A. (2001). *Green Political Thought.* London: Routledge.

Dogan, M. (1961). 'Political Ascent in a Class Society: French Deputies, 1870–1958', in D. Marwick (ed.), *Political Decision-Makers.* Glencoe, IL: The Free Press.

Dolez, B. and Hastings, M. (eds.) (2003). *Le Parachutage Politique.* Paris: L'Harmattan.

Döring, M. (2001). *Parlamentarischer Arm der Bewegung: Die Nationalsozialisten im Reichstag der Weimarer Republik.* Düsseldorf: Droste.

Downs, A. (1957). *An Economic Theory of Democracy.* New York: Harper & Row.

Dunleavy, P. (1980). 'The Political Implications of Sectoral Cleavages and the Growth of State Employment: Part I, the Analysis of Production Cleavages; Part II, Cleavage Structure and Political Alignment', *Political Studies*, 28: 364–83, 527–49.

Durkheim, É. (1993). *Éducation et Sociologie*, 1st edn. 1922. Paris: Presses Universitaires de France.

Duverger, M. (1951). *Les partis politiques.* Paris: Armand Colin.

—— (1954). *Poltical Parties, Their Organisation and Activity in the Modern State.* London: Methuen Wiley.

—— (1955). *The Political Role of Women.* Paris: UNESCO.

Eccles, J. S. (1994). 'Understanding Women's Educational and Occupational Choices', *Psychology of Women Quarterly*, 18: 585–609.

Eckstein, H. (1975). 'Case Study and Theory in Political Science', in F. I. Greenstein and N. W. Polsby (eds.), *Handbook of Political Science*, vol. 7. Reading, MA: Addison-Wesley, pp. 79–137.

Ehrlich, V. (1998). *Les Nouveaux étudiants. Un groupe social en mutation.* Paris: Armand Colin.

Ehrman, Henry W. (1983). *Politics in France,* 4th edn. Boston, MA: Little, Brown and Company.

Eley, G. (1990) 'Conservatives and Radical Nationalists in Germany: The Production of Fascist Potentials, 1912–1928', in M. Blinkhorn (ed.), *Fascists and Conservatives.* pp. 50–99.

Elgie, R. (1999). *Semi-presidentialism in Europe.* Oxford: Oxford University Press.

Eliassen, K. A. (1978). 'Mass Mobilisation and the Transformation of Parliamentary Elites in Norway', *Scandinavian Political Studies,* 1(2–3): 187–213.

—— and Ågotnes, J.-E. (1987). *Stortingsrepresentanter og statsråder, 1945–1985.* Bergen: NSD.

—— and Brosveet, J. (1977). *Politikerarkivet, 1814–1976.* Bergen: NSD.

—— and Pedersen, M. N. (1978). 'Professionalization of Legislatures: Long-Term Change in Political Recruitment in Denmark and Norway', *Comparative Studies in Society and History,* 20: 286–318.

—— and Sjøvaag, M. (2000). 'Democratization and Parliamentary Elite Recruitment in Norway, 1848–1996', in H. Best and M. Cotta (eds.), *Parliamentary Representatives in Europe, 1848–2000. Legislative Recruitment and Careers in Eleven European Countries.* Oxford: Oxford University Press, pp. 310–40.

—— and Sjovaag, M. M (2000). '*Democratization and Parliamentary Elite Recruitment in Norway*' 1848–1966. in Best, Heinrich, and Cotta, Maurizio (eds.): *Parliamentary Representation in Europe, 1848–2000.* Legislative Recruitment and Careers in Eleven European Countries. Oxford: Oxford University Press, 310–40.

Epstein, S. (1996). 'Extreme Right Electoral Upsurges in Western Europe: The 1984–1995 Wave as Compared with the Previous Ones', *Analysis of Current Trends in Antisemitism,* 8. Jerusalem: SICSA.

Estrade, M. A. and Minni, C. (1996). 'La hausse du niveau de formation. La durée des études a doublé en cinquante ans', *Insee Première,* 488: 1–4.

Étienne, J. M. (1968). *Le mouvement rexiste jusqu'en 1940.* Paris: Armond Colin.

Eulau, H. and Sprague, J. D. (1984). *Lawyers in Politics. A Study on Political Convergence.* Westport, CT: Greenwood Press.

Evans, G. (ed.) (1999). *The End of Class Politics? Class Voting in Comparative Context.* Oxford: Oxford University Press.

Eymeri, J. M. (2001). *La Fabrique des Énarques.* Paris: Economica.

Farneti, P. (1971). *Sistema politico e società civile.* Torino: Giappichelli.

—— (1978). 'Social Conflict, Parliamentary Fragmentation, Institutional Shift and the Rise of Fascism: Italy', in J. J. Linz and A. Stepan (eds.), *The Breakdown of Democratic Regimes: Europe.* Baltimore, MD: The Johns Hopkins University Press, pp. 3–33.

Farrell, D. (2001). *Electoral Systems. A Comparative Introduction.* London: Palgrave.

Faurby, I. and Kristensen, O. P. (1982). 'Conservatism in Denmark: A Profile of Party Activists', in L. H. Zig (ed.), *Conservative Politics in Western Europe.* London: Macmillan, pp. 83–102.

Ferguson, A. (1995; first pub. 1767). *An Essay on the History of Civil Society.* Cambridge: Cambridge University Press.

Field, G. L. and Higley, J. (1980). *Elitism.* London: Routledge.

—— and Higley, J. (1985). 'National Elites and Political Stability', in Gwen Moore (ed.), *Studies of the Structure of National Elites*. Greenwich u. London: publisher, pp. 1–44.

—— and Grøholt, K., and Higley, J. (1976). *Elite Structure and Ideology. A Theory with Applications to Norway*. New York-Oslo: Universitetsforlaget/Columbia University Press.

Flora, P. et al. (1983). *State Economy and Society in Western Europe, 1815–1975*. Frankfurt/London: Campus/Macmillan.

—— (ed.) (1987). *Growth to Limits*. Berlin: De Gruyter.

—— and Heidenheimer, A. J. (eds.) (1981). *The Development of Welfare States in Europe and America*. New Brunswick: Transaction Books.

Fogarty, M. (1957). *Christian Democracy in Western Europe*. London: Routledge.

Franklin, M. (1992). 'The Decline of Cleavage Politics', in Mark Franklin et al. (eds.), *Electoral Change. Responses to Evolving Social and Attitudinal Structures in Western Societies*. Cambridge: Cambridge University Press, pp. 383–405.

Frognier, A. and Matéo-Diaz, M. (2003). 'Le parachutage politique en Belgique', in B. Dolez and M. Hastings (eds.), *Le Parachutage Politique*. Paris: L'Harmattan, pp. 271–185.

Fuchs, D. and Klingemann, H.-D. (1990). 'The Left-Right Schema', in Kent Jennings et al. (eds.), *Continuities in Political Action: A Longitudinal Study of Political Orientations in Three Western Democracies*. Berlin: Walter de Gruyter, pp. 203–34.

Gal, R. (1979). *Histoire de l'Éducation*, 10th edn. Paris: Presses Universitaires de France.

Gallagher, M. (1988). 'Conclusion', in M. Gallagher and M. Marsh (eds.), *Candidate Selection in Comparative Perspective. The Secret Garden of Politics*. London: Sage.

—— Laver, Michael, and Mair, Peter (1995). *Representative Government Modern Europe*. 2nd edn. London: McGraw-Hill.

—— (2003). 'Ireland: Party Loyalists with a Personal Base', in J. Borchert and J. Zeiss (eds.), *The Political Class in Advanced Democracies*. Oxford: Oxford University Press, pp. 187–202.

—— Laver, M., and Mair, P. (2001). *Representative Government in Modern Europe*, 3rd edn. Boston, MA: McGraw-Hill.

Gambetta, D. and Warner, S. (2004). 'Italy: Lofty Ambitions and Unintended Consequences', in J. M. Colomer (ed.), *Handbook of Electoral System Choice*. New York: Palgrave Macmillan, pp. 237–52.

Garrigues, J. (1997). *La République des hommes d'affaires, 1870–1900*. Paris: Aubier.

Gaxie, D. (2001). 'Les critiques profanes de la politique. Enchantements, désenchantements, réenchantements', in J. L. Briquet and P. Garraud (eds.), *Juger la politique*. Rennes: Presses Universitaires de Rennes, pp. 217–40.

—— (2003*a*). *La Démocratie Représentative*, 4th edn. Paris: Montchrestien.

—— (2003*b*). 'Sur l'humeur politique maussade des démocraties représentatives', in O. Mazzoleni (ed.), *La politica allo specchio. Istituzioni, partecipazione e formazione alla cittadinanza*. Bellinzona: Giampiero Casagrande, pp. 109–36.

Gentile, E. (1973). *L'orignie dell'ideologie fascista (1918–1925)*. Rome: Laterza.

—— (1989). *Storia del Partito Fascista, 1919–1922. Movimento e Milizia*. Laterza.

—— (2003). *The Struggle for Modernity. Naturalism, Futurism and Fascism*. Westport, CT: Praeger.

Gergs, H., Hausmann, C., and Pohlmann, M. (1997). 'Political and Economic Elites in the Transformation Process in Eastern Germany', in H. Best and U. Becker (eds.), *Elites in*

Transition. Elite Research in Central and Eastern Europe. Opladen: Leske & Budrich, pp. 203–48.

Gil Pecharromán, J. (1994). *Conservadores subversivos. La derecha autoritaria alfonsina, 1913–1936.* Madrid: Endema.

Girvin, B. (ed.) (1988). *The Transformation of Contemporary Conservatism.* London: Sage.

Godmer, L. (2002). 'Les mutations du capital représentatif. La sélection des représentants régionaux', PhD dissertation, Paris-I Sorbonne University, Paris.

——(2004). 'La élus régionaux néo-communistes dans les territoires politiques issus de l'ex-RDA: domination du capital culturel et conditions de possibilité de sa conversion politique', *Transitions. Brussels*, 43(2): 43–58.

——(2005). *Le Principe Représentation.* Paris: L'Harmattan (forthcoming).

Golsch, L. (1998). *Die Politische Klasse im Parlament. Politische Professionalisierung von Hinterbänklern im Deutschen Bundestag.* Baden-Baden: Nomos.

Greenacre, M. J. (1993). *Correspondece Analysis in Practice.* London et al.: Academic Press.

Grèzes-Rueff, F. (1994). *La culture des députés français, 1910–1958. Essai de typologie.* Toulouse: Presses Universitaires du Mirail.

Griffin, R. (1991). *The Nature of Fascism, 1914–1945.* London: Pinter.

Gruner, E. (ed.) (1970). *Die Schweizerische Bundesversammlung, 1920–1968.* Bern: Francke.

Guarnieri, C. and Pederzoli, P. (1997). *La democrazia giudiziaria.* Bologna: Il Mulino.

Guerrero Serón, A. (1996). *Manual de sociología de la educación.* Madrid: Síntesis.

Guttsman, W. L. (1963). *The British Political Elite.* London.

Habermas, J. (1962). *Strukturwandel der Offentlichkeit.* Neuwied and Berlin: Luchterhand.

Hainsworth, P. (1992). *The Extreme Right in Europe and the USA.* London: Pinter Publishers.

Hakim, C. (1993*a*). 'Notes and Issues: The Myth of Rising Female Employment', *Work, Employment and Society*, 7(1): 97–120.

——(1993*b*). 'Segregated and Integrated Occupations: A New Approach to Analysing Social Change', *European Sociological Review*, 9(3): 289–314.

Hanley, D. (ed.) (1994). *Christian Democracy in Europe. A Comparative Perspective.* London: Pinter.

Hartmann, H. (1981). 'The Family as the Locus of Gender, Class and Political Struggle: The Example of Housework', *Signs*, 6: 366–94.

Hastings, M. (2003). 'Parachutages politiques et construction symbolique de la démocratie représentative', in B. Dolez and M. Hastings (eds.), *Le Parachutage Politique.* Paris: L'Harmattan, pp. 25–43.

Hazan, R. (1997). *Centre Parties. Polarization and Competition in European Parliamentary Democracy.* London: Pinter.

——(2002). 'Candidate Selection', in L. LeDuc, R. G. Niemi, and P. Norris (eds.), *Comparing Democracies 2.* London: Sage.

Hegel, G. W. F. (1821). *Grundlinien der Philosophie des Rechts.*

Heinen, A. (1986). *Die Legion 'Erzengel Michael' in Rumänien: sociale Bewegung und politische Organization: ein Beitrag zum Problem des internationalen Faschismus* (Südosteuropäische Arbeiten). München: Oldenbourg.

Helander, V. (1981). 'Lohkoutuminen, ministeriöpluralismi ja maatalouden konsultaatio', *Politiikka*, 23(4): 364–83.

—— (1997). 'Finland', in P. Norris (ed.), *Passages to Power. Legislative Recruitment in Advanced Democracies*. Cambridge: Cambridge University Press.

Herzog, D. (1975). *Politische Karrieren. Selektion und Professionalisierung politischer Führungsgruppen*. Opladen: Westdeutscher Verlag.

—— (1976). 'Partei- und Parlamentskarrieren im Spiegel der Zahlen für die Bundesrepublik Deutschlands', *Zeitschrift für Parlamentsfragen*. Heft, 1: 25–34.

—— Rebenstorf, H., and Wessels, B. (eds.) (1993). *Parlament und Gesellschaft. Eine Funktionsanalyse der repräsentativen Demokratie*. Opladen: Westdeutscher Verlag.

Hetherington, M. J. (2001). 'Resurgent Mass Partisanship: The Role of Elite Polarization', *American Political Science Review*, 95: 619–31.

Heywood, A. (1998). *Political Ideologies. An Introduction*, 2nd edn. Basingstoke, UK: Macmillan.

Higgs, D. (1987). *Nobles in Nineteenth Century France: The Practice of Inegalitarianism*. Baltimore, MD: The Johns Hopkins University Press.

Higley, J. and Gunther, R. (eds.) (1992). *Elites and Democratic Consolidation in Latin America and Southern Europe*. Cambridge: Cambridge University Press.

—— and Lengyel, G. (eds.) (2000). *Elites after State Socialism. Theories and Analyses*. Lanham: Rowman & Littlefield.

Hintze, O. (1970; orig. 1911). Das monarchische Prinzip und die konstitutionelle Verfassung', in *Staat und Verfassung. Gesammelte Abhandlungen*. Göttingen: Vandenhoeck & Ruprecht, pp. 359–90.

Hix, S. (1999). *The Political System of the European Union*. New York: St. Martin's Press.

Hoecker, B. (ed.) (1998) *Handbuch politischer Partizipation von Frauen in Europa*. Opladen: Leske & Budrich.

Hokkanen, K. (1996). *Maalaisliitto-Keskustan historia 3. Maalaisliitto sodan ja vaaran vuosina, 1939–1950*. Keuruu: Otava.

Hölmberg, S. (1989). 'Political Representation in Sweden', *Scandinavian Political Studies*, 12(1): 1–36.

Hubert, P. (1992). *Uniformierter Reichstag. Die Geschichte der Pseudo-Volksvertretung, 1933–1945*. Düsseldorf: Droste.

Huddy, L. and Terkildsen, N. (1993). Gender Stereotypes and the Perception of Male and Female Candidates', *American Journal of Political Science*, 37(1): 119–47.

Huntington, S. P. (1968). *Political Order in Changing Societies*. New Haven, CT: Yale University Press.

—— (1991). *The Third Wave: Democratization in the Late Twentieth Century*. Norman London: University of Oklahoma Press

Ignazi, P. (1989). *Il polo escluso. Profilo del Movimento Sociale Italiano*. Bologna: Il Mulino.

—— (1992). 'The Silent Counter-Revolution. Hypotheses on the Emergence of Extreme Right-Wing Parties in Europe', *European Journal of Political Research*, 3: 3–34.

—— (1994). *L'Estrema Destrai Europa*. Bologna: Il Mulino.

—— (2003). *Extreme Right Parties in Western Europa*. Oxford: Oxford University Press.

Ilonszki, G. (2000). 'Belated Professionalization of Parliamentary Elites: Hungary, 1848–1999', in H. Best and M. Cotta (eds.), *Parliamentary Representatives in Europe,*

1848–2000. Legislative Recruitment and Careers in Eleven European Countries. Oxford: Oxford University Press, 196–225.

Inglehart, R. (1977). *The Silent Revolution, Changing Values and Political Styles among Western Publics.* Princeton, NJ: Princeton University Press.

——(1979). 'The Changing Structure of Political Cleavages in Western Society', in R. J. Paltron, S. C. Flanagan, and P. A. Beck (eds.), *Electoral Change in Advanced Industrial Democracies, Realignment or Dealignment?* Princeton, NJ: Princeton University Press, pp. 25–69.

——(1984). 'The Changing Structure of Political Cleavage in Western Society', in R. J. Dalton (ed.), *Electoral Change in Advanced Industrial Democracies.* Princeton, NJ: Princeton University Press.

——and Norris, P. (2000). 'The Developmental Theory of the Gender Gap: Women and Men's Voting Behaviour in Global Perspective', *International Political Science Review*, 21(4): 441–62.

INSEE (Institut National de la Statistique et des Études Économiques) (1999). *Population de 15 ans ou plus par sexe et âge selon le diplôme* and *Population de 15 ans ou plus par sexe et selon le niveau d'études.* Paris: INSEE.

Inter-Parliamentary Union (2003*a*). 'Political will Indispensable for Steady Progress in Women's Participation in Parliament', *Press Release 155,* 5 March. Geneva (online publishing, http://www.ipu.org/press-e/gen155.htm).

——(2007). *Women in National Parliaments.* (online publishing http://www.ipu.org/ wmn-e/world.htm) (31.03.07).

Irving, R. E. M. (1979). *Christian Democratic Parties in Western Europe.* London: Allen & Unwin.

Jacobs, J. (1996). 'Gender Inequality and Higher Education', *Annual Review of Sociology.* Annual Reviews Inc., 22: 153–85.

Janos, Andrew C. (1989). *The Politics of Backwardness in Hungary, 1825–1945.* Princeton, NJ: Princeton University Press.

Janova, M. and Sineau, M. (1992). 'Women's Participation in Political Power in Europe: An Essay in East-West Comparison', *Women's Studies International Forum*, 11(1): 115–28

Jenkins, R. (2001). *Churchill.* London: Pan Books.

Johansson, J. (1999). *Hur blir man riksdagsledamot?* Södertälje: Gidlunds Förlag.

de Jouvenel, R. (1913). *La république des camarades.* Paris: Grasset.

Judge, D. (1999). *Representation. Theory and Practice in Britain.* London: Routledge.

Kaartvedt, A. (1964). 'Fra Riksforsamlingen til 1869', in A. Kaartvedt et al. (eds.), *Det Norske Storting gjennom 150 år.*, vol. 1. Oslo: Gyldendal Norsk Forlag.

Kailitz, S. (2004). *Politischer Extremismus in der Bundesrepublik Deutschland.* Eine Einführung, V. S. Verlag für Socialwissenschaften.

Kalyvas, S. N. (1996). *From Pulpit to Party. The Rise of Christian Democracy in Europe.* Ithaca, NY: Cornell University Press.

Kantrowitz, B. (2003). 'Learning the Hard Way', *Newsweek*, 15 September: 50–7.

Kaplan, G. (1992). 'Contemporary Western European Feminism', *UCL Press.* London: Allen & Unwin.

Karam, A. (ed.) (1998). *Women in Parliament: Beyond Numbers.* Stockholm: International Institute for Democracy and Electoral Assistance (IDEA).

Karvonen, L. (1988). *From White to Blue-and-Black, Finnish Fascism in the Inter-War Era.* Helsinki: Societas Scientiamum Fennica.

Kasekamp, A. (2000). *The Radical Right in Interwar Estonia.* London: Macmillan Press, Studies in Russia and East Europe in association with School of Slavonic and East European Studies, University of London.

Katz, R. (1980). *A Theory of Parties and Electoral Systems.* Baltimore, MD: The Johns Hopkins University Press.

——(1986). 'Party Government a Rationalistic Conception', in F. G. Castles and R. Wildenmann (eds.), *Visions and Realities of Party Government.* Berlin: de Gruyter, pp. 31–71.

——(1987). 'Party Government and Its Alternatives', in R. Katz (ed.), *Party Government: American and European Experiences.* Berlin: de Gruyter.

——(2001). 'The Problem of Candidate Selection and Models of Party Democracy', *Party Politics,* 7: 277–96.

——(2002). 'The Internal Life of Parties', in K. R. Luther and F. Mueller Rommel (eds.), *Political Parties in the New Europe.* Oxford: Oxford University Press, pp. 87–119.

—— and Mair, P. (eds.) (1992). *Party Organization. A Data Handbook.* London: Sage.

————(1995). 'Changing Modes of party Organization and Party Democracy: The Emergence of the Cartel Party', *Party Politics,* I: 5–28.

Kauppi, N. (1999). 'Power or Subjection? French Women Politicians in the European Parliament', *European Journal of Women's Studies,* 6(3): 329–40.

Kirchner, E. J. (1988). *Liberal Parties in Western Europe.* Cambridge: Cambridge University Press.

Kircheimer, O. (1966). 'The Transformation of the Western European Party Systems', in J. LaPalombara and M. Weiner (eds.), *Political Parties and Political Development.* Princeton, NJ: University Press, pp. 177–200.

Kitschelt, H. (1988). 'Left Libertarian Parties: Explaining Innovation in Competitive Party Systems', *World Politics,* 2: 194–234.

——(1994). *The Transformation of European Social Democracy.* Cambridge: Cambridge University Press.

——(1995). *The Radical Right in Western Europe: A Comparative Analysis.* Michigan: University of Michigan Press.

—— and Hellemans (1990). *Beyond the European Left: Ideology and Political Action in the Belgian Ecology parties.* Durham, NC: Duke University Press.

Kjær, U. (1999). 'Saturation Without Parity: The Stagnating Number of Female Councillors in Denmark', in E. Beukel, K. K. Klausen, and P. E. Mouritzen (eds.), *Elites, Parties and Democracy—Festschrift for Professor Mogens N. Pedersen.* Odense: Odense University Press.

——(2000). 'Representativeness and Local Politics in Denmark', in N. Rao (ed.), *Representation and Community in Western Democracies.* Houndmills, UK: Macmillan.

—— and Pedersen, M. N. (2004). *De danske folketingsmedlemmer—en parlamentarisk elite og dens rekruttering, cirkulation og transformation: 1849–2001.* Aarhus: Aarhus Universitetsforlag.

Knapp, A. (1997). 'Vers un gouvernement d'inconnus? Hommes politiques et hauts fonctionnaires en Grande-Bretagne', in E. Suleiman et H. Mendras (eds.), *Le Recrutement des Elites en Europe.* Paris, 128–57.

Knight, M. (1952). *The German Executive, 1890–1933*. Stanford, CA: Hoover Institute Studies, Stanford University Press.

Knutsen, O. and Scarbrough, E. (1995). 'Cleavage Politics', in J. W. van Deth and E. Scarbrough (eds.), *The Impact of Values*. Oxford: Oxford University Press, pp. 492–523.

Koole, R. and Leijenaar, M. (1988). 'The Netherlands: The Predominance of Regionalism', in M. Gallagher and M. Marsh (eds.), *Candidate Selection in Comparative Perspective*. London: Sage, pp. 190–209.

Kotler-Berkowitz, L. A. (2001). 'Religion and Voting Behaviour in Great Britain: A reassessment', *British Journal of Political Science*, 31: 523–54.

Krasner, S. D. (1999). *Sovereignty: Organised Hypocrisy* (chap. 1). Princeton, NJ: Princeton University Press.

Kreuzer, M. and Stepan, I. (2003). 'France: Enduring Notables, Weak Parties, and Powerful Technocrats', in J. Borchert and J. Zeiss (eds.), *The Political Class in Advanced Democracies*. Oxford: Oxford University Press, pp. 124–41.

Kriesi, H. (1998). 'The Transformation of Cleavage Politics. The 1997 Stein Rokkan Lecture', *European Journal of Political Science*, 33: 165–85.

Kristiansen, B. and Svåsand, L. (1982). 'The Conservative Party in Norway: from Opposition to Alternative Government', in L. H. Zig (ed.), *Conservative Politics in Western Europe*. London: Macmillan, pp. 103–30.

Kristjánson, S. (2002). 'Iceland: From Party Rule to Pluralist Political Society', in H. M. Narud, M. N. Pedersen, and H. Valen (eds.), *Party Sovereignty and Citizen Control*. Odense: University Press of Southern Denmark, pp. 107–66

Kuitunen, S. (2002). 'Finland: Formalized Procedures with Member Predominance', in H. M. Narud, M. N. Pedersen, and H. Valen (eds.), *Party Sovereignty and Citizen Control*. Odense: University Press of Southern Denmark, pp. 63–104.

Labatut, J. P. (1978). *Les noblesses européennes de la fin du XV à la fin du XVIII siècle*. Paris: PUF.

Lacko, M. (1959). *Men of the Arrow Cross*. Budapest: Akadémiai Kiadó.

Lane, J.-E. and Ersson, S. (1995). *Politics and Society in Western Europe*. London: Sage.

—— and Pennings, P. (eds.) (1998). *Party System Change*. London: Routledge.

—— McKay, D., and Newton, K. (eds.) (1997). *Political Data Handbook—OECD Countries*. Oxford: Oxford University Press.

La Palombara, J. (1964). *Interest Groups in Italian Politics*. Princeton, NJ: Princeton University Press.

La Palombara, J. and Weiner, M. (1966). 'The Origin and Development of Political Parties', in J. La Palombara and M. Weiner (eds.), *Political Parties and Political Development*. Princeton, NJ: Princeton University Press, pp. 3–42.

Laponce, J. A. (1981). *Left and Right. The Topography of Political Perceptions*. Toronto: University of Toronto Press.

Laqueur, W. (ed.) (1978). *Fascism. A Reader's Guide. Analyses, Interpretations, Bibliography*. Berkeley, CA: University of California Press.

Larsen, S. U., Hagtvet, B., and Myklebust, J. P. (1980). *Who Were the Fascists. Social Roots of European Fascism*. Bergen: Universitetsforlaget.

—— with the assistance of Bernt Hagtvet (eds.)(1998). *Modern Europe after Fascism 1943–1980's*, 2 vols. Boulder, CO: Social Science Monographs, distributed by Columbia University Press.

Lawson, K. and Merkl, P. H. (eds.) (1988). *When Parties Fail: Emerging Alternative Organizations*. Princeton, NJ: Princeton University Press.

Lawton, D. (1998). *Social Class, Language and Education* 1st edn. 1968). London: Routledge.

Layton-Henry, Z. (ed.) (1982). *Conservative Politics in Western Europe*. New York: St. Martin Press.

Leijenaar, M. (1997). *How to Create a Gender Balance in Political Decision-making: A Guide to Implementing Policies for Increasing the Participation of Women in Political Decision-making*. Luxembourg: Office for Official Publications of the European Communities.

—— and Niemöller, K. (2003). 'Netherland: Political Careers between Central Party Dominance and New Pressures', in J. Borchert and J. Zeiss (eds.), *The Political Class in Advanced Democracies*. Oxford: Oxford University Press, pp. 259–77.

Leonardi, R. and Wertman, D. ([1987] 1989). *Italian Christian Democracy: The Politics of Dominance*. New York: St. Martins Press, and London: Macmillan.

Lieven, D. (1992). *The Aristocracy of Europe, 1815–1914*. London: Macmillan.

Lijphart, A. (1968*a*). *The Politics of Accommodation. Pluralism and Democracy in the Netherlands*. Berkeley, CA: University of California Press.

—— (1968*b*). 'Typologies of Democratic Systems', *Comparative Political Studies*, 1: 12–24.

—— (1971). 'Comparative Politics and Comparative Method', *American Political Science Review*, LXV: 682–93.

—— (1977). *Democracy in Plural Societies. A Comparative Exploration*. New Haven, CT and London: Yale University Press.

—— (1994). *Electoral Systems and Party Systems*. Oxford: Oxford University Press.

—— (1999). *Patterns of Democracy. Government Forms and Performance in Thirty-six Countries*. New Haven, CT: Yale University Press.

Linz, J. J. (1976). 'Some Notes Toward a Comparative Study of Fascism in Sociological Historical Perspective', in W. Laqueur (ed.), *Fascism. A Reader's Guide*, pp. 3–124.

—— (1978). 'Crisis, Breakdown and Reequilibration', in J. J. Linz and A. Stepan (eds.), *The Breakdown of Democratic Regimes*. Baltimore, MD: The Johns Hopkins University Press.

—— (1980). 'Political Space and Fascism as a Late-Comer', in S. U. Larsen et al. (eds.), *Who Were the Fascists?*, pp. 153–89.

—— (1998). 'Fascism is Dead. What Legacy did it Leave? Thoughts and Questions on a Problematic Period of European History', in S. U. Larsen and B. Hagtvet (eds.), *Modern Europe after Fascism, 1943–1980's*. Boulder, CO: Social Science Monographs. New York. Distributed by Columbia University Press, pp. 19–54.

—— (2000). *Totalitarian and Authoritarian Regimes*. Boulder, CO: Lynne Rienner.

—— and Stepan, A. (eds.) (1978). *The Breakdown of Democratic Regimes*. Baltimore, MD: The Johns Hopkins University Press.

—— and Stepan, A. (eds.) (1996). *Problems of Democratic Transition and Consolidation*. Baltimore, MD: The Johns Hopkins University Press.

—— Gangas, P., and Jerez Mir, M. (2000). 'Spanish Diputados: from the 1876 Restoration to Consolidated Democracy', in H. Best and M. Cotta (eds.), *Parliamentary*

Representatives in Europe, 1848–2000: Legislative Recruitment and Careers in Eleven European Countries. Oxford: Oxford University Press, pp. 371–462.

Linz, J. J., Jerez Mir, M., and Corza, S. (2003). 'Ministers and Regimes in Spain: From the First to the Second Restoration, 1874–2002', in P. Tavares de Almeida, A. Costa Pinto, and N. Bermeo (eds.), *Who Governs Southern Europe? Regime Change and Ministerial Recruitment, 1850–2000*. London: Frank Cass, pp. 41–116.

Lipset, S. M. (1958). *Political Man. The Social Bases of Politics*. New York: Doubleday.

—— and Rokkan, S. (1967). 'Cleavage Structures, Party Systems and Voter Alignments: An Introduction', in S. M. Lipset and S. Rokkan (eds.), *Party Systems and Voter Alignments: Cross-National Perspectives*. New York: The Free Press.

Loewenberg, G. and Patterson, S. C. (1979). *Comparing Legislatures*. Boston, MA: Little, Brown and Company.

Lorwin, V. R. (1971). 'Segmented Pluralism', *Comparative Politics*, 3: 141–75.

Lotti, L. (1963). 'Il Parlamento Italiano 1909–1963, Raffronto Storico', in G. Sartori (ed.), *Il Parlamento Italiano, 1946–1963*. Napoli; Edizioni Scientifiche Italiane, pp. 142–200.

Lovenduski, J. (1986). *Women and European Politics: Contemporary Feminism and Public Policy*. Amherst, MA: The University of Massachusetts Press.

—— and Norris, P. (eds.) (1996). *Women in Politics*. Oxford: Oxford University Press.

Lucardie, P. and ten Napel, H. M. (1994). 'Betweeen Confessionalism and Liberal Conservatorism: The Christian Democratic parties of Belgium and the Netherlands', in D. Hanley (ed.), *Christian democracy in Europe. A Comparative Perspective*. London: Pinter, pp. 51–70.

Luebbert, G. (1991). *Liberalism, Fascism, or Social Democracy. Social Classes and the Political Origins of Regimes in Inter-war Europe*. Oxford: Oxford University Press.

McAllister, I. (1997). 'Australia', in P. Norris (ed.), *Passages to Power. Legislative Recruitment in Advanced Democracies*. Cambridge: Cambridge University Press.

Mackie, T. T. and Rose, R. (1982). *The International Almanac of Electoral History*, 2nd revised edn. London: Macmillan.

—— —— (1991). *The International Almanac of Electoral History*, Fully Revised 3rd edn. London: Macmillan.

—— —— (1997). *A Decade of Election Results: Updating the International Almanac*. Glasgow: Studies in Public Policy.

Magnette, P. (2003) 'Qu'est ce que le conservatisme politique?', in P. Del Wit (ed.), *Democratie Chretienne et Conservativisme en Europe. Une nouvelle convergence?* Bruxelles: Editions de L'Universitè.

Magone, J. M. (2000). 'Political Recruitment and Elite Transformation in Modern Portugal, 1870–1999: The Late Arrival of Mass Representation', in H. Best and M. Cotta (eds.), *Parliamentary Representatives in Europe, 1848–2000. Legislative Recruitment and Careers in Eleven European Countries*. Oxford: Oxford University Press, pp. 342–70.

Mair, P. (1993). 'Myths of Electoral Change and the Survival of Traditional Parties', *European Journal of Political Research*, 24(2): 121–33.

Manin, B. (1997). *The Principles of Representative Government*. Cambridge: Cambridge University Press.

Mannheim, K. and Stewart, W. A. C. (1997). *An Introduction to the Sociology of Education*. London: Routledge.

Mansbridge, J. (1999). 'Should Blacks Represent Blacks and Women Represent Women? A contingent "yes" '. *Journal of Politics*, 61(3): 628–57.

—— (2003). 'Rethinking Representation', *American Political Science Review*, 97: 515–28.

Manza, J. and Brooks, C. (1999). *Social Cleavages and Political Change*. Oxford: Oxford University Press.

Marques-Pereira, B. (1999) 'Quotas ou parité. Enjeux et argumentation', *Recherches féministes*, 12(1) 103–21.

Marshall, M. M. and Jaggers, K. (2002). 'Polity IV Project', *Political Regime Characteristics and Transitions, 1800–2002*. Dataset Users' Manual, University of Maryland: Center for International Development and Conflict Management (CIDCM).

Mastropaolo, A. (1993). *Il ceto politico. Teoria e prassi*. Roma: Nis.

Matland, R. E. (1998*a*). 'Women's Representation in National Legislatures: Developed and Developing Countries', *Legislative Studies Quarterly*, 23(1): 109–25.

Matland, R. E. (1998*b*). 'Enhancing Women's Political Participation: Legislative Recruitment and Electoral Systems', in A. Karam (ed.), *Women in Parliament: Beyond Numbers*. Stockholm: International Institute for Democracy and Electoral Assistance (IDEA).

—— and Studlar, D. T. (1996). 'The Contagion of Women Candidates in Single-Member District and Proportional Representation Electoral Systems: Canada and Norway', *Journal of Politics*, 58: 707–33.

Matthes, C. Y. (2000). 'Abgeordnete im Ungarn: Amtverständnis und Amtausübung', *Südosteuropa*, 49(3–4): 175–91.

Matthews, D. (1954). *The Social Background of Political Decision-Makers*. New York: Garden City.

—— and Valen, H. (1999). *Parliamentary Representation. The Case of the Norwegian Storting*. Columbus, OH: Ohio State University Press.

Mayer, A. J. (1981). *The Persistence of the Old Regime: Europe to the Great War*. New York: Pantheon Books.

Mayer, N. (1998). 'The French National Front', in Betz and Immerfall (eds.), *The New Politics of the Right*. Basingstoke: Macmillan Press, pp. 1–10.

—— and Sineau, B. (2002). 'France: the Front National', in H. Amsberger and B. Halbmayr (eds.), *Rechtextreme Parteien*. Leverkusen: Leske & Budrich.

Mellors, C. (1978). *The British MP. A Socio-economic Study of the House of Commons*. Farnborough: Saxon House.

Melucci, A. and Diani, M. (1992). *Nazioni senza stato. I movimenti etnico-nazionali in Occidente*. Milano: Feltrinelli.

Mény, Y. et al. (2000). 'The Future of Parliamentary Democracy: Transition and Challenge in European Governance', green paper prepared for the Conference of the European Union, Speakers of Parliament, Rome.

Merkel, P. (1980). 'Comparing Fascist Movements', in S. U. Larsen et al. (eds.), *Who were the Fascists?* Bergen: Universitetsforlaget, pp. 752–83.

Michels, R. (1989 orig. 1911). *Zur Soziologie des Parteiwesens in der modernen Demokratie*. Stuttgart: Alfred Kröner Verlag, 4th edition.

Miller, W. (1999). 'Elite-Mass Linkages in Representative Democracy. Introduction', in E. M. Warren et al. (eds.), *Policy Representation in Western Democracies*. Oxford: Oxford University Press, pp. 9–33.

Moore, B. (1966). *Social Origins of Dictatorship and Democracy Lord and Peasant in the making of the Modern World*. Boston, MA: Beacon Press.

Morlino, L. (1998). *Democracy Between Consolidation and Crisis. Parties, Groups, and Citizens in Southern Europe*. Oxford: Oxford University Press.

Müller, W. (2005). 'A Complex Electoral System with Subtle Effects', in M. Gallagher and P. Mitchell (eds.), *The Politics of Electoral Systems*. Oxford: Oxford University Press (forthcoming).

—— Jenny, M., Steininger, B., Dolezal, M., Philipp, W., and Preisl-Westphal, S. (2001). *Die österreichischen Abgeordneten*. Vienna: WUV- Universitätsverlag.

Müller-Rommel, F. (ed.) (1989). *New Politics in Western Europe: The Rise and Success of Greens Parties*. Boulder, CO: Westview Press.

—— (2002). 'Lifespan and Political Performance of Green Parties in Western Europe', in F. Müller-Rommel and T. Pogunkte (eds.), *Green Parties in National Governments*. London: Frank Cass.

—— and Pridham, G. (eds.) (1991). *Small Parties in Western Europe*. London: Sage.

Müller-Schneider, T. (1997). 'The Visualization of Structural Change by Means of Correspondence Analysist', in Michael Greenecre and Jörg Blasius (eds.), *Correspondence Analysis in The Social Sciences: Recent Developments and Applications*. London: Academic Press, pp. 267–79.

Musiedlak, D. (2003). *Lo stato fascista e le sua classe politico, 1922–1945*. Bologna: Il Mulino.

Myers, A. R. (1975). *Parliaments and Estates in Europe to 1789*. London: Thames and Hudson.

Narud, H. M., Pedersen, M., and Valen, H. (eds.) (2002). *Party Sovereignty and Citizen Control*. Odense: University Press of Southern Denmark.

Nationalrat (2003). *Ämtliche Verzeichnis der Abgeordneten zum Nationalrat, Stand 2003–11–07*. Vienna (available on www.parlinkom.gv.at).

Niven, D. (1998). *The Missing Majority: The Recruitment of Women As State Legislative Candidates*. Westport, CT: Praeger.

Nolte, E. (1966). *Three Faces of Fascism*. New York: Holt, Rinehart & Winston.

Noponen, M. (1968). 'Riksdagsmännens sociala bakgrund', in J. M. Jansson (ed.), *Studier i finländsk politik*. Stockholm: Läromedelsförlagen, pp. 63–113.

Norris, P. (1985). 'Women's Legislative Participation in Western Europe'. *Western European Politics*, 8: 90–101.

—— (1997a). 'Introduction: Theories of Recruitment', in P. Norris (ed.), *Passages to Power. Legislative Recruitment in Advanced Democracies*. Cambridge.

—— (ed.) (1997b). *Passages to Power: Legislative Recruitment in Advanced Democracies*. Cambridge: Cambridge University Press.

—— (1999a). 'Recruitment into the European Parliament', in R. S. Katz and B. Wessels (eds.), *The European Parliament, the National Parliaments, and European Integration*. Oxford: Oxford University Press.

—— (ed.) (1999b). *Critical Citizens: Global Support for Democratic Governance*. Oxford: Oxford University Press.

—— (2004). *Electoral Engineering—Voting Rules and Political Behaviour*. Cambridge: Cambridge University Press.

—— and Lovenduski, J. (1995). *Political Representation and Recruitment: Gender, Race and Class in the British Parliament*. Cambridge: Cambridge University Press.

—— and Lovenduski, J. (2001). *Blair's Babes: Critical Mass Theory, Gender and Legislative Life* (http://www.ksg.harvard.edu/wapp/research/working/blairs_babes.pdf).

Nyman, O. (1966). *Tvåkammersystemets omvandling. Samhälle och riksdag*, vol. 3. Stockholm: Almqvistt & Wiksell.

Oakes, A. and Almquist, E. (1993). 'Women in National Legislatures—A Cross-national Test of Macrostructural Gender Theories', *Population Research and Policy Review*, 12(1): 71–81.

O'Donnell, G., Schmitter, P. C., and Whitehead, A. (eds.) (1986). *Transitions from Authoritarian Rule*. Baltimore, MD: The Johns Hopkins University Press.

Offe, K. (1985). 'New Social Movements', *Social Research*, 52: 817–68.

O'Neill, M. (1997). *Green Parties and Political Change in Contemporary Europe*. Aldershot, UK: Ashgate.

Ortega, J. V. (ed.) (2001). *El poder de la influencia. Geografía del caciquismo en Espana, 1875–1923*. Madrid: Marcial Pons.

OSCE (Organisation for Security and Cooperation in Europe) (1995). *Education at a Glance*. Vienna: OSCE.

Otto, H-U., Rauschenbach, T., and Vogel, P. (eds.) (2002). *Erziehungswissenschaft in Studium und Beruf: Eine Einführung in vier Bänden*, vol. 4. Opladen: Leske & Budrich.

Panebianco, A. (1988). *Political Parties: Organization and Power*. Cambridge: Cambridge University Press.

Papini, R. (1997). *The Christian Democrat International*. New York: Rowman & Littlefield.

Passmore, K. (1995). 'Boy Scoutism for Grown-ups? Paramilitarism in the Croix de Feu and the PSF', *French Historical Studies*, 19: 527–57.

Patzelt, W. (1997). 'German MPs and Their Roles', *Journal of Legislative Studies*, 3: 55–78.

Paxton, P. (1997). 'Women in National Legislatures: A Cross National Analysis', *Social Science Research*, 26: 442–64.

Paxton, R. O. (2004). *The Anatomy of Fascism*. New York: Alfred A. Knopf.

Payne, S. G. (1995). *A History of Fascism, 1914–1945*. Madison, WI: University of Wisconsin Press (with extensive bibliography, pp. 523–77).

—— *Fascism in Spain, 1923–1977*. Madison: WI: University of Wisconsin Press.

Pedersen, M. (1966). 'Preferential Voting in Denmark: The Voters' Influence on the Election of Folketing Candidates', *Scandinavian Political Studies*, 1: 167–87.

—— (1975). 'The Geographical Matrix of Parliamentary Representation: A Spatial Model of Political Recruitment', *European Journal of Political Research*, 3: 1–19.

—— (1976). *Political Development and Elite Transformation in Denmark*. Sage Contemporary papers in Political Sociology.

—— (1982). 'Towards a New Typology of Party Lifespans and Minor Parties', *Scandinavian Political Studies*, 1:1–16.

—— (1988). 'The Defeat of All Parties: The Danish Folketing Election 1973', in K. Lawson and P. Merkl (eds.), *When Parties Fail*. Princeton, NJ: Princeton University Press.

Pedersen, M. (2000). 'The Incremental Transformation of the Danish Legislative Elite: The Party System as Prime Mover', in H. Best and M. Cotta (eds.), *Parliamentary Representatives in Europe, 1848–2000. Legislative Recruitment and Careers in Eleven European Countries*. Oxford: Oxford University Press, pp. 29–49.

Pedersen, M. (2002). 'Denmark: The Interplay of Nominations and Elections in Danish Politics', in H. M. Narud, M. N. Pedersen, and H. Valen (eds.), *Party Sovereignty and Citizen Control*. Odense: University Press of Southern Denmark.

——(2004). 'Journalister i Folketingssalen—redaktørernes og journalisternes indmarch og udmarch', in A. K. Petersen et al. (eds.), *Kære samfund*. Odense: University Press of Southern Denmark, pp. 148–59.

——Kjær, U. and Kjell, A. E. (2004). 'Institutions Matter—Even in the Long Run', *Tidsskrift for Samfunnsforskning*, 45: 335–53.

Petersen, J. (1975). "Electorato e base sociale del fascismo italiano negli quni venti", *Studi Storici*: Institute Gramsci editore.

Pelinka, A. (2004). 'European Christian Democracy in Comparison', in M. Gehler and W. Kaiser (eds.), *Christian Democracy in Europe since 1945*. London: Routledge, II, pp. 193–206.

Perkin, H. (1996). *The Third Revolution: Professional Elites in the Modern World*. London: Routledge.

Pesonen, P. and Riihinen, O. (2002). *Dynamic Finland: the Political System and the Welfare State*. Helsinki: Finnish Literature Society.

Peteaux, J. (2003). 'La métaphore et le processus. Genèse et réalité contemporaine du parachutage électoral', in B. Dolez and M. Hastings (eds.), *Le Parachutage Politique*. Paris: L'Harmattan, pp. 57–77.

Peters, B. G. (1989). *The Politics of Bureaucracy: A Comparative Perspective*. New York: Longman.

Petersen, J. (1975). 'Elettorato e base sociale del fascismo italiano negli anni venti', *Studi Storici*.

Pfeifhofer, E. (2002). *Die Abgeordneten Zur Nationalrat. Berufsprofil und Abhängigkeit von Partei und Fraktion*. Vienna: Wilhelm-Braumüller Universitäts-Verlagsbuchhandlung.

Pharr, S. and Putnam, R. (eds.) (2000). *Disaffected Democracies: What's Troubling the Trilateral Democracies*. Princeton, NJ: Princeton University Press.

Phélippeau, É. (1997). 'Sociogenèse de la Profession Politique', in A. Garrigou and B. Lacroix (eds.), *Norbert Elias, La Politique et l'histoire*. Paris: La Découverte, pp. 239–65.

Phillips, A. (1991). *Engendering Democracy*. Cambridge: Polity Press.

——(1995). *The Politics of Presence: Democracy and Group Representation*. Oxford: Oxford University Press.

Pierson, P. (2000). 'Path Dependence, Increasing Returns, and the Study of Politics', *American Political Science Review*, 94(2): 251–67.

——(2004). *Politics in Time*. Princeton, NJ: Princeton University Press.

Pitkin, H. F. (1967). *The Concept of Representation*. Berkeley, CA: University of California Press.

——(1984). *The Concept of Representation*. 2nd. edn. Berkeley, California: University of California Press.

Poggi, G. (1978). *The Development of the Modern State: A Sociological Introduction*. Stanford, CA: Stanford University Press.

Pogunkte, T. (2002). 'Green Parties in National Government from Protest to Acquiescence?', in F. Müller Rommel and T. Pogunkte (eds.), *Green Parties in National Governments*. London: Frank Cass.

Pollard, J. (1990). 'Conservative Catholics and Italian Fascism: the Clerico-Fascists', in M. Blinkhorn (ed.), *Fascists and Conservatives*, op. cit., pp. 31–49.

Polsby, N. (1968). 'The Institutionalization of the U.S. House of Representatives', *American Political Science Review*, 62:144–68.

Powis, J. (1984). *Aristocracy*. Oxford: Blackwell.

Pridham, G. (1977). *Christian Democracy in Western Germany*. London: Croom Helm.

Prost, Antoine (1997). *Éducation, Société et politiques. Une histoire de l'enseignement de 1945 à nos jours*, 1st edn. 1992. Paris: Le Seuil.

Przeworski, A. and Sprague, J. (1986). *Paper Stones: A History of Electoral Socialism*. Chicago, IL: University of Chicago Press

Przeworski, A. and Sprague, J. (1988). *Paper Stones: A History of Electoral Socialism*. The University of Chicago Press, 1988. 2nd edition.

Putnam, R. D. (1976). *The Comparative Study of Political Elites*. Englewood Cliffs, NJ: Prentice-Hall.

——(1993). *Making Democracy Work. Civic Traditions in Modern Italy*. Princeton, NJ: Princeton University Press.

Rae, D. (1967). *The Political Consequences of Electoral Laws*. New Haven, CT: Yale University Press.

—— and Taylor, M. (1970). *The Analysis of Political Cleavages*. New Haven, CT: Yale University Press.

Rahat, G. and Hazan, R. (2001). 'Candidate Selection Methods: An Analytical Framework', *Party Politics*, 7(3): 297–322.

Ramirez, F. O., Saysal, Y., and Shanahan, S. (1997). 'The Changing Logic of Political Citizenship: Cross-national Acquisition of Women's Suffrage Rights, 1890 to 1990', *American Sociological Review*, 62: 735–45.

Raniolo, F. (2000). *I partiti conservatori in Europa occidentale*. Bologna: Il Mulino.

Ranney, A. (1965). *Pathways to Parliament*. Madison, WI: The University of Wisconsin Press.

——(1981). 'Candidate Selection', in D. Butler et al. (eds.), *Democracy at the Polls*. Washington, DC: American Enterprise Institute, pp. 75–106.

Rantala, O. (1981). *Suomen puolueiden muuttuminen*. Valtio-opillisia tutkimuksia 40. Politiikan tutkimuksen ja sosiologian laitos. Turku: Turun yliopisto.

Reskin, B. F. and Roos, P. A. (1990). *Job Queues, Gender Queues*. Philadelphia, PA: Temple University Press.

Reynolds, A. (1999). 'Women in the Legislatures and Executives of the World. Knocking at the Highest Glass Ceiling', *World Politics*, 51(4): 547–72.

Rihoux and Rüdig (2006). 'Analysing Greens in Power: Setting the Agenda'. *European Journal of Political Research*, 45(s1): s1–s33.

Rintala, Marvin (1965). 'Finland', in Hans Rogger and Eugene Weber (eds.), *The European Right. A Historical Profile*. Berkeley, CA: University of California Press, pp. 408–42.

Ritter, G. (1990). 'The Social Bases of the German Political Parties, 1867–1920', in K. Rohe (ed.), *Elections, Parties and Political Traditions. Social Foundations of German Parties and Party Systems, 1867–1987*. New York: Berg.

Richardson, J. J., and Jordan, A. G. (1979). *Governing under Pressure*. Oxford: Oxford University Press.

Rintala, M. (1965). 'Finland', in H. Rogger and E. Weber (eds.), *The European Right. A Historical Profile*. Berkeley, CA: University of California Press, pp. 408–42.

Roberts, G. (1988). 'The German Federal Republic: The Two-lane Route to Bonn', in M. Gallagher and M. Marsh (eds.), *Candidate Selection in Comparative Perspective*. London: Sage, pp. 94–118.

Rogger, H. and Weber, E. (eds.) (1965). *The European Right. A Historical Profile*. Berkeley, CA: University of California Press.

Rokkan, S. (1967). 'Models and Methods in the Study of Nation Building', Paper presented to the Preparatory Meeting on Problems of Nation Building. Brussels: UNESCO.

—— (1970*a*). *Citizens, Elections, Parties. Approaches to the Comparative Study of the Processes of Development*. Oslo: Universitetsforlaget.

—— (1970*b*). 'Nation-building, Cleavage Formation and the Structuring of Mass Politics', in S. Rokkan (ed.), *Citizens, Elections, Parties*. Oslo: Universitetsforlager, pp. 72–144.

—— (1999). *State Formation, Nation-building, and Mass Politics in Europe: The Theory of Stein Rokkan*, edited by P. Flora with S. Kuhnle and D. Urwin. Oxford: Oxford University Press.

—— and Valen, H. (1964). 'Regional Contrasts in Norwegian Politics', in E. Allardt and Y. Littunen (eds.), *Cleavages, Ideologies and Party Systems*. Helsinki: Westermarck Society.

Rommetvedt, H. (2003). *The Rise of the Norwegian Parliament*. London: Frank Cass.

Rose, R. (1983). 'Disaggregating the Concept of Government', in C. L. Taylor (ed.), *Why Governments Grow*. Beverly Hills: Sage.

—— (1991). 'Comparing Forms of Comparative Analysis', *Political Studies*, 39: 446–62.

Rudaux, P. (1967). *Les Croix de Feu et le P.S.F.* Paris: Éditions France–Empire.

Rule, W. (1987). 'Electoral Systems, Contextual Factors and Women's Opportunity for Election to Parliament in Twenty-Three Democracies', *Western Political Quarterly*, 50(3): 477–98.

—— (2000). 'Patterns of Women's Parliamentary Representation', paper presented at the International Political Science Association World Congress, Quebec City, 1–5 August 2000.

Ruostetsaari, I. (1985). Maa- ja metsätaloushallinto, sidosryhmät ja konsultaatio. Unpublished Licentiate thesis in political science. Politiikan tutkimuksen laitos. Tampere: Tampereen yliopisto.

—— (1997). 'Julkinen sektori ja parlamentaarisen eliitin rekrytoiminen', *Hallinnon tutkimus*, 1: 27–46.

—— (2000). 'From Political Amateur to Professional Politician and Expert Representative: Parliamentary Recruitment in Finland since 1863', in H. Best and M. Cotta (eds.), *Parliamentary Representatives in Europe, 1848–2000. Legislative Recruitment and Careers in Eleven European Countries*. Oxford: Oxford University Press, pp. 50–87.

—— (2003). 'Finland: From Political Amateurs to Political Class', in J. Borchert and J. Zeiss (eds.), *The Political Class in Advanced Democracies*. Oxford: Oxford University Press: 107–123.

—— (ed.) (1985). *Public Employment in Western Nations*. Cambridge: Cambridge University Press.

Rush, M. (2001). *The Role of the Member of Parliament Since 1868: From Gentlemen to Players*. Oxford: Oxford University Press.

—— and Cromwell, V. (2000). 'Continuity and Change: Legislative Recruitment in the United Kingdom, 1868–1999', in H. Best and M. Cotta (eds.), *Parliamentary Representatives in Europe, 1848–2000. Legislative Recruitment and Careers in Eleven European Countries*. Oxford: Oxford University Press, pp. 463–92.

——(2004). 'L'évolution des élites Finlandaises après la crise des années 1990', *Nordiques. Printemps*, 4: 83–101.

Rustow, D. A. (1970). 'Transition to Democracy: Toward a Dynamic Model', *Comparative Politics*, II: 337–63.

Saarinen, A. (1992). *Feminist Research—An Intellectual Adventure*. Centre for Women's Studies and Gender Relations. Research Institute for Social Sciences, University of Tampere, Publication Series no. 4.

Sanbonmatsu, K. (2002). 'Political Parties and the Recruitment of Women to State Legislatures', *Journal of Politics*, 64(3): 791–809.

Sapiro, V. (1981). 'When Are Interests Interesting? The Problem of Political Representation of Women', *American Political Science Review*, 75: 701–16.

Sartori, G. (ed.) (1963). *Il parlamento italiano*. Napoli: ESI.

——(1976). *Parties and Party Systems*. Cambridge: Cambridge University Press.

——(1987). *The Theory of Democracy Revisited*. Chatham NJ: Chatham House.

——and Morlino, L. (eds.) (1991). *La comparazione nelle scienze sociali*. Bologna: Il Mulino.

Schmitt, K. (1990). 'Religious Cleavages in the Western German Party System: Persistence and Change, 1949–1987', in K. Rohe (ed.), *Elections, Parties and Political Traditions. Social Foundations of German Parties and Party systems, 1867–1987*. New York: Berg, pp. 179–202.

Schulz, G. (ed.) (2000). *Frauen auf dem Weg zur Elite. Bündiger Forschungen zur Sozialgeschichte*, 2nd edn. Munich: Oldenburg Wissenschaftsverlag.

Schumacher, M. (ed.) (1994). *Die Reichstagabgeordneten der Weimarer Republik in der Zeit des Nationalsozialismus, Politische Verfolgung, Emigration und Ausbürgerung, 1933–1945*. Dusseldorf: Droste.

Schumpeter, J. (1959). *Capitalism, Socialism and Democracy*. London: Allen & Unwin.

Schwarzmantel, J. (1998). *The Age of Ideology. Political Ideologies from the American Revolution to Post-modern Times*. London: Macmillan.

Secker, I. (2000). 'Representatives of The Dutch People: The Smooth Transformation of The Parliamentary Elite in a Consociational Democracy', in H. Best and M. Cotta (eds.), *Parliamentary Representatives in Europe, 1848–2000: Legislative Recruitment and Careers in Eleven European Countries*. Oxford: Oxford University Press, pp. 270–309.

Seltzer, R. A., Newman, J., and Leighton, M. V. (1997). *Sex as a Political Variable: Women as Candidates and Voters in US Elections*. Boulder, CO: Lynne Rienner Publishers.

Selznick, P. (1960). *The Organizational Weapon*. Glencoe, IL: Free Press.

Setta, S. (1975). *L'Uomo Qualunque, 1944–1948*. Bari: Laterza.

Seyd, P. and Whiteley, P. (1992), *Labour's Grass Roots. The Politics of Party Membership*. Oxford.

Sgier, L. (2003). 'Political Representation and Gender Quotas', paper presented at the ECPR Joint Sessions, Edinburgh, 28 March–2 April, 2003.

Shaw, M. (1990). 'Members of Parliament', in M. Rush (ed.), *Parliament and Pressure Politics*. Oxford: Clarendon Press, pp. 85–116.

Siaroff, A. (2000). 'Women's Representation in Legislatures and Cabinets in Industrial Democracies', *International Political Science Review*, 21(2): 197–215.

Smith. A. (1981). *The Ethnic Revival*. Cambridge: Cambridge University Press.

Sobral, J. M. and Tavares de Almeida, P. (1982). 'Caciquismo e poder politico. Reflexoes em torno das eleicoes de 1901', *Análise Social*, XVIII: 657.

Somit, A., Wildenmann, R., and Boll, B. (eds.) (1994). *The Victorious Incumbent: A Threat to Democracy.* Aldershot, UK: Dartmouth.

Sørensen, R. (2003). 'The Political Economy of Intergovernmental Grants: The Norwegian Case', *European Journal of Political Research,* 42: 163–95.

Spring (ed.) (1977). *European Landed Elites in the Nineteenth Century.* Baltimore, MD: The John Hopkins University Press.

Squires, J. and Wickham-Jones, M. (2001). *Women in Parliament: A Comparative Analysis.* Manchester: EOC.

Statistics Norway (2002). 'Sharp Increase in Educational Level'. Oslo (available on http://www.ssb.no).

——(2003). *Indicators on Education, in the OECD. Percentage of the Population of 25–34 Year-Old that has attained tertiary education, 1991, 1996 and 1998–2001.* Oslo (available on http://www.ssb.no).

Statistik A. (2002). *Bildungsstand der Bevölkerung.* Vienna: Statistik Austria.

Steed, M. (1985). 'The Constituency', in V. Bogdanor (ed.), *Representatives of the People?: Parliamentarians and Constituents in Western Democracies.* London: Gower. pp. 267–92.

Stengers, J. (1966). 'Belgium', in H. Rogger and E. Weber (eds.), *The European Right. A Historical Profile.* Berkeley, CA: University of California Press, pp. 128–167.

Sternhell, Z. (1986). *Neither Right nor Left. Fascist ideology in France.* Berkeley, CA: Berkeley University Press.

——Sznajder, M., and Ashéri, M. (1989). *La naissance de l'idelogie Fasciste.* Paris: Fayard.

Stokes, D. (1963). 'Spatial Models of Party Competition', in *American Political Science Review,* 57 (2) 368–77.

Stolz, K. (2003). 'Moving up, Moving Down. Political Careers across Territorial Levels', *European Journal of Political Research,* 42: 223–48.

Studlar, D. T. and McAllister, I. (2002). 'Does a Critical Mass Exist? A Comparative Analysis of Women's Legislative Representation since 1950', *European Journal of Political Research,* 41: 233–53.

Svasand, L. (1998). 'Scandinavian Right-Wing Radicalism', *The New Politics of the Right,* 77–94.

Szöllösi-Janze, M. (1989). *Die Pfeildrenzbewegung in Ungarn, Historischer Kontext, Emtwicklung und Herrschaft.* München: Oldenbourg.

Tarchi, M. (1997). *Dal MSI ad AN. Organizazione e strategie.* Bologna: Il Mulino.

Tavares de Almeida, P. (1991). *Eleições Caciquismo no Portugal Oitocentista.* Lisbon: Difel.

——(1995). A Construçao de Estade Liberal. Lisbon: Universitate Nova de Lisboa.

——and Costa Pinto, A. (2003). 'Portuguese Ministers, 1851–1999: Social Background and Paths to Power', in P. Tavares de Almeida, A. Costa Pinto, and N. Bermeo (eds), *Who Governs Southern Europe? Regime Change and Ministerial Recruitment, 1850–2000.* London: Frank Cass, pp. 5–40.

——Fernandes, P. J., and Santos, M. C. (2006). 'Os Deputados da 1ª República Portuguesa', *Revista de História das Ideias.* 27: 399–417.

The Economist (2004). 'Almost an Entitlement'. London, 24 January, 24.

Thiébault, J. L. (1988). 'France: the impact of electoral system change', in M. Gallagher and M. Marsh (eds.), *Candidate Selection in Comparative Perspective. The Secret Garden of Politics*. London: Sage.

Thomas, S. (1994). *How Women Legislate*. New York: Oxford University Press.

Tilly, C. (ed.) (1975). *The Formation of National States in Europe*. Princeton, NJ: Princeton University Press.

de Tocqueville, A. (1835–40) *De la démocratie en Amérique*. Paris: C. Gosselin.

Tusell, J. and Avilés, J. (1994). *Antonio Maura. Una Biografía Política*. Madrid: Alianza.

—— and Queipo de Llamo, G. (2001). *Alfonso XIII. El rey polémico*. Madrid: Taurus.

UNECE (United Nations Economic Conference for Europe) (2003). http://www.unece.org.

UNESCO (2002a). *Length, Starting, and Ending Age of Compulsory Education*. Report, UNESCO Institute For Statistics, Montreal.

—— (2002b). *Enrolment in Tertiary Education: Both Sexes*. Report, UNESCO Institute for Statistics, Montreal.

Urwin, D. (1973). *From Ploughshare to Ballotbox*. Oslo-Bergen-Tromso: Universitetsforlaget.

—— (1983). *Harbinger, Fossil or Fleabite? 'Regionalism' and the West European Party Mosaic*, in H. Daalder and P. Mair (eds.), *Western European Party Systems. Continuity and Change*. London: Sage, pp. 221–56.

Valen, H. (1988). 'Norway: Decentralization and Group Representation', in M. Gallagher and M. Marsh (eds.), *Candidate Selection in Comparative Perspective*. London: Sage, pp. 210–35.

—— Narud, H. M. and Hardarson, O. Th. (2000). 'Geography and Political Representation', in P. Esaiasson and K. Heidar (eds.), *Beyond Westminster and Congress, the Nordic Experience*. Columbus, OH: Ohio State University Press, 107–31.

Vanhanen, T. (1997). *Prospects of Democracy: A Study of 172 Countries*. London, Routledge.

Van Hecke, S. and Gerard, E. (2004). *Christian Democratic Parties in Europe since the End of the Cold War*. Leuven: Leuven University Press.

Van Kesbergen, K. (1994). 'The Distinctiveness of Christian Democracy', in D. Hanley (ed.), *Christian Democracy in Europe. A Comparative Perspective*. London: Pinter, pp. 31–50.

—— (1999). 'Contemporary Christian Democracy and the demise of the politics of mediation', in H. Kitschelt, P. Lange, G. Marks, and J. D. Stephens (eds.), *Continuity and Change in Contemporary Capitalism*. Cambridge: Cambridge University Press, pp. 346–70.

Verzichelli, L. (1998). 'Da un ceto parlamentaro all'altro. Il mutamento nel personale legislativo italiano', in R. D'Alimonte and S. Bartolini (eds.), *Maggioritario finalmente? La transizione elettorale, 1994–2001*. Bologna: Il Mulino.

—— and Edinger, M. (2005). 'A Critical Juncture? The 2004 European Elections and the Making of a Supranational Political Elite', *Journal of Legislative Studies*, 11(2): 254–74.

Volkens, A. (2004). 'Policy Changes of European Social Democrats', in B. Powell (eds.), pp. 21–42

Wal, J. T. (2000). 'The Discourse of the Extreme Right and Its Ideological Implications: The Case of Alleanza Nazionale', *Patterns of Prejudice*, 34(4): 37–52.

Walby, S. (2000). 'Gender, Nations and States in a Global Era', *Nations and Nationalism*, 6(4): 523–40.

Wallef, D. (1980). 'The Composition of Christus Rex', in Stein U. Larsen, Bernt Hagtvet, and Jan Peter Myklebust (eds.), *Who were the Fascists. Social Roots of European Fascism*. Bergen: Universitetsforlaget, pp. 517–23.

Wängnerud, L. (2000), 'Representing Women', in P. Esaiasson and K. Heidar (eds.), *Beyond Westminster and Congress: The Nordic Experience*. Columbus, OH: Ohio State University Press.

Ware, A. (1996). *Parties and Party Systems*. Oxford: Oxford University Press.

——(2001). *Political Parties and Party Systems*. New York: Oxford University Press.

Warren, M. E. (2003). 'A Second Transformation of Democracy ?', in B. Cain, R. Dalton, and S. E. Scarrow (eds.), *Democracy Transformed ? Expanding Political Opportunities in Advanced Industrial Democracies*. Oxford: Oxford University Press, pp. 223–49.

Weber, M. (1922). *Wirtschaft und Gesellschaft*. Tübingen: J. C. B. Mohr.

——(1919) 'Politik als Beruf', in H. Gerth and C. Wright Mills (eds.), *From Max Weber*. New York: Oxford University Press, pp. 77–128.

——(1921). *Gesammelte politische Schriften*. München: Drei Masken Verlag.

——(1994). 'Suffrage and Democracy in Germany' (first published in 1917). *Political Writings*. Cambridge: Cambridge University Press.

——(2004). 'A politika mint hivams', in M. Weber (ed.), *A tudomany es politika mint hivams* (first publ. 1919). Budapest: Kossuth, pp. 57–151.

Wessels, B. (1999). 'System Characteristics Matter: Empirical Evidence from ten Representational Studies', in Warren E. Miller et al. (eds.), *Policy Representation in Western Democracies*. Oxford: Oxford University Press, 137–61.

Wheare, K. C. (1963). *Legislatures*. London: Oxford University Press.

Whiteley, P., Seyd, P., and Richardson, J. (1994). *True Blues. The Politics of Conservative Party Membership*. Oxford: Oxford University Press.

Widfeldt, A. (2001). 'The Swedish Centre Party: The Poor Relation of the Family?', in D. Arter (ed.), *From Farmyard to City Square? The Electoral Adaptation of the Nordic Agrarian Parties*. Aldershot, UK: Ashgate, pp. 1–30.

Wildenmann, R. (1986). 'The Problematic of Party Government', in F. G. Castles and R. Wildenmann (eds.), *Visions and Realities of Party Government*. Berlin/New York.

Williams, Ph. M. (1970). *French Politicians and Elections, 1951–1969*. Cambridge: Cambridge University Press.

Willis, P. (1977). *Learning to Labour: How Working Class Kids Get Working Class Jobs*. London: Saxon House.

Wilson, F. (1998). *The European Centre-Right at the End of the Twentieth Century*. Basingtoke, UK: Macmillan.

Young, I. M. (2000). *Inclusion and Democracy*. Oxford: Oxford University Press.

Yrjölä, P. (1973). 'Ministeriura', in H. Hakovirta and T. Koskiaho (eds.), *Suomen hallitukset ja hallitusohjelmat, 1945–1973*. Helsinki: Gaudeamus, pp. 61–87.

Ysmal, C. (1996). 'Sociologie des élites du FN', in N. Mayer and P. Perrineau (eds.), *Le Front National à découvert*. Paris: Presse de Sciences Politiques, pp. 107–11.

Zuckermann, A. S. (1975). 'Political Cleavage: a conceptual and Theoretical Analysis', *British Journal of Political Science*, 5: 231–48.

——(1979). *The Politics of Factions: Christian Democratic Rule in Italy*. New Haven, CT: Yale University Press.

Index

Figures, notes and tables are indexed in bold, e.g. 228f.